Freedom Is A Constant Struggle

Freedom Is A

Constant Struggle

An Anthology of the
Mississippi Civil Rights
Movement

Developed and Edited by
Susie Erenrich

A Project of the Cultural Center for Social Change
Washington, D.C.

BLACK BELT PRESS
Montgomery, Alabama

Black Belt Press
P.O. Box 551
Montgomery, AL 36101

Freedom Is A Constant Struggle:
An Anthology of the Mississippi Civil Rights Movement

Edited by Susie Erenrich
Executive Director
Cultural Center for Social Change
3133 Connecticut Avenue, N.W., Suite 432
Washington, DC 20008

Cover photograph by George Ballis

The Cultural Center for Social Change is a non-profit organization located in the District of Columbia. It was established to educate the public through the arts about historical, social, and political movements in this country and abroad; to provide arts programming to underserved populations; and to collaborate with artists involved in projects for social change. For more information about the Center's 2-CD set, *Freedom Is A Constant Struggle: Songs Of The Mississippi Civil Rights Movement, The Long Walk to Freedom Reunion Concert* CD, or other organizational activities write:

Cultural Center for Social Change
3133 Connecticut Avenue, NW
Suite 432
Washington, DC 20008
(202) 462-4611

In loving memory of William Kunstler
July 7, 1919–September 4, 1995

Contents

Acknowledgments

Words can never adequately express my gratitude to all of the participants who have aligned in appreciating the value of this commemorative effort. This project would never have been possible without their memories, talent, and devotion.

A very special thanks to my best friend, assistant, and biggest supporter, Brad McKelvey. He stood by me through the best and worst of times.

I could never have completed this anthology without my wonderful parents, Wil and Louise Erenrich. They were always there when I needed them.

My dedicated attorney, Jay Rosenthal, who volunteered his time and expertise to the Center, deserves a tremendous amount of recognition.

I am grateful to Black Belt Press for recognizing the importance of covering this tumultuous time in American history. Black Belt's publisher, Randall Williams, along with the Cultural Center for Social Change, believes the civil and human rights struggle chronicled in this book reverberated well beyond the borders of the state of Mississippi. Let me add that the Black Belt editorial staff of Jeff Slaton, Drew Cotten, and Ashley Gordon deserve a world of thanks for their help in bringing this book together.

The Center has many friends who have generously contributed so much of themselves to insure the success of the Mississippi Civil Rights Movement project. There are too many of you to list, but I love and am indebted to each and every one of you. ❖

SUSIE ERENRICH

Introduction

Susie Erenrich is the
founder, executive
director, and
treasurer of the
Cultural Center for
Social Change. She
holds an MS in
Conflict Analysis and
Resolution from
George Mason
University, an MA in
Performing Arts from
American University,
and a BA in
Sociology from Kent
State University.
Susie has been
combining her work
as a community
activist with the arts
of social change for
more than two
decades. Her
teaching, performing,
choreographing, and
program develop-
ment have been
carried out in a
variety of settings.
These include
correctional
facilities, commu-
nity-based programs
for at-risk, low-
income populations,
the public schools,
and college
campuses.

Shortly past midnight on May 15, 1970, the Mississippi Highway Patrol and law enforcement officers opened fire on the Jackson State College campus. Thirty seconds and 230 bullets later, Phillip Gibbs and James Earl Green were dead. Gibbs, age twenty-one, was a pre-law major from Ripley, Mississippi. Green, seventeen, was a senior at Jim Hill High School in Jackson. Countless others were wounded by the fusillade and all of the witnesses were traumatized.

Blacks in Mississippi were accustomed to this treatment. The state has a long history of racist violence committed against its citizens—Emmett Till, Herbert Lee, Medgar Evers, and James Chaney, to name a few. The Jackson State tragedy would have gone completely unnoticed had it not occurred in the wake of shootings at Kent State University ten days earlier, when the Ohio National Guard claimed the lives of four white students—Allison Krause, Jeffrey Miller, Sandra Scheuer, and William Schroeder. The public outcry over the killing of white students at Kent State gave the Jackson State incident a significance it would not have attained on its own accord.

While a student at Kent State University, I became familiar with the names Phillip Gibbs and James Earl Green. "Long Live the Spirit of Kent and Jackson State" became more than a slogan, and in 1990 I edited my first anthology, paying tribute to the six students who were slain. Assembling articles for the Jackson State portion of that book was a difficult task. There was

little documentation on the Mississippi incident and what did exist was laden with untruths. As a result, there was disproportionate attention given to the Jackson State section of the book. The imbalance was very unsettling. *Kent & Jackson State, 1970–1990* was released on the twentieth anniversary of the Kent State shootings with only four articles from Mississippi.

One year later, the idea for this project, *Freedom Is A Constant Struggle*, was born while I was conducting graduate research on songs of the Civil Rights Movement. Digging through *Broadside*, a national topical song magazine from the early 1960s, I discovered that some of the most powerful and provocative material focused on the racism, segregation, and brutality committed against those who dared to dismantle the Mississippi system. Through this material, the history of the Movement unfolded before my eyes, and I had to share it with others.

I founded the Cultural Center for Social Change, a non-profit organization, and concurrently began to incorporate the information I had found into an arts empowerment curriculum for at-risk, low-income youth and children in the District of Columbia public schools. Most of the students had not been introduced to the songwriters in *Broadside* or to the participants of the Mississippi Civil Rights Movement. This was no surprise, because many had never even heard of the better known figures in African American history, such as Harriet Tubman, Sojourner Truth, or Nat Turner.

As a white woman, exploring African American history with my students always presented a moral dilemma, one I overcame with the assistance of an African American colleague. She helped me realize that history belongs to all of us, and that if I wasn't going to present the material to the students, they might never encounter it. So together my students and I took an artistic journey through Africa, the middle passage, slavery, and the Civil Rights Movement, paying special attention to Mississippi. We discussed how the past is intertwined with the present and future. The students made collages, wrote scripts, choreographed dances, recited poetry, composed songs, and created an African American history "Jeopardy" game. These activities sparked new energy and enthusiasm in many of the students. Empowered by the information and experience, many began to enjoy school for the first time in their lives.

More needed to be done. I wanted to reach policy makers, educators, and parents. I wanted to create new outlets for celebrating and commemorating struggles for social change throughout the world. Too often, these social change initiatives are forgotten or presented in ways that distort their significance and mislead the public.

So I devised an intensive national project on the Mississippi Civil Rights Movement where participants could document their memories and stories in a non-commercial and uncensored format. I could have selected another Southern state, such as Alabama, which shared Mississippi's reputation for brutalizing and killing its citizens over desegregation, but I chose Mississippi. Mississippi's past had haunted me for twenty years, and now I had an opportunity to do something about it.

For the next three years, I searched for Freedom Summer volunteers, members of the Student Nonviolent Coordinating Committee (SNCC), Civil Rights Movement leaders, native Mississippians, journalists, topical songwriters, artists, and photographers who were part of that historic period. Locating participants and gathering information for this project was not easy. It took months, and in some cases years, to track people down. I had never been to Mississippi and was in grammar school during the height of the Civil Rights Movement, so I couldn't rely on personal contacts. Busy schedules prevented the prompt arrival of materials. I was sometimes stood up and promised submissions that never came.

The Cultural Center for Social Change, the base of operation for this effort, had limited resources, which made the process even more cumbersome. There was no money in the organizational account, no computer technology, no fax machine, no paid staff members, and no clerical support. My passion for this project was the driving force. The telephone and an electric typewriter were the only tools which assisted in this mission to record an important era of American history.

Finding and choosing an appropriate publisher presented another problem. I forwarded outlines to ninety-one prospective publishers. The majority rejected the book. Some simply were not interested, or said it was too big or too narrow in scope. Others said it had no "commercial viability," or would cost too much, or prove too risky a venture. Many didn't trust the authors to convey their thoughts and feelings in an appealing fashion. While my "hands-off," no censorship policy dissuaded most publishers, Black Belt Press was one of the few to appreciate the concept and vision of the anthology—a work in which the participants and their experiences tell the story.

With contributions from more than eighty people, *Freedom Is A Constant Struggle* is one of the most comprehensive books ever published on the Civil Rights Movement in Mississippi. The articles and testimonials are of varying lengths and forms, including analytic essays and personal reminiscences. Each author chose a particular topic of interest and writing style. The only criteria was to cover some aspect of the Movement in Mississippi. Some authors submitted more than one article dealing with various points or issues. This was their prerogative, providing they limited their combined remarks to no more than twenty typed pages. Exceptions were made in cases where cutting an article would have detracted from its content. Alterations by me or Black Belt Press were prohibited unless the author consented or there was some glaring typographical error.

The anthology includes selected prints from one of the largest collections of photography from the Mississippi Movement. Some personal photos are also shown, along with drawings by children who attended the Freedom Schools that have not been seen by the public for more than thirty years. Eighteen sketches capturing the people and events of the time were done exclusively for this project.

Also included are the lyrics to forty songs which are part of a two-CD set, *Freedom Is A Constant Struggle: Songs Of The Mississippi Civil Rights Movement*. The album, which was released by the Cultural Center for Social Change in March 1994, showcases twenty-three artists. Included are fifteen songs that were re-recorded for the set, six songs that were never previously recorded, and two new songs composed specially for this project. The majority of the singers/songwriters featured on the album were involved in the Mississippi Freedom Summer of 1964. Aggie Friesen's original images from *Broadside* magazine accompany many of the songs in the anthology.

Thus, *Freedom Is A Constant Struggle* presents an unprecedented array of different media—articles, songs, photographs, and drawings. Each carries its own messages and each elicits a variety of responses from readers.

Much of the content is controversial, like Horace Doyle Barnette's confession to the FBI concerning his involvement in the murders of three civil rights workers; Dick Gregory's knowledge of their whereabouts; and Lawrence Guyot's scathing reminiscences of Allard Lowenstein. Issues that have never been resolved are aired with the hope that they will provoke dialogue among readers and the civil rights community, such as

Staughton Lynd's "Freedom Summer: A Tragedy, Not a Melodrama" and Doug McAdam's "Let It Shine, Shine, Shine."

Readers should also bear in mind that the words Negro, black, colored, and African American are used interchangeably throughout this anthology, reflecting the period in which the articles were originally written. The terms black and white, which were originally capitalized in some of the articles, appear throughout in lower case, reflecting the publisher's standards of stylistic and editorial consistency.

It is also important to point out that the anthology is not assembled in an obvious way. There are no chapters. Each entry is meant to stand on its own. The articles, songs, photographs, and artwork merge in a vibrant composite that celebrates the role each of the contributors played in Mississippi's Civil Rights Movement. This does not mean there is no order. Many of the articles and songs are arranged chronologically. For example, entries related to numerous events appear in the order that their respective subjects fall on the time line of the U.S. Civil Rights Movement, beginning with lyrics on the Civil War, "Hey Nelly Nelly," by Shel Silverstein and Joe Friedman, and concluding with a heartfelt "Thank You," by Chude Allen, on the thirtieth anniversary reunion in Mississippi in 1994.

Where possible, the photographs also carry readers through time. The first photograph, of Emmett Till and his mother, Mamie Till Mobley, comes from Mrs. Mobley's personal collection. The family did not have a lot of money, and the studio photograph was a special Christmas present they gave to themselves in 1954. The photograph is the last visual memory Mrs. Mobley has of her son before he was lynched the following summer while visiting relatives in Mississippi.

Matt Herron's and George Ballis's photographs and Sharon Riley's sketches are also strategically placed throughout the anthology, allowing readers to revisit the Freedom Schools, James Chaney's funeral, the Mississippi Freedom

Democratic Party's challenge at the National Democratic Convention in Atlantic City, the 1965 memorial march for the murdered civil rights workers in Philadelphia, Mississippi, the 1966 March Against Fear, and the aftermath of the 1970 Jackson State shootings.

Other groupings in the anthology include specific topics or events. For example, there is a whole section on the arts: the "Roots of the Singing Civil Rights Movement" workshop at Highlander; SNCC Freedom Singers; Mississippi Caravan of Music; *Broadside* magazine; Free Southern Theater; Civil Rights Movement photography; and an exhibit and drawings by Freedom School children. Other sections pay tribute to particular individuals like Medgar Evers, Fannie Lou Hamer, and Ella Baker. There are exceptions to these groupings, when the content of an article fits more appropriately in another section of the publication.

Three bibliographies, submitted by a few participants, are included to provide readers with additional sources of information and material. Every contributor also submitted a short biography, which appears next to his or her submission.

Despite the collection's breadth, I am saddened that it is not all-inclusive. Hundreds of people were never located and others never forwarded their materials. Nevertheless, I feel that *Freedom Is A Constant Struggle* is a fine project, one I have dedicated to Ella Baker. Ella's name is not widely known among the general public, but to those inside the Movement, her uncompromising mission and presence were a sustaining force. I am also proud to present this project in honor of Emmett Till, Medgar Evers, James

Chaney, Andrew Goodman, Michael Schwerner, Phillip Gibbs, James Earl Green . . . and all those who gave their lives to the ongoing struggle for racial equality and social justice.

This project has touched my life in many ways. The captivating power of the material and the wonderful people I met made it one of the most illuminating and emotional experiences of my life. I cried as I read many of the articles, finding it hard to accept America's horrific treatment of her own, such as Fannie Lou Hamer, who asked, "Is this America? The land of the free and the home of the brave?" Other times, I found myself heartened by the authors' defiance of Mississippi tyranny.

Thirty years is a long time. Many of the survivors of this struggle are gracefully aging now. Many have died. With each death a piece of American history descends, deep beneath the ground. *Freedom Is A Constant Struggle* attempts to capture and preserve as much of the history as possible. It is vastly different from other books on the Mississippi Movement because it was written by the history makers who stood up to an entire social system. All too often, the ordeals and accomplishments of ordinary citizens are conveyed in encapsulated information thirdhand. By the time an account of the event appears, the true essence of what actually happened becomes lost, or is only discovered years later by researchers who try to reconstruct the puzzle.

I am grateful that the participants have entrusted their most precious memories with me. I have learned so much through this process. Now I invite the reader to commemorate this exciting milestone with me and to share this valuable work with generations to come.   ❖

Freedom Is A Constant Struggle

Map of Mississippi

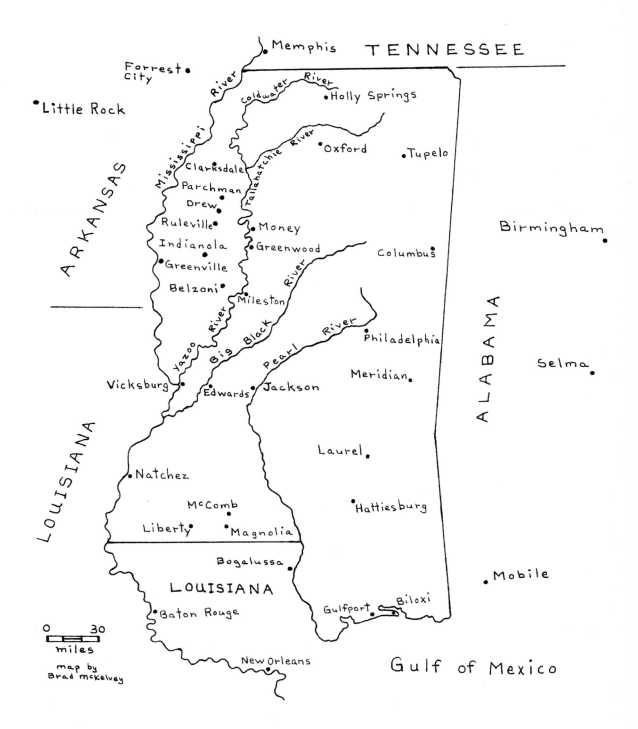

TENNESSEE

Memphis

Forrest City

Little Rock

Coldwater River

Holly Springs

Mississippi River

Oxford

Tupelo

Clarksdale

ARKANSAS

Parchman

Drew

Tallahatchie River

Money

Ruleville

Indianola

Greenwood

Columbus

Birmingham

Greenville

Belzoni

Mileston

River

Yazoo River

Big Black River

Pearl River

Philadelphia

ALABAMA

Selma

Vicksburg

Edwards

Jackson

Meridian

LOUISIANA

Laurel

Natchez

McComb

Hattiesburg

Liberty

Magnolia

Bogalussa

LOUISIANA

Mobile

Baton Rouge

Gulfport

Biloxi

New Orleans

Gulf of Mexico

0   30
miles

map by
Brad McKelvey

2

SHEL SILVERSTEIN AND JIM FRIEDMAN

Hey Nelly, Nelly

Hey, Nelly, Nelly, come to the window,
Hey, Nelly, Nelly, look at what I see.
He's ridin' into town on a swayback mule,
Got a tall black hat and he looks like a fool,
He sure is talkin' like he's been to school,
And it's 1850.

Hey, Nelly, Nelly, listen what he's sayin'.
Hey, Nelly, Nelly, he says it's gettin' late.
And he says them black folks should all be free
To walk around the same as you and me.
He's talkin' 'bout a thing he calls democracy,
And it's 1858.

Hey, Nelly, Nelly, hear the band a-playin'.
Hey, Nelly, Nelly, hand me down my gun,
'Cause the men are cheerin' and the boys are, too.
They're all puttin' on their coats of blue.
I can't sit around here and talk to you,
'Cause it's 1861.

Hey, Nelly, Nelly, come to the window.
Hey, Nelly, Nelly, I've come home alive.
My coat of blue is stained with red
And the man in the tall black hat is dead.
We sure will remember all the things he said,
In 1865.

Hey, Nelly, Nelly, come to the window.
Hey, Nelly, Nelly, look at what I see.
I see white folks and colored walking side by side.
They're walkin' in a column that's a century wide.
It's still a long and a hard and a bloody ride,
In 1963.

Recorded by Judy Collins:
"Jim Friedman sang this to me on a hot New York night, not so far from the Mississippi summer of 1964."

3

Emmett Louis Till

(JULY 25, 1941—AUGUST 28, 1955)

Emmett Louis Till, the only child of Mamie and Louis Till, was born on July 25, 1941.

At the age of five, Emmett was stricken with polio from which he recovered, except for a serious speech defect. Many visits to doctors, clinics, and speech therapists failed to cure his stuttering. Illinois Research Hospital finally advised that he would ". . . probably outgrow the problem."

Emmett was raised in Argo, Illinois, and attended school there until 1951. In Chicago, he attended the McCosh School until 1955, the year of his death.

Emmett was a humanitarian. Senior citizens were his main concern. They would depend upon him to run errands, shop, mow lawns, shovel snow, or whatever tasks they needed him to perform. At home, he voluntarily assumed responsibility for many household chores, including bill paying and laundry. He said: "Mom, if you can earn the money, I can take care of the house." This he did until his death.

Emmett attended the Argo Temple Church of God in Christ. In Argo, he would stay with his great-grandmother, Nancy Jane Carthan. She depended upon him to do her shopping and

Emmett Louis Till and his mother, Mamie. Photo submitted by Mamie Till Mobley.

mopping and other errands outside the home.

He was the chosen leader among his friends in Argo and Chicago. Emmett was known as the "mediator." He could move in and settle disputes and his judgment was acceptable. Parents depended upon his ability to steer the other young people in the right direction.

His ambitions were to build his grandmother, my mother, a church, and to be a motorcycle cop. He respected the officers of the law, and decided early in life to be one of them. Emmett was a peacemaker, full of life, full of fun, with a firm sense of direction.

Emmett was killed on Sunday, August 28, 1955, in Money, Mississippi. His confessed killers were J. W. Milam and Roy Bryant, plus others unknown. The jury's verdict was: *Not Guilty*. To this date, no one has been punished for Emmett's death or for his kidnapping.

J. W. Milam died of cancer in 1983. Roy Bryant, now legally blind, is bitter because, in his words, "Emmett Till ruined my life. He is dead, I don't see why he can't stay dead."

Both men were divorced by their wives shortly after the trial. Neither had the privilege of watching their two sons grow up.

On July 25, 1991, Emmett's fiftieth birthday, Mayor Richard Daley proclaimed the day to be Emmett Till Day in Chicago. Seventy-first Street was honorarily named Emmett Till Road from 71st and Kedzie to 71st and the Lake. Thirty-eight streets carry the sign: Emmett Till Road. The remaining streets are to be so designated in the near future.

Although it was a thirty-six-year struggle to get a memorial to Emmett in Chicago, the city of his birth, we recognize his fiftieth birthday to be the year of Jubilee. We know that his name represents healing, reconciliation, and a new beginning to universal brotherhood throughout this land.

To God be the Glory!!!!!!   ❖

Mamie Till Mobley is the founder and President of the Chicago-based Emmett Till Foundation dedicated to the memory of her son, Emmett Louis Till who was brutally murdered in Money, Mississippi on August 28, 1955. She is an active member of the Evangelistic Crusaders Church and directs a children's drama group called the Emmett Till Players. Mamie holds a Masters Degree in Administration and Supervision from Loyola University and is working on a Ph.D. in Philosophy through International Seminary in Orlando, Florida.

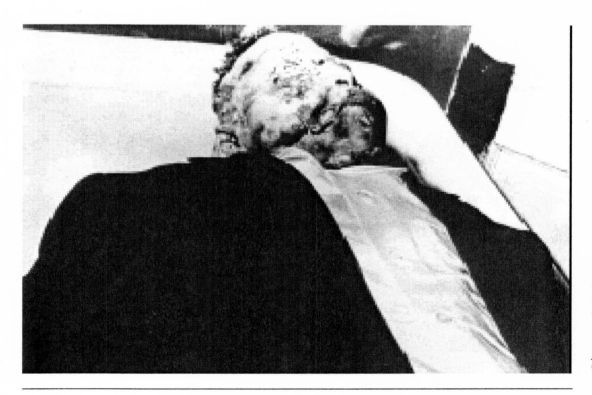

The remains of Emmett Till's bludgeoned body lies in his casket at Roberts Temple. (Photo used by permission of the Chicago Defender.*)*

A Letter from Emmett Till's Mother

A remembrance written by Mamie Till Mobley, Chicago, Illinois, March 3, 1994.

Dear Ms. Erenrich:

As I reflect upon the terror which reigned in the twilight hours of August 28, 1955, when my son, Emmett Louis Till, was forcibly taken from the home of my aunt and uncle, Elizabeth and Moses Wright, I realize that the purpose for which Emmett died has not as yet been fulfilled. Yet, nations of people realized that they had become tired. I understand now that my decision to hold a five-day wake, during which time six hundred thousand people were allowed to view my son's mutilated body, was not due to my genius, but was the guidance of a Higher Power. So powerful was the impact upon the viewers that protest meetings were held throughout the nation. Nearly every country in the world sent reporters to bring back the news. The Civil Rights Movement had begun!

Rosa Parks realized that she was tired of racial injustice, so she sat down. Dr. Martin Luther King, Jr., was so tired that he stood up, ending segregation on Alabama buses and interstate travel.

Uppermost in my mind is the "trial" which lasted five, hot days. The 118-degree temperature in the courtroom was mild compared to the hate which filled every inch. Not only was food and drink served to the accused, Roy Bryant and J. W. Milam, they were also allowed to play with their boys and use the judge's washroom. The black witnesses were unable to purchase, and had to walk two blocks to the nearest cafe to relieve themselves.

The courage of the black witnesses was unprecedented. Although some trembled with fear, they stood tall and told what they had seen. Moses Wright identified the kidnappers. Willie Reed dared to view the entire grisly beating and shooting through a crack in the boards of the barn. Amanda Bradley identified the truck which carried Emmett into the barn. She also told how J. W. Milam washed the blood from his person, and later from the bed of the truck. I was accused of collaborating with the NAACP to dig up a body, put a two-hundred-pound weight around its neck, and "planting" it in the Tallahatchie River. Although I had positively identified Emmett's body, the defense contended that Emmett was alive in Detroit, Michigan. The "not guilty" verdict came over the radio when we were about forty-five minutes from Sumner. The jury had been advised: "I know that every last Anglo-Saxon one of you will set these men free." They did. The foreman said it wouldn't have taken them one hour and five minutes to bring in a verdict, but they were told to make it look good. So—they drank soda water and told jokes to pass the time. Two months later, in November, they [the defendants] were also found "not guilty" of the kidnapping charges to which they had admitted.

Because of the reporters, the cameras, and the video tapes, we escaped with our lives. The locals thought the scenes were being instantly transmitted and were too cowardly to do us bodily harm with the world looking on.

PHIL OCHS

Here's to the State of Mississippi

Here's to the State of Mississippi,
For underneath her borders the Devil draws no line.
If you drag her muddy rivers nameless bodies you will find,
And the fat trees of the forest hid a thousand crimes,
And the calendar is lying when it reads the present time,
And here's to the land you've torn out the heart of,
Mississippi, find yourself another country to be part of.

Here's to the people of Mississippi
Who say the "Folks up North they just don't understand."
And they tremble in the shadows at the thunder of the Klan
All the sweating of their souls can't wash the blood from off their hands
For they smile and shrug their shoulders at the murder of a man.
And here's to the land you've torn out the heart of,
Mississippi, find yourself another country to be part of.

Here's to the schools of Mississippi
Where they're teaching all the children that they don't have to care
All the rudiments of hatred are present everywhere
Oh every single classroom is a factory of despair
And there's nobody learning such a foreign word as fair.
And here's to the land you've torn out the heart of,
Mississippi, find yourself another country to be part of.

Here's to the cops of Mississippi
They're chewing their tobacco as they lock the prison door
And their bellies bounce inside them when they knock you to the floor
No, they don't like taking prisoners in their private little wars
And behind their broken badges there are murderers and more.
And here's to the land you've torn out the heart of,
Mississippi, find yourself another country to be part of.

Phil Ochs was one of the musical spokesmen of the 1960s. His song, "I Ain't Marchin' Anymore" was one of the anthems of the anti-war movement. He was a committed activist who never compromised. Phil was a part of the Caravan of Music of Project Mississippi in 1964.

Aggie Friesen was born in 1945. For twenty years she contributed hundreds of drawings and graphics to Broadside magazine and participated in the layout of the publication. Aggie has a masters degree in Creative Writing. She lives in Berkeley, California where she is working on her second novel.

Here's to the judges of Mississippi
Who wear the robe of honor as they crawl into the court
They're guarding all the bastions of their phony legal fort
Oh, Justice is a stranger when the prisoners report
When a black man stands accused the trial is always short.
And here's to the land you've torn out the heart of,
Mississippi, find yourself another country to be part of.

Here's to the government of Mississippi
In the swamp of their bureaucracy they're always bogging down
And criminals are posing as the mayors of the town
And they hope that no one sees the sights and no one hears the sounds
And the speeches of the governor are the ravings of a clown.
And here's to the land you've torn out the heart of,
Mississippi, find yourself another country to be part of.

Here's to the laws of Mississippi
The congressmen will gather in a circus of delay
While the constitution's drowning in an ocean of decay
"Unwed mothers should be sterilized" I've even heard them say
Yes, corruption can be classic in the Mississippi way.
And here's to the land you've torn out the heart of,
Mississippi, find yourself another country to be part of.

Here's to the churches of Mississippi
Where the cross once made of silver now is caked with rust
And the Sunday morning sermons pander to their lust
Oh, the fallen face of Jesus is choking in the dust
And only Heaven knows in which God they can trust.
And here's to the land you've torn out the heart of,
Mississippi, find yourself another country to be part of.

PATRICIA MOSELEY

A Reminiscence

We boarded the bus in mid-July, 1960. That spring I'd been a junior in high school, taking part in advanced placement American History in a medium-sized New York high school. Our teacher was far to the left of anyone in authority I'd ever met, even though my own parents were liberal Democrats. In 1960, in New York, many liberal Democrats were holdover New Dealers, people who voted Democrat, believed in unions and Social Security, but rarely gave a thought to emerging social issues such as racial equality. That summer my eyes were opened to things I had seen before but not comprehended.

My participation in advanced placement history and as a member of the debate team put me together with the real student activists. I'd certainly never demonstrated or protested anything with any real vigor, but I sure did admire the kids who did. They were a source of stimulation, fascination, and in the end, they helped turn me in a direction I've never reversed. So when our teacher and my fellow students suggested we go into the deep South that summer after the Democratic convention (we never doubted John Kennedy would get the nomination that coming July) to help register black voters, I planned to go with only slight hesitation. We were all white.

I like to think I had voting rights on my mind, but actually, getting Kennedy elected was the real issue. I have to admit I might not have made a similar effort for any other candidate. That said, let me be fair to myself and say that a big reason we all wanted JFK elected was because of his civil rights position, indeed because of his position on all things that seemed fair and compassionate. Helping to put him in the White House was enormously important to us.

There were about fifteen of us, including I think about five adults. The history teacher was there, with his wife, and some parents. I really can't remember it exactly. It wasn't a school bus; it must have been chartered, but I can't recall. In any case, I was seventeen and I was on what I later romanticized as a freedom bus. It took us from New York to Richmond, where we picked up a few college-age white students. I don't know who they were, but one played the guitar, which was nice. It was very hot, and got hotter as we approached Lexington and then Nashville. The roads we traveled on were mostly two-lane, and went through farmland and small towns. Kentucky seemed very poor to me; I remembered the summer trips my family had taken by car to southern Florida, and how poor and miserable the black farm families of South Carolina, Georgia, and northern Florida were. In Kentucky the terrain was different, but the poverty was the same. Rural poverty and urban poverty seemed like separate issues in those days and I spent time thinking of all the differences.

Our destination was Mississippi. I guess we knew why, but I can't really remember the reasoning. I do know there was discussion of the spring student sit-ins in North Carolina that had spread to South Carolina, Tennessee, Alabama,

Patricia C. Moseley was raised in and around the New York area. Educated at New York University (Washington Square College), Bennington College, and American University, she has turned her professional attention to the environment since 1985. She remains a strong believer in old-fashioned liberalism and hasn't changed her position on the issues that matter.

Georgia, Louisiana, and Florida. Perhaps someone thought Mississippi needed a boost; I don't know. Originally I thought the social and critical sustenance issues were more important than something political. I needed someone to point out Frederick Douglass's 1865 thought, "Slavery is not abolished until the black man has the ballot." And someone always did point it out.

In Nashville we learned about the nonviolence training that was taking place there. We really didn't plan to break any laws, but some black older kids came to our motel and talked to us about it. I guess they were college students from Vanderbilt and Fisk, some of whom were probably in the process of establishing SNCC. We knew a little about Ella Baker; we knew who Martin Luther King was and that he was back in Atlanta. We also knew about CORE (one of the adults in our group was close to it in some way) and that there was some feuding between the various national groups pressing for racial equality. We also knew the students were somehow at odds with them all, but it didn't seem important to us at the time. To us there was a difference between local sit-ins and a national election. We were anxious to move on to Memphis, and then south toward Jackson.

We rested a couple of days in Memphis. Hot, hot, hot. Signs of segregation everywhere, as I'd seen as a child on those vacation trips. Motels and water fountains marked White Only, and several soda fountains closed since the sit-ins. We studied how Mississippi was organized, how and where voting jurisdictions were drawn, and learned how we would just go town-to-town, farm-to-farm, house-to-house, distributing literature about how to register to vote, and why it was important to vote for JFK.

Mississippi was a poor state, with low per capita income, low average education achievement levels, high infant mortality, and high illiteracy. It shocked me. Many white folks were poor too, but it was the black families that seized our minds and our hearts. We traveled down, and occasionally off, Highway 51 (I believe that's right). There was no interstate to hide the mis-

ery. The towns had poetic names like Avalon, Midnight, Eden, Black Hawk. There were dozens of them, small Southern crossroads, surrounded by farmland being worked by black field hands. I think many were tenant farmers; perhaps there were hired hands, too. But there were small kids in those hot fields, with rags on for clothes, and blood on their hands and feet. I wept for them, and wondered what in God's name John Kennedy could do about it.

More pertinent to the mission, I wondered what we were going to do next. Surely the house-to-house plan (which quickly translated into the shack-to-shack plan) needed some thought. For one thing, no one of voting age was usually at home during the day, except the very old folks, who were either too frightened or too amazed to even talk to us most of the time. But we persisted, there being no alternative plan, and no real suggestions from either the adults in our original party, from the Richmond college kids, or from the college students we picked up in Memphis. Some of them were black and they were as confounded as we were. We did distribute literature as best we could. Some friends of mine and I were shot at by white landowners when we ventured into the fields to talk to the workers. The white townspeople called us names and we were threatened by law enforcement people everywhere we went, who said they didn't need any help from the North, and that they sure felt no obligation to protect us. Well, it's true they didn't need any help. They had preserved a way of life that served them well.

Registering to vote in Mississippi turned out to be virtually impossible for many of the people we talked to. If you couldn't read, couldn't bring yourself to confront a white person on any issue, couldn't find transportation for the journey to the appropriate location, couldn't believe that democracy had anything to do with folks like you, couldn't leave your obligations for more than an hour, couldn't quiet your wife who screamed in panic when you told her you intended to go into town to register, couldn't think about anything except the hunger in your belly and in your children's bellies—you couldn't, wouldn't, didn't have the ballot.

There were a few who did register. They were incredibly courageous or they were closer to town or they were lucky enough to have bosses who looked the other way every once in awhile. We paid more than a few of them to do it, and we gave them rides in old cars the college kids got somehow. If they voted that November, I think they voted for John Kennedy, but I'll never know. In any case, what we did was a tiny effort, a minuscule drop in the beginning of a tidal wave. I got on with my life in the North. I was of course too young to vote for Kennedy, and anyway I got caught up in going to college, discovering the world of protest and folk music. Our rebel-

lion was verbal and intellectual, pursued while we followed (from a distance!) what the SNCC students were doing. In time I came to believe that voter registration issues in the South were best addressed by blacks themselves — the students, the churches, the emerging politicians.

But in my heart I felt close to the Freedom Rides of 1961, the trips south by Pete Seeger and Bob Dylan and Theo Bikel the following year or two. Later of course, like many young white liberals, I got caught up in the Vietnam protests. Civil rights became an almost de facto issue, something you gave money to, voted appropriately on, tried to practice in everyday life. Still, it all starts somewhere, and for me it started for real on a bus in July, 1960. ❖

GIL TURNER

Carry It On

*Gil Turner, singer/
songwriter, founding
co-editor of
Broadside magazine,
and actor, was born
in 1933. He played
12 string guitar and
5 string banjo. He
wrote numerous
songs, including
"Bennie "kid" Paret,'
about a young
Puerto Rican boxer
killed in the ring,
and "Carry It On"
which became one of
the anthems of the
Civil Rights
Movement. Gil was a
member of the New
World Singers along
with Bob Cohen and
they traveled down
to Edwards, MS with
Bob Moses in 1963.
There they gave a
workshop in freedom
songs to black
teenagers. Gil
helped lay the
groundwork with
Bob Cohen for the
Mississippi Caravan
of Music during
Freedom Summer
1964. In 1966, Gil
performed with the
National
Shakespeare Festival
in San Diego and
worked with actor
Will Geer on the
"Tribute To Woody
Guthrie." Gil died in
1974 as a result of a
life-long illness.*

Carolyn Hester: The "man
by my side a walkin'" is
Gil Turner's friend, Rev.
George W. Lee, who was
killed in Belzoni, Mississippi,
1955. I don't know the
year the song was written.
Besides Gil's recording of it
in the sixties with Bob
Cohen and the New World
Singers, I recorded it in
1965 at the Town Hall
concert.

There's a man by my side a walkin'
There's a voice inside me a talkin'
There's a word needs a sayin'
Carry It On, Carry It On, Carry It On
Carry It On.

They'll tell to you their lyin' stories
Send killer dogs to bite your bodies
Though they lock us into prison
Carry It On . . .

All their lies be soon forgotten
All their dogs gonna lie there rotten
All their prison walls will crumble
Carry It On . . .

If you can't go on any longer
Take the hand held out by your brother
Every victory gonna bring another
Carry It On . . .

AF

12

BOB ZELLNER

McComb, Mississippi

If Moses wouldn't come to the mountain, then the mountain would have to go to Moses. It was clear by now, after three or four weeks, that Bob Moses was simply not going to come to Atlanta, so all of the Atlanta SNCC staff packed up and headed for south central Mississippi—Klan country.

This was to be my first SNCC meeting and my first opportunity to meet some of these legendary SNCC heroes. The meeting started quietly enough in the upper room of the rather small Elks Hall in the Burgland community—what my grandfather would have called the "nigger quarter" of McComb, Mississippi.

James Forman was presiding. I had gotten to know him a little bit in Atlanta, and I already had an inkling that he was going to be very important in my life. Moses, on the other hand, was a blank in my mind except for his immense mystique which would continue to grow ever larger with the years. Today, when I had first come face-to-face with him, I was what . . . enchanted, mesmerized, astounded? Yes. He was quiet. He was roaringly quiet. Herbert Lee had been murdered two days ago and the town and the countryside was about to explode with volcanic fury. And here he was standing stolidly, equal weight on both feet, peering intently into my eyes. His eyes were deep brown and clear white, hooded slightly behind round gold-rim glasses. He said simply, "I'm glad you came. Thanks for taking my messages." He quickly made sure everyone had a place to sit, and nodding quickly to Forman he said, "We may

not have much time so we'd better get started."

"Everybody here doesn't know each other, Forman, so will you introduce everybody?"

Forman looked pointedly at me, which made me suddenly feel very white, and said, "Yeah, I see what you mean." Then he began the introductions. "Everybody here knows Chuck McDew, our 'esteemed chairman,' Charles Jones—direct action, Reggie Robinson—voter registration . . ." Forman went around the room in this fashion, and when he had gone all the way around, he looked down at me and said, "And this guy is Robert Zellner and he's really all right. His accent is a little on the peckerwood side, but it's okay because he is supposed to represent us on white campuses . . . hopefully."

"I suggested," Forman continued, "that he come to the staff meeting because if he's going to interpret what we are doing, then he needs to know what we are doing. Anyway, he's not so bad after you get to know him a little. I've already taped him for an hour or so, and I better tell you right now that his daddy was a Klansman . . . but I don't think he is." Forman's hand shot out, "Only kidding, of course," he said, and grinned at me.

"Anyway," Forman sighed, "back to the matter at hand. Moses, what's the situation?"

Moses gave a quick rundown. Herbert Lee was shot to death the day before yesterday by E. H. Hurst, a white Mississippi state legislator from Amite County. Hurst, Lee's next-door neighbor, had followed Lee to the cotton gin in Liberty. After parking behind Lee, Hurst got out of his

Bob Zellner, a white Alabamian, whose father, a methodist minister, was a klansman and whose mother was a school teacher, attended Huntingdon College in Montgomery, Alabama. While in college, Zellner met Martin Luther King, Jr., Ralph Abernathy and Rosa Parks who influenced him to join the Student Nonviolent Coordinating Committee (SNCC). The first white field secretary for SNCC, Zellner was arrested more than 25 times and was charged with everything from vagrancy to criminal anarchy. Today, Bob is completing a Ph.D. in Southern History at Tulane University, while conducting a national speaking tour on the Civil Rights Movement. A portion of his memoirs are being used in a forthcoming movie based on the early days of the Mississippi Civil Rights Movement.

pickup truck, walked up to Lee's truck and threatened him with a gun, telling Lee, "Get out of that pickup, nigger."

Lee said he wouldn't get out of the truck until Hurst put the gun away. Hurst refused to leave or put the gun away, so Lee got out of his truck on the opposite side to leave. Hurst walked around the front of Lee's truck and shot him one time in the head.

The body lay in the dust at the cotton gin for over three hours while a quickly-assembled coroner's jury found no cause of action against Hurst. Two black witnesses to the murder were forced to testify that Lee attacked Hurst with a tire iron.

After Moses convinced them to tell the true story to the FBI and John Doar of the Justice Department, the information was passed to the local police, and the sheriff broke the jaw of one of the witnesses. The other witness, Louis Allen, was shotgunned to death as he locked his front gate on his way out of the state. That was more or less the report from the voter registration wing of the SNCC staff.

McDew stood to make the report of the direct action project in the absence of Marion Barry, the project leader. "Hollis, Curtis, Brenda Travis and the others have just been released from over a month in jail for trying to use the white waiting room at the Trailways Bus Station in McComb," McDew reported matter-of-factly.

"Brenda," he continued, "returned to school yesterday and was expelled by the principal. Hollis Watkins and Curtis Hayes are going over there today with her to try to get her reinstated. If that Tom principal don't let her back in, the shit is definitely going to strike the rotating blade, and the kids are going to walk out on that handkerchief head."

I thought later how much like a movie it was when Chuck suddenly stopped talking, and everyone in the room held their breath because of an eerie sound someone had picked up. I didn't know what it was at first because I was not that familiar with the Civil Rights Anthem, but soon the words were unmistakable—I was listening to

young voices lustily singing "We Shall Overcome."

The singing got louder and someone in the room said quietly, "Holy Jesus!" Then the students were noisily tramping up the stairs. Without hesitating a moment, the students flooded into the small meeting room and, it seems in my memory, they immediately sprawled on the floor; poster boards and Magic Markers materialized from somewhere and they started making picket signs.

The plan, as near as I could make it out, was to march from McComb to Magnolia, the county seat, to protest the murder of Herbert Lee and the expulsion of Brenda Travis—six miles through hostile countryside!

Actually, I was fairly calm, considering the circumstances. I didn't realize at first that this march would be the first of its kind in the state of Mississippi since the days of Reconstruction a hundred years before. I was only minimally involved. After all, my job was to visit white campuses, and if I got mixed up in something like this march it would be highly unlikely that I would ever be able to set foot on a single white Southern campus.

Besides, I told myself, I can't go on this demonstration because my father, a Methodist preacher in Alabama, will lose his church and my mother will lose her teaching job. Also, I said to myself, I can't go (not that anyone's asking me, of course) because I'll be the only white person in the march and that might cause more violence than usual. (*More violence than usual*, I thought to myself. *How much violence is usual in these cases?*)

During this long colloquy with myself, the students finished their signs and began filing down the steps to form a line of march outside. This caused me to start talking to myself again. *I'm lucky*, I thought to myself, *I know what I'm going to do—or in this case, what I'm not going to do. I'm definitely not going to go on that march.*

For a fleeting moment I wondered how the other SNCC people decided who was going to go and who was going to stay behind to mind the store. Suddenly it hit me, "What the hell am I talking about . . . what about these kids . . . what's going to happen to them . . . and what about their parents . . . what about their jobs? This is Mississippi, for Christ's sake . . . in 1961 . . . these kids are going to be massacred."

About half the kids and some of the SNCC staff people had filed out when I slipped into the line and headed down the stairs. Nobody said anything to me, and I learned later that this was the SNCC way. Nobody ever suggested that such and such a person go on any particular action. Each person made up his mind each time. There were no orders.

Leaving the gloom of the Elks Hall, I was suddenly blinded by the sun of a glorious, brilliant October day. The date was October the fourth, 1961, and the black people of the Burgland community, McComb, Mississippi, were sky high. Smiling, laughing black faces lined the unpaved streets or hung over their front fences and whooped with joy to see this spectacle in deepest, darkest Mississippi. There was banter between the townspeople and the young marchers. We were the old guys, Forman, McDew, Moses, and I. I was all of twenty-one, Forman and maybe Moses a little older.

As we approached the railroad tracks, things began to get quieter until you could hear only the shuffle of feet on dusty gravel. Even the weather, it seemed, began to change as we crossed from "nigger town" to the sidewalks of white McComb. The sky seemed darker and the footfalls were quieter until this nervous quiet was shattered by a shout, "Zellner, I'll kill you . . . you dirty bastard. I'll kill you!"

At first I thought I was hearing things. Nobody here knew me. I'd never been to Mississippi before and even these kids, I was sure, didn't know my name. They knew I was one ever more standout eyesore of a white man in that all-black march, but they didn't know my name.

I kept looking for the source of the scream— "Zellner, I'll kill you." The scream seemed to get louder and louder until I finally located a red-faced, bald-headed white man leaning halfway out of a pickup truck. "Doc," I thought, "good ole

Doc from Huntingdon College—captain of the basketball team—my nemesis from school, the man who hated me most, the Klansman who always talked like my first two names were 'nigger lover,' as in 'nigger lover Bob Zellner.'"

"What luck," I thought, "I never knew where the son-of-a-bitch lived, and now by the greatest good luck, I've found out."

As I stared dumbfounded at Doc, it occurred to me that the whole town, maybe even the whole state, was rapidly mobilizing to annihilate us. Chains and pipes were materializing from nowhere. A speeding car cracked through our line trying to run someone down. The students would scatter in unison like a school of fish in the presence of a shark, then immediately come back together when the clear and present danger was passed.

One motorist ran his car into a telephone pole trying to hit some students, then leaped out with a pipe wrench, swinging it wildly over his head like a club. Our people were beginning to be hit.

When the line approached the City Hall, it was clear that our intention to pause briefly and then proceed to Magnolia was not going to work. Not only was it too late in the day to risk the open country, but our progress was blocked by a huge mob of white people which had formed in the street just beyond the City Hall.

What happened now, I was to learn later, was typical of SNCC—when in doubt, pray. Hollis Watkins, whom I could see from my place in line, stood up on the stoop of the City Hall, raised his left hand, bowed his head, and began to pray. I remembered that he was one of the ones who had just gotten out of jail. In a quavery voice Hollis said, "O Lord . . ." Just then a beefy, red-faced policeman reached for him and said loudly, "You're under arrest!" Hollis raised both hands over his head and shouted regretfully (I thought) "O Lord!" It was as if he were saying, "O Lord, here we go again ... How much jail time do I get this time?"

It wasn't actually very funny at the moment, but every time I tell this story I think of the incident with great merriment. Humor and religion—sometimes I don't know which sustained us the most.

While this was going on with Hollis, then with each marcher as he or she attempted to lead the group in prayer, a small mob of white men was beginning to gather around me. Without seeing him, I could sense that my old friend Doc was in this group somewhere. They'd reach over and shove me or lightly poke at me and then look at the police, who were by now standing around waiting their turn to arrest a praying marcher. Each time a member of this small mob would hit me, the cops would wink or look away, and their body language said very clearly, "He's fair game. Get him and get him good."

Later, when I reconstructed these events in my mind, I became convinced that the police could easily have stopped the violence at this point had they chosen to do so. I was standing quietly, determined not to show them any fear. My training in martial arts was coming in handy now because I was able, without showing much effort, to minimize the effects of these blows. I could do this by imperceptibly moving at the very last second, slipping a punch here, rolling with a punch there. At this point I had not even raised my arms to cushion the blows.

As the licks came faster and heavier now I became aware that Bob Moses and Chuck McDew had quietly moved to my side to absorb some of these punches. They were both stocky and solidly built and they seemed to have absolutely no fear. I would remember this moment as the time of bonding—a brotherly male bonding as fierce, I suppose, as any welded in war. When these two—one a dark, superbly trained and conditioned football player, the other (Moses) light skinned, with the raw power of a boxer—came to my aid, I experienced a wild moment of exhilarating insanity. "We can," I thought, "whip all these motherfuckers." Then, with some disappointment, I remembered we were supposed to be nonviolent. This nonviolence was certainly new to me because I was Southern born and bred and a pretty fair street fighter, as well as being

trained in boxing, wrestling, and fencing. The Zellner boys had had to fight their way into every little Southern town their Methodist preacher dad had ever been assigned to.

That moment with me, Moses, and McDew against the mob was fleeting, however. I was just in the throes of a most pleasant feeling of security, serenity, and absolute joy to find such brave stalwarts for companions when the cops came over and grabbed the two of them. To this day I remember the sound of the billyclubs and blackjacks the cops used as they thudded into Moses's and McDew's heads. I remember thinking, "How can one human do this to another human being—especially with everyone watching?" It was actually more ominous that they pounded these heads with all their strength, in the open. I thought, "If they act like this in public, what will they do to a person in their jail?"

At this point I became aware of a strange feeling of detachment. I was being beaten while I watched my new-found friends being brutally gashed and bloodied, and yet I felt at peace. I had a sense of standing above myself—of actually observing myself being harried by a small knot of men at the edge of a much larger mob in the street. My senses seemed (and now I am convinced they were) heightened to super proportions.

While Moses and McDew were being dragged off, I watched in grim fascination as the mob armed itself. They already had pipes and bats and wrenches, and now they were methodically tearing down a brick wall in order to fill their hands with missiles. I heard their screams now. The large mob—the one in the middle of the street—was pleading with the small mob around me, about twelve or fifteen men, to drag me out into the middle of the street. "Bring him here," they screamed. "We'll kill him. Bring him here." Their banshee screaming sounded like grief—a moan, then a shrill trilling like you hear sometimes in Middle Eastern countries during a time of mourning.

Then dutifully my little mob began to pick me up and move me bodily toward the street. Up to that point I had been rather passive. I still carried the Bible someone had given me. It seemed hours ago that someone had quickly hissed, "Hold this . . . I've got to go call the press." Suddenly a thought popped into my head. I heard very clearly in my father's preaching voice, "God helps those who help themselves." "Yes," I thought, "if they take me into that street there is no force on this earth that can save me. They will definitely kill me."

With this thought in mind I very deliberately placed the Bible on the steps and with both hands took hold of the railing pipe that ran down the center of the City Hall steps. It occurred to me that this railing was placed there to help old men and ladies ascend and descend the three tiers of steps to the City Hall. "I'll try to ascend," I thought quixotically.

Then it became a contest. I was showing resistance, and when I showed this first bit of resistance the mob, which I thought could not get any louder or more frenzied, exploded. My mind returned very rationally to the contest at hand. If I can hold on here, I have a chance to survive—if they pull me loose, I die. I don't know what held them back, but the large mob in the street continued to rely on the small group of men around me. "This is the vanguard," I thought. "These are the militant Klansmen." Their mettle was being tried now, so they set about with grim determination to detach me from my railing.

Several of them grabbed my belt while others took hold of my legs, stretching me out horizontally from the pipe which I clutched in both hands. There were, I estimated, two or three men holding each of my legs. Others attempted to pry my fingers loose from the somewhat rusty pipe. I was glad it was rusty because, I reasoned, it would improve my grip by providing friction. I calmly noted that my strength was incredible. How could this many men not pull me loose instantly? I was actually in pretty fair condition going into this fight, having just come off years of ballet dancing with the Montgomery Civic Ballet, exhibition diving, and the aforementioned boxing, wrestling, and fencing. "So," I thought, "this is a good contest. I certainly have good motivation, at any rate."

It didn't seem odd to me at the time that I would be having these rather detached, meandering thoughts, all the while trying to dodge the blows aimed at my hands now by a lead-filled pipe and the odd baseball bat and wrench. Things were happening fast, but my thinking and my physical actions seemed to happen even faster.

With lightning speed I would watch the pipe or the wrench descend toward my hands, and then at the last possible millisecond I'd release the grip of the endangered hand and grab the pipe in a different place. This would give me also a dry place on the pipe, free of blood, which would hopefully enable me to move further up the steps.

My mind seemed to be keeping up with many things at one time. The men pulling on my body fell into a rhythm. They'd pull hard and then let up momentarily to gather for another pull. When they leaned back, I'd move up the pipe and hold on for their next pull. It kept coming into my mind, "This is a great contest, and I think I'm winning."

This moment of hubris was shortlived, however, as one man behind me became suddenly more hysterical and went for my eyes. I felt particularly vulnerable there because my hands were fully occupied holding onto the pipe. This man slipped his hands over my head from behind and began probing into my eyes with his fingers. He seemed to have a purpose in mind beyond just putting his fingers into my eye sockets, and then I realized he was trying to get hold of my eyeball. He'd work the eyeball nearly out of the socket until it was on the surface of my cheek. Then he tried to grip it between his thumb and forefinger. This quickly developed into a contest inside a contest, with me thinking, "Will he really be able to get a grip on my eyeball?" My sociology training came into play at this point as I thought, "This is what they mean when they say 'eye gouging'— this is mayhem." Once again I decided to help myself if I could, without letting go of the rail. I'd wait until he just about got the eye where he wanted it, between his thumb and finger, and then I'd jerk my head in such a way to make the eye slip between his fingers and spring back into the socket. I remember thinking what an odd sound the eye makes when it hits the bottom of the eye socket—thunk! Then he'd start in again working the eye back out onto my cheekbone.

The hysteria of the men around me seemed to reach a peak, and they all started climbing on top of me. I supposed they reasoned that if they could not pull me loose from that hand rail then they could weigh me down enough to break me loose. So they played, "How many grown men can we pile on top of Zellner?" While they were piling on I realized I had reached the top of the flight. The last thing I remember was that my head was sticking out of the pile and resting on the top step. I literally could not move. I could do nothing to stop the big brown boot that crashed into my head again and again. Just before I passed out I thought, "So this is the way I die—like a football being kicked in a scrimmage."

The next thing I was aware of was a man's face in my face saying over and over again, "I oughtta let them kill you. I oughtta let them take you." Even before I realized I was in the police chief's office, I said in my calmest voice with as much authority as I could muster, "I'd like to make a phone call." There was a whoop of laughter but I recall one voice that said, "For goodness sake, let the man make a telephone call—nobody knows where he's at." When the man I later learned was the police chief, George Guy, said once again, "I oughtta let them take you," I noticed for the first time that the mob had filled the corridors of City Hall. The open door to the office was filled with rough-looking characters holding every known weapon. Both sides of the door were lined, it seemed, from top to bottom with squeezed red faces peering at me. One great joker kept hollering, "You think I can hit him between the eyes from here with this here wrench?" Then he'd shake his Stilson wrench at me and grin like he was a great friend of mine.

When my eyes cleared up a little I repeated that I'd like to make a call. We'd been trained to insist on a call and to never leave a jail willingly without first letting someone know where we were and where we were going. When I said that, the

chief said, "Why, you're not under arrest. You're free to go. Go on, get out of here." He motioned toward the door and the crowd in the door parted, leaving only the sweating faces stacked along the door jam.

I could tell the terror was about to begin again, and I didn't want to show fear, so I said rather loudly, "I do not choose to leave, and I insist on making a phone call."

"You insist, do you?" the chief said in a rage. He grabbed me by what was left of my shirt front and hurled me toward the door.

"Get out of my office, you dirty nigger-loving son-of-a-bitch. I only brought you in here 'cause you looked like a good nigger lover, a Goddamned dead nigger lover."

He shoved me into the hallway and I was swept down the hall and out the front door. I was thrown unceremoniously into a beat-up-looking car that quickly filled up with men from the mob. Other cars and some pickups roared to a start as if everybody was going to drive the Indianapolis 500. Off we went into the countryside.

My eye was really hurting now, but I immediately asked where we were going. Someone in the car said, "If you're lucky you might make it to the jail in Magnolia." I had never been to Magnolia and had no idea where it was until we got to the edge of town and a sign pointing to the left said, "Magnolia, 6 miles." The car I was in and the long caravan of pickups sped past the sign. Instead of turning left toward Magnolia we continued straight out into the country.

It was then that I became convinced I would not survive the day. Once again now, just like during the beating, a sense of peace descended on me and I marveled at the contradiction: when it seemed there was a chance I'd survive I'd become frantic and nervous, with an overpowering sense of dread. When it looked certain that I would die, I would become calm.

These people had been trying to kill me, it seemed, all afternoon, and now there didn't seem to be anything to stop them. At this point, however, I sensed some indecision on their part. Before, it was "Just let me at him—I'll rip him limb-from-limb." Now they didn't seem to know exactly what to do.

Somebody said, "Everybody saw us leave town with him."

"Yeah," someone else said, "but ain't nobody goin' to do nothing to us for doin' anything to him."

"That's true," another said, "but we can get some of the boys from Amite County to take him off our hands. We'll say we put up a fight, but they got him away from us anyway."

Another man from the front seat turned around and said with some glee, "Yeah, we can even black one another's eyes."

Every time I'd try to say something they'd say, "Shut up, nigger lover." A man who looked like my Uncle Harvey called me a nigger loving motherfucking Jew communist queer Goddamn Yankee from New York City. That was too much for me. "Look, friend," I said, "five out of six is not bad, but I'm not a Goddamn Yankee. I'm from further south than you are. I'm from East Brewton, Alabama."

That seemed to really piss them off, but it did get their attention. I figured that they must know that I wasn't a Yankee because Doc had been in the mob before and he must know these yahoos. "He's probably back there in one of those pickups," I thought.

I don't know why it seemed so important to me for them to know I wasn't a Yankee. Maybe it was because I was still convinced they intended to kill me. So I took the opportunity to look each of them in the eye and ask, "Do you think you are capable of killing me by yourself, or do you have to do it in a bunch like a coward?" This made them even madder, but I was certain they were going to kill me anyway, and for some reason I wanted them to think of me later as not being afraid.

I was getting more and more Southern as I went along, so I speculated out loud that there was not a man among them that could whip me in a fair fight.

They stopped the car then, and after removing some rails at a cattle gap proceeded to the

back of a cow pasture near some trees. Stopping under a field pine, a man from another vehicle, a rickety old flatbed wood truck, ostentatiously removed a rope with an elaborately tied hangman's knot. For the second or third time that day I heard myself saying under my breath, "These people are overreacting. They've got to be overreacting. This is, after all, for Christ's sake, my first demonstration."

For many years as I've told this story, I've left out the part about the hangman's rope because it sounded too fantastic even for me—the one who saw it. It is only now that I want to tell the whole story. (My resolve in this was recently boosted while talking to Hollis Watkins, a participant in that day's events. He described being confronted, on the same day, in McComb with white men carrying a hangman's noose. The hangman's noose Hollis described to me was decorated with a single red ribbon tied in a bow, just below the knot. When Hollis described the hangman's rope he saw, I realized for the first time that I probably hadn't imagined the rope they threatened me with that day.)

When they started arguing among themselves, I thought I had a chance. The few men and vehicles around me in the woods were outnumbered by the cars and pickups just beyond the ridge of the field back up on the road. I doubt if I'll ever know the reason, but after a number of urgent conversations on the squawking CB's (every pickup truck, it seemed, was equipped with gun racks and a long citizens-band radio whip antenna), they loaded me back into one of the pickups and off we went again.

This time they did take me to the jail in Magnolia, a low squat little brick building standing out in a yard under a huge live oak tree. It didn't look big enough to be a jail, but then it occurred to me I had never been in a jail before. Just because it looked like a jail you'd have in a photographer's studio to take joke pictures of Cousin Jane and Uncle Henry in prison stripes didn't necessarily mean it wasn't a jail. Anyway, it would have to do because it was the only one offered to me.

I remember feeling a great surge of relief when I heard the heavy door clang shut and the lock snap into place. I was in jail for the first time in my life, but I felt much safer than being out on the street.

By the time the caravan reached the jail, I realized that most of the entourage had quietly slipped away. I remember feeling some ambivalence toward the uniformed police who came forward to escort me to the cell. I wondered, "Are they protectors or not? ... Is this part of an elaborate charade still leading to my undoing?"

I didn't have long to collect myself and my thoughts in my cell before another uniform came to take me out. I had been trying to find a shiny surface to use as a mirror so I could assess the damage to my face and my body. The guard caused me to jump when he shouted, "Okay, let's go!" I really didn't want to leave that cell. My sense of time was totally screwed up. I didn't know if I had been in there ten minutes or two hours. The guard opened a door to the outside and the daylight streamed in. I immediately went limp and fell to the floor. I did not intend to leave that building without maximum resistance—no matter how nonviolent I was supposed to be.

The uniformed guard suddenly laughed and said, "It's all right. The Feds want to talk to you." Disbelief, fear, anger, relief—everything flooded over me at once, and I realized my system was finally overloaded. I felt like a package, highly prized and at the same time despised as something unclean. I felt that for hours since those moments on the City Hall steps I had simply been carried along by the tide, tossed here and there willy nilly wherever the force would take me. Now I finally put my foot down. "No," I shouted with determination, "I will not leave this building. I have not been allowed a phone call to a lawyer. If it is the FBI, as you say, then they can come here to me."

"Okay," the guard said with a grin and

stepped out the door. In a conversational tone of voice he said to someone outside, "Here he is, but you'll have to come get him."

At that, four crisply dressed look-alike white men with white shirts and ties peered in at me on the floor and said pleasantly, "We need the sun so we can take pictures."

They lined me up against the outside wall of the jail and asked me to face the low sun in the west. When they began taking pictures of my wounds, I stood there rather numbed and thought to myself, "All this because I had the audacity to march with some Mississippi black young people."

The sheriff and assorted deputies and a few remnants of the mob were standing a short distance away when one of the FBI agents sidled up to me and whispered, "It was pretty rough out there on the City Hall steps, wasn't it?"

"Yes," I said, "it was nip and tuck there for a while."

"Well," said the agent, "we didn't want you to think you were all alone out there—we got it all down—we took real good notes—we wrote it all down."

Years later when the FBI refrain "We can't protect. We can only investigate" had become a grim joke phrase with us in SNCC, I thought back on that afternoon and came to the conclusion that there were many times the cops could have stopped violence in its tracks with very little effort. The mob in McComb had constantly looked to the police for approval of their violence. The cops gave it, and apparently so did the federal officers.

When that little FBI agent whispered in my ear, I learned a valuable lesson—never depend on the federal government, especially never count on an agency headed by J. Edgar Hoover. I didn't really want to talk to them after that. I'd take my chances with my Southern haters—I knew where they stood. ❖

MARK LANE

A Southern Journey

The ride through the South was arranged by Rev. Callender. The Most Reverend Eugene St. Clair Callender arrived in central Harlem during the 1950s. There he established the less than elegantly, though certainly aptly named, Mid Harlem Community Parish. I soon became the attorney for his oppressed parishioners; we soon became fast friends, bridge partners and, Batman and Robin-like, together we sought out and confronted evil and discrimination wherever it lurked. We were busy; it was everywhere. One nearby church memorialized the continuing nature of the problem with a permanent notice on its bulletin board that read—Protest Meeting Every Thursday Night.

The national Civil Rights Movement was beginning to awaken. Like a sleeping lion it stretched, looked about and gave a mighty yawn-like roar. Pessimists or optimists, depending upon the observer's political perspective, differed as to its potential. Some heard and saw a sleeping beast that could never be roused. Others knew that there was a new force in the land and that the status quo was about to become an ancient relic.

Among the first to soldier forth in the untested bogs of Southern racism in a new era was the first Freedom Rider, Jim Peck. That slight, self-effacing, quiet man was beaten almost to death by a mob in a Southern town as he sought to exercise his right to travel in our land.

Two near miracles occurred almost simultaneously; another soon thereafter. That Jim

survived the cruel and prolonged attack and that the mental pre-Neanderthals, clubs in hand, had mastered prehensile skills were both astonishing.

From this attempted murder a movement was created reflecting a more successful effort made some two thousand years earlier.

The perilous trail that Jim had pioneered became a sacred path with the Holy Grail located somewhere south of Jackson, Mississippi.

Young people of principle, inspired by Jim Peck, embarked upon a trip through their country, often by bus. Black and white, together they journeyed to demonstrate that democracy might live in a multi-racial America. Always threatened and taunted, sometimes struck and wounded, invariably refused service by restaurants and lunch counters at every stop, they were each arrested as they reached the capitol of Mississippi.

A troubled nation responded. These few men and women were named the Freedom Riders and the prayers of millions rode with each of them as they embarked upon their dangerous mission.

In Harlem, Gene Callender had left the Mid Harlem Community Parish to be installed as the minister at the prestigious and powerful Church of the Master, upon the retirement of its famous leader, the Reverend James Robinson. That church, located on the fringes of Harlem, drew its parishioners not from the down and out but rather from the up and in. Gene often reminded them in his sermons about their responsibility to others.

Mark Lane is an author, lawyer, teacher, lecturer and filmmaker. He represented the American Indian Movement at the historic Wounded Knee trial, and tried numerous cases establishing the rights of minorities to serve on juries and grand juries in New York State and to utilize public facilities in Jackson, Mississippi. Mark served in the New York Legislature and was the only public official in the U.S. ever arrested as a Freedom Rider in the early 1960s. He is the author of many books and plays.

Saturday night, as Gene and I played in a bridge tournament, we had serious but non-specific discussions about the Freedom Riders. I sipped some Scotch as I saluted their courage. Casually my friend asked if I had ever considered joining their ranks. I was then a member of the New York state legislature and no public official had ever been arrested as a Freedom Rider. I said that in principle I had no objection to the concept, but that I could hardly go alone since the point was to illustrate the right of African Americans—I am sure that I then said "Negroes"—to travel together with white Americans from state to state.

Gene said, in a most disingenuous tone, one an accomplished psychiatric-social worker might refer to as non-threatening, "How about Percy?" He was referring to Percy Sutton, an elegant and accomplished black attorney who had become the president of the New York chapter of the NAACP and who later was to be elected Borough President of Manhattan. "Percy would be a wonderful companion," I offered.

Gene nodded, played a card, collected the cards, and smiled broadly. At the time I thought that he was pleased that he had taken a trick, not played one. When the evening ended, Gene asked me to be at his church the next morning. I agreed.

That Sunday morning was bright and brisk. Gene preached with emotion and skill to a full house. Then he paused, looked about at the audience and said he had an important announcement to make.

"Two dear friends of our church," he said, "have agreed to embark upon a historic mission for our nation." His deep, melodious voice took on added timbre. "This morning we acknowledge and honor our colleagues, Mark Lane—please stand Mark—and Percy Sutton—you too Percy—as they travel through the Southern states of our nation as Freedom Riders, to witness, for all of us, our commitment to freedom and equality. May God speed your way and keep you safe, dear brother Percy and dear brother Mark."

Before brother Mark could even catch his breath, to say nothing of uttering a demurrer based upon a defense grounded in a mistake in fact, the parishioners were participating in a blessed offering to cover the expenses anticipated for our travel. Several hundred dollars were raised and as they were pressed into Percy's hands and mine we began the noble task of comparing calendars and the ignoble thought of revenge to be exacted should we ever return from Mississippi and see our friend Gene again.

A few days later, the parishioners' impassioned praise still echoing in our minds, Percy Sutton and I arrived at Newark Airport. I had embarked from LaGuardia Airport and Idelwild Airport, later renamed JFK after the assassination of President Kennedy, on numerous occasions. This was my first flight originating in New Jersey. For years afterward, whenever I drove past that airport I thought of the flight to Atlanta, the gateway to a bus trip through Georgia and Alabama. I thought also of the fear hovering at the edges of my consciousness.

The point was to be together. A non-segregated taxi ride from the Atlanta airport was not all that difficult to arrange. Non-segregated accommodations in Atlanta were a different matter, a horse of another color one might have said.

Percy said he had the solution. He gave an address to the driver and soon we arrived at the all black YMCA in the middle of black Atlanta. As we walked up the steps, Percy leading the way, a hundred eyes focused upon me. I was, I felt certain, the first white person to enter that ancient building since it had been constructed.

We each requested a small single room. The clerk behind the scarred desk hesitated, began to warn me that I must have made some awful mistake and then finally gave me a key. I reached for my luggage but Percy, no doubt intoxicated by the moment, grabbed at it first, stating in a voice loud enough for all those in the lobby staring at me to hear "Dat's all right, Mista Mark, I take it fo' you." The spectators were puzzled but oddly reassured. Mista Mark had brought his Negro retainer with him.

Percy could not stop laughing for days. "You

should have seen your expression," he often began to say before collapsing into convulsions of howling roars and cackles.

My list, should we return from Jackson, had grown from one to two.

The bus trip to Montgomery, Alabama, was less amusing. Our presence had been anticipated and large throngs, not to say mobs, of white men swirled about as the bus pulled into a station in a small town. I had worked closely with Robert Kennedy during JFK's presidential campaign. Bobby had been named attorney general before Percy and I embarked upon our trip. I had called the attorney general to inform him of our proposed journey, and I had also requested protection from illegal acts that might be committed against us, including attacks from civilians and arrest by those acting under color of state law. His noncommittal reply, "We'll look into it," was less than reassuring.

This exchange had been publicized and therefore news of our visit had preceded us.

Several large and angry men, responding to the shouts from the crowd — "There they are," and "That's them, the nigger and the nigger-lover" — began to board the bus.

I had supported in spirit Dr. King's and Jim Peck's nonviolent philosophy. Now my commitment to it was to be tested. I grabbed my attaché case, prepared to strike the first would-be assailant with all my force as I looked across the aisle to Percy. He was equally positioned. We agreed, in a word or two, that we would inflict the most grievous bodily harm possible as a matter of self-defense.

The men who had been moving in single file in the narrow aisle toward us stopped as the one in front hesitated. Percy and I were each a bit over six feet, well-built, young, armed in a fashion and clearly determined. There was a discussion. Their name-calling and other indicia of bravado increased in volume and intensity as the potential assailants withdrew from the bus.

At the next stop, a larger town, reporters and photographers were present as well as the unruly protesters. Percy and I left the bus,

pushed through the crowd, entered the luncheonette and sat down at the counter. The waitress and waiter sought to give the impression that they did not know we were there but fascinated by our presence, they continued to sneak looks in our direction. During one of those indiscreet moments I caught the waitress's eye. "May we each have a cup of coffee, please," I asked.

She appeared amazed. I actually could speak. "Can't. He's a nigger and you're with him," was her entire explanation. It was clear enough. Flash bulbs exploded, photographers jostled each other to get that perfect shot. My request for two glasses of water was rejected with a shrug. I explained that facilities that serve interstate transportation are precluded from practicing racial discrimination. Passengers were boarding the bus and my arguments were not sufficiently persuasive. Percy and I rushed back to the bus through the disgruntled and muttering crowd. We settled in for the next part of the journey.

I looked at him. He seemed poised, elegantly dressed as usual, professional and calm. He had been born in the South. He knew its potential for violence far better than I did. Yet he was the personification of grace under fire, which in my mind, then and now, is the ultimate definition of courage.

At that moment I wondered if I had made the right decision, if the risks were justified by the possible benefits. Of one thing, I was certain. I could not have been more fortunate in the choice of a companion for the trip down freedom road.

We finally reached Montgomery many stops later without further incident and without a cup of coffee. We had tried to avoid the former; our efforts to secure the latter were universally rebuffed, often in anger, once in a while with regret, and from that small sign we took enormous encouragement.

In the Cradle of the Confederacy we were met by a number of young black lawyers. We ate with them; they offered their homes to us and together we spoke of a new South that might one day result from the efforts being made by so many. They expressed their gratitude to me, but I knew that my brief well-publicized trip through the South added but a drop to the mighty river of righteousness which Dr. King said would one day flow.

I knew that the real work for radical change was being done by those who lived there, the women and men, black and white, who engaged in voter registration drives, who fought each moment of racism which marked each day of their lives, who went to jail, walked to work, boycotted stores and lived at risk of imprisonment, poverty, and even loss of life. If our trip could help bring further attention to their struggle, the effort was sound. My doubts were forever resolved in the hours I spent in Montgomery with my new friends.

In the early hours of the morning, it was determined that while those who had preceded us were arrested at the Jackson bus station no one had tested the police reaction to a flight to that city. "Target the airport," they said, "it will provide a new experience." It was easy to convince me. The bus trip held no special charm for me. We might even get a drink on the plane and once airborne, when we looked out the window it seemed unlikely that we would be confronted by a mob made up of club-wielding, red-faced, angry men.

We landed in Jackson and entered the almost vacant, modern, relatively little airport building.

A few police officers and their chief stood off to one side silently observing us. Percy said he had to utilize the facilities. We found the white men's room. Percy preceded me. The officers moved slowly toward us. I was in a quandary. If I did not enter the rest room, Percy might be arrested alone for violating some ancient sacred Mississippi statute based upon the purity of white-sponsored urination. If I did enter, I might be arrested for some other crime existent at that time only in the minds of the local police. I opened the door and said, "Percy, for God's sake, let's get out of here. Do you want us to get busted

for disorderly conduct in a bathroom?"

Together we left the now forever-sullied facility and sat down in the waiting room. The chief of police walked up to us. He addressed only me.

"Mr. Lane, we have been expecting you." He paused. "You and this here—man—well, you cannot sit here together."

"Why is that?" I inquired.

"You could incite a riot!" he exclaimed.

I looked about. One woman, perhaps sixty years old, was sitting a few rows from us. She was concentrating on her knitting. She was, with the exception of the two future criminals and the police, the only other person present.

"Chief," I said, "I'm sure you can handle her if she gets out of line."

"I hate to do this, Mr. Lane," the Chief said, "but you and—well—your friend—you both are under arrest."

Percy had remained silent as he observed our little ritual exchange. He was precluded from it by reason of birth. I looked at him filled with respect. He was removed, perhaps above the small talk. He had come home to the South. He had made his silent witness.

The Chief sat in the front passenger seat, Percy and I in the back seat.

"Are you really a member of the legislature in New York?" he asked. I said that I was.

"You ever see our state capitol?"

I said I had not.

"Drive past the capitol," the Chief instructed the driver.

It was a magnificent building; I said so.

"Take 'em past the old capitol. It's not much out of the way," he said.

The old capitol building was charming; I said so.

I felt odd about our conversation. It was not that I had a cheerful, almost friendly, series of exchanges with the enemy; as an attorney that was not unprecedented. It was that Percy was being excluded.

"You know, Chief," I began, "we have been

together for several days. That is how we've been making our point."

"So I heard, Mr. Lane," he replied.

"On the bus for days, in the Negro YMCA, in homes in Montgomery, on the plane ride here, and even in your waiting room at the airport," I said.

"Negro YMCA?" he asked incredulously.

"Yes. But we never could figure out one problem."

"What's that?" said the Chief.

"How we could get an integrated ride from the airport to the center of Jackson. Chief, we both want to thank you for that," I said.

The Chief, who had been turned around in his seat—this was before the advent of seat belts in automobiles—slowly looked forward, never addressed another word to me, and was in fact silent until we reached the city jail except to say to the driver, "Let's go, put on some speed."

We were charged with disorderly conduct, placed in separate jail cells for some time, and ultimately released on bail.

Later in New York City, a meeting attended by more than one hundred Freedom Riders was convened by the Congress of Racial Equality (CORE), the organization led by James Farmer, which had largely financed and organized the campaign.

Percy and I were among the very few who had covered their own expenses or had been given traveling funds privately.

CORE was broke, we were all told. It had exhausted all of its funds in the effort. Therefore, since the State of Mississippi had set one day for us all to return to face trial, it had been determined by the CORE leadership that "when we are down there we will abide by all local ordinances."

When a young student asked what that meant exactly, he was told, "In the courthouse Negroes use the 'colored' restrooms and drink from the 'colored' fountains, while whites will use the 'white only' facilities."

Percy and I were less than pleased and we said so. We had not embarked upon that long and challenging journey to capitulate in the end to degrading Southern customs.

The CORE leaders argued that further challenges meant further arrests, higher bail, more return trips to court, all of which cost money, and there was none left for the continued struggle.

Percy said that he and I would return to Jackson, would violate indecent laws, and would remain in prison if need be until the Movement could afford to continue the effort or until the walls of racism came tumbling down.

The two of us returned as the advance army to the scene of battle. A friend met us at the airport and drove us to the courthouse. Before we entered the building we paused, shook hands, and I said, "It could be a long time."

Percy said, "I know it. Do we have a choice?" It was not a question.

We entered the courthouse together. Every "colored only" and "white only" sign had been removed by the authorities. In their place were newly stenciled cardboard plaques that read, "Men's Room, Defendants," and "Ladies' Room, Defendants." The State of Mississippi, too, was running out of funds and could no longer afford the confrontation. Our case was called. The charges were dismissed.

On the way home I said, "The signs were temporary. They'll be down soon."

Percy answered, "Yes. The cardboard signs will go now—but one day soon all the other signs will disappear also."

About two decades later, after I gave a lecture about the assassination of John F. Kennedy at a college in a small town in Alabama, I asked one of the students to drive me to the bus station. The same luncheonette was still there, although it had not aged graciously. I sat at the counter and read the menu.

I thought of Percy. For a moment he was there beside me, smiling now, as we saw a couple of black teenagers enter the restaurant, order hamburgers and Cokes, and laugh about some private matter. They had no idea of the drama that had been played out there twenty years ago.

I left without ordering. There was nothing more there that I wanted anymore.

Postscript

Now, as I write these words thirty years later, I think of friendships forged in that struggle. Of Jim Peck, who years later joined our war at Wounded Knee in South Dakota, of Phil Ochs, who joined hands with us and anti-war G.I.'s and officers at the Mountain Home Air Force Base in Idaho, of Harry Belafonte in the South and as he stood with the leaders of the Ameri-can Indian Movement at the federal courthouse in St. Paul, Minnesota.

I think of Pete Seeger and Dick Gregory, who were and are everywhere.

And I think of Barbara Dane. Oh, Barbara, where have we not been together? In the South, organizing at Army bases throughout the country against the war in Vietnam, helping to re-build the G.I. project in Idaho after it was burned to the ground.

When I remember you all, friends missing and friends present—how can I keep from singing? ❖

ED KING

Bacchanal at Woolworth's

Demonstrations in Jackson had to begin on Tuesday, May 28, 1963. With the breakdown of negotiation efforts on Monday, it was necessary to start direct action the very next day. The Jackson newspapers were already saying that despite all the threats, Jackson blacks could not produce any significant number of demonstrations. In the sense of strategic timing, this was the worst possible week to begin anything. Nothing could have started earlier because the bond money for anticipated arrests from the national NAACP did not come until late May. The period of speeches, mass meetings, attempted negotiations, and such was longer than we intended, but the tension had not worn down. But if there were no major demonstrations this week, then it would be hard to build up momentum again. And yet, Tougaloo College had just ended its spring semester and most of the students had left the campus. A smaller number would be returning for summer school which did not start for another week. On the high school scene this was the last week of school, the worst possible time for students to risk jail. But we had to begin.

The general strategy was to start out with a few small demonstrations each day. We would have to be careful about the number of arrests since bail bonds were scarce. We also did not think there would be very many demonstrators able to risk jail. We would try to take advantage of the recent Supreme Court ruling invalidating the arrests in the 1960 sit-ins and have selected, well-publicized sit-ins. A few picketers might be

arrested each day. With careful use of people and carefully selected sites for activity, a small number of demonstrators could keep the whole community aroused. In several weeks there might be more college students and high school students available. After many weeks we might reach the stage where we could have mass protest marches, composed primarily of teenagers out of school for the summer. As the children took a stand for civil rights and were jailed for their actions, we could count on their parents becoming involved. As it became clear that a significant movement existed in Jackson the time would come, perhaps in mid-summer, to call in Dr. Martin Luther King, Jr., for a really massive confrontation with Mississippi racism. Medgar Evers and Doris Allison agreed with John Salter and with me that eventually we would want to have Dr. King working in Jackson. We would need the help of every civil rights group in America. But initially this would be an NAACP project, the first major direct action campaign for the Association.

The plans for the first day of demonstrations were very carefully made; the goals were very small. There would be an integrated group of five pickets who faced certain, "instant arrest." There would also be a small scale sit-in at Woolworth's lunch counter. Three Tougaloo College students willing to risk arrest volunteered for this: Memphis Norman from Wiggins; Pearlina Lewis from Jackson; and Annie Moody from Centerville. Both of the women had been leaders in the campus civil rights movement the

Reverend Edwin King, an ordained minister of the Mississippi Conference of the United Methodist Church, is associate professor in sociology of health care at the School of Health Related Professions of the University of Mississippi Medical Center in Jackson. He has been with "Ole Miss" for over twenty years. He is also an adjunct professor at Millsaps College. Ed is a native of Vicksburg, Mississippi, who worked with the Mississippi Civil Rights Movement as Chaplain of Tougaloo College and as an organizer of the Mississippi Freedom Democratic Party. He has a dozen arrests there and in Alabama. His two daughters and their families live in the West. He has studied nonviolence with Gandhians in India and has written and lectured widely on nonviolence, social change, health care, and other issues as well as giving sermons in churches in the U.S., Europe, and India. Ed is presently working on a book on the origins of Freedom Summer.

past year. Memphis had not been very directly involved but had supported the movement. He was the student assistant to Borinski and had stayed on campus during this vacation week to make preparations for the sociology summer school program. When he realized the need for volunteers for the demonstrations, he quickly agreed to join up.

At 10:00 A.M. we were all gathered in the NAACP office on Lynch Street. We called the press to say there would be demonstrations on Capital Street after 11:00 that morning. We knew the press would notify the police. We did not give the exact locations of the demonstrations because we wanted some visibility before Captain Ray called in the "instant arrest" squads. Medgar Evers and John Salter would stay at the office to coordinate everything. I would go into town to observe the demonstrations and arrests. In this job of "spotter" I would avoid arrest so that I could make telephone reports to Salter and Evers. I wore my ministerial clerics (which SNCC people often called "bullet proof vests").

The police were watching outside Evers's office, but they did not know what to look for. Our promised demonstration might be a single demonstrator or might be some kind of mass march. All cars that left the office were followed into downtown Jackson. But all the passengers looked the same. Some non-demonstrators went into town to just walk around the streets looking in store windows. Police had to follow everyone and were not yet ready to arrest someone for just being in a car. The demonstrators went in different cars, and were let out at various places in the business area, in a very casual way. But everyone had watches and planned to meet at specific places at a certain time.

At exactly 11:15 A.M. the three students, who had been making casual purchases in different parts of the Woolworth's store, all walked up to the long white lunch counter, quietly sat down, and waited to be served. Most of the fifty-two seats were empty. but there were seven white customers. Five of them left the counter immediately, while two remained. One young white

girl casually finished her banana split, then quietly walked away. The white waitresses tried to ignore the new comers at first. Then one waitress finally asked them what they wanted. Annie Moody, selected as a spokesperson for the group, asked for service. The waitress explained that there was a separate counter for colored people, then hurried away to the back of the store where she was quickly joined by the other waitresses after they had turned off the lights at the lunch counter.

The remaining white customer, a middle aged woman, stayed at the counter for several minutes then walked over to the three blacks. No one knew what was going to happen. About ten white people were standing in the first aisle watching the demonstrators. I was standing with these people. A reporter for the *Jackson Daily News* was also there. We could all hear the lady speak in her calm, Southern voice, "I'd like to stay here with you, but my husband is waiting." As the lady left the counter a reporter asked her name and she refused to give it but said, " I am in sympathy with the Negro movement." The reporter went on over to the counter to talk with Moody and get the names of the demonstrators. I went up to the lady and introduced myself as the Tougaloo College chaplain and thanked her for what she had done. To my great surprise she told me she was from Vicksburg, my home town, but had lived outside the South for a time and now supported the Civil Rights Movement. There were too many very unfriendly whites standing around for us to continue the conversation. She left the store.

Store officials soon roped off the whole counter except where the three students sat. The colored lunch counter, with only thirty seats, was also soon closed. For the next forty-five minutes, the demonstrators sat silently at the deserted, darkened counter. Shoppers continued their business in other parts of the store, but frequently paused in little knots of muttering whites, a few aisles away from the lunch counter. There were even some shoppers, white and black, who would take just one look at the counter, abruptly look away, and go on making purchases as if nothing unusual was happening, at least nothing that could possibly involve them.

The *Jackson Daily News* managed to define the events of this first forty-five minutes as "trouble."

> Trouble broke out here yesterday at 11:16 A.M., thirty minutes after news services had been alerted that it would happen, when three Negro college students strolled into Woolworth's Capital Street store, made minor purchases, and took seats midway of the fifty-two-stool white lunch counter.

In the next two hours there would be more "trouble" here than in any sit-in during the history of the Movement. But the official white viewpoint was that the "trouble" did not start when white hoodlums violently attacked the demonstrators, but when the blacks peacefully sat down at the white lunch counter. A *Daily News* photo, showing the three students at the deserted counter, was labeled, "Incite Whites."

Captain Ray and a large number of Jackson policemen were standing outside Woolworth's. They could look through the glass doors and see the lunch counter demonstrators clearly. After just a few minutes, I realized that the police were abiding by the recent Supreme Court order and were not going to arrest the demonstrators. But pickets were another matter. I was talking to a friendly reporter, Kenneth Toler, Jackson writer for the *Memphis Commercial Appeal*. I told him that the pickets would soon be on Capital Street and he should see that. He said to me, "I think I had better stay here. This isn't over yet. We can't have a sit-in this quiet in Jackson. Something will happen." I had decided that the demonstrators were safe and would just be ignored at the counter until they were ready to leave. I wondered if they would stay until the store closed that evening.

I left the store to watch the street pickets, but I was too late. Another black student, also a "spotter," came over to me and whispered that the pickets had actually formed a single-file line and carried their signs ("Jackson Needs a Bi-ra-

cial Committee") for almost a full minute before being arrested. At exactly 11:30 A.M. the five picketers had unfurled their audacious banners. The integrated group was led by Rev. Eddie O'Neal, a black Baptist minister and the president of the Tougaloo student government. The two black women were Eddie Jean Thomas from Jackson and Doris Bracey, a student at Jackson State College; the two white women were both from Tougaloo College. One was Margrit Garner and the other was Jeannette King. They were arrested for "blocking the sidewalk." I was very proud of what Jeannette was doing and was disappointed that I was not able to see my wife holding her picket sign and being taken away to jail. So I returned to my post in Woolworth's.

A crowd of whites had been slowly gathering in Woolworth's. Shortly after noon they were joined by a number of white students, probably from nearby Central High School. About fifty people were standing in the aisles near the counter. They began cursing and taunting the demonstrators. None of the black students even looked around behind them, the three just held their heads down and glanced reassuringly at each other. Sometimes they seemed to whisper together. Suddenly several white men rushed forward and attacked the students. One man slapped Annie Moody, then pulled Memphis Norman from the counter. Memphis was hurled to the floor as the crowd shrieked in excitement and pushed forward for a better view. Both girls were knocked to the floor but quickly got back up to their seats at the counter.

Memphis Norman just lay on the floor, blood pouring from his mouth and nostrils, as a white man leaped up and down around his body, sometimes kicking his head from the side, sometimes stomping down on his face. The man's gyrations had a kind of style, almost like ballet or modern dance; his left arm arched gracefully over his head, as the other arm extended, pointing towards the black body being kicked with his ballet slippers, his soft, white tennis shoes. He would quickly turn a little circle, holding his right leg bent slightly in the air, then as the fingers of his left hand, held aloft, closed softly together like the silent snap of invisible castanets, he would stamp his white foot in the black face and prance around the body.

The shouting of the mob died down to a low giggle, a kind of communal snarl. The only other sound was low moaning from the body on the floor. Surrounding the man, like an obscene corpse de ballet, were about a dozen men in still, frozen pantomime positions, cigarettes dangling from their lips, waiting . . . The prima ballerina, a beautiful blonde belle, was poised in the wings in the next aisle. Watching patently over the whole scene were white FBI men observing the white Jackson policemen observing the white mob. There would be no "instant arrest" this time. Finally a plainclothes policeman intervened, arresting both Memphis Norman and his assailant on charges of disturbing the peace. Memphis was taken to jail and booked, still bleeding from head injuries, before finally being taken to a hospital. The white stomper turned out to be a former Jackson city policeman named Bennie Oliver. Ironically he had not adequately prepared for his debut performance. Had he been wearing hard soled shoes or boots instead of tennis shoes he probably would have killed Memphis Norman. As it was, the blood stains barely soiled his creamy white slippers.

All this took place in the glare of numerous floodlights from television camera crews. Individual newsmen added brilliant flashes of light from their cameras. The crowd grew swiftly in size, soon reaching over three hundred people. Most of them could not get to front stage to assault the two black women left at the counter. But they could provide the vital sounds of the orchestra and chorus. "Nigger bitch! Nigger bitch! Nigger bitch! Whore! Whore! Black whore! Communist, God-damned Communist! Go back to Russia!" The white ladies in the crowd sometimes joined the men in the cursing, sometimes just screamed out their hatred in high pitched shrieks, usually nonverbal but occasionally, like an emphatic piccolo, the shrieks came in a long, drawn out wailing, "She-e-e-y-i-i-i-t,

She-e-e-y-i-i-i-t!" While some older Southern gentlemen provided a ground bass, solid chord of "Gahd Dayumn, Gahd Dayumn, Gahd Dayumn," the teenage boys chanted a more rapid, "mothuh-fuckuh, mothuh-fuckuh, mothuh-fuckuh, mothuh-fuckuh."

As the music swelled, the beautiful blonde belle swirled out of the edge of the crowd and into the center spotlight. She swept up to the counter and picked up a plastic bottle of mustard. At first she grasped it so daintily it might almost be a fan as she struck Pearlina on the back. Twirling, she held the ugly yellow plastic above her head and its crown of long blond hair. Then she cradled the mustard jar in her arms, like a dancer with a bouquet; suddenly she was straining forward, standing on the tops of her toes, as a jet of mustard arched through the air to make a brilliant stain on the black hair of Annie Moody's head; then Pearlina's head was splattered. As the crowd burst into applause, the dancer turned towards them with a faint smile, almost made a little curtsy bow, then stepped off stage, back into the crowd. Next came three teenage boys. They grabbed up all the nearby food containers from the counter and showered the two black women with salt, pepper, and sugar. The crowd cheered their daring leaps, high into the air, and the sharp style with which they aimed their refuse at their victims. After a few gyrations, this pas de trois of frisky little ones, cute as cygnets, gentle as hawks, rejoined the mob. They usually held hands but this time their hands were too busy striking heads. The orchestra of hate played an interlude.

During all of this I was standing at the very back edge of the mob, walking around for a better view, and trying to get help. I went to the police standing outside the door. I asked Captain Ray to do something about the mob and to protect the girls at the counter. He seemed delighted at the situation and the fact that I had asked him for help. With his face in an even uglier grin than usual, he explained in a sort of whining voice, "But Rev. King, you know what the law is. Why the Supreme Court says that police can't interfere with a sit-in demonstration. Now the Jackson police are gonna do what is right, what the law says. That store is private property and I can't go in there unless the manager asks me. We'll just stay right out here on the sidewalk."

I tried to find the manager. The clerks told me several times he was not present. Finally I got to see one man who refused to give me his name or tell me if he was the manager or not. The clerks treated him as if he were some sort of authority, perhaps an assistant manager. I explained about Captain Ray. The man just looked at the mob and the scene at the counter and said, "That lunch counter was closed an hour ago. There's no reason for anybody to be sitting there. It's closed. That's all we are going to do." I told him we would find out his name and were going to sue both him and the Woolworth's store if he didn't help. He turned his back and walked away.

I went to a pay phone booth at the back of the store from where I could still see the counter. I called the office to report the situation to John Salter and Medgar Evers. Medgar wanted to come and join the sit-in but was persuaded to stay in his office and try to get national attention on the situation. I phoned Dr. Dan Beittel, the president of Tougaloo College. Beittel said he would try to reach the national offices of Woolworth's. I was really frightened for myself as I sat in the phone booth in the back of the store. Several white men stood watching me but never attacked me. They probably could not hear my conversations. I called Galloway Methodist Church trying to reach the Rev. Jerry Furr to ask him to try to get some white ministers to come to the store in an effort to get the police to break up the mob. But it was lunchtime and I could never reach any of the ministers.

Then I saw a white Methodist minister standing at the edge of the crowd. He was a man I had known for years. I knew that he was a conservative on theological and social issues, but thought that he must be shocked at the violence at the lunch counter. I rushed up to him. He

was not exactly pleased to see me. I explained the problem about why the police would not break up the mob, then asked for his help. I said that the mob was calmer now than a few minutes earlier. He agreed with that observation and said he had watched the whole thing. I suggested that he was the kind of person who could have great influence on the mob, if he would just go up to small groups of men and women at the edge of the crowd, introduce himself as a Methodist minister, and talk to them, he could begin to break up the mob. I said he could even tell the people he agreed with them about segregation but that this violence was no way to solve the problems. Then he should ask the people to leave the store.

He obviously wanted to get away from even talking to me. He finally said, "They're your demonstrators, why don't you tell them to leave? They're the ones causing the trouble. If they leave the counter, everything will settle down."

"But they can't leave," I replied. "If those girls even move, that mob will attack them again. They'll be killed before they could walk through all those people and get to the front door."

The minister quietly stated, "I will not do a thing for them—or you." He walked on over and joined the back ranks of the mob. I was absolutely convinced that he could have gotten the crowd to break up and go away. It could have been done by someone the whites would identify with. I looked at him, standing silently with the mob. I wondered if he would offer to hold the coats of some of the gentlemen so their arms would be more free to hurl the stones. I would have respected him more if he had at least shouted one curse word, but obscenity was beneath the dignity of a proper Methodist minister. I guess I should have been grateful that he did not identify me to the mob.

The crowd kept its focus on those sitting at the counter. But people on the edges kept trying to figure out who I was. I was dressed as a priest and I was white. But I clearly had not joined the mob. Several times people turned on me, "You're with them niggers. ain't you? I'll bet you're one of them." I would never answer these questions but welcomed the opportunity, little as it was, to try to talk with my accusers. "Those colored girls aren't hurting anybody. Why don't you leave them alone? Let the police take care of them."

"What kind of minister are you? Are you a Catholic? Are you with these nigger bitches?"

"I'm just a Christian minister, and I'm from Mississippi," I replied in my best Southern accent. "Those colored girls surely know by now what everybody in here thinks of them. If we all leave, I'm sure they'll leave the counter too. Why don't we just all go home or back to work?" A few whites, students and adults, did slowly leave the scene, but not my accuser.

The man turned away and back into the crowd joining the gentlemen who were shouting, "Go home, black bitches, go home!" This charming chant had a rhythm, almost a catchy tune, nearly irresistible. I know that a minister the crowd would listen to could have gradually broken up the mob in just the pattern I suggested to the minister I had spoken to. He was exactly the kind of person most of the white men present could identify with. They would have listened to him. The mob violence at the counter lasted almost three hours and was well reported in "live" broadcasts from the scene of the action on the Jackson radio stations. There must have been many white ministers in the city who knew what was happening. If they had come to the store, they could have calmed the mob. Some ministers could have influenced the mayor and the police captain. The offices of the Methodist, the Episcopal, and the Roman Catholic bishops were within a few minutes of Woolworth's. All the ministers of the White Mississippi Conference of the Methodist Church were in session at Galloway Church, less than three blocks away. That help never came.

But help for the demonstrators did eventually arrive. In one of the high moments of the entire nonviolent Movement's history, an incredible scene occurred at the Woolworth's lunch counter. While the mob stared, shocked into silence, several white people walked out from the edge of the crowd and up to the counter. They sat down on the filthy stools beside the two black girls. Then from the back of the store came three young black men to join the demonstration. Now there was an integrated group of eight, including two white women, sitting at the counter, smiling greetings at the two black women. The white women were Joan Trumpauer, a SNCC worker and student at Tougaloo, and Lois Chaffee, an English teacher from the college. The white man was John Salter who had decided, after hearing of the violence, that he had to be with the students and share whatever happened to them. The new black volunteers were George Raymond, a CORE worker, and Tom Beard and Walter Williams, high school students. Mercedes Wright, a black woman with skin light enough to "pass" for white and an NAACP staff member, joined me in the crowd.

The intermission was over. Now came the climax of the ballet, the great bacchanal. A terrible cry of white anger and hate burst from over three hundred white voices. The air was full of all the old music and obscenities, but this time there were new motifs, driving through the music with the intensity of a fugue: "Black bastards! Black bastards! Black bastards! Nigger lover! Nigger lover! Nigger lover! Go to hell! Go to hell! Go to hell! KILL KILL KILL KILL KILL! AAAAHHHHHHHH!!!!!"

The white men and teenage boys quickly lunged forward. Pearlina Lewis and Joan Trumpauer were grabbed from their stools and pulled by the hair towards the doors. They struggled loose and ran back to the counter but had to take stools separated from the other demonstrators. A white boy struck one of the black high school students on the head with some metal object, like a book end, that he had seized from a nearby sales counter. The black boy slumped forward over the counter, unconscious, then slowly, almost gracefully, slipped out of his seat and onto the floor into the ooze, and slime, and slop. He immediately regained consciousness before anyone could attack him while he was down. Holding onto the stool, he struggled back up to the counter.

A new male dancer came forward to replace Bennie Oliver in the cast. He leaped high in the air, hands outstretched above his head, brass knuckles flashing in the glare of the spotlights. He came down behind John Salter and struck him swiftly, once on the cheek, once on the back of the head. Salter never moved as the blood began pouring down his face and trickling in small streams down the back of his head.

The sight of blood inspired the blonde ballerina to come forward again, with even more grace than the first time. She did a slow pirouette holding aloft a dark red bottle of ketchup, as if it were a chalice of wine or blood. Then, her ritual dance concluded, she slowly poured the ketchup over Salter's bleeding head, mixing the crimson colors. Grandly, she bowed, as if towards an alter, and stepped back into the crowd. Now some more women, both young and old, rushed forward to join the men. One man emptied a salt shaker directly into Salter's wounds. A woman added pepper. A boy dashed up with a bottle of hot Tobasco pepper sauce, and a very young girl brought forth the vinegar. Salter's head and clothes looked like garbage. I could no longer distinguish the blood from all the other filth that clung to his hair, stained his shirt, or slowly slopped off his shoulders.

White boys darted behind the counter and soon had a fresh supply of the filthy looking mustard, an angry yellow color. Every demonstrator was soon adorned with a golden halo of mustard. (Salter's crown earned him the title, "Mustard Man," in the brilliant words of the *Jackson Daily News.*) All the lunch counter supplies were soon exhausted. White boys discovered cans of spray paint and came on to decorate the demonstrators in rainbow colors. One of the black boys wore a white shirt that soon bore the word "nigger" in bright red letters. "Hell" and "shit!" were other words easy for the mob to spell out in pretty shades of blue, and pink, and green on the backs of each person at the counter.

People in the corps de ballet, at the edges of

the mob, began to push and shove their way forward, with none of the grace of the earlier dancers. But those at the front were enjoying themselves too much to let others share the spotlight and the fun. Those at the back of the crowd began throwing metal ashtrays towards the counter. Most just sailed over the demonstrators, but a few heads were struck. Others in the crowd began ransacking nearby display counters for missiles and weapons. Whole counters of the plaster and plastic junk of America that Woolworth's sells as wall decorations for the modern home were available and soon in use. The counter with picture frames was next in line when the manager finally turned off the lights and began shouting that the store was closed. His stern voice

Tougaloo student Joan Trumpauer gives training in nonviolence to a group of northern clergymen who will attempt to integrate Jackson churches. Ed King in background. Both took part in the Woolworth lunch counter sit-in.

boomed out over a public address system suddenly put to use, calling on all the "customers" to please leave the store. "Woolworth's is now closed. I repeat, Woolworth's store is closed. Will all customers kindly leave. Please leave now. We are closed." When the sacred merchandise was seriously threatened, the responsible businessman decided to bring down the curtain.

Within ten minutes the mob had dispersed and cleared out of the store. Many left by the back doors as things were rather crowded at the front door, what with about fifty white policemen just standing around on the sidewalk. Only the newsmen remained in the store, still photographing the victim-visitors at the counter. Dr. Beittel came in and joined our people at the counter. I went up to John Salter and Joan Trumpauer and Annie Moody. I gave them a handkerchief, and the girls began to clean their faces as I started to wipe the blood and garbage from John's wound. The front page of the *Daily News* (and much of the world press, including the *Paris Match* which published color pictures of this sit-in) carried a picture of this scene, clearly showing the smeared demonstrators, but also identifying the chaplain and president of Tougaloo College at the lunch counter. Dr. Beittel asked Captain Ray to come into the store and protect the demonstrators until we could get cars for them. He refused. When we did come out of the store, the policemen formed a sort of line that held the white mob back, although the police made no effort to stop them from throwing the last few ashtrays and other souvenirs they had brought out of Woolworth's. We loaded everyone into Dr. Beittel's car and into my Rambler station wagon. The roof of my car would bear the stains of the mustard and ketchup and vinegar and salt for the rest of its days. The stains were a badge of pride for those who knew what they represented. We quickly returned to Medgar Ever's office. Those who needed medical help were taken to the nearby office of a black doctor.

That night on the Jackson television stations, a censored version of the events was shown.

National television carried vivid scenes of the violence, but Jackson had "cable trouble" and commercials during these scenes. When the local evening news came on, viewers were treated to the picture of empty seats at the lunch counter as a voice explained that this counter and all other counters in Jackson had been closed because of the sit-in demonstrations. No scenes of violence, of course. This was the normal pattern for both television stations. But, to our surprise, the local newspapers were full of pictures, front page even, some showing the wild dance of Bennie Oliver over the body of Memphis Norman.

The day after the Woolworth's riot, I received a special delivery letter from "A Friend in Christ." This "friend," possibly a minister of the Mississippi Conference of the Methodist Church, was probably some fundamentalist white minister who had been in the Woolworth's crowd along with the minister that I had recognized. I was not interested in knowing his identity. The letter was a perfect example of the epistles that appeared several times a week in both Jackson newspapers and is an excellent representation of the essence of the Religion of Mississippi. It may well have been written by a devout layman and not a minister. Accompanying the epistle were two clippings from unidentified religious publications. These were underlined in places and one was folded so that I could not miss the message on the back side:

JUDGEMENT [sic] hangs over the head of everyone, both saint and sinner, who trifles with God and with His WORD.

The major message was on the front side. It was titled:

CAN WE NOT SEE THE HANDWRITING ON THE WALL?

The heart of the lesson that followed was:

Repentance or Ruin! Christ or Chaos! Pray or Perish!

Only fast moving action on the part of Christians today will stop the fast moving conquests of the Communists tomorrow.

Along with the message was a smaller clipping. This one proclaimed:

WE NEED, THE AGE NEEDS, THE CHURCH NEEDS—Memorials of God's mighty power—Which will silence the enemy, dumbfound God's foes, strengthen weak saints—and fill strong ones with triumphant raptures!

Scissors had cut through the next sentence and I could only read part of the line.

STAND up on your feet and fight! Fight...

That final sentence seemed quite appropriate to the activity of the Magnolia Saints at the Woolworth's lunch counter.

Having read these inspired printed messages, I eagerly read the personal message in the epistle:

Dear Bro. King:

I have prayed much about this letter which I am writing to you, especially after the incident that I experienced yesterday at the Woolworth's 5 and 10 Store, where you were leading the sit-in demonstration. For some time I have been aware of your stand on this matter.

Let me say first, I am a Christian and stand for things of God; secondly, I am a true American, Democrat, and Southerner, and I believe with all my heart in our way of life, according to the Bible, and such action of which you were the leader yesterday is not according to the Word of God.

As I was reading my Bible last night, I came across some verses of scripture which spoke to me very plainly. Everyone seems to be seeking what they call "freedom." But according to this verse from the Word of God, there is only one way that a man can be free, and that is through Jesus Christ — the Lord and Savior. This does not imply in any way "social" freedom, as you and your followers are now seeking. It does mean "spiritual" freedom, and that we can be free from the wrath of God and judgements [sic] that follow.

Also, I was reading another passage, "He who lives by the sword shall die by the sword." This means that when a person lives with hate and murder in his heart for his fellow man, he will die that way. This is a spiritual death.

I would like to say , in closing, I am not writing you through any form of hate of race, creed, or color, for I do know God created everything in the beginning; but, also, that he separated everything according to its own kind—even the animals and the birds and the fish, and everyone has his own place [underlining mine] and duty to perform in God's world that he has made. I am also aware that everyone has a soul and that God so loved the world that he did give his only begotten son (John 3:16), that whosoever believeth in Him (Christ) shall not perish but have everlasting life.

Yours,

A Friend in Christ

I was to receive many such messages, from many different "Friends in Christ." These were the kind of Friends in Christ who loved the "old time religion," the "faith of our fathers," the old gospel songs, but somehow could never see any major difference between "The Old Rugged Cross" and "The Old Burning Cross."   ❖

JOHN R. SALTER, JR. (JOHN HUNTER GRAY)

Medgar Evers Speaks— May 1963

Excerpted from *Jackson, Mississippi: An American Chronicle of Struggle and Schism*

Exposition Press, 1979; and Kreiger Publishers, 1987.

John R. Salter, Jr., (John Hunter Gray), a half-blood Micmac/ Abnaki/Mohawk Indian grew up in Flagstaff, Arizona. Trained as a sociologist, he came to Mississippi with his wife, Eldri, in the summer of 1961 and became deeply involved in the developing movement. He was advisor to the Jackson Youth Council of the NAACP and chair of the Strategy Committee of the Jackson Movement, working very closely with Medgar Evers. Later he worked as a civil rights organizer for the Southern Conference Educational Fund and then as a grass roots poverty program activist.

Medgar had succeeded, with the assistance of the Federal Communications Commission, in securing equal time on television to answer the speech given by Allen Thompson a week before. He went down Monday and his seventeen-minute speech was taped for TV. Later that evening, following a brief strategy session, several of us, including Medgar, brought Cokes and went to a little home adjacent to the Masonic Temple where a television set was available. There we sat, crowded into a small room, and listened to one of Mississippi's greater public addresses:

I speak as a native Mississippian. I was educated in Mississippi schools, and served overseas in our nation's armed forces in the war against Hitlerism and Fascism. . . . Most southern white people, whether they are friendly or hostile, usually think of the NAACP as a "northern outside group." . . . At least one-half of the NAACP membership is in the South. There have been branches in Mississippi since 1918. The Jackson, Mississippi, branch was organized in 1926—thirty-seven years ago. . . .

Now the mayor says that if the so-called outside agitators would leave us alone everything would be all right. This has always been the position of those who would deny Negro citizens their constitutional rights. . . . Never

in its history has the South as a region, without outside pressure, granted the Negro his citizenship rights. . . . It is also in the American tradition to demonstrate, to assemble peacefully and to petition the government for a redress of grievances. Such a petition may legitimately take the form of picketing, although in Jackson, Negroes are immediately arrested when they attempt to exercise this constitutional right. . . .

We feel that Mayor Thompson will help Jackson if he will consult with a democratically selected bi-racial committee, some of whose members may be members of the NAACP. He would profit from the experience of other southern cities. . . .

Tonight the Negro knows from his radio and television what happened today all over the world. He knows what black people are doing and he knows what white people are doing. . . . He knows about the new free nations in Africa and knows that a Congo native can be a locomotive engineer, but in Jackson he cannot even drive a garbage truck.

. . . Then he looks about his home community and what does he see, to quote our mayor, in this "progressive, beautiful, friendly, prosperous city with an exciting future"?

He sees a city where Negro citizens are

refused admittance to the City Auditorium and the Coliseum; his children refused a ticket to a good movie in a downtown theater; his wife and children refused service at a lunch counter in a downtown store where they trade; students refused the use of the main public libraries, parks, playgrounds, and other tax-supported recreational facilities. He sees Negro lawyers, physicians, dentists, teachers and other professionals prevented from attending meetings of professional organizations. He sees a city of over one hundred fifty thousand, of which 40 percent is Negro, in which there is not a single Negro policeman or policewoman, school crossing guard, fireman, clerk, stenographer or supervisor employed in any city department or the mayor's office . . . except those employed in segregated facilities. He sees local hospitals which segregate Negro patients and deny staff privileges to Negro family physicians. The mayor spoke of the twenty-four-hour police protection we have . . . there are questions in the minds of many Negroes whether we have twenty-four hours of protection, or twenty-four hours of harassment. . . .

What then does the Negro want? He wants to get rid of racial segregation in Mississippi life because he knows it has not been good for him nor for the state. He knows that segregation is unconstitutional and illegal. . . . The Negro citizen wants to register and vote without special handicaps imposed on him alone. . . . The Negro Mississippian wants more jobs above the menial level in stores where he spends his money. He believes that new industries that have come to Mississippi should employ him above the laboring category. He wants the public schools and colleges desegregated so that his children can receive the best education that Mississippi has to offer. He believes additional Negro students should be accepted at Old Miss and at other colleges. He feels strongly about these and other items although he may not say so publicly.

. . . Jackson can change if it wills to do so. If there should be resistance, how much better to have turbulence to effect improvement, rather than turbulence to maintain a stand-pat policy. We believe there are white Mississippians who want to go forward on the race question. Their religion tells them there is something wrong with the old system. Their sense of justice and fair play sends them the same message.

But whether Jackson and the state choose change or not, the years of change are upon us. In the racial picture things will never be as they once were. History has reached a turning point, here and over the world. Here in Jackson we can recognize the situation and make an honest effort to bring fresh ideas and new methods to bear, or we can have what Mayor Thompson called "turbulent times." If we choose this latter course, the turbulence will come, not because of so-called agitators or presence or absence of the NAACP, but because the time has come for a change and certain citizens refuse to accept the inevitable.

Negro citizens want to help all other good citizens bring about a meaningful improvement in an orderly fashion . . . the two races have lived here together. The Negro has been in America since 1619, a total of 344 years. He is not going anywhere else; this country is his home. He wants to do his part to help make his city, state, and nation a better place for everyone regardless of color and race.

Let me appeal to the consciences of many silent, responsible citizens of the white community who know that a victory for democracy in Jackson will be a victory for democracy everywhere.

To anyone rational there could be no question regarding the sincerity of Medgar Evers, or the merit of his words. But the power structure of Jackson, and the system of Mississippi, were not rational on matters such as this. There were unquestionably those in the white community who subscribed to the essence of what Medgar had had to say, but they remained silent, choked

PORTRAIT OF

MEDGAR EVERS

BY SHARON RILEY

Sharon Riley was born in Washington, D.C., in 1950. She was trained at the Corcoran School of Art in her early years and was taught by numerous individuals outside of schools. Sharon has lived throughout the Americas, from Bluefields, Nicaragua, to her present home in Bar Harbor, Maine.

by the same mantle of fear that so long had strangled their community and state.

To the *Jackson Daily News* the next day, the speech of Medgar Evers was something from which to assemble a few scattered, out-of-context quotations, under the headline "Mix Drive Talked Up." ❖

JOHN R. SALTER, JR. (JOHN HUNTER GRAY)

Medgar Evers's Funeral

Excerpted from *Jackson, Mississippi: An American Chronicle of Struggle and Schism*
Exposition Press, 1979; and Kreiger Publishers, 1987.

We were up early Saturday morning, and weather forecasters predicted the hottest day yet. The news reported that a white youth had been shot in the shoulder while he and companions drove through a black neighborhood in the early-morning hours. Bill Kunstler and I, and Ed and Jeannette King, went to the Jackson airport to pick up Dr. Martin Luther King and the delegation from SCLC. A number of the NAACP staff were already there to meet others. The police were much in evidence in and around the terminal building, and a large number of newsmen were present.

I scanned the front pages of Saturday's *New York Times.* There was a long article on Jackson, datelined Friday and written by the veteran civil rights journalist, Claude Sitton, that dealt with the past two days, and it was clear that Sitton had determined the essentials.

His story pointed out that the NAACP had discouraged a mass march on Friday by telling people that "their almost certain arrest might prevent them from attending the funeral"; then it went on to indicate that there was "widespread sentiment for a proposed mass march after the funeral services," but that NAACP officials "feared that because of the repressive police tactics and the animosity among Negroes such a demonstration would lead to serious violence."

Claude Sitton had indeed figured things out:

Besides the feeling among participants, in a month-long desegregation drive here, and their sympathizers, the association officials

also were under indirect pressure from other civil rights groups. Representatives of the latter were urging Negroes to press for direct action . . . There were indications that adherents of the Rev. Dr. Martin Luther King were seeking to bring the Southern Christian Leadership Conference, of which he is president, into the struggle.

The article then had a brief discussion of Bill Kunstler and me, and mentioned our group as the "chief advocates of continued mass protest." But he neglected to mention the vigorous spirit at the grassroots.

With some understatement, Sitton went on. "Some association officials were said to be resentful of the efforts of the [M.L.] King faction to move into the Jackson picture."

By this time our plane was arriving. Followed by a large number of police, we stepped out of the terminal to the passenger gate. Several dozen white people joined the police in observing all of this. Newsmen pressed to the front. The plane landed and unloaded. Led by Dr. King, and with a whirring of television cameras, the SCLC officials arrived in Jackson. We greeted them, talked for a few moments, then went to the cars. Bill, I, Dr. King, and one of his aids got into my car, and the others rode with Ed and Jeannette King. The police, apparently fearing that an attempt might be made on Dr. King's life, formed to escort us to the Masonic Temple.

It had been understood, we felt, that our serious discussion of the internal problems of the

Jackson movement would take place after the funeral and any demonstration. Now, with the police moving us along very rapidly over the short distance from the airport to Lynch Street, we talked only of the general situation: the intense heat of Mississippi, the spirit of the people, and Medgar Evers. Within minutes we were at the Masonic Temple. Cars were parked everywhere for many blocks around, and a wave of humanity was pouring into the doors of the building. It seemed clear that several thousand people had come to the funeral. There was obviously no parking space. I let Bill, Dr. King, and the SCLC aide out, then drove down many blocks before I found a place to park. The sidewalks were full of people walking to the Masonic Temple. Police cars drove by, back and forth, but I could see none parked. I reached the door of the building at 11 A.M., the starting time for the services. Inside the corridor, where people were packed wall to wall, someone told me that even the standing room was gone inside the auditorium. The music was beginning.

I stood a long time in the packed corridor. Then the music stopped, and I could barely hear a prayer being given and after a time a speech. I attempted to move down the corridor toward the back, hoping to be able to hear what was going on, but I made little progress. After a time, the people around me began talking, and I joined in, asking them from where they came. They told me, naming many places besides Jackson: big towns, little towns, rural hamlets all over Mississippi. There were people from the Delta and from the hills in northeastern Mississippi, from the Gulf Coast area, and from the pine country down in the southwestern part of the state. The ripples of Medgar's death and the Jackson movement in general were reaching out a long, long way—stirring people and places into which no civil rights worker had yet set foot.

I saw several Tougaloo students and Youth Council leaders who were unable to get into the auditorium. It had occurred to me that many of the people on the outside might drift away from the funeral before it was over and miss the mass march. The youth leaders and I began to spread the word, asking people to stay around for the march. It became clear that everyone intended staying around; indeed most had heard that a march was to take place. I made my way slowly upstairs. The upper corridor had fewer people in it, and most were clustered around a Coke machine. I got a Coke. An insurance-office door opened and a man, a close friend of Medgar's, looked out. He saw me and motioned me inside. Several other men whom I knew well were also there. Through a small space in the wall, we could hear the speeches being given.

A great deal of the oratory tended, to the obvious disapproval of the men who were listening with me, somehow to blend Medgar, Mississippi, and the NAACP all together in such a way that the NAACP came out on top. But there were some good words spoken, among them those of Roy Wilkins, who said of Medgar:

> For a little while he loaned us and his people the great strength of his body and the elixir of his spirit. If he could live in Mississippi and not hate, so shall we, though we shall ever stoutly contend for the kind of life his children and all others must enjoy in this rich land.

Roy Wilkins called Medgar "the symbol of our victory," and said that "the bullet that tore away his life four days ago tore away at the system and helped signal its end. They can fiddle and they can throw a few more victims to the lions of repression and persecution, but Rome is burning and a new day is just over yonder."

As the funeral drew to an end, the announcement of the mass march was made. I went downstairs and made my way outside. There seemed to be even more people in the area than before. Then the funeral was over. A tremendous flow of people began to pour from the building. Many were crying. Bill Kunstler came out and suggested that I find someone who could take my car down to Farish Street, where the affair would conclude. I found a Tougaloo student who agreed to forego the march. The coffin was carried out of the Masonic Temple and was placed into the hearse.

A minister was calling on people to go out into the street and to line up three abreast. We walked out into the street. Police were out there, also giving directions. Someone remarked that the temperature was 102 degrees and due to go higher.

The head of the mass march began to take shape. Several of the Jackson ministers were in the front ranks, then the NAACP officials and Dr. King. I was in the sixth rank. Ed King and Bill Kunstler were a little behind me. Then, as soon as the first dozen or so ranks had formed, we were off, and the rest of the mass march began to organize behind us like a thin stream of water flowing from a great pool.

Newsmen were up in front beside us. Looking down Lynch Street, block after block, I could see the blue helmets of the Jackson police at every intersection. We marched on, and as we began to pass the groups of police, we could see the hatred in their faces. It seemed infinitely hotter than I had ever known it in my life, and my clothes were soaked with sweat. At one point, I turned for a moment and looked back and saw the long, moving line behind us. Then we marched through an underpass. Standing above us was one of the Jackson police officers who specialized in "identification." He looked bewildered. From his post, he could view a much longer line than we could see from the ground.

We marched on. Now Lynch Street was swinging over, and we were moving onto another street that cut over in the direction of the downtown area. The numbers of police seemed to have increased; they seemed as endless to me as we must have seemed to them. We passed into an area where white people lived. They stood in front of their houses and business places, women and children standing behind their men. There was shock and hatred and fear mixed together on all of their faces; but they were silent and so were we.

We were on Farish Street, still in the white section, and the numbers of white people were increasing; so had the silent shock, and the silent hatred, and the silent fear. The tall commercial buildings of downtown Jackson were rising around us as we moved toward the intersection of Farish Street and Capitol Street. At that junction solid walls of police, rank after rank, had formed a cordon through which we passed; and on the other side of each of the two police walls were hundreds of white people who had come to watch silently.

Then we were in the other portion of Farish Street, the beginning of the black business neighborhood. There, in front of businesses and on the sidewalks, people stood and watched, with solemnity, tears, and hope. Now there were not so many Jackson police. Block after block down Farish Street we went until finally we were in front of the Collins Funeral Home, to which Medgar Evers's body had been returned, there to await shipment by car to Meridian, and there to be loaded aboard a train and carried to Arlington Cemetery for another funeral service some days hence. One of the ministers up front held up his hand and told us all to spread out from the street.

I walked over to the lawn in front of the funeral parlor. The people were coming, rank after rank, and coming over to the sidewalks and the lawns. Rank after rank they came. A newsman from out of state walked up to me and said that he and others estimated that at least five thousand people were in the march. Even now, there was a huge number of people gathered around the area of the funeral parlor.

And inside was the body of Medgar Evers.

The Tougaloo student who had driven my car came up and, giving me the keys, said that it was parked right around the corner. I thanked him, but I was not planning to go anywhere. Ed King said that as nearly as he could tell no white Mississippians—other than he and Jeannette and Wofford Smith, Episcopal chaplain at the University of Mississippi—had been at the funeral. He was disappointed. Aaron Henry walked over, and we talked briefly. He was hoping for some direct action up in Clarksdale.

Rank after rank came the people. I could well believe that there were at least five thousand people in the mass march, and that probably many more than that had been at the funeral. Away up and down Farish Street, I could see the blue helmets of the Jackson police glinting in the sun.

It was very hot.

The ranks had stopped arriving. All the space around the Collins Funeral Home, including the street itself, was packed tightly with people who, sweat-soaked and quiet, said very little. All were just standing there. I looked around. Almost all the newsmen had left. I could see the NAACP officials walking together down the street. The affair was considered over. But the people were still there.

And inside was Medgar Evers.

It came to me that here was Mississippi—all together. The people around me were from every part of Mississippi. Inside was the man to whom they had come to pay homage, and he too represented Mississippi, as did that which had been dealt him. Up and down Farish Street were the police, and they represented Mississippi. The intense Mississippi sun was coming over the tops of the buildings to the west, and its heat had enveloped all of us. A great many things, all symbolizing the forces of Mississippi, were gathered together. Suddenly I recognized the feeling that flowed out to me from all of the forces meeting here, and I realized that the day was not yet over.

I was snapped out of this reverie by Bill Kunstler, who walked up with news that came as a great shock. Dr. King, he said, and the other SCLC people wanted me to take them immediately to the airport to catch a plane. He indicated that several of the SCLC staff had already caught rides to the terminal.

I looked at him and asked, very slowly, "Aren't we going to talk? The SCLC involvement?"

Bill Kunstler shook his head sadly. "I don't know what's involved," he said. "But they definitely want to go to the airport right away."

"What about Jackson?" I asked, still stunned.

"They've got to catch a plane," Bill repeated. "Maybe we can talk with them on the way to the airport."

I gave Bill the car keys and said that I wanted to stick around for a few more minutes at least, and asked if he could bring the car from around the corner.

I was still in a daze. No group that planned to involve itself in Jackson would be leaving now, not at this point. Ed King had seen Bill and me talking and made his way through the mass of people to ask what had occurred. I told him. He looked sick at heart.

People were still standing quietly. It was still hot. The police were still up and down the street. Medgar Evers still lay inside the funeral home. This was still Mississippi.

Bill Kunstler came up again. He had the car about two blocks away and Dr. King and an aide were in it. Steve Rutledge and Dave Dennis were going to ride to the airport, Bill said, and perhaps we could all talk with the SCLC people.

It was time to go, he continued, and he said it sadly.

Then the SCLC aide came through the crowd of people. He said that Dr. King could be shot, sitting in the car like that, and that they absolutely had to go immediately.

I told Bill to take the car, that I thought I would stay.

He hesitated for several moments. Then the SCLC man again pressed for immediate departure. Bill told me that he'd bring the car back and meet us at the funeral home. They left.

Something was beginning to happen out in the street—out where people were really massed together. It looked as if a woman was weeping and pointing toward the funeral parlor. Ed King and I moved closer.

Everything was suddenly very still.

Then someone—probably someone who had heard the song sung at our many mass meetings in the past month—began to sing, "Oh, Freedom," and it came softly and mournfully, over the people:

Oh, oh Freedom,
Oh, oh Freedom,
Oh, oh Freedom over me, over me.
And before I'll be a slave,
I'll be buried in my grave,
And go home to my Lord and be free.

Now we were all singing.

No more killing,
No more killing,
No more killing over me, over me.
And before I'll be a slave
I'll be buried in my grave
And go home to my Lord and be free.

There was a brief pause. Then, again suddenly, came another freedom song, a much more spirited one, "This Little Light of Mine":

This little light of mine, I'm going to let it shine.
Oh, this little light of mine, I'm going to let it shine.
This little light of mine, I'm going to let it shine,
Let it shine, let it shine, let it shine!

Everyone sang on—a mighty roar:

All over Capitol Street, I'm going to let it shine.
Oh, all over Capitol Street, I'm going to let it shine.
All over Capitol Street, I'm going to let it shine,
Let it shine, let it shine, let it shine!

Capitol Street! Capitol Street! and now all of the forces of Mississippi, all of the forces that were gathered together, began to react. *Capitol Street!* Out in the front of the funeral parlor, even as they sang, the people, in a great spontaneous surge, turned toward Capitol Street—object of the boycott, scene of many arrests, far off and inaccessible goal of the mass marches. In a mighty wave the people moved down Farish Street toward the heart of Jackson. Hundreds and hundreds of people poured from the sidewalks and lawns and porches to join the throng. Quickly I followed them, and so did Ed King and Jeannette, and Eddie O'Neal. Behind us came another great wave of people, and another, and another. We were all swept up in the stream of

surging Mississippi people, flowing down Farish Street—toward Capitol Street. There was sporadic singing, there were cries of "We want Medgar's killer! We want *freedom! Freedom! Freedom!*"

Ahead of us several blocks were a number of Jackson police, themselves running down toward Capitol Street—running from the huge, singing demonstration that had suddenly poured forth.

And far ahead of us, down at the intersection of Farish and Capitol streets, through which we had all walked only a short time before, we could see the massing of the battalions of blue and brown helmets.

There were people everywhere—in the street and on the sidewalks. Some were old and some were young; some were well dressed and some were not. But in all the faces, and in all of the singing, and in all of the cries of "*Freedom! Freedom!*" there was no fear, no fear-based apathy, no servility, no more of the past of Jackson and Mississippi, not even a spirit of violence—only the toughness bred by hard lifetimes combining with the hopes and the aspirations of generations into a determined and powerful forward thrust.

As we jogged along, occasionally pausing for a moment to catch our breath, Ed and I and Eddie O'Neal talked. This was the tremendous awakening of Jackson, maybe even of Mississippi, and this was the time to get Martin Luther King, now gone to the airport. He would come if he knew this was happening. But how to get him? We looked at a watch. Scarcely ten minutes had passed since everything began, and the car had left only fifteen minutes before. We pressed on with the people. Now we were close to Capitol Street. Directly ahead of us, blocking the entrance to the downtown area, slowing the momentum of the demonstration to a brief stop, then causing it to commence an ever so slow retreat, was Deputy Chief J. L. Ray and what appeared to be a huge army of many hundreds of lawmen of all kinds blocking all of Farish Street. Some people were pressing forward to get a closer view of the countless ranks of police; other people were moving back. Half a dozen freedom songs were being sung at the same time.

How to get Martin Luther King, now gone to the airport, before he left Jackson forever? The car must be arriving at the terminal.

We looked up. We were standing under a set of second-story offices used by black professional people, doctors, dentists, our lawyers. Some office must be open, some telephone available. There was still time! Still time for a call to the airport! Still time for Martin Luther King!

Quickly we mounted a flight of stairs—Ed, I, Jeannette, Eddie O'Neal. An office was open, its window overlooking Farish Street. We dashed in, looked for a telephone. There was none.

For a moment, before getting ready to try other offices in the building, we looked down at Farish Street and saw the tremendous throngs of milling people, saw the ranks of blue- and brown-helmeted police, saw the sunlight, felt the heat—all of the forces of Mississippi in motion. Then even as we were turning to seek elsewhere for the precious telephone, the police, having seen us either entering the building or looking out the window, poured into the building into which we were. They were at the top of the stairs in seconds.

Within two minutes both Ed King and myself were arrested, taken downstairs, prodded with clubs, and thrown bodily into a paddy wagon.

It had occurred with amazing speed, and we lay there stunned as the door closed on us. But there was still hope! Eddie and Jeannette had apparently not been arrested. Now all we could do was pray that they could in the next few minutes find that telephone.

There was a small, barred circular window in the paddy wagon. I looked out. All I could see were vast numbers of city police and highway patrolmen and contingents of sheriff's deputies—men with rifles and bayonets and shotguns and revolvers and police dogs—marching on Farish Street. I could hear shouts and yells and freedom songs. The paddy-wagon door opened

and a man was pushed in with us, his head bleeding where he had been struck with a club. He told us that the lawmen were not arresting many at all but were pushing the demonstration back and forcing the people from Farish Street. The door opened again. A woman, her dress ripped, was shoved in with us. She was crying. Ed King took out his Bible and began to pray.

We told her that, soon perhaps, the U.S. troops would come. The door opened again. A boy, blood all over his face, was pushed into the wagon. He was crying. Ed resumed his prayer.

Outside, we suddenly heard a volley of shots being fired, then another. Then we heard screams.

The others had expressions of horror on their faces, as I must have had on mine. I could think only "Sharpville." I could see nothing from the little window.

Again the door opened and a man with a bloody head was thrown inside. He had been clubbed and told us that the police were firing over the heads of the people, and that they were shooting out the windows above Farish Street. More time passed. There were more shots. More people were thrown into the paddy wagon. Ed read aloud from his Bible. I glanced out the little window. Suddenly I looked again.

Long lines of heavily armed lawmen were marching past into Farish Street. Police dogs were being led. Trucks were going past, loaded with police. But standing in the middle of all of this, leaning against a lamp post and looking as if he were observing passing traffic in New York City, was Bill Kunstler.

I yelled, "Bill! Hey, Bill!" Ed King came over and looked out the window.

Bill Kunstler was looking around. "Bill!" I called again. "It's me, John!"

"John!" he said. "Where are you?"

"In the paddy wagon!" I answered. He looked in our direction, and I pushed my fingers through the little window.

He saw them immediately and started over to us. A dozen men with rifles then stepped into view. They pointed their guns at Bill Kunstler.

"Who are you?" one asked.

"Gentlemen," he said, "I'm an attorney. I have clients in that wagon."

They moved toward him, rifles still pointing. He stepped back onto the sidewalk and moved down the street, out of view.

"Thank God he wasn't arrested," I said to Ed. "We need him." Then I realized something.

Eddie O'Neal and Jeannette King had not reached Martin Luther King. If they had, Bill Kunstler would have been with the SCLC leader, not by himself. I looked at Ed. His face showed the same realization. Neither of us spoke for a long time.

The paddy wagon was now almost full. The shouts and yells, even the shots, were much farther away. Then the engine started and the wagon gave a terrific lurch. We tried to sit on the floor, but the vehicle was maneuvered in such a fashion that we slid from one side to the other. We were traveling up Farish Street in the direction of the funeral home. I looked out the little window.

What had happened was obvious. Windows had indeed been broken by the police; glass was all over the sidewalks. Lawmen were everywhere. We passed a parked fire engine. I saw police holding groups of people at gunpoint, and nightsticks were drawn across the throats of several. I could not see the main body of the demonstration, although shouts and still some freedom songs were now very clear. Then the paddy wagon turned off Farish Street, and for a moment I saw Bill Kunstler and Steve Rutledge standing on a sidewalk.

Then we traveled fast, the driver taking each turn with screeching tires, sending all of us skidding back and forth. The injured people moaned. One woman appeared to have fainted.

We were passing through an edge of the downtown area. I looked out at Jackson, its commercial buildings shimmering in the late-afternoon sun. I hated it, at that point, more deeply than I had ever hated anything. Then I suddenly realized that Jackson was not *quite* as it usually was—there were scarcely any cars or people any-

where. The whole heart of Jackson was virtually deserted.

We were at the fairgrounds stockade. The paddy wagon stopped; the gate was opened; the wagon entered. The door was opened. I helped the woman who was almost unconscious to her feet. She climbed out. I stepped to the ground. The officer in charge pushed me over to one side, looked at me with a twisted face, and said, "Inciting to riot!"

Another said, "We ought to kill you right now!"

I stood there, slowly realizing for the first time that they felt that I, and perhaps Ed too, had organized and led the huge demonstration. Then I realized fully, for the first time, that these men, and unquestionably most of the white people, not only were totally incapable of realizing the role of Mississippi in producing protests but were totally unable to realize that black people could, themselves, lead themselves.

I looked around. There were dozens of police officers gathering where we stood. In the hot sun, leaning with arms out against the side of a long building, were about two dozen other people who had been arrested. Obviously the policy against mass arrests had been foregone.

We were searched, taken to a table, and one by one were booked. A number of lawmen, clubs in their hands, gathered around Ed King and me, cursing us continuously. It was clear that they hoped to provoke us into doing something, or even saying something, that would give them the "right" to club us into the ground. We stood there, saying nothing, looking at them. Ed and I were the last to be booked, and as I sat down in the chair by a table, I gave only my name, age, address, and occupation. The officer, who knew of course a great deal about me, went through, one after the other, all of the questions. As I refused to answer, he became increasingly angry. The muscles in his face jerked and he became very pale; finally, furiously, he pushed my arm from the table and cursed me as someone whom he would "dearly like to put a slug or two through." Ed went through the same routine.

When all had been booked, we were ordered to lean against the wall under the still-hot sun of late afternoon. Ed and I moved to join those who had been in our paddy wagon, but we were pushed by the police to a section of the wall by ourselves. As we leaned, arms out against the wall, the police walked back and forth behind us, still cursing, still threatening. I was drenched with sweat and I noticed that my coat was torn. A black mourning band that I had put on my arm for the funeral was hanging limply by a safety pin.

About an hour passed. From what we could hear, the police were holding various conferences behind us. Suddenly we were ordered to turn around. With several of those who had been in our wagon, along with a number from the other group, we were placed in a paddy wagon and taken to the city jail. One of the men with us was a Mr. Withers, whom I had met once months before, a photographer from Memphis, Tennessee, who did considerable work for black publications. He told us that he and other newsmen had left the area after the mass march from the Masonic Temple, then, hearing of what was developing, returned to the Farish Street area. But the police had blocked the newsmen from taking pictures and had threatened them, forcing several away at gunpoint. A TV cable had been cut by a deputy sheriff. Because he was black, Withers had managed to slip into the crowd and had begun taking pictures, but the police had broken his camera and had arrested him.

There were no Women for Constitutional Government at the city jail as there had been two days before, and it seemed clear that a wave of real fear must have swept white Jackson. We were formally booked again, and before I was led off, I gave Withers some cigarettes. The police officers in charge had evidently told the white prisoners in the cell block who I was because, as we passed their cages, screams came, "Give him to us! Let us get him!" But I was placed in a cell by myself.

I was extremely tired, but I could not sleep. What had occurred on this day in Jackson, es-

pecially the massive upheaval at Farish Street, had been the largest black protest in the history of Mississippi. It was inconceivable that it could not have a positive impact on the power structure, and the more I thought about it, especially the widespread police brutality, the more I felt that the federal government *must* be sending troops into Mississippi's hate-filled capital.

I knew that the developments of the day were going to have an effect upon the Jackson movement itself. I could not see how, after everything that had occurred, the effect could be anything but constructive: larger and more intensive mass marches. All of us, especially the people at the grassroots, had now reached the point where we could never, never turn back.

I heard the police coming down the corridor. I was taken from my cell into the main office. Attorney Carsie Hall was talking with Ed. The lawyer told us that we were being bonded out. The charges, which were disturbing the peace and interfering with officers, were, as he put it, "minimal, at this point." He went on to say that there might be additional charges levied against us. I asked about Withers and the others. He said that many of them were already out and that everyone would be out by nightfall. Several were receiving medical care. He told us that he would drive us to Tougaloo.

We went outside. Police gathered to look at us as we walked down the sidewalk, but once in the attorney's car, we relaxed. Soon we were going past the state capitol building, and I looked down Capitol Street, into the downtown area. Although it was Saturday evening, there was virtually no activity.

I asked Carsie Hall what had happened—the demonstration, the federal government, what had been going on?

He knew nothing except the fact that the demonstration had gradually dissolved and everyone had left the area, although large numbers of police were traveling through the black neighborhoods. Most of the prominent national figures who had come for the funeral, he continued, had either left before or during the Farish

Street demonstration, and others had left on the late-afternoon flights. He had been busy getting bail-bond money.

Then we were at Tougaloo and a large number of students and some faculty gathered to greet us. Jeannette King, Eddie O'Neal, Bill Kunstler, and Steve Rutledge had all made it through the Farish Street situation, were back on campus, and had a great deal to tell us. We went into the Kings' home to talk.

Immediately we wanted to know, although the answer seemed obvious, if Jeannette and Eddie had been able to get in touch with Martin Luther King. They told us that they had been unable to find any office open in the building. By then, hundreds and hundreds of lawmen were down on the street, and since they knew Dr. King's plane had left, they had logically enough stayed out of sight. Eventually they had joined forces with Bill and Steve.

I asked Bill Kunstler if anything had developed with Martin Luther King and the SCLC during the drive to the airport. He shook his head sadly. The degree of inter-organizational conflict that would develop between the NAACP and SCLC if SCLC involved itself in Jackson would, it seemed, be of a serious and drastic nature.

They told us about the demonstration.

It had gone on, they said, for at least forty minutes after we had been arrested, and police brutality had mounted steadily as the army of officers sought to disperse the people by forcing them back, block by block, along Farish Street. It had been by far the most brutally repressive situation since the beginning of the Jackson movement.

After a time, they said, following the shooting out of the windows and several very bloody and conspicuous clubbings, some youths began to throw bricks and bottles at the long lines of advancing police.

Bill and Steve told us that the NAACP officials had been many blocks away when the action had begun, arriving back on the scene well after the demonstration was under way. The

NAACP staff had attempted to persuade the people to go home but had been ignored, even after one staffer had borrowed a bullhorn from the police and had begun calling for everyone to leave the area.

When the bricks and bottles were thrown, Bill said, everything had become extremely tense. At that point the representatives from the U.S. Department of Justice, who had observed all of this, moved into the situation. John Doar, a key government man, had stepped out into the street and had pleaded with the people to go home. Finally, they did.

Governor Ross Barnett had gone on radio and television to call out the Mississippi National Guard to active duty on a standby basis, and at least five Guard units were at the Jackson armory.

But there were no federal troops, not even federal marshals.

Jeannette said that she had heard that Mayor Allen Thompson had gone on radio and television, telling all of the people of Jackson to stay away from the whole downtown area.

We were told that news media all over Mississippi were taking the position that Ed and I had instigated everything.

I began to tell them what the police had said to me at the fairgrounds stockade, but Bill Kunstler cut me short. "It isn't just the news media and the police that are taking that position," he said. Then he told Ed and me what had happened.

After the demonstration had been dispersed, Gloster Current and some other NAACP staff people had called an emergency meeting of the strategy committee and, with a number of the ministers, had gone to a church. Bill and Eddie had talked with several people on the street for a few moments. Then it had occurred to them that this was definitely one strategy committee meeting that they should not miss. They had gone to the church, arriving a few minutes after Gloster Current and the ministers had begun the meeting.

When he and Eddie walked in the door, Bill went on, Gloster Current was calling for the immediate expulsion of Ed and me from the strategy committee, charging that we had incited the "riot." Most of the ministers expressed shock and horror at the developments on Farish Street, especially at the Jackson black people themselves. But several of the clergy who had pressed Gloster Current and other NAACP staff people for tangible evidence of the involvement of Ed and me were told that the Jackson police had evidence to this effect. Indeed, it was even pointed out to the strategy committee that we had been arrested.

Bill said that he and Eddie had observed the course of the strategy committee meeting, interested in how it was being handled, and for a time kept silent. Several of the ministers were not certain that the Jackson police were the final authority on any of this, and a prominent NAACP attorney from New York had joined them in expressing these doubts. Someone had raised the point that perhaps Ed and I should be allowed to present our case to the strategy committee after we had been released from jail.

But Gloster Current had called again for our immediate expulsion from the strategy committee, and most of the ministers present appeared to support him.

At that point Bill Kunstler, who had defended me in segregationist courts in Mississippi, arose to defend me and Ed before the NAACP and the Jackson ministers. First, he pointed out that the Farish Street demonstration, a large part of which he had observed after returning from the airport, was not a "riot" in any sense of the word, and that whatever brick- and bottle-throwing had taken place, undesirable as that might be, had occurred only after the incredible police brutality.

He had then presented to the strategy committee his star witness, Eddie O'Neal, a minister himself, from Meridian, president of the Tougaloo student body, who had of course been with Ed and me up to the moment we had been arrested. Eddie O'Neal quietly told the strategy committee that the demonstration itself had been the purest expression of the feelings of the people—that it had been as spontaneous as any-

thing could be. He had talked at length, and when he sat down, the strategy committee took the position that neither Ed nor I would be expelled.

Bill and Eddie said that several hundred lawmen had cordoned off the black neighborhoods in Jackson.

I asked them about the strategy committee—what else had gone on?

They told me that the ministers, with sound trucks and under a police escort, were canvassing the black neighborhoods, pleading with the people to remain calm. No public mass meetings had been set for the next few days, but another strategy session had been scheduled for early Monday afternoon.

The whole account of the afternoon's strategy committee meeting made me angry. It seemed that in the final analysis not only white Mississippians, but the NAACP staff, and apparently a number of the Jackson ministers as well, could not really believe that the people could lead themselves.

It sounded as though the Jackson movement internally was by no means healthy, that many more crises lay ahead.

"The people are moving," I said, "and the Jackson movement will keep going. We won't let it stop."

Then Bill Kunstler indicated the he was returning to New York City the next day, Sunday. I asked him again if he felt that there was any chance the SCLC would involve itself in Jackson—especially in view of the huge demonstration of the afternoon. And even Bill's normally high degree of optimism failed him. Again, he shook his head sadly.

I walked outside. One of the Tougaloo administrative officials came up and we talked at length. A tremendous number of threats were pouring into the college, he said, concerning violence against me, against Ed, against the school. As we talked, a group of about twenty students came through the twilight. Many were carrying guns. We asked them what they were doing, and they indicated that they had set up a guard detail to watch the college that night. We nodded and thanked them. It seemed under the circumstances a logical enough step.

Steve Rutledge came out of Ed's house and said that a radio report indicated that the Women for Constitutional Government had levied quite a verbal attack against me.

Next, two FBI agents arrived, again to discuss the Thursday beatings on Rose Street. There was now, they said, considerable doubt that the police who had struck me and who had struck the others could be conclusively identified. I pointed out that every major television network had carried film sequences of my beating, at least, if not the other incidents, and that the faces of the police involved were clearly seen. They shrugged and indicated that there would still be difficulty.

I went back into the Kings' house. Jeannette was cooking supper for all of us. The telephone began to ring, and it was an unidentified white man reading scripture to us. We hung up, and the phone rang again. We answered with "Joe's Bar." He hung up. It rang again. "Madison County Dancehall," we said. He hung up. It rang again, and we took the telephone off the hook.

All were extremely tired and talked only briefly after dinner. Once again, there was no question but that the Jackson movement had to continue, with continuous mass demonstrations. Although we knew the position of the national NAACP, we were concerned about the attitude of the ministers and felt that they had reacted to the situation with panic. Obviously there was going to be no direct action on Sunday, but there would be a strategy session on Monday. And more important than anything else, the people were moving forward. One way or another, we decided, the Jackson movement would continue ahead—intensively.

By this time, the body of Medgar Evers was well on its way to Meridian, to the train that would carry him out of Mississippi forever. ❖

MYRLIE EVERS

Medgar Wiley Evers

(July 2, 1925–June 12, 1963)

Myrlie Evers-Williams was born March 17, 1933, in Vicksburg, Mississippi. In 1951 she married Medgar Evers and together they opened the first NAACP Mississippi state office. Following Medgar's death, she left Mississippi and became the director of planning and development at the Claremont Colleges, was the author of For Us, The Living (Doubleday, 1967), ran for Congress in 1970, and was one of the founding convening members—along with Gloria Steinem, Bella Abzug, Betty Friedan, and Frances Lear—of the National Woman's Political Caucus. Most recently, Myrlie was elected chair of the NAACP.

The morning of February 5, 1994, I heard the word that I had worked so long, so hard and prayed for over the past thirty years. GUILTY!!

The jury in the third trial of Byron de la Beckwith, the assassin of my husband, Medgar Wiley Evers, had rendered its verdict. Justice had finally prevailed. Now, perhaps our children and I could free ourselves of the ongoing nightmare of the early morning of June 12, 1963, when Medgar was killed; when we lost a husband, a father and provider; when his people lost a true friend and leader; and America lost a remarkable citizen.

Medgar had served his country in World War II only to return home and find that he was still considered less than a first class citizen. Medgar was still addressed as "boy"; he could not vote; although he paid taxes, he could not use public facilities such as libraries, swimming pools, parks, and recreational centers; he could not try on clothes or shoes at department stores or eat in restaurants; he could only sit in the "buzzard roost" at movie theaters; housing and jobs were sub-standard; and quality education was a joke. Those freedoms, taken for granted by so many, were denied us because of the color of our skin. Medgar Evers was determined to change those wrongs regardless of the personal costs involved.

As I reflect upon this unusual man and his work, I hope that history will not include him as a footnote but as a major volume in the documentation of the Civil Rights Movement of the fifties and sixties.

Medgar was a pioneer in the Movement. He was on the firing line when there were no cameras, no media to cover his bravery, when so many were afraid to be seen with or near him. He was pure in his desires and actions for he wanted nothing for himself—only freedom for his people.

Medgar was the first African American to apply for admission to the University of Mississippi (law school); to file a suit to integrate the public schools of Mississippi (*Darrele Kenyatta Evers v. State of Mississippi*); to investigate and secure witnesses in cases such as the Emmett Till murder; to boldly challenge a Mississippi system designed to forever keep "darkies in their place."

There are so many other contributions that Medgar made to the Movement, his people, his state, his country. For those of us who remember him, who love him, who believed in him and still know that the pursuit of justice and freedom is a constant struggle—we continue the fight. Medgar did not die in vain. He lives through each of us. ❖

TOM PAXTON

Death of Medgar Evers

The country is mourning the death of a soldier,
The death of a soldier who carried no gun.
A courageous soldier who died on his doorstep,
A soldier too brave to turn coward and run.
He never quit fighting,
He never quit trying,
He never lost courage and never laid down.
He never lost hope and he never feared dying and
Now they have laid him in Arlington ground.

The White Council boys made their black ugly phone calls,
Threatening his wife and his children with death.
He spoke to his wife in the dark of their bedroom
And decided to fight them till his dying breath.

The warnings increased and the threats they grew harsher
And once in the evening a firebomb came,
His wife put it out and nobody was injured
And the fire-bombers laughed at their hideous game.

Then young Medgar Evers instructed his children
And told them in case of a violent sound
They were not to run to see what was the matter
But instantly throw themselves down to the ground.

The threats drew the man and his wife close together
In his arms she would lie in the dark of the night.
And though she was frightened for her husband's safety
She never would ask him to give up the fight.

One night he came home to the point of exhaustion
The porch light was cheerfully brightening the night,
He walked up the steps as the sniper was aiming
The sniper who had him in his rifle sights.

Tom Paxton has been a much admired songwriter since he helped define the folk movement in New York's musical community in the early 1960s. With the world as his prey and lavish gifts of expression at his command, Paxton continues to find much to question, laugh about, and celebrate through words and music. He has been performing continuously for the past three decades and has produced 33 albums, including award winning records for children.

The bullet struck home and the sniper went flying
And Medgar's young children, they ran to the door,
His wife tried to stop them but they saw their dad dying,
They saw their dad dying on the living room floor.

Then sleep, Medgar Evers, your struggle is over,
They thought they could kill you but we know they were wrong,
They might lay you down in the quiet of Arlington
But while we're living the fight will go on.

He never quit fighting,
He never quit trying,
He never lost courage and never laid down.
He never lost hope and he never feared dying and
Now they have laid him in Arlington ground.

BOB DYLAN

Only A Pawn In Their Game

A bullet from the back of a bush took Medgar Evers's blood
A finger fired the trigger to his name,
A handle hid out in the dark, He hand-set the spark,
        Two eyes took the aim
        Behind a man's brain
        But he can't be blamed,
He's only a pawn in their game.

A south politician preaches to the poor, white man,
You got more than the blacks, don't complain,
You're better than them, you been born with white skin, they explain,
And the negro is named,
        Is used it is plain,
        For the politician's gain,
        As he rises to fame,
        And the poor white remains,
        On the caboose of the train,
        But it ain't him to blame,
He's only a pawn in their game.

The deputy sheriffs, the soldiers, the governors get paid,
And the marshals and cops get the same,
But the poor white man's used in the hands of them all like a tool,
He's taught in his school
        From the start by the rule
        That the laws are with him
        To protect his white skin,
        To keep up his hate
        So he never thinks straight,
        'Bout the shape that he's in,
        But it ain't him to blame,
He's only a pawn in their game.

Bob Dylan appeared alongside Pete Seeger and Theodore Bikel at a voter registration rally in Greenwood, Mississippi on July 6, 1963. It was there that he first sang his song "Only A Pawn In Their Game." Later that summer he performed the song during the great Civil Rights March on Washington. Bob Dylan arrived on the New York folk scene in early 1961 and signed with Columbia Records that same year.

From the poverty shacks he looks from the cracks to the tracks,
And the hoof beats pound in his brain,
And he's taught how to walk in a pack,
Shoot in the back,
       With his fist in a clinch,
       To hang and to lynch,
       To hide 'neath the hood,
       To kill with no pain
       Like a dog on a chain,
       He ain't got no name
       But it ain't him to blame,
He's only a pawn in their game.

The day Medgar Evers was buried from the bullet he caught,
They lowered him down as a king,
But when the shadowy sun sets on the one
That fired the gun,
       He'll see by his grave
       On the stone that remains,
       Carved next to his name
       His epitaph plain,
Only a pawn in their game.

PHIL OCHS

Too Many Martyrs

In the state of Mississippi many years ago,
A boy of fourteen years got a taste of southern law.
He saw his friend a hangin', his color was his crime,
And the blood upon his jacket left a brand upon his mind.

Too many martyrs and too many dead,
Too many lies, too many empty words were said,
Too many times, too many women and men,
Oh, let it never be again.

His name was Medgar Evers; he walked his road alone,
Like Emmett Till and thousands more whose names we'll never know.
They tried to burn his home and they beat him to the ground,
But deep inside they both knew what it took to bring him down.

Too many martyrs and too many dead,
Too many lies, too many empty words were said,
Too many times, too many women and men,
Oh, let it never be again.

The killer waited by his home hidden by the night,
As Evers stepped out from his car into the rifle sight.
The killer squeezed the trigger, the bullet left his side,
But it struck the heart of everyone when Evers fell and died.

Too many martyrs and too many dead,
Too many lies, too many empty words were said,
Too many times, too many women and men,
Oh, let it never be again.

We laid him in his grave while the bugle sounded clear,
We laid him in his grave when the victory was near.
While we wait for the future, for freedom through the land,
This country gained a killer, and this country lost a man.

Too many martyrs and too many dead,
Too many lies, too many empty words were said,
Too many times, too many women and men,
Oh, let it never be again.

JAMES FORMAN

Notes From Leflore County Jail

This journal entry was first published in *Black Protest History, Documents and Analysis, 1619 to the Present*, edited and with commentary by Joanne Grant, New York: Ballentine Books, 1968.

In 1890 or 1891 various Mississippi "bourbon" politicians, or very rich landlords, called a Mississippi state convention designed to take away the right to vote from black people and poor white people. They terrorized people and succeeded in imposing poll taxes and literacy tests before one could vote. Similar conventions were held throughout the South, resulting in the disenfranchisement of black people and poor white people.

In the 1960s members of the Student Nonviolent Coordinating Committee (SNCC), in coalition with other groups and individuals, attempted to reverse these decisions. Sections of the United States Justice Department objected to SNCC's insistence that within the 1964 Civil Rights Act all literacy requirements should be abolished as a requirement for the right to vote. SNCC and others lost this fight. The 1965 Voting Rights Law, however, was passed to correct the weaknesses in the 1964 Civil Rights Act.

The demonstrations in Greenwood that led to my writing "Notes from the Leflore County Jail" were sparked by the need to protest any demand that literacy tests were justified or that SNCC should agree to such proposals. For the first time in the modern Civil Rights Movement, the police in Greenwood, Mississippi, used police dogs against the demonstrators. Fortunately, I had a camera and took photographs of the police dogs which proved useful in the court of public opinion. As we were being arrested, I was able to give my camera to a co-worker for safe keeping.

We have been in jail one week today. Our morale is good, although there are serious undertones of a desire to be free among some members of the group. Now and then, the jokes of one or two turn to the outside. John Doar and the Justice Department received some sharp, but still humorous, comments from some of the fellows. They actually believed the Justice Department would have had them out by Monday. When we received news that the temporary injunction had been denied [we] were somewhat disappointed. Some of us tried to explain that

we must prepare ourselves psychologically to spend six months in this jail.

The cell in which we are being held is not bad so far as American prisons go. (The entire penal system needs reforming.) We are eight in a cell with six bunks. We have two mattresses on the floor. There is an open shower, a sink, a stool. It took us two days to get a broom and five days to get some salt for our food. The inner cell in which we are "contained" is approximately 15' x 12'. Not much room, is there? . . .

People outside send us food. When we were

James Forman, Ph.D. is a former Executive Secretary and International Affairs Director of the Student Nonviolent Coordinating Committee, SNCC. During the summer of 1964, he supervised the national office of SNCC which was located in Greenwood, Mississippi, and Atlanta, Georgia. He is currently the President of the Unemployment and Poverty Action Committee (UPAC) and the UPAC Fund, Inc., a 501 (c) (3) tax exempt organization.

in the city jail, we got food twice a day. Here we received a great deal Sunday, enough to last us till today. We are counting on someone to replenish our supply. However, [my doctor] has been to see me three times since I have been in the county jail. Each time she brings some food which I share with the fellows.

So far as my own diet is concerned, I have had sufficient eggs and bananas to sustain me. I must guard against giving these away since I don't want to become ill. They, the prison officials, have allowed me to take medicine and the doctor keeps me supplied. I am really not suffering due to my ulcers, although my sickness helps the group—through the visit of the doctor.

We are also improving our minds. We have been allowed to keep our books, and we have sufficient cigarettes. I even have my pipe and some tobacco. Personally, I have tried to organize our lives. Do you expect anything else of me? We have occasional classes. Moses gave us an excellent math lecture the other day. I gave one lesson in writing and English. Guyot has delivered several in biology. We are always having discussions. Sometimes one of us will read a passage from a book, and then we will discuss the meaning of it. We have had several stimulating conversations based on Thoreau's essay on civil disobedience and N'krumah's thoughts on positive action.

Around eleven o'clock we usually turn out the one large light in the middle of the room. We do not have sheets or blankets. We sleep in our underclothes. I suppose if it got cold we would put on our clothes.

In the morning when we get up we have grits, biscuits, and a piece of salt pork for breakfast. Then we sweep the cell. For the last two days, Bob, Guyot, and I have swept the cell and scrubbed it on our hands and knees. During the morning we usually have discussions, showers, play chess, talk, and wait for beans or peas and cornbread, which arrive around two o'clock. We do not have any more meals from the county until the next morning.

My personal opinions as to the significance

of our staying in jail follow. I am convinced that all the people connected with SNCC are busily engaged in protesting our unjust imprisonment. This is as it should be. I am also convinced that others sympathetic to the cause of Freedom are also alarmed at this travesty of justice.

Perhaps more important is that only our bodies are confined to this cell. Our minds are free to think what we wish, and we know our stay here will also pass away. Our imprisonment serves to dramatize to the nation and to the world that the black man does not even have the right to try to be an American citizen in some parts of our stalled democracy.

Our jail without bail may also serve to remind others in the Movement of the need for some of us to stay in jail to dramatize the situation.

On a local and state level, it is important that we stay in jail, for people are remembered more by what they do than by what they say. We have been telling Mississippians that we must prepare to die. We have encouraged them to accept our beliefs. Thus it follows that we must lead by example rather than by words.

Moreover, many acts of violence have been committed in Greenwood. The people are not afraid, but perhaps when they see our spirit and determination, they will have more courage. Then, too, the government must assume its responsibility for our release. If the Civil Rights Act of 1960 is ever to mean anything, then those arrested in connection with voter registration activities must be released by the efforts of the U.S. government.

When our people were arrested in Sunflower County for passing out leaflets announcing a voter registration meeting, it was really the government which should have sought their release. Instead of this, bond was posted, and then the government moved slowly to get the cases dropped and some consent agreement from the local officials about future arrests and interference with voter registration workers.

Perhaps more important than these social and political reasons is the personal significance that our imprisonment has for us. I have not yet asked each person for his personal reaction. As for myself, I am glad to make a witness for a cause in which I believe. I am glad for the chance to meditate, to think of many things, and to see the world continue as I sit here.

All of us are determined that once we are out we will walk to the courthouse with some more people. We have been discussing the dogs which most Mississippi officials try to use to halt demonstrations. I personally feel that I must be bitten by one of these dogs, for I don't believe we can continue to run from them. It must come to this, for the officials really believe, and the record proves them correct, that Negro demonstrators or peaceful citizens are not willing for dogs to bite them.

We sing of course. We are singing now. We love to sing "We'll never turn back." We have added a new verse.

"We have served our time in jail /with no money for to go our bail."

We place this as the second stanza.

Every night when the lights are out we sing this song. It is beautiful and it symbolizes our state—the entire song. Please tell Bertha [Gober, one of the Freedom Singers] to keep writing songs. She has a talent which should not be wasted.

There is a great deal of noise in the cell at times. We are trying to work out a schedule. Peacock suggested last night that our time might be better spent if we had a schedule. Concurrently with this idea Guyot was suggesting that if ever a dispute arose two people should take one side, two the other, and the remaining four should decide. Consequently, the question of a schedule was put before the floor. Surney and Smith objected to the schedule. Forman, McLaurin, and Guyot favored it. All arguments were presented as if we were speaking before a court. James Jones just consented to act as judge. He resigned and Peacock accepted the judgeship.

Smith presented some *reductio ad absurdum* arguments which were easily shattered. Finally the judge ruled in favor of the schedule. By this

time LaFayette was sleeping. The next incident around which there was disagreement was the light bulb. There is one light bulb in the middle of the room.

Each night it seems that someone has objections to it being turned out. Usually a compromise is worked out.

Interestingly, people are quoting Thoreau— "Government is best which governs least"—and then applying it to the cell. There are many divergent wills operating in this cell; a few people seek to have their own way at all times and seldom, if ever, indicate a willingness to understand others and give a little.

From these random notes you will perhaps catch a glimpse of what life is like in the cell. It is this that I am trying to portray.

We seem to have a morale problem. [One person] wants to leave the cell and says if he is not out by Sunday he wants bail. We have to constantly remind him and a few others that one cannot depend upon the Justice Department. One must prepare himself psychologically to stay here six months. If the government gets us out, fine. If not, then we ought to be prepared to stay for the reasons I mentioned earlier.

I am hungry; I just asked Guyot for a biscuit. It is cold, not very appetizing. I can only eat a small piece and drink two cups of water. I now have a plastic cup from which to drink. Last night Annelle Ponder sent Moses some tomato juice in a pitcher, along with a plastic cup.

We have just had breakfast . . . . Rice, biscuits, and a piece of oil sausage. I don't know if I am supposed to eat the sausage, but I did. I was very hungry. My supply of eggs is out. I have one left. I only have three small bananas. The next meal is at two o'clock . . .

John Doar paid us a visit this morning and said that we would probably be taken to Greenville this afternoon or tomorrow morning.

Doar felt that their complaint was not sufficiently prepared to get the order Monday.

Also they [the Justice Department] did not have affidavits supporting the events of last Wednesday. He takes the position that people working on voter registration have the right to peaceful protest of incidents such as the last shooting. He also suggested that Judge Clayton was not going to let anyone take advantage of us, but at the same time he was not going to allow anyone to be cute in his courtroom. Clayton is known to run a strict courtroom. We were also asked to be clean in the courtroom. Therefore we are sending for some more clothes, for we are in bad shape.

12:30 P.M.: Sather of the Justice Department interviewed me about the events, and while we were talking I heard some singing on the outside and our fellows yelling. Later we found out that nineteen more people had been arrested. We sang and sang. There are five women in the cell next door. One old woman is now praying as the old folks pray in the South. Her voice has a musical quality as she appeals and prays to God. She is praying for freedom in Greenwood, she is praying for mercy on Greenwood, she is praying for forgiveness in Greenwood. "Please," she cries, "go into the hospital, hold the church of God, you told us to love one another, there does not seem to be any love in this, look this town over, Jesus."

8:07 P.M. Wednesday, April 3, 1963.

We are now in the Washington County jail. We have been transferred so that we might testify in the injunction hearing tomorrow morning.

We were brought from Leflore County by federal marshals. When we came down from our cell, we saw these federal marshals with handcuffs and chains. Each person had a chain placed around him and was handcuffed to the chain. Serious protests were made about this treatment. Such remarks as "the powerful federal government" were uttered. It was somewhat ironic because upstairs we were all depending upon the federal government. It was even more ironic because I am sure the local officials were against the government taking us to Greenville and interfering with their so-called affairs. Perhaps it seemed strange to them that we were complain-

ing about the same forces to which they were opposed.

An interesting thing happened when the boys from the Justice Department were interviewing us this morning. Boll Weevil Styles also locked them up in the room. They were somewhat furious.

Well, when I was handcuffed, I asked the deputy marshal, Hubert Jones, to pick up my personal papers and my bag. He shoved the papers under my arms, put the tall shopping bag in my hands. I already had my suit hanging on my handcuffs. I had a hard time coming down the stairs trying to balance the bag. I asked Jones if he could help me with my bag. He simply gave me a slight shove on the back. The prisoners are now requesting that we sing songs.

Our plan has worked: we wanted to get them in the freedom mood. One wonders what the preachers are doing today. They are not in the Mississippi struggle, nor do they visit the jails. These prisoners are not really prisoners; they are starving for companionship and some fresh insights to make a dull, routine life more pleasant.

8:30 A.M.: Thursday, April 4, 1963. We have been up for two hours and a half.

8:45 A.M.: We are all dressed up in our best clothes, which is not to say very much, for most of them are borrowed clothes and hand-medowns. Clothes in the Movement are not very important. We often interchange from necessity. Most of the people working now complain that they have lost a few items in the Movement. Peacock says he came into the Movement with six pairs of shorts, now he has one. James Jones says that if Jessie Harris came up here now and demanded big clothes he would be naked.

Let us discuss sanitation. Last night we were given large clean towels here and a blanket. In Greenwood, we had to beg for toilet paper, and, imagine, they would never give us a towel. Frank Smith has a cold from the lack of a blanket in the Greenwood jail. There is something of a decent shower here, as contrasted with the shabby one in Greenwood.

11:45 A.M.: We are Free!

We sang this morning at the request of the prisoners. Many of them joined us. One of the things we have all discovered is that much prison reform is needed. There is absolutely no justification for the length of time people without bail must stay in jail waiting for their trial. I am reminded that I'm supposed to appear at some convention of criminologists in Louisville. I forget the date, but they are supposed to discuss some problems of race and jail procedure in the South.

I imagine there are many whites who must stay in jail a long time waiting for their trial.

We had a good breakfast this morning. Rice, butter, jelly, light bread, eggs, gravy, coffee, and an orange. Compared to the diet of the Greenwood jail, it was a sumptuous meal. There is no justification for not feeding prisoners a balanced diet. Greenwood should be ashamed. We never had a cup of coffee during the entire week we spent there. I shall speak to the sheriff about this.

PHOTOS BY

MATT HERRON

Matt Herron is a
photojournalist,
documentary
photographer,
researcher, writer,
activist, and author.
Matt's work has
appeared in
numerous publica-
tions including, Life,
Look, Time,
Newsweek, National
Geographic,
Smithsonian, New
York Times and the
London Mirror.
Matt's photographs
are in the permanent
collections at the
George Eastman
House, the
Smithsonian
Institution, and the
Schomburg Center
for Research in
Black Culture.

Jackson police dragging demonstrators to the "Nigger Wagon," 1965.

MALVINA REYNOLDS

It Isn't Nice

(Recorded by Judy Collins, who observed: "I hope when I am as old as Malvina is, I am as young as she has been all her life.")

It isn't nice to block the doorway,
It isn't nice to go to jail,
There are nicer ways to do it,
But the nice ways always fail.
It isn't nice, it isn't nice
You told us once, you told us twice,
But if that's freedom's price,
We don't mind . . .

It isn't nice to dump the groceries,
Or to sleep in on the floor,
Or to shout our cry of freedom
In the hotel or the store,
It isn't nice, it isn't nice,
You told us once, you told us twice,
But if that's freedom's price,
We don't mind . . .

Yeah, we tried negotiations
And the token picket line,
Mister Charlie didn't see us
And he might as well be blind;
When you deal with men of ice,
You can't deal with ways so nice,
But if that's freedom's price,
We don't mind . . .

They kidnapped boys in Mississippi,
They shot Medgar in the back,
Did you say that wasn't proper?
Did you stand out on the track?
You were quiet just like mice,
Now you say we're not nice,
Well, if that's freedom's price,
We don't mind . . .

It isn't nice to block the doorways,
It isn't nice to go to jail,
There are nicer ways to do it,
But the nice ways always fail,
It isn't nice, it isn't nice,
You told us once, you told us twice,
Thanks, Buddy, for your advice,
Well, if that's freedom's price,
We don't mind . . .
We don't mind!

PHOTO BY

MATT HERRON

Mississippi highway patrolman Hughie Kohler arrests Anthony Quinn, 5, son of Mrs. Aylene Quinn of McComb, Mississippi, during a voting rights protest. When Quinn refused to give up his small American flag, the patrolman erupted and wrenched it out of his hands. Winner, World Press Award, 1965.

Interview with Mrs. Mattie Pilcher

[Interview with Mrs. Mattie Pilcher, Greenwood, Mississippi, August 15, 1963, by Howard Zinn, with Roslyn Zinn. Mrs. Pilcher lived in the house just next to the SNCC Freedom House in Greenwood, and we went over to talk to her. She was ironing in the living room and she invited us to sit down.]

Howard Zinn: Well, Mrs. Pilcher, I will tell you what I wanted to talk to you about. Sort of about your experiences, and things about your family, and about what it has been like here in Greenwood, and if you lived any other places. And questions like that. I will ask you questions from time to time and you can just go on and say whatever you feel like . . . So let me ask you first, have you been living in Greenwood all your life?

Mrs. Pilcher: Yes I have, near all my life . . . When I married I had two—well, when my husband died I was with this girl, with the girl in the kitchen in there. And after he died that gave me two children. And he had a little social security . . . it was about $17 a month from that social security. So I would live off of that for eating and clothes the best way we could, you know. And then my Dad he would help me a little. And we were living in his house. But it was miserable living though . . .

Howard Zinn: Where was that? Right down the street there? What did your father do in Greenwood, what kind of work did he do?

Mrs. Pilcher: Oh, he farmed, well, he carpentered, he built houses, and filled manholes too . . . he went to cutting yards for people . . . just anywhere he could get a little job. They paid him fifty cents an hour to go to work at eight a.m. and work until four and five p.m. some days at fifty cents an hour. No way you can make a living.

Howard Zinn: It is certainly not much. Were you working all this time too?

Mrs. Pilcher: No, I wasn't working. I was at home. I was sick—well after I and him were married I had a set of twins and something happened to me and I was too weak to work, you know. And the doctor said that it would be a long time before I would be able to do any hard work. Well, I was working at home so finally one day I told him, well, it is so hard for you to get a job I believe I will see if I can't get me a job to help. So I got a job helping out a lady at work, white lady. I worked there until I and her couldn't agree. And why we couldn't agree? Well, she had wanted me to work for her and no one else. And she said, "Well, if you just can't work for me only," she said, "I just don't need you." So I didn't go back. She paid me off.

Howard Zinn: Do you do that work now, too, regularly? Or just off and on?

Mrs. Pilcher: I work out at the country club.

Howard Zinn: What do you do for them now?

Mrs. Pilcher: I can cook. Well, I help the cook and then we waits on the people, you know. Set tables, pick up dishes, you know, just anything that needs . . .

Howard Zinn taught at Spelman College and Boston University. He is the author of numerous books, his latest being, You Can't Be Neutral On A Moving Train.

Roslyn Zinn has been a teacher, social worker, activist and more recently a painter.

Howard Zinn: Do you like it? I mean how is it as far as the way they treat you?

Mrs. Pilcher: They don't like colored people. Because, I will tell you why. It is like any little thing you might do, break something or something, you know they don't like us, you know. And they are quick to call you "nigger."

Howard Zinn: Do they call you that to your face?

Mrs. Pilcher: Sure they call you that to your face! They don't mind it. They want to call you "nigger." They will jump on you, some of them...

Howard Zinn: Has there been any change in the way they behave toward you since all this business started with voter registration in Greenwood?

Mrs. Pilcher: Well, I will tell you about that. They don't want you to have anything to do with all them outside agitators or something like that. And they say, "Are you in that mess, or are you fooling with that mess?" What I said, I said, "I don't know anything about that mess." But if you tell them yes, well they don't want you to work . . . And they won't mention to you about this [civil rights activity]—they just get mad and find some fault around in the house now. That is the way they do it now . . . We colored people understand what it is all about. But you just can't say anything about it, because if you do then something might happen to you. Well, they just tell you, "You didn't do such and such things. Why didn't you do so and so and so?" . . . And say big word you know ... handle it just like . . . you were a little child . . .

Howard Zinn: Are you in better health these days, Mrs. Pilcher? You said you were sick for quite a while.

Mrs. Pilcher: Oh yes, I am. I feel good you know. And goes to work. Sometimes I will be sick, or I mean I will be sick just like a lot of folks from here. Well, I was picking cotton one year. I didn't know I had as much cotton in my sack as I did, seventy-some pounds of cotton. I went to pull it up and seems like to hurt me some way. And I went to the doctor and he said that I was all right and he gave me some medi-

cine. But sometimes I can feel it.

Howard Zinn: Which doctor was that?

Mrs. Pilcher: Dr. Percy.

Howard Zinn: He is a white doctor?

Mrs. Pilcher: He is the white doctor.

Howard Zinn: There is no colored doctor in Greenwood?

Mrs. Pilcher: I don't think there is.

Howard Zinn: I meant to ask you beforehand, when did you first get to be involved with the voter registration activity? How did you first get to know them?

Mrs. Pilcher: Well, my father has this building out here. And one day it was so cold—I had been hearing it talked around, you know. So finally one day, one morning, they said you know they burned the office up there, where the outside agitators had an office, you know.

Howard Zinn: You heard white people saying that?

Mrs. Pilcher: No, I just heard the people, the colored people were saying things. You know they had a big burning up there last night that it burned two places there. The next morning I was playing the radio and it come over the radio. I got it on the radio. And then that day, you know, people were talking about it . . . we didn't know what to think. Didn't know what to say about it because it was just something that was happening here that never had happened before. And me, myself, just going along working for the white people, taking what little they put on us, doing just whatever we had to do. I never had given a thought about freedom at all. And I was wondering what did it mean about freedom, you know, just kind of to myself and hearing people talk. Still I didn't know. . . . So one cold day after the building was burnt, Block and three other men, they came here.

Howard Zinn: Sam Block?

Mrs. Pilcher: Sam Block, looking for my father. So I told them, I showed them where he lived. So he was at home. So he brought them back over here and it was so cold. And we talked, and they explained it to us what it was all about.

Still I couldn't understand it, you know. But they was talking. So I said to myself, I wonder how in the world they are going to get up to these white folks here and they is putting people in the river and beating them and going about this work that they want to do, you know . . . I was all upset that night . . . Police—well, Sam Block had a car, they know that car. The car was sitting around out there and the police would just ride by. And I could see them ride by, and they would come back and go back around. I was so afraid that I just didn't know what to do . . . I went on to my daddy—he told them, he said, I don't guess I will rent it to you all because I might have much trouble out of the white people . . . So they went on, they didn't give up. The kept a coming back, talking to him . . .

Still he was afraid, we was, too. We were just afraid because we knew that the white people had been killing us, you know, beating us up and . . . well, they just walk in your house with guns and things, you know. Just five or six of them, like that, you know . . . So my daddy said, I just feel like I—I am too old a man to have a lot of trouble like that. Finally these two men in their car, they would come every evening, every day. Finally he let them [the SNCC workers] have the building.

. . . And so they went to give out food over here in a church, Wesley Chapel. Polices went over there and arrested them—well, they were going to register for voting. I don't know what occurred over there because I wasn't over there. I was afraid and then I was scared. They arrested a lot of them over there . . . So after they—they didn't have anywhere [for an office] after it got burned up there. They didn't have anywhere to put their typewriters and their things like that. So they told my dad, well, this is just all right. We will sweep and clean up and do around and work some after we get in here . . . So they did that. They just moved on in that old piece of building as it was. So finally they started their work going out registering people.

About three weeks after then . . . it was in the spring like, it had gotten a little warmer—

people who were going down to register they would start walking in a line. They [the police] started taking pictures and going around out there. The polices would block them off, you know, turn them around. Then they would get in cars and go . . . And started locking them up, too. . . .

And so a man named Dick Gregory, was that his name? He come up here, too. So he said that he was going to lead the marches . . .

Howard Zinn: Were you at that meeting, did you go to the mass meeting?

Mrs. Pilcher: Yes, I went to the mass meeting. And he told a lady that night, an old lady who lives right up the street here, he picked her out to march, to lead the line with him. So she told him, "Yes, sir, I will be there in the morning." And he said, "Well, you be there at seven a.m." She said: "I can get there at six a.m." It was cold, but she did, she got here before he did and she was ready! So when they got lined up and she was right there in front and marched right with him . . .

See, they were trying to get people that had never been down to register. So the lady [Martha Lamb] told me, she said I am going to start class. She came in here one Saturday and she told me, she said we want to learn people how to sign up for voter registration. And want you to read about Dr. Martin Luther King and other men, and different things, you know, in this book. I had some of the books. So I went to school out to her about two months.

So, finally, she said you are all ready good, she said . . . she wasn't afraid like we was. We was afraid. We was in there, but all the time we was afraid that they [the whites] would come in there . . . they would ride by. We didn't know what was going to happen at all. But we would still go . . . Were so shy that we would go in the back every time we would go, in the back way. They started mass meetings up again.

Howard Zinn: Let me ask you this, Mrs. Pilcher, what did you learn in those classes?

Mrs. Pilcher: Well, I learned how to—when we first started we read about Dr. King, and we read about freedom. And she learned us how to read, how to write, and how to use language, you know. And they started how to, how you could make out a check, and how you could fill out the registration blank. Well, she had us voting one day, too. After we filled out the blank that she had just like if we were going to vote. And filled out and passed the long envelope, and she had us fold them, you know, long way, and then fold them back halfway. And then she had us to write our name on the back and had a ballot box, drop it over in the ballot box. Oh, she just learned us lot of things.

Howard Zinn: Mrs. Pilcher, since you went down that morning to register have you succeeded in becoming registered?

Mrs. Pilcher: Oh, no, no. I have been down there twice. Next time when I went down there she said, now you didn't finish filling it out, so you didn't write anything about the Constitution. Well, I didn't know anything about the Constitution. She said: "Now, I just don't want you coming back here no more. No more. I don't see why you niggers, you don't know anything about the Constitution and you are trying to sign up for voter registration." Well, she talked so heavy to me about it. And so I said well I won't go back anymore . . . but still, I am going back . . .

Howard Zinn: Have you gotten to know the Movement better since they moved in next door?

Mrs. Pilcher: Well, I have. I have learned the Movement pretty good, what they say about it and what they want to do. They tell us you don't want to, you are not trying to fight against them, you are not trying to be mean to them. What you are trying to do, see, you just want to be as a brother and sister. What you want. We want to get equal rights. What that means—if you go and work, if the white man or white lady gets thirty-five or forty dollars, whatever he gets, you get the same. They say that we want to marry their daughters and their sons. But now in Mississippi, colored people, I don't think they ever want to do that. Because if it was just grown in

us they didn't do that in Mississippi.

Howard Zinn: Do you think they really believe that is what you all want? Do they really believe that?

Mrs. Pilcher: Well . . . what made us believe it so strong because we have children, this boy had been in the North where they associated together and he would just talk loud and be friendly. They killed this boy. He was visiting his grandmother and grandfather. And they went in there at night and they carried that boy out . . .

Howard Zinn: Wasn't that Emmett Till? That isn't too far from here.

Mrs. Pilcher: No, that is not anywhere from here. And several things . . . just like if they don't like a colored boy to smile at a white lady, not here . . . Only way to do that is if you are working for her and she is talking with you about something . . . But they don't like, they don't allow that here.

Howard Zinn: How old are your children now?

Mrs. Pilcher: I have a boy eighteen years old. And in March, the 16th of March, he will be nineteen years old.

Howard Zinn: What is he going to do? Is he going to school?

Mrs. Pilcher: He is going to college.

Howard Zinn: Where is he going?

Mrs. Pilcher: Tougaloo.

Howard Zinn: He is going to start in the fall? And he is all accepted and everything?

Mrs. Pilcher: He is all accepted and everything. I wasn't able to put him through school. I tried to raise my children without a father, my two biggest children. My husband, he is nice to them. But still he doesn't make enough to both have a home and to put him through college. One day, he says: "Mama, I will work my way through college." And I was worried, you know, about it. He said, "Mama, you don't have to be worried about me." He said, "I am going to Tougaloo College, because that is the only school I can go to, a school like that." Because you see, he joined the NAACP.

Howard Zinn: He did?

Mrs. Pilcher: Well, I didn't even know it. I didn't know anything about him really belonging to it until the Movement come up . . . he was the head of his basketball team. That is how he got his scholarship.

Mrs. Zinn: Is he a good student?

Mrs. Pilcher: He is a good student. They sent for him to come down to Tougaloo after school was out and he has been down there, you know, with them. And they think he is wonderful.

Howard Zinn: What is your son doing this summer?

Mrs. Pilcher: Well, he is not doing anything because there is nothing for him to do here.

Howard Zinn: There is no work for him?

Mrs. Pilcher: No work for him. The white boys and the white girls they get the jobs. They all go out there to the country club and caddy or something like that and make a little money . . . If they [the black kids] don't get up before daylight and catch a truck and chop cotton, or pick, well they just don't have a job . . .

[Mr. Pilcher arrives]

Howard Zinn: How are you? My name is Howard Zinn. Mr. Pilcher, this is my wife, Roslyn Zinn. We have been talking to your wife.

Mr. Pilcher: You taping what they say?

Howard Zinn: Yeah, yeah . . .

Mr. Pilcher: Oh, I ain't going to say nothing (laughter). Not going to let her say anything . . . (laughter) . . .

Mrs. Pilcher: And our boy, well, he likes the Movement, he really likes the Movement.

Howard Zinn: How about the younger ones? How old are your younger kids?

Mrs. Pilcher: Well, my youngest, she is seventeen. Well, that is both of my daughters (showing a picture). Both of those girls and both of those boys.

Howard Zinn: They are good-looking children.

Mrs. Zinn: They are beautiful.

Mrs. Pilcher: But my children been scared out, my youngest children, my girl is seventeen, she has been just scared out, you know, of the Movement, any kind of way. Now she likes it. She said, "Mama, I really like what is going on and I hope it will be one day." And she is kind of nervous, too.

Howard Zinn: Did something happen to scare her?

Mrs. Pilcher: Yes, it did. One day, you know, once the dogs went to biting, they came up there you know to register for voting and they put the dogs on them. A dog bit Reverend Tucker. They have had a time of it up there. And so that incident, and all of that, and the polices that you see, they would ride around here, you know. And they said that they had tear gas in the cars. And stopping and arresting peoples . . . And they could see it . . . and they were just afraid. They say, "Mama, I wouldn't want to go to jail at all." For them to put her in jail where lice and bedbugs, and all kinds of bugs and things to bite them . . .

Howard Zinn: The little ones, do they know what is going on?

Mrs. Pilcher: Yes, my boy, my baby, he is eight years old, he knows what is going on! (laughter) Well, he used to say, "Well, Mom, it is for us to go to school and we will learn more there, so we can have more." The Movement, that brought about food you know, clothes and stuff, come out there with a lot of food. And lots of clothes and they thought that was wonderful, all of that food, ooh man, this room wouldn't hold the food and clothes, you know (laughter). So they would get out there and jump around, and he says, "Mama" he says, "if freedom means plenty and clothes," he says, "we just be freed all the time." (laughter) He says, "Mama, we are going to have clothes, we aren't going to have to worry about washing clothes at night to have to go to school." He says, "Sam Block told us that we were going to have clothes and we could change and put on clothes like people and go to school like folks."

Howard Zinn: Mrs. Pilcher, let me ask you

this. When was the first time you got the idea that there were white people in the Movement who were trying for the same things?

Mrs. Pilcher: Well . . .

Mr. Pilcher: I reckon you got it from right there off that TV.

Howard Zinn: Off the TV? (laughter)

Mr. Pilcher: Every time they would arrest some, they would have white people in there arrested with them . . .

Mrs. Pilcher: . . . after they got into the office . . . it was white ladies and white men all around . . . The white men were talking with the colored ladies and the colored ladies were standing with hands on the white men's shoulders (laughter) talking. That is something that never had happened here. And the policemen would be riding by, acting, you know, like they were, they would look so funny and just ride, ride. They never would stop talking, you know.

Mr. Pilcher: Always know there was some good white folk and there was good colored people . . .

Howard Zinn: Do you have any criticism of the Movement, Mrs. Pilcher?

Mrs. Pilcher: No, I don't have any criticism of the Movement at all because I feel like they is doing all they know how, you know, to bring peace and freedom among us colored people and we people. And because they tell us they don't hate the white people, they just want to walk along by their side, they just want to be as free as the white man is . . . now the white people think that we want to get about them . . . But they don't want to do anything . . . .here in Mississippi. Colored people can't get too high in Mississippi or you will go to the river over there, or somewhere. You get drug behind a car right quick.

Howard Zinn: Have you thought about leaving Mississippi?

Mrs. Pilcher: Well, I did. I have thought about leaving Mississippi . . . I just wasn't getting anything, it looked like. Well, I wasn't the only one, there was other peoples, too. And I just worried a lot. Sometimes at night I would

just worry. I don't know why I did. We can't have money enough to buy clothes and food like the white people. Why our children can't have things like they have . . . Sometimes they don't be fit to go to school, you know, like other white children . . . But I never could figure it out. Well, I didn't have a job. So that is what made me marry him. (laughter)

Howard Zinn: Mr. Pilcher, I just want to ask you one question before you leave. Have you registered to vote?

Mr. Pilcher: No.

Howard Zinn: Do you expect to?

Mr. Pilcher: Yes, I just haven't had the time to go up there.

Howard Zinn: But you think you will one of these days?

Mr. Pilcher: Sure, sure, I am ready.

Howard Zinn: Well, I think we are holding up your dinner and things.

Mrs. Zinn: Yes, we certainly are.

Mr. Pilcher: You aren't holding up my dinner. I just see a fellow over there with some peas, and I am going to see if I can get some peas from him, that's all. You ain't holding up my dinner.

Howard Zinn: I think we have had a nice talk, Mrs. Pilcher.

Mrs. Pilcher: I just love the Movement so . . . just anything that I can do. Now I didn't know anything about the Movement or anything, but the people seem to be nice people. My husband and I, we just like it, and anything we could do to help the Movement, you know, we thought it is right. And we would do that, we would neglect things for ourselves, let them have it, you know, do without. My husband, he said, "Well, let them go ahead on and use it, I can do without it." And he just do without. And sometimes he says, "I will just omit taking a bath, let them all go in and take a bath." He said, "Get towels for them, give them what soap we have."

Food, they come in one morning they heard a whisper about they was going to bomb the

PHOTO BY

MATT HERRON

Ed King (left) with Aaron Henry at COFO meeting. King and Henry ran for vice governor and governor of Mississippi on the Freedom Democratic Party ticket in 1963.

building. So they stayed up out there all night. They didn't have a stove out there, anything to make coffee, you know. And it was so cold that morning, ooh, and so . . . I don't know how many pots of coffee I made, but I just kept making coffee until they drank it . . . I said well now, after I finish make you some coffee I will make some biscuits, lots of them. Lots of them weren't used to biscuits. I think they were used to white bread . . . I told my husband, "I know you have to work for what food you have . . . We don't have very much food, but I am willing to do without." He said, "Well, go ahead on and cook it." He said, "I have a dollar in my pocket, that will buy my dinner . . . just go ahead on and

cook it and let them have it. So I go ahead on and cook it and let them eat it all up. We just thought it was the wonderfullest thing we have ever heard of in our life, you know. And so now I enjoy it still better because they brought a lot food in and they said, "Mrs. Pilcher, you were so nice to us you just go out and get as much food as you want to."

Howard Zinn: Well, thanks very much, Mrs. Pilcher, it has really been nice talking to you.

Mrs. Zinn: Thank you so much.

Mrs. Pilcher: And I really enjoyed this. ❖

VICTORIA GRAY ADAMS

Mississippi, the Closed Society: Turning Points in the Life of a Christian Activist

From a presentation given at Trinity College,

Hartford, Connecticut, on April 15, 1988

On January 9, 1861, Mississippi seceded from the Union of the United States of America. And thus began the intentional journey of a state into a stance of regression that would earn it the reputation of being "The Worst of These"—in any area of civil and human rights you wish to consider. This journey into regression could, and did, lead only to stagnation and death—mentally, physically, and spiritually—of the majority of the inhabitants therein.

On November 5, 1926, at one o'clock on a cold Thursday morning, I am told that a baby girl was born to Mack and Annie Mae Ott Jackson (their first-born). With this event, a unique conscientious objector to the closed society became a member of the family called "Mississippians."

I trust that none hearing this statement will misread the declaration; because I promise you, it is not one of arrogance. However, you are the judges, I only hope that I can justify the statement in the time allotted for this sharing.

I've heard many stories about this child, Victoria, that took place too early for me to remember. But the first remembered incident that

I consider a turning point took place when I made a remark to my grandmother and my aunt following a visit of my aunt's white employers. I apparently had observed something that prompted this statement: "I sure wish we were white so we could be rich!" I remember clearly my sensing that I had said something that got their total attention. Thus began my education on the importance of the richness of being what and who God created you to be.

The second turning point came, as I can see it, when I was five or six years old. I had attended the baccalaureate service of the graduating class of the Depriest Consolidated School. Upon returning home that Sunday evening, I was sitting on the edge of the wood box in my grandparents' bedroom (which was also the family room, where family and friend alike gathered for social occasions when the weather did not permit us on the front porch). There were many people there, but I withdrew into a place apart—I had been really impressed with the baccalaureate ceremony. I haven't the faintest memory of what was said there, but that event evoked my first dream and formed my first con-

Victoria Gray Adams was born November 5, 1926, in Hattiesburg, Mississippi (Palmers Crossing). She attended Wilberforce University in Ohio for three years, Tuskegee Institute in Alabama, and Jackson State College in Mississippi. She was a charter member of the Mississippi Freedom Democratic Party, for five years served on the national board of the Southern Christian Leadership Conference (SCLC), and was the first woman to run for the U.S. Senate from the state of Mississippi. She has received numerous awards including the Fannie Lou Hamer Humanitarian Award.

Mississippi Freedom Democratic Party delegates during nomination rally for President Johnson. Victoria Gray (center) holding banner.

PHOTO BY

GEORGE BALLIS

George Elfie Ballis began photographing and organizing farm workers in the San Joaquin Valley, California, in the mid-1930s. He photographed and organized for SNCC in Mississippi and California from 1963–66 and for several years thereafter for the United Farm Workers Union. George shot and directed several prize-winning movement films—with stills—of Blacks, Chicanos, American Indians, and California agriculture. "I always photographed as an active partisan, not an observer." His civil rights and farm worker photos have been published in numerous books and magazines.

scious goal regarding my life: I was going to march up that aisle in that auditorium wearing one of those caps and gowns. I sat there on that wood box and saw myself marching up that aisle . . . at that point someone called me back to the present company and time, but that vision was indelibly stamped in my being, and I knew it would become a reality.

As I grew up in this little hamlet in Mississippi, I was told, directly and indirectly, time and time again, that God had plans for my life, and I must serve my people. I was also told by others in the community, both family and friends, that I would self-destruct at an early age. However, the prophecies for a positive life role impressed me far more than the negative predictions; and, in fact, the negative predictions only strengthened my resolve to live up to the expectations of the prophets and myself.

I was frequently in trouble with my peers as well as my elders because I had this habit of voicing my opinion on subjects and events. (This habit—the habit of a young person voicing her

opinions on various matters—all too frequently was not in keeping with the prevailing opinions.) I was keenly aware of the contradictions which existed in the family and the community, and I voiced and attempted to respond to those which limited and hurt people; and I was frequently ridiculed for those efforts.

To make a long story short, I was something of a misfit among my peers; and, according to the principal of the local high school (as told to my grandparents), a threat to some of the teachers and other elders in my environment.

In the meantime, things were happening in the country, in the world and, less perceptibly, in Mississippi. Other conscientious objectors were being born—like Lawrence Guyot, Curtis Washington, and Hollis Watkins! In the interim, I did many things: fulfilled that first goal to walk up the aisle, began a college education that was aborted due to a shortage of money to continue, entered the teaching profession, got married, became a mother, traveled and lived beyond the confines of the U.S.A., and upon returning to

America, decided to become a businesswoman.

And that is where I was when the modern Civil Rights Movement came into full bloom.

I had established a business that gave me the joy of recruiting others of my community to join me in a journey of financial freedom. And I was really enjoying this role, when along came two young men—teenagers—to Hattiesburg, Mississippi, in search of people who wanted an even more basic freedom, a freedom promised by the Constitution of the U.S.A. . . . in the persons of Curtis Washington and Hollis Watkins. Soon there were others: David Dennis, Lawrence Guyot, and others.

But one night, in the St. John Methodist Church, a meeting was called. St. John may have been considered the least of these, as churches went in that area and at that time; but, you see, all the other churches had joined the Closed Society, and St. John was the lone avenue to addressing the corporate community in an appropriate place, with the courtesy and courage of its pastor, L. P. Ponder, and its board (of which I was a consenting member). After a brief orientation/introduction period by Rev. Ponder, Curtis and Hollis shared their mission and then made the altar call—the "Invitation to Get on Board and Begin the Journey to First Class Citizenship." The meeting was sparsely attended. I looked around the sanctuary—Rev. Ponder's hand was lifted, Victoria's hand was lifted—but in that brief moment, I had another very clear vision of a major turning point—of a journey that was challenging and dangerous, but absolutely necessary!

I knew that my life would never be the same again; I knew that this decision might cost me my life, but I knew I had made the right decision; and I say to you, until this day—I had never turned back—nor shall I ever turn back—either in this world or the next!

There's more, but I know we must move on. However, just tolerate one more point of clarity: there was a mass meeting at the Star-light Baptist Church. [After St. John hosted the initial phase of the formation of the local Movement, others began to open up and give us more exposure to a wider audience.] By this time, the Council of Federated Organizations (COFO) had staged the big event that announced and invited the national leadership of the church, "The Clergy," to participate and give to the Mississippi Movement the weight of their support through their personal witness. Once this had begun, it first became evident that this was no one-day stand and we had to continue. The ministers, for the most part, simply couldn't pick up and leave (having performed their priestly duties and filled their one-shot commitment), once they experienced the Closed Society. They also experienced the Burning Bush, and the Damascus Road, and other pivotal experiences. (How do I know all of this? The bulk of the one hundred plus ministers who responded to our call were housed in the home of Victoria and Tony Gray, and the homes of the family of Victoria Gray. And so when we gathered at night or early A.M., we had to share the day's events from our individual perspectives; so I heard first-hand much of what was taking place.) The occasion of this meeting was to recruit more local people to join the demonstrations down at the courthouse. I was sharing with the audience and encouraging them—yes, pleading with them—to come and be baptized into "the Body of Seekers For First Class Citizenship," either for themselves or for others. Then, all of a sudden came a vision of another who preceded me, in the person of Isaiah; and in that moment I understood and envisioned clearly the meaning and application of his vision because it became mine. It was this: [Isa. Ch. 6] "In the year that King Uzziah died, I saw the Lord . . . and I heard the Voice of the Lord saying, 'Whom shall I send, and Who will go for Us?' Then I said, 'Here am I. I'll go, send Me'"—and so it has been, and so it is, and so it shall be! ❖

ODETTA

Movin' It On

Transcribed by Susie Erenrich

Any way you make it baby
won't you keep on movin' it on;
Any way you make it baby
won't you keep on movin' it on.

Now if you can't fly, run;
if you can't run, walk;
if you can't walk, crawl.

Any way you make it baby
keep on movin' it on;
Any way you can make it baby
keep on movin' it on.

My country tis for me; I've moved to right the right;
Ain't much to carry change sittin' down singing my song;
I sing to fight the spirit and keep him up bright and strong.

Any way you make it baby
won't you keep on movin' it on;
Any way you make it baby
won't you keep on movin' it on.

Now if you can't fly, run to the post tell them this too is your nation; if you can't run, walk and there won't be no resignation; if you can't walk, crawl to the polls and vote your determination.

Willie James Shaw, a SNCC worker, being arrested in Belzoni Mississippi, for encouraging local blacks to vote in a COFO "Freedom Election." Police said Shaw was parked too close to a fire hydrant.

Any way you make it baby
won't you keep on movin' it on;
Any way you make it baby
won't you keep on movin' it on.

Now if you can't fly, run; if you can't run, walk; if you can't walk, crawl.

Any way you make it baby
won't you keep on movin' it on;
Any way you make it baby
won't you keep on movin' it on.

PHOTO BY

MATT HERRON

JULIAN BOND

1964 Mississippi Freedom Summer

Julian Bond has spent the last three decades working for civil and economic rights. He was SNCC's Communication Director during Freedom Summer 1964, served four terms in the Georgia House of Representatives and six terms as a state senator. Since leaving public office, he has taught at Harvard, Williams College, Drexel University, and the University of Pennsylvania. He is currently a distinguished adjunct professor at American University, a lecturer in history at the University of Virginia, and a commentator on America's Black Forum, the oldest black-owned show on syndicated television.

Like the 1955-'56 Montgomery Bus Boycott and Martin Luther King's 1963 March on Washington speech, the 1964 Freedom Summer in Mississippi was one of the pivotal events of the Southern Freedom Movement; it has been written about, analyzed, and awarded credit or blame for the Movement's subsequent successes or failures.

For some, it caused the still-existing rift between black and white activists, forever sundering a movement which dreamed of black and white marching forward together, and it demonstrated the wrongness and futility of whites working in black communities and with black-dominated organizations. For others, it set the standard for black political organization and independence that had been long discussed but never achieved until the summer of '64. Many now believe it helped give an organizing impetus to the reborn women's movement. For all, the Mississippi Freedom Summer showed America its worst face, and America responded.

I had been working for the Student Nonviolent Coordinating Committee (SNCC) for three years as communications director—publicist and propagandist, seeking space in newspapers and minutes on radio and television, explaining our work to delegations of visiting journalists and others who swept through our offices on tours of the South.

From SNCC's Atlanta headquarters, I had seen the organization grow from a 1960 Coordinating Committee—a representative body of Southern black college students who tried to organize simultaneous protests from its Southwide university constituency—into an organization whose personnel had abandoned their educations to work full-time in the Movement. SNCC was the newest civil rights organization, created to harness—without suffocating it—the energy of the sit-in protests which had exploded across the South in early 1960.

In 1961, when CORE's Freedom Riders were beaten and their bus burned in Alabama, veteran sit-in students from Nashville dared carry the Rides forward into Mississippi. While serving thirty days in Parchman Penitentiary before being bailed out, they vowed to "put their bodies in the Movement," and a small cadre settled in McComb in southwest Mississippi to begin a pilot registration campaign. Their initial effort faltered when a local supporter was murdered, and high school students, striking in sympathy, were expelled from school, but the SNCCers regrouped in Mississippi's Delta and started anew. Dedicated to working with and for the communities into which they settled, the SNCC style insisted on "doing what the people say do." By 1963, several registration projects, most directed by a Mississippi-born staff, were scattered across the state.

My job for Freedom Summer would be to spread the word that the Civil Rights Movement was staging a confrontation with the nation's most recalcitrant state. The summer's events provided more than enough opportunity to contrast democracy's dream with its reality in Mississippi.

In the fall of 1963, few blacks were registered to vote in Mississippi, despite three years of hard work by the staff of the Council of Federated Organizations (COFO)—most of them from SNCC—and more than half a century of dangerous, anonymous work by scattered activists, many of them active in Mississippi branches of the National Association for the Advancement of Colored People (NAACP).

COFO had been established as a Mississippi umbrella organization—an amalgam of SNCC and Congress of Racial Equality (CORE) workers, local NAACP members, and various other activists.

A spring 1963 registration drive in Greenwood, where COFO efforts had focused, produced few results; after some initial publicity, the press had moved elsewhere. The federal government had intervened in Greenwood when violence by whites seemed imminent but made no further moves there or elsewhere in the state to help get Mississippi blacks registered to vote.

White freelance social activist Allard Lowenstein, a New Yorker long involved in liberal Democratic politics, suggested to Bob Moses, a SNCC staff member who was COFO's Voter Registration Director, that Lowenstein be allowed to recruit white students for the fall "Freedom Vote" campaign; they would provide needed manpower, and their white skins might provoke interest from the news media that black skins could not produce.

Lowenstein recruited one hundred Yale and Stanford students to come to Mississippi between late October and election day on November 4; they worked with the COFO staff to turn out black citizens for a mock "Freedom Vote" in which Dr. Aaron Henry, the black state NAACP president, and Tougaloo College chaplain Ed King, a white minister, were candidates for governor and lieutenant governor. The platform of this interracial team was radically different from standard Mississippi political fare—they called for school desegregation, fair employment, and a $1.25 minimum wage. Over eighty thousand blacks cast "Freedom Votes" in churches and stores, confounding all predictions, while journalists flocked to interview the white students, and FBI agents appeared where none had ever been seen before. For most purposes, the presence of the white students was a great success.

During a SNCC staff meeting in Greenville in mid-November, the idea of more white students coming to Mississippi for a longer time was considered. While no decision was made, it was not lost on those present that the white students did bring publicity and an increased federal presence into the state.

At the December COFO meeting, the idea was discussed again. There were suggestions that the number of whites be limited to one hundred. In late December, the SNCC executive committee approved the idea and sent SNCC staff to COFO's January 1964 meeting to lobby for it. The COFO staff gave its approval, despite warnings that these articulate, opinionated, better-educated white Northerners would overwhelm COFO's largely Southern black staff. Others warned that relying on whites to promote the Movement's goals perpetuated the very system of white supremacy the Mississippi project was intended to vanquish.

Moses had argued in favor of the project. "These students bring the rest of the country with them," he said, "They're from good schools, and their parents are influential."

Later James Forman, SNCC's executive director, would write, "We made a conscious attempt to recruit from Ivy League schools—to recruit a counter-power elite."

Thus the die was cast. For better or worse, the Mississippi Summer Project would begin. COFO divided Mississippi along the lines of its Congressional Districts—CORE would work in the fourth District; SNCC had the other three.

From the very first, COFO, SNCC, and the Summer Project faced political differences. Lowenstein had reportedly told Stanford students they would work during the summer under his direction; in Boston, Lowenstein recruiter

Barney Frank was saying those he recruited would be under the New Yorker's direction, too. Lowenstein further wanted the summer's work directed from New York. SNCC and COFO refused to allow him to dominate selection of the summer volunteers or direct their work. At Moses's insistence, SNCC moved its national headquarters from Atlanta to Greenwood, and all volunteer applications were routed through the COFO central office in Jackson.

SNCC's traditional poverty controlled its recruiting—the volunteers would have to be entirely self-supporting, limiting the number of blacks, few of whom could afford to spend a summer without salary working in Mississippi. It also meant that volunteers would be older than typical college students. Most recruitment was done by Friends of SNCC groups established to provide funds and political support. Other civil rights groups with campus chapters—especially CORE—did recruiting, too.

The summer's applicants were hardly typical Americans. Average median family income in the United States in 1960 was $5,600; the Freedom Summer's applicants' family income was almost 50 percent higher—$8,417. Median income for a Mississippi black family was only $1,444. Thus, the poorest people in the United States would play host for the summer to the children of the most privileged.

Applications came from 233 schools. Elite private universities—Harvard, Yale, Stanford, Princeton—provided 40 percent, or 123 of the 736 who applied. One hundred forty-five others came from elite public schools like Berkeley, Michigan, and Wisconsin. Students from the highest ranking public and private schools made up more than half of the applicant pool.

They were the children of the powerful, if not the rich. The children of Arthur Schlesinger and U.S. Rep. Donald Edwards (D-CA.) were volunteers. Other volunteers listed as their references Presidential counselors Eugene Rostow, Arthur Goldberg, and Bill Moyers; Yale Chaplain William Sloane Coffin; philosopher Herbert Marcuse; and U.S. Rep. Phil Burton (D.-CA).

Of the applicants, 10 percent were married, usually to another potential volunteer. Fewer than 2 percent were parents.

Ninety percent were white. The demand for those who could be self-supporting helped to place a racial limit on the applicants; equally decisive was that during the 1961-'62 school year, blacks were only 2.9 percent of all college students in America.

Forty-nine percent of the applicants were female, although in 1964, women were only 39 percent of undergraduate students in the United States.

Most of the students came from the Great Lakes, Mid-Atlantic, and Far West. Almost half—46.3 percent—came from Illinois, New York and California. Only 11 percent were from the South; most of these were black.

The financial requirement raised the applicants' average age to twenty-three. Twenty percent had completed their undergraduate education, and seniors and juniors outnumbered freshmen and sophomores by two to one. Twenty-two percent had full-time jobs; 70 percent of those were teachers.

Before the project began, the volunteers described themselves as optimistic and idealistic; religiously motivated; patriotic; and as conventional leftists, generally socialists. Forty-eight percent belonged to a civil rights group; 21 percent to a church or religious groups; 14 percent to a socialist or leftist organization; 13 percent to an affiliate of the Democratic or Republican Parties; 13 percent to an academic organization; and 10 percent to a teacher's organization.

Half belonged to a CORE chapter or a Friends of SNCC organization. Ninety percent claimed some kind of civil rights experience, and 25 percent knew another volunteer.

All those under twenty-one had to have parental permission. Most were interviewed on campus by a Friends of SNCC organization. Seventy were rejected—most because they were underage or applied too late. Twenty-five percent of the applicants were no-shows. When interviewed later, 25 percent of the no-shows said their parents had convinced them not to go.

In preparation for the summer, the city of Jackson, Mississippi, increased its police force from 390 to 450; they added two horses, six dogs, and two hundred new shotguns; stockpiled tear gas; and issued a gas mask to every policeman. They amassed three canvas-topped troop carriers, two half-ton searchlight trucks, and three giant trailer trucks to haul demonstrators to two large detention compounds at the state fairgrounds. The city's pride was "Thompson's Tank," named after the incumbent mayor—a thirteen-thousand-pound armored battle wagon built to the city's specifications at a dollar a pound.

The state of Mississippi the summer volunteers would enter had long relied on non-mechanized cotton farming. Its overwhelmingly rural black population lived in near-serfdom and was kept from any participation in public affairs through systematic state-sanctioned terror and sporadic violence from individual whites.

In 1960, 68 percent of all Mississippi blacks lived in rural areas. In the rest of the United States, only 38 percent of blacks were rural. Median non-white income in Mississippi in 1960 was $1,444, the lowest in the United States. Eighty-six percent of all non-white families in Mississippi lived below the federal poverty level. In 1960, the median years of school finished by Mississippi blacks over 25 was the sixth grade. For whites, it was the eleventh grade. Forty-two percent of Mississippi's whites had finished twelve years of school; only 7 percent of blacks had gone that far. In 1964, Mississippi averaged expenditures of $21.77 on each black child's education and $81.86 per white child. In Holly Bluff, Mississippi, education expenditures were $191.70 for each white child; each black child's schooling cost $1.26.

Infant mortality rates for blacks were twice as high as for whites. Two-thirds of all black housing was "deteriorated" or "dilapidated." Half of all black housing had no piped water; two-thirds of all black housing had no flush toilets.

In 1960, only 7 percent of Mississippi blacks old enough to register had actually dared to do so. Five counties had black population majorities and no black voters. In Coahoma County, 95 percent of the eligible whites were registered to vote.

Through the National Council of Churches, SNCC and COFO arranged for two week-long training sessions for the summer volunteers to be held at Oxford College for Women in Miami, Ohio from June 14-20, 1964. As volunteers arrived, I arranged for each to be photographed, front and center, and had each one list hometown newspapers. As the summer wore on, the SNCC communications staff began a daily ritual of reporting to Northern newspapers or feeding radio stations "actualities"—eyewitness interviews taped and edited to broadcast length—that "Mississippi Freedom Summer volunteer Mary Jones was arrested yesterday in Greenwood, Mississippi, while walking down a street in the Negro section" or "the McComb, Mississippi, Freedom House was raked with shots from a passing car last night."

One Oxford session speaker was the Justice Department's John Doar, who told the volunteers not to expect federal protection. "Maintaining law and order," he said, "is a state responsibility."

The volunteers attracted a great deal of media attention. They were white, young, attractive, heading into potential danger, willing to spend a summer living in primitive circumstances, the exotic elements from which media interest is born.

Two hundred fifty of them left Oxford College for Mississippi on June 20 and 21.

On the 21st, Bob Moses spoke to the volunteers. "Yesterday," he said, "three of our people left Meridian to investigate a church burning in Neshoba County. They haven't come back, and we haven't any word from them."

The three were Mickey Schwerner, a CORE worker from New York; James Chaney, a CORE volunteer from Meridian; and Andrew

Goodman, a New York volunteer. They were already dead when Moses made his announcement.

The original five hundred fifty volunteers were supplemented over the summer by about four hundred more; there were never more than six hundred in the state at one time.

There were originally thirty-two COFO projects spread out through the state. By the summer's end, COFO had established forty-four. The safest area proved to be the Gulf Coast—a tourist area more progressive than the rest of the state where illegal gambling and drinking had long been tolerated.

The most dangerous place was the third district in southwest Mississippi, where SNCC had begun its voter registration in Amite County three years before. Two-thirds of the summer's bomb attacks happened in the third district.

Workers were divided among voter registration efforts carried on in forty-two projects; Freedom Schools in thirty locations; and Community Centers in twenty-three projects.

Workers from SNCC and COFO helped to found the Mississippi Freedom Democratic Party (MFDP)—an alternative to the racist all-white state Democratic Party—in April 1964. In June, the MFDP fielded candidates in Mississippi's primaries running for the United States House of Representatives and Senate. All four lost and decided to run as independents in the November elections, but the state board of elections kept them off the ballot. They decided to run another "Freedom Vote" campaign like the previous fall. Many of the summer volunteers spent their time preparing for the "Freedom Vote" as well as in regular registration work, and in documenting the delays, obstructions, harassment, and terror which could become the evidence for lawsuits, the MFDP's convention challenge, and a congressional challenge in the fall.

Volunteers also helped to organize the complicated steps—from precinct conventions to county conventions to district conventions to state conventions—to establish the MFDP as a bona fide party. On August 6, sixty-eight delegates, including four whites, were elected to represent the party at the Democratic Convention in Atlantic City.

Freedom Schools, conceived by Charlie Cobb, were intended, in his words, to "provide an educational experience for students which will make it possible for them to challenge the myths of our society, to perceive more clearly its realities, and to find alternatives, and ultimately new directions for action." In March 1964, the National Council of Churches sponsored a meeting to develop curriculum: it consisted of remedial education, to make up for the paltry education black children had received from the segregated and under-financed public schools; leadership development, to find and discover future leaders for black Mississippi through studies of the Civil Rights Movement and black history; contemporary issues, to attempt to relate local, national, and world affairs to the children's current condition; and a non-academic curriculum which included arts and crafts, poetry and play writing, and establishing a student newspaper. Staughton Lynd, a Spelman College history professor, was the school's director.

Eventually, over 3,500 students attended.

At the summer's end, four project workers had been killed; four people had been critically wounded; eighty workers had been beaten; there had been over one thousand arrests; thirty-seven churches had been bombed or burned; and thirty black businesses or homes had been burned.

Eighty of the volunteers decided to stay after the summer was over; the majority of those who chose to stay were white women. The addition of these newcomers to a staff that had developed a familial closeness from three years of dangerous work under the most trying circumstances soon escalated the long-standing resentments and gender tension between black and white staff members which had threatened to stop the summer project before it began.

Although the Freedom Summer actually registered few voters, it built community centers, opened the minds and widened the horizons of some Mississippi school children, and invited America into Mississippi through the eyes and experiences of the summer volunteers. It established the MFDP, which would play an important role in Mississippi politics for years to come; the MFDP's lawsuits against the state's continual attempts to block, gerrymander, and otherwise interfere with the right-to-vote established important legal principles that had a widespread effect on reapportionment and voting rights throughout the nation. It inspired and trained a generation of white activists who took the Movement's message back to their campuses in the fall.

With the next year's Selma March, the 1964 Freedom Summer was the nonviolent, interracial Civil Rights Movement's last demonstration of organized mass activity; never again would black and white young people labor together to make American democracy work.

Thirty years ago, a small band of white and black Americans spent their summer in Mississippi; three decades later, America is a better place because of what they did and the sacrifices they offered there. Then, as now, much of the story has yet to be told.

The emphasis of journalists then was the attractive white Northerners and the sacrifices they were making to spend two months living in poverty and jeopardy in the most resistant state. Only recently have historians begun to tell the stories of the black men and women who risked life and safety to open their homes to these friendly strangers and who had worked to win freedom long before the summer volunteers arrived.

I teach history today to college students too young to have any firsthand memories of Freedom Summer. They are, however, the same age as the young workers from SNCC and CORE and the students from across the country who broke racism's back in Mississippi thirty years

ago. As we discuss the Civil Rights Movement, I often wonder whether they would respond as their mothers and fathers did in 1964.

Anyone wanting to learn more about Mississippi Freedom Summer should peruse the voluminous literature, beginning with Doug McAdam's *Freedom Summer* (New York: Oxford University Press, 1981) from which much of the information on volunteers in this essay is taken; for SNCC's participation, Clayborne Carson's *In Struggle* (Cambridge: Harvard University Press, 1981), Cleve Seller's *The River of No Return* (New York: William Morrow, 1973), Mary King's *Freedom Song* (New York: William Morrow, 1987) and James Forman's *Making of Black Revolutionaries*, (New York: Macmillan, 1972); for a detailed history of the murders of Goodman, Schwerner, and Chaney, Cagin & Dray's *We Are Not Afraid* (New York: MacMillan, 1988). Soon to appear are John Dittmer's comprehensive history of the Movement in Mississippi and William Chafe's biography of Allard Lowenstein. Anne Moody's autobiography *Coming Of Age In Mississippi* (New York: Dial Press, 1968) is a Mississippi-born participant's account of her life and the state's 1960s Civil Rights Movement. A firsthand account of Freedom Summer, written by a movement lawyer, is Len Holt's *The Summer That Didn't End* (New York: DaCapo Press, 1993). Elizabeth Sutherland's collection of *Letters From Mississippi* (New York: McGraw Hill, 1965) tells the story in the volunteer's own words; and Nicholas Von Hoffman's collected *Chicago Daily News Columns* expanded and reprinted in *Mississippi Notebook* (New York: David White, 1964) give a journalist's view. Sally Belfrage's *Freedom Summer* (Charlottesville: University Press of Virginia, 1990) is a British volunteer's story of the summer. ❖

Folks approaching courthouse building to attempt registration.

ARTWORK BY

SHARON RILEY

JACK NEWFIELD

Amite County

Excerpted from *A Prophetic Minority: The American New Left,*
New American Library, 1966.

I'm going back out before the rain starts a-falling;
I'll walk to the depths of the deepest dark forest
where the people are many and their hands are all empty
where the pellets of poison are flooding their waters
where the home in the valley meets the damp dirty prison
where the executioner's face is always well hidden
where hunger is ugly, where souls are forgotten
where black is the color, where none is the number

—Bob Dylan

When you're in Mississippi, the rest of America doesn't seem real. And when you're in the rest of America, Mississippi doesn't seem real.

—Bob Parris

In the mythology of the Movement, Amite County is a synonym for the Ninth Circle of Hell.

It was to impoverished, remote Amite County, in southwest Mississippi, that SNCC's Bob Parris came in August of 1961 to attempt SNCC's pilot project in voter registration. Beaten twice and jailed thrice, Parris left for the state capital in Jackson after four melancholy months.

It was in Amite that Herbert Lee, a fifty-two-year-old father of nine children, was murdered by E. H. Hurst, a member of the Mississippi state legislature.

It was in Amite that farmer Louis Allen, a witness to Lee's slaying, was shotgunned to death in his home, after he had spoken to the Justice Department about the Lee murder.

It was Amite that saw not a single white volunteer during the 1964 Summer Project because of its legacy of lawlessness.

It was Amite that until July of 1965 had only one registered Negro voter in the whole county, despite a Negro population majority of 55 percent.

It is Amite that twelve years after Brown v. Board of Education does not have a single classroom desegregated, two years after the 1964 Civil Rights Act does not have a single public facility desegregated, and a year after the 1965 act does not have a federal voting registrar.

It is Amite that has never experienced a civil-rights march, a sit-in, or even a picket line.

It is in rural, red-clayed Amite that the Movement has bled itself dry trying to break the century-old reign of terror, poverty, and fear.

Amite is about eighty miles south of Jackson on the Louisiana border. Its county seat is the hamlet of Liberty, population 652.

Jack Newfield was born in the Bedford-Stuivesant neighborhood of Brooklyn. His first book, A Prophetic Minority *covered the rise of SNCC and the Civil Rights Movement. He worked for 24 years for the* Village Voice *and is now a columnist for the* New York Post. *In 1992, he won an Emmy for a PBS television documentary on boxing promoter Don King.*

More than half of the total population of the county is Negro, but only 40 percent of the 13,000 eligible voters are Negro. Because of the hopeless cycle of poverty, many Negroes escape to Baton Rouge, New Orleans, and Chicago while still in their teens. Sociologists have estimated that Negro emigration from Mississippi is 40 percent. Amite is becoming a place for the very old and the very young.

Although many Negroes in Amite own their own farms, most of them are marginal. Attendance at all-Negro Central High each autumn falls below 50 percent because so many children are required to chop cane and pick cotton on the farms. While this makes the farmer less vulnerable to economic reprisals, it does lead to frequent acts of physical violence.

More than 90 percent of the Negro homes have no heating system or indoor toilet. Only a few have telephones. Almost all rely on hand-dug wells for water. Food must be purchased in Liberty, where Negroes are still beaten up on the street on whim, and where no white has ever stood trial for violence against a Negro.

The sheriff of Amite is six-foot, five-inch Daniel Jones. His father, Brian Jones, is the Klan leader in the county.

Amite does not have a white, business-oriented middle class that has made Greenville, in the delta, an oasis of decency, or a merchant class that finally, in 1965, helped halt the reign of terror in nearby McComb. It was Hodding Carter's *Greenville Delta Democrat Times*, and later Oliver Emmerich's *McComb Enterprise-Journal*, that spread the message of compliance and moderation. The only newspaper in Amite is a racist sheet called the *Liberty Herald*.

Amite seems outside the flow of history, a backward enclave insulated from the passage of time. It has not only missed the Civil Rights Movement, but the Industrial Revolution as well. There are no factories, no shopping centers, no unions in the county. The longed-for educated, civilized white moderate isn't in hiding; *he doesn't exist in Amite.*

This chapter is an attempt to chronicle the descent of three young Dantes into this one particular hell. This trio of pioneers did not abandon hope, but brought hope to this Ninth Circle.

Liberty is one of the oldest towns in Mississippi, its founding dating back to 1805. Among the earliest settlers in Amite were the poor whites—the "peckerwoods"—who were pushed out of the area around Natchez by the cotton-plantation-owning class of aristocrats. As the South moved toward the Civil War, great tensions developed between the rural peckerwoods of Amite and the affluent, genteel planters of Natchez. When the war began, the residents of Natchez voted to remain in the Union, while the poor whites of Amite chose secession.

After the Civil War, Amite was over 60 percent Negro. There were Negro sheriffs and a powerful Republican Party organization. But after the historic Compromise of 1876 ended Reconstruction, the pattern of Negro disenfranchisement came to Amite, as it did to all of the South. Negroes were lynched, driven off land they owned, beaten, and their right to vote taken away. Most Negroes who own their own land in Amite today do so only because one of their ancestors fought for it with guns or fists. Most of the Amite Negroes, however, fled to the rich soil of the delta, where cheap labor was needed to clear the swamps for the future plantations.

The diminution of Negro power in the county has continued all through the twentieth century. The only Negro resistance to this trend came during the 1930s when several of Huey Long's Share the Wealth Leagues sprang up in the area, but they were violently suppressed. The remote rurality and the backward poverty of Amite have been the jaws of the vise that has bled the Amite Negro since Reconstruction.

Robert Parris Moses grew up in a housing project on the edge of Harlem. But somehow he was not swallowed up by the squalor and violence of the ghetto like so many of his contemporaries. Instead, gifted with a philosophical and poetic mind, he went downtown at age thirteen, as a result of high grades on a competitive examination, to virtually all-white, academically superior Stuyvesant High School. There Parris not only compiled outstanding grades, but was captain of Stuyvesant's championship basketball quintet and vice president of his graduating class.

Parris then went, on a scholarship, to predominantly white Hamilton College in Clinton, New York, where again he excelled in both scholarship and sports. It was at Hamilton that a French instructor introduced him to the writings of Albert Camus, whose melancholy morality was to make a lasting impact on his thinking. Almost a decade later, addressing volunteers at Oxford, Ohio, for the Mississippi Summer Project, Parris compared racism to Camus's plague, and the volunteers to the sanitary squads.

From Hamilton, Parris went on to graduate school at Harvard and received a master's degree in philosophy in 1957. Afterward Parris began to teach math at one of New York City's elite private schools—Horace Mann, in the Riverdale section of the Bronx. Nothing in his first twenty-four years—spent increasingly in the white world—seemed to indicate that Parris was destined to become a myth-shrouded legend to thousands of young radicals, and to have his picture hang in a sharecropper shack in the delta next to Abraham Lincoln's and John F. Kennedy's.

Folksinger Bob Cohen, who lived with Parris in Manhattan from September of 1960 until he left for Amite in July of 1961, remembers him as "extraordinarily quiet, gentle, abstract . . . really involved with his students and reading a lot—Bertrand Russell and Camus in French. . . . Yet, I always had the sense he was very busy in his head all the time."

Cohen met Parris at the Maine Folk Dance Camp in June of 1960, and recalls, "One of the few times I can remember Bob's face really lit up was when he was folk dancing. He loved it. I remember sometimes we would be coming home late from a party or something, and if Bob had had a good time, he would start dancing down Amsterdam Avenue. He could be very free and gay then."

Cohen, who named his first child after his roommate, says, "Bob hardly ever talked about going back South after his trip in June of 1960. . . . The only hint I got of the deep feeling he had about going back South was that he would sit for hours and listen to a record of Odetta singing, 'I'm Going Back to the Red Clay Country.'"

Nineteen hundred and sixty-one, when Parris went back to the red clay of Amite and Pike counties, marked the first time a SNCC worker tried to live in and become part of a community. It was the first time SNCC engaged in voter registration. It was probably the most creative and heroic single act anyone in the New Left has attempted. Certainly much of the subsequent history of the New Left has flowed from that existential act of Parris disappearing alone into the most violent and desolate section of Mississippi.

As a consequence of that deed and his own selfless personality, Parris occupies a legendary niche in the New Left. He has been compared to Danilo Dolci, Hesse's Siddhartha, and Prince Kropotkin. Perhaps the reverential feeling about this shy, often sad prophet was best expressed by Dick Gregory when he introduced Parris to the mammoth Berkeley teach-in in May of 1965 with these words:

> I refused to do my act a few minutes ago because it was too light. Now it's dark enough, but I looked over my shoulder and found some light that I must get rid of first. This is a young man who has done more for my life without even knowing it to make me commit my life for right over wrong. Thank goodness I happened to be in the right place at the right time when he was speaking in his own little way. Many times I listened to him when he thought I was asleep in jail; many times I overheard him in the sharecropping fields of Mississippi. I'd like to postpone my act for another few minutes and bring to the stand a man who, to me and to many people, will stand up among the greatest human beings who have ever walked the face

of the earth. I don't have to say any more. I would like to present to you a *man* —Bob Parris.

The series of events that propelled Parris into the Ninth Circle of Amite began during the summer of 1960. It was then that Parris, while traveling through Mississippi trying to recruit Negro students to attend SNCC's October founding conference, met Amzie Moore, the indomitable leader of the NAACP chapter in Cleveland, Mississippi. In the course of several conversations Moore convinced the twenty-five-year-old SNCC field secretary he should quit his teaching job and return to the delta the following summer to begin a voter-registration campaign. Parris agreed, and in November the popular Negro magazine, *Jet,* printed a short item describing the projected venture. Amite County's NAACP founder and leader, E. W. Steptoe, saw the *Jet* item, and along with Pike County leader C. C. Bryant, wrote a letter to Parris in New York, suggesting he change his plans and try to organize a project in southwest Mississippi. At that point only thirty-eight of nine thousand Pike County Negroes were registered to vote, and one of fifty-five hundred in Amite was eligible to vote, according to Civil Rights Commission figures.

Parris, who was encountering unexpected difficulty in finding a church willing to house a voter-registration school in the delta, agreed to come to the Amite-Pike region.

Civil rights workers had not even tried to enter Mississippi until 1952. According to Elizabeth Sutherland in her *Letters from Mississippi,* the "first 'agitator' was shot and killed, the second was shot and run out of the state." Next came Bob Parris in July 1961, without a grand scheme, lacking concrete experience in voter registration.

On August 7 the SNCC Pike County voter-registration school opened up in a hamlet called Burglundtown in a two-story structure, which included a grocery below and a Masonic meeting hall above. The only teacher was Parris, and the student body consisted of about twenty

Negroes, half of them too young to vote.

After the first class, four persons went to the registrar's office in nearby Magnolia, the county seat, and three of them registered without incident. Three Negroes went down on August 9, and two registered successfully. Nine journeyed to Magnolia on August 10, and one was registered. The next night one of the Pike County Negroes who had attempted to register was shot at by a white farmer. The next day only two people showed up at the voter-registration school.

Parris then went into Amite, living on Steptoe's farm. On August 15, he accompanied an old farmer named Ernest Isaac and two middle-aged women, Betha Lee Hughes and Matilda Schoby, to the courthouse in Liberty. The trio managed to fill out a form but not to take the test. As they were driving out of Liberty toward McComb, their car was flagged down by a highway patrolman, who told Isaac, the driver, to get out and come into the police car. Isaac quickly complied, but Parris also got out of the car and asked the officer why. He was pushed and ordered back into the car. At that point the patrolman arrested Parris for "impeding an officer in the discharge of his duties." Taken to McComb, Parris was fined fifty dollars, and for the first of many times saw the inside of a Mississippi jail, as he spent two days in prison, fasting, rather than pay the fine.

On Monday, August 28, Parris started a voter-registration class at Mt. Pilgrim Church, the first in the history of Amite County. The next day he went with Reverend Alfred Knox and Curtis Dawson to the courthouse in Liberty to try to register. A block from the courthouse they were met by Billy Jack Caston, a cousin of the sheriff and the son-in-law of state representative E. H. Hurst. Without saying a word, Caston walked up to Parris and knocked him down with a punch to the temple. He then proceeded to pummel Parris for several minutes with punches to the head and ribs. Parris just sat in the street trying to protect himself as best he could in the traditional nonviolent position, his head between his knees and his arms shielding his face. Reverend Knox tried to pull Caston off his victim, but white bystanders ordered him not to intervene.

Knox and Dawson never made it to the courthouse. Instead they picked up the semiconscious Parris and drove him to Steptoe's farm. Steptoe later recalled, "I didn't recognize Bob at first he was so bloody. I just took off his teeshirt and wrung out the blood like it had just been washed." Then Steptoe drove Parris to a Negro doctor in McComb, who sewed eight stitches in his scalp.

The next day Amite experienced another first: Parris filed assault and battery charges against Caston, the first time in that area a Negro had challenged the right of a white man to beat him up at will. The warrant was made out by the county district attorney after the county judge refused.

The trial was held in the Liberty courthouse on August 31. More than one hundred whites, many of them openly armed, jammed the courtroom for the spectacle. While on the stand, Parris was asked by Caston's attorney whether he had participated in riots the year before in Japan or San Francisco. After his testimony Parris—the plaintiff—was told by the sheriff he had better leave the courtroom because he could not guarantee his safety. So before the trial ended in Caston's acquittal, Parris was given a police escort to the Pike County line.

Meanwhile, two other crucial events were happening during the month of August. One was a SNCC staff meeting at the Highlander Folk School in Tennessee. At that meeting the fledgling organization was divided into two camps: one favoring direct action on the order of the sit-ins and the freedom rides, and the other suggesting the innovation of voter registration. Hints from the Kennedy Administration that it would look favorably on voter-registration activities, plus financial support from the New World and other foundations, strengthened the voter-registration group in SNCC. After prolonged debate, SNCC decided to adopt "an all-

out revolutionary program encompassing both mass direct action and voter registration drives."

The second thing to happen during August was the gradual emergence from jail in Jackson of the first group of Freedom Riders. Four of these freedom riders, Reggie Robinson of Baltimore, John Hardy of Nashville, Travis Britt of New York, and MacArthur Cotton of Jackson, were to join Parris before the month was over. Also, direct-action partisans like Marion Barry came to McComb during August and sparked a series of sit-ins and protest marches. A fifteen-year-old McComb highschool student, Brenda Travis, and five friends sat-in and were arrested. Her companions were sentenced to eight months for "breach of the peace," and Brenda was turned over to juvenile authorities and sentenced to one year in the state school for delinquents. Later, more than one hundred of Brenda's classmates at Burgland High School marched through McComb to protest her severe sentence and expulsion from school. They were all arrested as they knelt praying at the steps of the city hall.

More violence in Liberty.

On September 5th, Parris and Travis Britt accompanied four Negroes to the courthouse. In his pamphlet, *Revolution in Mississippi,* Tom Hayden recorded Britt's terse description of the events that followed:

> There was a clerk directly across the hall who came rushing out while we were waiting, and ordered us to leave the hallway. He said he didn't want a bunch of people congregating in the hallway. So we left and walked around the building to the courthouse, near the registrar's window. By the time we reached the back of the building a group of white men had filed into the hall. . . . They were talking belligerently. Finally one of the white men came to the end of the hall as if looking for someone. He asked us if we knew Mr. Brown. We said no. He said, you boys must not be from around here. We said he was correct. This conversation was interrupted by another white man who ap-

proached Bob Moses (Parris) and started preaching to him: how he should be ashamed of coming down here from New York stirring up trouble, causing poor innocent people to lose their homes and jobs, and how he (Bob) was lower than dirt on the ground for doing such things, and how he should get down on his knees and ask God forgiveness for every sin in his lifetime. Bob asked him why the people should lose their homes just because they wanted to register and vote. The white gentleman did not answer the question but continued to preach. He said that the Negro men were raping the white women up North, and that he wouldn't allow such a thing to start down here in Mississippi. . . . At this point Bob turned away and sat on the stoop of the courthouse porch, and the man talking to him took a squatting position. Nobody was saying anything. I reached into my pocket and took out a cigarette. A tall white man, about middle-aged, wearing a khaki shirt and pants stepped up to me and asked, "Boy, what's your business?" at which point I knew I was in trouble. The clerk from the hallway came to the backdoor leading to the courthouse with a smile on his face and called to the white man, "Wait a minute, wait a minute!" At this point the white man, who they called Bryant, hit me on my right eye. Then I saw this clerk motion his head as if to call the rest of the whites. They came and all circled around me, and this fellow that was called Bryant hit me on my jaw and then on my chin. Then he slammed me down; instead of falling I stumbled onto the courthouse lawn. The crowd (about fifteen, I think) followed, making comments. He was holding me so tight around the collar, I put my hands on my collar to ease the choking. This set off a reaction of punches from this fellow they called Bryant; I counted fifteen; he just kept hitting and shouting, "Why don't you hit me, nigger?" I was beaten into a semiconscious state. My vision was blurred by the punch to the eye. I heard Bob yell to cover

my head to avoid any further blows to my face. . . . Bob took me by the arm and took me to the street, walking cautiously to avoid any further kicks or blows. The Negro fellow that had been taking the registration test gave up in the excitement, and we saw him in his truck. . . .

This incident, in the heart of the hell Bob Parris says isn't real unless you're there, went unreported in the national press. This was still three years before the Summer Project, and such beatings administered to blacks were so commonplace as not to fit the definition of news. Such beatings, however, turned out to have considerable news content in 1964, when the bloodied recipients were white students from "good families" in the North. In 1961 the blood of Parris and Britt was invisible.

The beating had its desired effect. Attendance at meetings and voter-registration classes dwindled to almost nothing. The small group of SNCC workers walked the back roads from dawn to dusk in a vain search for Negroes willing to try to register in Liberty. "But the farmers were no longer willing to go down," Parris later recalled, "and for the rest of the month of September we just had a rough time."

Amite's unchecked, legally sanctioned violence became murder on September 25 when Herbert Lee was shot to death in front of the Liberty cotton gin by E. H. Hurst.

The day before, Parris had met with Steptoe and John Doar of the Justice Department at Steptoe's farm. Steptoe had told Doar that Hurst, whose land is adjacent to his, had publicly threatened to kill him and Herbert Lee. Lee had attended voter-registration classes and had volunteered a few days before to attempt to register in Liberty, the first individual to do so since the beating of Britt.

Lee was shot once in the brain by Hurst's .38 caliber revolver. It happened about noon in front of a dozen witnesses, including several Negroes. Lee, wearing his farmer's overalls and field boots, was sitting in the cab of his pick-up truck, and fell out into the gutter when he was shot. For two hours his body lay in a pool of blood, uncovered and swarmed over by insects. Finally, a coroner's jury in Liberty met and ruled that Lee was killed in self-defense.

Parris felt responsible for Lee's death, just as three years later he was to feel himself responsible for the deaths of Goodman, Chaney, and Schwerner. For the next three nights, from sundown till almost sunup, he walked and rode through the mist-shrouded rolling hills of Amite, knocking on strange doors, seeking the three Negro witnesses. Fighting off exhaustion, waking up families that had to get up at 5 A.M., Parris finally found the Negro farmers who had witnessed the slaying. But none was willing to tell a grand jury the truth. Instead they told Parris that the sheriff and deputy sheriff had warned them to tell everyone that Lee, who was about five feet four, had tried to hit Hurst, who is six feet three, with a tire iron.

One of the three witnesses was a farmer named Louis Allen. Late in October a federal grand jury convened to consider an indictment of Hurst. It was then that Allen drove to McComb to inform Parris that he had changed his mind and would tell the truth about Lee's death if he were guaranteed federal protection.

Parris called the Justice Department in Washington but was told it was "impossible" to provide Allen with protection. So Allen testified to the federal jury that Hurst had killed Lee in self-protection. Six months later a deputy sheriff told Allen he knew he had contacted the Justice Department, and he broke Allen's jaw with a flashlight. On January 31, 1964, Allen was found dead on his front porch as a result of three shotgun blasts.

Tormented by the shadows of guilt, Parris has tried to make Herbert Lee a symbol for all the hundreds of Mississippi Negroes who have been lawlessly murdered by whites. Whenever he spoke in the North in 1962 or 1963 he would talk about Herbert Lee, and soon thousands of young people knew of this one murder out of many. Lee was also memorialized in a song, "Never Turn Back," written in 1963 by Bertha

Gober, a wide-eyed teenager from Albany, Georgia. For a while the song, a dirge sung at a slow, elegiac tempo, was the "We Shall Overcome" of the SNCC workers in Mississippi. Its final verse goes:

> We have hung our heads and cried
> Cried for those like Lee who died
> Died for you and died for me
> Died for the cause of equality
> No, we'll never turn back
> No, we'll never turn back
> Until we've all been freed
> And we have equality
> And we have equality

The murder of Lee broke the back of whatever had been stirring in Amite. Few Negroes were willing to be seen talking to Parris or to the other "Freedom Riders," as they were called by both Negroes and whites. The tiny flicker of hope from Parris's candle went out, and Amite's Negroes were left to curse the darkness.

A month later Parris went to jail for two months in Pike County for leading a march of one hundred eighteen highschool students to the McComb city hall. From the Magnolia jail he smuggled out a note to the SNCC office in Atlanta. The last few paragraphs illuminate Parris's speculative and poetic turn of mind.

> Later on, Hollis [Hollis Watkins, now a member of SNCC's executive committee] will lead out with a clear tenor into a freedom song, Talbert and Lewis will supply jokes, and McDew [Chuck McDew, then SNCC's chairman] will discourse on the history of the black man and the Jew. McDew— a black by birth and a Jew by choice, and a revolutionary by necessity—has taken on the deep loves and the deep hates which America, and the world, reserve for those who dare to stand in a strong sun and cast a sharp shadow.
>
> In the words of Judge Brumfield, who sentenced us, we are "cold calculators" who design to disrupt the racial harmony (harmonious since 1619) of McComb into racial strife and rioting; we, he said, are the leaders

PHOTO BY

GEORGE BALLIS

Bob Moses (Parris), 29, during MFDP meeting, 1964.

who are causing young children to be led like sheep to the pen and be slaughtered (in a legal manner). "Robert," he was addressing me, "haven't some of the people from your school been able to go down and register without violence here in Pike County?" I thought to myself that Southerners are most exposed when they boast. . . .

This is Mississippi, in the middle of the iceberg. Hollis is leading off with his tenor, "Michael row the boat ashore, Alleluia; Christian brothers don't be slow, Alleluia; Mississippi's next to go, Alleluia." This is a tremor in the middle of the iceberg—from a stone that the builders rejected.

In January, Parris left southwest Mississippi, melancholy and depressed, to begin a pilgrimage that was to lead to the Mississippi Summer Project, the Freedom Democratic Party, and a 100 percent rise in Negro registration in the state by the end of 1965 (25,000 to 50,000).

But for three years Amite was to remain that base of the iceberg most submerged beneath the ocean of terror. Nobody tried to register in Liberty after the murder of Herbert Lee. No SNCC project was attempted in the county. No summer volunteer was sent into the hills and woods of Amite. For three years a pattern of life incomprehensible to an outsider endured without assault. Negroes were beaten and killed. Whites, a minority in the county, continued to make every political and economic decision. No word was written about the iceberg, and the tiny crack Parris had made froze over.

E. W. Steptoe, a small, reed-like man with a time-trampled face, has lived in Amite all his fifty-six years. He was there trying to register before Parris came; he was there after Parris moved on to Jackson and Greenwood; and he is there today, shaming, cajoling, bullying Negroes into registering.

Steptoe is not a saint. He is a violent man and an egotistical one. He can be demagogic at meetings, and he can con reporters and naive visitors. But there are few men like him in the

whole state of Mississippi. His courage, his common-sense wisdom, his bittersweet wit and love are the special qualities of the rural Mississippi Negro, who lives by his wits to survive, and whose life depends on human bonds with others.

Steptoe first tried to register in 1953 and was told he flunked the test. In 1954, after reading about the Supreme Court's desegregation decision, he organized an Amite County chapter of the NAACP. Its third meeting, however, was broken up by armed Klansmen with the help of the deputy sheriff.

"My uncle was so scared after that meeting," Steptoe recalls, "he ran into the woods and stayed there for a week, living on raw food. Then he finally came out and left the county."

In June of 1964 Amite sheriff Daniel Jones visited a score of Negro homes, making it clear there would be reprisals if they put up white summer volunteers. Steptoe was the only Negro in the county who said he would house "as many white civil rights workers that will fit in my house." The final decision not to send any volunteers to Amite County was made in Jackson after Goodman, Chaney, and Schwerner were reported missing in Neshoba County.

One of the 650 summer volunteers was a rabbi's son from Bakersfield, California, named Marshall Ganz. During the summer Ganz worked in McComb on one of the more effective SNCC projects, along with Curtis Hayes, Mendy Samstein, J. D. Smith, and Dennis Sweeney. Their freedom house was bombed in August, and Hayes narrowly escaped death. At the end of the summer Ganz was one of the 150 who chose to remain.

Elizabeth Sutherland remembers the first time she met Ganz in July of 1964:

> As soon as I saw him I knew he would be one of those volunteers who would stay in the state. Marshall seemed more mature and more sophisticated than most of the other volunteers. He was an economic radical, but more important, he had a sensitive, literary kind of mind. He was the type of person who

was driven to become a part of people's lives in a deep way. He seemed more concerned with human relationships than with staging big demonstrations. I think Marshall could be a fine novelist if he ever had the time to reflect on his experiences.

So in January 1965 Ganz moved to Steptoe's farm to become the first full-time SNCC worker since Parris in Amite County. Miss Sutherland now suspects it was Ganz's "passion for human contact" that led him to abandon the "impersonalization of a city like McComb to live directly with the poor farmers in Amite."

In McComb, Ganz had lived in a freedom house with about ten other staff members and had been somewhat removed from the rhythm of life in the Negro community. But at Steptoe's farm, he was at the vortex of it and intimately involved in people's everyday lives.

For six months Ganz canvassed alone in Amite; tedious, repetitive, frustrating drudgery. Hour after hour, day after day, he would walk the deserted gravel roads of the county, talking, visiting, joking with people who had never seen a friendly white face before in their lives. For six months all he did was try to find local Negroes who were willing to act against the system that emasculated them.

Early in July two more SNCC staff members—both girls—joined Ganz and Steptoe in Amite. One was twenty-year-old Hazel Lee, a Negro from Panola County and a veteran of six arrests and a hundred picket lines. Hazel came, she says, "because I heard that Amite was a really tough place where there had been a lot of killings. I felt I had to go there."

The other was a Jewish girl from Brooklyn named Carol Rogoff, a 1963 graduate of Beaver College near Philadelphia. Carol did not come to fashionable Beaver a rebel. But during the summer of 1963 she became active in the SNCC-ignited movement in Cambridge, Maryland. She was almost expelled from college, and there were tensions with her conservative family, but she continued to work in the Movement after the summer in Cambridge.

In 1965 Carol was in charge of organizing high school students in New York City. During the Easter vacation she escorted a group of those students on a visit to McComb, repaying a trip made by a group of McComb students to New York the previous Christmas. While in McComb, Carol made a few trips to Steptoe's farm and was so touched by the pure, slow movement being built in Amite that she decided to return there as a SNCC field secretary in July.

Ganz, Rogoff, and Lee were all part of the SNCC faction most committed to decentralization and grass-roots decision making and most antagonistic to flashy demonstrations and leader-oriented mass rallies. All agreed the Movement in Amite must be built slowly and with care, from the bottom up.

"A big influx of volunteers would smother the Movement here," said Carol, "as it did in McComb. If anything is to be built in Amite it must be inward, rather than outside-oriented. What has to be done is to build a community of local people who trust each other and are willing to act on their grievances; local Negroes who are willing to take responsibility and make decisions democratically."

After weeks of canvassing and church meetings of thirty and forty people, it was finally decided a group of Negroes would try to register on July 22 at the Liberty courthouse. By then the Voting Rights Act was about to be signed by the president, and the Mississippi legislature had passed a new law liberalizing the procedures for voter registration to prevent application of the federal law of Mississippi. Marshall Ganz called the Justice Department in Washington and the FBI in McComb to inform them of the registration bid, but in order to thwart dependence on whites, none of the SNCC workers accompanied the twenty-two Amite Negroes to Liberty on July 22.

At 9 A.M. they were lined up outside the courthouse, only a few yards from the spot where Herbert Lee's body had lain for two hours. The group included Steptoe, making his eighth attempt to register; Reverend Knox, who had made that first bloody trip to Liberty with Bob Parris in 1961; Ben Faust, a seventy-seven-year-old farmer who once spent five years in the infamous Parchman Prison for allegedly stealing a cow; and William Weathersby, a militant farmer who had attended registration classes in 1961.

"Okay, who's first?" asked Sheriff Jones, his hand ominously fingering his gun.

Silence.

Then William Sibley, a farmer, stepped forward and announced, "Me."

By dusk all twenty-two had been registered to vote.

A month later about two hundred Negroes were registered, including the widow of Herbert Lee and one of his nine children.

All summer Ganz, Rogoff, and Lee worked hard, winning slowly the confidence of the community, then its respect, and finally its love. When they ate, it was a meal forced on them by the community, by those who had less than enough to feed their own families. Local whites began to spread dozens of nails each night in Steptoe's gravel driveway, and the project's one beat-up car suffered from a series of flat tires. The car was a necessity in the completely rural county, and calls would go out in the middle of the night to friends in New York and California, asking for money needed to fix the flats so that as few days as possible would be wasted.

In September Marshall left Amite, planning to return after a few months' rest, perhaps with a tape recorder to document the saga of the Ninth Circle. But instead, Marshall went to California to help in the dramatic grape-pickers' strike near Delano. He quickly involved other SNCC workers in the strike and became a close aide to strike leader Cesar Chavez, whom *The New Republic's* Andrew Kopkind has compared to Bob Parris.

In November I visited Amite.

As one drives from Jackson to Amite along fog-clouded Highway 51, the abstract sociological term "rural" becomes concretized. The sense of desolation and backwardness grows with each

mile on the odometer. There are no cities except for McComb, whose thirteen thousand inhabitants make it a metropolis by Mississippi standards. Next to Jackson, the capital, the biggest city in the state is Meridian, population fifty thousand. Perhaps one of the reasons for Mississippi's primitive racism is the absence of a cultured urban center that might civilize the population from within. Georgia has Atlanta, Louisiana has New Orleans, even Alabama has Montgomery. But Mississippi has Meridian, where the killers of Goodman, Chaney, and Schwerner are still free.

Even a short stay in Amite is a bruising experience. Old Negroes with bent spines and work-swollen fingers lie to the SNCC workers, inventing ailments and appointments rather than face the local registrar in Liberty. A meeting in a broken-down shack called a church approaches Gandhian *agape* with the singing of religious hymns and the preachments of love thy enemy. A home with no toilet, no telephone, and no heat, and with six children crowded into three small rooms is spotlessly clean, and a magnificent meal is prepared for a dozen people in two hours. An old farmer named Willie Bates recalls how his cousin was castrated in 1962 and asks whether "there is any place on earth where colored peoples is treated meaner than in Amite County?"

Fear and Love

These are the two polarities upon which the fragile, embryonic movement in Amite rests.

The Movement in Amite is at an earlier stage than anywhere else in Mississippi. Even the most rebellious local Negroes think a public demonstration in Liberty must wait for another age. The protest in Amite is pure and religious, uncontaminated by organizational in — fighting or Mau Mau militancy. It is just two outside organizers and perhaps 200 or 300 local Negroes. The *right* to protest has not yet been won, much less the tokens of desegregation or the utopian goal of equality. For a Negro to talk to another Negro active in the Movement requires courage; to come to a meeting is authentic heroism.

There is not much talk about Herbert Lee, but there is a lot of remembering.

The daily routine of Steptoe, Carol, and Hazel is "boring, shitty," work, as Carol puts it. It is canvassing from sunup until twilight, and then often a meeting in a church. There is nothing dramatic about the work. There are no emotional releases. The tension is constant: every passing car is a threat, every white face a mask for violence, every back road a potential trap. There is no freedom house in Amite, where drink, talk, or sex can be shared with other organizers. There is nothing more intellectual than the *McComb Enterprise-Journal* to read. By November both Carol and Hazel had been there for five months and both were preparing to leave, burned-out by the tension, the exhaustion, the frustration, of day-to-day work.

Religion is the source of love in Amite. Baptist churches are the only possible places to hold meetings. Several of the indigenous leaders developing in Amite, like Reverend Knox, are ministers, or, at least, deacons in their church, like Curtis Dawson. The people themselves are deeply religious.

There is no tradition of freedom singing in Amite. Few Negroes even know the words to "We Shall Overcome." The four meetings I attended while in the county were all begun with the singing of Baptist hymns and a prayer. There were none of the fiery call-and-response chants of "Freedom Now" or of the improvised freedom songs that characterize the Movement in urban centers.

One of the meetings I attended was in Mt. Pilgrim Baptist Church on Steptoe's land, where Parris had conducted his first voter-registration class in 1961. Herbert Lee is buried in the churchyard, and his handsome fifteen-year-old son, Herbert Jr., was among the fifty people present at the meeting.

Mt. Pilgrim has no pulpit. There are just ten rows of spare wooden benches in the center and four rows on either side. It is lighted by only three bulbs. Outside it was 45 degrees, and until the warmth from the small heater spread throughout the room, few people took off their jackets. A hand-drawn tablet with the Ten Commandments was on the wall.

One by one, individuals began drifting in, some in blue denim field overalls and mud-caked boots, others in sports jackets and shirts open at the neck. The men and women segregated themselves by sex.

The meeting began with the singing of two hymns: "Lord, Come By Here," and "Jesus, Hold My Hand While I Run This Race." Then there was a prayer by Reverend A. D. Hackett, an itinerant preacher without a permanent church. "God is going to cure our troubles through somebody," he said in a prophecy that synthesized the Bible with the Movement.

I had come to Amite with young folk singer Eric Andersen. We, along with Carol, were the only whites at the meeting, and Steptoe used our faces as his text for the evening. (Steptoe is one of the few local Negroes who is not religious.)

"White people come down here and do everything for us," he began. "But you have to do just one thing for them—and that's to redish."

Chants of "Amen" and "That's right" welled up from the benches.

"We're going through something here now that should have happened years ago. I've been in this struggle since 1953 and now I can see the first change happening."

More amens greeted that affirmative observation.

"You all have to go down and redish now. You should want to make this a better county to live in. You have to take that first step. You get the key to freedom when you redish. To be a redished *voter* means you are an American, a first-class citizen. It will keep bullets out of your body and clubs away from your head."

Curtis Dawson, with a morose, bespectacled face not unlike Bob Parris's, spoke in the same vein of civic virtue and racial reconciliation. It was a sermon of love no Harlem hustler could comprehend.

"We must love everybody," he started.

From that opening statement he began to build, the way a blues singer states, restates, and then embroiders on a basic theme.

"White people care more about us than we care about ourselves," Deacon Dawson added, the counterpoint of amens and "Say it, brother," rising from the benches.

"They do everything for us. They go farther with us than we go with ourselves. But we have to redish for our own selves."

With that, the amens swelled up again.

And then, as is often done in Amite, a political point was cloaked in a biblical analogy.

"God told Moses," Dawson said, "to pick up a stick. But Moses said it was a snake. But the Lord insisted he pick it up, and when Moses did, it turned out to be a sword. Right now it looks like picking up a snake. But once you pick it up, it will become the sword of freedom."

Then Carol Rogoff, sitting in the last row, began to sing, "This Little Light of Mine." And the younger people in the church, some of whom had gone to jail in Jackson in June, joined in, and Eric Andersen began to contribute a guitar accompaniment.

> This little light of mine/we're gonna let it shine . . .

The words filled the church and spilled out into the frosty night. With modulating fervor, each new chorus was sung.

> All over Mississippi, we're gonna let it shine. . . . All over the courthouse, we're gonna let it shine . . . All over Sheriff Jones, we're gonna let it shine . . . All over the highway, we're gonna let it shine . . . All over Liberty, we're gonna let it shine/oh, we've got the light of freedom/we're gonna let it shine.

Most of the older people had left, since Amite farmers must get up at 5 A.M. But a cluster of teenagers remained around Eric, singing the songs they had learned in jail.

After a while Herbert Lee, Jr., began to sing: *"Oh, my father was a freedom fighter/I'm a freedom fighter too. . . ."*

Fear

That's the other emotion always just beneath the surface of life in Amite. It is there whenever you stop for gas in Liberty; whenever the dogs start barking in the night and someone is approaching the house; whenever you notice the gun Steptoe always keeps within reach.

One incident that happened to me helped demonstrate the total vulnerability of Amite Negroes to random violence. Four of us—Carol, Hazel, a local woman named Juanitta Griffin, and I—were nailing up posters on trees for the Agricultural Stabilization and Conservation election. The ASC county committees decide local cotton allotments, who gets extra acreage, and who gets community credit corporation loans. Until Carol and Hazel came to work in Amite, Negro farmers didn't know they were eligible to run in this election even if they weren't registered to vote in political elections. The federal government hadn't bothered to inform them of their right to participate.

I had just nailed a poster to a tree and we were driving away when we noticed a pick-up truck stop, and the driver tear down the poster. For about a quarter of a mile the truck followed us on the deserted, narrow gravel road. We noticed it had no license plate. The driver had a woman, a child, and a Negro in the cab with him. Suddenly he came up on us very fast, trying to drive us off the road. He barely missed. He drove on a few hundred yards to discharge his three passengers. Then he began to come up on us again from behind, making a second pass, again coming very close to forcing us off the road. By this time we were growing frightened, realizing that we didn't know where we were and that the driver of the tagless pick-up truck had us at his mercy.

Carol, who was driving, suggested we try to make it to a paved road less than a mile away. Just then the pick-up truck bore down on us, head-on, at about 60 miles an hour. Carol swerved, and our car landed in a ditch.

We were destroying all the lists of local Negroes we had in the car when the driver of the truck pulled up alongside. He had a face from central casting, like all the faces I had watched in newsreels spitting on little girls in Little Rock and unleashing snarling police dogs in Birmingham.

"You-all need any help?" he asked mockingly.

"No, thank you," Carol replied.

"Well, if you-all did, I'd tell you-all to call Martin Luther," the face said and drove off to a dairy barn up the road.

The four of us quickly got out and began to walk as fast as we could in the direction of the main road. As we walked past the dairy barn, the driver, now with a friend and a pack of dogs, began shouting at us.

"White trash . . . nigger lovers . . . degenerates . . ."

We kept walking, heads down, and he began following us cursing and threatening.

Before he caught up to us we reached the main road and flagged down a log truck with three Negroes. But the Negroes were afraid to pick up our integrated group. Only several minutes of pleading convinced them to take us to a nearby home, where Carol called FBI agent R. L. Timmons, stationed in McComb.

Agent Timmons said he was busy just then but would come to Steptoe's farm the next morning to hear our stories.

Within a few hours the grapevine in the Negro community reported back that the man who had chased us was named Dan "Buster" Wells, and that he had a long history of brutality against Negroes. The Negro originally in the truck with Wells was also spoken to, but he wouldn't talk to us, much less to the FBI. The Negroes in Amite remember Louis Allen, too.

The next morning Agent Timmons arrived exactly on time, wearing a businessman's blue suit. He carefully took down all our statements but added he didn't think "anything would come of them."

"We don't have any jurisdiction," he said, incanting the phrase that has made FBI agents despised by civil-rights workers. "Why didn't you call Sheriff Jones when this happened?" he asked.

Carol reminded Agent Timmons that many local Negroes believed that Sheriff Jones had personally murdered Louis Allen, and that he had never arrested a white man for violence against a Negro.

The next day, on the street in McComb, we accidentally ran into Timmons's assistant, Sy Hoglund. While Timmons grew up in Louisiana and is clearly hostile to the Movement, Hoglund is a Northerner who went to law school at the University of Wisconsin. He reluctantly admitted that since we were working on the federal ASC election when the incident occurred, "there might be jurisdiction . . . but we will not do anything more than file a report unless the Justice Department specifically instructs us to proceed further in the case."

Bob Parris, Marshall Ganz, and Carol Rogoff are all complex, city-bred, middle-class intellectuals. That Amite should attract and sustain such people is, I suspect, an insight into one of the New Left's most tangled threads. That thread is the revolt against the IBM card, against urban impersonalization and the alienation of mass society; a revolt rooted in the void, which cries out for the kind of human generosity and vitality that exists among rural Mississippi Negroes.

Many civil-rights workers in the state rage passionately against the life style they left behind in the comfortable North: suburbia, status commodities, nine-to-five jobs. But in Amite people are judged not by their manners, or their fathers' income, or what fraternity they belong to, but by their integrity, their work, and their courage.

Although it is too often sentimentalized, there is a special quality to the Negroes of Amite County that is missing elsewhere. The routinized middle class doesn't have it, the cynical Northern-ghetto Negro doesn't have it, and the violent, poor Southern white doesn't have it. In part this distinctive quality comes from living in a totally rural environment, removed from the criminality, corruption, and violence in the cities. In part it derives from the strength of the Baptist Church with its embracing of the values of both the Sermon on the Mount and the Ten Commandments. And in part it comes from a people that has achieved an authentic nobility in one hundred years of stoic suffering.

In *Letters from Mississippi*, a few of the volunteers reached for an explanation for their love of a culture they had been taught, in America's best schools, was slow and primitive.

"One sees freedom here," one volunteer wrote, "that is so much more than the ironical fact that enslaved people are, at least relatively, the liberated ones. Some 'white' people sit at their feet wondering at this sorrow freed and made beautiful . . ."

Another summer worker wrote home: "When I see these simple people living lives of relative inner peace, love, honor, courage, and humor, I lose patience with people who sit and ponder their belly buttons . . . "

Still another volunteer observed: "There is some strong ambivalence which goes with this work. I sometimes fear that I am only helping to integrate some beautiful people into modern white society with all of its depersonalization (I suppose that has something to do with its industrial nature). It isn't 19th century pastoral romanticism which I feel, but a genuine respect and admiration for a culture which, for all the trouble, still isn't as commercialized and depersonalized as our Northern mass culture."

What I am trying to suggest is the ultimate irony of the New Left's assault on the Closed Society. It is that the liberators have so far benefitted more from the struggle than those in bondage, that for all the enormity of their heroism, Parris, Ganz, and Rogoff have gotten more than they have given. And it may be an enduring paradox that all through Mississippi the lives of the white volunteers have been more enriched, and more fundamentally changed, than the lives of the maids and tenant farmers whom they came to help.

Such a tentative suggestion, finally, flows from a suffocating pessimism about the future of Amite County.

Pessimistic because Amite is such a desperately poor place to begin with. Pessimistic because so many of the young Negroes leave, and the bright and rebellious handful that stays is likely to be recruited into the Government's million-dollar anti-poverty Headstart program or else die in Vietnam. Throughout the state the potential second generation of the Movement is being absorbed by such programs and the draft. Pessimistic because SNCC probably left Mississippi a year too soon, and the MFDP has expended too much of its energy in Washington and not enough in remote outposts like Amite.

Nevertheless, three young Dantes, all under thirty years of age, have helped bring substantial change since July of 1961. The right to hold meetings and the right of civil-rights workers to move freely around the county have been won. The pattern of fear and submissiveness in the Negro community has been broken. Local leadership is developing. About five hundred Negroes are registered, and at least one thousand will be on the voting rolls by the time of the next countywide election in 1967. Such voting strength is, at least, enough to dilute the arbitrary terror.

Still, no Negro's life has been materially improved. Nor is there any visible possibility of such improvement. Amite remains the bottom of the iceberg, which only massive outside intervention, backed by the federal government, can shatter.

On my last night in Amite, an old Negro preacher asked me what could possibly change the "conditions of my people?"

The only answer I could give him was the absurd fantasy that one day Lyndon Johnson, traveling in disguise as did Peter the Great, might come to Amite and live for a few days on Steptoe's farm. ❖

TRADITIONAL SPIRITUAL

ARRANGEMENT BY JULIUS LESTER

Wade In The Water

(Transcribed by Susie Erenrich)

Wade in the water, wade in the water,
children, wade in the water,
God's gonna trouble the water.

I said wade in the water, wade in the water,
children, wade in the water,
God's gonna trouble the water.

Well there ain't a hymn that I've been told,
God's gonna trouble the water,
Well the streets up there are paved with gold,
God's gonna trouble the water.

I said wade in the water, wade in the water
children, wade in the water,
God's gonna trouble the water.

Well, who's that yonder all dressed in white,
God's gonna trouble the water,
well, it looks like a host of the Israelites,
God's gonna trouble the water.

I said wade in the water, wade in the water,
children, wade in the water,
God's gonna trouble the water.

I said wade in the water, wade in the water,
children, wade in the water,
God's gonna trouble the water.

Julius Lester was a photographer, writer and folksinger for SNCC. He has published more than twenty books and teaches in the Judaic Studies Department at the University of Massachusetts at Amherst.

Well who's that yonder all dressed in red,
God's gonna trouble the water,
Well it looks like the children Bob Moses led,
God's gonna trouble the water.

I said wade in the water, wade in the water,
children, wade in the water,
God's gonna trouble the water.

ERIC ANDERSEN

Under A Dark Pink Moon:
A Story of Mississippi

I was twenty-two years old when Jack Newfield, a writer for the *Village Voice*, invited me and my musician girlfriend, Debbie Green, to accompany him down to Mississippi to meet the people there and observe first hand the voter registration drive underway in Amite County. It was early November, and as of the previous July, not one black American had been registered to vote. But it was not from lack of trying, as we soon found out. We flew into Jackson from New York, and it was almost 11 P.M. when the plane touched down. Amite, the county we were heading to, is adjacent to the Louisiana state line, and its county seat and main town, where all the local roads meet, had the unbelievable name of Liberty, Mississippi. This was the Deep South but *this* county, Amite, had the worst voting registration record in the entire country, almost non-existent. Black people there were beaten, threatened, shot at, and killings were still common. The concept of law and justice had drifted right over the place. I imagine if I had known this before I boarded the plane with Debbie and Jack, I would have had second, third, and fourth thoughts about traveling there at all. Amite County was a dangerous place in 1965.

We stayed at E. W. Steptoe's farm which, depending on how you looked at it, was either the eye of a hurricane or the rim of a sleeping volcano. But it quickly became our sanctuary. Steptoe was in his fifties, a short man with a deeply lined face and eyes that could quickly evaluate a situation or penetrate a truth. He was

Amite's fearless leader of the voting drive who had first tried to register alone in 1953 but had "failed" the written test.

Steptoe was joined and inspired in 1961 by a young northerner, Bob Parris, a black man from the Bronx who had come down to help organize the county. Bob had worked in SNCC and before that had only recently received his degree in philosophy from Harvard. A lot happened, good and bad, during Bob's stay, but no one got to register. Some residents did begin to have courage until people got killed. Bob had chosen Amite County because it was the worst in all America and known in civil rights workers' lore as the "Ninth Circle of Hell," an allusion to Dante's *Inferno*. Steptoe was born on the land, and he had no intention of ever leaving it; he wanted instead to change it.

We stayed at Steptoe's farm over a week with him and his daughters. In New York, the day before we flew down, I cut all my hair off and took a light tweed collegiate sports coat, thinking at the time it might make me less conspicuous or even invisible to the local whites. It didn't. They knew where I was from before I even opened my mouth.

I might add that this was the first of three times in my life I ever looked at my own race as the enemy to be *feared*. I felt the same thing when I read about Wounded Knee and John Neidhardt's book *Black Elk Speaks*. The last time was more recent: watching the Nazi skinheads in full-force action in Germany and other parts

Eric Andersen is a songwriter, poet, and recording artist who has released eighteen albums. He was discovered by Tom Paxton in San Francisco and got his start in Greenwich Village along with Phil Ochs and Bob Dylan. He divides his time between New York and Norway, where he writes and lives with painter Unni Askeland and their four children.

of Europe. In Amite I never spoke to one local white person. Not even for gas.

Although that memory and time spent in Mississippi now swims in a distant dream, some images are as vivid as the paper in front of my eyes. Here are those that come to mind.

Jackson, Mississippi.

Collecting our luggage and standing at the Jackson Airport rent-a-car counter with Jack and Debbie; filling out forms and showing our I.D.s and licenses to a thin Southern clerk barely old enough to shave, who examined them like it was a customs check; and our feeling as immediately out of place as three souls wearing yellow stars of David on our sleeves in 1942 Berlin.

Walking outside to find the car in the balmy November night and seeing an enormous dark pink moon hanging in a bare Mississippi sky; then driving at that late hour, few cars on the road, down Highway 51, the main road from Memphis to New Orleans—immortalized in so many Delta Blues songs—and seeing wisps of cold fog drifting over the road from the dark pines alongside. The moon was hanging right above the highway, and we aimed right for it until fog smothered it. Over whishing sounds of tires, imagination became enchanted as the heart began to be frightened. A seeping, eerie feeling pervaded the car as we drove on, the feeling of driving into the maybe too-well-known that waited ahead. Hearing the buzz of our own fears in the silence of the night and seeing the reflections of our faces glowing in the dashboard lights that began to act like a little fireplace, keeping us safe and warm from the strange danger outside. Hearing our own hearts beating out a primitive hope that the car wouldn't break down here, not now.

Arriving safely at last, after driving through the dark streets of Liberty, to the house where we would meet the people who would help and shelter us. There we met Hazel and Carol, two out-of-state organizers, one white from

around Philadelphia and the other black from another nearby county. After whispered greetings and a quick rundown on what was happening, we left and parked in front of a small barbecue shack that doubled as a juke joint on the weekends, where we were made welcome, fed, and given cold beer. More brave people and more big smiles. A sense of humanity returned, and a small feeling of safety and relief set in as we relaxed with these beautiful sons and daughters of those who were once sharecroppers. From that oasis, more driving into the dead night, threading the car carefully along red backpine roads till we turned into a driveway, and on a clearing we saw the lights of a house. Inside, Steptoe was waiting for us. He saw we were tired and sent us to bed.

Waking up, rubbing our eyes, seeing the wispy blue sky through the bare window; smelling bacon and sitting down to it with eggs and coffee and canned milk. New smells and new light. Beautiful light over a beautiful land. All around us, in every window pane, the soft red of the earth and the pale green of the pines.

Seeing, that first morning, Steptoe's wizened face sitting across from us over coffee cups on his worn pine kitchen table in a wood-frame house that didn't have a kitchen, just one big room. He paused for thought and began explaining to us what was happening in the county and recounted some of its recent violent history. He told us how his neighbor E. H. Hurst, a sitting member in the Mississippi state legislature, whose driveway faced Steptoe's own, had killed Steptoe's friend with a bullet to the head at point blank range near the local cotton gin a few years back because he had tried to register to vote. There were witnesses followed by silent voices who had been warned not to talk, or else. The body had lain on the ground in the middle of town for over two hours. E. H. Hurst got off on the grounds of self-defense. Steptoe also told us that a little time later one witness did come forth secretly to the Justice Department to tell what he saw. That was a man named Louis Allen. But Louis Allen got blasted away by a shotgun on his front porch soon afterwards.

Hearing how he, Steptoe, had to drive a different route anywhere he went to avoid possible ambush. I kept thinking about E. H. Hurst's driveway that faced Steptoe's.

Listening while he outlined the things we would be seeing and doing as we rode with him, Hazel Lee, or Carol Rogoff to canvass the countryside to get people out to register, a fearsome journey for these humble, eligible, but unwelcome prospective voters because it meant showing their faces and giving their names at the Liberty courthouse. Steptoe was grateful for the use of our car, but we all knew that the memories of Herbert Lee and Louis Allen were never far from anybody's minds.

Grinning as we witnessed Steptoe's inborn genius for survival with a sense of the comic and an ability to hustle, cajole, frighten, humor, and convince already scared people to get the power to get over their fear. Often it worked, but not always. Navigating with him down red clay rutted roads into poor dirt farms hidden by canebrakes and pine groves. Greeting the smiles with smiles and seeing the fearing eyes of his flock who suddenly would have a visiting relative or a mysterious stomach ailment that would prevent them from going in to register that week. This was hard work all around, but Steptoe kept on them, and they knew it was only a matter of when, not if. Yet voting for most ran a close second to fear of dying.

Suddenly being overtaken by clouds of terra-cotta dust from wildcat, outlaw pick up trucks, loaded shotguns sticking out from their mounts behind the rear windows, driven by surly white faces, and getting the distinct impression those guns weren't intended for hunting squirrels or rabbits.

Seeing Jack Newfield's shaken face after he, Carol, and Hazel, had been run off the road by one of them because they were hanging farm election posters and had to walk for miles to the highway to hitch a ride back. Then watching the blue, non-descript car of FBI Agent Timmons come up the drive, and seeing Steptoe tell him what happened. Overhearing agent Timmons ask Steptoe why he hadn't called the local sheriff, Daniel Jones, for help; knowing, of course, that most of the locals believed the sheriff had personally blasted Louis Allen off his front porch, and whose father was the head of the county Klan chapter.

Almost believing Steptoe's story, as most whites *and* blacks did, that he had a direct line to the Attorney General's office in Washington. And maybe he did. They didn't come much craftier than Steptoe. He had both guts and guile.

Browsing in the Liberty drugstore, looking for toothpaste, and while going to the counter to pay, hearing the soft drawl of the white lady cashier asking me, "What part of New York are you Yankees from?" I paid her, smiled, and shoved the toothpaste and change into my pocket, jumped into the car, and high-tailed it back to Steptoe's, making a point not to go back to Liberty for *anything*. I had no direct line to the Justice Department, and they knew it.

Arriving as we did in the dark to Mt. Pilgrim Church on Steptoe's land to attend a late night church service with the group whose courage was drawn from a deep religious faith. Sitting together with them on the rough plank benches under a few bulbs, listening to the Deacon Dawson and singing spirituals together. Seeing each other's scared but joyful eyes as the service commenced, while knowing three of us would soon leave and they would remain behind. Admiring the beauty of their faces and their inner strength and feeling sick from my own weakness in the face of it all. Still trying to overcome fear and hoping that by overcoming fear to maybe overcome death. Standing and singing spirituals, then being asked to get up front and play my guitar along with the voices and even to sing my own song, "Waves of Freedom," and hearing how small my voice sounded in the room and how big the wilderness really was.

Meeting those two parents and going into that simple house, smelling the woodstove burning; and looking into their clear eyes, their broad smiles of strong, perfect teeth, and absolutely black, beautiful skin; tall muscular people whose ancestors were brought in chains from far over the sea against their will; and knowing those kids had never seen a white person at their house before. Looking into those beautiful, generous faces that still had the power to open their hearts to us; and wondering and probing my own heart and asking myself how anyone could ever hate them. Or hate anyone.

And looking out the window or walking around Steptoe's house on his beautiful land on paths strewn with pine needles almost the color of the red earth, while humming to myself that minor refrain from an old folk song I remembered that went: *in the pines in the pines, where the sun never shines, and I shivered the whole night through.* And thinking of the danger that always lurked, as though I had been walking on the beautiful, copper-colored diamonds of a coiled rattlesnake.

Dancing the last night at a party in another house on stilts, no running water or indoor toilet, but the lights worked and so did the little 45rpm record changer, where these black Mississippi teenagers played for us the coolest, hippest records out of Mem-

phis and New Orleans, things I'd never find in New York. We danced and ate and laughed til our hearts broke from joy. Getting quick lessons on ham hocks, black-eyed peas, corn bread, and collard greens, which were explained to me as a cuisine created from what the owners of the plantations discarded. And my tongue taught me different. And thinking that the true power of the Great American Dream should have been the other way around.

And making fearful love to Debbie under a bare bulb on the floor of Steptoe's bathroom, looking over my shoulder because the windows were shiny night black with no curtains and feeling we were marked like two slow-moving targets.

Embracing to only let go the greatest joy of having met these beautiful, kind, brave angel souls; and feeling the terrible sorrow of parting when the time came for us to leave them and say our final farewells. Driving down Steptoe's long drive, looking back and waving goodbyes, while intent on making a beeline for Highway 51 North to the Jackson Airport, knowing the killers of Goodman, Chaney, and Schwerner still roamed free in Meridian, some seventy miles away.

Reading later the hand-penciled note Steptoe sent to us from Liberty to New York, on yellowed, lined grammar paper, thanking us for caring enough to take the time to visit him and for our kindness in letting him use our car to help enroll voters; and smiling as the memory of that week that seemed like a year came back; and feeling the pins prick my eyes as I saw his face in my mind.

Klofta Sept. 1993

ERIC ANDERSEN

Waves of Freedom

Transcribed by Susie Erenrich

They say we are but strangers
That we've been so all our lives
We've seen a lot of trouble
Yes we've seen a lot of strife
But I will make one promise
Before I take my leave
We'll ride the waves of freedom
And that you can believe
That you can believe, That you can believe

Now the weather might be stormy
And the waves may see no light
The winds will be bending
Down with all their might
And the rains will fall in anger
For there's soon to be a fight
But the dawn is not for breaking
Behind the darkest night
Behind the darkest night, Behind the darkest night

Oh they tried in Rome of ages
To tie and chain the free
Napoleon and Hitler
Yes they tried most bitterly
Rock the waves of freedom
Defy their slavery
For all the crest was rolling
The tides to victory
Tides to victory, Tides to victory

Now the clouds may cough confusion
And laugh in mockery
So the waters twist and darken
But the waves swell endlessly
They'll brave the loudest thunders
Till the clouds fall endlessly
And the storm gates fly open
And the waves they fall on free
Clear waters we shall see
Clear waters we shall see

Yes they say we are but strangers
That we've been so all our lives
We've seen a lot of trouble
Yes we've seen a lot of strife
But I will make one promise
Before we take our leave
We'll ride the waves together
And that you can believe
That you can believe
That you can believe

PHOTO BY

MATT HERRON

Hazel Brannon Smith checking final copy at the type desk of her newspaper, the Lexington Advertiser. *Smith won a Pulitzer Prize for taking the highly unpopular stand in favor of fairness in Mississippi race relations.*

GEORGE W. CHILCOAT AND JERRY A. LIGON

Developing Democratic Citizens: The Mississippi Freedom Schools

Edited from: *Theory and Research in Social Education,* Spring, 1994, Volume XXII, Number 2, pp. 128-175. © by the College and University Faculty Assembly of the National Council for the Social Studies
Used with permission by George W. Chilcoat
Original title: *Developing Democratic Citizens: The Mississippi Freedom Schools As A Model For Social Studies Instruction*

George W. Chilcoat and Jerry Ligon are currently editing a problems-issues models book that demonstrates fifteen instructional models for elementary and secondary educational use. They have written several articles on the Mississippi Freedom Schools and are planning on writing a book on the Freedom School experience. Chilcoat is an Associate Professor at Brigham Young University, Provo, Utah, who is interested in the study of various historical radical educational and theatrical experiences that can inform contemporary educational practice. He is writing a social studies text based on the 1960s concept of participatory democracy as evidenced in radical education and theater. Ligon is a Professor of Education at National Louis University, St. Louis, Missouri, who is interested in a problems-issues approach to social studies instruction.

Historical Background

Active change in the white Southern social, political, and educational infrastructure began with the Supreme Court's 1954 landmark decision of *Brown v. Board of Education,* and continued through limited federal intervention and active civil disobedience by members of various civil rights groups organized around the goal of eliminating white social and political injustice. The Student Nonviolent Coordinating Committee (SNCC) formed in 1960 was one of the most effective of these groups (Forman, 1972; Sellers, 1973; Zinn, 1965).

As the first organization of the Civil Rights Movement controlled by university students, SNCC was committed to nonviolent, direct action for social change (Sellers, 1973). Its leaders staged numerous sit-ins at all-white eating establishments and participated in freedom rides to Alabama and Mississippi to protest segregated bus terminals. Between 1961 and 1963, SNCC focused on the political and social life of Mississippi's African American communities by instructing residents on community planning and voter registration. Retaliation by whites was swift and brutal, manifested by arrests, beatings, prison sentences, and even the murder of African American community leaders and SNCC activists (Zinn, 1965).

Responding to increased white repression as well as fragmentation and competition among several civil rights organizations, SNCC helped organize in 1963 the Council of Federated Organizations (COFO), an umbrella organization that coordinated activities of the Congress of Racial Equality (CORE), the National Association for the Advancement of Colored People (NAACP), and the Southern Christian Leadership Conference (SLC). In November of that year, members of COFO and SNCC conceived the Mississippi Freedom Summer Project, a major political action program involving approximately 1,000 chiefly white volunteers (Student Nonviolent Coordinating Committee

[SNCC] Papers, 1982, Reel 38) designed to promote African American equality and basic democratic rights through a variety of strategic activities:

- A massive drive for voter registration among disenfranchised African Americans;

- A mock election in defiance of an all-white state Democratic party run by the newly created Mississippi Freedom Democratic party (MFDP or FDP) to represent African Americans in the upcoming national Democratic convention;

- Community centers providing weekly instruction and entertainment for African American adults and preschool children;

- A summer school program providing teenage African American students with a richer educational experience than was available in schools and hopefully committing these students to become a force for social change in Mississippi (State Historical Society of Wisconsin [SHSW], R. Hunter Morrey Papers; SHSW, Rev. Richard Gould Papers; Rothschild, 1982; Perlstein, 1990).

Charles Cobb (SHSW, Henry Bowie Papers; SNCC, Reel 68), a field secretary for SNCC, proposed the idea of freedom schools as a war against academic poverty. He claimed that the Mississippi school system was the worst in the nation, and that the segregated black schools were the worst in Mississippi. He also claimed that these schools were intellectual wastelands with "a complete absence of academic freedom" meant "to squash intellectual curiosity" (SHSW: Henry Bowie Papers, unpaginated).2

Cobb advocated an educational system for African American students that related to everyday experience. He also conceived of schools as a political organizing tool to train students to become local civil rights workers and organizers (University of Washington Libraries, Otis Pease Papers). Freedom schools were designed to "offer young black Mississippians an education that public schools would not supply; one that both provided intellectual stimulation and linked

learning to participation in the movement to transform the South's segregated society" (Perlstein, 1990, p. 297).

To make these schools a reality, the National Council of Churches sponsored a curriculum conference in New York during March, 1964 (Fusco, 1964; SNCC, Reels 67, 68, 69). Approximately 50 people participated, including SNCC staff members; public school teachers from the New York Federation of Teachers Union who had participated in a small-scale freedom school project in Virginia during the summer of 1963; Myles Horton, director of the Highlander Folk School, who had helped organize citizenship schools in black Sea Island communities off the coasts of South Carolina and Georgia; Noel Day, a junior high school teacher who had organized and designed curricula for one-day residential freedom schools during the 1963 Boston schools boycott; and Staughton Lynd, professor of history at Spelman College, who later was appointed coordinator of the freedom schools.

The major focus of this conference was formulating a core civic curriculum to prepare young African Americans for full citizenship in a democracy (SNCC, Reel 35). The four main components of the student-oriented curriculum were:

- Problem-solving case studies that related political, economic, and social forces to direct experience;

- A focus on discussion as means for achieving a new society;

- Use of *Guide to Negro History,* a comprehensive survey of African American history, and

- Reliance on personal experience as the basis for studying civic and social issues.

Because African American students were not offered a solid academic program in the segregated public schools, freedom schools were intended also to provide remedial reading and writing instruction; a humanities curriculum emphasizing English, foreign languages, art, and creative writing; and a general science and mathematics curriculum. In addition, the conference recommended numerous progressive, democratic teaching techniques emphasizing self-discovery and self-expression and encouraging students to think critically, to question Mississippi's oppressive social order, and to participate in social change (SNCC, Reel 27; Lauter & Perlstein, 1991).

Two week-long orientation meetings also sponsored by the National Council of Churches were held in June 1964 on the campus of Western College for Women at Oxford, Ohio, to train the freedom school volunteers (SHSW, Rev. Richard Gould Papers; SHSW, Joann Ooiman Papers; SHSW, Lise Vogel Papers). These volunteers included both teachers and nonteachers, all of whom received intensive course training in Mississippi politics, race relations, the SNCC philosophy of nonviolence as both a momentary tactic and a life commitment, practical safety procedures (Lake, 1964; Rothschild, 1982), pedagogical techniques, and use of the core curricula. During this time, participants prepared for the specific situations they would encounter and examined the existing educational structure of African American schools.

On the last night of the orientation, Bob Moses, a SNCC field secretary, spoke to the teachers "about the prospects, the dangers, and the rewards that the summer might bring" (Rothschild, 1982, p. 406). He implored them "to be patient with their students. There's a difference between being slow and being stupid. The people [the teachers would] be working with aren't stupid. But they're slow, so slow" (Sutherland, 1965, p. 39). On completing the orientation, volunteers traveled to locations throughout Mississippi to open their six-to eight-week freedom schools. The organizers had planned initially for 20 schools with a total population of 1,000 students (SHSW, Robert Starobin Papers); however, the program met with unanticipated success and enthusiasm, resulting in 41 schools in 20 communities with a total of 2,165 students (SNCC, Reel 38). Although high school

students were originally targeted, the project attracted a number of elementary and adult students as well (Holt, 1966).

The following schedule for the Jackson, Mississippi school was typical for many of the other freedom schools throughout the state:

Morning

8:15–8:30 Freedom songs and devotions

8:30–9:20 History of the Negro in America (on a rotating basis of two and three sessions per week per subject)

9:30–10:20 Citizenship curriculum (two general sessions per week and three small group discussions), also including films related to citizenship

10:30–12:00 Special subjects

Afternoon

1:30–3:30 Afternoon activities:

1. Arts and crafts

2. Playwriting, producing, acting

3. Writing, editing, publishing the freedom school newspaper

4. Mondays-sessions on how to prepare and mimeograph leaflets for mass meetings, voter registration campaigns, etc.

5. Typing, one hour per day, times to be arranged (SNCC, Reel 68).

The culminating event for all freedom schools was a three- day statewide student convention held in August, 1964, in Meridian, Mississippi, planned and administered by student delegates, who formulated and adopted a detailed platform on issues ranging from job discrimination to civil liberties (SHSW, Robert Parks Papers; SHSW, Howard Zinn Papers; Grant, 1964; Lynd, 1965). This was the first time African American students from around the state had gathered to discuss common goals and concerns (SHSW, Jake Friesan Papers).

Although the members of COFO and SNCC hoped that freedom schools would continue beyond the summer project, only a few were able to sustain enough study and activism to do so. The original planners had not intended the schools to become permanent institutions, merely a vehicle for effecting immediate change (Lauter & Perlstein, 1991), but many students and teachers found that the short six-to-eight week freedom school experience had a significant impact on their lives. In a newspaper interview (Millstone, 1964), Staughton Lynd, the freedom schools coordinator, voiced this impression:

Mississippi is never going to be the same. There are 2,000 youngsters who know now that they can relate with white people on the basis of equality. These kids want to be educated; they reach out for it. If the Negro gets the vote, these are the people who will be in the legislature in future years (p. 6).

Goals

When asked if her efforts to help African American students learn to think for themselves and take control of their own lives constituted indoctrination, one freedom school teacher replied, "Yes, I suppose so. But I can't think of anything better to indoctrinate them with. Freedom. Justice. The Golden Rule. Isn't there some core of belief a school should stand by?" (Zinn, 1964, p. 374). This core was the driving force behind the freedom school experience, embracing an overriding desire for equity, justice, and social change with education as its medium. By educating youth in new subjects, new attitudes, new methods, and new convictions of their own abilities and potential, SNCC hoped to provide them with the tools to change their world (SNCC, Reel 73).

The general goal of the entire Mississippi Freedom Summer Project—the center of its core of belief—was to promote a new power structure, one based on equity and social justice (SHSW, Sandra Hard Papers). If any major changes were to take place in Mississippi, they would have to begin with African American youth (Howe, 1965). Freedom schools were intended to convert these young people from passive observers of their society to active, critical participants able to undertake solutions to community problems and to create a better society

for both African American and white citizens (SHSW, Robert Starobin Papers; Lauter & Perlstein, 1991). As Cobb wrote, "The overall theme of the school would be the student as a force for social change in Mississippi" (SNCC, Reel 27). The introduction to the citizenship curriculum stated it this way: "It is not our purpose to impose a particular set of conclusions. Our purpose is to encourage the asking of questions, and hope that society can be improved" (SHSW, Christopher Hexter Papers).

Asking questions became the vehicle for converting attitudes from passive to active; questioning facilitated the core of belief. On the simplest level, students needed to learn to ask questions in the classroom. Liz Fusco said of the Mississippi black schools of the era:

What . . . [the students] learn in their schools is to be alert to what the authority [teacher] wants and to come up with that, and that is always a fact you can memorize. So you learn to copy, you learn not to think, you learn not to ask a question that you don't already know the answer to or that you're not sure she knows the answer to, because the worst sin is embarrassing the teacher (SHSW, Liz Fusco Papers).

Ingrained teaching and learning patterns are difficult to change; however, for the goals of the freedom schools to be realized, change was imperative. Jane Stembridge, who participated in organizing the curriculum conference, wrote to the freedom school teachers:

This is the situation. You will be teaching young people who have lived in Mississippi all their lives. That means that they have been deprived of decent education, from the first grade through high school. It means that they have been denied free expression and free thought. Most of all—it means *that they have been denied the right to question.* The purpose of the freedom schools is to help them begin to question. This is not an easy job. Neither is it impossible. Deep inside, these young people possess great creativity . . . the desire for knowledge . . . and the wild hopes of all young people. You have to reach deep and tap these resources (SNCC, Reel 39).

Freedom school teachers and administrators hoped that by learning to question freely and thoughtfully in the class situation, students would "develop a new way of thinking and be awakened to their powers of analytic reasoning" (SNCC, Reel 27). As one SNCC field secretary affirmed, "More students need to stand up in the classrooms around the state and ask their teachers a real question" (SNCC, Reel 27). Freedom schools enabled students to articulate the desire for change awakened by the questions they were now being empowered to ask (Noel Day interview).

In addition, the civic curriculum was designed to give students respect for human diversity and dignity and an enhanced self-identity based upon an understanding of the roots of their oppression culled from their personal experiences and from black history (SNCC, Reels 27, 38). With these new perspectives and communication skills, African American teenagers were expected to return to their communities, teach other students (Fusco, 1964; SNCC, Reels 6, 65, 68), and hopefully form local and statewide student action groups for voter registration, school boycotts, and community leadership. Expectations in the various schools ran high among the project organizers (Zinn, 1964; Gillard, 1965, SHSW, Staughton Lynd Papers; SHSW, Elizabeth Sutherland Papers; Aviva Futorian interview).

The organizers also realized that the volunteers would bring their own personal objectives for teaching in the freedom schools, and each individual would need to reconcile his or her personal goals with those prescribed by the curricula and the pedagogy (SNCC, Reel 67). Cohesiveness and cooperation among faculty, administrators, and other staff members was vital. To promote this cooperation, freedom school staff needed to agree upon a set of goals that would pedagogically drive their respective schools. "Hopefully, before the opening of each school, there will be time for the staff to agree on overall aims and to apportion individual responsibilities" (SNCC, Reel 67).

The Schools

Gulfport Freedom School. Within the core beliefs embraced by all of the freedom schools, Gulfport emphasized helping African American youth to discover themselves as human beings. Teachers stressed racial pride, critical thought, and social action. The school was "a place of social, political, intellectual, and recreational development," a place to "fill the large void in the Negro youth's life" (Gillard, 1965, p. 24). The school also provided students with opportunities both in and out of class to examine the conditions in which they lived, to identify problems, and to develop better ways of life for themselves, their families, and the Gulfport community (Gillard, 1965).

Jackson Freedom School. Teachers in this school focused on changing the negative approach to education that was prevalent at the time. Florence Howe (1965), a teacher at Jackson, asserted that some instructors in the public school system were ill-prepared, and as such were either timid or hostile, often dictatorial, and sometimes even vengeful toward their students. Both timid and hostile instructors taught only rote learning and expected their classes to be passively receptive: "You learn this . . . and you get along. Get used to the violence, get used to being stuck, get used to taking orders, for that is the way life is on the outside" (Howe, 1965, p. 145). Howe also noted that these teachers would not allow students to question the status quo or to protest the poor living conditions of the African American people.

In contrast, the Jackson teacher assumed the role of a student among students, acting as a concerned questioner and listener who did not always have the right answer, but who was anxious to help students control their own lives and contribute to self-determination in their communities (Howe, 1965; SHSW, Frederick Heinze Papers). Staff members reinforced this role when they stated that "academic experiences should relate directly to . . . real life in Mississippi and since learning that involves real life experiences is, we think, most meaningful, we hope that the students will be involved in the political life of their communities" (UWL, Otto Pease Papers).

Holly Springs Freedom School. Teachers at Holly Springs perceived two problems preventing changes in the oppressive power structure: (1) Students had repressed their mistrust and hostility toward whites, docilely addressing them as "Mr.," Mrs.," or "Miss," and passively accepting a second-class position, after "years of being automatically second and automatically wrong" (SNCC, Reels 6, 65, 68); and (2) students had suppressed their own ideas and feelings and as a result had little confidence; thus, the teachers developed two major goals adapted from the core principles: (1) to help African American students and white teachers view each other as people whose sole difference was cultural experience and (2) to provide students with opportunities to practice creative thought through a variety of expressive outlets (SNCC, Reel 6).

To assist in achieving the first goal, teachers asked students to address them by their first names (SNCC, Reels 6 & 65). They also shook hands with students to show a genuine concern for them as equal human beings (Pam Allen questionnaire). Many African American students were stunned by these verbal and physical symbols of friendship used to break down old prejudices and fears. To overcome African American students' lack of confidence, Holly Springs teachers provided a number of creative, motivating opportunities for them to express themselves (SNCC, Reel 6; Pam Allen questionnaire; Aviva Futorian interview). They wrote and published a freedom school newspaper containing their own articles, poems, news stories, and editorials. These activities also extended beyond the school when students and teachers produced and staged a one-act play together; it was performed a number of times in Mississippi and later in New York.

Ruleville Freedom School. Within the core principles, Ruleville focused on education as a tool for solving problems and effecting positive change. Dale Gronemeier, the school librarian, wrote to a friend that the school was intended "to remedy the educational dearth education" (SHSW, Dale Gronemeier Papers). As Kristy Powell, teacher and coordinator at Ruleville, wrote in one weekly report, the purpose of the school was to be a center for real education, not just an academic institution (SHSW, Staughton Lynd Papers). Academics had its place—to provide students with solid research skills to solve problems—but if education was to have a lasting impact on African American students, they needed to apply what they learned in school to create positive change in their community. True achievement in learning was considered to have occurred only if students were involved in exploring ideas, applying reasoned options to life's problems, making choices, and promoting community involvement. To accomplish these objectives, teachers worked closely with students, both academically and socially, to solve problems and effect improvements.

Mileston Freedom School. Like the teachers at Ruleville, the teachers at Mileston believed that the academic components of the project were important but not as important as the social and political changes they were charged to effect. Mileston had a strong focus on political consciousness with an emphasis on the oppression experienced by African Americans (SNCC, Reel 65). These teachers felt that if students could understand how exploitation and injustice were blocking their personal and community development and could learn how the white system worked, they would be able to engage in the kind of dialogue, cooperation, risk taking, and ultimately the democratic action necessary to initiate change (SNCC, Reel 65; SHSW, Staughton Lynd Papers).

Curriculum

The March 1964 Curriculum Conference sponsored by the National Council of Churches (SNCC, Reel 64) proposed two progressive curricula targeted to strengthen African American students academically and to prepare them for greater social and political activity. Most African Americans had had limited exposure to most academic subjects; many needed remedial help in basic reading, writing, and mathematics skills, and many had merely a flagging interest in learning due to their negative experiences in school; therefore, an academic curriculum of reading, creative writing, mathematics, science, English, foreign languages, and art was created. The major thrust of the freedom schools, however, was the civic curriculum designed to relate directly to student experiences and life situations. It consisted of three components: (1) case studies of social issues, (2) the *Guide to Negro History*, and (3) a citizenship curriculum (Fusco, 1964; SHSW, Robert Starobin Papers).

Case Studies

The case studies were structured specifically to help African American students learn to contend with and solve problems in their communities. Teachers were to focus not on teaching facts but on teaching students to draw upon their own experiences, to relate the case studies to current situations in Mississippi, and to derive suggestions to solving problems in their own area. Writers of the case studies each agreed to outline a week's study (approximately 5 one-hour lessons) providing a set of concepts with material for each lesson relevant to each concept, to indicate sources teachers could utilize for further information, and to offer ideas for effective ways to present case content (SNCC, Reels 37, 67).

Although 14 cases were originally planned, only 7 were developed fully due to time limitations. The following case studies were incorporated in the freedom schools: (1) the impact of the congressional campaign of Fannie Lou Hamer, Ruleville resident and active member of the Mississippi Freedom Democratic Party, on the Mississippi movement (Sugarman, 1966); (2) the impact of the Mississippi judicial system on African Americans; (3) the Mississippi power structure; (4) the ramifications of poverty for African Americans and whites; (5) the parallel histories of Nazi Germany and the white power structure of the South; (6) the Southern education system; and (7) the passage of the Civil Rights Bill of 1963 (SNCC, Reel 64).

Although all seven case studies were substantial lesson plans, pedagogical quality varied (Perlstein, 1990); for example, the case study on the power structure in Mississippi provided insightful information on the structure of the working class: blacks plowing, planting, and picking cotton, and poor whites working in factories. It also included important features of dominant social, political, and economic policies and entities in the state: banks, utility companies, the White Citizens Council, and the white Mississippi Democratic Party. It did not, however, provide instructional guidelines; thus, teachers received no help in presenting the information or in guiding students to use the information to improve their own lives under such a structure (SHSW, Pam Allen Papers).

In contrast, the case study comparing the Nazi German power structure and the power structure of the South (SHSW, Joann Ooiman Papers) provided content, teacher guidelines, and suggestions for instructional strategies. Teachers were given instructions on how to help students use historical experience to generate possible solutions to current situations. Organized into five sections, this case study began with an overview comparing the power elite of Nazi Germany with that of Mississippi, noting the comparison of concentration camps to Mississippi's communities as closed societies and emphasizing the importance of active community resistance. The remaining four sections provided historical narratives illustrating the major points of the lesson. A discussion/role-play format gave teachers and students opportunities to explore ways that African Americans might avoid mistakes made by those who suffered under Nazi persecution. Lesson designers hoped that students would develop critical thought in the following areas: (a) the danger of cooperating with persecutors; (b) the importance of maintaining individual identity, exercising initiative, and resisting attempts to reduce race to group status; (c) the goal of maintaining inner convictions and choosing one's own attitudes; and (d) the significance of group solidarity, avoiding divisions manipulated by rewards or privileges (SHSW, Joann Ooiman Papers).

The Guide to Negro History

The *Guide to Negro History* (SHSW, Pam Allen Papers; SHSW, Joann Ooiman Papers; SNCC, Reels 38 & 67) was developed to teach African American students about their heritage so they could construct a positive image of themselves as a people with heroes and positive role models (Fusco, 1964), and realize that they were participating in a historical reform movement to achieve social, economic, and political justice (Gillard, 1965). Consistent with the overall freedom school goal of making learning meaningful in a real life context, lessons were focused to help students understand the relationship of history to their daily lives. Students could "grow and develop new insights as they (1) master relevant information; (2) relate this new knowledge to the information they already have; and (3) attempt to apply these insights to current problems" (SHSW, Joann Ooiman Papers).

The introductory lesson in the guide introduced students to black history by describing a slave revolt known as the Amistad incident, which occurred in 1839. Students then learned about a series of historical episodes comprising their heritage: the slave trade; the institutionalization of slavery as reflected in the Constitution of the United States; attempts at black resistance; the Haitian revolution; the abolitionist movement; Southern reconstruction; and the civil rights laws. These lessons also emphasized the positive changes that occur when people devote their time and energy collectively to causes of justice and equity.

The Citizenship Curriculum

To help students examine their life situations critically in terms of what they wanted to achieve and how they could work toward a more just and equitable existence, the freedom schools implemented the citizenship curriculum (SHSW, Christopher Hexter Papers; Noel Day interview). Teachers explored with their students two sets of questions that formed the foundation to understanding the content of the citizenship curriculum:

Primary set of questions

1. Why are we (teachers and students) in freedom schools?

2. What is the freedom movement?

3. What alternatives does the freedom movement offer us?

Secondary set of questions

1. What does the majority culture have that we want?

2. What does the majority culture have that we don't want?

3. What do we have that we want to keep? (SHSW, Christopher Hexter Papers)

Lauter and Perlstein (1991) assert that these questions were essential to understanding and reshaping society—then and now—as they shift from an individual to a collaborative outlook:

First, these questions do not ask "What does the majority culture have that I want?" but "What does the majority culture have that *we* want?" The distinction is critical and yet very difficult to comprehend within the framework of American educational institutions, for virtually everything in our schools and colleges, except for some team sports, is calculated to reenforce the idea of individual advancement, private accumulation of knowledge, grades, degrees. Freedom school students were quite clear about this matter [that] the discrimination they encountered every day had little or nothing to do with them as individuals;...it had everything to do with them as black people. And thus the question was not only the knowledge, the sense of self . . . an individual might accumulate...but also how the social definition . . . as an "ignorant nigger," or, more politely, a "culturally deprived" black . . . might be changed by joining with others who shared a similar fate (pp. 4- 5).

The citizenship curriculum consisted of seven units. Each lesson posed a series of questions to stimulate class discussion. The first compared the lives of African Americans with whites in their community, including schools, housing, employment, and medical facilities. The second lesson compared the lives and experiences of northern African Americans with southern African Americans, demonstrating that geographical region made little difference in the realities of black second-class citizenship, and students were urged to remain in Mississippi to work to change the reality rather than to leave the area in hopes of escaping it. The third lesson examined some of the myths perpetuated by white culture to suppress African Americans through low expectations and negative self-images. The two subsequent lessons deepened this exploration of others, particularly how African Americans and poor whites were being exploited through money, power, fear, and inferior laws. The sixth lesson, "Material Things versus Soul Things," and the first half of the seventh lesson taught the principles of nonviolence as a philosophy for personal life and as the dominant methodology of the Civil Rights Movement. Teachers presented various civil rights experiences as examples of ways in which nonviolence helped to create "the atmosphere in which reconciliation and justice become actual possibilities" (SHSW, Christopher Hexter Papers). In the second part of the seventh lesson, teachers urged students to participate actively in changing the existing society and described specific steps to effect change.

The curriculum committee stressed the concept that both the civic and the academic curricula should be applied constantly to existing conditions and events in students' lives (Howe, 1984). Although teachers were urged to use the designed curriculum, they were given the option of modifying or altering it if the existing situations or the experiences and abilities of the students warranted such change (SHSW, Jerry Demuth Papers). Despite the fact that many of the volunteers were inexperienced teachers with inadequate knowledge of African American history and civil rights issues, the curriculum designers believed that they should have opportunities to make their own curricular and instruc-

tional choices (UWL, Otis Pease Papers; SNCC, Reel 39).

The Schools

Gulfport Freedom School. Gulfport offered the full curriculum advocated at the curriculum conference (SNCC, Reel 68), but from the first day of class, individual student needs, concerns, and desires demonstrated that modifications were necessary to increase its effectiveness; for example, during one discussion in the citizenship curriculum students were asked about the weaknesses and needs of their own schools. Students responded that school was a waste of their time, and they were not learning what they needed to qualify for jobs. When the teacher pressed them to be more specific, they replied that they wanted clerical jobs, so arrangements were made to offer business courses, including typing, to all interested students (Gillard, 1965).

Even the recreational program developed from student needs and experiences (Gillard, 1965). It was designed to provide enjoyable activities and to make students conscious of the differences between the African American and the dominant white Mississippi culture; for example, to help students examine critically the conditions of their neighborhood, the teachers suggested a game of baseball. The students readily agreed and took their teachers to their playing field—a rutted path running beside their homes. After the game, the teachers guided the students in a discussion of why white children had playing fields and African American children played on a rutted road. After the discussion, they went to look for a better field. This activity was designed deliberately to lead students to think from a base of their own everyday personal and community experiences, to examine what was represented by these experiences, and ultimately to consider why and how their society needed to be changed.

Jackson Freedom School. (Howe, 1965; Zinn, 1964) on the Jackson school reflected a program containing the citizenship curriculum, the seven case studies, and African American history taught in the mornings with a series of elective courses including chemistry, biology, English, French, and typing taught in the afternoon. An additional curriculum was designed around local conditions, events, and even movies as bases for discussion (Paul Lauter interview).

Howe (1965) recalled a specific experience where she was able to apply the citizenship curriculum to local conditions with her 11- to 14-year-old students. She asked them to describe their houses, comparing them to the houses of whites in Jackson and to the houses where they or their mothers worked as domestics. Howe then asked what changes the children would like to make in their own homes. Answers varied from adding rooms to increasing yard space; however, the children did not want what they perceived to be the grand homes they described in the white community. They perceived their own homes as comfortable. When the discussion turned to public schools, the reaction was different; they became angry. Although their school was new, it was inferior to the white school. The students resented the second-hand textbooks, the inadequate teachers, and the repressive atmosphere that permitted no questions or discussions about topics they felt were important.

Similarly, teachers in Jackson monitored local events to link the curricula and the goals of the freedom schools; for example, a newspaper editorial charged that civil rights workers were teaching African American people to break the law. After students read the editorial, the teacher asked them if they thought it was true, leading the discussion toward a purposeful learning experience. An observer reported her words and the children's responses:

"If you could write a letter to the editor about it, what would you say? . . . Here's paper and pencil, go ahead. We'll pick out one or two and really send them to the editor." This was not education for grades, not writing for teacher's approval, but for an immediate use: It was a learning surrounded with urgency. And the students responded with seriousness, picking apart

the issues: Are we for the law? Is there a higher law? When is civil disobedience justified? Then the teacher explored with them the differences between statutory law, constitutional law, and "natural" law. (Zinn, 1964, p. 372).

Applications of citizenship instruction to actual events extended beyond local conditions into national issues, policies, and events. One teacher involved students personally, using the Civil Rights Bill of 1963 case study (Zinn, 1964). The reasons that Barry Goldwater, Arizona senator and Republican presidential candidate, gave for voting against the bill were listed on the blackboard: The bill was unconstitutional; it would not end prejudice; it could not be enforced; and it violated what were considered to be states' rights. The class then played out the arguments, one student acting as Goldwater and defending his viewpoint with vigor, while another classmate developed strong arguments against Goldwater's assertions.

Holly Springs Freedom School. Holly Springs offered a variety of different elective classes based on the interests and needs of the individual students; however, core classes of citizenship and African American history were required of everyone, and teachers worked to help students experience racial identity and pride (Pam Allen questionnaire; SHSW, Sandra Hard Papers). Curricula were scheduled as follows:

9:00–9:15 Civil rights folk songs
9:30–10:30 Core classes: Negro history and citizenship curriculum
10:30–11:30 Choice of dance, drama, art, auto mechanics, guitar and folksinging, or sports
12:00–2:00 School closed
2:00–4:00 Classes in French, religion, crafts, music, playwriting, journalism
4:00 Seminar on nonviolence

Pam Allen recorded an experience while teaching a lesson from the *Guide to Negro History* that reflected her own and her students' feelings and reactions to a historical event about which her students knew nothing:

Let me describe one of my first classes and one of my favorite classes. I gave a talk on Haiti and the slave revolt that took place there at the end of the eighteenth century. I told them how the slaves revolted and took over the island . . . how the French government (during the French Revolution) abolished slavery all over the French Empire . . . and . . . that the English decided to invade the island and take it over for a colony of their own. . . . They knew that the Negroes always lost to the Europeans. And then I told them that the people of Haiti succeeded in keeping the English out . . . [that] Napoleon came to power, reinstated slavery, and sent an expedition to reconquer Haiti. . . . But when I told them that the French generals tricked the Haitian leader Toussaint to come aboard their ship, captured him, and sent him back to France to die, they knew that there was no hope. . . . Former slaves, Negroes, could not defeat France, which had the aid of England, Holland, and Spain, especially without a leader. When I told them that Haiti did succeed in keeping out the European powers and was recognized finally as an independent republic, they just looked at me and smiled. The room stirred with a gladness and a pride that this could have happened (SHSW, Pam Allen Papers).

Ruleville Freedom School. Prior to the opening of the freedom school at Ruleville, the teachers decided that the overall curriculum should be structured cooperatively by the entire staff. In addition to the required citizenship and black history curricula, each teacher had the right to develop his or her own curriculum (SHSW, Staughton Lynd Papers). When school began, the initial class schedule was similar to that of the other freedom schools (SHSW, Jerry Tecklin Papers); however, the teachers soon realized that their classes were very academic and many students were not excited about most of them, so they decided to revise the curricula. The citizenship curriculum remained, but three revisions were made to bring it closer to student needs and interests (SHSW, Staughton Lynd Papers).

First, they added a class in world geography (SHSW, Jerry Demuth Papers). The teachers chose Australia, Egypt, and Africa for study, emphasizing black cultures. Second, they added a general motivational session prior to scheduled classes. Speakers for this session included members of the freedom school staff, individuals involved with voter registration, and SNCC visitors who spoke on topics such as the white southerner, the black in Mississippi, Gandhi and nonviolence, and the Mississippi Freedom Democratic Party.

The third revision was the most innovative. The staff organized the freedom school into an active student forum for community change (SHSW, Staughton Lynd Papers; SHSW, Jerry Tecklin Papers; SNCC, Reel 40). One of the most striking activities developed from students' concern that the African American teachers in their public schools were afraid to register to vote, and thus could not take the lead in demanding better, integrated schools (SHSW, Ruby Davis Papers). Students wanted to picket their public school in order to help their teachers realize that they too could become active change agents. Freedom school teachers helped students practice picket strategies and act out interviews with their public school teachers on how to register to vote. Together they wrote a pre-picket letter to the public school principal and faculty presenting their demands, and they produced leaflets urging students in the public school to join the picket. Although threatened with suspension, a number of public school students joined the freedom school students in a successful picket of the local high school.

Mileston Freedom School. Even more sweeping changes in the freedom school format occurred at Mileston. The goal of the teachers at this school was to create an active approach to developing student leadership for community activism (SNCC, Reel 65). As teachers and students worked, those activities began to take up a greater proportion of school time. Utilizing their learning experiences from the citizenship curriculum and the *Guide for Negro History*, students wrote and produced a play promoting positive community change, created and staffed a freedom school newspaper, and prepared and participated in a mock precinct meeting in preparation for the Meridian freedom school convention. Because students wanted to spend more time implementing the civic lessons, the teachers decided that the short time they had to spend with the students would be better put to use for activist purposes than for passive study of the proposed academic curriculum; therefore, the academic curriculum was eliminated.

Instruction

Charles Cobb stressed that teaching methods should promote classroom activities and discussions as "an outgrowth of [student] experiences" (SNCC, Reel 27). Traditional teaching in Mississippi had served as a form of oppression. Authoritarian in nature, it relied on rote learning where a teacher lectured and then tested solely on content. Students were expected to be passive and subservient. Under this form of education, African American youth learned not to trust others (particularly whites), to be cynical, and to expect inadequate preparation for functioning in society (SNCC, Reel 67). The possibility that students should someday serve as active agents for social change was unheard of—and it was undesired. Such was the mentality of the black public education system and of the Mississippi society at large (Holt, 1966).

In contrast, freedom schools rejected these practices and relied upon progressive instructional methods designed to promote "student participation in learning, a sense of the worth and equality among students, and the need to connect lessons to life." (Perlstein, 1990, p. 319). Freedom school teachers demonstrated that they could be trustworthy and honest in teacher-student relationships, and that they respected students and their experiences. A handout entitled "Notes on Teaching in Mississippi" distributed to the freedom school volunteers prior to their teaching experiences included the following advice:

What will they demand of you? They will demand that you be honest. Honesty is an attitude toward life which is communicated by everything you do. Since you, too, will be in a learning situation, honesty means that you will ask questions as well as answer them. It means that if you don't know something you will say so. It means that you will not "act" a part in the attempt to compensate for all they've endured in Mississippi. You can't compensate for that, and they don't want you to try. It would not be real, and the greatest contribution that you can make to them is to be real (SHSW, Pam Allen Papers).

Discussion

Organizers suggested to teachers that discussion should form the basic method of instruction, and it was expected to promote effective, cognitive results among students (Holt, 1966; Noel Day interview). They praised this method for the following strengths:

1. Encouraging expression;
2. Exposing feelings (bringing them into the open where they may be dealt with productively);
3. Permitting the participation of students on several levels;
4. Developing group loyalties and responsibility; and
5. Permitting the sharing of strengths and weaknesses of individual group members. (SNCC, Reel 39)

Two volunteer teachers explained ways in which the freedom school discussions differed from traditional classroom recitations:

In the first place, they were "open"—that is, there were no single, prepackaged answers that teachers were to listen for or to require students to memorize. The idea was, indeed, that no one could have a single, ultimate answer to any or all of the questions, for the questions' purpose was to evoke not only response but also students' search for definition and identity. In the second place, the questions were based on what the students already knew from their own lives—that is, they could begin to respond, and they were already equipped. And third, essential to such questions and such response is the process of discussion itself. The hidden assumptions behind a reliance on discussion are, first, that talk—saying the words—is a necessary step for discovery of self and social identity. Further, the public discovery—saying the words in a group—might lead to action, if not at once, then later (Lauter & Howe, 1970, p. 42).

Creative Activities Combined with Discussion

Other progressive methods were suggested, including drama, art, singing, films, guest speakers, role playing, creative writing (with an emphasis on poetry), school newspapers, and social action projects (Sutherland, 1965; SNCC, Reel 67; Paul Lauter interview; SHSW, Pam Allen Papers). Discussion was used as a follow-up technique for these other methods "to make certain that the material has been learned" (SNCC, Reel 39).

Role Playing. Freedom school teachers found that role playing was very popular with students and very effective instructionally, because it brought out hidden attitudes that teachers and students could then examine (SHSW, Sandra Adickes Papers). Pam Allen found in her teaching experiences that role playing would "permit the expression of a wide range of feelings by the students, involve their total selves, stimulate creativity, provide the teacher with insights about the students and at the same time get across the content material" (SHSW, Pam Allen Papers). Others confirmed the potential of role play to measure comprehension, particularly of the civic curriculum (SNCC, Reel 67). In addition, role play was stressed as a means of developing critical consciousness (Zinn, 1964).

Journalism. Local newspapers published exclusively under white ownership often presented articles favoring white issues and condemning black civil rights (Mabee, 1964). In response, many freedom schools "spurred an indigenous black press" (Rothschild, 1982, p. 407). One teacher in Clarksdale described the operation of the school's newspaper.

Most of the week was spent working on the *Clarksdale Freedom Press.* Getting all the inter-ested kids in the basement of Haven Methodist Church, examining possible articles, editing them, typing them, etc., was great! The place looked like a newspaper office with people running in and out, with typewriters going, and newsprint everywhere. It was excellent experience for the kids too. . . . They did most of the work and made most of the decisions. (Sutherland, 1965, p. 97).

Lecturing. Occasional lecturing was suggested in the citizenship curriculum, but its role was limited (SNCC, Reel 67). Teachers were cautioned to use it rarely, and not allow it to replace the other methods. Reports indicated that some teachers lectured for a variety of reasons. At the New Bethel Freedom School, lectures "gave out information . . . at a much faster rate" (SNCC, Reel 67), and teachers at Gluckstadt Freedom School lectured primarily because of a lack of student materials and resources (SNCC, Reel 67). Clarksdale reported that one of its freedom schools was conducted "on a somewhat formal level, as opposed to roundtable discussions . . . but this does not seem to be particularly detrimental to the school" (SNCC, Reel 67). One school in Madison County devoted the first hour and a half of each day's schedule "to Negro history with the entire student body attending a lecture given by one teacher and then individual groups of students discussing the lecture with their respective teacher" (SNCC, Reel 68). In Pleasant Green, the school "experimented with letting the students take over the lectures and discussion-leading, and were excited by the good results" (SHSW, Joann Ooiman Papers).

The Schools

Gulfport Freedom School. At Gulfport, many of the suggestions from "Notes for Teaching in Mississippi" were incorporated (Gillard, 1965). Discussion and creative writing were the dominant modes of instruction, and students actively discussed, debated, and raised questions related to their way of life. They became so enthusiastic and successful that debates were organized with other freedom schools. Lively discussions on the theme of nonviolence as a philosophical approach to freedom followed film viewing. To provide students a way to express deep feelings about their personal experiences, teachers encouraged creative writing, so that all could find their own voices. To train them in more public, utilitarian forms of writing, the curriculum included opportunities for students to write letters to federal officials about the depressed conditions of the black communities. As a specific training ground for active community participation, the school published a newspaper, *The Press of Freedom,* containing student work including poetry, critical essays, editorials, personal experiences, and news reporting (SNCC, Reel 39). Working together, the students also created a short play entitled *Memories of Freedom School,* that emphasized one of their favorite activities—singing.

Singing songs about freedom and deriving lessons from songs were very important activities in the Gulfport freedom schools. Teachers would begin classes each day by asking which freedom songs the students wanted to sing. Students chose songs like "I Woke Up This Morning with My Mind Stayed on Freedom"; "They Say That Freedom Is a Constant Struggle"; and "Ain't Gonna Let No Segregation Turn Me Round" (Jones, 1964). Each session began with a different song, but at the close of school the song was always the same. One observer described its significance:

There was one special song, a very solemn song. It requires everyone to gather in a circle and join hands for a time, each thinking in his own mind about the meaning of freedom and about people like Medgar Evers, Herbert Lee, and the three civil rights workers in Neshoba County, and all the others who have died fighting for freedom in Mississippi. . . . Someone begins. "We Shall Overcome. . . . We are not afraid. . . . Truth shall set us free." Everyone knows that overcoming will be difficult because there are many white and Negro people who are afraid of freedom. The song lets students and teachers know the pattern of their lives, that all the great number of years which comprise a life

isn't so many after all when there is freedom to be fought for (Jones, 1964, p. 5).

Jackson Freedom School. Discussion was the dominant instructional mode at Jackson (Howe, 1965), and it was based usually on varied learning experiences, i.e., as a follow-up to films; to readings of authors James Baldwin, Ralph Ellison, and Richard Wright; or to presentations by guest speakers like Pete Seeger, a nationally known folksinger who sang, taught, and discussed songs of other countries with the children. To promote the discussion relationship, setting was important. The traditional style of students sitting in rows with a teacher standing in front was inappropriate. This not only interfered with free expression, it stressed inequality between teacher and students—a negative relationship that characterized the students' earlier experiences in the black public schools. To break down the authoritarian tradition physically as well as emotionally, students and their teacher sat in a circle facing each other. Discussions usually followed a three-step pattern after the teacher and students were seated comfortably in the circle (Howe, 1965). The teacher first asked introductory questions and then asked probing ones. Finally, as the discussion progressed, the teacher would draw more critical thinking from the students: "How do you feel about this idea?" or "How do you feel about her experience?"

Writing was also important in the political education of the Jackson student. Writing experiences were structured to give students a feeling of self-worth, a sense of being in control, and an understanding of their power to achieve something. These students also wrote and published their own newspaper. Howard Zinn (1964) taught his students to react to news articles and editorials in a local newspaper by writing editorials of their own. Florence Howe (1965) read and discussed poems by Langston Hughes and e.e. cummings with her students, and encouraged them to express their personal reactions and feelings. With this motivation in place, she taught them the elements of poetry and asked them to write individual and group poems based upon their personal experiences and aspirations. Students shared these with one another, and intense discussions often followed.

The Jackson school not only encouraged students to express themselves, it urged them to become involved in their community. "Students had direct evidence that their [freedom] school experience had led them to create something that was lasting and profound" (Howe, 1965, pp. 156-157); for example, during the third week of freedom school it was announced that African American first-graders for the first time would be able to register to attend a formerly all-white elementary school. Apprehension ran high in the African American community. To encourage parents to register their children, 36 local African American ministers announced that a prayer meeting would be held. To prepare her own students to share in the experience, Howe (1965) initiated a discussion about the myth of black inferiority. Her efforts, however, were greeted with silence.

Wanting her students to be honest about their feelings, Howe asked, "What am I going to say to my friends back north when they ask me why Negro mothers haven't registered their children in white schools? That they like things the way they are?" (p. 186). Students then began to explore their real feelings and fears: Jobs might be lost, personal safety was threatened, and the possibility of failure in white schools loomed high. After this, the discussion began to shift. They began discussing reasons why first-graders should integrate the white elementary school. One student suggested that class members go out into the neighborhood and talk to parents who were reluctant to send their first-grade children to the white school. Howe suggested that they practice the dialogue they might have with hesitant parents. In the practice conversation, the father wasn't convinced, but the mother thought that she would try to enroll her child. Students then made plans to go out into the neighborhoods.

One of the freedom school teachers and a number of student volunteers spoke to over 70 families about attending the prayer meeting and provided transportation. Although 27 parents agreed to go, only one mother came. Undaunted, the freedom school students began revisiting the 70 families the next day. Their efforts were rewarded; 11 out of 43 eligible African American first-grade children in Jackson registered to attend the previously all-white public elementary school.

Holly Springs Freedom School. A variety of teaching methods were used at Holly Springs. Pam Allen, who taught the citizenship curriculum, religion, nonviolence, and also assisted in the drama class, shared her adaptation of the techniques:

> [Lectures] I shared what I was learning. I am an excellent speaker, a storyteller actually....I enjoyed the verbal sharing, and the girls' enthusiastic responses kept me at it.
>
> [Stories] My lectures on Negro history were really telling students to share experiences, but we didn't tell myths or legends.
>
> [Discussion] It was fun, very exciting and alive. We always had discussion after my presentation. I believe it was spontaneous and easy—no pulling teeth or trying to pull ideas out of the students.
>
> [Creative writing] For self-expression and sharing.
>
> [Resource People] We utilized the voter registration men. Someone spoke every morning before classes began.
>
> [Drama] The kids developed their own play. [They] chose the topic of the Medgar Evers killing, divided up the parts, and the characters role-played their parts.
>
> [School newspaper] We mimeographed a newsletter made up of student writings.
>
> [Community action] It's what the school was about—educating students for involvement in changing the social conditions. [The] main work was registering people into the MFDP (Pam Allen questionnaire).

Through the freedom school newspaper, students had opportunities to express their personal feelings as well as their critical analyses of individual, community, and national experiences. In addition, they honed their leadership skills and involved themselves in community affairs (Pam Allen questionnaire; SHSW, Sandra Hard Papers; Aviva Futorian interview). This first freedom school newspaper in Mississippi, the *Freedom News,* published four editions with students doing most of the work and making most of the decisions. They published articles on national and community news, critical essays on why African Americans should vote and why whites ought to accept African Americans, and a feature article on the efforts of the Holly Springs mayor to discourage the freedom school volunteers. They also published a story on how a local white businessman learned to accept African American workers as equals, a poem on the J.F.K. assassination, and a tribute to the freedom schools.

Drama was also important to the development of students at Holly Springs and to their involvement in civil rights work. Some became involved personally in the movement for the first time by writing, producing, and performing plays (Aviva Futorian interview; Roy de Berry, Interview). One student recalled: "In fact, I'd say that was the first time I really became personally, deeply, emotionally involved in the Movement. Up to then, it was sort of a job, something that had to be done and so we did it. But this was different" (Lukas, 1968, p. 86).

The idea of producing a play began in the writing workshop (SNCC, Reel 6) and the students chose to portray the life and death of Mississippi civil rights leader Medgar Evers. Deborah Flynn, a New York public school teacher, suggested that they develop the story and dialogue by improvising, a technique which their role-playing experience taught them to do well. Flynn explained:

The dialogue . . . except for the quotes, is indicated or simply outlined as a series of suggested ideas to carry forward the action of the play. Dialogue in this type of play should never be considered as words to be studied by heart and repeated by rote. This play form is particularly well-suited to present ideas of action (SHSW, Pam Allen Papers).

Flynn provided the historical facts of Evers' life and death, and for two weeks the students acted out the story until the scenes were scripted. During a class discussion, one of the girls remarked, "I don't think of him as really dead. I feel that from his grave is growing a huge tree which is spreading seeds of freedom all over" (Lukas, 1968, p. 84). Her analogy, the seeds of freedom, became the title of the play.

The 50-minute project began with the actor-students sitting in the audience, and entering the stage at designated times to portray their part in their own words. The narrator tells the audience.

And this is a play about freedom . . . about us! Yes, us, because every step we take along the freedom road, every time we act, every time we do something to move forward . . . we plant a seed. And seeds are blowing in the wind today (SHSW, Pam Allen Papers).

Ruleville Freedom School. Many of the methods used at Gulfport, Jackson, and Holly Springs were used at Ruleville as well (SHSW, Staughton Lynd Papers). Instructors here were focused on helping students prepare and carry out a protest picket against their public high school. Artwork consisted of making picket signs; creative writing took the form of designing and writing leaflets to persuade other students to join; and letters presenting student demands were composed and sent to the school principal and teachers as well as to newspapers. Role playing was used to practice picketing procedures and encounters, and an original play with a 20-member cast depicted the story of the picket proceedings.

One of the striking features of the Ruleville school was the number of outside resource people who participated in directing attention to civil rights issues; for example, Caravan of Music, a touring group of folksingers, visited on six different occasions, providing entertainment and ideas as they sang songs about the Movement. On another occasion, 13 women from various national women's organizations gave a one-day workshop followed by a student discussion. A particularly popular event was the presentation of a historical play, *In White America,* acted out on the back porch of the freedom school building by the Free Southern Theater, a Mississippi touring company (SNCC, Reel 38; John O'Neal interview). Freedom school teacher Kristy Powell described the experience:

> The audience almost became a part of the play. Small boys climbed on to the porch to go to the bathroom in the middle of a scene; dogs and hens paraded in front of the stage, and there was an intimacy and informality about the performance that underlined for me the impression that the play was woven out of the very stuff of these people's lives (SHSW, Staughton Lynd Papers).

In her weekly report, Powell (SHSW, Staughton Lynd Papers) provided a description of her own experience attempting to integrate a progressive curriculum with traditional teaching methods. She taught two classes in African American history to 13- and 14-year-olds and remedial reading to students at or above a fifth-grade reading level. When teaching history, she introduced each topic by telling a story, showing pictures, and asking students then to read something on the subject. She would find as many resources on the topic as she could and for the next two or three days, allowed the students to interact freely with the topic through these resources. Some students, as Powell recounted, "did [some] historical [or] some creative writing; some drew pictures, copied poems, or copied historical documents" (SHSW, Staughton Lynd Papers). At the end of each unit, she displayed all of the student work on the back porch of the school building.

Powell's remedial reading class exemplified the attempt to incorporate aspects of the civic curriculum in a class focused primarily on basic skills. Her goal was to help students learn not only to read but to read critically and in so doing to examine pertinent issues of their society.

Content included African American history from *Ebony* (a popular magazine); articles by Frederick Douglas; Martin Luther King Jr.'s "I Have a Dream" speech; poems such as Margaret Burrough's "What Shall I Tell My Children Who Are Black?"; and copies of the freedom school newspaper, *Freedom Fighter.* Powell focused both the reading content and her teaching methods so that students participated in pertinent and relevant discussions comparing reading content to the conditions in Mississippi in which they lived.

Mileston Freedom School. The theme that permeated Mileston's instructional methodology was collective student involvement (SNCC, Reel 65). Students wrote and published a school and community newspaper, created and performed a play for the community, recruited and registered African American adults to vote, and prepared themselves to participate in the Meridian student convention.

At least three four- to six-page editions of the school newspaper, the *Mileston Minute,* were published (SNCC, Reel 65) containing stories of local people involved in community work, critical essays about labor conditions for African Americans and poor whites, articles on African American history, editorials on beliefs and concepts of freedom, and poems ranging from thoughts on African American history to African American self-discovery. Activities associated with the paper were designed deliberately to involve students: interviewing others, observing, and participating in community experiences. Teachers hoped that by reflecting and writing upon these experiences, students would be able to serve the community more effectively.

The Mileston play, *The American Negro,* was meaningful for the students who produced it, and it was well received by the community. (SNCC, Reel 65). Presented as the culminating activity of a community meeting urging African Americans to become politically involved, the play depicted experiences and conditions of African Americans in a historical context. The first scene showed a variety of native Africans—free, happy, and proud. It then turned to the issue of slavery and depicted a mother and child chopping cotton, speaking of freedom, and being whipped for harboring such ideas. Scenes moved from the Civil War to the segregated South, and then to the conclusions of both world wars—wars to make the world, but not the South, safe for equality and democracy. The play then depicted two African American men talking of lost sons and lost freedoms as the Ku Klux Klan rushed into their shanty and killed them both. At the end of the last scene, the narrator stepped onto the stage and spoke directly to the audience:

I am the American Negro.

You have seen my past; you have known my past.

And you have seen the trouble I've seen.

Today we have seen many men die

Because they stood for their rights.

Today we have seen three men disappear

For joining in our fight.

Tomorrow many more will die.

And many more will suffer,

But we've begun and we are not turning back

And someday, somehow, we shall overcome!

(SNCC, Reel 65).

The narrator then invited the audience to join in singing "We Shall Overcome." Edith Black a volunteer teacher who attended the performance, wrote that the audience was very moved (SNCC, Reel 65).

Many Mississippi communities involved in the summer project were served by groups of both freedom school and voter registration volunteers. In some communities, the two groups found themselves in conflict as each accorded its own program the top priority (McAdam, 1988). This conflict did not exist at Mileston (SNCC, Reel 65) as both groups worked together to help the community overcome repression. After classes, freedom school students canvassed African American neighborhoods, showing adults how to fill out voter registration forms and obtaining commitments to go to the courthouse and complete the registration to vote. In

class, students discussed the need to contact African American laborers on the plantations surrounding Mileston. They organized the Mileston Action Group (MAG) to ensure that voter registration would continue after the summer volunteers had gone.

In preparing for the Meridian student convention, Mileston students found opportunities to develop leadership skills, including the ability to propose and implement change and the ability to articulate a variety of ideas (SNCC, Reel 65). The entire school worked to write a political platform for three chosen delegates to present at the convention. To facilitate this, mock precinct meetings were staged in class so that students and teachers could discuss local conditions and political issues. Small groups discussed, researched, and prepared motions on the issues that students felt were most important. The small groups then merged into larger ones to debate positions and to construct a representative platform, one that was eventually presented, voted on, and accepted at the Meridian convention; thus, the students practiced and honed the skills they would need for future political participation and, at least on this occasion, were rewarded with public success.

Evaluation

Sandra Adickes (SHSW, Sandra Adickes Papers), a Hattiesburg teacher, claimed that one of the reasons freedom schools were such an exciting educational adventure was that there were no report cards. The curriculum designers felt that traditional evaluation/testing methods were as oppressive as traditional teaching methods because both caused fear, submissiveness, and loss of self-respect among students (SHSW, Pam Allen Papers). Accordingly, one curricular report suggested that teachers not test students formally because it was not effective as a teaching device (SHSW, Pam Allen Papers). Another report adopted a different perspective, suggesting that testing was an unfortunate part of life for students; therefore, it should be used to demonstrate the concepts of domination and submission, and teachers should help students learn to counteract test results (SNCC, Reel 67).

Although freedom school teachers appeared to use little or no formal testing (see SHSW, Joann Ooiman Papers; Aviva Futorian interview), they did find it necessary to assess what students knew in order to help them build better lives (Sutherland, 1965). Deborah Flynn (SNCC, Reel 6) felt that she should evaluate student writing to help them increase their language and communication skills, and she involved her students in the evaluation process by having them critique each other's writing. Placed in this collaborative role, her students helped strengthen their responsibilities for their own learning.

In addition to informal teacher and peer evaluation, some teachers stressed self-evaluation. To promote growth, they felt that students needed to examine their ideas from different perspectives and in light of new knowledge. Jerry Tecklin (SHSW, Jerry Tecklin Papers) explained this position with a specific incident. One of his students, Deloris, writing on the topic "What are some problems Negroes will face in the future," expressed the opinion that if African Americans were to become equal and gain their freedoms, there would need to be a war. Based on the principle that all people are created equal, "as written by Abraham Lincoln," she claimed that whites kept African Americans from being equal. She wrote, "But when it [equality] does happen, it is going to be a lot of trouble in the state of Mississippi."

Tecklin made grammatical corrections and noted that "'All men created equal' [was] written by Thomas Jefferson," but his real concern was helping Deloris deal with her hostility. He did not criticize her feelings, but asked her a number of questions to help her examine her thoughts critically:

> Is war between whites and blacks the only way to get your freedom? Do you know of another way? You have a good idea of what is wrong in Mississippi but might there be a better way of improving conditions? Why don't whites want Negroes to learn? Keep trying to ask yourself these questions (SHSW,

Jerry Tecklin Papers).

The teacher needed to confirm for Deloris that her feelings and opinions were valid, even though he wanted to correct some of her misconceptions. By asking questions, Tecklin provided the necessary knowledge without making a judgment. Deloris needed to make her own judgment and then make the corrections that this entailed.

The only freedom school that reported discussing the role of evaluation was Gulfport (Gillard, 1965). Although they had no formal evaluation procedures, teachers assessed student development using informal criteria that they considered to be more democratic: (1) teacher observations of changes in student behavior; (2) public presentations of student work; (3) evidence of student writing skills; (4) debates and discussions showcasing speaking skills; and (5) book reviews and discussions evidencing reading ability. No formal examinations were given.

Although not formally described as an evaluative activity, the Ruleville freedom festival held on the last day of school might be considered an informal assessment of what students had learned (SHSW, Staughton Lynd Papers; SHSW, Jerry Tecklin Papers). The program included the following creative student presentations: (1) a puppet play in which the valiant knight Bob Moses (SNCC field secretary) fought the wicked witch Segregation; (2) a student play, *Uncle Tom's High School,* telling the story of the Ruleville student protest and picket; (3) choral readings of Eve Merriam's poems; (4) three freedom songs written by students; (5) two readings of student poems about the Montgomery bus boycott; and (6) a finale in which everyone sang "We Shall Overcome."

Classroom Management

Although little discussion of evaluation in the freedom schools took place, even less was articulated about classroom management. Many teachers claimed that because the students were highly motivated, there was little need for discipline (Norma Becker questionnaire; Francis

Howard questionnaire; Howard Zinn questionnaire; Pam Allen questionnaire; Aviva Futorian interview). Attendance was completely voluntary; in fact, in some areas, freedom schools operated concurrently with public schools so students attended only if they wished to be there (Pam Allen interview). At first, many students sat passively as teachers taught, not knowing what to expect or how to act (Sugarman, 1966), but as they began to feel more at ease and free to participate, the curriculum and the teaching methodology appeared to occupy them and keep them motivated. "Our school," noted Sandra Adickes, "was by any definition a fine school—no attendance sheets, absentee postcards, truant officers, report cards—just perfect attendance" (SHSW, Sandra Adickes Papers).

Motivation and discipline problems did occur (SNCC, Reel 64 & 68), but some problems may have occurred because teachers attempted to be too strict; for example, Joann Ooiman described a situation where three students protested a structured classroom environment in their freedom school as being a dehumanizing, authoritarian situation:

> One daytime encounter worth recording [is] that with two professional women teachers (late 20s) who have driven away two fellow teachers and are in deep conflict with a third. They are disciplinarians, very structure-conscious and appallingly unsuited for a freedom school situation. They've suspended three students. Incredible. They insist on a this-hour-we-do-this-and- as-the-next- hour-strikes-we-change-to-this-setup. The long-suffering fellow working with them now (only a college sophomore) promises not to quit, but neither will he remain silent in his protests, sticking up for the suspended students, arguing for a more flexible, relaxed program that won't smack so much of school in its formidable senses—[I have] very mixed feelings about those women (SHSW, Joann Ooiman Papers).

No classroom management problems were

reported in the five freedom schools described here, except for a minor incident at Jackson when two boys entered into a fist fight. After they were separated, their teacher, Florence Howe, talked to them about resolving problems. Her counsel typifies the classroom management outlook in the freedom school plan: "Now look here, we have few rules in this school, but we do have one important one, and that is we do not hit each other—we talk. Understand? We talk here. . . . Whenever you feel like hitting someone, remember to talk instead" (Howe, 1965, p. 147).

Conclusions

The Mississippi Summer Project produced lasting changes in the lives of its participants as well as in the communities where they served. In a sociological study of freedom summer volunteers that included both teachers and voter registrars, Douglas McAdam (1988) found that many remained socially and politically active through the antiwar and women's liberation movements and continue to be active today. The number of nonteacher volunteers who later became teachers is not known. Numerous nonteacher volunteers who were interviewed for this study are also currently involved in other careers or community activities.

Teachers

The evidence suggests that most of those who were professional educators prior to the summer project returned to the profession. Some, however, did not. Aviva Futorian, a Chicago public school teacher, returned from her experience in Mississippi and enrolled in law school believing that she could make a stronger social and political impact as an attorney than as a teacher (Aviva Futorian interview).

Those teachers who left Mississippi and returned to their former classrooms were changed by their experiences in the freedom schools. Dan Hudson, a high school history teacher from Hartford, Connecticut, who taught in a freedom school in Belzoni, Mississippi, was impressed deeply by the impact of the civic curriculum and of the progressive instructional strategies on his Mississippi students. He returned to his school with a personal commitment to adopt goals and implement strategies with his history students similar to those he had experienced in the freedom school. Hudson stated:

> The SNCC . . . approach will have some influence on my teaching. I'll be getting away from an authoritarian lecture posture to some kind of attempt to create an atmosphere conducive to freer discussion. It would be . . . the group working out problems and having discussions instead of my spoonfeeding them. I'll certainly make a much greater attempt to incorporate Negro history into American history. . . . I want to work it in so it becomes clear and natural that Negroes played a part in building this country (SHSW, Jerry Demuth Papers).

Florence Howe (1972, 1984), trained and experienced as a teacher in the traditional sense, wrote that the curriculum and strategies of the freedom schools were a revelation to her; they challenged and contradicted her understanding of teaching. She was amazed by the physical arrangement of freedom school classrooms, with the teacher sitting inside a circle of students rather than standing in front of orderly rows, and she had to adjust to her new role as a resource drawing out student experiences and knowledge rather than reporting her own. As she helped students find their identities, she found her own as well. When she returned to teach in a women's college at the close of the summer, she began quickly to integrate many of the principles she learned in Mississippi into her women's studies and writing classes. Her goals for her college students were similar to those of the summer project: to promote equity for women; to build upon students' experiences as women; to raise student consciousness of personal and social identity; and to encourage her students to become agents for social change. Howe created a meaningful curriculum for her students, choosing literature related to their lives, moving their

chairs into a circle, asking questions based upon their experiences, and having them write creatively about who they were and what they read. Looking back, Howe realized that her freedom school experience taught her that the classroom should function in response to the real-life needs and questions of the students.

Students

The effects of the freedom schools on its students are difficult to discern. Apparently no study has recorded subsequent events in their lives or detailed the influence of the summer experience. Aviva Futorian (Aviva Futorian interview) has kept in contact with many of her students, and she believes that the freedom schools affected them positively. Most have remained in Mississippi, although one who became a lawyer now lives in the North. Most have remained socially active, and participate in a variety of political and educational matters. One of Futorian's former students is director for Head Start in her county. Another is in an advisory position to the governor of Mississippi. When contacted by telephone, several of her students recalled positive memories of their freedom school experiences; they believed that the freedom schools helped them develop active concern for the well-being of their communities and state.

Freedom school classes had an obvious immediate effect, as manifested in the community projects, the academic achievements, and the public activities such as production of newspapers, publications, and plays. As Liz Fusco reflected:

> To think of kids in Mississippi expressing emotion on paper with crayons and in abstract shapes rather than taking knives to each other; to think of their writing and performing plays about the Negro experience in America rather than just sitting in despairing lethargy within that experience; to think of their organizing and running all by themselves a Mississippi Student Union whose program is not dances and fundraising but direct action to alleviate serious grievances; to think even of their being willing to come *after school,* day after day when their

whole association with school had been at least uncomfortable and dull and at worst tragically crippling—to think of those things is to think that a total transformation of the young people in an underdeveloped country can take place, and to dare to dream that it can happen all over the South (SHSW, Liz Fusco Papers).

The experience of the freedom schools was exhilarating, but when most of the teachers returned north, some SNCC staff members wondered how lasting the effect would be on the lives of African American students. Was a six-to eight-week period long enough to combat years of past oppression and to fortify students for years of oppression to come?

Liz Fusco, who remained with a few other teachers to continue teaching in freedom schools through the fall and winter, believed that the summer freedom schools had a short-term positive effect, but she feared it would not be lasting, particularly in promoting community change. Although deeply committed to the principles practiced in the freedom schools, Fusco maintained that to promote permanent change, at least one 9-month term was necessary. Unfortunately, few of the students and teachers had this opportunity.

Social Studies Education

The principles promoted and practiced by the freedom schools are not new in social studies education (see Tanner & Tanner, 1900). The fact that they were applied in unusual, often hostile circumstances is unique, however. The public school system in Mississippi at the time was authoritarian; textbooks were the dominant instructional tools, and teachers were the domineering authorities. Discipline was structured to promote acceptance of and obedience to societal norms, and there was little or no promotion of active thinking or of other forms of inquiry. Students were expected to memorize factual information, and they were tested and graded on what they could recall. Mississippi schools were not the only such schools, however. Cuban's (1991) study of social studies classrooms from 1900 to 1980 demonstrated that many class-

rooms lacked any semblance of democratic teaching. Teacher talk, textbooks, testing, and traditional chronological content were dominant far beyond Mississippi.

Shaver (1987) notes a number of reasons why social studies classes have been boring to many students. Detriment, however, extends beyond boredom. Students become passive and cynical when social studies classes have no meaningful connections to their own needs, interests, or community values (Shor, 1992). Indeed, these were the very concerns that prompted SNCC to create and operate the freedom schools in the first place (SNCC, Reels 27 & 68; Holt, 1966).

Freedom schools provided a brief exception to this damaging pattern. They exemplified a democratic approach to instruction that appeared to work on a short-term basis, and that may have worked with at least a few individuals on a long-term basis as well. One can only speculate at the changes that might have occurred if the freedom schools had operated on a nine-month basis, as advocated by Liz Fusco, and had been sustained over a number of years.

The Future

If social studies educators are truly concerned with helping students develop the critical and reflective skills necessary for full and meaningful participation in today's society, they must begin to question whether the present educational system has the capability of achieving this goal. Perhaps the fundamental paradigm upon which social studies education is currently based should be revised extensively. For six to eight weeks during the summer of 1964, freedom schools revised this paradigm in the intellectual wasteland of Mississippi, with a project designed to promote student self- discovery and to articulate a vision of social justice. Abandoning the traditional approach to education, these schools focused on the minds and abilities of students, encouraged them to think, to express, and to participate, and offered them a chance to make a difference in their world:

The students were taken seriously in the freedom schools. They were encouraged to talk, and their talking was listened to. They were assigned to write, and their writing was read with attention to idea and style as well as to grammar. They were encouraged to sing, to dance, to draw, to play, to laugh. They were encouraged to think (Fusco, 1964, p. 18).

The ideas of Charles Cobb and the other freedom school planners were not implemented consistently in every school, but within the overall experience, changes and achievements are evident that contain profound implications for social studies instruction today. Howard Zinn (1964), one of the freedom school teachers, suggested that the freedom schools provide a model from which to scrutinize prevailing educational ideas and practices that are rooted in an unjust society:

> [The freedom school project] was an experiment that cannot be assessed in the usual terms of "success" and "failure," and it would be wrong to hail it with an enthusiasm which would then lead it to be judged by traditional criteria. But that venture of last summer in Mississippi deserves close attention by all Americans interested in the relationship between education and social change (p. 371).

Zinn hoped that the freedom school concept could be applied more widely to correct antiquated beliefs concerning education and in turn to correct prevailing social ills:

The freedom schools' challenge of the social structure of Mississippi was obvious from the start. Its challenge to American education as a whole is more subtle. There is, to begin with, the provocative suggestion that an entire school system can be created in any community outside the official order, and critical of its suppositions. But beyond that, other questions were posed by the Mississippi experiment of last summer. . . . Perhaps people can begin, here and there (not waiting for the government, but leading it) to set up other pilot ventures, imperfect but suggestive, like the one last summer in Mississippi. Education can and should be dangerous (Zinn, pp. 374-375).

Today in the 1990s, social studies education seems to have become listless, with little energy or direction. A conservative historical movement dominates classrooms, and academic knowledge is dispensed and accepted with limited critical examination. Dialogue between those who create academic policy and those who carry it out is limited. To put a spur to this lethargy, we urge renewed discussion. The freedom schools provide an example we should all explore. ❖

Appendix

Unpublished Document Collections

State Historical Society of Wisconsin Archives (SHSW):

Sandra Adickes Papers
Pam Allen Papers
Jacqueline Bernard Papers
Henry (Harry) Bowie Papers
COFO Papers
Ruby Davis Papers
Jerry DeMuth Papers
Jake Friesan Papers
Liz Fusco Papers
Aviva Futorian Papers
Rev. Richard Gould Papers
Dale Gronemeir Papers
Sandra Hard Papers
Fred Heinze Papers
Christopher Hextor Papers
Eugene Hunn Papers
Staughton Lynd Papers
R. Hunter Morrey Papers
JoAnn Ooiman Papers
Robert Parks Papers
Robert Starobin Papers
Elizabeth Sutherland Papers
Jerry Tecklin Papers
Lise Vogel Papers
Howard Zinn Papers

Manuscript and University Archives

University of Washington Libraries (UWL):
Otis Pease Papers
Mary Aicken Rothschild Papers

Interviews

Noel Day
Roy de Berry
Aviva Futorian
Paul Lauter
John O'Neal

Questionnaires

Pam Allen
Norma Becker
Francis Harris

Howard Zinn

References

Angell, A.V. (1991). "Democratic Climates in Elementary Classrooms: A Review of Theory and Research." *Theory and Research in Social Education,* 19(3), 241–266.

Barr, R. D., Barth, J.L., & Shermis, S. S. (1977) *Defining the Social Studies.* Arlington, VA: National Council for the Social Studies.

Cherryholmes, C. (1980). "Social Knowledge and Citizenship Education: Two views of Truth and Criticism." *Curriculum Inquiry.* 19(2), 115–141.

Cuban, L. (1991). "History of Teaching in Social Studies." In J. P. Shaver (Ed.), *Handbook of Research on Social Studies Teaching and Learning* (pp. 197–211). New York: Macmillan.

Engle, S. H. & Ochoa, A. S. (1988). *Education for Democratic Citizenship: Decision Making in the Social Studies.* New York: Teachers College.

Fancett, V. & Hawke, S. (1982). "Instructional Practices in Social Studies." In I. Morrissett (Ed.), *The Current State of Social Studies: A Report of Project SPAN* (pp. 207–263). Boulder, CO: Social Science Education Consortium.

Forman, J. (1972). *The Making of Black Revolutionaries: A Personal Account.* New York: Macmillan.

Foshay, A. W. & Burton, W. W. (1976). "Citizenship As the Aim of the Social Studies." *Theory and Research in Social Education,* 4(1), 1–22.

Fusco, L. (1964). "The Mississippi Freedom Schools: Deeper Than Politics." *Liberations,* 9(10), 17–19.

Gillard, M. L. (1965). "The Concept of the Mississippi Freedom School and Its Implantation in Gulfport, Mississippi." Unpublished master's thesis, Newark State College, Newark, NJ.

Giroux, H. A. (1980). "Critical Theory and Rationality in Citizenship Education." *Cur-*

riculum Inquiry, 10(4), 329–366.

Goodlad, J. (1980). *A Place Called School.* New York: McGraw-Hill.

Grant, J. (1964, August 29). "Freedom Schools Open a Door to the World." *National Guardian,* p. 5.

Harris, I. M. (1988). *Peace Education.* Jefferson, NC: McFarland.

Hepburn, M. A. (Ed). (1983). *Democratic Education in Schools and Classrooms.* Washington, DC: National Council for the Social Studies.

Hertzberg, H.W. (1981). *Social Studies Reform, 1880–1980.* Boulder, CO: Social Science Education Consortium.

Hinman-Smith, D. (in progress). *Does the Word Freedom Have a Meaning?: The Mississippi Freedom Schools, the Berkeley Free Speech Movement and the Search for Freedom through Education.* Unpublished doctoral dissertation, University of North Carolina, Chapel Hill, NC.

Holt, L. (1966). *The Summer that Didn't End.* London: Heinemann.

Howe, F. (1965). "Mississippi's Freedom Schools: The Politics of Education." *Harvard Educational Review,* 35(2), 144–160.

Howe, F. (1972). "Why Teach Poetry/ An Experiment." In L. Kampf & P. Lauter (Eds.), *The politics of literature* (pp. 259– 307). New York: Pantheon.

Howe, F. (1984). *Myth of Co-education: Selected Essays, 1964–1983.* 1983. Bloomington, IN: Indiana University.

Jones, F. (1964, September 18). "Freedom Teacher." *New Zealand Listener,* p. 5.

Kickbusch, K. W. (1987). "Civic Education and Preservice Educators: Extending the Boundaries of Discourse." *Theory and Research in Social Education,* 15(3), 173–188.

Lake, A. (1964, November). "Last summer in Mississippi." *Redbook,* pp. 64-65, 112–117.

Lauter, D. & Howe, F. (1970). *The Conspiracy of the Young.* New York: World.

Lauter, D. & Perlstein, D. (1991). "Mississippi Freedom Schools: Introduction." *The Radical Teacher,* 40, 2–5.

Longstreet, W. S. (1985). "Citizenship: The Phantom Core of Social Studies Curriculum." *Theory and Research in Social Education,* 13(2) 21–29.

Lukas, J. A. (1968). *Don't Shoot—We Are Your Children!* New York: Random House.

Lynd, S. (1965). "The Freedom Schools: Concept and Organization." *Freedom Ways,* 5(2), 302–309.

Mabee, C. (1964, September 10). Freedom schools, north and south. *The Reporter,* pp. 30–32.

Maxcy, S. J. & Stanley, W. B. (1986). "Reflective Inquiry, Reconstructionism, and Positivism: A Re-examination of the Process of Social Education. *Journal of Research and Development in Education,* 19(3), 62-71.

McAdam, D. (1988). *Freedom Summer.* New York: Oxford University.

Millstone, J. (1964, August 18). "Mississippi's Freedom Schools to Remain on Permanent Basis." *St. Louis Post-Dispatch,* pp. 6–7.

Oldendorf, S. B. (1989). "Vocabularies, Knowledge and Social Action in Citizenship Education: The Highlander Example." *Theory and Research in Social Education,* 17(2) 107– 120.

Oliner, P. (1983). "Putting Community into Citizenship Education: The Need for Prosociality." *Theory and Research in Social Education,* 11(2), 65–81.

Parker, W. C. & Jarolimek, J. (1984). *Citizenship and the Critical Role of the Social Studies.* Washington, DC: National Council for the Social Studies.

Parker, W. C. & Kaltsounis, T. (1986). "Citizenship and Law-Related Education." In V.A. Atwood (Ed.), *Elementary School Social Studies: A Research Guide to Practice* (pp. 14–33). Washington, DC: National Council for the Social Studies.

Perlstein, D. (1990). "Teaching Freedom: SNCC and the Creation of the Mississippi Freedom Schools. *History of Education Quarterly,* 30(3), 297–324.

Popkewitz, T. S. (1977). "The Latent Values of the Discipline-centered Curriculum." *Theory and Research in Social Education,* 5(1), 41–60.

Purpel, D. E. (1989). *The Moral and Spiritual Crisis in Education: A Curriculum for Justice and Compassion in Education.* New York: Bergin & Garvey.

Remy, R. C. (1978). "Social studies and citizenship education: Elements of a changing relationship." *Theory and Research in Social Education,* 6(4), 40–59.

Rothschild, M. A. (1981). *A Case of Black and White: Northern Volunteers and the Southern Freedom Summers,* 1964–1965. Westport, CT: Greenwood.

Sellers, C. (1973). *The River of No Return: The Autobiography of a Black Militant and the Life and Death of SNCC.* New York: Morrow.

Shaver, J. P. (1981). "Citizenship, Values, and Morality in the Social Studies." In H. D. Mechlinger & O. L. Davis, Jr. (Eds.), *The Social Studies* (pp. 112–138). New York: Longman.

Shaver, J. P., Davis, O. L., & Helburn, S. W. (1980). "An Interpretive Report on the Status of Pre-College Social Studies Education Based on Three NSF-Funded Studies." In *What are the needs in pre-college science, mathematics, and social studies education* (pp. 3–18). Washington, DC: National Science Foundation.

Shermis, S. S. & Barth, J. L. (1982). "Teaching for Passive Citizenship: A Critique of Philosophical Assumptions." *Theory and Research in Social Education,* 10(4), 17–37.

Shor, I. (1992). *Empowering Education: Critical Teaching for Social Change.* Chicago: University of Chicago.

Stanley, W. B. & Nelson, J. L. (1986). "Social Education for Social Transformation." *Social Education,* 50(7) 528–530, 532–534.

Strike, K. A. (1988). "Democracy, Civic Education and the Problem of Neutrality." *Theory Into Practice,* 27(4) 256–261.

Student Nonviolent Coordinating Committee. (1964, August 5). "Mississippi Freedom Schools." *The Student Voice,* pp. 2–3.

Student Nonviolent Coordinating Committee. (1982). *The Student Nonviolent Coordinating Committee Papers, 1959–1972.* [Microfilm Reel No. 6, 27, 35, 37, 38, 39, 40, 64, 65, 67, 68, 69, & 73]. Stanford, NC: Microfilming Corporation of America.

Sugarman, T. (1966): *Strangers at the Gates: A Summer in Mississippi.* New York: Hill & Wang.

Sutherland, E. (1965). *Letters from Mississippi.* New York: McGraw-Hill.

Tanner, D. & Tanner, L. (1990). *History of the School Curriculum.* New York: Macmillan.

Teitelbaum, D. (1990). "'Critical Lessons' from Our Past: Curricula of Socialist Sunday Schools in the United States." *Curriculum Inquiry,* 20(4), 408–436.

White, C. S. (1982). "A Validation Study of the Barth-Shermis Social Studies Preference Scale." *Theory and Research in Social Education,* 10(2), 1–20.

Wood, G. H. (1985). "Schooling in a Democracy: Transformation or Reproduction?" *Educational Theory,* 34(3), 219–239.

Wood, G. H. (1985). "Education for Democratic Participation: Democratic Values and the Nuclear Freeze Campaign." *Theory and Research in Social Education,* 12(4) 39–56.

Wood, G. H. (1993). *Schools That Work.* New York: Plume.

Zinn, H. (1964, November 23). "Schools in Context: The Mississippi Idea." *The Nation, 199,* 371-375.

Zinn, H. (1965). *SNCC: The New Abolitionists.* Boston: Beacon.

Zinn, H. (1970). *The Politics of History.* Boston: Beacon.

Zinn, H. (1990). *The Politics of History.* Urbana, IL: University of Illinois.

Edie Black, summer volunteer, teaches a Freedom School class in the community church near Mileston, Mississippi, summer 1964.

PHOTOS BY

MATT HERRON

A summer volunteer teaches a science class to students at the Mileston Community Center in the Mississippi Delta, summer 1964.

CHARLIE COBB

Organizing Freedom Schools

I'm thinking of freedom songs, almost obscure now, or viewed as quaint musical icons of a different era; but three decades ago their vital lyrics provided much sustenance to the Southern Civil Rights Movement: *Ain't gonna let nobody turn me 'roun,* we sang. *We'll never turn back,* and *Keep your eyes on the Prize.*

All the songs affirm. They express what we are going to do. They assume that "freedom" is affirmative, that freedom starts with deciding what you want to achieve and is reached by finding the ways and means of organizing toward that goal or goals. You'll find no reasoning that the struggle for human and civil rights is in any way determined by what cannot be done. Only, as the old song goes, . . . *that freedom is a constant struggle.* Always, a constant faith in human ability and possibilities.

We tend to analyze the Movement in terms of strategy and tactics, especially because it is true that the effectiveness of those strategies and tactics did indeed break down the barriers preventing blacks from exercising voting rights and brought an end to at least the legal justifications for racial segregation in public schools and public accommodations. But such a narrow approach misses the point, or perhaps more exactly, is only a half-right portrayal of what was unfolding in the Deep South during the sixties.

As powerful and rigid as the structures of white supremacy were, they were more easily defeated than the manner in which thought— and with thought, behavior—imprisoned the

communities in which we worked.

Yes, we wanted an end to segregation, discrimination, and white supremacy. However, at the core of our efforts was the belief that black people had to make decisions about and take charge of the things controlling their lives; the effective movement was grounded in grassroots local leadership. We were organizers in Mississippi, not leaders, even if at moments we led. The distinction was important to us, and a practical necessity.

Most of us organizing soon learned that our main challenge was getting black people to challenge themselves. Stated another way, people would have to redefine themselves. That was the foundation on which white supremacy could be effectively challenged. As SNCC organizer Larry Guyot, a native Mississippian, put it once: "To battle institutions we must change ourselves first."

While the ever present threat of economic reprisal and personal assault was of genuine concern to any black person considering an attempt at voter registration, the words an organizer heard most often in a sharecropper's home were: "Register? That's white folks business, boy." And it reflected something more than fear. In Issaquena County, a narrow, almost all-black strip of cotton plantation land along the Mississippi River, Henry Sias, well into his sixties when I met him in 1963, cautioned me in two ways during a long conversation. Be careful was the first. "These white folks know you're here."

Charlie Cobb was a SNCC field secretary in Mississippi from 1962–1967. Now a writer based in Washington, D.C., he has written extensively about Africa and the Caribbean.

Then later and more tellingly: "We could do [register, vote, take county offices], but to tell you the truth, we don't know what we could do. Won't think on it. That's what I mean when I say we down far."

The most important struggles in Mississippi were within the black community: whether to allow a movement worker to speak in church or use the church for mass meetings and voter registration workshops; whether to trust that worker with your life, your family's life, or your family's economic survival. Every step in the fight against racism and discrimination was preceded by a deeper and more profound struggle that involved confronting oneself.

The Freedom Rides to Jackson notwithstanding, SNCC and CORE organizers were working in Mississippi because a handful of Mississippians had already confronted themselves in this way and had decided to risk everything for change. They were the virtually underground NAACP chapters, sometimes at odds with the national organization, working invisibly at voter registration; the Amzie Moore's who had to guard the filling station he owned with rifles simply because it was a black-owned gas station in the white-ruled Delta; the Herbert Lee's pressing for school desegregation, and he paid for it with his life. There were others, young and old.

They trained us in how to listen to people and talk to people. And to measure risk. What they thought in urging us to work in Mississippi was that if we listened and learned we could help the communities *they* led see a way toward change.

The arguments for and against the 1964 Mississippi summer project framed the issue of change in terms of race, nonviolence, and the need for national pressure on the state. But at its most basic, the debate was over whether hundreds of white college students would take over the Movement and, with what was presumed to be their superior resources, education, and connections, stifle local black leadership, some of it just developing. Or, did the inarguable and im-

mediate facts of terrible violence, economic reprisal, and the low level of national concern outweigh this? After all, violence *was* on the increase. Federal authorities still insisted their hands were tied in responding to it. Media, for the most part, did not get to the out-of-the-way rural counties where SNCC and CORE organizers worked. And, insofar as success could be measured by attempts at voter registration, few in the prevailing climate of terror were attempting it.

In a sense, the debate was never resolved, although by default, plans for the summer project went ahead; the students were on the way. If SNCC/COFO didn't bring them down, the National Council of Churches said it was going to. Organizers, no matter where they stood in the complex debating about the summer project, finally said, if they're coming down, we'll organize them. It was in this ambivalent context that the idea of "freedom schools" emerged.

One of the things you learn as an organizer is to constantly be on the lookout for issues and openings that encourage people to challenge their ideas and habits. The person who may not see the value of attempting voter registration, or who may see the value but not be willing to run the risk, might eagerly embrace the idea of a farm workers union. Many more people attended church "mass meetings" than braved the danger of going to the voter registrars office at the county seat.

In Mississippi, as was the case throughout the South, on education there was broad black consensus: black schools were inferior to white schools; and along with this, the almost contradictory belief that education was one of the main avenues to greater opportunity and a better life.

The oppressive narrowness of Southern black public schools still seems almost unbelievable today despite the grim problems confronting contemporary public education. In the Mississippi Delta, the fall school term was delayed while cotton was picked. New brick school buildings built to give the illusion of "separate but equal" contained virtually bookless libraries and science labs with no equipment.

But more than the inadequacies of the physical plant, the idea of ideas, thought, and creativity among black people, was ruthlessly suppressed. As we wrote in the original freedom school proposal: "Here, an idea of your own is a subversion that must be squelched; for each bit of intellectual initiative represents the threat of a probe into the why of denial. Learning here means only learning to stay in your place. Your place is to be satisfied—a 'good nigger.'" It is true that many teachers struggled heroically against these conditions, giving inspiration and imparting knowledge in spite of the state. However, the schools as institutions remained part of the apparatus of repression. Indeed, the police were likely to be called if an organizer showed up on school grounds.

Few parents would accept a direct challenge to the existence of even these public schools. For although black schools were more like sandbars than islands of hope, they were something in a land of nothing. Something that offered some chance of a better life.

What if, it occurred to some of us, we could extend the worlds of possibilities opening up to us through activism, in a broader, more institutional way in the communities where we organized? What if we showed what was possible in education? We had already been approaching this through "literacy workshops" within the context of organizing for voter registration. And SNCC itself had created a "nonviolent high school" during the 1961 protests in McComb, Mississippi. A few of us had even begun to experiment with programmed learning materials in Selma, Alabama, as well as the Mississippi Delta. But we hadn't really tackled education as an approach to community organizing in and of itself.

Significantly, the model for how to do this emerged from a specific political organization that also grew out of grassroots organizing: the Mississippi Freedom Democratic Party.

The Department of Justice had long claimed that apathy was one of the important reasons for the low number of blacks registered to vote. We argued that in Mississippi and throughout the blackbelt South, to ask blacks to enter a hostile white county seat was to guarantee that few blacks would attempt to register.

A "freedom registration" and "freedom vote" was one result of our effort to prove the point. Blacks were registered at home with simple forms. Candidates were selected to run for state offices. Thousands of blacks both registered and voted within this "mock" but meaningful framework. And thus the MFDP was born.

Freedom schools were a variation of this idea. We could "parallel" the state structure "to fill an intellectual and creative vacuum in the lives of young Negro Mississippians."

Although the actual planning of the freedom school project was delegated (among those key early planners were Myles Horton of the Highlander Center, SCLC's Septima Clark, a former schoolteacher, New York teacher and United Federation of Teachers activist Norma Becker, Noel Day who wrote a citizenship curriculum in question and answer format, and Staughton Lynd who wrote "A Guide to Negro History" and later became statewide director of the freedom schools), the idea of the bringing schools into existence became integrated with the daily work of field organizers in the months leading up to the summer project. For those of us still trudging plantation roads, it offered an additional route by which the paralysis freezing black Mississippians in a place where they were acted upon instead of acting could be challenged.

Traditional and widely embraced notions of education were transformed by placing programs—whether remedial reading or African American history—in the arena of social change. As with the voter registration drive and all other organizing in the state, the essence of the schools was that black people could begin to rethink in their own terms the ways and means of shaping and controlling their own destiny. Fannie Lou Hamer put it to me this way, "We can start learning to learn."

About two thousand students attended

classes in some forty schools. If the number seems small, it was twice what we had estimated attendance would be. There were remedial classes as well as courses in literature, the humanities, creative writing, foreign languages, art, drama, typing, and Afro-American history and culture. Discussion of civil rights and social change was continuous. It should be pointed out that many students were attending public schools in the summer, for cotton was picked in the fall.

As a practical matter, the schools effectively struck a balance between the reluctance of organizers to use inexperienced, white student volunteers in the dangerous rural areas of the state and the need to deal with the reality that they were coming and would have to be used in some manner that was concretely beneficial during the summer.

That the program in some respects seemed to accept traditional liberal concepts and approaches to education, which in many ways did not then—and does not now—grapple with the deeper flaws in education and society, does not negate the important benefit of the schools' contribution to expanding the idea in black Mississippi that black people could shape and control at least some of the things that affected their lives. Perhaps the fact that the schools existed at all was their greatest success. As Staughton Lynd noted in a report to COFO that summer, the schools helped "to loosen the hard knot of fear and to organize the Negro community."

The freedom schools hardly broke down hundreds of years of oppression, but near the end of the summer when freedom school stu-

dents from around the state convened, they reflected a substantial growth of political awareness. Their resolutions asked for slum clearance, low-cost federal housing, jobs programs, and even sanctions against South Africa among a long list of proposed reforms.

After the summer, some freedom schools continued. But never would the number of schools or the number of students attending them equal those of that first summer. For a variety of reasons the Movement was changing. In part it was a victim of its success. We had in one sense accomplished what we set out to do: a public accommodations law had been passed; a voting rights law seemed certain. Mississippi was now prominently on the political map. New organizations, like the Mississippi Child Development Group, with deeper financial pockets were establishing themselves.

Many of us were unsure of what to do next. Grassroots organizing—the lifeblood of the Movement—diminished. Many organizers scattered. Some were shattered and never recovered. Others took advantage of the opportunities they had helped create. Increasingly, black elected officials filled the vacuum. And at the first dinner of the Congressional Black Caucus, one congressman proclaimed, "We are the new Civil Rights Movement." That, of course, was not and is not true. The "new" Civil Rights Movement, like the "old," is still made up of the people organizing in many black communities today, often as invisible as the Movement was thirty years ago. ❖

Freedom school student Eddie Carthan learning to type. Years later Carthen became mayor of nearby Tchula. His economic development programs so challenged local whites that he was framed on murder charges, jailed, and later released.

J. WASHINGTON LANDRÓN

Freedom School

Five ones are five
Five twos are ten
Five threes are fifteen
Five fours are twenty
Five fives are twenty five
Six fives are thirty
Seven fives are thirty five
Eight fives are forty

In colony days we had a king
And he passed laws for everything
Back when we had a king
And it was yes, king and no, king
Please, king and thank you, king
To everything we said yes, king.

Well, because we wanted our Liberty
We fought that king so we'd be free
Just fighting so we'd be free.
We didn't want to say yes king and no, king
Please, king and thank you, king
We had to get away from the king.

Five ones are five
Five twos are ten
Five threes are fifteen
Five fours are twenty
Five fives are twenty five
Six fives are thirty
Seven fives are thirty five
Eight fives are forty

Jack Landrón was a student at Emerson College in Boston, Massachusetts, in 1964. He was under contract to Vanguard Recording Society and enjoyed a reputation as one of the outstanding folksingers of that era. He was then known as Jackie Washington and performed across the United States and Canada as well as on national television with a featured role on the NBC series The First Look. *Today, he is an actor based in New York and in addition to radio and television commercials and voiceovers, he occasionally appears in concert.*

Well, after we had made the grade
We got some ships and set up trade
And other nations came around to trade
And a Spanish ship* came to our port
Selling stuff of every sort
Selling stuff of every sort

And they had a bunch of Africans
And they sold them to the Americans
They sold them to the Americans.
They bought those folks. Just think of that
To plow the fields and feed the cat
They called them slaves. What d'ya think of that?

And all they said was yessuh and no, suh
Please, suh and thank you, suh.
To everything they said yessuh.

Five ones are five
Five twos are ten
Five threes are fifteen
Five fours are twenty
Five fives are twenty five
Six fives are thirty
Seven fives are thirty five
Eight fives are forty

So now we're fighting one more war
To make us free for evermore
Free for evermore
'Cause we don't wanna say yes, sir and no, sir
Please, sir and thank you sir
We don't want to say yes, sir.

Five ones are five
Five twos are ten
Five threes are fifteen
Five fours are twenty
Five fives are twenty five
Six fives are thirty
Seven fives are thirty five
Eight fives are forty

Following the release of the album in which this song was originally recorded, I had a phone conversation with Pete Seeger. In my life he is one of the men I most admire, so I was flattered to learn that he had heard the song and even more thrilled when he said some nice things about it. However, he pointed out that it was not the Spanish that introduced slavery to the Americans. I think he said it was the Dutch, but I was so embarrassed to find out that I had been teaching those kids the wrong thing, I must have blocked out what he told me. Besides, as a Puerto Rican I've been quite happy to be pissed at the Spanish, so the song is being transcribed here without correction. Sue me! ❖

Children dancing at a Freedom School

ARTWORK BY

SHARON RILEY

GUY & CANDIE CARAWAN

Carry It On: Roots of the Singing Civil Rights Movement

Let this conference be a springboard for a cultural revival in the South at a community level.

—We must do serious and loving research into the basic forms of expression of the Negro people—into the sources of the spiritual, the epic sermons, the work songs and field hollers, the blues, and the dance music which express the particular genius of this people.

—We stand firmly opposed to those who hold that because the Negroes are winning the Civil Rights fight that they must be assimilated into the sterile ways of Main Street America. We intend to encourage the Negro community to come alive in its own spirit and on its own terms.

—We intend to show both young and old that the Negro folk artists and their songs show as much complexity, beauty, and cultivation as any other cultural tradition.

—In our folk music, we will discover a bridge toward a prideful and democratic meeting ground with the white people of the South.

Statement of purpose by participants in a cultural workshop at Highlander, 1965

By the mid 1960s many youthful freedom fighters had reached the conclusion that their own cultural heritage could be a weapon in the struggle for liberation. It hadn't always been true. In the beginning stages of the Movement, many young people felt that older folkways had held their parents back. Spirituals, folktales and beliefs, grassroots wisdom, were often seen as symbols of backwardness and stumbling blocks to progress. In other liberation struggles, too, it is not always immediately obvious that cultural strength—particularly older forms of expression—can build resolve, unity, hope, and the passion to win.

There are many factors which deepened the understanding of the importance of culture in the Civil Rights Movement, but in the summer of 1964, and throughout the period of 1960 to 1965, some very specific work was focused on

an attempt to nurture the cultural roots of the Movement. During those years we were working with the Highlander Folk School in Tennessee. Highlander, an adult education center dedicated to social change, began in 1932. In the late 1950s and early '60s, it served as an important gathering place for strategists and activists from Southern communities challenging segregation. It also had a long history of supporting regional culture—drawing songs and stories from people and teaching and circulating songs, poetry, and skits that supported whatever social struggles were on the agenda.

Beginning in the summer of 1960, Highlander sponsored a series of cultural workshops with the general theme of "singing for freedom." These would take place at Highlander, in Atlanta, Georgia, and in Mississippi. There would also be a series of festivals in the sea islands off

Guy and Candie Carawan, based at the Highlander Center in Tennessee for more than thirty years, have worked as cultural organizers in the South, and have performed nationally and internationally. They have produced four books and a dozen documentary albums reflecting both traditional cultures of Deep South African American and Appalachian communities; and the adoption of these cultures into social movements. They have also produced 12 albums of their own music. Guy is best known for spreading "We Shall Overcome" throughout the South in the early 1960s. He plays guitar, banjo, and hammered dulcimer. In addition to singing, Candie is an artist and potter.

the coast of South Carolina, where Highlander was conducting a literacy program around voter registration and full citizenship for black people. I worked with Highlander as a cultural organizer and educator, building on the work of Zilphia Horton who died in 1956. Candie joined me after our marriage in 1961.

One goal in each of the cultural workshops was to spread the repertoire of freedom songs springing up in isolated communities. There were also sessions for encouraging songwriting and adapting songs and for strengthening songleading skills. In later workshops we made a conscious effort to include an older layer of African American culture, the root of the freedom songs, to draw upon its strength and its richness.

Between 1960 and 1965 we saw the freedom repertoire grow from a limited number to seventy-five or eighty songs—thirty or so widely known throughout the South. Different types of songs evolved for every kind of situation, expressing a full range of emotions. There were songs for mass meetings and demonstrations— stirring and hopeful; there were angry, serious, and determined songs; songs for jail cells; songs for parties and celebrations—full of humor, satire, jubilation; there were songs which expressed grief and sadness—songs in a minor key. It is difficult to imagine the Civil Rights Movement without its powerful component of song. Many of the songs have moved through time, adapted by subsequent movements and are still used today. The Movement in Mississippi provides a good setting to examine one way in which youthful freedom fighters made a leap in understanding and embracing the cultural underpinnings of their struggle.

Following the Freedom Rides in 1961, Mississippi became an important target area for the Movement—the state with the most deeply entrenched segregation and repression, perhaps the biggest challenge for the Movement. As the youthful organizers moved into Mississippi, they needed all the tools and skills they could muster, not the least of which were courage and a

basic optimism that things could change. They also found that songleading was an asset.

As the Movement moved into grassroots organizing, civil rights workers used songs as a basic introduction to the communities in which they worked. The song identified what the struggle was about. The presence of organizers with this body of material made for a high level of exchange between them and the communities they sought to organize. . . . One of the first reactions was the immediate elevation from within the community of those persons who were most skilled in the art of songleading.

In most cases, they took over the role of songleading from the organizers by demonstrating how songs functioned in relationship to the experiences of the group. This involved the fine art of knowing what song to sing at which occasion, when it was necessary to change lyrics, and when songs could be used as they had existed for years in the black community.

—Bernice Reagon (doctoral dissertation, p. 179–80)

Hollis Watkins, Sam Block, James and Willie Peacock, and James Bevel, one of the songwriting preachers and activists of the Nashville Movement now returned to work in Mississippi, were to emerge as powerful indigenous songleaders and organizers.

The central organizing tactic in Mississippi was voter registration, though many other abuses of people's basic rights were also confronted. There was a long history of opposition to black voting, and in the early 1960s most black people in rural Mississippi felt there was no chance that they could register and vote. For a variety of reasons, including an upsurge of violence and intimidation by a power structure resistant to change, Greenwood was to become the testing ground for voter registration, and in 1963 most of the civil rights workers in the state positioned themselves there.

There was a great deal of harassment as

Gathering of Mississippi freedom workers at a SNCC meeting at Tougaloo College in Jackson. Left to right: Curtis Hayes, James Jones, Jesse Harris, Willie Peacock, Charles McLaurin, Sam Block, Jimmy Travis, MacArthur Cotton, Hollis Watkins, unidentified woman, Charlie Cobb. Front row: James Forman.

PHOTOS

SUBMITTED BY

GUY CARAWAN

people began to go to the courthouse to attempt to register. Trained dogs were used to frighten and attack people. A major task was to help people get over their fear, and to convince them that there was support for them and concern about their situation. Here the music was crucial. Songs were used at mass meetings and in smaller gatherings and became an underpinning to the voter registration drive. Sam Block and Willie Peacock were the first organizers in Greenwood, and both were excellent singers. They knew and taught the freedom songs; they evolved new words that spoke directly to the situation in Greenwood.

Most of the organizers in Mississippi used music. When you're dealing with a group, if you're able to tune in and communicate with them, you can tell when the monotony is getting to people, and the spirit or the morale is beginning to die down. So you can sing a song and lift them back up to build that spirit to a point where they're willing to accept what you have to say to them. One of the things that made it easier for me is that singing was a part of me.

Hollis Watkins, 1983 interview

Perhaps most important of all, these young organizers heard and appreciated the deep longing and strength in the people's own music, and they used that strength to help bolster people's courage. In the mass meetings in Greenwood, the old long-meter hymns, spirituals, and gospel songs, and prayers were very important. And several years later, when the value of the older layer of black culture would be discussed and argued about, the freedom workers who had organized in the Mississippi Delta and in other communities deep in the Black Belt, would be the ones to speak eloquently about the power of black culture and its importance to the freedom movement.

People did rise above their fear in Greenwood. By the spring of 1963, in spite of violence and intimidation, three thousand people had lined up to register, though most were not accepted.

During this time we were living on Johns Island in South Carolina, working with Highlander's citizenship school program and concentrating on the older layer of folk expression there. We did not leave our concern for the active Civil Rights Movement behind, nor our interest in how the newer songs were evolving. In addition to inviting some of the young freedom singers over to the sea island festivals, we began to work on some southwide conferences which would focus specifically on the use of music in the Movement and the older roots of that music.

The first took place in Atlanta in May of 1964. It was organized jointly by Highlander, SNCC, and SCLC, with Bernice Reagon, Dorothy Cotton, and Andrew Young helping with the planning and I was serving as coordinator. It brought together freedom singer/activists and songleaders from all across the South. The primary goal was to spread the repertoire of songs from one area to another, and to learn from each other how music was strengthening the Movement. There were additional goals. We wanted the young freedom singers to meet and to hear some carriers of an older layer of culture and experience at the workshop, and to consider the relevance of that culture and experience to the current movement. To allow this to happen we invited Bessie Jones and the Georgia Sea Island Singers, and Doc Reese, a singer of work-gang songs from the Texas prison system. Aware of a growing number of northern topical songwriters who were commenting about the Southern freedom struggle in their songs, we felt it would be good for them to have a chance to hear about the struggles firsthand and the Southern songs that were so important to the Movement. We knew the freedom singers would also be interested in sympathetic northern songs. Tom Paxton, Phil Ochs, and Len Chandler, all prolific topical songwriters, attended the gathering. Theo Bikel from the Newport Folk Foundation, long interested in the Civil Rights Movement, also came.

Josh Dunson wrote extensively of this workshop in his 1965 book, *Freedom in the Air:*

> There was that tremendous impact that only occurs when fifty to sixty songleaders bring their voices and clapping together in thunderbolts of song for twenty, twenty-five minutes, just on and on and on. The north-

ern guests were out of breath, for they were not used to twenty minutes of letting your whole body explode into song.

> . . . There are two forms of music that seem strange alongside the freedom songs—the northern "broadside" songs and the traditional Negro songs and stories ...There are murmurs whenever Bessie Jones and the Sea Island Singers act out songs with dances or tell the old slave stories...and tension builds until Saturday morning when Charles Sherrod questions "Why? Why these songs here?" and a heated discussion ensues.

> The debate was the most important single event at the "Sing." Bessie Jones defended her songs as the culture of the slave who, despite the master's attempts to force him into an animal's life, succeeded in making his own system of songs which not only provided a form of expression, but also served as signals for escape, She told the young people, "Your children are gonna call your music old later on, too. . . . You should know the bottom before you come to the top."

> Len Chandler commands great attention, for, to many, his knowledge of guitar and his classical background is a model for success. When he effectively dissected the brainwashing that a hostile white society forced on the Negro people, it moved many in the audience: "I went through this scene man. I was ashamed of my Grandmother's music. I went to school to get a degree and things were all put in a nice little box, a package of the Western World's music. But there was nothing in that box about my music. . . . This music [Bessie Jones's] is great, and the boys on the radios and the TVs have stopped you from hearing it—but this is it, man, this is the stuff."

> Still, others had doubts. One woman stated: "I came here to sing and hear freedom songs. I can hear the old songs anytime I want back home." There was still a strong feeling by a number of young and old against

The Georgia Sea Island Singers with freedom corps volunteers

the very music that had provided them with the basic melodies and words for the new freedom songs.

Amanda Bowens, her eyes flashing with anger, just let loose: "I'm tired of going to church and listening to teenagers giggle and laugh when the old songs are sung. I want to know what the old songs are. I want to sing them. I want to know that my parents were working for 15 cents a day. What these songs are is what most of this means."

. . . Although not everyone was convinced, there was a realization by many young songleaders of the importance of their own traditions. The Movement was beginning consciously to tap the strong and militant Afro-American heritage.

Following the Atlanta workshop I was invited to organize a group of singers to take part in the national Newport Folk Festival that summer. This was the period when the struggle in the South, with its powerful music, had come to national prominence. In 1963 the festival had

ended with some of the most popular and well-known folk figures—Pete Seeger, Bob Dylan, Joan Baez, Peter, Paul, and Mary—linking arms with the Albany Freedom Singers to sing "We Shall Overcome." Now in 1964, an even larger and more diverse group of freedom singers representing several Southern communities was heard by thousands of people.

The commitment of some of these northern folk performers reached beyond the concert stage. Some of them came south during the summer of 1964 to take part in the Mississippi Caravan of Music. The Caravan sent musicians and singers to freedom schools, mass meetings, and the freedom houses where the summer volunteers and regular freedom workers stayed. They spread a variety of musical styles and new songs around the state that summer, and they lifted spirits and helped give the message that people from far away do care what happens in Mississippi. But perhaps in the end, they learned even more than they shared. Coordinator Bob Cohen wrote in *Broadside* magazine, when the summer was over:

The struggle in Mississippi is what this great country of the United States is all about. It's what the songs we sing are about. If people are jailed, beaten, murdered, and their houses and churches bombed and burned, just because they wish to sing their life's song with a straight back and a strong voice, then as long as this is happening, none of us are truly free to sing out, be it in nightclubs, concert halls or even in our own homes.

At Christmas time in 1964 we organized another Sea Island folk festival. Bob Moses and several other people from COFO—the Council of Federated Organizations, a coalition of civil rights groups working in Mississippi—came over to Johns Island. They were by now particularly interested in the process of finding, and supporting, the traditional music and culture in the communities where they were working. Bob particularly felt that holding grassroots festivals in communities where there were civil rights activities going on would add another dimension to COFO's main objective, which was to convince the people in these communities that they have a lot to offer, politically and culturally, and that they can make their own decisions and struggle to gain more control over their lives. Bob invited us to hold a workshop in the Mississippi Delta similar to the Sing for Freedom in Atlanta.

The workshop took place in May 1965, at Edwards, Mississippi, and Willie Peacock and Willie McGhee helped plan and organize it. It was designed to present to the "Freedom Corps" trainees (native Mississippians between the ages of eighteen and twenty-five who had signed up to spend a year working in various Mississippi communities) a range of African American folk music as well as contemporary freedom songs. The folk artists participating included Doc Reese from Texas, the Georgia Sea Island Singers, the Moving Star Singers from Johns Island, and Ed Young, a Mississippi fife player. Taking part also were folklorists Alan Lomax and Ralph Rinzler from the Newport Folk Foundation, each with a keen interest in encouraging an appreciation of folk heritage. Highlander, the Newport Folk Foundation, and the Delta Ministry of the National Council of Churches financed the gathering.

It turned out to be a complicated, but important, weekend. The folk artists shared a wide variety of experiences, skills, and talents; play—parties and games, folktales, spirituals, gospel songs, and worksongs from the Georgia Sea Island; complex shouts from Johns Island, the amazing fife playing of Ed Young; and the gang labor songs, field hollers, and intense experiences from the Texas prison system.

These songs came to me at the close of a period in Texas prison life when the mark of a good guard was how cruel or brutal he could be to his prisoners. Usually he was the lowest class of man that could be found, whose only desire was to get the feel that goes with somebody calling you Boss Man.

Everyday but Sunday was work day. If it was raining we'd work in the mud—some eleven miles in a fast trot. The horses was the only thing they was concerned with because they say if you kill a nigger, we'll get another; if you kill a mule we'd have to buy another, so don't kill the mule.

They worked us from the very peak of day until black dark and would've worked us later but there was a danger of losing somebody. Each squad was guarded by a man who had a six-shooter or a winchester or a double-barreled shotgun. Each twenty squads had two squads of dogs, one in front and one behind, and there were at least two dog sergeants and an assistant captain that followed us wherever we might be working.

—Doc Reese, speaking to the Freedom Corps, Edwards, Mississippi

The young Mississippians took it all in. They also sang, loudly and proudly, the new freedom songs.

Alan Lomax, who had given a lot of thought to the potential for a major program linking the

Fife player Ed Young with Ralph Rinzler.

freedom struggle to a real cultural revival in Mississippi, spoke movingly about the history of black music in America and with great determination about the necessity of nourishing it.

> . . . Continual cultural development should go hand in hand with political and educational development. The healthiest cultural growth always is rooted in the resources native to the people of an area. It is a fortunate thing that along their way the Negro people have created a rich lore of tales, dances, songs, oratorical techniques, ways of praying, recipes, riddles, forms of greeting, lullabies, and a thousand other ways of doing and speaking which give Negro life a special flavor. Why should all this be given up in return for economic betterment? It need not be. The Negro people should be encouraged to be themselves, to develop themselves in their own way as they move along freedom's road. But here they must draw upon their own past, as all people have done before

> them. They must not be ashamed of their forefathers, but proud of them for their courage, the wit and the beauty that they continually expressed, even though they were for a time in bondage. . . . SNCC, composed as it is of individuals who are unashamed and flexible and unhampered by stuffy middle class prejudice, must provide the leadership and sponsorship that will nurture this cultural movement.

His words met with mixed reaction. Some of the older folk material was new to the young freedom workers, and they were dubious of its relevance. They were caught up in the immediate—the power and outspokenness of the new songs. Some were at a place in their own development, in their own growing self-esteem and anger, that they could not easily take the advice of a white man—particularly a white Southerner who spoke with such self-assurance and vigor. Others reacted to Doc Reese, a Baptist preacher, who represented to them an adult authority figure, though they identified with his experiences in the Texas prison. There was some arguing and belligerence, for here was a sampling of a new generation of Southerners breaking out of the old submissive patterns.

It was somewhat confusing to the older folk artists who had come to freely share their music and experiences. Some of the young people seemed a bit brash to them, and their outspoken behavior raised concerns about their safety in the repressive South. Still, it was a rich weekend. Many thoughts and questions were raised, and in the end, people left with a new understanding about Mississippi and what was possible there.

Bob Moses and COFO staff people were more convinced than ever that this cultural component had real importance. Sam Block, Willie Peacock, and Willie McGhee were determined to do something about supporting the older culture. They went back to their communities and organized the first grassroots Mississippi festival, which took place in Mileston that August. To help defray expenses they applied for a grant from a new fund which had been set up from the royalties from the song "We Shall Overcome." The two-day gathering included an art show by Africans and African Americans, a slavery-time cook-out, old-time secular and religious music, and buck dancing. This would be the first of several festivals in different parts of the state organized by this trio, and the antecedent of an important Delta blues festival which continues to this day.

> Through song and dance a people are able to share their burden, triumph, sadness and gladness of heart. People sing songs of heroism. They sing songs about the common oppressor or exploiter. The smallest and the greatest desires of a people are brought out in folk music. These songs can be used to draw people together and unite them in one common aim, goal, and purpose.
>
> —Willie Peacock, Report to the We Shall Overcome Committee

The Newport Folk Foundation continued its interest and support of the cultural work in Mississippi and in other parts of the South. They funded a traveling resource person to encourage the Southern work. Julius Lester had been a student at Fisk during the sit-ins in Nashville, had worked at Highlander on the cultural program in 1961–62, and was a writer, singer, and songwriter based in New York. He was a sensitive and energetic person to take on the work for Newport, and he would provide important support for the civil rights workers who were now turning to cultural work.

In October of 1965 there would be one more important southwide cultural conference—this time at Highlander Center in Knoxville. It was called by Bernice Reagon, by then a student at Spelman College in Atlanta, and organized by Bernice and me. Its purpose was to draw together the growing number of people in the Southern states who were beginning to focus on the cultural heritage and traditions of black communities and tying that heritage in with the freedom movement.

There were people from Georgia, Alabama, Mississippi, South Carolina, and Louisiana. Alan Lomax was there as was Dr. Willis James, a folklorist working with Bernice in Atlanta. There were indigenous folk artists, grassroots community leaders, and young freedom workers. This time there was more agreement about the importance of grassroots cultural work.

Specific plans were drawn up. There would be festivals on Johns Island and in Charleston organized by Bill Saunders and Esau Jenkins. Sam Block, Willie Peacock, and Willie McGhee would continue their work in Mississippi, organizing a festival in Greenwood at Christmas time. Mable Hillary of the Georgia Sea Island Singers would organize a blues sing in her home community in Cayete County, Georgia, and a festival in Brunswick near the group's home on St. Simons Island—again the forerunner of a festival which is going strong today. There were plans made for Albany, Georgia; Gadsden, Alabama; and Atlanta as well.

Bernice Reagon would in the next few years join forces with Anne Romaine, a white singer and activist from Gastonia, North Carolina, to start what became the Southern Folk Cultural Revival Project, organizing concerts of older and younger black and white Southern artists and presenting them at college campuses, churches, and community centers. The idea that grassroots cultural work is important and is relevant to social change dovetailed with a growing pride in black culture that was becoming evident in the Southern freedom movement and would eventually have a very large impact on American culture as a whole.

Other movement activists went on to become lifelong cultural organizers and teachers. Hollis Watkins stayed on in Mississippi and is currently director of Southern Echo, a political and cultural community organization. Worth Long became a prominent folklorist continuing to document Southern culture and to organize cultural events. Willie Peacock, Len Chandler, Betty Mae Fikes,and Cordell Reagon all live on the West Coast and use their cultural knowledge and skills to educate and work for social justice. Chuck Neblett of the SNCC Freedom Singers has worked as a city official and youth choir director in Kentucky. This year he organized a reunion tour of the freedom singers throughout the state. Carlton Reese, Rutha Harris and countless others have stayed in their home communities, using the power of song to carry their work forward. Dr. Bernice Reagon has written extensively and has organized major conferences on civil rights culture through her work as cultural historian at the Smithsonian Institute. She produced an excellent collection of recordings of freedom songs released by the Smithsonian. In her album notes she wrote:

I grew up in Dougherty County, just outside of Albany, Georgia, in a community steeped in Black Southern cultural traditions. These traditions came alive for me as they shaped the cultural structures of the Civil Rights Movement. From the late 1950s through the mid-1960s, I celebrated and participated in the wedding of our traditional culture with our contemporary struggle for freedom. All the established academic categories in which I had been educated fell apart during this period, revealing culture to be not luxury, not leisure, not entertainment, but the lifeblood of a community.

Bernice Reagon

Voices of the Civil Rights Movement:
Black American Freedom Songs;
1960–1966—Smithsonian Institution ❖

OSCAR BRAND

Which Side Are You On

When I was small in Manitoba and there was no television or radio, we sang our fun with ballads, dances, and play-parties. One of the ballads was called "Lay The Lily-O." It told of a wealthy young lady who refused to marry the high-born men who courted her because she loved a simple sailor boy. In the years of balladry this was a very revolutionary idea. It coupled feminism with an attack on class distinctions:

> She said, "Tho I am courted by men of high degree.
> None but Jack the sailor boy can win my heart from me."
> Lay the lily-o
> Lay the lily-o.

When we moved down across the border, I wandered around the States singing and listening. In Harlan County, Kentucky, a woman named Florence Reece had turned our old ballad into a miners union rallying cry, "Which Side Are You On?" with such verses as:

> They say in Harlan County there'll be no neutrals there.
> You'll either be a union man or a thug for J.H. Blair.
> Which side are you on?
> Which side are you on?

At first I was annoyed. Then I was captivated by the new words, and I sang them around without much coaxing. Then, on one of my civil rights excursions into the Deep South, I heard a new version of the song. This time it was lead by Martin Luther King, Jr., who had a strong sweet voice.

With slight changes, the song began to pop up everywhere. Finally, one sad day in Mississippi, where we were marching to protest the murder of Medgar Evers, I heard a new set of lyrics. The message, however, hadn't really changed:

> You got to choose in Jackson,
> Whenever things look dark,
> You'll be a Freedom Rider,
> Or Uncle Tom for Charlie Clark,
> Which side are you on?
> Which side are you on?"

A few years thereafter I was asked to act as music director for *In White America*, the first black history play at Sheridan Square in Greenwich Village. I needed a powerful song to close the evening. Of course, I chose "Which Side Are You On" just as the Reverend King sang it. And Moses Gunn, Gloria Foster, and Fred Pinkard made the theater ring with what was still a love ballad but had taken on the overtones of liberty. ❖

Oscar Brand was born in Winnipeg, Manitoba and came to the U.S. when he was very young. Oscar was heavily involved in the folksinging movement and the Civil Rights Movement. He has a wife, Karen, who is a lawyer, and four children.

Young people clapping and chanting freedom

ARTWORK BY

SHARON RILEY

MATTHEW A. JONES JR.

Freedom Fighter

Matthew Jones was one of the leaders of the Nashville student movement while a student at Tennessee State University in 1960. He wrote his first freedom song in 1961, and in 1963 developed the Danville Freedom Voices to go into the tobacco fields of Virginia and sing freedom songs. In Danville, he wrote many songs including the "Ballad Of Medgar Evers." In the fall of 1963, Matthew went to Atlanta to reorganize the SNCC Freedom Singers. He remained with them until 1967. Matthew was arrested twenty-nine times while in the Movement.

In 1994 the words *Mississippi Freedom Summer* ring in the ears of America and the world. It gives you the feeling that Mississippi was the only place that significant Movement activity took place. As a member of SNCC and also as one of the directors of the Freedom Singers, it was necessary for me to look at the Movement in its entirety. I cannot see Mississippi and not also see Alabama, Georgia, Tennessee, Arkansas, South Carolina, North Carolina, Virginia, Louisiana, Florida, and the rest of the South. The volume of information written about Mississippi would lead people to think that problems in other sections of the South were secondary. The media concentration on Mississippi was the direct result of the deaths of Mickey Schwerner, Andrew Goodman, and James Chaney. In 1964 we knew that the country would not react to black students being killed. We felt that with white student involvement the country would pay attention. We were right. It was sad to find out that this country would only respond to the death of its white youth. It is even sadder to me that in 1994 the white establishment is still only interested in the history surrounding the death of its youth. James Chaney would not have been known had he not been killed with Andrew and Mickey. (It bothered me that James Chaney's mother lived in a housing project in New York City, wishing that she could have a house of her own.) Why can't we fertilize our own flowers? Why do we let our flowers wither on the vine?

After reading this article I hope you will see that the Movement was a powerfully interwoven tapestry of people, ideas, and resources from all over the United States. It drew its moral force from the personnel and ideas of the entire Southern student movement: from Greensboro, North Carolina, and the beginning of the sit-ins to the development of the philosophy of nonviolent direct action in Tennessee; from the beginning of SNCC as a permanent organization in the fall of 1960 to the sending of SNCC field secretaries to all sections of the South; from the field reports of these freedom fighters to the nation's awareness of the disappearance of James, Mickey, and Andrew. All these Movement trends and the deaths of many freedom fighters across the South were needed to set the stage for the Mississippi Freedom Summer. The Freedom Summer could not have happened in a vacuum, it would not have been possible without this great university of freedom. Through my experiences as a field secretary of SNCC and a member of the Freedom Singers, I will try to set the stage for the Mississippi summer. I will also try to show how these experiences have affected my life.

On a warm day in the spring of 1943, as I was sitting on my front porch in Littleton, North Carolina, watching the people go by, a short familiar woman walked by the house. Her name was Ella Baker. Every time she would come home people in town would say "Ella's back." I now know what a fearless woman she was. People couldn't express their feelings, but they recognized that she was different. However, according to my father, her fearlessness was not a surprise. Ella's mother was a powerful woman who did not keep her beliefs about racism secret.

Ella's mother, Mrs. Baker, lived next door to my family when I was five years old. One day Mrs. Baker came to our house to protect us because she saw a white man walk into our house. Carrying a stick in her hand, she asked him why was he there. As I remember he left in a hurry.

In 1943 my father was the principal of the county school in Littleton, N.C. He wrote a letter to the *Raleigh News and Observer* which was printed in the winter of 1943. The letter said that Negroes of this country are forced to sit in the back of buses, go through the back doors of white people's homes, while Japanese at that time had no such problem (World War II had just started). The newspaper printed every word my father wrote.

As a result of that letter, the KKK came for my father one night. Fortunately, he had been warned by a white drunk whom he befriended. After discussing the incident with a white city councilman who was a personal friend, he was told that we would be protected until he found suitable work in another state. I can still see those strange white men coming to our door as I held the hem of my mother's dress. They said, "Where's Matthew!" My mother answered, "He's gone." Then they left. I was too young to be afraid. We left town a few days later.

During that period, Ella Baker was doing great work in the struggle and yet the KKK did not come for her. They wanted to kill my father, however, for writing a letter to the editor of a newspaper about the conditions under which black people lived in the South. When a black man spoke out with opinions of his own he was killed or had to leave town. Depending on the nature of his opinions, a black man's career and his life are still in danger even today. Black women, even during those times, were not treated the same way.

On February 1, 1960, some students at A & T College in Greensboro, North Carolina,

had a sit-in at a Woolworth lunch counter. I remember my reaction, "I know that these sit-ins are right. What will our parents, teachers, and preachers think? What will they do?"

Students from all over the South began to sit-in. I was a senior at Tennessee State University when sit-ins broke out in Nashville, Tennessee. Dr. W. S. Davis, president of Tennessee State University, called for a meeting with the students. I thought that he might be prepared to lead us or at least lend his emotional support. I was naive to assume that he would give his approval. He said, "If you students don't sit-in, Governor Buford Ellington will give us two thirty-thousand-dollar buses with water fountains on them for our track, football, and basketball teams."

When I heard the president of TSU tell us not to fight for our freedom, I knew that the older generation was not going to lead us and we would have to lead ourselves. I stood up while the president was speaking and walked out. I walked from Tennessee State University to Fisk University to meet Rev. C. T. Vivian, who was sending students to Cain-Sloan Department Store's lunch counter. He sent me. In four hours I was in jail. I never felt better. I could fight for freedom and live to talk about it. I never felt more relaxed.

It was a new day! We now had the leadership of activists such as Rev. C. T. Vivian, Jim Lawson, Ella Baker and others. We all know that without the administration, leadership, and guidance of the great Ella Baker, then the NAACP, SCLC, and SNCC would not have developed into the great civil rights organizations they were soon to become.

It was in Nashville that I became a freedom fighter. I went to jail along with John Lewis, James Bevel, and Bernard Laffayette of the American Baptist College (Bernard is now president of that college); Diane Nash, Angeline Butler, and Marion Barry of Fisk University; Lucretia Collins, Katherine Brooks, Paul Brooks, Lonnie Hubbard, and John Hardy of TSU and many, many more.

I consider Nashville, then called the Athens of the South, a primary influence in providing the setting for the development of nonviolent, direct-action philosophy in the western hemisphere. With the help of the examples of Gandhi and Christ and the insights of Jim Lawson, a nonviolent think tank was developed by James Bevel, John Lewis, Bernard Lafayette, Diane Nash, myself and others. A nonviolent, direct action philosophy was developed by this student movement. Bernard Lafayette and James Bevel became very adept at using these techniques. When they became a part of SCLC they gave to it our nonviolent philosophical insights and the direct-action techniques made in the fiery furnaces of the SNCC experience. Bevel became one of King's main strategists. The march on Washington was Bevel's idea.

I graduated from Tennessee State University in August 1960. I worked in Appalachia (East Tennessee) as a music and mathematics teacher. My father, being president of the Knoxville NAACP, and my being in the sit-in movement led to my being fired and arrested in 1961. There is almost no account of the pain and suffering caused by the witch hunts the FBI carried out against early veterans of the Civil Rights Movement. The FBI terrorized entire neighborhoods. After they came into neighborhoods asking questions, some of us lost our jobs and were no longer able to visit our loved ones and friends.

I had to leave Elizabethton, Tennessee. I found out what it was like to be blacklisted. I had a wife, two children, and one on the way. These incidents destroyed my marriage. I was being forced to live in a racist society as an Uncle Tom. I was very sad about my future. I decided to try teaching in another state. My father, who got me my first job, got me my second job. (Give credit where credit is due.)

In the fall of 1961, I was teaching at Ballard-Hudson Junior High in Macon, Georgia. Every day I had to ride on a segregated bus. One afternoon as I came from work, the bus driver told me to go to the back of the bus. I don't know what possessed me, but I walked to the front of the bus and said to the driver, "I'll go to the back of the bus today, but this is the last time." There was a bus boycott being planned in Macon at that time. I met with the principal of the school and told him that I wanted to go to the rally. He advised me not to make any speeches or say anything that would cost me my job, but suggested that I sing a song instead. For that occasion, I wrote my first freedom song:

FREEDOM ROAD
What is this road we travel on
It looks so dark and gloomy
We chose this road because we know
it'll lead us to equality.

This, this is Freedom Road
That Jesus guards so I am told
Haste, haste along this path
Although this walk may be our last
God bring us strong nonviolent men
Men who have Christ in front of them

And as this road through Macon goes
Where it'll stop nobody knows

This, this is Freedom Road
That Jesus guards so I am told
Haste, haste along this path
Although this walk may be our last
God bring us strong nonviolent men
Men who have Christ in front of them

And as this road through the Southland winds
It'll never stop 'til the end of time

This, this is Freedom Road
That Jesus guards so I am told
Haste, haste along this path
Although this walk may be our last
God bring us strong nonviolent men
Men who have Christ in front of them

© 1994 Wisdom Train (ASCAP)
© 1961, 1964 Matthew Jones (ASCAP)

The congregation went wild. They had probably never heard words and music rendered in that fashion before. Neither had I. I knew the song had been effective because I was told my contract would not be renewed for the coming year. I was fired.

It seemed to me that someone or something did not want me to be a man. I knew that I had to change course. Ironically, I received a draft notice from the U.S. Army Services. Imagine a country that does not want you to be free while demanding that you fight for it. At the end of the school year, I immediately returned to Knoxville, Tennessee, and enrolled in graduate school at the University of Tennessee. In those days, you did not have to fight in the war if you were in school.

It was in the summer of 1962 that I enrolled at UT. Marion Barry, one of the leaders of the Nashville sit-ins and the first chairman of the Student Nonviolent Coordinating Committee, had been awarded a fellowship in chemistry and was attending UT. In the previous school year he had founded a group called the Students for Equal Treatment. I was glad Marion was there. I was comfortable being in a group that understood the nature of scientific nonviolence.

We began direct-action demonstrations of all kinds. Marion and I were the oldest and had the experience of the Nashville sit-in movement to rely on. The movement in Knoxville was very effective because of our presence and the moving of the Highlander Folk School to the area. With the help of Highlander and its director, Myles Horton, we felt secure. Myles Horton was a great man that many leaders in the Movement owe thanks for his contribution to their development. Highlander and my father's church were the only places blacks and whites could meet for the purpose of planning our daily movement activity in Knoxville.

One of our daily activities was to organize boycotts of certain Knoxville stores that practiced segregation. We demonstrated in front of these stores. Demonstrating was either dangerous or boring. It was for these demonstrations that I wrote my second freedom song. However, this was my first freedom song written on the picket line:

DON'T BUY DOWNTOWN

All you Negroes in Knoxville
Don't buy downtown
Let Mayor Duncan know how you feel
Don't buy downtown

Don't buy downtown
Don't buy downtown
Let Mayor Duncan know how you feel
Don't buy downtown

We know segregation's a killer
Don't buy downtown
Don't bring packages out of Miller's [department store]
Don't buy downtown

Don't buy downtown
Don't buy downtown
Don't bring packages out of Miller's
Don't buy downtown

We are walking up the freedom path
Don't buy downtown
If we catch you we will take your photograph
Don't buy downtown

Don't buy downtown
Don't buy downtown
If we catch you we will take your photograph
Don't buy downtown

We will fight 'til Duncan twitches
Don't buy downtown
Don't bring packages out of Rich's [department store]
Don't buy downtown

Don't buy downtown
Don't buy downtown
Don't bring packages out of Rich's
Don't buy downtown

We know what we have to do
Don't buy downtown
To see a picture at the Bijou
Don't buy downtown

Don't buy downtown
Don't buy downtown
To see a picture at the Bijou

Don't buy downtown

You can be a blocker or you can be a talker
Don't buy downtown
Don't let us catch you in Cas Walker's
Don't buy downtown

Don't buy downtown
Don't buy downtown
Don't let us catch you in Cas Walker's
Don't buy downtown
(Cas Walker Market—Cas Walker was a
legendary segregationist in the Knoxville area)
© 1993 Wisdom Train (ASCAP)
© 1962, 1994 Matthew Jones (ASCAP)

This movement was very effective because of the commitment of a small group of dedicated students, both black and white, including Marion Barry, who always wound up being the president or chairman of every group he was ever in; and Avon Rollins, a dynamic, young, fiery engineering student, who was from Knoxville and very sincere and religious. When we picketed a Catholic hospital for not accepting Negroes (our name at the time) as patients, Avon carried his rosary counting its beads as we walked. The mother superior approached us, cursed us, and tore up our picket signs. "Love thy neighbor as thyself" could be seen very clearly by any one who came by. The Bible verses on the signs stood out like doves in a sea of buzzards. Avon looked confused and shaken. He was so upset by the conduct of the nuns that he never used his rosary again.

Marshall Jones, my brother, was studying opera and according to certain music experts had the possibility of entering the Metropolitan Opera Try-Outs and winning. Marshall, my sister Brenda, and I were in the music education department at UT. There were very few blacks at UT. There were so many whites that I got a headache. Marshall was a very close friend of Marion's. I was too serious to have many close personal friends. However, Avon Rollins became my closest friend and remains so today.

It was in Knoxville that I met some sincere, dedicated white people. My relationship with these white people was very therapeutic for me. They were Southern born and bred. They understood the South and its ways. They had been separated from family and friends because of a belief in freedom. Phillip Bacon was a white student who took an inheritance he received at the death of one of his relatives, placed it in the hands of a local minister and said, "We are ready to go to jail until all this money is gone." We were arrested numerous times. I was arrested eighteen times. Every time Phillip went to jail, he was beaten and harassed by inmates. It just dawned on me that I don't know if he ever got his money back.

The first time I was jailed in Knoxville, I was thrown in a cell with hardened criminals. One man had been in jail so long he had his own chest of drawers in his cell. I talked about the Movement until the lights went out. When I awoke the next morning this man said, "Matthew, do you see those bars over there. The jailer told me that if they found you hanging from those bars this morning, he would let me go free. I couldn't do that because I know you are doing the right thing." I knew at that moment that I was in a struggle that meant something to everyone. That same night, Stephen Wagner, a white comrade of mine, was severely beaten in another cell in the same jail. Some of the other Southern whites jailed constantly were Harry Wersima, Bambi Sharp, Larry Yates, Mary Ann Wade, and Ed Hamlin.

On one afternoon we had a sit-in at the mayor's office. I was arrested by a black police officer whom I had known since he was a kid. I felt that we had failed him and others like him. We were taken to jail and placed in cubicles called grapefruit boxes. These boxes gave you no room to stand and no room to lay down, with a small can in the corner for your waste. These boxes were made of cement and had slits in the side for air. I began to sing and started demanding better conditions. After eight hours they let me out to use the restroom. Because I came out of the cubicle with confidence, the jailer became very angry and hit me with a slapjack on the right side of my head. A slapjack is a piece of steel covered by leather used to subdue you. My head was throbbing, but I maintained consciousness. Marion said, "You didn't have to do that."

The jailer turned to Marion and said, "What did you say?" Marion just looked at him. I was glad he didn't say anything. That jailer would have killed him.

My father, Rev. Matthew A. Jones, Sr., was the surrogate father to the students. I will never forget the day my father and I were arrested together. I didn't think anything of it at the time. I came from an activist family. My father had always been outspoken. As I mentioned before, my father was run out of Littleton, North Carolina, by the KKK. He became a welder on the shipyards of Wilmington, Delaware, during World War II. He later finished theological seminary and became an Episcopal priest. His uncle before him, William Claude Chance, Sr., had taken the Pullman car industry to the Supreme Court and had the curtain between blacks and whites removed in all dining cars. Uncle Chance was a cousin of Paul Robeson. Fighting for freedom was in my blood. However, at that time I did not know my history.

In early 1963, Avon left Knoxville to work for the Student Nonviolent Coordinating Committee [SNCC]. I was happy that he had developed into such a fine organizer. They sent him to a hell-hole of a town called Danville, Virginia. We missed him, but we continued to destroy segregation in Knoxville with nonviolent, direct-action techniques. The Movement had spread to Knoxville College and with the increasing numbers we began to demonstrate all over Knoxville. My father and other ministers set up their own organizational structures. They organized Knoxville to the point that my father could run for mayor of the city.

After June 10, 1963, Avon sent me a letter that had enclosed within it a newspaper clipping that would radically change the course of my life. The clipping showed the picture of a woman who had been hit in the breast with a billy club. The policemen had sprayed the people with a fire hose so strong that they rolled down the street like leaves. Avon wrote in his letter, "Dear Matthew, I need you. Come to Danville. You have to see it to believe it. I am now the director of the Virginia field office of SNCC." The letter and clipping disturbed me. How could anyone be so brutal to a woman? I decided I would put everything on hold and go to Danville for a week.

When I arrived in Danville, I could tell that I was in a battle zone. Some of the people still carried the scars of the June 10 demonstration. Avon took me to the home of Sylvester Walton, where Avon and I stayed for the duration of my time in Danville. SNCC had just carried out a major offensive there. I had a lot to learn. Avon and others began to tell the story of June 10. From this story came my third freedom song:

LEGEND OF DANVILLE

In Danville on June the tenth
In the year of sixty-three
From Bibleway Church to the court house
Some people marched to be free

The night was dark and the journey long
As they marched two abreast
But with the spirit of freedom songs
They didn't need no rest

Move on, Move on, Move on with the Freedom Fight
Move on, Move on, We're fighting for equal rights

As they fell down on their knees
Led by Reverend McGhee
He looked up and cried, "Lord, please
We want to be free."

They heard the voice of Chief McCann
As it cut across the prayer
I'll never forget those violent words,
"Nigger, get out of here."

And as they heard those brutal words
They didn't turn around
The water from the fire hose
Knocked them to the ground

And as they fell down on the ground
They were hit with billy sticks
I'll never forget that terrible sound
As the people's heads did split.

Move on, Move on, Move on with the Free-
dom Fight
Move on, Move on, We're fighting for equal
rights

Don't you stumble brother don't you falter
Oh Mother don't you weep,
We're climbing up to our freedom
Although the road is steep

On June 13 we marched again
They used the tear gas bombs
The grand jury indicted us
On five thousand dollars bond

In Danville town's corrupted courts
We got no justice done.
We were found guilty before the trial
And the judge, he wore a gun

Move on, Move on, Move on with the Free-
dom Fight
Move on, Move on, We're fighting for equal
rights.

I went to the Movement office, which was a store front that at one time had been a shop. This storefront had the name *The Danville Christian Progressive Association* painted on the display window. As I walked in, I saw people that I would later share life and death experiences I could never have imagined at the time: SCLC's Wyatt T. Walker, James Bevel, and James Orange; from SNCC, Avon Rollins, Bob Zellner, Dottie Miller (Zellner), Ivanhoe Donaldson, Sam Shirah, J.V. Henry, Mary King, Annie Pearl Avery, Bruce Baines, and Claudia Edwards for The Congress of Racial Equality (CORE).

There was a lot of Movement activity in Danville. Press releases were being sent out daily. Sessions on how to protect yourself in a nonviolent fashion were given frequently. That night I went to my first mass meeting. People were singing freedom songs and praying with an en-

ergy I had never heard before. In Nashville it had been students. In Danville it was people of all ages and classes. I was hooked. I told Avon I wanted to stay.

My job was to teach nonviolent technique and to organize the high school student demonstrations. SNCC veterans like Cordell Reagon and Jim Forman had left a good foundation on which I could build. I developed a group of nonviolent guerrillas who could strike a target and return to the office without getting arrested. They only had to have their picket signs, their blue jeans on, and their toothbrushes.

Dan River Mills, a textile manufacturer, was a major employer in the Danville area. It would only hire black people in menial jobs. I decided to use the students to stop Dan River Mills employee shifts from changing. Avon always gave me the freedom to handle the students as I saw fit. That's why I was able to do a good job.

The students had been trained to meet me at a moment's notice. They were taught never to divulge what they were about to do. To make sure they would not talk, I never gave them the final details until just before the demonstration.

I called four of my best-trained students one morning and asked them to come to the movement office prepared to demonstrate. When they got there I laid out the plan: they were to go to Dan River Mills and block traffic in such a way that the employees could not get to and from work. They were told to bring cloth picket signs that they could fold and put in their pockets. When they got to Dan River Mills they were to wait for the traffic lights to turn red, then stand in front of the car, facing the driver until the light changed three times, take the sign out, show it to the driver and then sit in front of the car. It worked. Traffic was blocked for ten miles. They were told to move if the police asked them to. The police had to approach the demonstration on motorcycle. The policeman asked them to move. They moved. We had completed our objective without an arrest.

One of the abilities I had that I was most proud of was being a nonviolent warrior. I liked being faced with danger and then watching the danger disappear. I liked being with warriors. The person I liked being with the most was Annie Pearl Avery. When I went on a demonstration, I wanted Annie Pearl with me. She was so fearless in the face of danger. She was very strong and very young. She was from Birmingham and as a child had faced the fire hoses, the jails, and Chief Bull Conner—sixteen years old and ready to rumble. One day we were being arraigned in front of a judge who found us guilty. However, it was clear that we were not guilty. In protest, we decided to "go limp" in front of the judge. We lay on the floor. The judge cited us for contempt and jailed us. They picked us up and carried us to the elevator. Once on the elevator, they were going to beat me. They saw me as being the problem. As they drew back the billy club to hit me, Annie Pearl put her leg across my body and pointed her finger in the officer's face and said with force, "Don't, don't you hit him!" The officer had to hit her to hit me. He withdrew the club. They took us to solitary confinement. I could hear Annie Pearl's voice ringing through the jail, "Don't touch me. Back off or I'll hit you with my shoe." They soon took me out of solitary and placed me in a cell. I was shocked when I saw my lawyer, Len Holt, in the cell with me. Len was black, and we were proud of him.

> *In Danville town's corrupted courts we got no justice done.*
> *We were found guilty before the trial and the judge he wore a gun.*
> (Legend of Danville)

We were bailed out by local black residents who could mortgage their homes to get bail money. For years after the Danville movement, I would have to come back to settle a legal problem. I had to go back because our people were in danger of losing their homes.

In later years, when I heard people talk about the rights of women in the Movement and how they were so under-utilized, I didn't understand what they were saying at first. I was too busy working and demonstrating. I knew when I wanted to go on demonstrations that women were the most fearless and the most dependable in times of crisis: Annie Pearl Avery, Fannie Lou Hamer, Prathia Hall, Dorie Ladner, Ruby Doris Robinson, Emma Bell, Brenda Travis, and many more. I hate to mention names because you always miss somebody.

One dark night we demonstrated for the right to register to vote. Martin Luther King had come to town to march with us. We were afraid. This was the first major march since June 13, and Chief McCann had vowed to stop us again. Everyone was visibly shaken, including King. We marched two abreast. M. L. King was behind me. I don't know why he was not in front. I guess we were protecting him. I marched near the front with a Danville freedom fighter named Thomas Holt. When we saw Chief McCann with his bright lights we knew the end was near. He told us to stop. He told us to go back. We did not retreat. He arrested us.

We were sent to the Danville County Farm that was run by a man named Captain Price. We were all placed in a large room with cots in them. Before we could settle ourselves, Chief Price separated the leaders from the others. Thomas Holt, Samuel Giles, and myself were removed from the room. I was placed in solitary confinement. I was there only a short while. Suddenly, a young soldier named Buford Holt was brought into the cell. I asked him why was he there. He began to tell a story that became my fourth freedom song.

DEMONSTRATING G.I.

I'm a demonstrating G.I. from Fort Bragg
The way they treat my people makes me mad
You know that I couldn't sit still
Because my home is in Danville

I came home one Friday night
I saw my sister fighting for her rights
I said, "Keep on Sis, and I'll be back
Standing tall with my boots so black."

While sitting in camp I read the paper
I said to my sergeant, "I'll see you later,"
I caught the bus and came on home

"I told you, Sis, you wouldn't be alone."

I got arrested on a Sunday eve
The police said, "You ain't overseas,
And don't you forget one simple fact,
That your skin is still black."

I was bound in jail for over a week.
All I got were some beans to eat,
Out of a rusty tray, I was fed
And I slept on an iron bed.

Secretary of Defense McNamara
Said, "Colored Boy, what's the matter?
I don't care if you fight for your freedom
But please take off that uniform."

I said, "Well I'm an American fighting man,
I'll defend this country as long as I can,
And If I can defend it overseas,
Then why don't you set my people free?"

To the Army, Air Force, and the Navy,
Come on soldiers, don't be lazy,
If you want to integrate,
Then come on out here and demonstrate.

© 1994 Wisdom Train
© 1963, 1994 Matthew Jones

Captain Price said sarcastically, "Matthew, you're going to work today." They put me on the back of a truck and took me to a rock quarry. That's a place where you break big rocks into little rocks. After the rocks are broken as small as possible, they are put into a gravel machine. I was given a twenty-pound sledge hammer with which to work. I had been identified as a leader. The foreman looked at me and said, "Go behind that gravel machine to work." The gravel machine made a lot of noise. The sound it made churning small rocks into gravel was like a cement drill breaking up the sidewalk of a New York City street.

When I got behind the machine, an inmate with a twenty pound sledge hammer on his shoulder was standing there. He said, "Are you one of them freedom niggers?"

I said, "Yes, but I'm not a nigger." I looked him in the eye with love. At that time of my life, I believed totally in nonviolence. He dropped the hammer and hit me in the eye with his fist. I was relieved that he dropped the hammer. He trembled as he looked at me with anger. He looked like an outlaw who wanted to pull the trigger and couldn't.

I was taken from the rock quarry and put back into solitary confinement. I was alone again. They gave me a crust of bread and a cup of water three times a day. My clothes and the mattress on the bed were taken away. On the fourth day, they brought me a plate of food. I told them I had already eaten. Captain Price was very angry that his method of breaking me down did not work. I was supposed to grab that plate of food like a mad dog.

Price seemed to have more respect for me now. He had a doctor examine my eye. The doctor was astonished that the eye seemed healed after a few days. Price got scared. He wanted me broken. I began to chant Bible verses late at night to bug him. He said, "I know you think you're like Jesus, but I can't let you run my jail."

Price came in a few days later and said, "You're going home. Get ready." I was happy. I took messages from the other freedom fighters to give to their families. They took me out of that cell and placed me in another cell behind some real redneck crackers. Price had fooled me. There was a flimsy lock on the door. The experience of the eight hours behind that door was the most hair-raising. They would say, "Let's break this door down and get this nigger." I was scared. I was upset at myself because I had fallen for Price's ten-cent penal mind game. They moved me from that room and took me to another county. I thought they were going to lynch me.

When I arrived at the other jail, as an act of self-preservation, I did not cooperate with the work schedule. They threw me into solitary confinement. I wanted solitary this time. I did not have to deal with people I did not know. I could control my environment. They took my clothes, put a high-voltage light bulb in my cell, and placed towels under the door. This cell had no bars, only a big iron door. The cell was very hot. Luckily, they left my shirt. I told time by waving a wet undershirt in the air until it dried. If I began waving my shirt in the air after breakfast, I found it would be dry by lunch time.

They came to my cell the next day and said, "It's time for you to go home." They placed me in a police car and took me back to Danville. When I arrived, I expected to see a lot of us in the holding room. To my surprise only thirteen people had been arrested. I said, "What happened? We had two-hundred-fifty people in the march?" What happened to King?

"He had to catch a plane. His schedule was too tight to get arrested," someone said. I was disappointed because I had assumed that he was going to be with us.

Being out of jail, I shared the songs I had written in jail. I began to teach the students freedom songs. At times we went into the tobacco fields and sang freedom songs in churches. I called the students the Danville Freedom Voices. Gradually, I became known for my singing and songwriting. Jim Forman came to Danville and asked to see me. He asked me to leave Danville and raise funds for SNCC. He wanted me to travel around the country and sing about the Movement and write songs. I asked him, "Why do you need me, don't you have the Freedom Singers?"

He said, "Bernice is pregnant, and Ruthie is going back to school." I thought the Freedom Singers should not stop functioning. I was interested in rebuilding the Freedom Singers, but not in going out on the road alone. He said, "I'll take care of that. I don't think you should get involved in that, but I will look into it. I want you to go to the SNCC projects in Mississippi and get a feeling of how SNCC works." Avon thought I should go, so I bid him goodbye and was on my way.

I rode a Greyhound bus into Mississippi. It was so beautiful, but I could see a klansman's image in every clump of beautiful shrubs. I went to Yazoo City, Greenwood, Canton, and Jackson. In Canton I was told the story of a sheriff who went to the house of a Negro man and his wife and said to the husband, "I want your wife. I will come here to see her next Thursday." The husband said, "Yes, sir." Canton was so bad they would kill a Negro and leave him on the steps of a Negro funeral home. That husband had the choice to submit and live, or object to the sheriff's behavior, then leave town, or die.

Mississippi was hard to tame. SNCC was trying to civilize it. My years in South Carolina had toughened me. South Carolina was the only state tougher than Mississippi. Sometimes I feel that the state of Mississippi is scapegoated. I would dare anyone to comb the swamps of South Carolina looking for old bones.

I came to Atlanta in the fall of 1963 to reorganize the Freedom Singers. It was there that I met Charles Neblett, a man I would work with for the next three years. Our first job was to find new personnel. The Freedom Singers had been on the road for part of the spring and summer of 1963. The personnel were Bernice Johnson, Ruthie Harris, Cordell Reagon, and Charles Neblett. From that group's experience, we learned the lesson that when young men and women traveled alone on the road, complications develop. That is why we specifically wanted young men who could sing, were committed, and were punctual. We found Emory Harris, Ruthie's brother from Albany, Georgia, and James Peacock from Charleston, Mississippi. We needed a good tenor voice. I knew Marshall, my brother from Knoxville, Tennessee, could do the job, but he had a promising opera career if he continued studying. I called him and begged him to come. I knew SNCC needed funds, and we needed competent people who could deliver the goods. I knew Marshall could deliver the goods. I had no problem in asking him to leave school. I thought the only job in the world worth having was a job as a field secretary of the Student Nonviolent Coordinating Committee. I still consider myself a SNCC worker.

My years with the Freedom Singers were some of the best years of my life. I traveled across the country with Charles "Chuck" Neblett,

Emory Harris, Marshall Jones, and James Pea-cock. Later a Venezulaian named Rafael Bentham joined the group. Rafael brought the guitar and his South American rhythms. With-out Rafael, *Oginga Odinga* (1963) would not have sounded the way it did. Cordell came back. Cordell had left the group to form the Freedom Voices. Cordell was one of SNCC's best orga-nizers and a very good singer. Cordell was a per-son you had to experience. He had a very un-usual personality. Once you met him you did not forget him. When Peacock got sick, Carver "Chico" Neblett joined the group. When Rafael left, Jim Forman knew we were looking for a guitarist. One day he was discussing the group's needs in the New York SNCC office. Lucille Perlman, one of SNCCs' most important con-tributors, overheard Jim and said, "My son Bill plays a guitar."

Forman said, "Contact Matthew Jones."

Bill Perlman came to see me. I liked him immediately. I told him that I liked his musi-cianship, but it was not my decision. The group was waiting to hear him if I thought he would fit in. I gave him some songs to learn. We dis-cussed the group's musical style and how I thought the music should be played. Bill went away to practice. When he left, I did not know how it would work out. He came back with the music and the guitar style memorized. I was happy. I set up a meeting with Chuck, Chico, Marshall, Cordell, Bill, and myself. The group liked Bill. At first I was concerned that he was only eighteen years old, but it didn't matter. Bill was an old soul. Bill was the only Caucasian to ever sing in the Freedom Singers.

I will always regret not being able to sing with Bernice and Ruthie in a group setting. Both of them have such fine voices. I sometimes won-der what type of music I would have written for their voices. Bertha Gober sang with the group in the early, early days. I never met her, but her song, "We'll Never Turn Back," stays in my heart always. Her song was SNCC's "We Shall Over-come."

Members of SNCC probably have always wondered what life was like for the Freedom Singers on the road. We traveled in a station wagon that was our home away from home. All of our belongings were in that car: our instru-ments, our clothes—everything. We traveled over three-hundred-thousand miles in a station wagon. We could go across country in two and one-half days. How did we do that? Marshall, Chuck, Chico, and Emory took turns all night long. We were highly Zorzed. We usually left a town the night after a concert to get to the next town by the following morning. That morning we would usually have a radio show, a concert at a school in the afternoon, and a concert that night. Occasionally, we got an extra day in a town. In King of Prussia, Pennsylvania, we did twenty-one engagements in one week. We all got sick. We never did that again.

My job in the Freedom Singers was being the business manager on the road. My contact in the SNCC office was Dinky Romily, who supplied us with a $400 expense account to buy gas and take care of the car. It was my job to be sure the money was used for the car. I was re-quired by SNCC to keep receipts for every penny. I would collect the money from the school and send it to the SNCC office. I can remember sending as much as $5,000 in one week to SNCC. I also was the musical arranger for the group and either wrote or arranged most of its material.

Singing freedom songs was a spiritual expe-rience. Freedom songs are mantras and chants for freedom, constantly placing visions in your mind how courage should overcome fear, how love should overcome hate, making a previous weakness a present strength. We repeated words of freedom over and over again until the ideas within these words became a reality. If you hold hands and sing "Ain't Gonna Let Nobody Turn Me Around" enough times, you begin to be-lieve nobody can turn you around. I had not realized how scientific our approach had been until I got involved in Ayurveda, a natural heal-ing system from India. In order to retain their knowledge, they learned it in the form of sutras.

Sutras are discourses in song and or rhythm that made it possible to retain knowledge without memorization. We owe Gandhi and India more credit than we would think on the surface.

The creation of freedom songs always came from the Movement experience of the writer or singer. One case in point was Bertha Gober's "We'll Never Turn Back." That song shows that she had a familiarity with the classical spiritual. A classical spiritual is merely a spiritual arranged in parts for choruses and choirs to sing. John Work and Hall Johnson are examples of the most prolific and most sung black choral arrangers of that time. These spirituals made up a large part of the choral music of the Southern black college. "We'll Never Turn Back" is a mixture of two of these spirituals: "I've Been 'Buked and I've Been Scorned" and "I'll Never Turn Back No More." Gober uses the titles of these songs to weave her own personal magic: *We've been 'buked and we've been scorned, we've been talked about sure as you've born. But we'll never turn back. No we'll never turn back, Until we've all been freed and we have equality.* Another case in point was the classical spiritual "Soon Ah Will Be Done." The end of the chorus in the original spiritual is *Going home to live with God.* I changed it to *Going home to Freedom Land* (1964 Matthew Jones Mercury Records *Freedom Sing Of Freedom Now*)

Next to the classical spiritual, there was the church song. "This Little Light Of Mine"; "Come By Here, Lord"; "Get On Board, Children Children"; "I'll Be Alright"; "Do What The Spirit Say Do"; and "We Are Soldiers In The Army" are examples of songs that were used to describe the settings and activities surrounding our demonstrations.

The songs gave the names of the policemen who beat us and the mayors and governors who oppressed us. *Oh Prichette, Oh Kelly, Oh Prichette open them cells* are words to a freedom song based on the classical spiritual "Oh Mary, Oh Martha." This song gives Chief Pritchett and Mayor Asa D. Kelly of Albany, Georgia, an infamous place in the history of the Civil Rights Movement. In

this song the students are actually having a conversation with their jailers. Their love for their oppressors seems clear. Gober makes Pritchett and Kelley seem human: *I hear God's children crying for mercy, I hear God's children praying in jail. Oh Pritchett, Oh Kelly, Oh Pritchett open them cells.*

We used spirituals, gospel songs, church hymns, popular songs, rock and roll, rhythm and blues—any song that was a part of our consciousness. All over the South you heard these melodies with words indigenous and powerful; in Mississippi—Greenwood, Jackson, McComb, Charleston, Holly Springs, Meridian; in Georgia—Albany; in Tennessee—Nashville; in Alabama—Selma; in Virginia—Danville; and in Arkansas—Little Rock. Each area chewing up segregation and spitting it out. We threw Jim Crow into the quicksand of justice and sang freedom songs, his head seemed to disappear under our feet as we were marching, Freedom's coming and it won't be long.

But Jim Crow's head did not disappear. He just went into the back rooms of Congress and corporations and came out with a new head. We didn't know what to do. Some of us saw that we were not going to win the battle as fast as we thought. We figured that when the white man saw us as human, the battle would be won. That was not the case. The nightmare had begun. We began to explore socialism, Malcolm X, Mao, and armed struggle. We attached ourselves to everything and anything that would relieve us of the migraine that our naivete had given us. Well-meaning activists came from the north with their ideas of scientific revolution spewing from position papers foreign to us. They didn't seem to mind. We were the people they were going to liberate. Our direct-action philosophies slowly gave way to many other approaches that led to SNCC moving from the South and getting involved in the ghettos of the north. It was like Rutherford B. Hayes taking the soldiers out of the South. I was devastated. If SNCC had maintained its Southern base, it probably would be training the thousands of youth that now languish in the streets and in prisons with no leadership and no purpose.

In the spring of 1964, we went on a tour with Dick Gregory. We had tremendous respect for him, and we appreciated all of the efforts he made to support us. Both Dick Gregory and Harry Belafonte gave financial and moral support through their active presence. The most important concert we gave on that tour was at Miami University in Oxford, Ohio. While we were singing and Dick was performing, someone burned a cross on the lawn. Nothing phased us at that time. We left a lot of organized students in the area. Those students made it possible for us to meet at Western College for Women in the summer of 1964.

The importance of our work in the summer of 1964 was very clear. I knew most of the students who were there. We had sung and organized at most of the colleges where the volunteers came from. I felt responsible because of the role I played in the students' being there. Chuck and Cordell had gotten there early and had helped in giving the students nonviolent defense training. Chuck, Cordell, and I had trained many students. Those students needed all the support, training, and confidence they could get. We heard that Andrew Goodman, Mickey Schwerner, and James Chaney were missing, and I got scared. I sat under a tree where we had been training students and wished they would go back home. *The white folks down in Mississippi will knock you on your rump and if you holler freedom you'll wind up in the swamp.* ("Oginga") I watched the buses as they pulled off and thought, "Please go home." Bob Moses was inside making everything clear to the students. He was always good at making things clear. Bob had a way of enveloping you with a few words and an eloquent silence.

The infusion of black and white students from the north and the lack of time to adequately train them weakened the concepts of nonviolence, and we became more defense minded. Self-defense became the major topic. Nonviolence was no longer discussed seriously. It was

looked on with disdain, and its exponents thought of as stupid. Jim Bevel, in particular, tried to shock people into understanding the power of nonviolence, but his efforts did not work. They were too extreme for most people. However, I always knew what points Bevel was trying to make. John Lewis was never understood. His sense of nonviolence was so developed that his thoughts were always either misinterpreted or misunderstood. We had lost the power that made us unique and there was no way to regain it. Bevel and I would sometimes talk for hours about what actions could remedy the problem. I told him to forget about it, because the moral force needed to correct the situation was long gone.

Voter registration was the order of the day. Lawyers and Marxist writers of every persuasion had taken over the philosophical development of SNCC. The Southern student was sent back to the cotton fields from whence he came. The SNCC veterans who counted were position paper writers and rhetoricians who met for hours on end to spout their individual versions of which philosophical direction SNCC should take.

Some of this "intellectual masturbation" was good for us. We began to read works of Franz Fanon, Marx, Mao, Lenin, and with their help researched the course of people's revolutions. We connected our struggle to other struggles for liberation around the world. But we had lost something we had in the beginning—fearlessness and a sense of a personal power to change things.

We began to look to other people to guide us. This new-found knowledge affected everything we did. On December 21, 1963, Oginga Odinga, a Kenyan diplomat came to Atlanta on a State Department tour. We did not know him personally, but we did know that he was a black man important enough to be on a State Department tour. Several of us went to the Peachtree Manor, a hotel in which Mr. Odinga was staying. We brought him some SNCC pamphlets and other literature. Members of SNCC decided to buy stock in a restaurant named the Toddle

House to show Oginga Odinga that in America they would arrest black people trying to eat in a restaurant where they owned stock.

We were arrested. SNCC workers continued to demonstrate. I was thrown into solitary confinement. I had found, through experience, that solitary was the best place for me. I wrote "Oginga Odinga" in this cell:

OGINGA ODINGA

We went down to the Peachtree Manor
To see Oginga Odinga
The police said, "What's the matter?"
See Oginga Odinga
The police he looked mighty hard
At Oginga Odinga
He got scared 'cause he was an ex-Mau Mau
To see Oginga Odinga
Oginga Odinga, Oginga Odinga,
Oginga Odinga of Kenya, Who?
Oginga Odinga, Oginga Odinga
Oginga Odinga of Kenya
Uhuru Ha! Uhur Ha!
Freedom Now Ha!
Freedom Now Ha!
Oginga said, "look-a-here,
What's going on down in Selma?
If you white folks don't straighten up,
I'm, gonna call Jomo Kenyatta"
Oginga Odinga, Oginga Odinga,
Oginga Odinga of Kenya, Who?
Oginga Odinga, Oginga Odinga
Oginga Odinga of Kenya
Uhuru Ha! Uhur Ha!
Freedom Now Ha!
Freedom Now Ha!
The white folks down in Mississippi
Will knock yo' on your rump
And if you holler freedom,
You'll wind up in the swamp
Oginga Odinga, Oginga Odinga,
Oginga Odinga of Kenya, Who?
Oginga Odinga, Oginga Odinga
Oginga Odinga of Kenya
Uhuru Ha!
Uhur Ha!

Freedom Now Ha!
Freedom Now Ha!
© 1993 Wisdom Train [ASCAP]
© 1963, 1993 Matthew Jones [ASCAP]

On December 20, 1964, we saw Malcolm X at a church in Harlem. We were touring northern cities to gain support for the Mississippi Freedom Democratic Party. Mrs. Hamer spoke. We sang. Malcolm X was sitting on the dais looking through his notes. When we sang "Oginga Odinga," Malcolm X stopped looking at his notes and looked at us. He seemed startled, as if he couldn't believe his ears. When he spoke he said, "I couldn't help but be very impressed at the outstart when the Freedom Singers were singing the song, 'Oginga Odinga,' because Oginga is one of the foremost freedom fighters on the African continent. . . . The fact that you are singing about him is quite significant." After the church service, he took us to the Audubon Ballroom, where his organization had a program each Sunday. It was exciting. I was surprised at Malcolm's response to us, and it made me feel significant. The complete speech can be found in *Malcolm X Speaks: Selected Speeches and Statements* by Grove Press.

On July 4, 1964, Forman walked into the SNCC office on Raymond Street and said, "George Wallace is having a political rally today, and some of you should go." Forman was a brilliant organizer, and I had made it a habit to at least listen to him. Thirteen of us got in a van and went to the Lakewood Stadium. I remember getting out of the van with Chuck Neblett, Wilson Brown, Karen Haberman, and James Peacock. We left Marshall and others in the van as lookouts. When we got inside the stadium, we knew we were in trouble. This was not just a political rally. It was a meeting of the heads of the White Citizens Council and the Ku Klux Klan. We looked for a way out. There was none. We were caught between ten thousand red-necked racists and an eight-foot fence. The action against us started when a white lady screamed and threw a Coke on us. Men began to stand with metal chairs in their hands and emit an indescribable sound that sounded like a death yell. They began to hit us with chairs. Chuck, Wilson Brown, and myself were beaten while the people chanted, "Kill the niggers, kill the niggers." This experience changed my way of thinking. I had finally been convinced that some white people were devils and beyond help. But it took a possible subdural hematoma for me to be convinced. Chuck, Wilson, and I all had head injuries.

I have talked about this incident many times, but I find it difficult to write about. I remember the whites closing in behind me. I remember Chuck climbing that fence trying to get out and being knocked down by chairs. I remember Wilson Brown holding on to a policeman and racists hitting him with chairs. The racists were so incensed that they beat the policeman while trying to hit Wilson. I remember being knocked to the ground and an eighty-year-old man getting on the ground. I thought he was going to help me, but he began to hit me, hollering, "Nigger! Nigger!"

The policeman guarding me turned his back so that the mob could finish me. An Asian photographer took a picture of me on the ground and the policeman standing up. He kept alternating first taking a picture of the policeman, then me. The policeman saw this and immediately began to protect me. I have always wanted to thank that photographer. He saved my life!

We were taken out of the stadium over an eight-foot fence, placed in a police van, and driven to the hospital. We consoled each other not knowing of our condition. Being July 4, many accident victims were at the hospital. Everywhere I looked there were black people bleeding from holiday activities. I needed fifteen stitches in my head. I became very frightened because I knew a redneck cracker was going to perform surgery on my head. When I went into his office I said, "Doc, my wife hit me in the head with a frying pan."

The doctor said in his Southern drawl, "I know why you are here and by God I agree with you." I would never again make assumptions

about a person's character based on a stereotype.

This experience with the KKK brought me closer to the philosophy of Malcolm X. The Freedom Singers began to sing "A White Man's Heaven Is A Black Man's Hell," written by Louis X, later to be named Louis Farahkhan. Farahkhan was a calypso singer in his youth. The Freedom Singers had both extremes, from the most militant to the most nonviolent.

I walked around Atlanta waiting for my skull to heal. I would walk from the SNCC office on Raymond Street to where I lived as if by radar. As I walked, my life would pass before me. I began to relive the trauma of the many nonviolent wars of which I had been a part. If I was in a restaurant and an unfamiliar white person walked near me, I would immediately go into a nonviolent defense posture. I was suffering from what they call today post-traumatic stress syndrome. There should have been studies done analyzing the effects of the Civil Rights Movement on its participants.

I still remained noviolent but my approach changed. I now believe that a highly evolved nonviolent practitioner should be able to control his environment in such a way that violence does not happen unless he wants it to happen. If violence happens in your presence and you are involved in it, you are participating in violence. It does not matter whether you threw the blow or not. You were there to receive the blow. How do you so confuse an opponent that he forgets his aggression, redirects it, turns it inward, or transforms it into a positive energy?

I was arrested twenty-nine times and do not regret a single arrest. It made me strong. I am sick and tired of being sick and tired. I will not allow anybody to violate my body or my mind in any shape, form or fashion. If they do they will have to deal with me immediately. Freedom! Freedom! Freedom!

When Arthur and Carolyn Reese, two young black teachers, arrived at the Oxford, Ohio, orientation, they didn't know how they were going to be used. According to Carolyn, Staughton Lynd decided that they would run a freedom school in Hattiesburg, Mississippi. The philosophy of that school was a mixture of Arthur Reese's "Africentric" ideas and Charlie Cobb's ideas of keeping youth off the streets. Africentric is a term coined by Arthur Reese to symbolize the most ancient of African thought and behavior. These two teachers were dedicated to the education of black youth. The theme of their school was "Freedom is a Constant Struggle." They took the slogan to the Meridian Freedom Conference held at the funeral for James Chaney. The other schools began to use the slogan as well. According to Carolyn, she and Arthur made the freedom schools Africentric.

I first heard the song, "Freedom is a Constant Struggle," in 1963. The Freedom Singers began to sing it in early 1964. The final version was the result of the Freedom Singers concertizing the version that had been sung by Sam Block and Willie Peacock in 1963. Guy Carawan gives the Freedom Singers the credit for its copyright in the 1968 printing of the song book, Freedom is a Constant Struggle. However, when Guy printed a combination of his classic, "We Shall Overcome" (1963), and a later classic, "Freedom Is A Constant Struggle" (1968), under the name "Sing For Freedom" (1990), another person is credited with the copyright. At the Freedom Summer orientation in Oxford, Ohio, after Bob Moses spoke about Goodman, Schwerner, and Chaney being missing, Jean Wheeler began to sing "Freedom is a Constant Struggle", a song already well known by the Freedom Singers.

I always felt that the Freedom Singers should sing all the songs of the Movement as well as songs written by people outside the Movement. One of the most important songs that I collected was "Hartman Turnbow." This song was brought to me by its author, Mike Killen, an actor. In 1964, Mike Killen came to a concert we were giving at the Ash Grove in Los Angeles. After the concert he approached me with this song. I was thrilled because it was about a Tchula, Mississippi, black man named Hartman Turnbow, who was not exactly nonviolent and was a member of the Mississippi Freedom Democratic Party. I arranged it, and it became one of our favorite songs:

HARTMAN TURNBOW

My name is Hartman Turnbow, and I belong to me
I live in Mississippi down in Holmes County
There're bullet holes in my front door,
They've set my house on fire.
But I'm gonna vote this fall,
Because it's freedom I desire
Last spring I went to register
To cast my one man's vote
They called me "boy" said, Tip your hat
But they didn't get my goat, then come the very next morning
when the clock was striking three
I heard this noise, I saw this fire
I knew they'd come for me
My name is Hartman Turnbow, and I belong to me
I live in Mississippi down in Holmes County
There're bullet holes in my front door,
They've set my house on fire
But I'm gonna vote this fall,
Because it's freedom I desire
Now down in Delta County, we got no running water
So the Mrs. filled some buckets
and passed them to my daughter
While I greeted my guests with buckshot
'Til the four of them drove away
Then I went to see the sheriff
As soon as it was day
My name is Hartman Turnbow, and I belong to me
I live in Mississippi down in Holmes County
There're bullet holes in my front door,
They've set my house on fire.
But I'm gonna vote this fall,
Because it's freedom I desire
I told him how it happened
He said, "Boy you're a liar"
He said I, Hartman Turnbow
had set my own house on fire
He threw me in the jail house

But he had to set me free
'Cause there's a law in this here country
And that law means liberty
My name is Hartman Turnbow, and I belong
to me
I live in Mississippi down in Holmes County
There're bullet holes in my front door,
They've set my house on fire.
But I'm gonna vote this fall,
Because it's freedom I desire
      © 1964 Mike Killen, arranged by
      Matthew Jones, Freedom Singers

Women in the Civil Rights Movement, by and large, did not get a chance to develop their potential. I did not realize the depth of ability of the women in the Movement until the '70s. It has been said that if you want to get something done, call a woman. When you want to ask a question, call a man. This axiom is true. If you want something done, call a woman. Call Dorothy Dewberry. Call Dottie Zellner. Call Gloria Richardson. Call Dinky Romily. Call Carolyn Goodman. Call Martha Norman. Call Ruth Howard Chambers. These are brilliant women, capable of moving mountains. There are many women that need to be appreciated but space will not permit it.

Dorothy Dewberry Aldridge remains a SNCC worker today. During the '70s she taught the history of the Movement to the youth of Detroit by having me come to Detroit and sing freedom songs and talk about my experiences. She used her vast knowledge of Movement sites, like Lowndes County, to set up networks between Lowndes County, Montgomery, and Selma in Alabama; Albany and Atlanta in Georgia; Memphis, Tennessee; Little Rock, Arkansas; Jackson, Ruleville, Money and Philadelphia, Mississippi. Dewberry would arrange for hundreds of students to travel the roads of SNCC field secretaries and get a feeling of the Movement by visiting the grave sites or memorials for Viola Liuzzo, Jimmie Lee Jackson, Martin Luther King, Fannie Lou Hamer, Emmett Till, Medgar Evers and many more. I accompanied her on most of those trips. I liked those trips because it gave the students the opportunity to meet Movement heroes from different states. We made sure that they understood the Movement from different perspectives.

I rejoiced when the students met Bob Mants, Charles Sherrod, Ruthie Harris, Emory Harris, John Lewis, Hollis Watkins, and Wazir "Willie" Peacock. Dorothy and I shared the feeling that the students needed to meet some of the people who, by their blood, had made the students' lives easier. She made it possible for the Michigan Coalition for Human Rights and the University of Toledo to send students into Mississippi and the rest of the South. The students were then able to learn about the history of the Movement and to see first-hand what had been done and what needed to be done.

I worked night and day with Ruth Howard Chambers and Martha Prescod Norman to free Curtis Hayes, a SNCC worker from McComb, Mississippi, from a Liberian jail. I enjoyed working with them. They were dedicated to the task of freeing Curtis. Without their work he would not have been freed.

Dottie Zellner, Dinky Romily, and Gloria Richardson are always involved in the celebration of many Movement ideas and principles. The most important activity in which they participate, in my view, is being actively concerned about our leader and teacher, Jim Forman. They have been a great support to me.

Without the leadership of Carolyn Goodman, I don't think we would know the names Goodman, Schwerner, and Chaney today. Carolyn's ideas and commitment to keep the names of these three young men in the public eye has made all of our lives more productive. She works for us all. I wonder what it would have been like to work under the leadership of any of the above women in the '60s.

In 1972, I took my first lessons in boxing. Those experiences helped me understand nonviolence. Gandhi said that nonviolence in the hands of the weak turns into passive resistance and in the hands of the strong it turns into love. One day an opponent was throwing punches at me. I was always good at defense. I relaxed in my defense and it seemed that his punches were moving in slow motion. I knew what he was going to do before he did it. I was amazed that I was able to stay out of harm's way by being relaxed and fearless. I had a relaxed, alert, firm, concentrated, and loving attention to all that surrounded me. I began to spar regularly. I could box men who were a lot younger and stronger. I learned to take their aggression away from them. The only way to remove aggression is with humility and love. I have found that the greatest boxers are the most humble. Gandhi was right. There is power in being humble, forgiving, loving, and uncompromising in the face of injustice.

I am still boxing and training boxers in 1997. I am still writing freedom songs, singing freedom songs, running the Open House Coffee House, where people learn to write freedom songs. I never stopped. During the '60s—SNCC. During the '70s—the Hey Brother Coffee House with Rev. Fred Kirkpatrick. During the '80s—freeing the Birmingham Six in England; Sierra Leone in West Africa; fighting Siaka Stevens, a true dictator, and having freedom songs delivered to his desk in Freetown; going to Belfast, working with Bernadette Devlin. I am a Freedom Fighter. I know nothing else.

I am happy to be involved in this project and to lend my song "Ballad of Medgar Evers" (1963), and to be involved in helping my friend Bob Cohen with "Shadows on the Light." I heard from Susie Erenrich that Bob had written an article for the anthology and that Bob, because of his incarceration, could not complete "Shadows on the Light." I decided that if Bob wanted me to, I would complete the song. I contacted Bob's former wife, Susie, who contacted Bob and forwarded his OK. It was a great experience. Bob was a member of a caravan of folksingers that sang in Mississippi during the Freedom Summer. I think it is one of the most important songs in the collection.

This project has been a positive force in my life. It has been a positive force in my brother Marshall's life. His song "In The Mississippi River" is such an important contribution to the Movement. I want to thank my wife, Shelly, for all her love and support. Every man needs a good woman. Thank God for Shelly. I want to acknowledge my three sons, Matthew, Gerald, and Ellis. Through this article they will learn more about their father.

I am very happy that after thirty years Byron de la Beckwith, the murderer of Medgar Evers, has finally been convicted. Justice has rolled down like waters from a mighty stream.

BALLAD OF MEDGAR EVERS

In Jackson Mississippi in 1963
There lived a man who was brave
He fought for Freedom all of his life
But they laid Medgar Evers in his grave
They laid Medgar Evers in his grave
They laid Medgar Evers in his grave
He fought for freedom all of his life
But they laid Medgar Evers in his grave
He spoke words of truth for all men to hear
Black and white alike for to save
Then a hate-filled white man named Byron de la Beckwith
Laid Medgar Evers in his grave
He taught words of love, dignity, and freedom
He'd die before he would be a slave
Then a high-powered rifle tore out his heart
And laid Medgar Evers in his grave
And laid Medgar Evers in his grave
And laid Medgar Evers in his grave
Then a high-powered rifle tore out his heart
And laid Medgar Evers in his grave
Medgar had some company in his heavenly home
Those three children from Birmingham
Like Christ they died for you and for me
They died for you to be free
They died for you to be free
They died for you to be free
Like Christ they died for you and for me
They died for you to be free

© 1963, 1993 Matthew Jones [ASCAP]
© 1993 Wisdom Train [ASCAP]

Over the years, whenever an ex-SNCC worker made a historical achievement or made a mistake, I felt like it was I who had the achievement or made the mistake. In conclusion here's a song that I wrote in 1986 in tribute to all my brothers and sisters in SNCC who gave of themselves in a struggle for a better world.

WE MUST RISE AGAIN

My life has come and gone
And new life is a-dawning
But I can't take no rest
Until I see the morning
I know that I must come again
If we are going to win
I don't see how we can take a rest
Until we pass the test
You can't count us out
You think that you have bought us
Now don't forget our pass
There is a lot our past has taught us
I know that I must come again
If we are gonna' win
I don't see how we can take a rest
Until We pass the test
If you're feeling kind of low, brother, sister
Here is one thing that I know, brother, sister
Together we defeated the army of the Klan
We can do the same today, I hope you understand
I know that we will rise again
A new day is dawning, we see the morning
We will see the morning

Together we will rise we will see the evil crumble
So tell us no more lies
Or you will take a tumble
I know that we must come again
If we are gonna win
I don't see how we can take a rest
Until we pass the test
We will breathe new life
We will see the light a-dawning
We will take no rest
Until we see the morning
If you're feeling kind of scared, brother, sister
Don't close the eye inside, brother, sister
Our children don't know the truth
They are watching the video
But if we rise again
They will surely knowI know that we will rise again
A new day is dawning We will see the morning

© 1986 Matthew Jones (ASCAP)
© 1994 Wisdom Train

We will rise again in the work of Bob Moses, John Lewis, Carolyn Goodman, and many more. Transform yourself. Rise again!!

I am a freedom fighter. I am all oppressed people rolled into one. I am African, Native American, Jew, Palestinian, Irish—all rolled into one. We all should be. Freedom! Freedom! Freedom! ❖

MARSHALL R. JONES SR.

1938–

In the Mississippi River

A member of the SNCC Freedom Singers from the
latter part of 1963 to the latter part of 1965.

Prior to the Freedom Singers, I attended the University of Tennessee and was active in the civil rights struggle there. I was a part of the Students for Equal Treatment, a student group organized at the university headed by a chemistry student from Memphis, Tennessee, Marion Barry. This was a growing Civil Rights Movement both on campus and in the downtown area of Knoxville. I was arrested twice, once marching towards the downtown area with other marchers in the vicinity of the Knoxville Civic Center. The second time, I was again arrested with a group protesting the racial segregation in a downtown cinema.

My brother Matthew at this time was very actively involved in the Movement in Danville, Virginia. Avon Rollins, a friend and a neighbor, headed this Danville movement. Avon and Matt would go back and forth from Danville to Knoxville, being involved in both struggles.

I heard that Matt was playing a major role in this vicious movement in Danville and was spending time in solitary confinement. I, along with some other members of the Students for Equal Treatment, felt it necessary to pay Danville a visit due to our concern for Matt's welfare.

A racially mixed group, we arrived in Danville on the heels of one of the most brutal demonstrations of police brutality imaginable. People were severely injured by the police, many people were hurled down the streets and gulleys,

hit by the power of the fire hoses. The water was so powerful that it injured people upon contact with the water. Dan River Mills, a textile factory, was the focus of the civil unrest.

We arrived in Danville in one private car belonging to Stephen Wagner and his wife, a white couple also attending the University of Tennessee. We were stopped by the city police after we drove past Dan River Mills and arrived in the vicinity where Matt was supposed to be. The police officer began to question Steven, who was the driver of the car.

The officer asked us to get out of the car. Steven moved his arm to the door to get out but was interrupted by Matt, appearing out of nowhere, who stated that the police officer had no right to ask us to get out of the car because we had not committed any crime and that the police officer should be ashamed of himself; then he told us to stay in the car. I thought at this moment we surely would be shot or lynched.

The police officer must have been totally thrown off balance at Matt's complete disregard for his own safety. He told us that we had better leave town if we knew what was good for us. Matthew encouraged us to go ahead and leave, that he would be alright. So we did. We returned to Knoxville and to our academic endeavors. We did not hear from Matthew for at least a month, but his whereabouts were closely monitored by the SNCC office in Atlanta.

Marshall Jones was involved in the Civil Rights Movement in Knoxville while studying at the University of Tennessee. His brother Matthew encouraged him to join the SNCC Freedom Singers in 1963 to work full-time against social injustice and inequality. Marshall composed "In The Mississippi River" to pay tribute to Goodman, Schwerner and Chaney and all of the others who were killed in the struggle.

I was at this time fully committed to a career in opera. I was only thinking of the Metropolitan Opera and New York City. My voice teacher at the university was Edward Zambara. He believed that after a year of voice lessons and coaching, I would have a very good chance of ending up on the Metropolitan Opera stage.

I mention the above mainly to dramatize the seriousness of my operatic endeavor. Approximately one month into my preparation, my brother called me from Atlanta and stated: "Hey man, you need to come to Atlanta right away. The Movement needs you!" I thought at first that he was joking because he knew that I was studying for the opera. I reminded him of this and he responded without a pause, "But the Movement needs you more." Well, to make a long story short, within a couple of days I was standing in the SNCC office along with my brother and Jim Forman, the executive director of SNCC. Only one week earlier he had summoned Matt to Atlanta, away from the movement in Danville. Matt brought many songs written while he was in jail. Jim Forman appointed him the leader of the group which was called The Freedom Singers. The previous group remained on the road for approximately three months and did a considerable amount of traveling and singing for such a short period of time. Because of internal problems in the quartet, made up of two males and two females, it came off the road and was not able to return—thus the recruitment of my brother out of Danville, and the recruitment of yours truly out of Knoxville and the University of Tennessee. One member of the first group, Chuck Neblett, joined us. The three of us became the total nucleus of what came to be known as the "second group." The three of us are featured in the first selection on the B side of the album, *The Freedom Singers Sing of Freedom Now*, on the Mercury label.

We visited the field offices of SNCC in the South, participated in demonstrations, carried songs and messages to the back dark roads in this racially charged land. By the time this group was ready to strike out for the West, North, East,

Canada, and Nova Scotia, three members would be added—one gentleman from Mississippi, James Peacock; a gentleman from Albany, Georgia, Emory Harris; and Rafael Bentham, a student at Morehouse College from Venezula. These gentlemen joined the group at different times within its traveling life. Bill Perlman, a singer/guitarist, Chico Neblett, the brother of Chuck, and another from the previous group, Cordell Reagon, who was in and out for one reason or another, contributed to the final tour of the Freedom Singers. Bill Perlman became an integral part of the final sound and musical character of this group. Songwriting had become the thing of the day which began very early in the game before Bill came on board but solidified itself with the very timely mastering of concert material. Bill's presence gave Matt more time to focus on harmony and arrangements.

The fact that this group, unlike the previous one, wrote and arranged its own songs, but also sang the songs written and performed by other folksingers and popular groups did not sit well with many in the folk world. Due to petty jealousies, a previous member of the Freedom Singers preceded us on our road trips, telling our concert organizers that we could not sing. Even though he later returned to the group, the negativity generated at that time followed the group's history into the 1990s.

The efforts to quiet this group, mainly by some members of the previous one, were short lived because our presence was felt throughout the folk world. Recordings of past concerts, which still continue to surface, reveal the true artistry that was indeed evident. Many famous groups that were born during this time and afterwards share many similarities to this group of the Freedom Singers.

After our initial Southern tour, we returned to Atlanta. We lived together so that we could rehearse everyday. Sometimes we would go to the SNCC office to try our songs out on the office staff and always got rave reviews from them.

The Freedom Singers started out on our

North Eastern tour of the U.S., arranged by the SNCC office, with many small groups called the "Friends of SNCC," who would coordinate the concert or activity in their particular city. Our mode of travel was a small Buick station wagon used by the previous group. We parted company with the car on a snow and ice-covered road somewhere in Pennsylvania. It was a miracle that no one was injured. We all walked away from the faulty Buick and caught a bus back to the SNCC office on 15th Street and Broadway in New York City.

A larger and more up-to-date Ford station wagon was purchased. Within a couple of weeks, we were on the road again.

There were always at least three drivers in the group so this new vehicle kept on the move as the drivers took turns at the wheel. We were then traveling constantly without any let up, from city to city, from state to state.

Early in the year of 1964 Mildred Forman, the wife of Jim Forman, contacted the famous comedian, Dick Gregory. He gladly gave of his time, audience, stage, and money to the Civil Rights Movement as he and the Freedom Singers appeared in concert hall after concert hall, all over the country, dramatizing and spreading the message of the Movement. "Thank you, Dick Gregory."

Other singers and celebrities who shared their experiences with the Freedom Singers were, to name a few, Buffy Sainte-Marie, Nina Simone, Leon Bibb, Carmen McRay, Joan Baez, Gwendolyn Brooks, Pete Seeger, Lena Horne, Odetta, and, without a doubt, Harry Belafonte.

In the beginning of the summer of 1964, news was spreading over the country that three civil rights workers were missing. When the news mentioned that the rivers of Mississippi were being dragged, it was a collective speculation that numerous bodies may be pulled out. Rather than let the dragging continue, the police officials drew the focus from the rivers, where they had already found several unidentified bodies. They indicated that, for some reason, the bodies of the three were not in the rivers but somewhere else. Hearing that, my mind went back to when I was a child and a teenager.

The fear, the lynchings, the hangings, the selective killings of blacks by white racists, Emmett Till and many others whose existence upon this earth ended without opposition for fear that a whole family might be slaughtered— all seemed to indicate this way of life would hold to its most murderous path. As I returned from my reflections, I realized that we had paid the supreme price in the loss of these courageous and heroic three—Michael Schwerner, James Chaney, and Andrew Goodman. What was most apparent was that the senseless disregard for human life was not only prescribed for the blacks of the South, but also for anyone who questioned or tampered with continuation of this total victimization of one group upon another. In the midst of my anger and feelings of helplessness, I wrote "In the Mississippi River" within an hour's time. I attempted to say as much as I possibly could without being too wordy.

I must make reference to the ending of "In the Mississippi River," the line that reads: Well, you can count them. It tells us that you can still count them because there were many who found their graves in the rivers. This is a song of struggle, a song of grief, a song of declaration, and a song with a promise to "stop them from going in the river."

In The Mississippi River

Words and music by Marshall Jones

In the Mississippi River
Lord, Lord, Lord, Lord
In the Mississippi River
Lord, Lord, Lord
In the Mississippi River
Well, you can count them one by one
It could be your son
Well, you can count them two by two
It could be me or you
Well, you can count them three by three
Do you wanna see?
Well, you can count them four by four
Oh, well—a into the river they go

Oh, well—a into the river they go
Well, you can count them five by five
with their hands tied
And they don't come out alive
And their feet tied
And you can count them six by six
Holes throughout the body
In Mississippi, they got it fixed
Like Goodman
And you can count them seven by seven
Like Schwerner
The Mississippi River sure ain't heaven
And Chaney
And you can count—a them eight by eight
Ummm—the people
And we are thrown there because of hate
Yes, like you and me
And you can count them nine by nine
In the Tallahatchie River
In Mississippi this ain't no crime
You can count—a them ten by ten
And we wonder when the right will win

In the Mississippi River
Lord, Lord, Lord, Lord
In the Mississippi River
Lord, Lord, Lord, Lord
In the Mississippi River
Yeah, Yeah, Yeah
We gonna stop them from going in
We gonna stop them from going in
We gonna stop them from going in
With their heads cut off
We're gonna stop them from going in
We're gonna stop them from going in
Tied by the feet
In the Mississippi River
Lord, Lord, Lord
In the Mississippi River
Lord, Lord, Lord, Lord
In the Mississippi River
Yeah, Yeah
Well, you can count them
Well, you can count them
In the Mississippi River

❖

BOB COHEN

Sorrow Songs, Faith Songs, Freedom Songs: The Mississippi Caravan of Music in the Summer of '64

Through all the sorrow of the Sorrow Songs there breathes a hope—a faith in the ultimate justice of things. . . . Is such a hope justified? Do the Sorrow Songs sing true?

The result is still distinctively Negro and the method of blending original, but the elements are both Negro and Caucasian.

. . . When, struck with a sudden poverty, the United States refused to fulfill its promises of land to the freedmen, a brigadier-general went down to the Sea Islands to carry the news. An old woman on the outskirts of the throng began singing this song [Nobody Knows The Trouble I've Seen]; all the mass joined with her, swaying. And the soldier wept.

W. E. B. DUBOIS
The Souls of Black Folk

We sat in the hot humid auditorium in the Oxford State College for Women, Oxford, Ohio. Robert Parris Moses, Bob to all of us and my former roommate, stood in front of us and said: "They are dead, they have been murdered." For a couple of days we had heard rumors that Mickey Schwerner, James Chaney, and Andy Goodman were missing. They had gone to Philadelphia, Mississippi, to investigate a church burning and reported violence to civil rights workers there. We were the second wave of northern volunteers in the Mississippi Freedom Summer of 1964. We had learned how to curl up in the fetal position and take the batons of

cops, as well as how to ignore the verbal abuse. We had held hands and swayed as we sang "We Shall Overcome," and we had seen a weary, red-eyed, very thin Rita Schwerner walking around the campus. The newspapers reported the mysterious disappearance of the three civil rights workers—two of whom had trained in the very rooms we trained in and sat in the seats we were sitting in and sang the songs we were singing. But for Bob Moses there was no mystery. He knew from three previous years' experience in the labyrinth of that tropical state that the three had been killed. And in his soft, almost disappearing voice and with his large brown eyes, he

Bob Cohen was born in 1939. He belonged, along with Gil Turner, Delores Dixon, and Happy Traum, to the New World Singers. They sang in the '60s raising funds for SNCC and were the first to record "Blowin' In The Wind" (Broadside Records), having helped give birth to this song when Bob Dylan, listening to them singing the old civil war freedom song; "No More Auction Block For Me," borrowed part of the tune for his song. The New World Singers also recorded an album for Atlantic Records for which Dylan wrote the liner notes. Bob taught folk music in private schools and the Bank Street College of Education. He then made some bad choices in his life and wound up spending three years in a New York State Prison for Medicaid Billing Fraud. He took it as a challenge and, while incarcerated, wrote over 70 faithsongs, including "Shadows On The Light." He is currently out on work release and has already appeared at Caffe Lena and other coffee houses. His latest song, "The '90s Are The '60s Turned Upside Down" says: "I still believe we can change the world/ with acts of love/not hatred hurled."

177

assured us that is what had happened, even though there was no clue as to what had happened. Then he said we should all think long and hard about what we were getting into. I remembered what my high school classmate Steve Max, son of *Daily Worker* satirist Alan Max, had said to me when I told him where Susan and I were going. "Oh," he said, puffing on his pipe and speaking out of the side of his mouth, "so you're going to be cannon fodder for the Movement." As Susan was pregnant with our first born, I did not find his observation amusing but attributed it to his rather taciturn nature. Now I sat sweating with fear, the taste of spaghetti sauce in my throat, wondering what others around us were thinking, were feeling. There was silence, not even a murmur from the two hundred or so people, trainees in nonviolence. Then suddenly, from way back in the large college auditorium, came a woman's rich alto voice singing slow and mournful a true song of sorrow:

> *They say that freedom is a constant struggle*
> *They say that freedom is a constant struggle*
> *They say that freedom is a constant struggle*
> *Oh Lord, we've struggled so long*
> *We must be free, we must be free.*

Some of us craned our necks, looking backwards, to see who it was, but the auditorium was packed. The minor-mode melody and the slowness of its tempo entered our viscera, and we all started to sing with an almost detached, floating, goading voice. The form made it easy to catch on to—a line repeated three times and then a prayerful fourth line. She sang more verses by only changing one word. Pete Seeger used to call this a "zipper" type song: ". . . a constant walking . . . a constant talking . . . a constant weeping . . . a constant singing." By the end of the meeting no one had turned back. We were determined to go down to the "red clay country."

A year earlier Bob Moses had put on my Odetta record and played the song she sang, "I'm Going Back to the Red Clay Country," over and over again. There was Odetta, a middle-class

California black woman studying to be an opera singer turning to folk music, and here was Bob, a middle class black man, Harvard graduate, Bible-thumping fundamentalist in the middle of Harvard Yard, turned into a Camus-reading (in the original French) existentialist, turned into one of the leaders of the Student Nonviolent Coordinating Committee, planning to turn Mississippi upside down. Bob and I shared a delight and an enthusiasm for the variety and aliveness of all cultures, as particularly experienced through their music. I had met Bob at a folk dance camp in Maine run by the politically conservative aficionados of folk dance. The campers were a strange mixture of young folkies, older WASPs, anti-communist emigres from eastern Europe, and other unusual suspects sharing in common a love of English contra-dances and Yugoslavian circle dances with much the same passion as many young people were to bring to rock music, still only on the horizon. Bob was the only black person in the camp but felt comfortable as he bent the knee or kicked out or followed the myriad patterns of the caller or instructor. We felt in those days, and I still do now, that the ingesting of other people's cultures strengthened rather than weakened one's own, causing one to define that which was universal and that which was special, feeling less isolated and more in communication with the rest of humanity.

I was planning to move out of my parent's home and, being an only lonely child, was looking around for a community of kindred souls to set up house with in New York City. We were joined by the son of probably the only Jewish psychiatrist in Grand Rapids, Michigan, at the outer fringes of the Diaspora, and a young lady folk dancer who hailed from Connecticut. We took a railroad flat on the upper West Side, which later turned into an R & R pad for the veterans of Mississippi and other points south—including Julius Lester, Charles McDew and many others passing through—some staying a night, some staying for months. By the summer of '63 we were joined by my soon-to-be-wife,

Susan Beecher. She is a descendent of "the little lady who started the Civil War" (according to Abe Lincoln), Harriet Beecher Stowe (author of *Uncle Tom's Cabin*), and Julia Ward Howe, who wrote "Mine Eyes Have Seen the Glory of the Coming of the Lord" out of her abolitionist and religious beliefs (and which song I sang as I stood isolated in my own prison cell some thirty years later).

Susan just recently sent me some of her remembrances of Mississippi in the summer of '64. Susan and I worked together giving an informal orientation to the musicians who "came down"; and while I was driving them around the State of Mississippi, she was helping to run the COFO office (Council of Federated Organizations) in Jackson, the state capitol. I have taken the liberty of arranging the shards of memory (Susan is a professional and wonderful artist of pottery) into poetic form because that's how I hear her clear, bell-like voice across these thirty years.

Remembrances of Mississippi

Let me just run some stream of consciousness
by you
Mississippi
Just that word can still run shivers through me
truly another country
when we were there I really felt that we were
not
in the USA
I, too, remember the singing of "Freedom is a
Constant Struggle"
after we heard the news of the three missing
when we were still in Oxford
I remember
the piercing sadness in my heart
realizing they were dead
sadness turning to rage
as we read and clipped the newspapers
page after page
"incident"
"the so-called missing civil rights workers . . ."
I remember
the blinding heat

wondering how the blacks survived at all
working in the fields in that heat
day after day
the love the local blacks gave us
and the acceptance
despite the fear and the consequences to their
lives
that befriending us could bring
I remember
traveling to McComb
shortly after a terrible bombing
sitting and talking with the local black civil rights
workers
how young they were
the black girls
shyly asked me
if they could touch my hair
as they had never touched the hair of a white
woman
and they talked about their feelings
(negative)
about their own hair
and I tried to tell them that their hair
was just as lovely as my own
and how I felt my own hair was stringy and flat
and we laughed
I remember
day after day the news
would come into the COFO office
over the phones we were handling
our lifelines
to each other
how important those phones were
for safety
for keeping track of each other
the news would invariably be
of other beatings
bombings
feeling incredulous that this was happening
I remember
a young man coming into the office
the dazed confused look in his young blue eyes
we tried our best to sooth him
clean the blood from his face
and ears
I remember

getting into our old red Chevy
thinking that all the racists in Mississippi
knew this car
and what they would do
The best remembrances are of the music
little wooden churches
literally rocking
with the force of huge round sounds
of the freedom songs
ringing in our throats
singing until we could sing no more
singing because that was the only way
to sooth our troubled minds
the only way we could keep going
day after day
Fannie Lou Hamer
the force
this always brings tears to my eyes
And I remember
Bob Moses with the eyes of
deep understanding
deep pain

Our "Chevy convertible" was given to us free by my Dad's nephew, Marcus Aurelius Goldman (only recently did I read about what a wild and woolly emperor Marc was named after from the days of Rome). There was a back seat but no floor—in those days we didn't seem to need such luxuries. The old red Chevy had difficulty starting most of the time except, thank God, for the time Bob Moses and I went to meet Harry Belafonte and Sidney Poitier at the Jackson Airport. Belafonte and Poitier had come down (as had we all) to lend their moral (and in some cases, musical) support to the Movement. That night they were driving on to another town so we were just there to greet them. As we were leaving the airport, Bob and I saw some heavyset white men giving us that strange "what are these aliens doing here on the planet of Mississippi" look and heading toward us to find out, or worse. We quickened our step without breaking into a run. In my mind was the reliable reluctance of the little old red Chevy never to start at the turning of the key. I saw our own red blood mixing

with the chipped rusty red of the old sputtering auto. We got in the car, slammed the loosely hinged doors, just as the two or three good citizens were coming out of the airport doors. I turned the key with my shaking hand—and miracle of miracles—the old dear roared in response and off we drove into the threatening night.

A year earlier, 1963, we had headed down to Mississippi in a beat-up old Buick. We were Gil Turner and Delores Dixon of the original New World Singers, Bob Moses, and myself. We were headed for Edwards, Mississippi, to give a workshop about freedom songs. As the New World Singers, Gil, Delores, and I had been busy singing at fund raising activities for the Student Nonviolent Coordinating Committee (SNCC) on college campuses around New York City and its environs. We were regulars at Gerde's Folk City in NYC and used to bring up Bob Dylan on stage to join us in his songs. Every night we were on stage Delores (a black music teacher and singer) would do a stirring version of the post-Civil War freedom song, "No More Auction Block for Me—Many Thousand Gone". Dylan took a liking to her and the song she sang. Pretty soon he called us down to Gerde's rat-infested cellar to hear his "Blowin' in the Wind," which was based on the "Auction Block" tune. In those days Bob (like Woody Guthrie before him) based the tunes for his songs on folk tunes (many Irish folk songs, etc.). "Blowin'" along with "We Shall Overcome" and Gil Turner's "Carry It On" (written after the bombing of the black church in Birmingham, Alabama, resulting in the death of four young girls) became anthems of the Civil Rights Movement. Our group was the first to record "Blowin'" for Moses Asch on Broadside Records (on which Blind Boy Grunt, A.K.A. Dylan, appears along with Happy Traum, who was soon to join our group). We had all been eager participants and contributors to the topical song movement of which *Broadside* magazine was the organizing force. Many an afternoon was spent listening to Phil Ochs, Dylan, Tom Paxton and others sing their latest, ripped right out of that morning's headlines. With all our dedication to SNCC it was natural for us to say yes when Bob suggested we go down to give a workshop and "teach-back" the songs that had originally come from the Southern black culture—the songs of faith with the double entendre of freedom were now being put into use again as the Movement grew. Actually, knowing what I know now about faith, in the minds of the faithful there wasn't (and isn't) any real dichotomy between "Steal Away to Jesus" and steal away to freedom, except perhaps in the minds of their white masters or today's fundamentalist atheists (of which I used to be one, Oh God).

So there we were on the road to Edwards. Somewhere in Tennessee we stopped for some coffee and pie and got our first taste of Southern hospitality. (well, maybe not the first for Bob). After waiting a good fifteen minutes for what we ordered, a man, maybe the cook/owner, came out with a hatchet and told us to get our or . . . We beat a quick retreat, a bit shaken. I mentioned to Bob sometime later that as it was happening I did not feel personally threatened, almost removed from the actuality. He said he had experienced the same thing and that part of it was not living with this violence every day— sort of "observer" status that made these confrontations sometimes seem unreal, though scary.

Months before that, Gil and I had spent some weeks on John's Island off the coast of Charleston, South Carolina, at an early version of the folk festival. We joined Alan Lomax and Guy and Candie Carawan plus the residents of the island who, led by a lively and energetic Bessie Jones, celebrated their religious culture through songs, dances, and games. At the Moving Star Hall wooden church, we were literally rocked as the parishioners "shouted," which means they stamped one rhythm with their feet, clapped another with their hands, and sang a third with their voices. The effect of the polyrhythms, the shaking of the floorboards, and the air filled with sound was the very essence of faith

in a freedom unseparated from a devout belief in an almighty God.

Guy and Candie, along with Pete Seeger and others, had been a small force to revive and capture the essence of these "sorrow" spiritual, gospel songs and put them to work again as the backbone of the Civil Rights Movement. We had also spent some time around them at the Highlander School where, under the leadership of Myles Horton, much of the training of the original cadre of leaders and agitators had taken place. I remember standing in the Smoky Mountains of Tennessee with Myles and Sarah Reed* as she told us of the violent struggle of the miners in Harlan County. Then in her flat but expressive old lady's voice, she sang her composition written back in the 30s, "Which Side Are You On," based on the folk tune, "Oh the Lilies—O." As she sang, I noticed her husband make a sudden move toward the bushes. After she finished the song, he blandly mentioned that he had just killed a rattlesnake. I thought back to how I used to torture my father with the verse from that song: *Don't listen to the bosses/Don't listen to their lies.* He was a boss of a small furniture manufacturing firm brought down by the lethal combination of the union, who saw him as Rockefeller V, and his competition, which took him for a shnook. Dad was neither, nor was he ever a liar. But what does youth know of reality?

So with all these experiences behind us, we attempted to pay our dues back to the people from whom all these beautiful heart-felt songs had come from. On our first night in Edwards it was very hot and very full of mosquitoes. Aside from singing and clapping to the freedom songs, the young folks seemed to be slapping another rhythm, or non-rhythm. Bob Moses got a bit upset with them, telling them that these folks (us) had not come down there to listen to them

* I don't have the resources to check out my memory—but Pete or some other folklorist— or *Sing out!* magazine should know. I think "Sarah Reed" is accurate as her name.

slap at the mosquitoes. Actually it hadn't bothered us that much, and we felt a bit chagrined. Perhaps the song of the mosquito took priority at that moment over the songs of freedom!

I didn't realize then that I would be back in Mississippi the next summer along with hundreds of other young folks from "up north" in a project that, as I look back on it now, came out of the Judaic tradition (prophetic) of social justice and the Christian tradition of being a witness. After listening to Bob Moses listen to Odetta's singing about the red clay country, it became obvious that he was committed to working down there, and I asked what or in which way I could be of help. He suggested that coming down to sing and bringing others to do the same would be a creative act of witnessing that would, in addition, help focus the media's and the nation's attention on the injustice and violence there, and also be a morale booster for all those putting their lives on the line to exercise basic American rights.

And so that spring, with the help of Harold Leventhal and others, we got commitments from performers to come down and travel around the state to sing at rallies, lending their voices, names, and presence to the devilish inferno of the delta.

Susan was pregnant with our first child, whom we would name Sean Moses (after the Irish playwright, Sean O'Casey, and our friend, Bob Moses). We traveled to Oxford College for Women in Ohio in the aforementioned red Chevy. On campus were hundreds of young people. Robert Coles remarked on Susan's being pregnant and our still heading for Mississippi. We met Sally Belfrage, who was to write a book about the experience, *Freedom Summer,* and participated in most of the training which consisted of talks, discussions, nonviolent physical strategies, and evening sings. Vincent Harding was an especially inspiring speaker. One afternoon we were harangued by a young black, saying only by changing the "system" would anything really be changed. I think he meant the system of segregation, but he never did define it. He had been through the beatings and shootings that were happening in many places in the state and seemed a bit unhinged. I remember Bob leading a bunch of us in a Yugoslavian line dance to a record he had brought with him. Later, in Mississippi, I taught the Israeli dance for rain, "Mayim," to a group of young black children and Howard Zinn joined the circle dance.

One of the "dos and don'ts" impressed on us was to always go 5 miles below the speed limit. We practiced that on the way down, slowing down as we came into each town, from 45 to 40 to 35 to 30 to 25 to 20 to 15 and back up again as we left the town. In the dead of night going through one town near Memphis, Tennessee, we were followed for a while by a police car but fortunately it finally turned off onto another road. In order to avoid unneeded incidents, we were told, avoid black and white together (a favorite verse of ours to the song, "We Shall Not Be Moved") in one car. When we finally got to Jackson we were housed along with Paul and Rachel Cowan at Mrs. Jefferson's house. She was a matronly black lady, active in the NAACP (one of the COFO organizations) who welcomed us in. Later we lived in a building that was part of the Tougaloo College campus.

In trying to recall those days in detail, I wish to insert here an article I wrote for *Broadside* magazine of October 20, 1964. It was meant as kind of a recruiting piece to get other folks and topical song singers to continue our summer effort, but I think it pretty accurately captures a lot of what we did.

Broadside #51 Oct. 20, 1964
The Mississippi Caravan of Music

By Bob Cohen
Director, Summer 1964

Twenty-two artists participated this past summer in the Mississippi Caravan Of Music. Those taking part were: Len Chandler, Bob Cohen, Judy Collins, Jim Crockett, Barbara Dane, Alix Dobkin, The Eastgate Singers (Adam and Paula

Cochran, James Mason, Jim Cristy), Jim and Jean Glover, Carolyn Hester, Greg Hildebrand, Roger Johnson, Peter LaFarge, Phil Ochs, Cordell Reagon, Pete Seeger, Ricky Sherover, Gil Turner, Jackie Washington, and Don Winkelman. They came down for varying periods of time all summer long, traveling to and performing at all of the over thirty projects in Mississippi.

The Caravan is a cultural arm of the Mississippi Freedom Project—the most ambitious civil rights project ever. Over eight hundred volunteers, students and professionals, spent the summer opening up the "closed society"—manning freedom schools, community centers, helping to form the Freedom Democratic Party, researching federal programs, bringing people down to the courthouses to register to vote, answering telephones and mopping floors. Singing is the backbone and balm of this movement. Somehow you can go on in the face of violence and death, cynicism, and inaction of the FBI, the indifference of the federal government—when you can sing with your band of brothers:

"They say that Freedom is a constant struggle,
Oh Lord, we've struggled so long, we must be
free . . .
"They say that Freedom is a constant dying . . ."

or

"This may be the last time . . . may be the last time
I don't know."

or

"This little vote of mine,
I'm gonna let it shine . . .
I've got the light of freedom,
All in the Citizens Council . . .
All in Mississippi, Lord . . .
All in the White House . . .
Let it shine, let it shine,
let it shine."

The first song helped many of us get over the paralyzing fear we felt when the news came of the disappearance of the three civil rights workers in Philadelphia, Mississippi. We sang it just before we left the orientation session at Oxford, Ohio, to go to the South.

But it wasn't only freedom songs that kept us going. I remember one very busy day in the office when someone started singing a Hebrew round, "Hava Na Shira" ("Sing Hallelujah")— slowly the rest of us picked it up—and soon three parts were going with everyone continuing about their work, phones ringing and typewriters clicking. The rest of the afternoon was spent in working and singing—"Dona Nobis Pacem" and "Hey Ho, Nobody Home" (an old English round which was very close to Mississippi 1964 reality: Meat nor drink nor money have I none . . .)

Those Caravan singers who could stay for a longer period than a week spent two or more days at each project. Others went from place to place on a rather hectic schedule. A typical Caravan day would begin with the singers participating in a class on Negro history at the freedom school. They showed that freedom songs were sung back in the days of slavery—and how some songs even blueprinted the way to freedom on the underground railroad. The singers demonstrated the important contribution of Negro music in every aspect of American musical and cultural history. For children who have been educated—or rather brainwashed—by the public school system to accept the myth of their own inferiority, this was an exhilarating revelation. For the majority of adults, as well as children, it was the first time they had heard of such great musical artists as Leadbelly and Big Billy Broonzy. For many the music they had learned to be ashamed of was given new stature by the visiting musicians.

Completing a program at one freedom school, the Caravan group would travel on to another, usually a trip of one or two hours. There they would hold a workshop informally with the students in the afternoon. These workshops generally wound up with whatever the singers and children were mutually most interested in—anything from folk dancing to African rounds to English ballads to learning the guitar chords for

Broadside #51

THE NATIONAL TOPICAL SONG MAGAZINE   OCT. 20, 1964   PRICE -- 35¢

ROLL, FREEDOM, ROLL

"ROLL, FREEDOM, ROLL" is one of many songs sustaining the Civil Rights movement in the SOUTH, of which HOWEVER has said: "History has never known a protest movement so rich in song." This BROADSIDE is part of a Special Broadside Issue with a number of such songs, created by the Negro people in the heat of their struggle for freedom. Also several songs by Northern songwriters Justin Gabler and Len Chandler written while they were in Mississippi last summer, and articles about the Mississippi Summer Project itself.

NEW YORK POST

Terror in Miss.

Washington

Bombings and burnings of Negro churches and homes in Mississippi have become epidemic especially in rural areas where violence was breakout at the city of Canton in recent Negro voting.

184

"Skip To My Lou." After time out for some dinner, there would be a mass rally to sing for or a hootenanny that might last three hours.

It seemed to me that the farther out in the country and the more ramshackle the wooden church the greater was the singing. I'm thinking particularly of a mass rally in Ruleville, home town of Mrs. Fannie Lou Hamer (more about her later), where the singing nearly blew off the roof. I'm sure the other singers all have illuminating experiences to tell of their travels over Mississippi. One thing, I believe, we all shared. That was returning to Freedom House late at night and then singing on into the early hours of the morning with the civil rights workers who had little other opportunity just to relax and let off steam. In ways like this the Caravan, in addition to its educational and cultural work, served an important function as a morale booster for the others in the Civil Rights Movement, both volunteers from out of state and local rights workers.

Another aspect of Caravan activities was that they sometimes stimulated local white people to participate for the first time in an integrated function (nonviolently, that is!) A number of white Mississippians turned out for concerts that Julius Lester, Len Chandler, and Cordell Reagon gave on the Gulf coast. When Pete Seeger sang in McComb, two white college students came to hear him. Several days later they had dinner with some of the civil rights workers. Soon afterward when Pete sang in Jackson four students from Ole Miss attended. They, too, were so impressed that they showed up a few days later in the Jackson Council of Federated Organizations (COFO) office, expressing interest in the freedom schools. All this, of course, took considerable courage on the part of these white local youths. One of the main aims of the Citizens Councils and their ilk is to intimidate and terrorize local whites so that they will suppress any decent instincts and remain immobilized. You might say that the above was another example of the power of music!

My own job was to direct and coordinate throughout the summer, as well as traveling around and singing myself. The phone, a map, and a calendar were the main equipment in the Jackson office where I and my wife, Susan, were stationed. Singers came into Jackson, and I would spend a few hours trying to orient them to the unreality of Mississippi—an almost impossible but necessary effort. Then I would plan a tour for them, sending them north, south, east, and west (not all at once). Everyone traveled with groups. As far as these singers went, there were only two instances of police harassment—one person arrested for reckless driving and the other fined for blocking traffic. This was extremely good luck, considering the amount of traveling done. Unfortunately, it was not typical for most of the other volunteers and the Negro Mississippians.

A word about Mrs. Hamer, who is not only a dynamic leader but a great singer as well. Actually there is no contradiction here. When Mrs. Hamer finishes singing a few freedom songs one is aware that he has truly heard a fine political speech, stripped of the usual rhetoric and filled with the anger and determination of the Civil Rights Movement. On the other hand, in her speeches there is the constant thunder and drive of music. Mrs. Hamer had a job sharecropping for eighteen years. She lost it immediately after attempting to register to vote. On top of losing her livelihood she was beaten almost to death. Yet her spirit is indomitable and her humor as rich as the soil of the delta. When she was running for the U.S. Congress earlier in the year one of the verses of one of her campaign songs went: (To the tune of "Oh Mary")

"If you miss me in the Missus' kitchen,
And you can't find me nowhere,
Come on over to Washington,
I'll be Congresswoman there."
And another went:
"If you miss me in the Freedom fight,
And you can't find me nowhere,
come on over to the graveyard,
I'll be buried over there."

Yes, Mrs. Fannie Lou Hamer "knows her song well."

There are many ways to contribute to this Freedom struggle—money, food, clothing, etc. But perhaps the most important contribution is your physical presence in Mississippi. The Mississippi Freedom Project is continuing through this winter and on into next summer. Freedom schools and community centers continue to be open. Now, more than ever, your presence is needed, not only to contribute your talents but to help focus the attention of the nation on this truly new frontier, a frontier being carved out with the courage and lives of Negro and white people. Take along your guitar, harmonica, banjo, broken bottle neck (for playing only), autoharp, bass, car, songs, drums (Jim Crockett brought down a whole set of drums the kids went wild over), kazoos, jugs, voices, and all the other hootenannies and thingamajigs you can find—load 'em up and head down to the Magnolia State. Leave behind the people with "barrels of money who don't know how to sing" and join hands and voices with those from whom came the songs we sing.

If this is beginning to sound like a recruiting message addressed to all of you reading this article and those you can reach with the "good news"—well, that's exactly what it is. Once you decide on the amount of time you can spend, and when you can do it, contact Wendy Heyel, Caravan of Music, c/o COFO, 1017 Lynch Street, Jackson, Mississippi. She will then plan out a tour for you and expect you on the day you have specified. If you're in the New York area and have more questions, call me at TR 3-9118 or Julius Lester at OR 5-8581. The struggle in Mississippi is what this great country of the United States of America is all about. It's what the songs we sing are about. If people are jailed, beaten, murdered, and their houses and churches bombed and burned, just because they wish to sing their life's song with a straight back and a strong voice, then as long as this is happening none of us are truly free to sing out, be it in nightclubs, concert halls, or even in our own homes.

The addresses and phone numbers at the end of the article don't mean anything anymore except that it's interesting to note the main headquarters of the Movement were on Lynch Street. Not even Charles Dickens might have thought of a more ironic location.

This article names most of the musicians that came down and is more reliable than my memory, but I hope it does not leave anyone out; if so, I apologize for any such lapse. I do remember driving Pete Seeger up and down the roller-coaster hilly roads to McComb and up into the delta. He was a bit concerned that I was not giving the people on the side of the road a wide enough girth. Pete realized that many of the young people would not know him or his songs, so he decided to always open with "If I Had a Hammer," which had become a recent hit by Trini Lopez in a semi-rock and roll version that, as Pete said, had Lopez singing the harmony line rather than the melody. Pete always ended with his marvelous telling of the African folk tale, "Abiyoyo," which people of all ages had fun with and joined in the singing of the lively chorus. Pete sat in the back seat with his long legs up on the back of the front seat. I think he was a bit wary of my driving at which I was relatively new. Susan and I would go pick up the singers when they arrived at the Jackson Airport and on the way back to the city gave them some orientation. Some of the performers behaved a bit like "artists" in saying they already knew what to do, but Carolyn Hester stood out as one of the most humble and loving of people who, perhaps, coming from Texas was a bit more realistic about having to tone down one's '60s lifestyle in order to survive and not cause yourself or any others trouble. Some of the singers went from town to town and some, like Julius Lester, stayed for a while at one movement house. Staying over in Vicksburg one night (the city of a famous Civil War battle) I heard a dull thud. The next morning I was told someone had shot some bullets into the house but no one had been injured. I remember Judy Collins and Barbara Dane singing Malvina Reynolds's new song "It Isn't Nice": It isn't nice to block the door way/It isn't nice to go to jail/there are nicer ways to do it/ but the nice ways always fail... which with its rhythm and bluesy tune was popular. Phil Ochs was there with Jim and Jean, who were singing Phil's melancholy and moving song, "Changes." The Freedom Singers were around singing a number of songs written by one of their members and a fine jazz singer, Matt Jones. They sang a cappella and were warmly received wherever they went. All the performers pitched in to play for the inevitable singing of freedom songs which, in addition to "We Shall Overcome," included: "We Shall Not Be Moved," "If You Miss Me at the Back of the Bus," "Keep Your Eyes on the Prize," "Hold On," "Freedom is a Constant Struggle," "This May Be the Last Time," "Ain't Gonna Let Nobody Turn Me Around," "We Will Never Turn Back," "Woke Up This Morning With My Mind Stayed on Freedom," "Oh, Freedom," "I'm On My Way," and the ever-rousing "This Little Light of Mine."

Since I have been in prison and become a cantor for, in addition to the Jewish Services, the Catholic Mass and Protestant and 7th Day Adventist Services, I keep meeting these songs sometimes in their former versions, i.e. "Woke Up This Morning With My Mind Stayed on Jesus," or "Keep Your Hand on that Plough, Hold On." The vibrancy of the Protestant hymns combining the African American rhythms and melodies with the European rhythms and melodies makes for the greatest of inspirational singing even today in the '90s, especially among young black males who sadly make up such a large proportion of the prison population, at least in New York state. I have found that part of my mission, thirty years later, is to re-relate these songs back to these young folks who have very little sense of their recent past history and sometimes seem to be trapped-off (a prison term) in the often rollicking rhymes of rap to the exclusion of almost everything else. There is great creativity in much of rap and in the constant rhyming that goes on in the effort to put daily experiences into the rhythm of rap speech with elements of humor and frankness. It reminds me of those days in the topical song movement where our raw material was what was happening to us and our world. One of my attempts has been to combine a '50s talking blues form strained through a '90s rap style along with a singing chorus to tell the story of the summer of '64 ("Shadows on the Light") It has met with some success, with a number of guys coming up to tell me they like the words. I think, here I am recruiting again, it is or should be a vocation for some of us veterans of '64 to go back into the streets and talk and sing about the history of those times. True, these times are very different and much of the rhetoric no longer makes sense. But that was a time when black and white people did work together for a common cause and where hatred was considered a sin and not explained away solely as the expression of frustration and protest.

And may I say, as one for whom the very word God was a profanity, that there is a richness in the faith of our brothers and sisters of whatever religious practice. It was this richness that we shared, expanded, utilized, that as Susan says, was "the only way we could keep going." We can't and shouldn't forget the history of the misuse of religion but should separate out the essence of human glimpses of the grace of God from the sordid and often violent attempts of humans to control what they perceive as just one more form of power. The songs we sang and still sing were inspired by faith, grounded in sorrow, and given wings by a belief in being "free at last."

I grew up on the "sorrow songs" as they were sung concert-style by Marian Anderson and Paul Robeson. The beauty of their voices, combined with the poetry and grandeur of the melodies, touched me deeply in my soul. Little did I suspect that I was learning so much about my own people's faith and history through "Go Down, Moses," "Oh, Mary Don't You Weep," "Deep River," and "Swing Low, Sweet Chariot," and about the faith of others that carried the faith of my people even further—as Robeson sang the songs from his reverend brother's A.M.E. Zion Church: "On Christ the Solid Rock I Stand," "Someday He'll Make It Plain to Me" or the Middle Eastern call of the meuzzin as he calls his people to prayer. The best of our history is in these songs. I gather that Bob Moses is now going around the country teaching young people algebra/mathematics as a second language. He knows there is still much more work to do. I would teach music as the first, second, and third language, the tongue of the heart, the speech of the soul, God's song in us all.

Shalom.

Shadows On The Light

Words & Music by Robert Cohen (c) 1993
("Freedom Is A Constant Struggle," words and music traditional)

To King and Moses: Followers of God, Leaders of Men

In Oxford College for Women in O-hi-o
We were getting ready, ready to go
Down to the land of the kudzu vine and old man river
Tho it was hotter 'n hell, the word "Mississippi" made us shiver

We were learning the techniques of non-violence
For we would no longer keep the conspiracy of silence
As our brothers who tried to vote were beaten and slain
We could no longer bear the burden of this shame

Phil and Bobby sang it so right
Whenever some people ain't free they cast shadows on the light
Power and glory was blowin' in the wind
Too many thousand gone, and God said: Hatred is a sin

When we heard that James, Michael, and Andy had disappeared
Their absence summed up everything we feared
We can be pretty certain, Bob Moses said,
If they are missing, most likely they are dead

Now is the time if you wanna turn back
No one will blame you if you pack up your sack
And return to the North where there's still much work to do
Its a never ending journey and to your own self be true

Then a woman's voice rose in the warm spring air
Filled with the mystery of compassion, the weariness of care
The melody was sad, but the words sang wisdom
It went through us like fire, the fire of freedom

They say that freedom is a constant dying
They say that freedom is a constant crying
They say that freedom is a constant trying
Oh Lord, we've struggled so long, we must be free, we must be free!

They say that freedom is a constant talking
They say that freedom is a constant walking
They say that freedom is a constant struggle
Oh Lord, we've struggled so hard, we must be free, we must be free!

So we were soldiers in the army of '64
Songs and love our only weapons in a summertime war
And whether we knew it or not, God was on our side
We lit His little light of Freedom and took it for a ride

Fannie Lou Hamer sang it so right
Whenever some people ain't free they cast shadows on the light

This little light of mine was blowin' in the wind
Too many thousand gone, and God said: Hatred is a sin

We sang "We Shall Overcome" and prayed they would come over
And if they attacked us we hoped God's grace would be our cover
We put our bodies and souls on the line
Sometimes they threw us in prison tho we had committed no crime

Joan and Judy sang it so right
Whenever some people ain't free they cast shadows on the light
Carry it on was blowin' in the wind
Too many thousand gone, and God said: Hatred is a sin

We traveled around the state singing in churches and Freedom Schools
Those filled with hatred called us "Nigger lovers," "Yankee fools"
But we brought back the songs to the folks from whom they sprang
Long ago they had turned the Bible into songs that now the whole world sang.

Carolyn and Julius sang it so right
Whenever some people ain't free they cast shadows on the light
10,000 candles were blowin in the wind
Too many thousand gone, and God said: Hatred is a sin

Later things fell apart as things tend to do
When hatred is driving some rowers in your crew
On this spinning ship the Captain's high above
When you're looking for justice, keep your eye upon the dove

Pete and Harry sang it so right
Whenever people ain't free they cast shadows on the light
If I had a hammer was blowin' in the wind
Too many thousand gone, and God said: Hatred is a sin

Martin and Malcolm said it so right
Whenever people ain't free they cast shadows on the light
I have a dream was blowin' in the wind
Too many thousand gone, and God said: Hatred is a sin

August 1964 In Mississippi

To sketch a week I spent in Mississippi, August, 1964, I need to begin with Gil Turner. Somewhere in his 30s then, Gil was a peace activist, civil-rights advocate, musician, songwriter, husband, parent, poet at heart, and brother figure to me. Gil was also burly, warm, and passionate on social issues, kind of too careful around me, I thought, and hiding a drinking problem. He was going to be my lifeline, nonetheless, in some life-and-death matters, I trusted him even if I didn't trust his car. He had phoned me late that spring to let me know that his dear friend, Bob Cohen, was going to be a coordinator for the Mississippi Summer Music Caravan and asked if I would like to drive down to Jackson to lend a hand in the voter-registration activities.

As a folksinger, song leader, and songwriter, I always thought that what looked like front-line political impact was misleading. Indirect pressure was the best, I thought, that me and my kind could apply. So the idea that Gil, myself, and thousands shared was that here, in 1964, was a crack in the door of prejudice, and we wanted to jam that door open Right Now. Civil Rights was our agenda and our musical interests were taking a back seat for the moment. Our connectedness to our generation was intact—but our pride in our country was at stake.

The turmoil of our Nation over civil rights issues was at a boiling point—in June, activists Andrew Goodman, Michael Schwerner, and James Chaney were declared missing and feared dead. I didn't think I could live here any more if I didn't do what my conscience told me to do. I was going to go home to the South and be a witness to anything that happened there. If enough witnesses and spotlights were present, it had to make a difference, it must make a difference.

My family back home in Texas wasn't going to know the truth concerning my whereabouts that week. They would probably think that I was out on the concert trail as usual. My lawyer father and especially my civil-servant mother would have liked to have been with us—my mother has been a freedom rider her life long. But I didn't want them to know the specifics—I didn't want them to waste time worrying about "what might happen." Also, in a very practical sense, this was not a moment when I was even going to consider turning back.

Bob Cohen was one of Gil Turner's best musical compatriots. Their group, the New World Singers, was the source of a great deal of my familiarity with protest songs. I learned "Carry It On" that summer from Gil. Bob, as Coordinator of the Mississippi Summer Music Caravan was in the office of the Council of Federated Organizations. COFO was the umbrella that connected the Student Nonviolent Coordinating Committee, SNCC; the Congress of Racial Equality, CORE; the Southern Christian Leadership Conference (headed by Dr. Martin Luther King, Jr.), SCLC; the National Association for the Advancement of Colored People,

Carolyn Hester is a folksinger/ songwriter. She came to attention through the unusual path of being presented by rock n' roll hero Buddy Holly. She, in turn, participated in the discovery of Bob Dylan and mentored Nanci Griffith. Pete Seeger has always been her biggest inspiration. Carolyn and her husband David Blume continue to tour the U.S.A. and England. They have two daughters, Karla and Amy.

NAACP; and all other groups joined in the voter-registration effort. One Man, One Vote. Trouble was, Bob Cohen and his wife, Susie, had explained, the pressure which had been brought to bear on our black brothers and sisters to accept the status quo—the prevention of blacks from seizing their own personal power—had to be fought on the turf of greatest resistance—the South. Illiteracy and economic bondage were in cahoots with intolerance and prejudice. In my view, it was not only the black population who was being controlled—but also the attitude of generations of Southern whites, trapped in ignorance and fear. Bob Cohen's job was to bring singers and music makers together with the voter-registration workers and leaders. We were needed to lead songs at meeting halls, churches and in fields, if necessary, in the attempt to keep up the morale of those brave souls doing the slug work, house to house.

Then, a few days before our trip, the bodies of Goodman, Schwerner, and Chaney were found on Tuesday, August 4. Something that haunts me still is that all three families wanted their sons buried together. It was a poignant and even heroic request. The state of Mississippi refused. It only strengthened the resolve of freedom riders from everywhere.

That weekend we left New York City about midnight. One small suitcase each, one guitar each, some cash, a few sandwiches and apples. We stopped for water, coffee, soft drinks and restrooms along the way. Otherwise, we drove nonstop, straight through to Jackson. Certain moments stand out in memory—driving through Washington, D.C., past the Lincoln Memorial, all lit up. Gil let me drive that early morning out of Washington, along the Appalachians past Charlottesville. Gil slept about two hours in two days—I slept about four.

In Jackson, at the motel, we met up with Alix Dobkin, my good friend and a greatly talented writer, singer and instrumentalist. She was married at the time to Sam Hood, who along with his father, Clarence Hood, ran The Gaslight in Greenwich Village. Late in the afternoon

of our arrival, Alix, Gil, and I went to eat dinner, and when we returned to the third floor hotel rooms, we had a message waiting. It hadn't been there when we'd left an hour or so before. To our astonishment, on the doors of our rooms was scrawled KKK in huge, black letters. "My guitar," I thought—I hoped my guitar was OK. After carefully opening our doors we found all the instruments and our other belongings intact.

We were in shock. The evening newspapers and the TV news were full of items concerning the impact of the voter registration on the locals. We left a wake-up call with the operator for 6 a.m. I was exhausted but frightened that we already had been singled out as civil-rights workers. I lay there wondering if I would be able to sleep in Mississippi at all.

The next morning, I jumped when the wake-up call came but realized thankfully that I had fallen asleep after all. Cancel that comforting thought—the voice on the other end of the line said, "OK, nigger lover, time to get up." I hung up quickly, told Alix, and we dressed immediately, fearing that an unfriendly knock on the door would soon follow. Not only had our operator scared the wits out of us, but it was only 5:30 a.m. We woke Gil anyway and made a hasty exit, looking neither right nor left. I was strangely calm and tried to put Alix at ease. She was a street-wise, Philadelphia Art Institute-educated young lady, but I was a couple of years older.

We found a cafe that opened at 6 a.m. No one approached us. Gil phoned Bob Cohen after breakfast, about 7:30 a.m. Bob met us, and we proceeded to the COFO office, located in some storefronts in the middle of Jackson. As we approached the building, walking on the opposite side of the street, Bob Cohen said: "See that car there—that's a local plain clothes from the Sheriff's Department. And the next car, that's a deputy from the Justice Department. Now, of course, that's a Jackson Police car—you see how they slow down in front of the COFO office. We think they are taking photos of everyone.

And, of course, the FBI and the KKK know us, too."

"But Bob," I said, "Your wife is pregnant. Isn't this a terrible place for her to be?" Bob replied, "Susie and I just didn't want to be separated right now. We'd rather be together. There's just no other place on the planet we'd rather be.

The COFO office was friendly and busy. We were given our "traveling papers"—schedules and a list of addresses where we could stay, plus a map. I don't recall any financial arrangements, per diems, or travel money. We were to be hosted by families along the way—sorry to say, no white families. I was to find out that for the first time in my life I was going to be truly safe and really secure on the black side of town. We were made so welcome. We felt so honored to be there.

Our assignment was to travel to Moss Point, Biloxi, Hattiesburg, Meridian, and back to Jackson. One rest stop that morning was at Wiggins. When we were ready to start out again, we discovered that the car had a dead battery, but the station attendant refused to help us. Looking at the map we saw that Wiggins is not far from Philadelphia, Mississippi, where Goodman, Schwerner, and Chaney had been found the week before. Gil lost no time phoning back to the COFO office in Jackson, and we got a jump-start from a man who, I believe, was a minister. Our instruments were, of course, covered up. It was just that we had "Yankee" license plates.

The four days spent in Moss Point, Hattiesburg, Meridian, and Biloxi have merged in my mind. In each town we enjoyed the camaraderie of the voter-registration workers. They worked quietly and intensely. On the streets, at work, they dressed and conducted themselves conservatively. At night, they, like ourselves, enjoyed the safety of churches and the homes of black families.

Our host families seemed genuinely happy about our presence. Their friendship and hospitality soothed our fears. In some instances, we knew that people were taking risks by being seen with us, by taking us in. The family in

Hattiesburg asked me for a snapshot of myself. I complied, with a silent prayer that no one would be penalized for having the photo in their home. I had tripped over into paranoia.

It was a great pleasure hearing Gil and Alix play and sing all week. I met lots of new songs. "They Say That Freedom Is A Constant Sorrow . . ." and it was unforgettable being part of a living folk music process.

At the end of our "tour of duty" we headed back to Jackson. A "music caravan" performance was held that evening, and we enjoyed hearing Barbara Dane, Len Chandler and Jackie Washington.

I saw that year's electoral activities from another angle as later that month I met Aaron Henry and Fannie Lou Hamer at the Democratic Convention in Atlantic City. The Mississippi Freedom Democratic Party made a powerful impact in their efforts to be seated at the convention, so as to truly represent the mass of newly registered black voters. Dr. Martin Luther King, Jr. was at the convention, as well, and his presence was inspiring and calming at the same time. I had been invited to the Convention to sing at a gathering of the Young Democrats for Johnson and Humphrey. . . . "Which Side are you on, boys, Which side are you on?"

This is August 31, 1993. As I write, remembering the summer of almost thirty years ago, I think of Goodman, Schwerner, and Chaney. The song I wrote for them:

Three Young Men

Three Young Men are sleeping now
The word has gone from town to town
One in the South and two in the North
A generation is left bowed down
So now, now, now.
Three Young Men came down the highway
Though struck silent, walk louder still
The lessons of Gandhi inspiring them
To conquer Goliath, but not to kill
So now, now, now
When all is known at story's end
When the ashes of murderers toss on the wind
A sigh and a singing will still be heard

The song of the gift of three young men
So now, now, now

And in today's *Los Angeles Times* there is an article telling how last Sunday, Amy Elizabeth Biehl, twenty-six years old, a Californian and Fulbright Scholar at the University of the Western Cape, was stabbed to death, mistaken for a white South African. To quote the Times: "Much of her time in South Africa Amy spent working on human rights. She had also been developing voter-education programs for the township (of Guguletu). On Sunday, Father Basil von Rensburg urged the congregation to make Biehl's death a catalyst for the peace she sought. "Nothing can bring Amy back, nor the many others who have died," he said. "But their deaths should inspire us and our political leaders to make this country safer for visitors and for its own people. Let us put an end to hateful language and anger, which thwarts reconciliation."

At such moments you cry because you know your generation was brave and fought the battle, and yet we still hunger for justice and must work for it everyday.   ❖

BARBARA DANE

I'm On My Way

Adaptation of a Traditional Song

Traditional call and response pattern first thought to be a form invented in slavery time. Now known to have been used in Africa for centuries. It probably was invented by pre-literate societies as a way of teaching, and in modern times it proves to be a valuable tool for situations where the singer needs to pass on what the group needs to know in order to participate fully.

I'm on my way (I'm on my way)
and I won't turn back (I won't turn back)
I'm on my way (I'm on my way)
and I won't turn back (I won't turn back)
I'm on my way (I'm on my way)
and I won't turn back (I won't turn back)
I'm on my way, glory, I'm on my way.

I'll ask my brother (I'll ask my brother)
to go with me (to go with me)
If he says no (if he says no)
I'll go anyhow (I'll go anyhow)
If you won't go (if you won't go)
don't hinder me (don't hinder me)
'Cause I'm on my way, glory, yes, I am on my way.

I'll ask my sister (mother, father, friends) to go with me
I'll even ask my boss to go with me
If he says no, I'll go anyhow
If you won't go, let your children go
I'm on my way to the freedom land.

Barbara Dane is a blues and jazz singer who has lent her voice to the cause of racial and economic justice since 1945. She began singing union organizing songs which brought her to the shop gates of the '40s, freedom songs which carried her to Mississippi and antiwar songs which took her to storefronts and cellars on the outskirts of military posts. Barbara has toured extensively throughout the world, including Hanoi, Havana and Japan.

ALIX DOBKIN

Pages From Mississippi

Having spent much of my twenty-four years in fear of "missing something," there was no way for me to pass up an invitation to join the Folk Music Caravan in 1964 for the Mississippi "Freedom Summer." Besides that, my politically activist Communist parents had named me after a heroic uncle killed fighting Franco in Spain, and had trained me to be a political trouble maker. Some of my folkie friends from Greenwich Village, namely Gil Turner and Len Chandler as I recall, recruited me along with other Gaslight Cafe regulars like Peter LaFarge, Tom Paxton, Eric Andersen and Carolyn Hester. And of course Pete Seeger would be there, as he was on behalf of every cause worth singing for.

In addition to presenting a program featuring four or five folksingers each night (except Mondays) the Gaslight served as homebase to those of us not on the bill that week. Conventional wisdom of the time dictated that "two 'chick singers' back-to-back" was "bad programming", while fifty consecutive boys—with guitars—was not. Nobody ever questioned this logic, certainly not I or Carolyn. Although unable to appear at the same club on the same night, we did enjoy a close friendship which lasted for many years. Seasoned and comfortable in our separate folk niches, Carolyn and I admired each other's work, liked each other's company, lived short blocks apart in the West Village, and often hung out together when off the road.

We, and almost everyone we knew, stood squarely behind equal rights and against racism. During the early sixties, as now, most members of the folksinging community, like Pete, regularly performed in order to benefit various political causes. The whole country knew about the murders of Medgar Evers and Goodman, Schwerner and Chaney. At the Gaslight, Phil Ochs was singing, "Here's to the State of Mississippi," a few blocks away at the Village Gate, Nina Simone was singing, "Mississippi Goddamn," and there was a good chance that Bob Dylan might be found at any club he wished singing his powerful and popular, "Oxford Town." Voter registration and The Student Nonviolent Coordinating Committee were hot. Bob Cohen, director of the "Folk Music Caravan" for "Freedom Summer," along with friends and colleagues like Gil, Len and Jackie Washington, were spending the summer months working in Mississippi. We signed on with them to spend some time in support of voter registration workers in churches, community centers, and Freedom Schools.

And early one evening, there I was. The image of me and Carolyn having a good laugh together in a hotel room somewhere in downtown Jackson, Mississippi remains in my memory. We were feeling wired up and a bit nervous, but mostly eager and curious about the people and events in store for us as we faced each other; I, perched on the lower end of a twin bed, she, sitting upright in a chair with wooden armrests, her long blonde hair illuminated by

Alix Dobkin is in the process of writing her memoirs after 20 years largely spent on the road visiting and singing for lesbian communities all over the English speaking world. She has had the unique privilege of helping to lay the foundation for a rich and thriving lesbian culture. Alix's sixth album, Love & Politics, a 20-song compilation, summarizes thirty years of writing and entertaining. Her first album, Lavender Jane Loves Women was produced in 1973 with Kay Gardner and holds the distinction of being the first internationally distributed lesbian album.

the fading southern sunlight from the window to her left. Carolyn, who was a sweet singer, could hit the highest note heard on the east coast. Texas had conferred upon her a charmingly soft twang, cousin to a drawl, and personal knowledge of the south. But it was new to me.

An easterner my whole life except for two numbing teenage years in Kansas and one week in Virginia, I was immediately overwhelmed. Beneath its exalted ceiling, the atmosphere in the room was palpable. A sensation of being judged from above with watchful distrust, not unlike my own, mingled with impressions gathered from movies like "The Little Foxes," and writers like Eudora Welty and William Faulkner. I could almost feel the "Deep South" as it drew a long, humid breath, hazy with lush romance and decay, punctuated by the sharply held, secret breath of tragedy and shame. I had read and heard about "The South," but I was unprepared for the sheer physical impact of it.

My most vivid impression of the hotel was the "KKK" scrawled in red across the dark brown panel on the outside of our door. We noticed it the next morning on our way out. Serious and sobering, we agreed, but not surprising. Of course the Klan would know and disapprove of our presence in Jackson. Of course they would try to bully us, scare us away from their domain. Naturally this respectably seedy hotel was riddled with them. Every black person here endured far greater, even life-threatening risks on a daily basis. Year after year they confronted threats more perilous than a vandalized door.

As it turned out for us, the grafitti proved more validating than intimidating; the unfriendly public notice of our small role provoked a larger personal drama; that of insight as it deepens and conviction as it strengthens. Here was a powerful credential, a red badge of courage, written proof that we had put ourselves on the line.

Feeling more righteous and angry than fearful, we waited for the elevator, rode down to the lobby, and walked over to the desk. We eyed the clerk suspiciously. His cronies, lounging silently,

eyed us back. Static hostility crackled above the grand old carpet in the lobby between us. We completed the process of checking out and turned to walk, with measured step, toward the cheerful sunshine beckoning outside. A venomous "Y'all come back now" followed us out through the door.

Thankful to be out of there, we headed directly to SNCC headquarters where we belonged, where instead of the brittle silence of the hotel, a warm, rich cacophony of voices welcomed us. It's a whirlwind in my mind, a swirling impression of images and activity: pamphlets and papers, books and manuals stacked onto shelves, heaped on tables, some funky furniture haphazardly arranged throughout a series of small dark rooms, flurries of movement in and out, men speaking intently into phones, a casual exchange here, an intense discussion there.

Outside the door on the street, an assortment of organizers and supporters congregated. A colorful mix of students and other young people loitered or rushed about, relaxed or met in small groups in the brilliant, lazy, morning sunshine, a sharp contrast to the darkness and urgency inside SNCC headquarters. We spotted Gil, who welcomed us to Jackson in his typically warm, slightly distracted way. We found Len, always energetic, but here exploding with even more volcanic enthusiasm than usual. They introduced us to other SNCC workers.

A few blocks away a car was parked at a curb underneath a tree. We squeezed in and huddled with the veteran organizers who brought us up to date, intent upon the exchange of information and alert to movement outside. Knowing looks were exchanged as Carolyn and I shared the morning's, "KKK-on-the-hotel-door" story. We got some general instructions: traffic laws were to be strictly obeyed, no one was to travel alone, and someone was always to know our whereabouts. Carolyn and I would be escorted and transported through rural Mississippi, with one exception. SNCC allowed only a very few elite, highly trained and experienced organizers to go to "the Delta." In one part of my mind I was intrigued and challenged, and in another part I was relieved at the restriction. People were getting murdered in the Delta.

Slowly we cruised the neighborhood, coming to a full stop at every stop sign, signalling for every turn, always mindful of activity wherever white men were likely to congregate, especially at places like gas stations. We noted what they were doing and whether they were alone or in how large a group.

The next day, Carolyn and I began our backwoods tour, singing for meetings and rallies, visiting families in one community after another who treated us to spectacular meals consisting of endless courses of home cooked, crispy fried chicken and ham, luscious mashed potatoes, sweet potatoes, biscuits, gravy, corn, black-eyed peas, greens and beans cooked in lots of salt pork, and unfamiliar chitterlings and okra which I sampled and praised politely, coffee with evaporated milk, pies, cookies, jello, fruit and much more. Were we quite sure that we didn't want another helping? My stomach was completely full, but my mouth wanted to eat that southern food forever, and I've been a fan ever since.

Our week was spent driving many miles on two-lane highways and dirt roads, going from churches to schools, from simple, comfortable houses on the outskirts of small towns to isolated, run-down wooden shacks stuck way out in a lonely field. We talked with people about the importance of voting, and how their vote would make a difference. I remember standing in front of a mailbox listening to one resolute, old woman, her eyes glittering as she declared that nothing could keep her from exercising the right to vote on election day. Then she turned and made her painstaking way down the narrow, potholed road, leaning on a cane for support. She was awe-inspiring, like Fannie Lou Hamer was awe-inspiring.

But some people were reluctant to register. We understood why and asked them to think about it and contact a worker if they changed their minds, wanted to talk, or needed a lift to the polls. Children sat quietly attentive, or peeked out from around a doorway or their mother's legs. Even though we must have looked strange to them, although I can't now picture what we looked like then or what we wore, and even if they were hesitant about our purpose, everyone treated us kindly and cordially. We spent the days exchanging many handshakes and conducting many hunkered-down conversations with barefoot children, each a radiant jewel, each endangered, like the four girls killed less than a year earlier by a bomb in the basement of a Birmingham, Alabama church. We asked and answered questions about our lives and shyly touched each other to affirm the extraordinary occasion.

Particularly vulnerable after a meeting or rally, we practiced vigilance leaving buildings. As many as a dozen of us would get into cars and follow each other to the house where we were staying for the night. A lookout would be dispatched to watch for trouble outside, while inside we laughed at funny stories and quieted down for sad or scary ones. Smart, entertaining, and always gracious community activists, neighbors, relations, and newly signed-up voters, their lives in constant jeopardy, came by to meet us, their allies from "up north," and to express their gratitude for our presence. Married couples insisted on giving us their bed for the night, or else we slept on couches and floors, often within feet of a loaded shotgun propped up behind the door. Except for the revolver on a policeman's belt, I hadn't seen real firearms close up before. These people were genuine heroes to us with their brave, upbeat attitude, and we quickly formed mutual admiration societies.

We said, "thanks," "goodby", "keep voting," and kept moving, often driving at night along dark, deserted dirt roads. We'd fill the gas tank, make grim jokes and pray against a breakdown or flat tire. A couple of times, cars filled with white men followed us for miles. A couple of our guides had recently been beaten up and jailed. The following March, civil rights activist

Viola Liuzzo was murdered driving on just this kind of road.

At night the Mississippi countryside appeared menacing, but by daylight, exhilarating. In four years of fine arts training I hadn't encountered such a rich palette of greens. They were layered throughout the neat fields and acres of diverse woodland surrounding the small towns. The charming, elegant neighborhoods we drove through in Mississippi belonged to a world apart from the one we had come from and were going to. Lofty, graceful trees lined smooth streets, providing shade for trim lawns neatly outlined by arrangements of orderly flowerbeds; a perfect setting for homes far more grand and prosperous than the houses we stayed in. Like most of the world, this exquisite country has been stolen by racist criminals and belongs to racist criminals, I reflected sadly, and across my vision luscious greenery, flashing the raw injustice of it, rolled by.

The days were non-stop travelling, meeting, talking, laughing, singing, and eating with new people. We gathered in dim churches and bright community centers, in small and large groups, to listen to eloquent speeches and plain-spoken anecdotes. Occasionally we crossed paths with other musicians, like the Freedom Singers.

Many of us had been singing Dylan's songs in our shows for years but the general public was just learning about his genius. At the time I was performing my own arrangement of "The Times They Are A-Changin'," and probably sang it in Mississippi, along with "The Jug O' Punch" from Ireland by way of Tommy Makem and the Clancy Brothers, "Coplas" from Mexico via Cynthia Gooding and Theodore Bikel, and "Vegetable" from *Sing Out* magazine:

> *"Tell me what to do*
> *Tell me what to say*
> *Tell me what to think, or if I may*
> *I'll obey, 'cause I'm the perfect citizen*
> *I'm a non-protesting, status-quoting*
> *true-to-the-norm conformist*
> *I'm a Vegetable . . ."**

Our performances were met with appreciation and enthusiasm, but we were accorded celebrity status not because we were "famous folksingers," which may or may not have been true, but because we had made the trip. It wasn't clear when our presence helped protect local people or when we increased their risk, but the point was to be strong and united, not intimidated.

I had come to sing for the people, but what I remember is singing with them. Despite my diehard, lifelong aversion to religion and its symbols, when the people sang songs I knew I joined in with everything I had. The importance of the Church in organizing and sustaining this community was considerable, and I had learned to respect it. The language of a song might be gospel, but its meaning was "Freedom" and its effect was empowering and unifying. I could feel the force of spirit, like the force of conscience, alive in each of us when we sang together, confident that we all understood what we were singing and why. A thrilling strength vibrated upwards from my heart and out through my throat. Happily, I had learned some hymns on my visit to Virginia with a friend whose aunt was a fundamentalist preacher and whose church we had frequently attended. We sang, "Amazing Grace," I Woke Up This Morning (with my mind stayed on freedom . . .)," "We Are Soldiers In The Army (We've got to fight, although we have to cry . . .)", and others.

Church music was absent from my childhood, and I have never felt entirely comfortable singing it. However the union songs, adapted by civil rights workers, had traditionally served as "spirituals" to me growing up in my community. As I joined in with the familiar chorus of "Which Side Are You On?" I felt more strongly entitled, more deeply connected. Meetings ended, as did virtually every political gathering of the time, with, "We Shall Overcome," hands joined, bodies swaying, and hearts aligned.

*"Vegetable," by Art Samuels, ©1959 by Stormking Music, Inc., NYC

I loved having the chance to meet and sing with the people of beautiful Mississippi. I was complimented by the genuine welcome they gave me and honored by their appreciation of my brief effort. They told me that my presence was important to them. I hoped they knew how important it was for me. ❖

PHOTOS BY

MATT HERRON

Hollis Watkins sings with folk group at Tougaloo Chapel. Tougaloo student Austin Moore was responsible for cancelling virtually the entire season of Jackson civic (segregated) concerts. In response, folk groups performed at black Tougaloo College to integrated audiences, 1964.

JUDY COLLINS

Mississippi

Sunday P.M. August 1

We arrived in Jackson on the plane at 5 o'clock in the afternoon, after flying in from Newark Airport. There was a purple and deep red sunset that nearly covered the sky of Jackson like a cloak of blood; the light of the sun passed through it to the wet pavements and the thick green grass. The humidity was high. Walking in the air was a little like swimming. Bob and Sue Cohen picked us up at the airport. We drove to the COFO office in their little red car. Driving along, Bob began to talk about what was going on, and the seepage of understanding and fear soaked into my mind. He started with the basic rules about traveling, (never travel integrated, for instance,) no mingling with Negroes in most public spots, with the exception of one or two spots in Jackson that are integrated restaurants. All the instructions given in the legal guide were restated. Barbara Dane was with me, I neglected to mention. Those first couple of days in Jackson were made really better by her being there with me. When I first planned to go, I didn't know who would be going along; finding she was going on Saturday, August 1, I decided to go with her, saving the people at the office in Jackson a trip to the airport and providing some great company for the short, but somehow long, trip to Jackson.

The office of COFO in the city is located in a Negro neighborhood on Lynch Street, of all things. I first saw the address and thought someone was being funny. But there it is, and I had my first feeling of the security I was going to learn to feel when I reached a Negro neighborhood. The most frightening thing of all is to be in a white neighborhood in Mississippi. You know exactly where people are, and they certainly are not with you. Communist is probably the most widely used term for the whites and Negroes that are working in the Movement. It is a catch-phrase, in this country anyway, for anyone who doesn't hold the view that this country is all-good and all-pure. There is that particular feeling in Mississippi that these "outside agitators" are directed by Communist front people. It seems to give them an excuse to do anything they please to the people in the Movement.

The COFO office in Jackson is fairly large, with shelves and files and telephones everywhere, and people going about all kinds of business. Somebody donated some electric typewriters for the office, and the work is a little easier because of them. There is a mimeograph machine in the back room that is used almost constantly. The Jackson office steers the activities of the whole Mississippi project, and each day every freedom school office in the state is called three times, as a standard security practice; this is in addition to the calls that come in and go out continuously all day and sometimes all night.

A system of security is arranged for all people traveling from one place to another in the state. When you leave one office, you estimate your time of arrival at the next stop, and when you

Judy Collins is well known on the political front. She was a participant in the Civil Rights Movement and in 1964 went to Mississippi with the Caravan of Music. She began studying classical piano at the age of five, but it was the music of Woody Guthrie and Pete Seeger and the traditional music of the folk revival that fired her love of lyrics, and by 16 made her move from playing the Steinway to playing the guitar. Judy has recorded 26 albums, written two books, and co-directed the documentary film Antonia: A Portrait Of A Woman.

arrive you call your original base to let them know you have arrived safely. If you don't call within the prescribed time, the office begins to call hospitals and jails in the area in which you are traveling to find out if you have been arrested, etc.

I was immediately struck by the dedication of the people that are working in the Movement. I knew up front that they must surely be good people. But their goodness really supersedes anything I imagined. Their job is a unified effort to register Negroes in the state of Mississippi to vote. That is the simple purpose. All the complications, the bad living conditions, the heat, the terrible opposition from the white communities in almost every city, simply add to the strain on their lives there.

(As I write this, from the notes I kept on the tour, I sit at an old wood desk in an 18th-century house in New England, listening to the songs of Bob Dylan—"The Times They Are A-Changin'"—and I marvel at how painfully, how slowly, they do indeed change. The narrow minds who fear change in Mississippi are the same kinds of minds who always fear change. Only there, in that police state, where violence is the weapon on only one side, the resistance to change is so open, so frightening. The countryside here is so calm. It so belies the hatred that I know is in the place I have just come from.)

Barbara and I stayed at a motel that first night in Jackson. A place called Sun and Sand, of all things. Almost as ludicrous as Lynch Street. It was only recently integrated. Out of about 300 rooms in the motel, 197 of them were taken by people who were working in various capacities in the Movement. There were doctors who had come down for two or three weeks, and lawyers who had set aside some time to come and give their time to defend the people who got arrested and put in jail on trumped- up charges. I felt very strange staying there, with the big pool and the room-service, on my first night in Jackson. I would have preferred to be in the office, using the sleeping bag I brought for just that purpose. But there were so many people in the

city that there was just no room for us to stay except there. So Barbara and I had a swim and listened to the long Southern drawls of the people who were guests. We wondered at their ability to accept and dance to the rock-and-roll music that they played, and at the same time refuse simple human rights to the people who were, and still are, the basis of that music. They dig it, and think its theirs. Not looking at where it came from, really, nor caring.

I felt very afraid of all the people who were white and were there at the motel but not connected with the Movement. You can feel the animosity immediately. There we were in a plastic motel room in Jackson, with the impersonal decor that could place it anywhere in the fifty states, maybe Canada, too.

Sunday morning I woke up feeling stranger than when I went to bed. Barbara and I went to a church to have lunch with some of the workers. Someone from the north is providing money to the women of the church so that they can prepare lunch every day for the workers at the office. Nobody has any money. The ladies put up a great lunch, with fried chicken and rice and salad and peas and desert. Barbara and I sang for the first time there. It was great, and everyone joined in on all the songs. This was the first taste I had of how really vital the music is to the Movement. Later on things happened which made it even more obvious, but here was the first feeling of the good that the music does. (The fraternizing of Negro and white friends must take place in offices and churches and the freedom houses—not in cars, seldom on the street. A young boy called "Bull" asked me if I needed cigarettes (he was Negro); I said yes.

"I'll go get them for you," he said.

"Is it cool for me to come with you?"

"No." I stayed.

After the lunch and the singing we drove to the COFO office, where we stayed for the rest of the afternoon, listening and talking to and with the people there. The Eastgate Singers arrived, after a week's traveling through the northeastern part of the state. They were really ready to call it a good job and head for Chicago. But after talking for about two hours about the transportation situation (there is a grave shortage of cars, and no one can travel alone) and the anticipation of our traveling together, they decided that it would be good to stay. And so I was to travel with them. In their VW bus. We planned a temporary schedule of travel, and then all of us went to the staff party at the freedom house. They don't very often get out of the routine of work and eating and sleep, and so it was very festive for everyone. About two hundred people were there. The food, (hot dogs, potato salad) was gone in five minutes and the singing started, in the back yard, with people standing and sprawling on the lawn. Barbara sang the new song, "It isn't Nice," a rock-and-roll song, with her melody and Malvina Reynolds's words, and the place really rocked. They are so thirsty for music. It was so great, singing, with the sweat just pouring off, and the people just singing out with all their might. That's one thing you see right away; just start a song, and everyone is right there, singing out. The evening finished with all of us singing "We Shall Overcome," and you know, even though you know it is true all the time, when you sing it together, there is something that happens that makes you just as sure as you live that it is going to happen, and happen when you will see it happen. It was very beautiful.

It was after I sang that Heidi came up to me, and something special happened there in the Mississippi heat, in the night. Sometimes I wonder in spite of my convictions, if what I sing really means something to people. And what she said removed any doubts I might have ever had. She said, "Did you ever sing at City College?" I said yes. She said, "I came into the foyer the afternoon you were singing; your back was to me. That's why I didn't know who you were right away. You sang a song—that one you sang tonight about Medgar Evers. It was because of hearing that song at the concert that I decided to come to Mississippi." She was crying. The next morning she told me how the sequence of

things hung together. She decided upon hearing the song, and the next day in the mail the letter came from SNCC inviting her to participate in the Summer Project. I guess she and I really have Henriette Yurchenko to thank for that, since she arranged the concert and kept after me until I set a date to do it, committed myself.

When the two-thousand-year-old man was asked what mode of transportation was most frequent in the old days, he replied, "Fear." It must still be true. I have never lived with actual, tangible fear in my life, on a consistent level. It is painful. It is necessary here in Mississippi because, as in a war, it is a protective device. The sound of a siren, only annoying or interesting in any other place, is a cause for real alarm.

Greenville, Mississippi. August 2

We left for Greenville from Jackson today at about 11:30. The Eastgate Singers and I packed ourselves into the VW bus, the bus that was going to really become home for the next few days. We went to the COFO office, where the activity was heavy. All the office was talking about the party the night before. They really dug it. Heidi told me a lot about the situation in Jackson with the voter registration and, as she found out after about twelve hours in Mississippi, your own problems just cease to be important when you are faced with the problems that these people have.

A little about the workers here in the Summer Project. They have all volunteered their services and taken on the responsibility of paying for all expenses during their stay, including any jail bail they might incur. This works out in most cases, since I think some of the people come from families where there is not a lack of funds. But it is not always the case. There is no permanent bail fund, and in one instance in Ruleville the bail money had to be raised among the workers, from funds they could have put to other uses, because they wanted the worker out of jail so that he could do canvassing in voter registration. Every person working means that just that much more gets done. It is terribly important to have every worker out and able to do voter registration. Some of the workers in Greenville and other places are living on nine dollars a week. There is a shortage of cars, as I mentioned before.

We got to Greenville after a trip through the lovely countryside of northeast Mississippi. Every pickup truck carries a double gun rack in the back window. We drive under the speed limit, and it is extremely hot. It is like going on outpost expeditions in a war. The difference is that we carry no weapon but the Constitution and whatever state laws might possibly protect us. Only the enemy is armed, and he has everything from Thompson's tank in Jackson to people loaded with hate and guns in all the other parts of the state. It is a very tough battle.

Monday

Greenville is very quiet. The progress in registration seems to be at a standstill because it is so quiet. This is a fairly progressive town, and people are just not interested enough in what is going on to really care about getting the vote, or joining the Freedom Democratic Party. There is hardly any security in Greenville. We walked about freely, integrated, going to cafes and even drinking beer in the freedom house.

Charles Cox is the head of the COFO office there. He is from Howard University and will probably go back to school this fall after having been here in the state for two years. He is very warm and inspires a feeling of great confidence. There is a minister here from one of the Southern colleges. He must be about sixty, and he and his wife are here with the Council of Churches volunteer force. He seems to be a good man, too, and his wife is motherly and white-haired and very patient.

The Activities at Greenville

Afternoon singing at the freedom church to the children and some of the workers. Then a mass meeting in the evening for adults. This was not a terribly large gathering, and not nearly as enthusiastic as some of the other meetings we were to sing at during the week. The people seem

a little lethargic. We had a fine party after the meeting was over and sang our heads off for the staff. I began already to feel the vocal effect of all the singing.

We went to bed late and slept at the freedom house in our sleeping bags. It was awfully hot. A train went by in the middle of the night, and the light came shining in and the noise of the whistle was hideous. I think I finally went to sleep about four in the morning. I just couldn't stop the wheels from spinning in my head long enough to get gone. We woke up about 10 o'clock, hot and sticky and uncomfortable.

On the way to Ruleville we stopped off in Indianolla. This is a little town that has only had its freedom school for about three weeks. The enthusiasm of the Negro children there is encouraging. I gave Al Gargonie's little Washburne guitar to the girl who runs the school there—Liz Fusco. She plays and can teach the children to play, and they will have a guitar to use. She was so excited and thanked Al for sending it. They need all kinds of things there, from instruments and books to clothing and money. The Negro children have to go to school in hot buildings, poorly equipped, all summer, because they must be free to pick cotton in the fall. We like to think child labor laws have been enforced. No humane laws dealing with the Negro's way of life have even been broached in Mississippi. And these little kids often go to school from seven in the morning—the ones who do come to school—all through the afternoon to the freedom school. There they are taught some of the real history of their ancestors and skills of various kinds and are probably beginning to understand that there is dignity and pride in being Negro; something the Mississippi school system would not have them even suspect.

3:00 P.M. Tuesday

ain't gonna let nobody turn me 'round . . .

We arrived in the Negro neighborhood of Ruleville thankfully. There about fifty children were waiting for us in the 100 degree heat. We started to sing, and soon our voices had given out, and the kids carried on and on into the afternoon. It got hotter, and the children pretty much took over the singing. There were some good group singing leaders; we played and they sang. We met the people who are working there: Len Edwards, Dale and Jerry, and Ellen Seigel, the girl I stayed with. More of that in a minute. The water tank sat on the porch, and it refreshed us and tasted so cool and good, the water. We were all together there.

When the meeting was over Paula and I went to the house where Ellen is staying, the house of a woman I will call Mrs. Carlton. She is old enough that she really doesn't understand what these young people are doing. But I heard her say once during the afternoon, "Ellen is my girl as long as she is here." Paula and I took a bath and felt refreshed. Ellen said, "It is so hard to keep clean here. We just can never get really clean, and the reporters come and look at us and go back to their modern motel rooms and say that we are dirty and don't dress so well...and they don't have to contend with the heat and the dirt and the lack of facilities we are faced with." They don't see how hard it is just to keep a shirt clean and a shaven face.

Returning at 5:30 to the office, we were told we were going to Drew, a nearby town, to sing at a voter registration meeting. (In Sunflower County, 68 percent of the population is Negro. Out of twenty-five thousand eligible voters, less than two hundred are registered to vote.)

I have mentioned fear before; we were told that Drew is a dangerous place to go. We were told that we should expect to go to jail; the police had said that after the COFO workers accused them of harassing and not protecting, they were prepared to look on at whatever might happen to the people who went there—that they would not even attempt to protect us. The girls who work for COFO in the Ruleville office were not allowed to go with us. It is a policy there that the men go when there is actual threat of danger. But we were the singers, there to make music at the meetings, and we piled into the truck, without having eaten, and eaten at the

same time by total fear and the understanding that what we were doing was dangerous. I knew that I would probably be shot at or killed or beaten. We sang in the bus on the way "Ain't Gonna Let Nobody Turn Me 'Round." It is something to know that there is nobody that can turn you around except yourself, and the singing, the music is what makes a lot of this conviction possible. (Someone wrote an article recently about the difference between the labor movement songs and the songs of the freedom movement in which they pointed this out, how vital the songs are to the freedom movement: in jail, on the picket line, in a bus riding to Drew, in the county of Sunflower, in the state of Mississippi.)

I sat in the bus and changed the strings on my guitar to keep my hands from trembling. Their trembling made the task longer than it normally takes. Mrs. Hamer came out pretty soon and got in the car in front of us. We followed the car out of Ruleville and into Drew. I found that the only way to settle the terror—direct it—inside me was to sing. And so we sang softly *ain't gonna let nobody . . .* The conviction that some Southern white bastard with gun racks and an aerial whip and a rifle was going to shoot us was positive. (Do I repeat this too many times? I wish I were inspired with the kind of prose that would make the saying of it once enough.)

We drove into Drew and into the Negro neighborhood. It is a relatively small town. Strange that it should house such hatred. The home where the meeting was held was owned by a woman whose son was beaten nearly to death only a few months ago by the sheriff, who sat outside the house in his car during the whole time of our meeting—their meeting, for it is not ours. They need some herb to remove fear, some substance of support from somewhere—the government, the system—that will say, "It is alright for you to vote. You are human beings and you are entities in our system." So Mrs. Fannie Lou Hamer spoke to them, and to us; she who has been beaten and arrested and harassed for saying that she has a right to vote. To vote, man. Fired from her job the day after she registered in 1962 in Indianolla in Sunflower County, the lady of dignity who stood up and sang with us "This Little Light of Mine." She led us in singing that song while the police cars roamed the neighborhood and the cars of the Klan circumnavigated the block and the town stood in horror at the gall of seventy-five Negroes who had come to sing about freedom and listen to a beautiful woman talk about the right of a man to be human.

Mrs. Hamer sat down in a chair in the heat on the lawn. So few people were there because of the intimidation of being there. She walked over to where we stood with our instruments, and she opened her mouth and sang the first line, *This little light of mine . . .* We sang for about 45 minutes. Then she spoke to the people. She spoke so strongly, so beautifully. We felt purged and united.

The sun was setting when we got back to Ruleville. We were glad to be there.

After dinner we went back to the office. In the heat, all the workers were gathered, fanning themselves with brochures, and in the middle was a man dressed in an orlon shirt and Bermuda shorts. A white man. He had come to talk to the workers. He came in the night, on a bicycle. The heat was nearly unbearable. The sweat was dripping from every face, and this man was asking questions of the COFO workers (I say this all the time, and what I really want to say is how beautiful they are. I want to know all of them well; they deserve more than the title "worker"). He wanted to know why they were there. He was raised in Ruleville. He knew the problem. How could they, outside agitators, possibly know what the problems were? I must indicate to you that he really was the best of the lot in that place, that city of white supremacy. He was curious. He had the guts to come to see them, knowing that he would be persecuted, in whatever way was available to the people he knew. But he was to leave the state next week to move to Nevada. This may have had a great deal to do with his courage in coming there.

Here was a man who was raised on the myths of the white society in the South. He probably would have gotten ill at the thought of drinking out of the same fountain a Negro had used. He nearly said as much. But his thoughts were clearly stated, and he acknowledged the fact that the Negro should have the vote. He kept saying, "I think you people are sincere. You seem sincere, but why do you think you are needed here?"

(The other two white men who came to talk to the office people: one was arrested by the police for being drunk—he wasn't—and the other was arrested for some trumped up charge.)

I listened to the conversation for the better part of three hours. It was terribly frustrating. This was the best of the crop. And he was a bigot, in spite of all the out-of-state college education he had had. It kept getting in the way. Two or three of the people at the office talked to him, stabbing away at his prejudices, giving him credit for being a "good" person, for having courage; they were so beautiful, so patient. They went into great detail. They discussed their reasons for being there. They made a point of saying that they were asked by the Negro leadership of the state to come in and help them in their voter registration campaigns. They softened his frightening remarks by offering him facts about the community in which he had grown up; they chided him so gently for his lack of knowledge about the situation of Negroes in Ruleville. They taught me more about the Project than I would have known.

He was the best of the crop. And he really didn't understand. He could not get going beyond the fact that he was filled with fear of the Negroes. Little things kept coming up . . . "Do you want to intermarry with Negroes?" I kept wondering if he heard anything that was said.

When we had listened to about all we could listen to, we went out in the yard in front of the office and sang songs under the Mississippi stars about how the world is full of woe and the times are very hard. It is true. I walked home on the dusty foot road to Ellen's house and lay for a long time in the dark in Mrs. Carlton's house; the fan hummed air into the stiflingly hot room. Once in a while a dog would bark at the police wagon as it bumped over the dirt roads in the neighborhood. Everything else was quiet except my rambling thoughts.

The next morning there were twelve ladies from the north that came to listen to the workers and the Freedom Democratic representatives talk about the problems in Mississippi. We listened, too. We drank hot coffee and ate bread and heard Mrs. Hamer talk to these people. These ladies are part of a project called "Wednesday in Mississippi." Each week twelve come down to talk to some group in Mississippi, and go back north to do what they can in the way of fund-raising, etc., for the project. After spending the whole of the morning listening and watching, we piled into the bus and headed out for Clarksdale.

When we got into the office there, all the staff was in an emergency conference; the kids went to eat, and I stayed around to listen to Lafayette (I don't recall his last name) and the rest of the group talk about the trouble in Marx, a little town nearby, where they had gone the day before to start canvassing for voter registration. The police and the White Citizens Council had literally chased them out of town and threatened them, as is their wont everywhere in Mississippi. They managed to get seven names on the register; the police came and took down all the names and the next day I heard that two or three of the people had already been fired from their jobs. It's really the way to hit people right in the stomach, and that is the least that they can expect from their friendly, white, Southern- hospitality-filled neighbors.

When their staff meeting was over and they had decided the tactics that they would use, we went to sing in the church across the street. We had a really good sing; we all felt stronger and better afterwards. We went to eat at the restaurant down the street. Lafayette came with us. We all drank a little beer and talked a lot. He spoke of the feeling of responsibility; he is the head of the office there in Clarksdale. That same day the bodies of the three boys had been discovered near Philadelphia, and he knows, as everyone else does, that this is a possibility for anyone anywhere in the state who is involved with the Project. It must be a terrible weight to bear, to have to tell people where to go and how to pursue the goals we are all after. When we went back to the office there were about fifty people gathered outside; little kids and COFO workers. A pickup truck pulled up by the office and sat there; the man driving the truck has threatened to kill Lafayette. We all stood and sang right at him "It Isn't Nice," the song Malvina Reynolds wrote that Barbara Dane set to a new rock and roll melody. Afterwards we went to the church for a rally. It ended late, and we all went home with no voices left at all; we had sung until there was nothing left. It was the best way in the world to loose your voice. It means so much, the music.

The next day was the last in Mississippi for this trip. We left, rolling down the highway into Tennessee, and I got a plane for New York. I'm going back as soon as I can. Meanwhile, think of the strength of those people there who hold up their share with little help and much pain. I wish I could just go and stay there, doing whatever there is for me to do. But the sensible thing, I recognize, is the raising of the money to allow them to do more, for me and for all of us who suffer under the delusion that we are living in a democracy. ❖

LEN CHANDLER

A Long Introduction To A Long Poem About The Long Summer of '64

Len Chandler is the co-founder/director of the Los Angeles Songwriter's Showcase and Senior Editor of the Songwriter Musepaper. Chandler's freedom songs were recorded at the Smithsonian and stored in the National Archives. Two songs he wrote on the Selma-to-Montgomery March are in the documentary film "King." He recorded for Columbia, Folkways, Broadside, Blue Thumb, FM, and King Records and wrote 15 topical songs a week for a year on KRLA's Credibility Gap. Chandler's songs were also featured on KLET-TV's Musical Muse and Earth News Radio, syndicated to over 400 markets worldwide.

Pop—pop—pop—pop—pop. That didn't surprise me, after all it was the Fourth of July and my first day in Vicksburg, so I thought they were trying to freak me out with some firecrackers. If they were joking they were doing a good job, diving off the porch and going flat on the floor. But when the fifteen-year-old who had insisted on carrying my guitar said, "You better get your ass down Mr.," I hit the floor just in time to hear the next volley punch several small holes in the wall behind my chair. After lying in the dark in silence for a long time, someone said, "Welcome to Mississippi."

I had missed the SNCC field workers' orientation in Oxford, because I was held over for a week with Hoyt Axton at a gig at a coffee house called the Buddhi, in Oklahoma City. (Hoyt had a hit song called "Greenback Dollar.") I figured the money I'd make would cover expenses for much of the summer. On my last day in Oklahoma, not only did the club owner stiff me for my week's wages, but a local eatery refused to serve me. As I walked out the door, I saw a huge sign in the sky. It said Liberty. The sign was an advertisement for a bank. The irony helped steel my resolve to win some liberty. I was ready for Mississippi.

I flew into Vicksburg from New York and was supposed to meet Cordell Reagon, who was driving. However, I was there several days before Cordell arrived with Jackie Washington and Julius Lester. The head of the Vicksburg Freedom House was a quiet guy named Mario Savio, who later became a leader in the Berkeley free speech movement. The day after the shooting there was a lot of discussion about security. The Vicksburg Freedom House was surrounded by woods and thick underbrush. It also sat nearly three feet off the ground on cinder blocks. Their so called watch dog loved everybody and wouldn't even bark if you stepped on his tail, so they devised a plan. Armed with flashlights, sentries were to patrol the grounds all night in shifts. That night some locals invited me to hang out with them at the black VFW. When I returned at about three in the morning, I asked them to drop me off down the road just to test the newly instituted security program. The sentry with the flashlight was sitting on a mattress outside the house, asleep. I petted the dog, tied the sentry's shoelaces together, and took his flashlight. I covered the flashlight with a blue bandanna and crept through the house. Everyone was sleeping. I left notes that said, "You're dead...your throat was cut in your sleep." They didn't like the joke, and they didn't learn the lesson. About four months later, the Vicksburg Freedom House was severely damaged by a bomb blast. Fortunately, there were no injuries.

Before Cordell arrived, the whole mood of the Vicksburg project seemed depressed. I had been in Tennessee, Georgia, Arkansas, and Alabama, and the camaraderie and joy that permeated all those movements seemed to be absent here. When Cordell heard that no one was supposed to go anywhere in integrated cars, he said, "I didn't come down here to practice segregation. I'm going to town. Who wants to go?" That was the end of that policy.

We went back to the VFW, and the owner offered to throw a party for the SNCC staff and all the freedom workers. The VFW resembled a fort with thick concrete walls and slit windows. It had clear visibility in every direction. The man who owned the place said, "I got some questions for y'all before we can do this thing." He brought out several rifles, pistols, and a shotgun, spread his arsenal on the counter and said, "Now if you freedom riders are up in here partying and some rednecks decide that it's time for us to die, are you going to practice nonviolence or will you shoot?" My answer came quickly, "I'll shoot." My commitment to nonviolence was only tactical, not philosophical. We partied hard, and the next day there was a lighter spirit in the air.

When I look back now, I know that I'm lucky to have ever gotten out of Mississippi alive. It's not that we didn't recognize the real and present danger that faced us all. The fact is, we were ready, eager even, to challenge anyone or anything that even appeared to deny us the freedom and liberty that other citizens enjoyed.

My mother forced me into action in the North nearly ten years before Cordell Reagon introduced me to direct action in the South. It was a pivotal experience that helped prepare me for the struggles to come. It was my eighteenth summer. My mother said, "Len, I want you to go to the Sunday School picnic." I resisted. She said, "A Negro has never been allowed to go swimming in the Crystal Pool at Summit Beach Park. The Negro churches are renting the whole park for their picnic. If we're paying for the whole park, we should be able to use all the facilities."

When I tried to enter the pool area, the gate keeper said the pool was closed. I asked about the twenty people who were swimming in the pool. He said they were members of a private club and that a member had to sign for any new members. I found the park manager's office and went in. After a heated discussion he tried to leave his office, but I wasn't finished talking to him. He used his stomach to push his way to his car. Then used his car to slowly push against me until he got to the gate. The church mothers were saying, "Now son, we just come out here to have a good time and we don't want no trouble." I said, "I don't want any trouble either, I just want to get all we're paying for." As he pushed me out of the front gate with the bumper of his car, the last thing he said to me was, "Before I let a nigger swim in this pool, I'll fill it up with cement." This was the only outdoor public swimming pool in Akron, Ohio. I wrote a letter to the *Akron Beacon Journal* describing my experiences. They printed it, and I got a call from the NAACP. With their help, we organized a challenge using three black couples and three white couples. We rehearsed, synchronized our watches, and took our notebooks to record all conversations verbatim. The whites were admitted, the blacks were rejected. We sued and won, and they filled the Crystal Pool of Summit Beach Park with cement.

Back to Mississippi. I was thinking about the SNCC office in Jackson and the sound of the voices. Above the cacophony of the clattering machines was a new kind of music. You could hear the heavy influence of that master virtuoso orator James Forman. Some of the young SNCC workers even emulated his gestures. Ruby Doris, Ivanhoe Donaldson, Lafayette Cherney all spoke SNCC. There was a pace, a measured thoughtfulness, a SNCC sound. It was a mellow, front porch-comfortable, Coleman Hawkins-like embrace.

Talking about sound, next door to the office in Jackson was a bakery. It had a huge rotating tub they mixed batter in. Some of its ball-bearings were defective, so it pounded out a strange beat that had an even pulse but wildly random accents. I used to stand in front of it and play my guitar.

I had heard the staff talk about the patience and the time it took to register people to vote. I believed the vote to be the source of real power and the reason we were there. I had always wanted to do voter registration, but they drafted me to play at mass meetings and rallies. Consequently, I traveled from place to place all the time, sleeping in cars, on church benches and on the floors of freedom houses. I got my registration chance one day quite by accident. I was walking down a dirt road outside Hattiesburg. I can't recall where I was going. I passed a house that must have been about fifty yards off the road. A woman came to the edge of her porch and said, "Boy, didn't your mama ever teach you to say 'howdy do' to old folks? You must be from up North." I went up and introduced myself, and we talked for a while. She asked me if I could play that box I was carrying. I played and sang, and she went in the house and got me a glass of lemonade and asked me did I know how to string beans. Well, at stringing beans, I'm an expert. My Alabama-born grandma grew plenty of string beans in our victory garden during World War II. Instead of just snapping them one by one, I would line up the ends of about four and snap them with one move. She said she had been stringing beans for nearly seventy years but she had never seen anyone do them like that. She laughed and said it looked like it could save some time, which was always a good idea.

We talked about the dirt road that ran in front of her house and how she had to carry her good shoes to church in a paper sack and put them on when she got there because the road was so dusty. We talked about how the road turned to blacktop as soon as it crossed the railroad tracks to where the white folks lived and

how maybe voting could change things like that. She talked about how crazy dangerous the white folks were and how all the Movement people would be leaving soon. She asked me to come back the next day to eat some of the beans I helped her string. She would cook them with a ham hock and some white potatoes and make some corn bread. I told her I was going that night and I didn't know if I'd ever get back that way again. She said she had lived a hard life and that she was old and hadn't seen too much of the world. But there was one thing she thought she would like to see. I asked her what that was. She said she wanted to see the inside of that voting booth that they were so busy trying to keep her out of. The next day SNCC workers took her to vote.

Cliff Vaughs, an ex-Marine from Boston, lived in Tupelo. When I first walked into his house he had a Harley-Davidson engine disassembled on his dining room table. It was gleaming. Cliff was one of the craziest people I had ever met. He gave me a ride on another one of his bikes and, without warning, popped his suicide clutch and did a wheely down this bumpy dirt road. I almost tore my arms out of the sockets trying to hold on.

We stayed at Cliff's house while we were working in that area. Every night or so, sometimes twice a day, we would sing at a mass meeting. Sometimes we sang in churches with three or four hundred people and no amplification. Sometimes we sang on a flat bed truck, in the middle of a field, with a mike taped to a rake. I grew up in a Baptist church, I even led the junior choir, but they wanted the youth to be sophisticated and would not let us rock the gospel songs like the old folks. They made us sing anthems.

So I had never experienced singing like the singing of Mississippi. Those people could kill you. It would be humid, 100+ degrees, and a song would start. People would be standing and rocking—children, teenagers, old people in their sixties and seventies, playing tambourines and swaying and shouting on one song for over thirty minutes.

I was playing my guitar and singing with sweat splashing on my boots, when this small, stout lady locked me with her eyes. She was short and heavy but you couldn't call her fat. She had on a stingy-brim, straw hat and a flowered cotton dress that seemed to be designed to test the strength of buttons. I swore that I was not going to let some little old lady wear me out. The whole church was rocking, verse after verse. We made up verses then started at the beginning again. Somewhere I turned a consciousness curve and was transported. I became a transcendental surfer riding the crest of a never-ending musical wave. I had joined them in *the zone*. I didn't know it then, but I had just met the soon-to-be-legendary Fannie Lou Hamer and we were singing her favorite song, "This Little Light Of Mine."

I don't know how many times I went back and forth to Mississippi that summer. After the first time, I always drove. I had a blue Hillman Minx convertible, seven or eight years old. When I was getting ready to leave New York, a SNCC worker named Alma Bosley gave me a five-pound jar of peanut butter to take on the trip because, after you got into the South, it was really dangerous to stop to get anything to eat. We called it the "backup peanut butter and bread." That jar of peanut butter in a brown paper bag went back and forth across the country many times with many people. Somehow it got broken and when it was given to the next group going south they said, "Are you crazy? We're not going to eat this." We told them, "Take it anyway. Take it for good luck. Take it because it's a tradition." They took it.

I just read Wallace Terry's *Bloods: An Oral History Of The Vietnam War By Black Veterans*. Most of the stories recounted soldiers' brushes with death. Nothing makes you pay attention to what's going on more than thinking this might be the last thing you hear or see on earth. There were many times like that in Mississippi.

I was with Cordell in my Hillman Minx and we had to stop for gas. I had to use the toilet. I asked the attendant for the key that was hanging on the wall marked "men." He said, "You don't need no key. Yours is 'round the back and it's open." I went to the rear and it said "colored." Well, I had to go real bad. I mean sit down go. The place was filthy and flies were everywhere. I said, "No way," went back into the station, walked behind the counter, took the key and headed for the door. Mr. Double-Beer-Belly said, "Hey boy, that ain't for you." I said, "Yes, it is. I wouldn't let my dog go back there." I went to the white men's room and it was clean, had two urinals and a stall. As I was sitting in the stall the outside door opened. I saw Double-Beer-Belly's boots from under the stall door. He said, "You better come out from there, boy; we got something for you out here." Then I heard Cordell yell, "Len, it's getting hot out here." I was thinking, they're going to have to shoot me on the toilet, because I'm not going out there. Then I saw what I thought was a hornet nest near the ceiling over the toilet. I figured if I could get them stirred up, maybe I could get away. I decided that first I'd better see if anyone was home. I took off my belt and stood on the toilet and did a Zorro windup and hit the nest. The nest was empty, and I was pissed. I said, "Well, it *was* a good idea." Then I said, "It's *still* a good idea." I hit the door running, waving my arms over my head yelling, "Hornets!" I blew passed them so fast I was in the car and Cordell was speeding away before they could move. I described the nest to Cordell and he said, "Man, that wasn't no hornet nest, that was just a wasp nest. If it had been an active hornet nest, you might not have made it to the car." We spent hours worrying about every car we saw. We were afraid they had called ahead to arrange a reception for us.

In Jackson, we picked up a young white kid from the SNCC office. We were taking him to the Sun 'N Sands Motel. Cordell was driving and the kid had very long legs, so he was sitting in the front seat. We were waiting for a light to change when a car pulled up on the right side. All of our windows were down. Mr. Deep-Tan-

Crew-Cut in the car on our right gave a colorful rendition of the famous "Scum Bag Nigger Lover" speech, then tried to smash the kid in the face with the police-style night stick that he held in his left hand. The light changed, and we peeled away. Two blocks later, the light caught us again and Mr. Deep-Tan-Crew-Cut pulled up in the same position. By then, we had rolled all the windows up so he started banging on the side of the car with his billy club. I'm yelling, "Go Cordell! Drive!" And he's saying, "The light, man!" I say, "Screw the light. Get us out of here." As we sped away, out of the back window I saw Mr. Crew-Cut give me the finger and show me the pistol he had in his right hand.

I had not slept in a bed for weeks. So when my wife, Nancy Rose, came to town and got a room at the Sun 'N Sands Motel, I thought it was time the place was integrated. Nancy was white. We'd been together since 1958. She phoned the SNCC office with her room number, and I sneaked into the Sun 'N Sands. Clean sheets, hot shower, it was great. I hid in the toilet when room service came. I got in and out without being detected. If I had been, you would have read about it.

The Hillman Minx's dash lights didn't work, so we had to use a flashlight to check the speed and gas at night. Foreign auto shops are not on every other corner in Mississippi. Coming back from Canton one night, the headlights went out and we had to drive down the pitch black country roads holding a flashlight out the window. I found a foreign auto service station in the yellow pages and went there to get the work done.

The owner was a white man in his late fifties or early sixties with suspenders, a little round belly, and glasses on the end of his nose. He had to tilt his head back to see. I couldn't tell if those were laugh lines or squint lines at the corners of his eyes. He was talking with a mechanic when I came in. I heard that soft, slow white Southern drawl that I imagined must have filled the offices of White Citizens Councils as they plotted to bomb churches, to crush boycotts, to fire the uppity niggers who had registered to vote. I

heard those saccharine sweet tones echo through the hardware store as he added that extra length of rope to the bill along with the 30/30 rifle shells that would soon seal another freedom worker's fate. No, maybe not. This was not the voice of red neck, six-pack Bubba with the pickup truck and rifle rack. This was a bourbon and branch-water, it's a dirty job but I can always get somebody else to do it voice. This was the voice that set policy, that owned, that controlled, that managed, that manipulated. This was the voice of disenfranchisement that first said "poll tax" and "grandfather clause." The voice that X'd people off their land. After the Civil War, former slave owners left many tracts of prime real estate to recent ex-slaves. They were told that the government was going to give them seed, lard, and molasses to get them started, and all they had to do was to make their sign. Since it was illegal to teach a black to read, most could not. So instead of signing a receipt for free goods, they were signing quit-claim deeds to their property, thus X'ing themselves off their land.

I imagined these were the luscious, honeyed tones that compelled the Grandma-house keeper to let them call her Mamie even though her real name was Emma, "Cause we had our Mamie for so long, we just got used to the name 'Mamie.' I hope you don't mind," as if this was a new dog out of the pound, with no past and no life outside of their presence. We can call *it* what we want whenever we want. "Oh no!" the voice would have said. "The fact that my wife's best friend is named Emma has nothing to do with it." This was the voice of quality, of refinement that offered to pay $1.50-a-day plus car fare and lunch. This was a voice that was understood and appreciated. It never had to be raised. When it spoke, all other voices were silent. This voice did not discuss, it pronounced. Its suggestions were mandates that set actions in motion. So when Emma's (alias Mamie's) son, who'd won that scholarship to Howard University, got his degree and a good government job in Washington, came back home with his brand new car, no one had to tell him he couldn't drive his mother all the way to work. He knew it would be best to drop her off a couple blocks away. He didn't know she would be seen, that the neighbors would report back to the voice. The "all" voice. There would be no dispute, no debate. No demands for explanation. When the voice pronounced, "Mamie, we won't be needing you anymore," they understood. They knew the meaning of *unseemly*. It would be *unseemly* to have a housekeeper with a son whose car rivaled the quality of theirs. Everyone understood. Nothing more needed to be said.

This was the voice on the board of education that was determined to transform the sweet plums of expectation into the leather prunes of disappointment. This voice administered schools where children learned to read upside down because of the shortage of hand-me-down, antiquated books, where the rain came in and the wind blew through, and teachers' salaries were only a fraction of their white counterparts; where the economic reality that the voice helped to create called them back to the fields where they only hoped to survive, instead of challenging them to achieve the academic excellence they knew they would need in order to thrive. This was the Tennessee Williams meets William Faulkner voice resonating from incestuous closets, repeatedly scanning variations of a homophobic nightmare featuring black genitalia. "Power! We must always, in every way, remind them who's on top. We'll make 'colored only' water fountains shorter, no chrome, and don't bother to clean them. They dare not complain. Let them order their food from the window out back. Make the window high so they have to reach up. No, don't waste concrete for pavement in front of it. Let them stand in the dirt."

I know this voice, this person, this past and present. This is my enemy. Within those tones with all their nuance and subtlety, I heard the seductive song of death. I thought I saw generations of repression and exploitation combining with lust and self-loathing merge into rivulets of infectious saliva forming at the corners of what should have been lips. I thought I saw the cor-

rosive acid of the passion for power and a fear of the inevitable fall popping to the surface of his skin like bubbles to the surface of a toxic waste dump. I'm in the lion's den without a toothpick for protection. But hey, I've got a ball point; if the rap goes rancid, I'll go for his eyes.

I wanted to run. I wanted to fight. I wanted to scream. I wanted to do anything but what I did. I planted my feet and put my face in neutral as he wiped the sweat from his upper lip and said." May ah hep you, suh?" "I hope so, sir," popped from me. I started to explain my problem when he said, "Why don't we step into my office, suh. I got air condition and it sho is hot today." We walked into his office, and he introduced himself and extended his hand. I shook it without hesitation. I was surprised, but I was on automatic. "Miss Dawson, could I ask you to bring Mr. Chandler here a cold drink." He "suhed" me. I "sired" him. Every sentence from each of us was liberally seasoned with appropriate politeness. I had a wiring problem that took over three hours to repair. By the time the work was completed, I had acknowledged my involvement with the Movement, and he had confessed that the golden rule was the guiding principle of his life and the standard by which he evaluated everything from race relations in the U.S. to the Vietnam War. During our conversation, a black mechanic came in to ask that some additional parts be ordered. He treated him with the same respect that he had been extending to me. He said the South was going to change because the South was wrong and must change. "Do unto others as you would have them do unto you." I asked how he was able to harbor such radical and locally unpopular ideas and still have good relations with the business community. He said that he had been in business many years and ran the best foreign car place in the state. He said he tried to avoid conversations with fools, but he was known for having a mind of his own.

I had enjoyed a wide range of positive experiences with all kinds of people and knew I would never fall into the ignorant pit of racism.

But he had just proved I had become a regionalist. When I left, we shook hands and he gave me a card that had variations of the golden rule translated from about ten different languages, quoting major world religions. It was a good day, a day of growth.

Many SNCC cars had two-way radios with long aerials that extended from the front fender to the back of the trunk. It was great for keeping in contact, but it also made the cars easy for anyone to identify. One day we were rolling down the highway, and I saw fifty or sixty people in the cotton fields, standing facing us with their hoes held in a vertical position high above their heads.

Cordell told me that they recognized us as freedom workers and this was a salute to us. They held their salute until we were out of sight. Click—another picture I would hold in my heart forever.

Cordell and I bought the big straw hats that the cotton pickers wore in the fields. Then Bobby Fletcher, Cliff Vaughs, Worth Long, James Orange, and many of the other workers started getting them until it became a part of the uniform. CORE started selling them with a band that said Freedom Hat.

Nancy Rose had become an expert leathercrafter. I think it started when I was carrying a sweat sock filled with all my gear. I stuffed the sock with things like my pipe, tobacco pouch, lighter, autoharp tuner, tuning fork, finger picks, glasses, notebook, pen, little flashlight, phone book, and my hay fever pills. I asked her to make me a leather pouch resembling those in medieval paintings that I could wear on a drawstring around my waist. She made one in the early sixties, and I wore it out. She reworked the design so you didn't have to take the pouch off to get into it and made them out of beautiful suede. By that time, she was also making great women's handbags, sandals, hats, book bags and many other things. Several of the SNCC workers got her to make bags we called hip-pouches for them.

Many people (who had been working as sharecroppers most of their lives) got kicked off the land when they registered to vote. Nancy Rose got some New York manufacturers to donate two vans full of leather sewing machines. We drove them south in one of my life's roughest rides. They were cargo vans with no insulation, carpet, air conditioning, or seats. We had a single mattress to sit on. The floor got so hot, the mattress started smoldering several times. We put out the fire with our sweat. (Just kidding.) When we finally made it, Nancy joined a craft co-op and set up a leather workshop. She taught people how to make products and arranged to have them sold at the Freedom Outlet House in New York's Greenwich Village.

Abbie Hoffman set up the Freedom Outlet House to sell handicrafts that displaced sharecroppers made in the South. The money went to the people who had created it and to the Movement. Nancy told a gray-headed former field worker that his finger nails were too long and they were scratching up the finish on the leather. The man told Nancy that he couldn't cut his nails because he needed them to pick cotton. Then he looked at his hands for a long time and said, "I don't think I'm ever going to pick cotton again," and cut his nails.

James Brown had a hit called "Papa's Got A Brand New Bag." So when I heard that he was coming to Jackson to do a concert, I asked Nancy to make him some very special bags. At the concerts, some SNCC workers went back stage during intermission and gave him the bags. He came out wearing one of the bags, performing his hit and threw the other one into the audience. People went crazy. SNCC made a deal with him to have a SNCC representative travel with him and sell the bags, with all the money going to SNCC. The arrangement worked great for several weeks. Then Brown sent the SNCC rep home, had a Detroit manufacturer knock off the design, and had his people sell the bags and kept the money. That broke my heart. I lost all respect for the man. So when Brown went to prison, I didn't feel bad.

Biloxi, Mississippi, has some of the most

beautiful white sand beaches in the world. We were in Biloxi for some big meeting. I don't recall what it was about, but there were representatives from all over Mississippi, both black and white. Some of the people stood up and told stories about how they had become involved in the Movement and what they had been doing. I heard some very moving accounts from students who had dropped out of school, broken with their families, and were risking their lives daily to put an end to the injustice of legalized segregation. At the end of the meeting we joined hands to sing "We Shall Overcome." A young fisherman, whose story had been extremely compelling, came up and told me his wife had been standing beside me when we sang. He said it was the first time she had ever touched a Negro. I ran into him again, a year or so later, and he told me his wife had filed for divorce because of his Movement activities. I asked him how he felt about that and he sang, *Ain't going to let nobody turn me 'round turn me 'round, turn me 'round. Ain't gonna let nobody turn me 'round. I'm gonna keep on a walking, keep on a talking, marching up to freedom land.*

In Biloxi, someone loaned me a motor bike. I was very comfortable on the bike because I had years of experience driving a motor scooter in New York. As a part of my defensive driving skills in New York, I had learned to always look at a car's front wheels. You can tell what they're going to do before they can do it. As Cordell and I were riding through town, a city bus pulled up on our left side. The bus driver looked over at us and smiled. I smiled back, then looked at his front wheel just in time to see him cut it toward us. He forced us to jump the curb and lay the bike down to avoid going head first into a tree. Had the tree not been there, I believe he would have followed us over the curb.

Aaron Henry and others were busy organizing the Mississippi Freedom Democratic Party to challenge the regular Democrats for their seats at the National Democratic Convention. This would be the focal point for all the voter registration programs that swept Mississippi all summer.

One scene will always remain fresh in my memory. The bus leaving for Atlantic City was filled with freedom workers and representatives of the Mississippi Freedom delegation. We were singing, *You should a been there, you you you should a been there, you should have been there to Roll Freedom Roll. Roll Freedom Roll, Roll Freedom Roll, I've got to get my freedom before I die, so Roll Freedom Roll.* We were singing "This Little Light Of Mine," "Ain't Going To Let Nobody Turn Me 'Round," and "Freedom Is A Constant Sorrow." Then someone started singing *This May Be The Last Time. This May Be The Last Time. This May Be The Last Time, I don't know.*

The fact is, we did not know if we would be alive to sing, to work, to pray, or play together again because this was a war. Although most of us had embraced the principles of nonviolence, the white racists that we opposed had not.

I had never been to a convention before, nor had I been to Atlantic City. Security was very tight around the convention hall. The Mississippi Freedom delegation was going to try to be seated, and I knew it was something that I didn't want to miss. Of course, we had no credentials to get down to the floor. We didn't even have spectators' tickets. So we came into the convention center through an underground service entrance, hiding behind garbage bins, ducking into utility closets until we worked our way up to a spectator's area. I saw a girl who was with the Young Democrats For Freedom, I later learned her name was Posey Lumbard. I asked if she was going to be in the area for a while. She said she was, so I asked her to hold my leather vest and my freedom hat and said I would get it from her later. I introduced Posey to other SNCC members and that radically changed the direction of her life. Posey joined the Movement, went South, fell in love, got married, had three children. She continued to work in Movement oriented activities until she was killed in a car accident while visiting her parents in the north.

I kept a small pair of scissors in my pouch to trim my beard. I used them to liberate a pass from a Mississippi delegate who had been holding it hostage. I jumped the rail and ended up standing next to Fannie Lou Hamer as she threatened to sit down in the lap of one of the delegates if he refused to relinquish his seat. The failure of the Democratic Party to recognize the Mississippi Freedom delegation marked a low point in the history of representational democracy.

Flashback to Biloxi. This was a grand hotel. The drapes were super-plush green velvet and I had to think of Scarlet O'Hara. Sis Cunningham of *Broadside* magazine had asked me to write an article about my experiences in Mississippi. I had been keeping notes. I had pages of observations virtually written on the run. I ordered a pen with a light in it from Hammacher and Schlemmer. I wrote notes at night in moving cars, while walking, anytime and all the time. I had met the courageous and the cowards, the defiant and the defeated, the nonviolent and the undefiled.

The undefiled were rare, perhaps nonexistent. Who has been beaten and not been corrupted by dreams of retribution? Who has been pierced by the fangs of public humiliation without succumbing to the fantasies of vengeance?

The smaller me, who still lives in a house I can afford, dreamed for years of vengeance. As I write this, Byron de la Beckwith is on trial again for the murder of Medgar Evers. Some say they want justice. Okay, I'll call it justice as long as it makes him hurt as intensely as we, who have waited for justice deferred, have hurt. Perhaps he should hurt more, since he will not live enough to hurt as long.

Even with all its frustration and disappointment, the Movement years were some of the best years of my life so far.

Here's "Random Thoughts On A Mississippi Muddle," written on the cold tile floor of a bathroom in that hotel in Biloxi.

Printed in *Broadside,* July 1964

> The muse has put a fire brand in my throat
> A new kind of passion has put the pen back in my hand
> Cornered now and risking all
> Counting all my empty pockets
> Cursing every pinched mouth promise
> With a gun in my pen and my brain on the trigger
> Baby I'll try to tell you one more time

LEAVING AND ARRIVING

> I left my house in the usual mess
> That I leave it in when I am leaving
> I knocked on the door of the lady next door
> To say goodbye to her and her children
> Johnny kissed quick with his eyes all a-wonder
> At the suitcase in my hand and guitar on my shoulder
> Ronnie all wide-eyed and really not knowing
> That the kiss meant goodbye and the guitar meant going
> Johnny who's older said, "Where is he going?"
> "To the wars," said I and his mother together
> "To the wars," and we said it together.
>
> I strapped on my suitcase and started my scooter
> I'd too little time to go search for a taxi

I raced it 'cross town for my last look at Nancy
I hope not last look
Just last look before leaving
I hailed me a cab and got caught in the traffic
All tense now with fear that I'd miss my connection
I climbed in the side of a sleek silver eagle
That could pierce darkest clouds and could make its own thunder
Though the patchwork quilt earth is a sight worth beholding
I dreamed on the brink of the nightmare I raced to

The turbulent air tossed me out of my dreaming
I saw cloud banks that looked like some cruel kind of sculpture
Where are the clouds with the feather soft edges?
Thunder clouds gathered in dread somber warning
In pillars of black from the sky to the swamp lands
No smoking and fasten your seat belt was flashing
I land in a land just one spark from explosion
Where freedom fired fervor has just started glowing

THERE ARE MANY HERE AND EVERYWHERE

Who pretend to defend but deform the defenseless
With the cruelty of cancer lay waste to the gentle
Who turn a deaf ear to the pleas of the helpless
Who buckle their belts 'round the throats of the hopeful
Who hit in the heart with their hate fashioned hammers
Who sign first the pledge and proclaim their allegiance
Whose harvest of hate bears new seeds ripe for sowing
Whose marshes and swamps hold a triangle secret
Whose mothers are mothers of pale insurrection
Whose offerings of peace are a sheath for a dagger
Who own all the wells but have never drawn water
Who scatter the pieces
Who burn and dismember

THERE ARE MANY HERE AND EVERYWHERE

Who dying of thirst pollute an oasis
Who spit on the hand that is held out to help them
Who rend their last garments to prepare for the winter
Who gnaw at the hurdle they should lightly leap over
Who fetter the feet of the swift and the eager
Who keep for their counsel the leech and the carrion
Who'd rather eat crow than fly with the eagle
Who gasping for air keep their head 'neath the pillow

MAYBE THERE ARE MANY HERE,
THERE MAY BE MANY EVERYWHERE

Who long for some liquor to help blur the image

Whose eyes have grown dull out of fear, out of focus
Whose brain is all scarred from those long psychic beatings
Whose waiting no more for the reign of King Jesus
Whose life has been labor to fill other's coffers
Who have but one crime and one transgression
Who was born in a land that would give him no blessing

HERE IS ONE

Condemned to the quarry he's as hard as a rock now
With nothing to lose but his body and person
Squinting at last now to focus the vision
Seeing he'd spent all his life bound in prison
Seeing now clearly who'd done all the beating
Hearing new threats from the bullies who'd beat him
Saying they'd leave him there dead without gender
Knowing they would, not be too young to remember
The violence they'd done to his brain and his body
Having learned well all the lessons they'd taught him
Tempered like steel in the fires that had forged him
He took the dare now to get what was owed him

He joined with the others and heard all the speaking
The old songs they sung now all had a new meaning
The prayers they prayed were a new kind of praying
All circled in youngsters, the lean, clean and gentle
He heard of nonviolence, a new kind of weapon
He knew of the weapons the racists were using
He couldn't believe what the others were saying
He told of the knife and the gun he'd been keeping
They preached and they pleaded and tried to convince him
With love he must bear all the blows of the brutal
And armed without arms bare his throat to the jackal

Clenching his teeth in a vise-like unyielding
Spitting out words in a stream of hot rivets
He told them that all he had left was his body
And he would give that in a real fight for freedom
But before he would fall he would take a great number
They said, "Thanks for coming, but your gun isn't needed."
He wondered how thick was their old constitution
Would it fit in a hat to save heads from cracking?
He's standing in wait on the edge of the circle
Knowing nonviolence is the bait for all bullies
There's no sanctuary where nothing is sacred
He'd kill the first one who'd lay hands on his body
Then he'd keep on shooting and cutting and shooting
His last shot he'd save it to make himself brainless

If they caught him they'd burn him and the good death is painless.

I HATE HATE!!

The white heat of hate now consumes the consumer
The hat band of hate stops the flow of their thinking
Hate is the source of the greatest subversion
And the halls of our congress are filled with contagion
The counterfeit king holding high the brass scepter
The house boy turned whore writhes in counterfeit pleasure
With charm bracelets choking the life from our infants
They bargain for brand names worth more than the garment
What hope has the lamb where the wolf is made shepherd?

WILL THE CIRCLE BE UNBROKEN?
BY AND BY!!

Ring around the rosies picket full of posies
Ashes to ashes we all fall down

With hope for the future should I lay my heart open
Where hate sears the hair of my chin and my eyebrows
Where it reeks now of reckless to walk where I want to?

Ring around the steak house pocket full of pennies
Bashes to crashes we all fall down

When the maker of whips is the first to be beaten
When I open my eyes and I'm glad to see morning
When I don't fear the food that is set on the table
When knife is a tool just to cut out a cancer
When gun is a fear that's been long since forgotten
When bomb is a bad word not fit for good company
When law breakers gently are cared for in clinics
When borders are not even counted in crossing
When birth is a blessing and babes are born smiling
When death is a quiet that comes to the aged
Then justice . . . will grant us . . . the peace . . . we've been seeking.

❖

Folksinger Len Chandler playing for summer volunteers in Mileston, Mississippi, 1964.

LEN CHANDLER

We Will Not Bow Down To Genocide

I heard a young boy say
No, my dad's not here today.
The police came and took him for a ride,
They put him in a cell
Without charges, without bail
'Cause he would not bow down to genocide.

We will not bow down
We will not bow down
We will not bow down to genocide

If you tell folks what you know,
If you point your finger at the foe,
Then the graves and the jails and the canons open wide.
I've got a feeling in my brain,
A feeling that I've gone stark raving sane
'Cause I will not bow down to genicide.

We will not bow down
We will not bow down
We will not bow down to genocide

It's not only in the south
They try to put a gag in freedom's mouth,
But that gag is wearing thin this whole world wide.
And there are many in jail for me,
They fight for justice and liberty
'Cause they would not bow down to genicide.

We will not bow down
We will not bow down
We will not bow down to genocide

BARBARA DANE

Michigan to Mississippi: A Journey

For me the Mississippi Summer of 1964 really began nearly twenty years before, in Detroit where I was born. It was part of the grim reality back then that a black person couldn't get a cup of coffee, let alone a meal, in most parts of the city because of a notorious and well-established pattern of home-grown apartheid. Nobody seemed interested in enforcing the Michigan Equal Accommodations Act, already on the books for years, and well-known racists such as Gerald L. K. Smith (head of the Black Legion, Michigan's own version of the Klan) and Father Coughlin (a rabid right wing, Catholic priest with a large radio following) had been setting the tone for race relations for far too long on the local scene.

During the Great Depression, all this seemed to be accepted as commonplace in the part of town where I grew up. But it had upset me for a long time, although I didn't know what anyone could do about it. I was just out of high school in 1946 when I found out about a group of young people who were planning to test the Equal Accommodations Act at the Barlum Hotel Coffee Shop and decided to join up with them. The test consisted of something one takes for granted today, just a group of black and white friends meeting for lunch. But when the management tossed us out of the place, as they routinely did any black would-be patrons, the real action started. What we had done was part of a plan to kick-off a major campaign to end Jim Crow in the restaurants of the city.

Beginning immediately, we mobilized a picket line in front of the Barlum Hotel which was to appear again every Saturday for weeks on end, each time larger than the last. The location for the test had been well chosen, because the hotel occupied nearly all of one side of Cadillac Square, the familiar gathering point of so many of Detroit's union organizing and other historic struggles. With our signs, shouts, and songs, our numbers grew into the hundreds, drawing support from a coalition of community, union, and church groups spearheaded by the AYD (American Youth for Democracy).

It was there and in the many other picket lines, rallies, and demonstrations of those postwar days that I found my real voice as a singer. In the fine old organizing tradition of adapting familiar tunes and reworking or replacing yesterday's texts to get across today's message, I discovered that no text or tune was sacred. I also discovered that the dainty soprano sound suitable for the Sunday School choir was good for practically nothing in the streets, so I opened up and let my natural sound come out—not pretty, but it carried over the crowd. It was there I met a whole range of audacious people who became my closest friends. It was a moment that set me free in ways I would better understand as the years unfolded.

By the time the early '60s arrived with their lunch counter sit-ins and Freedom Riders, I had an intensively active singing career and three small children to support with it. The kids grew up thinking that painting picket signs and marching in front of the 5 & 10 Cent store or in peace demonstrations was just what everybody did. Like most mothers, I used to worry about what effect all this activity would have on them, but as adults they've expressed the feeling that being part of a community of people committed to something greater than themselves was a privilege and in many ways a joy.

When in 1964 I heard about a caravan of singers being organized to support the literacy and voting rights campaigns of the Freedom Summer in Mississippi, I began to prepare myself a way for the journey by talking about it at every opportunity and in every performance. To raise money for the trip, I started selling off household and personal items through signs on local bulletin boards, and I'm sure some people bought more things than they needed. I went to buy a suitcase and when I told the man in the store what it was for he wouldn't let me pay. A wonderful artist named Earl Newman created a handsome silk- screen portrait of me singing and gave me a box-full to sell as a fund raiser.

I walked up and down Telegraph Avenue with a canister that said "Send a girl to jail!" (meaning me). People actually put money in it! A dear friend in Venice Beach invited my children to stay with her for the summer as her contribution to the struggle. In short, it seemed like nearly everyone felt proud to know someone who was actually planning to go to Mississippi to help in any way at all, and wanted through that contact to somehow send a part of themselves.

Suddenly the shocking news that three young volunteers, James Chaney, Andrew Goodman, and Michael Schwerner, had been kidnapped was flashed across the nation. A caravan of "folksingers" was being quickly assembled to tour the Freedom Schools, which had been set up in spare bedrooms, church basements, and store fronts up and down the state to teach literacy and voter registration techniques. There was the idea that this would attract more of the national public spotlight to events in Mississippi,

thereby making it more difficult for the night rider types to carry out their mayhem under cover. The search for the three civil rights workers was in full swing, tensions were at bursting point, and new violence could break out at any moment.

I got in touch immediately with the Caravan committee in New York, quickly organized a great many logistics with children and career and lover and landlord and ex-husband and bill collectors, etc., and was on my way. I felt I carried a great responsibility, as if my whole community was going with me and all my audiences too. In the end, I was only in Mississippi a bit over two weeks, but it was part of a continuity in my life that would have been disjointed forever had I not gone. It was worth every bit of risk involved.

SNCC workers met us at the plane in Jackson and took us immediately to headquarters. There they briefed us on the frightening situation surrounding the kidnapping of the three volunteers, details of the ongoing search, as well as what security measures we should follow. Clearly, whatever had happened to the three had been done to try to intimidate the rest of the volunteers in the hopes they'd all go home. But one of the key songs on everyone's lips was "We'll Never Turn Back."

We were to split up in teams to drive to various parts of the state, where we would present for the most part informal programs of songs at the Freedom Schools, sometimes held in yards, sometimes in church halls, living rooms, or back bedrooms, or simply in fields. We were singers, and we would sing, whenever and wherever the Movement workers decided we could be of use. There was Judy Collins, Len Chandler, Phil Ochs, Davy Sear, Gil Turner, and who else? I really can't reconstruct a list because we arrived at different moments and were sent off in many directions without meeting all together, but it was a sizable group.

Why had we come? Each of us had our own perceptions and priorities, of course. Some of mine: to bring from a distance a message of solidarity and identification with the struggles be-ing waged by this time all over the South and spreading north; to listen and to learn, and to gather tools from this with which to help build greater solidarity; to witness some of the work of these often anonymous but nevertheless au-thentic American heroes, working to liberate themselves and in the process saving an impor-tant part of the American soul.

To be confirmed in the rightness of this his-toric struggle. To help break the isolation of Mississippians, in 1964 still living under bru-tally enforced barbaric social and economic rules invented in feudal times. (Most black Missis-sippians depended on work in cotton and earned, according to SNCC field secretaries Charles Cobb and Charles McLaurin, $300 to $400 for sharecroppers and $150 to $160 for day laborers annually. I'm talking about for a whole year's work.) To help lift a curtain of si-lence that prevented most Americans from knowing about this fact, a silence fostered and endorsed by the very men who represented the state in Congress and who benefited most from the nation's ignorance. Most of all because (to quote John Hulett, then chairman of the Lowndes County Freedom Party), "You cannot become free in California while there are slaves in Lowndes County. And no person can be free while other people are still slaves, nobody."*

We're talking about things that happened thirty years ago, so I can only offer a kind of mosaic now. Rising images are soaked in sweat, crusted with dust, floodlit with sunshine, green and leafy and grassy. There is Bob Moses and a handful of other SNCC office volunteers relax-ing from all the tension by dancing the twist, the mashed potato, the hitchhike, and the dog on a patch of cement just outside their office door, still wet with puddles from a sudden down-pour. Blue chambray work shirts everywhere, uniform of the Movement volunteers, simple but reassuring because of the coordination implied.

A whole mixed gang of us recently arrived folks invading a black-run restaurant for fried chicken dinners, and what courage it must have

taken for the proprietors to let this noisy bunch, which included a lot of white strangers, gather there. Joanne Grant, there to report on events for the *Guardian* newspaper, having to cover her hair with a scarf lest its outline in the rear win-dow call unnecessary attention to her presence in a car full of whites. Len Chandler passing potato chips from one car of friends to another while riding through the streets of Jackson, just to show he couldn't be intimidated into unchar-acteristically low-key behavior.

I wound up in a car with a SNCC volun-teer and a singer-songwriter from New York, who insisted on riding hunched down on the floor of the car the whole way. As soon as we arrived at the humble home of a supporter in the crossroads town where we were to stay that night, I overheard the singer on the telephone detailing our entire itinerary to someone at the top of his lungs. This was the very thing we'd been warned not to do, for fear more of us would be kidnapped on the backroads, so I shouted at him to shut up at once. "Leave me alone, I'm talking to *Newsweek*!" was his reply, indicating a unilateral plan he'd worked out. I avoided riding with him from then on.

A dusty country ride and there is burly car-penter Abe Osheroff with the sun behind him, high up in some scaffolding he'd just built, an older Jewish guy from L.A. who had fought fas-cists as a volunteer in the Spanish Civil War now volunteering to build a community center for the Movement in Mississippi. And wouldn't you know, he chose to build it right across the road from the home of Hartman Turnbow, a hero of the voter registration drive in the town of Har-mony, whose place, with his family in it, had been shot into just a few nights before.

More miles in another direction and there is the broad manicured green lawn of some black folk who, having somehow managed to make it into a middle class set-up themselves, hadn't let that stop them from allowing us to hold a large inter-racial fund raising party at their home. And every single night, at every stop on those tense and dangerous journeys between the kidnapping of Goodman, Schwerner, and Chaney and the discovery of their mutilated bodies at the bottom of a dam, we met black Mississippians with next to nothing of space or possessions who shared whatever they did have with us strangers, mostly white, in a time and place where white folks and strangers mostly meant big trouble.

Up in the hills to the north of the capitol we visited a proud people I never knew existed: black independent small farmers who had never been a part of the plantation system. These were people who had survived from Reconstruction times clear up to the mid-sixties by using hand labor and mules, horses and wagons instead of relying on cars, trucks, and tractors; kerosene lamps instead of electricity, homegrown food and homemade clothing wherever possible. They ran a TV on occasion with a generator, and I observed some of the young people as they watched the nightly news. To an outsider, they seemed to be looking at the live news coverage of a civil rights demonstration just a few miles away in Jackson as if it was a Hollywood movie, as if it had only the remotest connection with them.

But it was the Delta that was calling me all the while, the cotton country where so many of my musical heroes were born, and where Fannie Lou Hamer was fast becoming a legend. Among the first to attempt to register to vote, she had been badly beaten in jail and had risen up stronger than ever, singing, organizing, and preaching freedom. I remember sitting under some trees in a little park in Ruleville where she lived, talking with a group of elders and singing a blues for them learned in Chicago from local son Muddy Waters, trying somehow to convey the enormous value the world outside places on this music created out of the very pain they were living through.

I remember ordering a quilt from the little cooperative Mrs. Hamer had set up in Ruleville as a fund raising effort. These work-worn older ladies without proper spectacles for hand work or the money to invest in materials had "found

a way where there was no way" by piecing together scraps the best they could. When it arrived by mail in New York many months later, the quilt was a mute testimony to the sacrifices with which the commitment to make it had been fulfilled, and how nearly everyone managed to find a place in the struggle.

Most of all I remember the power of Fannie Lou Hamer among her people, weaving together song and talk and song again, making the spirits of her weary, sweaty neighbors visibly rise as their hearts connected. She seemed the perfect fulfillment of the concept "singer:" not just one who sings, not only a great voice, but a shaman, preacher, teacher, healer taking responsibility for community and continuity, making sure that life itself will go on with any sense of the reasons for it. As she reminded them again of the rightness of their struggle and led them into the cadences of call and response so old and yet so new, you could almost touch the ties that bound them ever closer into a community with the strength to resist and triumph. Why was this brilliant, dedicated, and capable woman not in charge of running the country, or at least the state, rather than being beaten and harassed, forced to live a precarious day to day existence?

The urgent demand for change, for an end to segregation, was a cry taken up and supported by millions upon millions of Americans. Integration was the word that swept the land. But inside the black community a debate went on about which the likes of me knew nothing. Local black leadership, with agendas and strategies developed over many decades and through many struggles, saw itself sidestepped in some cases, or not sufficiently consulted or taken into account in others, or they sometimes simply didn't feel the respect that was merited.

Who invited all these northern white students and their friends to mess about here anyway? It wasn't only white segregationists who asked this question. Integration into what? Some black leaders were asking why anyone would want to be part of the rotten system and culture that white society represented for them. Tactics and strategies, nonviolence versus preparation for self-defense, objectives and personalities of all sorts were being discussed and struggled over. Both blacks and whites were raising a host of questions, and we haven't seen an end to it yet.

But regardless of these debates, the shining reality of the student sit-ins, the Freedom Rides, and the marches had already altered the country to its core, believers and antagonists alike. Nothing would be the same again. There was a larger question on the agenda which had been decided not in discussion but in action. Without a vote or an edict, a campaign or a slogan, but with an unspoken mandate made manifest by what took place, the country was becoming a place of citizens at last, no longer a nation of subjects.

The long cold war of the heart had begun to thaw. People emerged who could not only speak out about injustice but who could act— and even act in concert—to do something about it. What was unleashed by the so-called "Civil Rights Movement" helped give birth to a renewal of the age-old struggle for women's rights, new movements for lesbian and gay rights, for immigrant rights, for the rights of the disabled, for the right of self-determination for the widest possible variety of people. The movement against the war in Vietnam was indispensably strengthened and enriched by the empowerment people discovered through that earlier movement.

An important part of the power of a Martin Luther King, a Fannie Lou Hamer and, yes, a Malcolm X, was that they could articulate that for which a great many Americans, both black and white, have long yearned. A more just society, yes, and right now, but an America where we could begin at last to practice what we've always said we were about: all for one and one for all. *E Pluribus Unum*, look, it's right there on our money. Justice under the stars and stripes and also under the dollar sign. An end to hypocrisy, one of the ugliest of our national social diseases. A place where we could begin to practice the golden rule. The freedom to admire, respect, and learn from one another without fear.

The promise of a "Freedom Summer" is still a long way from fulfillment, but it was a start. Passage of the Voting Rights Act a year later was a clear response to the voter registration campaign which was the centerpiece to all the marching, organizing, singing, and insisting. It was also a belated effort to clean up our nation's image before a world which had seen all too many photos of police in the act of beating and hosing down children, snarling police dogs attacking elders, people who were merely attempting to exercise rights long taken as guaranteed by foreign admirers of the United States of America.

A major upsurge in African American representation in Congress, state legislatures, and local governments followed. Similar assertions of self-determination and empowerment among Latinos, Native Americans, and Asian Americans were encouraged by these successes. Ethnic studies departments were fought for and won on major university campuses and, for a while at least, the nation seemed to be committing itself to affirmative action as a way of correcting past injustices.

True, cynical politicians like Richard Nixon and Ronald Reagan were able to unleash a backlash which allowed them to ride into office by promoting and encouraging mean-spirited attitudes among many whites. And this tide, some days, seems to be the rising one. Those who would posture as "protectors" of lives in which they have no interest after birth, those who hack school budgets to death and jack the cost of higher education up out of reach in order to build more and bigger prisons, the proponents of anti-immigrant measures of every description, these are just a few of the actors in this essentially white supremacist drama. And they have powerful friends.

Racism is still pervasive in American society, as the beating of Rodney King revealed so dramatically in case anyone was sleeping. Resistance is everywhere and will be as long as conditions are as far from equal as they are today for the vast majority of people of color. But important gains were made by the Movement whose

"Freedom Summer" we are discussing here which have not been rolled back, and it isn't likely that they can be. The days are gone when the wealthy white men who have controlled this country could sleep peacefully in the assumption that the train and the right-of-way are theirs and the rest of us only riders (or worse yet, porters). New generations of Americans are—despite the ravings of many of their unreconciled elders—growing up as part of a multicultural country in a multi-colored world. This is a historical process that no power can stop. And Freedom Summer helped to clear the way. To this extent, all who took part in it can call themselves shapers of history.

* "Black Protest: History, Documents and Analyses, 1619 to the Present (1968)," Joanne Grant's important collection of documents and recollections of the period.

PETE SEEGER AND LEE HAYES

The Hammer Song

Adapted by Barbara Dane

Well if I had a hammer,
I would hammer in the morning,
I would hammer in the evening,
All over this world
I would hammer out danger,
I would hammer out a warning,
I would hammer out love between my brothers and sisters,
All over this world.

Well if I had a bell,
I would ring it in the morning,
I would ring it in the evening,
All over this world.
I would ring out danger,
I would ring out a warning,
I would ring out love between my brothers and sisters,
All over this world.

Well if I had a song, yeah,
I would sing it in the morning,
I would sing it in the evening,
All over this world.
I would sing out danger,
I would sing out a warning,
I would sing about love between my brothers and sisters,
All over this world.

Well I got a hammer,
And I got a bell, yeah,
And I got a song to sing
All over this world.
It's the hammer of justice,
Yeah, the bell of freedom,
And it's a song about love between my brothers and sisters,
All over this world.

PETE SEEGER

A Few Words About the Civil Rights Movement

Maybe there has been a social movement without songs or chants, but I never heard of it. In North America the union movement, the peace movement, and others have been famous for songs.

But surely never was there a movement like the Civil Rights Movement to make music such a central part of it's meetings, rallies, marches, sit-ins, mass imprisonments.

African and European traditions mixed as singers with various tinted skins, from north and south found themselves putting new words to old tunes and singing them together.

It was a time of history I'll never forget, and my family and I will always be glad to have been a part of it in some way. Of course the victories were not as complete as we hoped. But we made it, up another rung on Jacob's Ladder. Halleluya.

❖

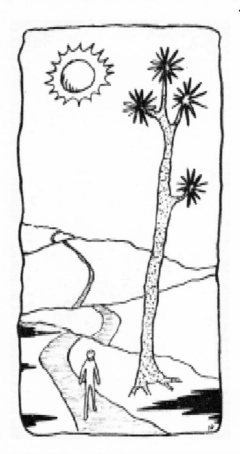

Pete Seeger has been singing for more than 50 years at civil rights marches, peace rallies, for unions, schools and colleges. He is best known for songs he has written or helped to write, such as, "Where Have All The Flowers Gone," "If I Had a Hammer," and songs he adopted and introduced such as, "Guantanamera" and "We Shall Overcome" which are known worldwide. Pete helped start the Clearwater organization which sails a 106-foot traditional sailboat on New York's Hudson River educating tens of thousands of school children every year to problems of pollution. He has recorded many albums available on Folkways and Columbia Records and has published numerous books, including his musical autobiography, Where Have All The Flowers Gone, a Sing Out publication.

Folksinger Joan Baez performing at Tougaloo College near Jackson, Mississippi. Jackson excluded blacks from all civic concerts so entertainers performed at Tougaloo, a black college. Her audience included a significant number of local whites drawn by Baez's reputation—the first integrated public event in Mississippi history, 1964.

PHOTO BY

MATT HERRON

Tribute to Phil Ochs

In 1964 I was a housewife and mother, taking care of my family and going to college at night. I had participated in the March on Washington on August 28, 1963, and that had been my first overt political action. I remember two weeks before the march hearing on the radio that there would probably be violence in Washington, so I thought that maybe I should stay home. After all, I had two small children to care for. Then I thought, "That's exactly what they're trying to do—scare off people so that the march will be a failure."

In June of '64 I heard the news about the three young men missing in Philadelphia, Mississippi. On the evening of August 3, I attended a rally at Woodmere High School at which the guest speaker was Nathan Schwerner, father of Michael Schwerner. I went into labor that evening, and when I awoke after giving birth to my son, the first news I heard was that they had found the three bodies.

I was so angry, sad, and frustrated, not knowing what I could do to help stop the sickness in the South. I finally came up with an idea to help raise funds for the voter registration drive. I handmade birth announcements for my son which read as follows:

> Here I am, born white and free
> In a land of opportunity.
> I need no clothes—no finery,
> So won't you contribute to SNCC for me?
>
> Jonathan Michael Tanzman
> Born August 4, 1964

We raised several hundred dollars which helped me to feel that at least I had done something to help with what was happening.

Other people were doing various things to help the cause. On April 9, the New York Council of Performing Artists was created by a small group of folksingers. They planned to act as a clearing house for benefits throughout the nation for civil rights, employment, and other causes as well as going to the scene of conflict itself and participating in direct action as artists. It was through this organization under the chairmanship of Gil Turner that artists were recruited to take part in the Caravan of Music of Project Mississippi between June 15 and August 30. Artists would be asked to spend one week in Mississippi to play before integrated audiences.

Requests for support were published in *Broadside* magazine which was quite popular at that time, and in *Sing Out* magazine, which is still in existence today. Among the people who responded and who went to Mississippi as musicians were Len Chandler, Bob Cohen, Judy Collins, Barbara Dane, Alix Dobkin, Carolyn Hester, Gil Turner, Jackie Washington and my brother, Phil Ochs.

Some of them stayed for a week, while others such as Len Chandler and Jackie Washington ended up staying for the whole summer. The idea was to put on a concert in a church and then, after singing and having fun, suggest that the people in attendance register to vote. The

Sonny Ochs resides in upstate New York where she teaches middle school, produces Phil Ochs Song Nights and other concerts, and has a radio show on WRPI. In her spare time, she reads and takes long walks in the woods.

church was the natural place to hold these events because it was the only place where African Americans could congregate, so it was the only place to speak to a group.

Phil did a couple of these concerts with Jackie Washington. Telling me about these occasions, Jackie was amazed at how well folks received Phil's performances, considering Phil's songs were geared toward an urban white audience. Here was Phil playing to audiences of unsophisticated country people—churchgoing farmers who were generally wary of voter registration because of possible (probable) reprisals. Yet they came, apparently seeing Phil as a very sincere young man who really cared about their plight.

Before Phil headed for Mississippi, he would often visit Sis Cunningham and Gordon Friesen at the *Broadside* office (which was really their apartment), and he would be very excited. He kept talking about "social realism," and how exciting this was for him to actually be doing something concrete—going into the field of battle where things were actually happening, instead of just talking and writing about it from a safe distance.

This experience opened up a whole new field of thought and activity for Phil. It boosted his topical protest writing and gave him a big shove forward. I remember talking with him when he got back and asking him what it was like. He said that one of the churches in which he sang had been bombed the next night. He jokingly said that he hoped that the bombing wasn't a reflection on his performance.

When he returned from Mississippi, he wrote some really strong songs, among them "Here's to the State of Mississippi" which caused a lot of controversy. Some people objected to the line, "Mississippi, find yourself another country to be part of.", which was equated with, "America, love it or leave it." Another criticism was that there were many good people in Mississippi, so that line wasn't fair. I consider the criticism valid, but I feel that the verses are so strong that they make the song worth listening to.

Another song Phil wrote before he went to Mississippi was "Goin' Down to Mississippi" which appeared in B*roadside* #48. He dedicated it as follows: "This song is written partially for the three project workers who disappeared, partially for the rest of the students going down this summer, and partially for myself." (7/1/64) The song was released a couple of years ago on an album titled T*oast to Those Who Are Gone* (Rhino Records).

Unfortunately I don't really know much about Phil's experiences in Mississippi. I am very proud of him for taking part in what could have been a fatal undertaking. He was an idealist like so many of the students and musicians who traveled to Mississippi from all around the country to try to make a difference. I wish there were more of that idealism alive today.

For those of you who may never have heard of Phil Ochs, I'll give you some background. Phil was the middle child of a middle class family living in middle America (Ohio) when the '60s began. He was very patriotic but saw that all was not right in this country. He felt some injustice first hand while majoring in journalism at Ohio State University. Some of his writings were censored by the school paper because they were pro-Castro, so he quit college and headed for New York City.

When Phil arrived in New York, folk music was becoming very popular and there were numerous places where a musician could play around Greenwich Village. Phil started writing topical songs at an amazing rate, many with a humorous twist. His first recording was with Vanguard Records, where he had one quarter of an album which also featured Eric Andersen, Bob Jones, and Lisa Kindred.

Phil played concerts all around the country, many of them at anti-war rallies. He had three sold-out concerts at Carnegie Hall. He traveled all around the world—Australia, Europe, South America, and Africa. He was so vibrant, and got such a kick out of life. He made several albums on Elektra and A&M Records.

With the passage of time and his growing disillusionment with the political system of this country after the 1968 Democratic Convention, Phil started to have bouts of depression interspersed with short manic bursts. During two of those manic bursts, he produced "A Tribute to Salvador Allende" at the Felt Forum and "The War Is Over" concert in Central Park.

On April 9, 1976, Phil committed suicide at my home in Far Rockaway, Queens, New York. It was not totally unexpected. He had been very depressed for quite awhile. He was thirty-five years old.

About ten years ago, someone suggested that we do a "Phil Ochs Song Night" at the Speakeasy in New York City. We got a few performers to sing some of Phil's songs. It was a very successful evening, and since then we have done more than twenty of these shows in places such as Washington D.C., Boston, New York City, Philadelphia, Columbus, and Albany.

The bad news is that some of Phil's songs are still timely today—thirty years after they were written as topical songs. The good news is that performers such as Magpie, Kim and Reggie Harris, Nancy Tucker, Pat Humphries, and many more are carrying Phil's songs all around the country. Phil's songs cry out against war and racism, and many of today's topical writers are producing new songs which do the same. Phil would be thrilled if only he knew that he had influenced so many songwriters. ❖

PHIL OCHS

Goin' Down To Mississippi

Broadside Number 48, July 20, 1964

This song is written partially for the three project workers who disappeared, partially for the rest of the students going down this summer, and partially for myself. —Phil Ochs, July 1, 1964

I'm goin' down to Mississippi,
I'm goin' down a southern road,
And if you never see me again
Remember that I had to go,
Remember that I had to go.

It's a long road down to Mississippi
It's a short road back the other way
If the cops pull you over to the side of the road
You won't have nothing to say
No, you won't have nothing to say.

There's a man waitin' down in Mississippi
Waitin' with a rifle in his hand
And he's lookin' down the road for an out of state car
And he thinks that he's fightin' for his land
Yes, he thinks he's fightin' for his land.

And he don't know the clothes I'm a-wearin'
And he don't know the name that I own
But his gun is large and his hate is hard
And he knows I'm comin' down the road
Yes, he knows I'm comin' down the road.

It's not for the glory that I'm leavin'
There's no trouble that I'm lookin' for,
But there's lots of good work that's callin' me down
And the waiting won't do no more
No, the waiting won't do no more.

Don't call me the brave one for going
Don't pin a medal to my name
For even if there was any choice to make
I'd be goin' there just the same
I'd be goin' there just the same.

For I'd rather take the chance in Mississippi
Than never learn how to stand
And hide my head in a television world
And wonder what it is to be a man
And wonder what it is to be a man.

I'm goin' down to Mississippi, I'm goin' down a southern road,
And if you never see me again
Remember that I had to go,
Remember that I had to go.

Freedom Summer... Freedom's Blowin' In The Wind

Peter, Paul, and Mary (Travers) have exemplified the folk tradition in their grassroots approach to both music and political change ever since their 1961 premier performance at the Bitter End in New York's Greenwich Village. These three distinctly different artists, each with his or her own separate interests and solo projects, have managed to successfully combine their varied talents into a creative and ever-evolving whole. Today, with the release of their latest project, Peter, Paul, and Mommy, Too, *the trio's inspiring message of idealism and hope is reaching a fourth generation of fans.*

For many of my contemporaries, Freedom Summer was not just the summer of '64, but it was the summer that most Americans realized that change was definitely blowing in the wind. My involvement in the Civil Rights Movement did not begin that summer, nor did it end in the dreadful summer of '68.

I had been raised and taught very specifically, by both parents and school, that the dreams of equality were much sturdier than a moment in time or the eloquence of one man or woman; that the struggle for freedom and equality would resurface again and again. But to be truthful, it was the men and women who fueled the early 1960s with their passion, courage and sometimes their blood, who confirmed in reality those ideals and inspired the songs I sang with Peter and Paul.

Songs and traditions are kept alive by people loving and living them. In the early years of the Civil Rights Movement, songs like "If I Had a Hammer," "Go Tell It On The Mountain," and "Blowin' In The Wind" took on an urgency as well as a relevance. As we sang "If I Had a Hammer" on the campus of Ole Miss while the National Guard defended James Meredith's right to attend school in 1962, I realized a frightening truth. My idea of "... love between my brothers and my sisters" was different from most of the students we were singing to. They were singing along with gusto about love between white brothers and sisters only.

The song that most identified the Movement for me was Bob Dylan's "Blowin' In The Wind." We sang it at marches—Washington; Selma-Montgomery; Frankfurt, Kentucky. We sang it for Martin Luther King, Jr., and both Presidents Kennedy and Johnson. We sang the line, "How many years can a people exist before they're allowed to be free?" with anger and entreaty all at the same time.

Then at the memorial service for Andrew Goodman, one of the three young men killed in that Freedom Summer, we sang the lines from "Blowin' In The Wind," with tears running down our faces, "How many deaths will it take till they know that too many people have died?" I still don't know the answers to the questions the song poses, but because the struggle for equal rights and justice continues, I do know we'll have to keep singing those songs. ❖

BOB DYLAN

Blowin' in the Wind

How many roads must a man walk down before you call him a man?
Yes,'n how many seas must a white dove sail before she sleeps in the sand?
How many times must the cannon balls fly before they're forever banned?
The answer, my friend, is blowin' in the wind,
The answer is blowin' in the wind.

How many years can a mountain exist before it's washed to the sea?
Yes,'n how many years can some people exist before they're allowed to be free?
How many times can a man turn his head pretending he just doesn't see?
The answer, my friend, is blowin' in the wind,
The answer is blowin' in the wind.

How many times must a man look up before he can see the sky?
Yes,'n how many ears must one man have before he can hear people cry?
How many deaths will it take till he knows that too many people have died?
The answer, my friend, is blowin' in the wind,
The answer is blowin' in the wind.

WAZIR PEACOCK

Reflections

Willie (Wazir) Peacock was born in Tallahatchie County, the same county where Emmett Till was lynched. He graduated from a high school in Charlestown, Mississippi, in 1958 and went to Rust College in Holly Springs, Miss., where he joined SNCC. After graduation, Wazir became a full-time Field Secretary for SNCC in 1962. He was one of the original SNCC song leaders. After a stint doing graduate research at Tuskegee (Alabama), he returned to Mississippi to organize the Community Cultural Revival, the folk festival which was a forerunner to the Delta Blues Festival. Today, Wazir teaches independent living skills to developmentally disabled children.

I. Why Do You Do It

I was born in Mississippi during the time that our country was engaged in World War II. In the early years of my life, I experienced a strong sense of community. It was safe for me to go anywhere without fear of being molested. I remember feeling loved, cared for, and protected by the elderly and young adults.

As a child it was easy to find someone who would talk about how well they knew your parents or grandparents, uncles, and aunts. Why? Because they had grown up together—a continuum of community from generation to generation.

As World War II wore on, these communities began to disintegrate. Families began to migrate to the north to have better protection under the law, and more political, educational, economic, and social freedom. I remember how sad it made me to see so many of my friends moving away to the North, some of whom I never saw again. I suffered a great loss.

This raised questions in my mind that were to take me on a life journey seeking answers and solutions to problems that could change the situation. As I was seeking, I found a wealth of fellow warriors who had things in place to do battles with the evils of society. I took my place among them and have kept up the struggle ever since.

I think that social change organizing is the bringing together of individuals affected by a central need. It is the work of those individuals to raise the consciousness of the populous to a level where organizing can be effective enough to eradicate the need. One of the best examples of this kind of organizing to date is the "Algebra Project," founded by Robert P. Moses in 1982. Bob Moses could not have picked a more critical need—one which must be transformed into an issue to be addressed by our nation's government if the U.S. is to remain a competitor in the high technology field. Mathematics at the middle school level must be dealt with effectively in order to have a domestic work force with adequate qualifications. That which was relegated to the elite must now be given to the masses in abundant doses.

The most important issue facing my community is under-employment and unemployment, conditions which cause wounded pride and self-hate, feelings that manifest in drug dealing, turf war murder, and self-destruction.

II. What Have You Done

As an activist, organizer, and field secretary for the Student Nonviolent Coordinating Committee (SNCC), the first task before me was organizing black people in Mississippi and Alabama to register to vote.

Due to unconstitutional laws in Mississippi and Alabama, black people were disenfranchised. They were not allowed the rights of citizens to register and to vote. I became active in 1960 in Holly Springs, Mississippi, where I was a student at Rust College, one of the two local, black colleges. This is where we began to work going

Willie Peacock, Matt Jones, and Sam Block in the SNCC office in Greenwood Mississippi.

PHOTO BY

DANNY LYON

door to door educating the people of their rights under a constitutional form of government. This effort inspired more and more people to attempt to register to vote. I graduated from Rust College in the spring of 1962 and stayed on as a full-time organizer for SNCC.

I left Holly Springs (Marshall County), Mississippi, for the Mississippi Delta. I entered Greenwood (Letlove County), Mississippi, to become co-organizer of the Voter Registration Project. The fear of the people was greater than any other place I had been. As soon as black people there became aware of my and Samuel Block's aim and purpose, they would literally cross over to the other side of the street to avoid being identified with us in any way. It was quite understandable why people had so much fear and hated to see us coming: this was the home of the National White Citizens Council. After the people saw that we meant business and that we were not going to leave or run out on them, they began to open up to us. After several months of day to day walking and talking to people in every conceivable place where black people gathered, came February of 1963. Black people in Greenwood started going down to the county courthouse in hordes to attempt to register to vote.

While I have done other things since that time, I think that my participation in that project was my greatest accomplishment because the fear of the people was broken, and this led to the formation of the Mississippi Freedom Democratic Party (MFDP).

My greatest disappointment came in 1964 in Atlantic City, New Jersey, at the Democratic National Convention. As MFDP organizers, we had really done our homework. We had done our caucusing and had lobbied the members of the Credentials Committee of the Democratic Party. We had proved our case: that the regular Mississippi Democratic party was disloyal to the national Democratic Party and that it practiced racial discrimination. But when it came time to vote, they seated only the white Mississippi Democratic party. For me, this was a demonstration of how powerful the Southern white politicians were at the national level. I learned that politicians moved according to what would get them elected and re-elected, and not necessarily according to the rules or what was morally right. I learned that there may be many defeats preceding the victory. You must prepare for the long haul and make struggle a way of life.

❖

GUY CARAWAN

Ain't You Got a Right to the Tree of Life

Title from an old Johns Island, South Carolina, chant.

Ain't you got a right, ain't you got a right,
Ain't you got a right, ain't you got a right,
Ain't you got a right to the tree of life,

Ain't you got a right to the tree of life.
You can tell all of my sisters,
You can tell all of my brothers,
Tell it to the world 'bout the tree of life.
Ain't you got a right, ain't you got a right,
Ain't you got a right to the tree of life.

Ain't you got a right, ain't you got a right
Ain't you got a right to the tree of life.
You can tell all of my sisters,
You can tell all of my brothers,
You can tell it to the world 'bout the tree of life.
Ain't you got a right, ain't you got a right,
You can tell all of my sisters,
You can tell all of my brothers,
You can tell it to the world 'bout the tree of life.

We come from a distance,
We come from a distance,
And we got a right to the tree of life.

Rocky was the road,
And dangerous the journey,
But we got a right to the tree of life.

Our lives will be sweeter,
Yours and mine and our children's lives will be sweeter,
'Cause we got a right to the tree of life.

Ain't you got a right, ain't you got a right,
Ain't you got a right, ain't you got a right,
Ain't you got a right to the tree of life.
You can tell all of my sisters,
You can tell all of my brothers,
Tell it to the world 'bout the tree of life.

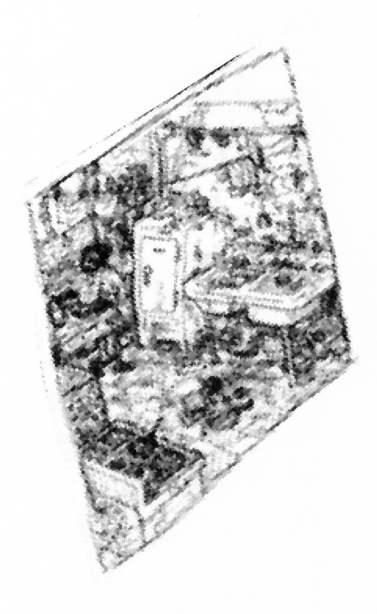

SIS CUNNINGHAM

Broadside Magazine as it Related to the Mississippi Summer Project

Sis Cunningham was born in 1909 in western Oklahoma's farm country. She taught public school in the area for four years. Sis was active in various Unions, was a member of the Red Dust Players, and joined the Almanac Singers in 1941. She co-founded Broadside magazine in 1962 which folded in Dec. '88. She produced five books, the two most recent of which are basically her own songs. Presently, Sis is a member of the Disabled In Action Singers of New York.

Broadside magazine, a journal beginning in the early 1960s which focused on the activities and works of topical songwriter-singers, was in full swing at the time of the Mississippi Freedom Summer Project. A considerable number of our contributors and volunteer staff members participated in this notable event. I was co-founder and co-editor of the magazine along with my husband, Gordon Friesen, and we published the accounts of several of these participants, notably Bob Cohen's "Mississippi Caravan Of Music," Len Chandler's long poem "Random Thoughts On A Mississippi Muddle," plus his introduction (transcribed from a tape) to his beautiful and memorable song "I'm Goin' To Get My Baby Outa Jail," (all in *Broadside* #52, Oct. 1964).

The introduction was as follows:

There was a lady, a schoolteacher from Orangeburg, South Carolina, at this benefit up here, and she told about how she had gone into this white hospital waiting room when she was pregnant, and they came and arrested her because she refused to move to the Negro waiting room. This young rookie cop came and arrested her, just like off the street, without consulting the chief or any other superiors. So when they got her in there and saw she was pregnant, they got sort of uptight and they wanted to get rid of her because it was, you know, sort of a bad mark against them. She wasn't the usual kind of hotel guest they liked to have in the jail. And so they gave her a low bond. She was well-known in the area anyway as being a very big civil rights worker.

But she wouldn't pay her bail. She just wouldn't pay it, because she said that she was innocent, and refused to participate. They gave her one of those quick, hokey-pokey trials and gave her like a very low fine—five dollars or something—just to get rid of her. So she wouldn't pay the fine. So then she was in jail, and everybody else shoved her court case up on the dockets and it went to the Fifth Circuit Court of Appeals, and there the decision was reversed in her favor: they said to turn her loose, right? And so I wrote this song as though I were her husband at home waiting to come and get her.

She, by the way, and her husband were fired from their respective jobs. She was a schoolteacher and he was teaching at the university. They were both fired for their participation in the Movement.

Other memorable comments were Tom Paxton's on the writing of his song "Beau John," and Julius Lester's on the Freedom Singers (both in *Broadside* #52, Nov. '64). We received some letters from Broadsiders while they were down South, but for the most part they were too involved in the activities to do much writing; we listened to their reports when they returned. Nearly all were enthralled by their first experience in political action—and greatly stimulated.

Mainly we printed songs which poured into our office: songs which were constantly being sung on the many marches and demonstrations. Peter Seeger sent us a raft of them, including "Roll, Freedom, Roll," cover song of *Broadside* #51. In earlier issues we had printed "Oh, Pritchett, Oh, Kelly" by Bertha Gober, a black teenager, written while she was in jail in Albany, Georgia, her fourth arrest, and "If You Miss Me At The Back Of The Bus." One of the most moving songs we printed during this whole period was another by Bertha Gober, "Never Turn Back." Bob Dylan's early "Ballad of Emmett Till," about the brutal murder of a fourteen-year-old black youth, and "The Lonesome Death Of Hattie Carroll" are examples of great writing on events preceding the Summer Project. Phil Ochs wrote (among many) "The Ballad Of Oxford, Mississippi," "Freedom Riders," "Goin' Down to Mississippi," and "Here's To The State Of Mississippi," the latter being one of the strongest songs politically ever to scorch the pages of our magazine. Phil went south that summer and wrote us moving letters from there. Somewhat later we received a song from Nina Simone, "Mississippi Goddam!," also a very strong and jolting one. Our standby, the truly prolific topical songwriter Malvina Reynolds, sent us "Singin' Jesus," which has the verse lines:

> *And his song said Men are brothers*
> *And it rang out clear and great*
> *And what the color of the brothers' skin*
> *He did not stipulate.*

And "Jailhouse Buddy," with the chorus:

> *Jailhouse buddy, we walked together*
> *We walked together that Freedom Line*

> *Jailhouse buddy, we walked together*
> *We'll walk together till the end of time!*

This song of Malvina's calls to attention one we had in #30, "I Ain't A Scared O' Your Jail," introduced by a group calling themselves Freedom Fighters (well before Reagan misused the term). The very young loved this song and did a twisting dance to it.

Women songwriters new to the topical music scene were coming forward. Debby Lewis sent in "Talkin' Civil Rights." Janis Ian, then a fourteen-year-old *Broadside* volunteer, brought us her song "Baby, I've Been Thinking," about a white teenage girl being attracted to a black teenage boy, and the problems that ensued. This song later won national recognition when re-titled "Society's Child." Some time later Anne Romaine's heart-wrenching "Backstreets Of Downtown Augusta" came to our attention, a ballad picturing the grief of a black mother whose young son was beaten to death in jail. The most moving song of Fannie Lou Hamer, the great leader and singer of the Civil Rights Movement, was "Go Tell It On The Mountain." She is remembered also for having made this statement in one of her speeches: "I'm sick and tired of being sick and tired!"

"Freedom Is A Constant Struggle," a great traditional song reintroduced during the Mississippi Freedom Project, was printed on the cover of *Broadside* #50, Sept. '64. On a "notes" page appearing in this same issue co-editor Gordon assessed this song as the most widely sung of all. A note we printed along with Julius Lester's "Dead And Gone" is entered here as it has a reference to the three murdered civil rights workers, Goodman, Schwerner, and Chaney:

> "Last summer a fisherman on the Pearl River (boundary between Mississippi and Louisiana) hooked half a human body. Parts of a second body were found a few hours later. This is not uncommon in that part of the U.S.: streams are regular dumping places for murdered and lynched Negroes (Emmett Till, Mack Parker). But interest was aroused in this instance because the search was on

for the three Mississippi civil rights workers, two of whom were white. This interest quickly waned when it was found that these two were not connected with the case; they were two Negroes, just part of the regular toll."

From 1964 through the rest of the sixties we were receiving great songs inspired by the Summer Project: Matt Jones's "Legend of Danville," Tom Paxton's "Goodman, Schwerner, And Chaney," Rev. Fred Kirkpatrick's "Everybody's Got A Right To Live," to mention a few. There were more, many more. Covered here are only the highlights of *Broadside*'s focus on the Civil Rights Movement's Great March toward Freedom.

For more information on *Broadside* write to:

Sis Cunningham
215 W. 98th Street # 4-D
New York, NY 10025

❖

DENISE NICHOLAS

Birth and Life of the Free Southern Theater

Denise Nicholas's passion for acting took flight during her two years as a performer throughout the deep South with the Free Southern Theater. The experiences that took root there have remained with Nicholas, who has established a successful career as an actress and writer. Nicholas is best known for her portrayal of guidance counselor Liz McIntyre on the hit ABC TV series Room 222, *on which she made her television debut. And for four seasons, Nicholas starred with Carroll O'Connor on the CBS-TV drama* In the Heat of the Night, *in which she portrayed coucilwoman Harriet DeLong. In feature films, Nicholas has starred with Bill Cosby and Sidney Poitier in* Let's Do It Again *and* A Piece of the Action—*for which she earned NAACP Image Awards as Best Actress—and in the film* Ghost Dad, *again with Cosby. Nicholas will also soon star in the upcoming family*

We propose to establish a legitimate theater in the Deep South with its base in Jackson, Mississippi. . . . Through theater, we think to open a new area of protest. One that permits the development of playwrights and actors, one that permits the growth and self-knowledge of a Negro audience, one that supplements the present struggle for freedom.

While it is true that the theater which we propose would by no means be a solution to the tremendous problems faced by the people who suffer the oppressive system in the South, we feel that the theater will add a necessary dimension to the current Civil Rights Movement through its unique value as a means of education.

—FROM A GENERAL PROSPECTUS FOR THE ESTABLISHMENT
OF A FREE SOUTHERN THEATER

With that, the Free Southern Theater was founded in 1963 by Gilbert Moses, John O'Neil, and Doris Derby at Tougaloo College in Jackson, Mississippi.

By Freedom Summer (1964), the FST was ready to launch its first tour. With the help of an active New York fund raising committee headed by Carol Feinman and Joy Manhoff, enough money was raised to mount a production of Martin Duberman's *In White America*. Tour sites (sixteen in Mississippi) were selected based on COFO activity in the town. Memphis was also a stop on that first tour, as was New Orleans. By the end of the tour, it was clear that Mississippi was too oppressive an environment in which to pursue the processes of the theater. The Free Southern Theater relocated its operational base to New Orleans in the fall of 1964 and prepared its next tour.

"We had begun. Now we had to figure out

a way to continue to exist. We needed a black community in the South large enough to support the theater, and even before the first tour we knew we would end up in New Orleans.

"Relocation of the FST headquarters from Jackson to New Orleans, however, was regarded in the back of our minds as a cop-out. New Orleans has a large middle-class black section which we hoped to tap as backers. Richard Schechner (then editor of the *Tulane Drama Review*) lived in New Orleans and could involve himself fully in FST if New Orleans was chosen as our operating base. We as actors felt we could use the distance from the Movement to concentrate on our art. We went to New Orleans.

"Idealistically, however, we felt that we were beginning to separate ourselves from the Movement, and the people to whom we were first committed. Still, there was a great deal of excitement and a lot of work to be done. A theater building had to be located, living facilities found, a local board formed, actors hired, money raised, the Mississippi tour planned." (Gilbert Moses)

During the early fall of 1964, the Free Southern Theater went into rehearsal for its second tour. Ossie Davis's *Purlie Victorious* and Samuel Beckett's *Waiting For Godot* were selected for production. A new group of actors, technicians, and volunteers descended upon our humble quarters, and we groaned once again into high gear.

The COFO projects in Mississippi were eager to have us return with our new slate. Project volunteers worked with us to secure places for the performances, homes to house our company members in each town, and helped with publicity. The Free Southern Theater became the focus of a community event involving everyone and open to everyone.

The second Free Southern Theater tour was more ambitious. After a week of performances in New Orleans, we headed to Mississippi, hitting twenty-three cities. We also went to Atlanta, Memphis, and ended in New York with performances at the New School for Social Research and the American Place Theater.

Letter to the New York Fund-Raising Committee, December 11, 1964

Our plays have been presented under all imaginable conditions.

Last month in Indianola, we gave an outside afternoon performance of *Purlie Victorious.* We set up our playing area on a field next to the Indianola Freedom School which had recently been condemned by city officials due to a fire which had "mysteriously" broken out in the building. COFO workers say that firemen watched the building burn, and that after finally deciding to put the fire out, they destroyed a lot of equipment in the building with water hoses and axes. During the two hours it took us to set up we attracted a crowd of over two hundred people. We invited children to help us lash our flats. The atmosphere was a circus, where actors and

their make-up were the attractions. The outdoor setting was especially appropriate for the character Gitlow, who, for the first time, literally ran on stage from the cotton field spewing cotton from his pockets. That afternoon's performance was one of the most exhilarating thus far.

Questions from the people after the performance rejuvenate us. Of course, there are some who listen to the discussion much in the same manner that they have watched the play; there are some who wait on others to formulate their thoughts. But there are those who ask a lot of questions, who have a great deal to say.

The Free Southern Theater exists for all the people here and, in particular, for those people who are just beginning to express themselves.

We arrived in Mound Bayou yesterday morning, the only all-Negro community in Mississippi. It was raining. The rain had washed the dirt roads clean to the gravel underneath, filling the deep draining ditches on both sides, churning the dirt roads into mud moats.

Entering the COFO office here, we saw some local people filling out forms to receive old clothes. They said, "We're coming to the performance tonight." In the rain, driving in their trucks for miles to come to our church/theater, over muddy roads, they come.

For these people, and for us, we extend our thanks.

Respectfully,

The Free Southern Theater Company

We arrived in New York, exhausted, exhilarated, and full of fight. We came to strut our stuff for the New York literati and to prove to those who were working so hard on our behalf that we were very serious about theater.

"Our performances in New York attracted

drama, Ritual, *with Clarence Williams III. As a writer, Nicholas has scripted seven one-hour episodes and one two-hour* In the Heat of the Night *movie and is currently at work writing the feature film* Legacy, *a contemporary drama about romance and vengeance in the world of politics. A native of Detroit, Michigan, Nicholas is a graduate of the University of Southern California where she earned a B.A. degree in drama.*

a lot of attention and interest; many more actors and directors applied to join the FST; we found a theater and we organized a new company, a larger one, to undertake the 1965 tour." (Gilbert Moses)

Progress Report

Free Southern Theater, Summer 1965

OPERATIONS:

1. The Repertory. After three months of rehearsal under Robert Cordier's direction, FST has previewed Bertolt Brecht's *The Rifles of Señora Carrar* and Martin Duberman's *In White America* in New Orleans at Dillard, Tulane, and Xavier Universities, the Dryades YMCA, Sacred Heart Church, Guste Homes, St. Peter Claver School Auditorium, First Unitarian Church, the Jefferson Parish Harlem Gym, and at Tougaloo College in Mississippi... Performances of *Carrar* and *In White America* have been enthusiastically received and often cheered.

2. Community Project. In conjunction with the Tulane University Summer School, the FST staff will offer a lecture series in children's creative dramatics aimed at public school teachers. . . .

3. Playwrights' and Actors' Workshop. Part of each working week is devoted to this workshop in which new scripts are tested and evolved. Gilbert Moses provides improvisations, parts of scripts, etc., to be performed by the company. In this way, plays related to our own and our audiences' experiences are evolved. This phase of the FST program is just now beginning. Moses wrote the song being used in *Carrar*.

4. Training. Speech and movement classes are held regularly in the company and are mandatory for all actors. A special seminar on modern theater has been conducted by Richard Schechner.

THE COMPANY:

The company is almost entirely professional and Equity. Although salaries are well below Equity levels (maximum $35 per week), an informal arrangement with Equity permits the employment of union actors at what are exploitative

wage rates. Hopefully this situation can be remedied soon. The company is more than double the size of last year's, and a significant number of hold-overs assure ensemble continuity. The object of the FST is to build an organic ensemble over the next several years. . . .

The company will leave New Orleans on August 1 and remain on tour until December 19. Two week-long vacations will be used for rest, and many in the company will return to New Orleans during these off-periods. Experience in past tours has shown that uninterrupted touring is too exhausting both physically and mentally. The nature of the theater is such that the tour is as wearing as it is challenging. . . .

The 1965 fall tour was cut short for lack of funds.

The Free Southern Theater, like the Civil Rights Movement itself, was unraveling. In our desperate gasps, we managed, in 1966, to mount *An Evening of African and Afro-American Poetry* (assembled by the actors), *Roots* by Gil Moses, *Does Man Help Man?* by Bertolt Brecht, and William Plomer's "I Speak Of Africa." We toured, fussing, cussing, and discussing all the way. Some of the overwhelming issues that faced us were: to be or not to be a black theater, a community theater, an integrated theater, a professional theater, a political (as in agitprop) theater, a museum (as in regional) theater. Gilbert Moses left in the midst of this agonizing turmoil, never to return.

"Despite our conflicts, it was a productive summer (1966). We played in Mississippi, Alabama, Georgia, and New Orleans, capturing for many the spirit of black pride and consciousness that the Movement was undergoing at that time. Many of the discussions after performances were fantastic, unforgettable. . . .

"Gil Moses' *Roots* evoked good comments on the role of black men and black women. It was performed brilliantly by Roscoe Orman and Denise. Plomer's short puppet play, "I Speak of Africa," brought hoots of delight from black kids who saw themselves portrayed as heroes for the first time, and whites as crude villians. Brecht's *Does Man Help Man?* almost caused a fight in Atlanta at Morehouse's Sale Hall." (Tom Dent)

August 1966 Letter from Gil Moses

To the members of the Free Southern Theater:

The reflection I get from the FST up here is one of having "grown up." People no longer take a patronizing attitude towards it; but rather they think it is fantastic. And it is more. More than they realize.

I have admiration for all of you who stuck it out—thru-out all the hassles—'cause I know how frustrating it is to take the time; to live thru idea becoming reality.

You, this season, really have shot thru the arguments of all bullshit artists who are concerned, yet "steady making it." You have shot thru a whole history of the Western concept of theater. In a sense, this season, you have done the most simple, yet impossible thing: provided an opening for young black artists; called into existence a theater which ignored commercialism; attempted to build an audience for expression where there was none . . . and you know all the other clouds and fog you have cut thru . . . precisely.

Personally, when I think of returning, the effort involved in the FST appears so great. It is such an effort.

A theater so open that the internal and constant struggle between politics and art, between nationalism and internationalism, manifested itself externally—no other theater in this country can boast such scars and pain. I'm very proud that my play was part of your program. I was afraid you weren't going to do it. (And hey, can someone send me a few programs from the different cities?) The problem is obviously staying together. After this year's experience, the art you could finally produce is fantastic. I am all of a sudden overcome with the meaning of the theater, and the work of the people in it . . . and all I can finally say is: you deserve as much respect as any group or anybody I have ever known, heard of, or read about in my life; as much respect as a flower, as the sea, as change, as motion itself. . . .

Gilbert

The Free Southern Theater lived on in one form or another, including a 1967 tour. The FST was finally put to rest in grand New Orleans fashion in 1984. But this way of crossing over rests on a concept of community; of secrets and symbols, of continuity, of history. The genius of the FST can't be measured. It touched an entire community of people and changed everything it touched. ❖

(Excerpts from *The Free Southern Theater* by The Free Southern Theater, edited by Thomas C. Dent, Richard Schechner, and Gilbert Moses, The Bobbs-Merrill Company, 1969)

John O'Neil in a performance of Purlie Victorious. *The troupe staged the production in an open field after local segregationists burned the church where the theater was scheduled to perform.*

DENISE NICHOLAS

The Free Southern Theater

I have laid over my memories of the Free Southern Theater a romantic veil. I was very young, full of idealism, looking for truth, looking for adventure. What I learned during my two turbulent, incredible years in Mississippi and Louisiana has been the spine of my personhood ever since.

Perception through time feels like virtual reality of the mind. My roommate at the University of Michigan was from Grosse Pointe. She said, "The only black person I ever knew was the maid." My dad always said, "White people have the problem, not you, baby."

I was reading *The Strange Career of Jim Crow,* listening to the winds of change coming from the South and running full tilt to my Art History classes coveting the framed, contained bliss of the Impressionists.

People visited our campus with stories of what was going on down South. I listened. There had always been a deep political strain in my soul and a great sense of fairness. The issues of race and power hadn't hit home with the big wallop because I refused to let them in. In my mind, some people were stupid and some people weren't.

Grandma Hines had marched on the Dayton, Ohio, police department when a young black boy was beaten. Grandma Waddy B. got fired from a job as a maid in Detroit when my dad drove her to work in his new car. Daddy kept saying he'd never work for no white man cause the white man didn't want to see you with nothing. In high school Ameri-

can history class, I argued forcefully with the teacher about slavery which got a meager two paragraphs in the textbook. I stood alone.

Slowly, the pieces fit into a wall in my mind, and I began to see that this race/power thing was not about a few dumb individuals. I left school to go south.

The train trip south from Ann Arbor, Michigan, to Jackson, Mississippi, was time travel, hurtling back to a primeval awakening. The trip itself was the entry. A plane ride wouldn't have allowed the aura, the people, the sounds, the colors, the history to congeal in my mind slowly enough . . . so that I could step into that vast terrifying place with the hairs on the nape of my neck quite appropriately raised. I needed to have fear. This was my first trip to the Deep South. I arrived June 1964, wide-eyed, expectant.

"Why you down here? You don't look like the kind of girl whose parents'd let her be a voter registration worker. You down here looking for something to fill your hot pussy or you here to get these niggers off their asses and on their feet?" The skin on his bare arms looked moist, luminous. It was red, yellow copper, black. "Since you don't know a damned thing about me or my family, why don't you just wait and see. If we're fighting for rights, I guess that includes my rights, too, hot pussy and all." Silence. In Ann Arbor, a white boy had pointed to a blond coed, looked at me and said, "Don't you wish you looked like that?" I was stunned. It had never entered my mind. Chasm.

In White America by Martin Duberman . . . our first tour through Mississippi. In McComb, a bomb was thrown near the stage. People scattered but came back when the smoke settled. No one was hurt so we continued the performance. Had I taken leave of my senses? I was afraid but so was everyone. In Indianola, the White Citizens Council came out to "see" our show. People were hanging from the rafters of the building. We gave them a performance they'll never forget.

That the Free Southern Theater changed the course of my life goes without saying. That I have fed my mind and soul from that plate till this day may not be so obvious. What was it that dug so deep? The moral certitude of the Civil Rights Movement? The right and wrong of how a society deals with its people? I cut my political/artistic teeth on the grandest scheme America has experienced since the Civil War. It is the only baggage I fight to hold on to.

In Milestone, the people had the light of fear and the light of courage in their eyes. We performed in a half-built community center being built by a white carpenter/builder from California. We sang to the heavens, to the trees, to the air. We sang until we dropped. We harvested hope everywhere we went.

> *The men sat up on their porches with shotguns so that we might sleep. No Klan riding through here anymore, blowing up our cars and shooting into our homes. We are ready to resume life in the world beyond the bondage, poverty, and ignorance of this place called Mississippi. Please help us.*

The police arrested me on a corner in downtown Jackson for handing out flyers announcing our performances. The elevator doors at police headquarters closed, and I nearly fainted from the terror of what I'd heard was coming. The beatings, the rapes, the whole horrid history of abuse flashed through my mind. They took me to an office, asked me some questions (bad English and not a clue about theater) and then it was back down the elevator, back into the police car, back to the precise point they'd picked me up.

We rode the highways and roads of Mississippi from Mound Bayou to Gulfport, from Canton to Clarksdale, from Greenville to Hattiesburg. We pitched our dreamy tent of theater to provoke, to entertain, to give laughter, and even more tears than were already there. Mississippi waded in tears. We were there when the curtain rose. We were there helping to pull the cord that brought the light of the 20th century to a place in hiding.

> *The moss swung from tree to tree on the road to Vicksburg when the Klan robes caught the wind and rose like a specter as their car sped by us on the highway.*

In Ruleville, Fannie Lou Hamer spoke on *Waiting For Godot*. "We been waitin' and waitin'!" She brought that play home to our audience. There was an existential quality to life in Mississippi, frozen in time, a moonscape with Spanish moss like looping dreads. The slave connected to the master and the master connected to the slave in an arc of never ending energy. Slavery changes everything forever. When all is gone, there is genetic memory.

Dew Drop Inns all over Mississippi. Thundering juke boxes with funky rhythm and blues. You loosened up just walking in the door. Aretha, Bobby Bland, the Impressions. We shot pool, drank moonshine, and smoked Pall Malls. We danced the fear out of our bodies, off our backs. The tension used to bear down on us forcing a frenzy of release. Then walk out into the thick night air, fire flies, mosquitoes nipping and zipping, finding our way in a strange town, in a strange land.

> *It's so hot and humid most of the time. Slippery wet skin, glowing, and we're walking in slow motion, raising our young arms to the gods, singing freedom songs and knowing we are right.*

You cannot convince me that what happened between 1954 and 1968 in America was not a revolution . . . nonviolent/violent . . . a wrenching change in direction, an unprecedented amplification of document. The Constitution, the Bill of Rights were made recognizable by the blood and guts of those who held them so dear they would die to live the principles. Those people were the quietly mumbling, shining black people who lived the nightmare of America's duplicity, and the black and white youth who joined them. They were the people I met and loved in Mississippi and Louisiana.

They found Schwerner, Chaney, and Goodman dead. Time stopped again. My mouth went dry and my eyes narrowed. We cried, eyes burning with anger. We burned with the hatred we were trying to rid ourselves of. We stared off into the future. When would the dying end. Probably never.

The Magnolias made me nauseous until I embraced their fruit, the giant flowers white and sweet and the hanging, charred black bodies, in one deep long breathe.

We trapped ourselves in a moot point; what plays to do before a largely rural, unsophisticated audience who'd never seen a play before. What difference does it make? The experience of live theater is a truth in itself. In *Purlie Victorious*, Gitlow ran in from a real cotton field, cotton spewing from every part of his oversized coveralls. We laughed till we cried. Somewhere, in a tiny church, a man came quietly up onto the stage from the audience to help me open a jar I was trying to open in Gil Moses's play *Roots*. It was the kindest gesture. We wrestled on with that point through Brecht's *The Rifles Of Senora Carrar*, O'Caseys's *Shadow Of A Gunman*, Gil Moses's *Roots*.

I stayed in a house on a cold long road with no plumbing. I walked outside in winter to get water. The woman of that lonely house became mythic to me. In a story, she became the first black woman to register to vote since Reconstruction. When the registrar tried to stop her, she beat him with a bag of canned peaches. Later, she became "Odessa Robbins" in my Odessa script for In The Heat Of The Night.

Mississippi was even more oppressive than we could have imagined. In time, we moved the Free Southern Theater to New Orleans for our rehearsals and classes, then toured back into Mississippi and Louisiana.

In the French Quarter, a young police officer pointed a gun at my head and said, "Take one more step and I'll blow your brains out." What madness was in his mind? I was unarmed, helpless, and standing in front of my own apartment. SNCC photographers were staying over to rest. The police wanted their film and their cameras. Where am I?

The old man from Marseilles lived in the garret across Burgundy street. He sat in his window painting pictures of Provence on tiny match boxes. He used to yell his hellos down to the street in French. He was always there, watching.

A mouse in a cello? Severn Darden, master improvisationist, came to do a workshop with us. Before my eyes, he was a mouse in a cello. I was enthralled. We worked at our craft—the arts of the theater: scene study, dance, voice work.

We developed improvisational pieces involving the local people and their struggles in a particular town, i.e. Bogalusa, Louisiana, (Indian named creek: Bogue Lusa, meaning smoky or dark waters. Company: Crown Zellerbach). These pieces were miracles. The audiences reveled in seeing themselves and their plight up on the stage nearly overnight. Gypsies.

In Jonesboro, Louisiana, I saw an "officer of the law" pick a lawyer up and throw him down a hallway because the lawyer was trying to get one of our vehicles out of the pound.

The Deacons for Defense took to the gun for self-defense. We felt safe in their custody. Sleep.

New Orleans rains. I left the movie theater after Truffaut's *Jules And Jim*. Truffaut. Something was changing in me. Film. I saw Fellini, Bunuel, Antonioni. I pined over *Black Orpheus*. Where were the Americans? What was happening? Nothing seeped into my consciousness. Bruno Mello and Marpessa Dawn were so beautiful on the big screen, so beautiful it took one's breath away. I saw how we looked on the screen and I knew somehow I'd go to that. I didn't know what lay ahead. How could I know America didn't want us beautiful on the big screen. . . .

Pop's Big Time Crip. On the edge of the Garden District. Already this is different. Talk politics, lis-

ten to Billie Holiday mourn. All jazz. Red beans and rice. No moonshine here. Pop's went to North Africa in World War II and lost both legs. The Army gave him two artificial ones. Lop-sided pool table . . . work that into your game. His peg-legged buddy used to stand on his hands on a table and tap dance on the ceiling. This place is insane and suits me fine.

A few of us went to lunch at a famous French Quarter restaurant. The waiter set the table, took the orders, but served only the blacks. When questioned, the manager said, "That's the law. We gotta serve you but we don't gotta serve them!" as he pointed to the whites in our group. What new insanity is this? Call the lawyers, here we go again.

The Ghetto of Desire, the 9th Ward, New Orleans. The Free Southern Theater in a new place. I've seen poverty in the country and I've seen it in town.

Tony, eleven, rode his souped-up bike to burn rubber at every stop, to run you down at every turn. There when you came, there when you left. Tattered and sometimes dirty, he would tilt his head, scream in frustration when you didn't recognize his power, when something in his skin, right beneath the surface, ached. Face burnt black, eyes jumping out, full of want of warmth, full of joke, accusing you of betrayal of the unspoken vow to be committed to no other but him. He sat proudly by the door of the car, silent, trusting you to give him a tool to fight rough life hand to hand, tooth and nail. He would fight life before submitting to the streets of this sprawling ghetto. He would swing a stick in pain because you knifed his image, told him to be cool and stop cussing, told him to stop being himself, told him to throw away the image he was fast building but didn't give him another that would insure his survival, stripped him in a

cold wind because you didn't like his clothes but didn't give him anymore or show him how to get. He'll smile, embarrassed, knowing you love him. He'll smile, holding a cigarette, choking, playing with it. "I can do it."

We did *An Evening of Afro-American Poetry and Song.* CBS came down and filmed it for TV. The Ghetto of Desire went national and so did I.

One day, I reached down for some energy. Empty. Burn out. It was already September 1966. I had been in the Deep South for two years. I had grown from girl to young woman. New York was calling and I left, feeling like I was being shot out of a rocket.

New York was a whole different thing. No doubt, it was liberating. I became immersed in "sophisticating" myself. I had been in the Deep South a long time. My accent had changed, my demeanor had changed, and my eyebrows were so thick, I looked like a charming werewolf. I took speech, drama, dance, went to movies, went to plays and tried, when I could afford it, to eat in elegant restaurants. But I missed the South. I had become a strange conglomeration of influences. . . . I still am. But more, I missed the soul of the South, the gentleness of the people, the clarity of the situation, the blood in the soil. I missed the irony, the history at close hand, the years of depth in people's eyes, the insanity of it all. I missed space, trees, rivers of dread, Magnolias, live oaks, and the constant shadowy presence of my people everywhere. ❖

Los Angeles, California
February 7, 1994
Copyright 1994

The cast of Free Southern Theater getting ready for a performance at the dedication of the community center at Mileston, Mississippi. Facing the camera are Gil Moses and Denise Nicholas.

John O'Neil in a performance of Purlie Victorious. *The Troupe staged the production in an open field after local segregationists burned the church where the theater was scheduled to perform.*

MATT HERRON

Photography in Difficult Times: Documenting the Civil Rights Movement

In 1962 and 1963 my wife, Jeannine, and I were organizing peace demonstrations in Philadelphia and helping to found the first local CORE chapter, which picketed Woolworth stores in support of Southern lunch counter sit-ins. Our feet were firmly planted in the Northern peace movement, but our eyes were on the South. We sensed the power unleashed by student demonstrators in Atlanta, Greensboro, and other centers of action, and we compared it with the somewhat ritualized activities of the traditional peace groups we were working with.

In the spring of 1963, a few days after organizing a highly successful demonstration that brought a thousand soberly suited Quakers with neatly lettered signs to surround Philadelphia City Hall, I woke in the middle of the night to the realization that all our efforts didn't make a damn bit of difference. As peaceniks, we were as much a part of the establishment as the police with whom we communicated so carefully. If anything, our demonstrations gave people a chance to feel good about opposing war making without having to risk anything very significant. And meanwhile, reports came in daily that convinced us a revolution was in the making south of the Mason Dixon Line. It drew us like a magnet.

In June, Jeannine flew to Mississippi to join the funeral march for Medgar Evers, but also to investigate whether a young family with two small children could live safely in Jackson and work with the Civil Rights Movement. The answer was "probably"—so long as we lived in a white neighborhood and were discrete. In August we moved to Jackson, the only family ever to do so.

At that time I was just beginning a career in magazine photojournalism. I had published in *Life,* and *Look* had just printed my eight-page picture essay on a new treatment for brain damaged children, a story that triggered the greatest reader response of any in *Look*'s history. My plan was to suggest stories to the mass circulation magazines from a Mississippi base that would have greater depth and background than the somewhat superficial news accounts these magazines were beginning to print. I also offered my services to the Civil Rights Movement, both to record demonstrations and other Movement activities (primarily for SNCC), but also to get the message out to my growing list of mainstream magazine clients. As time went on, I added a third agenda: I began to document the everyday patterns of black life in the South, and normal aspects of Southern white culture that often seemed bizarre to my Northern eyes.

Thus I found myself walking a thin line, with a foot as it were, in three camps: Movement photography with a frankly propagandistic purpose, supposedly "objective" magazine photojournalism, and social documentary. It wasn't always easy to keep a balance. Although my soul kept company with the Movement, to actually become a member of SNCC would have blown my credibility with the straight world of journalism, so I kept a certain independence. And although my chosen career was magazine photography, my background as a political radical caused me to view the world through a very different lens from most of my professional colleagues. Even where social documentary was concerned, when I organized a project to chronicle life in Mississippi during the summer of 1964, the greatest documentary photographer of them all, Dorothea Lange, kept herself at arm's length because she perceived in me a certain "lack of objectivity."

I don't know of other photographers who attempted to straddle this wall—most were firmly planted in one camp or another, but my schizophrenia of purpose sometimes led to interesting opportunities. Routine news assignments that gave me special access allowed me to use my cameras in probing ways. I particularly remember covering the inaugural of Mississippi Governor Paul Johnson for *Time*. The folkways of Southern politicians were so strange to me that I felt I was witnessing a ceremony on Mars, but as a news photographer I was virtually invisible and I made the most of it.

By the time I began working in Mississippi, SNCC's own relationship to the media had become pretty well established—due largely to the vision of its executive director, Jim Forman, who understood from the beginning that using the press effectively could be a powerful tool in the Civil Rights struggle. Forman, a former schoolteacher from Chicago with a solid academic background and some experience as a journalist, saw the wisdom of devoting a portion of SNCC's meager resources to communications,

both as a fund raising tool and as a means for bringing pressure to bear on the federal government, and by extension, on Southern political institutions.

With Julian Bond as its communications chief, SNCC learned by doing—discovering that recalcitrant Southern reporters could be prodded into covering an event if a sympathetic Northern editor requested their coverage; that news releases with no chance of reaching print might be picked up if they included a letter to an important official. And pictures were worth literally bushels of words. A single shot of teenage girls languishing in a gulag-like jail brought action where dozens of indignant reports accomplished nothing. Sometimes photographers (or field organizers posing as photographers) would be assigned to cover a demonstration simply to defuse violence—the police were less likely to use their clubs if cameras were present.

Photographer Danny Lyon joined SNCC in 1962, covering actions from Cairo, Illinois, to Albany, Georgia, to Danville, Virginia. A darkroom blossomed in SNCC's crowded Atlanta offices, and Danny's pictures began appearing in news reports and on the pages of the *Student Voice,* a SNCC paper that began appearing regularly in 1963. Transformed into posters and sold for a dollar, Lyon's pictures began to increase the flow of money into the impoverished organization. Francis Mitchell, a photographer for the Johnson publications, came on board along with Norris MacNamara, and now the newest and poorest of the civil rights organizations also had the first photography department. Working with donated equipment and improvising from shoestrings, they made it work.

News of these exploits reached the New York workshop of Marty Forsher, the most expert professional camera repairman in the country, and soon Marty was collecting Pentax cameras from New York studio photographers, reconditioning them, and shipping them south. SNCC photographers would use the cameras until they broke and then mail them back for repairs—a seemingly endless cycle. In no small measure

Marty kept our cameras alive.

Out of our experience photographing in the streets, a lore of survival emerged. Civil Rights photography was usually difficult and frequently dangerous, but some of us were fortunate to live charmed lives; others walked into brick walls. I was pretty lucky. During the three years I was actively involved I was jailed only once, and clubbed a few times, but never seriously injured. These were my simple rules for survival.

1) *Never be a hero.* My job was to get the pictures and get out safely with the film, not to become a martyr to the cause. Any slight of hand that furthered this end was perfectly acceptable. Most SNCC photographers collected bogus press cards or printed their own. At one point I supplied SNCC with legitimate passes from Black Star, my picture agency. Since being taken for a Southern newsman was usually our best option, the Birmingham Police Pass quickly became the Cadillac of credentials. Those of us who managed to acquire one felt fortunate indeed. I remember being stopped by Jackson police one night in the middle of a riot and feeling envious of the credentials of my companion, *Newsweek* Bureau Chief Karl Fleming, until I saw him haul out what I was showing: the trusty Birmingham Police Pass.

2) *Be inconspicuous.* I shaved my beard the day I entered Mississippi, and tried to look as white bread Southern as possible from that day on. Since I could never master a true Mississippi accent, I was usually from "N' Orleans" when responding to that familiar and threatening question: *"Where You From!"* I never carried cameras in the open unless I intended to use them immediately. Even stopping on a deserted country road to photograph a sharecroppers shack could provoke an unexpected confrontation. Each situation was a judgment call. The best cover I knew belonged to Bob Fletcher, a black photographer who survived in Mississippi for years. Bobby drove a battered commercial van with Atlanta plates and a faded sign attesting to "Water Softener Repairs." He was never stopped.

3) *When necessary, apply chutzpah.* At demonstrations we usually stood with the police, not the demonstrators, and tried to act as if we owned the place. Often the police assumed we did. In perfect application of chutzpah, Danny Lyon arrived one morning in a deserted forest clearing to photograph a recently burned church. The ashes were still smoldering. A few moments later a sheriff's car burst into the clearing, siren sounding and lights flashing—a potentially bad situation. Danny went directly to the car, showing his credentials and saying, "Hello, I'm Danny Lyon. The FBI will be here in five minutes." In response the sheriff hauled out his wallet and showed Danny *his* credentials!

4) *Travel light, keep moving.* Shortly after arriving in Mississippi I made myself a leather belt case for lenses and film. My design specifications required that I be able to run flat out without losing film or equipment from the case. After that I never worked with a bulky camera bag, and when a situation looked bad, I shed the belt case as well and simply stuffed lenses in my pockets. In photographing demonstrations I made it a practice never to stand in one place more than a few seconds, and always to plan my next move so that when I got to a new position I was ready to shoot. Constant movement produced more picture situations, but was also protective. If the locals decided to beat up on me, it usually took them a few moments to gather resolve, and by that time I was elsewhere.

Fear was the one problem I dealt with continually. Fear is inhibiting. It clouds the eye and leads to bad pictures. It must be overcome if one is to work, and I did it mostly by simply strapping on my cameras like chest armor and walking into the center of things. If I was shooting I automatically had a reason for being there and I was less afraid. I don't know why it worked, but it did. Looking back, I think I was probably afraid every hour I lived in Mississippi, although it didn't seem so at the time. I know it took three years living in New Orleans to lose the habit of constantly watching my rear view mirror to see who was following my car.

My paranoia was a rational response. In those days segregationists in the Deep South enjoyed an informal license to kill and frequently did so with impunity. Black people went missing all the time, and occasionally whites. When FBI agents dragged the Yockanookany River in the summer of 1964 for the bodies of murdered Civil Rights workers, they didn't find Mickey Schwerner, James Chaney, or Andrew Goodman, but they did find the bodies of nearly a dozen anonymous black men, some weighted down with chains and bearing marks of torture. I have often wondered how the SNCC organizers I knew found the courage to do some of the astonishing things they did. I think the resources they drew on may have been fueled by anger and outrage.

I have lived a relatively privileged life. I have never been subjected to systematic humiliation, denial, or degradation, and I did not have those reservoirs of outrage to draw upon when I strapped on my cameras. Mostly I worked from the conviction that what I was reporting was important, that my pictures had the power to change the course of events, and that I was pho-tographing history. It did not always give me the courage I longed for, but it was usually enough to get the job done.

Civil Rights photography is part of a long and honorable lineage of photography in the service of social justice. Beginning with Louis Hine's turn-of-the-century pictures of immigrant sweatshops (which resulted in the first child labor laws), Dorothea Lange's photographs of dust bowl America, Charles Moore's gripping pictures of Birmingham police dogs attacking demonstrators (which speeded passage of the Voting Rights Act of 1965), and countless pictures of Vietnamese peasants brutalized by war, photographs have created laws, righted wrongs, and changed the way we see ourselves.

I am proud to be part of that tradition, but the bonds of Mississippi go deeper and are more personal than that. For a brief moment in the midst of the Movement while carrying on what was certainly a war, I experienced what it was like to live in a truly loving, truly integrated society. It was the finest moment of my life. I will never forget it. ❖

© 1995 Matt Herron

Art Show and Sale for the Mississippi Freedom Schools

ART SHOW and SALE
FOR THE
MISSISSIPPI FREEDOM SCHOOLS

Sponsors:

Mr. & Mrs. Abram Chayes
Congressman & Mrs. Don Edwards
Rev. Stuart Gast, Jr.
Mrs. Dorothy Goldberg
Congresswoman Edith Green
Mrs. Gilbert Harrison
Senator & Mrs. Jacob Javits
Rev. Richard McFarland
Mr. Clarence Mitchell, III
Dr. James Nabrit, Jr.
Mr. Drew Pearson
Congressman & Mrs. William F. Ryan
Mr. & Mrs. Leo Silberstein

Please address correspondence to:
GEORGETOWN GRAPHICS GALLERY
3307 O Street, N.W.
Washington, D.C.
LINDA GORDON

Dear Fellow Artist:

I hope you have watched with as much interest as I the development of the Mississippi Freedom Schools. Beginning last Summer and continuing to the present, civil rights volunteers—teachers, students, people from all walks of life—have been conducting a series of voluntary schools, designed to supplement the terribly inadequate Negro school system in Mississippi. Beyond their academic work, however, the Freedom School is a new concept in the state: an island of freedom in the midst of oppression and fear and ignorance, where young people can test ideas, ask questions, and acquire the tools to participate in the process of bringing democracy and freedom to the South.

These schools must be continued—and to do so costs money, for supplies, books, subsistence for teachers, etc. A group of interested persons in Washington, D.C., has decided to support the schools by holding an Art Show and Sale, the proceeds of which will go to the Student Nonviolent Coordinating Committee, the mainstay support of the Freedom Schools. It will be held for a week in late March, at the Grace Episcopal Church, a historic landmark in Georgetown.

A special feature of the Show will be an exhibit of paintings and drawings by children in the Freedom Schools, which will most certainly draw interest and critical attention. The show will be a financial success, however, only if we artists will contribute work to be sold at the Show, and I am asking you to join with me in providing this support. I hope you will be able to give a saleable work outright. If this is not possible, please contact the committee for the Show and other arrangements can be made.

Such a Show and Sale will attract a varied audience, from friends of SNCC of limited means to art patrons. Keep in mind both audiences when considering a contribution—we would like to receive prints and drawings as well as paintings and sculpture. But please consider seriously making as much of a contribution as possible.

We are asking that the works be no larger than 24"x30". Prints and drawings can be matted or unmatted. If a work is not sold, it will either be returned or kept for a future sale, at your discretion.

Please respond by contacting Mrs. Beverly Silberstein at the Georgetown Graphics Gallery, 3307 O Street, N.W., Washington, D.C., 333-6608 Noon to 5 P.M. I hope you will be able to participate with me in this significant expression of support.

Sincerely yours,

Leonard Baskin

Beverly Silberstein and her daughter, poet Andrea Sexton have been involved in progressive politics for many years. In 1957, Ms. Silberstein founded the Georgetown Gallery of Art in Washington, D.C., which is still in existence. The gallery sponsored a major art exhibition by prominent artists and Mississippi Freedom School students in order to raise funds for the Freedom Schools project.

ART SHOW AND SALE FOR THE MISSISSIPPI FREEDOM SCHOOLS

Grace Episcopal Church, 1041 Wisconsin Avenue, N.W. (at the canal)

OPENING: April 23 8 PM

Daily through May 2: 1 to 10 PM

Artists

Samuel Adler
Leonard Baskin
Isabel Bishop
Samuel Boskats
Sister Mary Corita
Robert D'Arista
Jim Dine
Jules Feiffer
Sam Gilliam
Robert Goodnough
Robert Gwathmey
Sid Hammer
John Heliker
Robert Kulb
Eugene Larkin
Pietro Lazzari
Francis Luxrato
Hans Moller
Bavo Radulovic
Al Reinhardt
Karl Schrag
Nikolai Shchurchenko
George Schneider
John Alross
Moses Soyer
Raphael Soyer
William Walton
Eugenia Woolman
Len Zion
   and many more

Sponsors

Mr. Leonard Baskin
Mr. and Mrs. Abram Chayes
Congressman and Mrs. Don Edwards
Rev. Stuart F. Gast, Jr.
Congresswoman Edith Green
Mrs. Gilbert Harrison
Senator and Mrs. Jacob Javits
Rev. Richard MacFarland
Mr. Clarence Mitchell, III
Dr. James Nabrit, Jr.
Mr. Drew Pearson
Congressman and Mrs. William F. Ryan
Mr. and Mrs. Lee Silberstein
Student Nonviolent Coordinating
                    Committee

Special Display

DRAWINGS AND PAINTINGS BY CHILDREN FROM THE
MISSISSIPPI FREEDOM SCHOOLS

The public is invited - - - Browsers are welcome

You are invited to attend an exhibit of paintings, prints, and drawings to be sold to benefit the Mississippi Freedom Schools

OPENING—Friday, April 23, 8–10 P.M.
DAILY—April 24–May 2, 1–10 P.M.

Grace Episcopal Church of Georgetown
1041 Wisconsin Avenue, N.W.
below M Street at the Canal
Washington 7, D. C.

Donation $1.00

SPONSORS
Leonard Baskin
Mr. and Mrs. Abram Chayes
Congressman and Mrs. Don Edwards
Reverend Stuart Gast, Jr.
Congresswoman Edith Green
Mrs. Gilbert Harrison
Senator and Mrs. Jacob Javits
Reverend Richard McFarland
Mr. Clarence Mitchell III
Dr. James Nabrit, Jr.
Mr. Drew Pearson
Congressman and Mrs. William Ryan
Mr. and Mrs. Lee Silberstein
Washington, D. C. Office,
Student Nonviolent
Coordinating Committee

Special exhibit of paintings and drawings by children in the Mississippi Freedom Schools

You are invited to attend an exhibit of paintings, prints, and drawings to be sold to benefit the Mississippi Freedom Schools

OPENING—Friday, April 23, 8-10 P.M.
DAILY—April 24-May 2, 1-10 P.M.

Grace Episcopal Church of Georgetown
1042 Wisconsin Avenue, N.W.
  below M Street at the Canal
Washington 7, D. C.

Donation $1.00

SPONSORS

Leonard Boudin
Mr. and Mrs. Abram Chayes
Congressman and Mrs.
  Don Edwards
Reverend Stoney Cook, Jr.
Congresswoman Edith Green
Mr. Gilbert Harrison
Senator and Mrs. Jacob Javits
Reverend Richard McFarland

Mr. Clarence Mitchell III
Mr. Isaac Nehrie, Jr.
Mr. Drew Pearson
Congressman and Mrs.
  William Ryan
Mr. and Mrs. Lee Silberman
Washington, D. C. Office,
  Student Nonviolent
  Coordinating Committee

Special exhibit of paintings and drawings by children in the Mississippi Freedom Schools

The artwork shown on these two pages is representative of student artwork included in the Mississippi Freedom Schools Art Show and Sale.

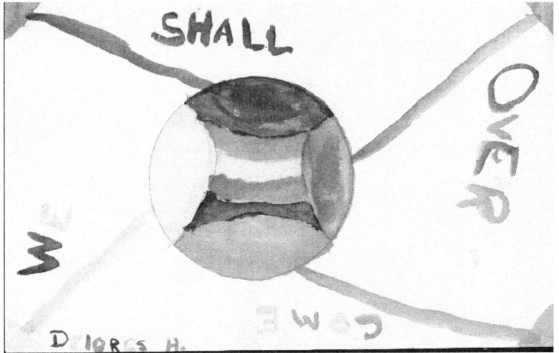

Reporter

MISSISSIPPI, THURSDAY, JULY 30, 1964   NUMBER 31

Colored Youth Drowns Friday

[text largely illegible]

Youth Talent Show Planned

[text largely illegible]

LOCAL CIVIL RIGHTS WORKER HAS COMMUNIST BACKGROUND

Senator James O. Eastland asserted in a Senate speech last week in Washington that much of the civil rights activity in Mississippi this summer is being pushed by those with Communist or Communist-front backgrounds. Senator Eastland, who is chairman of the Senate Internal Security subcommittee, said recent arrests in Moss Point, Holly Springs and Drew have made it possible for Communist participation and leadership to be brought into the open.

Christianity And Communism Cannot Mix

[text largely illegible]

[He cites in particular an address book taken from LARRY RUBIN by authorities in Holly Springs, which turned out to be filled with names and addresses of Communists and Communist organizations.]

[text largely illegible]

LARRY RUBIN was photographed as he led the voter registration drive here last Friday. He appears to be unhappy about something.

Photo by South Reporter

Part of the front page of the Thursday, July 30, 1964, edition of The South Reporter *in Holly Springs.*

LARRY RUBIN

A Walk in Holly Springs, Mississippi Winter 1964

Going into downtown Holly Springs was like stepping off a safety island in the middle of Broadway with the light against you. If you know how to dodge the cars, you can survive.

I never went downtown too often—my work was in the rural areas where most Negroes lived. But the day I'm telling about was a Saturday, when everybody came to town. They would buy supplies and overcome the System in the traditional way—in bars. Saturdays I would go where the people were to explain the voter registration test and to talk to the various leaders of the Freedom Democratic Party precincts.

This particular Saturday, I was walking the five blocks from our office in the Negro section to downtown. I was feeling the sun beating down on my head.

Someone yelled: "Cum heah, bawh." ("So," I thought, "my day starts.")

I turned around—on the opposite side of the street in a gas station an elderly white man was yelling and cursing at me. He was standing with three or four others. I knew him. He owned a plantation. Several days before, he had come to our office. He had pulled out a pistol and had told me he'd kill me if I didn't leave his "niggers" alone. ("His niggers"—that's the System summed up.)

Anyway, I stopped walking and decided whether to go over to him. I turned my back to him and continued walking. My legs felt wobbly, but I forced myself to walk straight, and I even slowed down.

"Ya Red sun-nuva-bitch, cum heah!"

My stomach tightened up—but I continued walking.

A beer bottle whizzed past my head. I felt a great sense of relief—he wouldn't be coming at me. If he were going to chase me, he wouldn't have thrown anything. I continued walking.

When I first worked in the South, I acquired the freedom worker's walk—you sort of slouch and walk to one side of the pavement. Your eyes shift from side to side to see who's following. I had been in the South the largest part of three years, and I had learned how to make myself inconspicuous. That Saturday I walked slowly, registered no expression, and looked straight ahead.

I arrived in the business district. A white person yelled at me from a passing car: "Fuckya." A storekeeper saw me and raised a clenched fist, extending his middle finger. White people in cars stared at me.

The whites knew me. I had been in Holly Springs for eight months. Senator Eastland had

Larry Rubin was elected to the Takoma Park, Maryland, City Council in November, 1994. Between 1961– 1964, he was a field organizer for the Student Nonviolent Coordinating Committee in Southwest Georgia and Mississippi. For the past 30 years, he has been an organizer or communications staffer for a variety of unions and community organizations, including stints with the National Jewish Community Relations Advisory Council and the Philadelphia Urban Coalition. In Philadelphia, he helped organize white neighbor- hoods to prevent violence in case of court ordered busing. He lives with his wife, Fran, and his two daughters, Ariel and Allison.

Black citizens filling out voter registration forms at Forest Cy Courthouse office of registrar Therand Lind. Sign on wall indicates ordeal of public exposure applicants face.

PHOTO BY

MATT HERRON

mentioned me at some length in a speech which was broadcast on television. My picture had been on the front page of papers throughout Mississippi under the headline *No Room Here For Communists.*

The stares I got were expressions showing hate, disgust, and curiosity. The people who stare consider civil rights workers to be obscene. And because they think this, they have a compulsion to look—like an American Legion member who sees police pulling prostitutes out of a home.

The stares are not directed at me as an individual, but at a class of monsters invented by the white Southerner. The stares used to reduce me to a state in which I was grabbing for my individuality—I would repeat my name to myself. But that Saturday I waved to the cars to enjoy the confusion this caused. The white people were afraid I would consider it an acknowledgement of my gesture if they continued to look at me. But looking away would also be an acknowledgement of me, so most people tried to do both at once.

Downtown Holly Springs is nothing but the courthouse square surrounded by five or six streets radiating at right angles to the square. I went to the street where many Negroes were sitting on benches. Everybody waved a greeting. I felt protected, even though the gang of white men who hung around the courthouse moved to the side facing me.

A woman asked me to help her with the registration test. As I was explaining it, five or six others came over. After we were through, they all crossed the street to take the test in the courthouse.

Mr. Gipson, the head of a Freedom Democratic Party precinct, asked me for sample voter tests to give to families who had requested them.

Mr. Totten, another leader, drove up in his pickup. We talked for a while. I was standing on his running board. Suddenly, the druggist from across the street came over. The corner became silent with the approach of the white. However, Mr. Totten and I continued talking.

"Bawh, ah whunt t' tahlk t' ya."

"Yassuh," and Totten got out of his truck and went with the druggist to his store.

The man who had been sitting beside Mr. Totten in the truck drew out a shotgun and pointed it towards the drugstore. We waited. Finally, Mr. Totten came out. He was shaking. He said he'd meet me back at the Freedom office.

There, he explained that the druggist threatened him, telling him not to talk to me any more. Mr. Totten was frightened, but he said that he had faith that somehow he would be safe.

After he left, another leader of the Freedom Democratic Party came to the office. He said that his church had just been burned down. We had been holding voter registration classes there.

I had talked that church's deacon board into using the building for the Movement. They had been reluctant. They were afraid it would be burned down.

The precinct leader said that he had faith that somehow the church would be rebuilt. ❖

Excerpts from Larry Rubin's Mississippi State Sovereignty Commission File

LARRY RUBIN

239 Park Avenue, Takoma Park, Maryland 20912
Work: (202)260-0410 Home: (301)270-2130

April 25, 1997

Mississippi Department of Archives and History
P.O. Box 3979
Jackson, MS 39207-3979

Dear Sirs,

My name appears in the files of the Mississippi State Sovereignty Commission, of which I was a "victim" as per the classification in the ruling issued in the case of *U.S. District Court — Southern District of Mississippi in the case of ACLU et al* v. Fordice, et al, Civil Action No. J77-0047 (B)

As per that ruling, I wish to review all files containing my name.

I am exercising the right granted to me in the above cited case, but I wish to state for the record that I have no objection whatsoever to making all the State Sovereignty Commission files, including those containing my name, available to the public without restriction. Regardless of what I learn upon review of my files, I will continue to have no objections to making all the State Sovereignty Commission files public

Sincerely yours,

[signature]

Larry Rubin

Personally appeared before me on the 22nd day of April 1997 Larry Rubin, satisfactorily proven to me be the person whose signature is affixed hereto

[signature]

TITLE: Lafayette - Marshall Counties

* *

DATE OF INVESTIGATION: May 6, 7, 1964

* *

DATE OF REPORT: May 19, 1964

* *

INVESTIGATED BY: Tom Scarbrough, Investigator

* *

TYPED BY: Elizabeth Arnold

* *

        On Wednesday morning, May 6, 1964, about 10:30, Sheriff Boyce Bratton
of Lafayette County called me by telephone to advise that about 2:30 A.M. the
same date a city policeman of Oxford stopped a small Studebaker Lark bearing a
Georgia tag, pulling a large U-Haul-It trailer loaded with something. He stated
that the policeman stopped the driver because there was no tail light on the
trailer. He said there were six men inside of the small Studebaker - three Negroes
and three whites. He said the white men gave their addresses as Philadelphia,
Pennsylvania, and London, England; and two of the Negroes gave their addresses
as Hattiesburg, Mississippi; the third gave his address as Shaw, Mississippi.
Sheriff Bratton stated that he needed advice, as he felt the entire crew were
up to no good. He asked me to check with Attorney General Joe Patterson and the
Governor's office and determine, if possible, if there were not additional charges
he could prefer against the master as he felt they should be held for further investigation to determine what they were hauling and the nature of their business.
Otherwise, he stated, he was going to have to release all of them pretty soon. I
advised Sheriff Bratton, I would make the contacts as requested and call him back.

        I talked with General Patterson and Honorable Herman Glazier, the
Governor's Administrative Assistant, and apprised them both of what the sheriff
had on his hands in Oxford and of his request. Both General Patterson and
Mr. Glazier recommended that their proof of ownership of the automobile should be
established by the occupants and that the rental agreement should be thoroughly
checked as to who rented the trailer, where it was destined to go, etc., and
of course, tags and weight limit should be checked.

        I called Sheriff Bratton back and told him what General Patterson and
Mr. Glazier had advised being done. The sheriff stated he had already established
all of these facts which checked out all right. He asked me if I could not come
right on up there. I advised the sheriff I could if he felt my services would be
of any assistance to him. Bratton asked me to come on and he would hold the sextet

2-19-34

until I got there. I asked the sheriff if he had heard any rumors that the U-Haul-it trailer might contain weapons, whiskey, or literature which could be designed for the purpose of overthrowing our government. He stated he had heard rumors that perhaps they were hauling guns and might possibly have whiskey in the trailer. I advised the sheriff since he had heard these rumors, I believed he would be within his legal rights to obtain a search warrant and proceed to give the contents of both automobile and trailer a thorough and complete search and that he could perhaps attend to this while I was getting there.

The sheriff followed this procedure, that is after he served each occupant of the automobile with a copy of the search warrant which he had the County Attorney to prepare. He had the occupants of the car to unload the trailer and automobile. This took quite some time as the trailer and contents alone weighed over 9,000 pounds, and it was estimated that they were hauling between 3900 and 4200 books.

The sheriff had just finished unloading all the contents of the trailer when I arrived. There was quite an odd collection of books. These books were destined for delivery to Rust College, so Richard Frey, white male, stated. Frey was one of the six arrested. He further said this was the second load that had been carried to Rust College. When questioned further as to what they would be used for, he said they would be used to teach the schools which are to be conducted this summer in various sections of Mississippi.

—o—

Arrested with Richard Frey was Larry Rubin, white male, address Philadelphia, Pennsylvania, born June 23, 1943. Rubin appeared to be the one in charge of money matters. He had on him at the time of his arrest $418.00. He said his father is a plumber and that he gave him $950.00 when he left Philadelphia. Rubin is a blonde, blue eyed Jew and admitted being a worker for SNCC working for world peace and better understanding among the races he stated. He said he did not believe Jesus Christ was the Son of God, but did believe that he was a good man and that Christ did at one time live here on earth. I asked Rubin where he had been living since he left Philadelphia, Pennsylvania. He stated he came by SNCC headquarters in Atlanta, Georgia, and from there on into Mississippi. I asked him if he had been living among the whites of this state or with the Negroes. Rubin stated he had been living with the Negroes. I asked him how he expected to bring about a better understanding between the races and peace and tranquility in Mississippi if he did not fraternize and visit with the white communities. He stated it appeared that his presence was resented by the whites. Whereupon, I asked him since he was from Philadelphia, Pennsylvania, and that Chester, Pennsylvania, was near by why he did not exert and put forth all of his charming personality and talents toward bringing about peace and a better understanding among the races where he came from and in his own home town. He said there were others there to do the same type of work he was doing here. He then added we misunderstood his and his companions type of work. When asked to explain he refused to talk anymore. Rubin has a B. S. degree from Oberlin College in Ohio.

I next tried to converse with Richard Frey. His attitude was one of insolence and silence. This is not my first acquaintance with Richard Frey and his attitude has changed considerably as to his talking and demanding his constitutional rights. The first time I saw Frey was in Indianola, Mississippi,..

last fall when he was locked up in the county jail and charged with distributing political propaganda within the city limits without a permit. This propaganda was urging Negroes to participate in a local election in behalf of Aaron Henry's candidacy for governor. On this occasion he was very vocal in demanding his constitutional rights. He requested the Chief of Police of Indianola to permit him to call his father, who is an attorney, in Philadelphia, Pennsylvania, so that he could talk with him. The Chief of Police granted his request and Richard Frey talked with his father. His father later talked with the Chief of Police and made inquiry about what his son had gotten into. The Chief told him what he had done and who his associates were and where he was living. Richard Frey's father told the Chief of Police at that time that he had tried to straighten Richard out and tried to give the boy a good education, but the boy had gotten out of his control and that he was not going to intercede for him, that Richard would have to suffer the consequences of whatever the penalty might be for any law he violated.

Richard Frey also was locked up in Greenwood, Mississippi, during the last voter registration demonstration there. He was charged with picketing in a restricted zone and failing to obey the orders of an officer. Richard Frey has had two years of college at Yale University. He is a field worker for SNCC and is paid out of the Atlanta office.

I next talked to John Papworth, white male, height 5'8", weight 150 pounds, born December 12, 1921, in London, England. Papworth was the most talkative of all of the group. He said he is a member of the "Committee of 100" in London, England. He had passport stubs in his possession which depicted he has been all over most of Africa as well as Pakistan in Asia, and parts of Europe. He is presently here in this country on a three months' visa. This, however, is not John Papworth's first visit to America. It is not known how many times he has been in this country, but no doubt several. He acknowledged having been locked up in a number of jails throughout the country and also in England for demonstrating. He was a member of the crew which set out marching from Canada to Cuba in the interest of peace and a better understanding between America and Cuba. This crew was composed of both Negro and white males and females. They were all locked up in Albany, Georgia, and spent some time there. Although he said that the beginning of their march was for the purpose of establishing good relations between Cuba and the United States, their plans were changed when they reached the south and that he and his crew have been working since their release from the Albany, Georgia jail in the Negroes' civil rights. Papworth is a "one worlder" and thinks the world should be run by one harmonious, peaceful government with equal rights and privileges for all. He denied being a communist, but he said he did not believe in capital punishment. When asked if his organization participated in the demonstration protesting the experimentation of the H-bomb in the South Pacific, he stated they did. When asked further if his organization did not sponsor propaganda insisting on fair play for Cuba, he said he was not sure that they participated in this project but admitted his organization endorsed it. Notes were found in his possession which indicated he was in Jacksonville, Florida, at the time that racial disturbance and violence occurred this spring. When asked what he did for a livelihood, he said he did not believe in working. Papworth has the appearance of being a dope, but he is everything else but stupid. He is hard of hearing and has a sallow complexion and wears dirty slouchy clothes.

-j-

Papworth stated he had been living among the Negroes ever since he came to the south. When asked how he expected to convince the white people we are wrong in our belief in segregation when he himself spent all of his time with the Negroes, he laughed and said "you folks are all right but need to get a broader vision in your minds." I asked Papworth how he felt Africa should be ruled. He stated the white man should get out of Africa and let the natives run their own country. When asked why he did not stay in Africa and get the natives straightened out in his travels over there, he laughed again and said "you do not understand." I asked him for a news paper in which he had several items he had written. He gave me the one which is attached to this report. In reading one of his stories concerning his account of his stay in the jail in Albany, Georgia, I detect a familiar ring which we are entirely accustomed to in the south and which follows the same line as all the rest of the agitators, based on the big lie such as demonstrations, constitutional rights, police brutality, and voter registration drives. I asked Papworth where he expected to go when he left America. He said he planned to go to Mexico and laughed when he said "and visit the Aztec Indian ruins" after which he planned to visit in Cuba for awhile.

The three Negro boys would not talk much, but rather looked to Papworth to answer questions. They did say they were working for SNCC and each was being paid $9.64 per week. This seems to be the standard wage for the mediocre agitators as that is what is being paid down at the COFO headquarters on Lynch Street in Jackson. I recognized one of these Negro boys at a glance. His name is Alvin Earl Packer from Hattiesburg. He was a regular participant in the demonstration in Hattiesburg. We have his picture in our files and it looks quite different to the way he looks at present. He had a feminine appearance in the line at Hattiesburg and local police told me he was a well known sex pervert. Packer has been expelled from the Negro high school in Hattiesburg; so have the other two Negro boys. Packer is 6' tall and weighs 145 pounds. He was born August 18, 1946. Douglas Clinton Smith, Negro male, address Hattiesburg, Mississippi, was born August 12, 1946. We probably have Smith's picture in our files. He is 6' 2" tall and weighs 160 pounds, black in color, and does not seem to have too much sense. Will Henry Rogers, the third Negro male, is from Shaw, Mississippi. He was born June 1, 1946, is 5' 6" tall and weighs 120 pounds. All three of the Negro boys said they were promised they would be sent to college by SNCC for working for civil rights.

I am attaching a photostatic copy of a picture of this group which appeared in the Oxford Eagle.

I do not know what part the three Negro boys played in the plans of the three white agitators in having them along, as in my opinion, they are too ignorant to teach anybody anything on any subject. They probably brought them along to load and unload the books.

Some of the books were addressed to Robert Moses, Greenwood, Mississippi, Field Director for CORE. The books consisted of school books from the 2nd grade on up and appeared to have been used in some other state. The state's name had been removed from the inside of the book covers; however, there were several books which did not appear to be ordinary text books. The titles of some of these were "The Marxist" by C. Wright Mills; "Negro Slaves Revolt in the South" by Herbert Aptheker; "Negroes with Guns" by Robert F. Williams; "Geography of a Modern World - Revised

-4-

for Distribution in Africa," "Living in our Democracy,""The Girl from Scotland Yard,""The Bobbsey Twins," and the "Prints of Gravstork." I would not consider any of these books as standard textbooks in grammer school or high school. These books which these racial agitators were hauling are to be used by COFO in what they call the Mississippi Project this summer in teaching Negro schools in various sections of the state their rights and importance of citizenship, etc. Of course, the object of this Council of Federated Organizations (COFO) is to create racial unrest, sit-ins, drive-ins, equal job opportunities, civil disobedience, and to conduct voter registration drives and have all of their masses which they are teaching to participate in the local election for the Negro candidates running for the United States House of Representatives and Senate. These converts also will distribute campaign literature for the Negro candidates. The entire operation of this gang of trouble makers will be carried on by a mixed group of white and Negro college students. Some of the white students are already in Mississippi working at this time at the Mississippi Free Press turning out political propaganda for the Negro candidates' use this summer. The group of white college students are expected to come from the north, east, and west out of liberal schools and will live among the Negroes while in Mississippi.

This happy crew of unAmericans will be partially financed and supported by the National Council of Churches. The NCC has already made arrangements with a bonding company to make bond for any of the agitators who violate our state and local laws and who may get in jail. This was done in order to avoid tying up so much cash for bonds.

After the books were examined and other contents that the six agitators were carrying outside of the jail at Oxford, it was decided by Sheriff Bratton, Chief of Police Collins and I that it would be best to release all of them and let them proceed on to Holly Springs, Mississippi. This decision was reached mostly for the reason that state scales are available at Holly Springs and state tag- men are also on duty there. It was our belief that the U-Haul trailer was improperly tagged and perhaps overloaded.

After paying a $19.50 fine, this group headed out for Holly Springs about 4:30 P.M., Wednesday afternoon. Unfortunately for them, Sheriff Flick Ash happened to be coming on to Highway 7 as they passed by. The small Studebaker car he said was squatted in the rear to the pavement and looked like an ant trying to pull a betsy bug. Both vehicles he said were swerving back and forth from one side of the road to the other in a very dangerous and reckless manner. The sheriff stated he was in unmarked car on this occasion and after following them for some distance and observing them violating the safety rules of the traffic laws, he pulled up beside the group and motioned them over to one side of the lot and gave them a ticket for reckless driving and directed them to follow him to the county jail in Holly Springs, Mississippi. He said after looking the motley crew over he became suspicious of the whole gang and locked them all up in the county jail for further investigation. The sheriff said they all were in accord that they were guilty of reckless driving and stated in court they could not drive otherwise since the load was too heavy for the small car to pull. There were six adults in the small Lark Studebaker, plus all of their suitcases and personal effects. In addition to the load in the Studebaker they were towing a very large U-Haul trailer which weighed over 9,000 pounds; however, their tag was

-5-

was sufficient to take care of the item, but it was not the proper tag they needed for conveying a product for public use. Therefore, they were required to buy the proper tag, pay damages, etc.

While this gang was being held in jail for investigation, it was determined they were involved in an accident before the sheriff arrested them. They also failed to report having been involved in an accident. Sheriff Ash told me that he could not afford to discriminate against these people just because they were from out of the state, that he had recommended to the Justice of the Peace in the case of two white Marshall County citizens that week that they pay $100.00 fine and cost for reckless driving, and that he had made the same recommendation for these people. Altogether they paid out in fines and costs a little over $300.00 on three charges, ie., reckless driving, failure to report an accident, and improper tag.

I personally observed the condition of the automobile at the jail in Holly Springs. I know that it was totally unsafe to go even a short distance on a street or highway. The back bumper on the car was almost pulled off and I could barely stick the toe of my shoe between the tail pipe and the ground. I did not talk to any of this group at Holly Springs after they were arrested. I felt it best that I did not since I had questioned them earlier at Oxford, Mississippi. I had to leave Holly Springs before they were arrested due to the fact I had a speaking engagement at 7:30 P.M. at Houston, Mississippi, at which time I talked with all county and city officers of Calhoun, Chickasaw, and Pontotoc Counties.

This group of officers met at the courthouse in Houston. The meeting was called by the sheriffs of the three counties to discuss ways and means of enforcing the law and keeping the peace if and when outside trouble makers come into any of the three counties. A meeting of this kind was held on Friday night before this crew was arrested Wednesday morning and Chief Collins states had it not been for the meeting on Friday night before this motley crew of agitators probably would have gone on through Oxford unnoticed.

I advised Sheriff Ash that I felt it would be a good idea after he released this group to escort them all the way to their destination at Rust College, and I further told the sheriff I felt it would be well for him, with perhaps Sam Coopwood, the Mayor of Holly Springs, to discuss just what part Rust College is going to play in aiding this group of outside agitators. I told the sheriff I felt that our state officials would be interested to know the policy of Rust College and that furthermore, the Methodist churches of this state would like to know what the policies are at Rust concerning cooperating with this outside bunch of civil rights agitators. Sheriff Ash told me that he would talk to President Smith of Rust College.

The names and addresses of people and organizations throughout the United States were found among this group's belongings. Photostatic copies were made of them and are on file with this department. More activity can be expected from this trio of white men. It is my belief they will figure in the middle of the groups of agitators which are expected to come to Mississippi this summer. We know that 600 white college students have already signed up for the Mississippi Project. We know that the National Council of Churches plan a big memorial service in memory of Medgar Evers in Jackson on June 12, 1964. Charles Evers has stated

-6-

perhaps they would have a large scale demonstration also at this time. We know that James Farmer will be in Canton on June 23. We also know that plans are being made by Farmer and his motley crew to stage a large scale demonstration in Canton on June 29. No doubt this trio will also figure in Robert Moses' plans.

Mississippi officers are well alerted to the fact that they will be tested to the limit this summer by these groups. They also know that these people will be supported by the Justice Department in whatever agitation they may create; however, they are well prepared to see that the peace is maintained and no state laws are violated. They appreciate very much the assistance this department has given them by organizing them into one coordinated group and advising them as to what is to be expected from these agitators. All Mississippi officers whom I have had the pleasure of being with in the last three months feel that they have the full power of the state from the Governor on down behind them, and therefore, will not hesitate to enforce the laws and will not use brutality in any form except as a last resort. I am proud of the part this department has had in training our county, city and local state officers in preparing them for whatever emergency may arise.

-7-

TITLE: Marshall County

DATE OF INVESTIGATION: July 24, 1964

DAYS OF REPORT: July 29, 1964

INVESTIGATED BY: Tom Scarbrough, Investigator

TYPED BY: Elizabeth Arnold

On Thursday night, July 23, 1964, Senator George Yarbrough of Red Bank, Mississippi, in Marshall County called me at my home and inquired if I would come to Holly Springs the next day, Friday, to give information which he felt I had to the Editor, Grady McAlexander, of the Holly Springs newspaper "The South Reporter." Senator Yarbrough owns the newspaper. He stated they were doing a feature story on known communists who are affiliated with the Mississippi project and who have been active in Marshall County. I advised Senator Yarbrough I would be in Holly Springs the next morning by 9:00.

Agreeable to our conversation, I arrived in Holly Springs around 9:00 A.M., Friday, July 24. I carried along with me copies of reports of investigation I personally had made which I felt would aid the editor in his item concerning communist activities in Mississippi and in Marshall County. In addition to my own personal investigations, I gave him other documented articles concerning known communists, who have been active in what is known as the "Mississippi Project."

On my arrival, I also learned that a voter registration drive was scheduled to take place that morning, and that the Holly Springs auxiliary police were on duty along with a number of special deputy sheriffs which Sheriff Flick Ash had trained for emergency purposes. The information the Sheriff's Department had received from the voter registration drive leaders was that a number of Negroes would assemble at the Negro Asbery Church, which is located in Holly Springs several blocks from the courthouse, and march in a mass group to the courthouse. Of course, this group was to be spearheaded and lead by Larry Rubin, white male from Philadelphia, Pennsylvania, and who has been exposed by previous investigation by this department as being a young communist. Rubin it seems is the main ranked behind the voter registration drive in Holly Springs. The sheriff went down to the church and advised Rubin and his group of Negro voters that a mass march to the courthouse would not be permitted, but he further advised if those who were qualified to register to vote in Marshall County wanted to register they could either walk or be transported to the courthouse in groups of not more than four. He further advised Rubin and his group that if they insisted on coming in large numbers they would be arrested. The sheriff also advised

2-20-82

that as long as they vote in an orderly, quiet manner they could proceed to take the voter registration test just like everybody else. He further advised that this test was available to all of those who were interested in taking it every day at the courthouse and it was not necessary to put on a big show. The agitators complied with the sheriff's request in not coming to the courthouse in groups of more than four.

There was no incident of any kind which took place in Holly Springs all day long. Around 25 or 30 Negroes were brought to the courthouse to take the voter registration test. It is now known how many of them were able to pass the examination. From the caliber of Negroes I saw that came to the courthouse, I would say very few of them qualified to vote.

A copy of a poster announcing the beginning of the registration drive, which was put out by COFO, is attached to this report. It was learned that COFO did not plan to continue the voter registration drive the following Saturday or Monday. A copy of another circular put out by COFO is attached to this report announcing a meeting at the Parker School house, south of Byhalia, on Monday, July 27; however, COFO had to change the plans for this meeting after Superintendent of Education of Marshall County, Mr. Appleban, forbade the meeting to be held in the school house. This meeting was for the purpose of electing delegates for the Freedom Democratic Party to represent Marshall County in the statemeeting which was to be held in Jackson to elect delegates to send to the National Democratic Convention in Atlantic City. Also attached to this report is a copy of "Searest" which is the official school paper published at Rust College. It is evident from reading the contents of this college paper that Rust College is tied in with COFO activities in Marshall County and this state. I am also attaching to this report a list of persons who have purchased Mississippi tags and tag numbers. These people are all connected with the freedom school project going on in this state. On this same report is a list of names and tags purchased in Leflore County. This group of agitators which have moved into Mississippi were advised before coming here to purchase Mississippi tags as soon as possible after they arrived. This was done in order to throw Mississippi officials off track of identifying this natty group.

Larry Rubin was active in bringing Negro voter registrants to the courthouse. He wore a dark pair of sun glasses and was very camera shy. Several tried to take his picture but did not get a very good shot of him. Rubin has not made any inquiry whatsoever about the loss of his little black address book, which Senator Jim Eastland exposed as being filled with names and addresses of known communists; however, he did complain to the Justice Department that his civil rights were violated by Sheriff Ash and his deputies and this investigator. As the result, the officers mentioned were questioned by the FBI.

A close surveillance is being kept on activities carried on by this natty, beatnik looking crowd of agitators by local officials in Marshall County.

All kinds of rumors can be heard everywhere one goes concerning indecent conduct by Negro males and white females, who are traveling about over this state. It is obvious that the white male and female outside invaders are carrying this conduct on to infuriate our citizens. I am advising all county and city officials to keep cool heads during this summer's crisis and to prevent, so far as is humanly possible, acts of violence which can be avoided. Of course, they are advised to do this in a legal way without sacrificing any of our customs and traditions.

-2-

It was told to me that Edward Barry, white male from Dayton, Ohio, graduate student of the University of Ohio, is staying in COFO headquarters at 100 Rust Street in Holly Springs. He is said to be Larry Guyon a bodyguard. There are other white agitators out at Rust College which can be seen daily on the campus.

Two civil rights workers in the Mississippi project recently were invited to talk to the sociology students at the University of Mississippi. This course is being taught by Joseph H. Bowling and Vaughn Leroy Grisham at the University. It is supposed that these two university professors invited the man and woman to address the sociology class. I have not yet been able to obtain the names of this pair. Their talks were allegedly made to the students in a sociology class Wednesday, July 29. I am going to try to obtain the names and home addresses of these people so that their background and affiliations can be checked.

I gave all the officers copies of the laws passed by the recent Legislature and signed by the Governor concerning racial agitation, riots, boycotts, etc. These laws have been compiled by this department along with other laws relating to the same subjects which had been passed by previous legislatures. All officials were very appreciative of these copies of laws which we have compiled.

I do not believe I have ever seen all officers, city, county, and state, so concerned about our present racial situation and the attempts which are expected to be made by the federal government to implement the civil rights laws which were recently passed by our national Congress. Mississippi officers at this time appear to be leaning heavily on the assistance of all state officials in helping them to solve their problems; however, everywhere I have been local officers are doing a magnificent job in combatting these Mississippi project communists and beatnik outside invaders.

PHIL OCHS

You Should've Been Down in Mississippi

Pardon me, all you people
Who enjoy your peace of mind
You say everybody's equal
Everybody is doin' fine

You should've been down in Mississippi
In the summer of sixty-four
If you were down in Mississippi
You wouldn't say that anymore

Pardon me, Mister Backlash
You say you're worried about your home
Say we're goin' too far too fast
Say you wanna be left alone

You should've been down in Mississippi
In the summer of sixty-four
If you were down in Mississippi
You wouldn't say that anymore

Pardon me, Mister Policeman
While you're shinin' up your shield
Say you stand for law and order
You wouldn't do no dirty deal

You should've been down in Mississippi
In the summer of sixty-four
If you were down in Mississippi
You wouldn't say that anymore

Pardon me, Mister Soldier
While you're marchin' down the road
Say you're fightin' for your future
And the freedoms that you hold

N

You should've been down in Mississippi
In the summer of sixty-four
If you were down in Mississippi
You wouldn't say that anymore

Pardon me, Mister President
You want your place in history
Say you're doin' all you can do
To make all the people free

You should've been down in Mississippi
In the summer of sixty-four
If you were down in Mississippi
You wouldn't say that anymore

Pardon me, all you people
Who enjoy your peace of mind
You say everybody's equal
Everybody is doin' fine

You should've been down in Mississippi
In the summer of sixty-four
If you were down in Mississippi
You wouldn't say that anymore

PATRICIA BARBANELL

Mississippi Freedom Summer

A Personal Story

Someone once asked me what decision had most affected my life. I surprised myself by answering, with little hesitation, "Joining Mississippi Freedom Summer."

Ironically, I have faced hundreds of life-altering choices in my half-century of experience. Many have had radical influence on the paths I have traveled. Yet, I knew as the words left my tongue, that I answered the truth from the heart—that the one choice that most profoundly influenced who I am was the choice I made in the spring of 1964.

For me, the story is not what it was like or what happened in Mississippi Freedom Summer. When asked, I tell some stories—the facts as they come out on a given day. Then, if the energy is right, I try to tell the real story as I lived it. A story of personal growth and life change. A story of not what I did, but what I gained that summer.

In 1964 I was a muddle-headed hippie child of nearly twenty-one years, spouting radical rhetoric, singing protest songs, and creating visions of change. In retrospect, I hardly knew who I was and certainly didn't know where I was going in life. In 1964 it didn't seem to matter. As my sophomore year in college ended, I packed my gear and headed with my guitar-plucking boyfriend to the Newport Folk Festival.

There, amid the masses and the music, was a table recruiting people to sign up for Mississippi Freedom Summer. My boyfriend promptly signed up, having no doubt that his parents would sign the permission slip needed and give him the travel and expense money required. Not wanting to be left behind, I promptly signed on too, seriously doubting whether my parents would sign my thing, let alone give me money.

The personal trauma this act created at home is still painful to remember. To make a long story short, I ended up borrowing the money, leaving the day after my twenty-first birthday (when permission was no longer needed) and waiting two full years until my father talked to me again. This decision was the first truly independent action of my life. And it changed my world in ways that I never could have envisioned in 1964.

It is not surprising that I had no idea of the journey on which I had embarked. At the age of twenty-one I had little experience with the world outside of school and family. To me, if I thought about it then at all, life was simply a road to be traveled, stopping for a while and moving on, leaving people, places, and things behind. Little did I suspect the larger truth—that some paths remain alive in us, shaping our lives years after we have traveled on them.

Over the years, I have tried many times to define exactly what happened to me in the summer of 1964. On first analysis, it seemed that it was the specifics of experience that affected me.

For the first time, I encountered a reality different than my own. The poverty and the legal deprivation of services astonished my young mind. Pictures of black and white water foun-

Dr. Pat Barbanell is currently Coordinator for Arts in Education for the Schenectady City Schools, where she works to expand students' visions in all curriculum areas through direct encounters with the arts and artists. She administers many funded programs which focus on multi-cultural issues, serving the needs of the diverse populations in Schenectady's inner-city schools. She has published articles and often speaks to other educators, promoting a multi-cultural, multi-disciplinary approach to restructuring education. She is married to Mark Edelstein who shares a vision and a hope for the just future of this society.

tains and bloody Freedom Riders had done little to prepare me for the simple reality of no access to libraries or bookstores or supermarkets.

My visions about many things were challenged.

I came to Mississippi to make a revolution but found that what most people wanted was simply to attain the comfortable middle-class life that I adamantly rejected.

I came believing that if I did right to people, they would do right to me, but like many others, I encountered anti-white and anti-semitic sentiments among some co-workers. At first, the pain and confusion of this brought me to my emotional knees, but with strong guidance from other co-workers, I found clarity and understanding of myself and others as I struggled for balance.

Never having encountered real danger in my life, I arrived with a certainty of personal invulnerability. As I experienced life-threatening vigilantism, the illusion left forever.

When I returned to school, I was asked to speak publicly about my experience. In my mind, I changed from one who "says" to one who "does." I came to believe that the experience had redefined and improved my self-image.

Now at the distance of thirty years, my view is different. I believe what changed most was not my vision and not my self-image, but rather my frame of reference to the world. I have come to realize that since the summer of 1964, three

things which I gained in Mississippi live in me to touch my every action.

No matter what the opposition, I have no hesitation to stand up for what I believe to be right. Sometimes people think I have "guts" in facing daunting opposition on difficult issues, but I know better. Such positions come easily. After Mississippi Freedom Summer, most situations seem "Micky Mouse."

I can't be intimidated where my commitment or my values are concerned. The experience in Mississippi put my personal ghosts to rest. I can't count the times that this fact has helped me to cut through levels of nonsense and enabled me to arrive at common ground and productive dealings with a diversity of people.

My commitment to being an agent of positive change has become an underlying theme of my life. Before Mississippi Freedom Summer, I carried my social activism as a flag, creating more noise than anything else. The rhetoric found a place in my inner reality that summer and became the foundation for the path I have followed since.

I would best sum up the Mississippi Freedom Summer by noting that on Veteran's Day each year, I find myself celebrating veterans like myself who served in our domestic wars. I am eternally grateful for the experience which I live with every day, and I work to give some of the fruits of that experience back to the communities of people that I encounter in my journeys.

ERIC ANDERSEN

Take Off Your Thirsty Boots

Broadside #55, February 12, 1965

Transcribed by Agnes Cunningham

You've long been on the open road,
You've been sleeping in the rain,
From the dirt of words and the mud of cells your clothes are smeared and stained,
But the dirty words, the muddy cells will soon be judged insane,
So only stop and rest yourself till you are off again.

Then take off your thirsty boots and stay for a while,
Your feet are hot and weary from a dusty mile,
And maybe I can make you laugh,
Maybe if I try,
Just lookin' for the evenin' and the mornin' in your eyes.

But tell me of the ones you saw as far as you could see,
Across the plain from field to town a marching to be free,
And of the rusted prison gates that tumbled by degree,
Like laughing children one by one who looked like you and me.

But take off your thirsty boots and stay for a while,
Your feet are hot and weary from a dusty mile,
And maybe I can make you laugh,
Maybe if I try,
Just lookin for the evenin' and the mornin' in your eyes.

283

I know you are no stranger down the crooked rainbow trails
From dancing cliff-edged shattered sills of slander-shackled jails
But the voices drift up from below as the walls they're being scaled
All of this and more, my friend your song shall not be failed.

Then take off your thirsty boots and stay for a while,
Your feet are hot and weary from a dusty mile,
And maybe I can make you laugh,
Maybe if I try,
Just lookin' for the evenin' and the mornin' in your eyes.

You've long been on the open road,
You've been sleeping in the rain
From the dirt of words and the mud of cells your clothes are soiled and stained.
But the dirty words, the muddy cells will soon be hid in shame,
So only stop and rest yourself till you are off again.

Then take off your thirsty boots and stay for a while,
Your feet are hot and weary from a dusty mile,
And maybe I can make you laugh,
Maybe if I try,
Just lookin' for the evenin' and the mornin' in your eyes.

FRANCES O'BRIEN

Journey Into Light

It had been rather a quiet summer in Vicksburg, at least compared to other Mississippi towns in 1964. There had been one shooting but no one got hit. Numerous threats were made but not carried out. Sinister looking men visited the Freedom School from time to time—once while one of my students was reciting the Gettysburg Address—although they did nothing but look around and leave. So perhaps we had become complacent. Or naive. In any case, we were careless.

I was delighted with the work being done by my three-to-thirteen-year-olds. Several "slow learners" were improving in reading. All were showing real insight in their art work and group discussions.

Moreover, there was the belief that my friends and I were helping to change the world, or at least the United States. We were making history. In the words of Saint Paul, we were not overcome by evil, but were overcoming evil with good.* It was a heady feeling.

One night reality intruded. Six of us walked down the long driveway of the Freedom Center to meet the car that would take us "home" to the various houses where we were staying. I don't remember why the drivers didn't come up to the house on that particular night. Maybe someone had heard rumors of a Klan meeting and was in a hurry. Perhaps a recent rainstorm had made ruts in the driveway. Anyway, we were supposed to go down six at a time, but there was a mix-up. This car would hold only five

passengers. I was left out.

"Can't I just squeeze—"

"No you can't!" The driver interrupted. "We can't risk overloading the car after dark. Don't worry—someone else will be along in a minute."

The door slammed, and the car was gone. I felt like crying and at the same time told myself not to be a baby. It was true we couldn't squeeze five people into a back seat and risk being stopped by a policeman. That would mean all seven would go to jail—and being arrested after dark was a freedom worker's nightmare. Night was when people mysteriously "disappeared" from Mississippi jails, as had James Chaney, Michael Schwerner, and Andrew Goodman only a few weeks before.

I'd been told to expect another car right away, and sure enough, there it was. Headlights slowed and came to a stop a few feet away only minutes after the first car had left. That wasn't bad at all. With a joyful cry I skipped toward the stopped vehicle. In it were four men in white robes and hoods.

Before I could recover from my horror, one of them jumped out, clapped a hand over my mouth, and dragged me inside. They all seemed to think it was a hilarious joke—capturing a little nigger-lover like that without even the trouble of hunting. I gathered they were on their way to a meeting but would be "a trifle late" because of me.

In a lonely field or vacant lot—it was too dark to tell which—the car jerked to a stop. The

Frances O'Brien has taught children with special needs in Bakersfield, California, for the past 28 years. She lives in a small mountain community and is active in various volunteer projects which include the Cesar Chavez Memorial March from Delano to Sacramento in the spring of 1994. She also does a little writing on the side. Frances spent the summers of 1964 and 1965 in Mississippi.

man holding me spoke as if to an erring child, "Now you just be a good little girl and do what we say. We've gotta teach you a little lesson so you'll go home to your mama and daddy and mind your own business after this."

By this time the driver had yanked open the rear door and ordered us out. One of the men took two segments of rubber hose out of the trunk. I tried to drop into the defensive position but the man holding me was too strong. "No you don't, little lady! You bend over that hood and don't try any more funny business."

He pushed me up against the front of the car. I bent over the hood and covered my head with my hands.

"That's a good little girl. Stay nice and still now, so we can whup you."

The four men shouted with laughter. But when the next man spoke, he was serious, "See here little girl, we're going to make you sorry you ever came to Mississippi, and we're going to make you say you're sorry. Any time you want us to quit, just speak up and we'll let you get down on your knees and beg our forgiveness."

I vowed to myself I'd go to the bottom of the river first. But the man obviously wasn't a mind reader. Almost gently he continued, "You can even do it now, if you want. Save us all a lot of trouble."

I clenched my teeth. Someone yanked up my skirt. I was too terrified to think clearly, or even to think at all. Nevertheless, the words of Bob Moses at the Oxford training session flashed into my mind: "Girls, your life is more important than your modesty. Never mind keeping your dress down during a beating; *keep your head covered!*"

It proved to be sound advice. The Klansmen took turns, two of them beating until they were tired, then passing their hoses to the other two. Each blow stung harder than the one before. After what seemed a long time, the pain began to grow duller. The jeering voices faded away . . .

The next thing I knew, I was lying on the ground in the driveway of the Freedom Center. It was like waking up from a nightmare, except

I was not in bed and the smart of my skin was very real. Feeling myself over, I was amazed to find there wasn't any blood. (I had heard that a rubber hose leaves little or no incriminating evidence, but I didn't think of that at the time.) I believed I had been gone for many hours and it must be almost daylight. My first thought was to get back to the Freedom School and let people know I was still alive. I ran up the hill, or at least got up there as quickly as I could.

Several volunteers who stayed at the Freedom Center were on the front porch, casually chatting and laughing. One of them looked up and saw me.

"Oh, hi, Fran. I thought you'd left."

I couldn't believe it. Here I'd been kidnapped and beaten and these people acted as if nothing had happened. I started to stammer something about the car not holding seven, and one of the young men began to lecture: "You should have come back right away. Don't you know it's dangerous to wander around alone at night? This is Mississippi, you know. A lot of things could happen."

I cried then. The sensible thing would have been to explain that something did happen, but I was beyond being sensible. The words simply wouldn't come—at least not with any coherence.

The other workers gathered around, caring and sympathetic. However, they seemed to be talking to each other rather than to me: "Something scared her, I think." "Her dress is all dirty." "Did she fall down the hill?"

"There was a car circling around here about half an hour ago—right after those other guys left," someone volunteered. "Was that it?"

I managed to express some sort of affirmative, but could not elaborate. At the time I thought the others were giving me no chance. It is more likely they were just trying to make sense of what they heard coming out of my mouth.

Bessie, a mother of six who lived at the Freedom House, hurried out and put her arm around me. Unlike the white northern college students, Bessie was a veteran civil rights worker of several years. She and her children were made homeless by a bomb.

"It's ok," Bessie whispered in my ear. She demanded no explanation, her manner implying I didn't have to tell anything if I didn't want to.

Perhaps the real problem was that I did not want to tell. I didn't want to admit having run up to the car without knowing who was in it. I was ashamed of having waited at the bottom of the hill "like an idiot" instead of running back up to the Freedom School. Moreover, there was a feeling of unreality about the whole episode. From what was said, I gathered I had not been gone much over half an hour—forty-five minutes at the most. Yet it still seemed like many hours to me.

I don't remember how I got to the home of my hostess that night nor what, if anything, I told my roommate. Beverly must have been there ahead of me, and it seems unlikely she failed to notice anything wrong. But I have no recollection.

I wanted to forget the episode as quickly as possible. It seemed the sensible thing to do. Why dwell on such unpleasantness when there were many positive things to talk about? I wanted to recapture the euphoria I felt at the beginning of the summer, and I almost succeeded.

Had the SNCC workers in Mississippi known what I was suppressing they would have been annoyed, to put it mildly. The whole point of involving white college students in the Summer Project was to focus national attention on the brutality of white supremacists. However much the liberal press might deny its own racism, Klan violence was always more "newsworthy" when directed against white people.

I did not feel at all guilty about depriving the American public of one more horror story. It seemed to me they had more than enough already. Throughout the summer, reporters and public alike pounced on every account of violence with an eagerness I considered downright ghoulish. Thus I felt a mischievous satisfaction in concealing something I knew the media would love to know. The possibility that I might

be hurting myself did not occur to me.

I kept quiet for twenty-five years. During part of that time I was able to banish the Klan incident entirely from my conscious memory. I even came to believe the comforting story I told my parents: "Vicksburg is so concerned about having a good reputation that nothing really bad ever happened."

But subconscious awareness was never far away. In the early 1970s I wrote a novel set in postwar Germany. The central character is a professor who, having opposed the Nazis and his own family, is plagued by flashback and guilt. Much of my own experience is in it. I found the writing to be therapeutic, even though doing the necessary research gave me nightmares.

Any mention of American slavery or the Civil Rights Movement gave me worse nightmares. Those triggered by the television miniseries *Roots* were the worst. After watching the episode in which the hero, Kunta Kinte, is flogged until he calls himself "Toby," I woke myself up screaming. The next day I was nervous, angry, and impossible to get along with. I did not know why. I accepted both dreams and irritability as inevitable reactions to certain stimuli—like allergies.

The first questionnaire I received from a sociology professor named Douglas McAdam went straight into the wastebasket. Was I supposed to suffer nightmares and emotional turmoil just so some sociologist could write a thesis? No way! I didn't even bother to send a negative reply.

Later a very nice letter from Mr. McAdam arrived, accompanied by a duplicate questionnaire. This time I grudgingly filled out and returned the latter. Although I didn't know it then, I had taken the first step along a path that would lead out of the dark wilderness of repressed anger into the light of understanding.

It may have been while answering Mr. McAdam's questions that I first began to realize not all the effects of the Mississippi summer were negative. Certainly it made me a better teacher. Having learned virtually nothing about Afro-

American history in school, I saw to it my students were not so deprived. I could understand readily the tendency of some minority students to take offense where none was intended. And I was able to respond with insight to a little girl in my class who had been abused and molested.

There was a personal gain as well. Before Freedom Summer I was a timid person, afraid of the dark and of strangers among other things. In Mississippi I was given something to be fearful about. I have been able to tell the difference ever since.

Once a mother complained to me that her eleven-year-old son was "afraid of his own shadow." I couldn't help thinking that I knew a very good cure for that but I wouldn't recommend it. Of course I did not say that aloud, but gave a suitably professional reply to the parent.

By the time Doug McAdam's book, *Freedom Summer*, was published in 1989, I was more receptive to reading and even talking about the Mississippi experience than I had been for many years.

Reading Doug's book was like turning on the lights in a dusky room. Delightful incidents, long forgotten, sprang into consciousness like children after a game of hide-and-seek. Faces came to mind; so did whole conversations. I decided I really wanted to attend the twenty-fifth reunion of summer volunteers in June. I could hardly wait to share experiences with other veterans, and if it brought on a nightmare or two that was just too bad. I felt it would be worth it.

It was. Shared experience made talking about Mississippi with other volunteers easier than trying to educate people who had never been there. Some veterans said they simply had avoided the subject for years in order not to "open old wounds." I could relate to that.

But when a wound is festering beneath the surface, opening it is the sensible thing to do. The process of cutting and cleansing may be painful, but it leads to healing. That was how I felt about the 1989 reunion and about other gatherings that followed throughout the summer.

Healing cannot be hurried and change may come very slowly indeed. Yet I have noticed several changes in myself in the last five years. I can look at Freedom Summer in its entirety; celebrate the good and be honest about the bad. It still is difficult for me to talk about the Klan incident, but it is not impossible.

Probably younger readers will wonder why I didn't express more anger toward the Ku Klux Klan, or at least to the men involved in my abduction. It is necessary to understand that the Klan's activities were expected, not only by freedom workers but by the whole country. Klansmen were "supposed" to do things like that and everybody knew it. One might as well hold a skunk morally accountable for spraying or a rattlesnake for striking.

The Klan itself unwittingly endorsed this idea. Flyer after flyer proclaimed that if we "outside agitators" got hurt in Mississippi we had no one to blame but ourselves. The White Knights had no choice but to respond with violence. It was inevitable. I don't suppose it occurred to the Grand Dragon, or whoever wrote the flyers, that this attitude placed him in the same category as a rattlesnake or skunk.

Today it appears the White Knights have plenty of company. One can hardly pick up an "Opinion" page or tune in a talk show without being bombarded by someone's animosity for someone else. Not only ethnic minorities but political, religious, and alternate lifestyle groups get targeted for hate. Sometimes it is very difficult not to respond in kind. Like an unchecked epidemic, hatred infects even the kindest of people with bitterness and a tendency to regard certain other individuals as animals or worse.

But all who hate (or hate back) have one tragic thing in common: in dehumanizing the person or thing despised, we dehumanize ourselves. More than thirty years ago Martin Luther King, Jr., wrote: "hate multiples hate; violence multiples violence; toughness multiples toughness in a descending spiral of destruction."**

We see this happening today. Reading a newspaper or listening to the radio may well cause good people to throw up their hands and cry in despair, "What can we do?"

In the summer of 1964, about six hundred college students thought we had the answer. We were dedicated to the cause of equality for all. If necessary, we were willing to die for it. In some ways we were much like the young men of an earlier generation who believed that their suffering would make the world safe for democracy.

Recently I talked with the ninety-three-year-old widow of a World War I veteran. As she described the eagerness with which her husband and his friends set out for the trenches of France, I could not help comparing it, in my mind, with Vietnam. I remarked wistfully, "My generation was never that idealistic."

"Oh, really?" Nell responded with a smile. "What do you call sacrificing yourself to rid the country of racism?"

My nephew, who was born in 1963, said of our efforts, "It was worth a try."

Perhaps that best sums up all serious attempts to overcome evil with good. No one can change the whole world, but anyone can change a tiny part of it. The consequences of different groups hating each other are painfully obvious. The results of people reaching out to one another in love and understanding are less spectacular. They occur quietly, in little-known places, and do not have the same publicity appeal as wars and riots.

Look for them. Like sprouting bulbs in spring, they seem to increase the more one seeks them out. Can they be expanded? Can all of us who truly wish to see an end to the "Us vs. Them" mindset dividing our society join hands and cooperate to make that happen? I hope so. It's worth a try.

*Romans 12:21
**"Loving Your Enemies" in *Strength to Love*, 1963 Harper & Row, NY   ❖

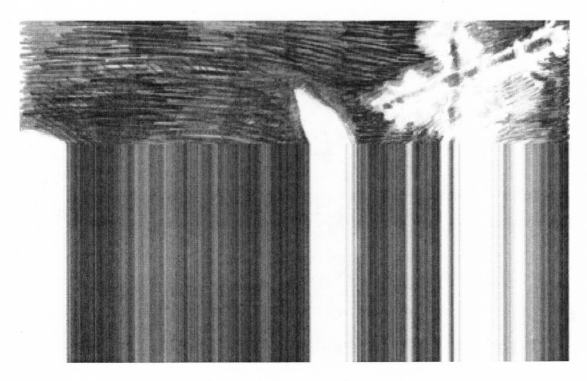

ARTWORK BY

SHARON RILEY

LEN CHANDLER

Going To Get My Baby Out Of Jail

I'm going to get my baby out of jail
I'm going to get my baby out of jail
She said she wasn't guilty and wouldn't pay her bail
I'm going to get my baby out of jail

My baby wouldn't let me pay her fine
My baby wouldn't let me pay her fine
She said she wasn't guilty and wouldn't pay one dime
But I'm going to get my baby out of jail

I must have walked a valley on my floor
I must have walked a valley on my floor
Just waiting for her footsteps and her knocking at my door
No I'm going to get my baby out of jail

They phoned and said the word had come today
They phoned and said the word had come today
I'm meeting all the lawyers at the courthouse right away
I'm going to get my baby out of jail

The highest courts all honored her appeal
The highest courts all honored her appeal
They said she wasn't guilty that she'd got a dirty deal
So I'm going to get my baby out of jail

Every police in this county knows her name
Every police in this county knows her name
But I'm going to get my baby just the same
Yes I'm going to get my baby out of jail

One thing more keeps working on my mind
One thing more keeps working on my mind
Those high court costs and lawyers fees aren't something like a fine
I'm going to get my baby out of jail

ARTWORK BY

SHARON RILEY

Protesters in Jackson assisting each other into a police van.

Mississippi Summer 1964

Robert Dahl is a Sterling Emeritus Professor of Political Science at Yale University, where he taught in the Political Science Department for many years. He is the author of numerous books on democratic theory and practice. Robert lives in New Haven, Connecticut.

James Tobin is a Sterling Professor of Economics Emeritus at Yale University. He has been on the Yale faculty since 1950. He retired from his teaching position in 1988. James graduated from Harvard College summa cum laude in Economics in 1939, received a Ph.D. in Economics from Harvard University in 1947 and was a Junior Fellow of the Society of Fellows from 1947–50, the last of which he spent at the Department of Applied Economics at the University of Cambridge, England. In 1961–62, on leave from Yale, he was a member of President Kennedy's Council of

We went to Mississippi together in late June 1964 on the urging of several Yale students who were members of a group organizing the local effort to send volunteers. We had attended a meeting in one of the residential colleges where the student organizers explained the crusade and sought student and faculty recruits. For us the most persuasive recruiter, the one who remains most sharply etched in our memories, was a graduate student on a visiting fellowship from England, Nicholas Bosanquet (who is now a Professor of Political Science at the University of London). Why would an Englishman involve himself so deeply in such a campaign in the United States? His answer was straightforward: what happened to Negroes (the term then used and therefore used by us here) in the United States had importance far beyond its boundaries.

In any case, we were told, the presence of two senior Yale professors, even for a short visit, would raise the morale of the young volunteers, provide white Mississippians a measure of the seriousness, respectability, and peaceful intentions of the students, and perhaps add a bit of security.

As it turned out, we encountered neither Nick Bosanquet nor any other Yale students while we were in Mississippi. Whether our support buttressed the morale of the other volunteers we did encounter is doubtful.

We arrived in Mississippi the last week in June. As we boarded in Atlanta our connecting flight to Jackson, each of us felt the same anxi-

ety of adventure he recalled from his first trip over the Iron Curtain or into the Soviet Union, which was considerably heightened by the fearful event that occurred two or three days before. The mysterious disappearance in Philadelphia, Mississippi, of the three civil rights workers, James Chaney, Andrew Goodman, and Michael Schwerner, cast a shadow over our visit and over the whole project. They were believed to have been murdered, but their bodies were not found until August.

Much of our mission was to be ambassadors to the white community, so far as possible the white establishment. In Jackson, we were put up for three nights at the comfortable home of a white family who failed to fit our stereotypes. Our host was a white upper-middle-class professional and a World War II veteran. He was a well-informed Southern New Deal liberal, a chronic dissenter from Mississippi orthodoxy. He supported the Civil Rights Movement.

Perhaps through his connections, our first venture in attempting to cloak "our" student volunteers from the North in an aura of respectability was a lunch meeting with members of the city and state white establishment. It took place at a posh downtown club, attended by city officials, business men, lawyers, and other local bigwigs. As we remember, they were polite but suspicious. They were defensive and resentful of invading Northerners seeking to reform or overturn long-standing institutions the invaders do not understand. They admitted sins of the past and said they were in the process of reforming Mississippi; they warned that their efforts would be set back by unruly external pressures. As we described "our" well-meaning, pacific, conscientious students and explained what was on their minds and ours, our local hosts regretted that our young people could not meet and talk with their young people, presumably at their country clubs. Nevertheless our liberal escort thought we had made a difference.

At Jackson State University we met with students and faculty who told us how the state discriminated against the black university, and against its graduates seeking to continue their educations at other state institutions. The private black college Tougaloo, outside Jackson, we found to be a central focus of the statewide campaign, too busy to give us much guidance for the rest of our trip.

We went on to Greenwood, where we had been given the address of the Movement's local headquarters. To reach it, we drove through unpaved streets without sidewalks, street lights, and sewers. The houses in the Negro residential section were small and primitive but well-kept. The civil rights camp was bustling with young civil rights workers of both races and by neighborhood residents who were lodging and feeding them. A crisis atmosphere, engendered by the Philadelphia disappearances, prevailed. The young leaders at the camp were cordial to us but perceptibly embarrassed: What can we do with these graying professors, and how can we assure their safety? They came up with the idea that we should go talk to the local sheriff, whom they regarded as a threat.

This Southern sheriff was out of central casting. He looked like Bull Connor. He listened to our spiel with thinly disguised hostility: Why are your young friends stirring things up in our town? Just tell them to obey the law. They have nothing to fear from this office if they do. If not, . . . We could not, on the other hand, get from him any assurance he and his force would protect the volunteers from white townspeople. We carried this message back to the camp and returned to get lunch downtown. The patrons at the lunch counter already had word of our visit. One of them told us the local joke: to determine whether the missing civil rights workers had drowned, put a welfare check on the surface and see if they rise to it. Driving north from Greenwood to Clarksdale on a lightly traveled highway, we had the distinct feeling we were being followed. (Our rental car was conspicuous by its out-of-state plates.)

The next day we visited Ole Miss at Oxford. The highlight was Professor James Silver, a well-known historian of the South, who shared with us his impressive knowledge of the structure of terror on which Mississippi politics had long been based and still was. (He describes it in detail in his book *Mississippi,* which appeared that year.) Then, after a brief visit to a small and quiet college in Holly Springs, we went on to Memphis and our flight home.

Whether our visit made any contribution to Mississippi Freedom Summer is hard to say. Surely it was very little. The greater contribution was to our own awareness and feelings. To be sure, our stay had been brief, our exposure to life in Mississippi, for Negroes and whites, superficial. Yet we both clearly recall today the strong sense of relief with which we crossed the border into Tennessee. The journey had left a deep and lasting impression of Mississippi's reign of terror—physical, psychological, social, economic, political, symbolic—a life that Mississippi Negroes knew all too well. ❖

Economic Advisors in Washington. James was President of the Econometric Society 1958, of the American Economic Association 1971, and of the Eastern Economics Association 1977. in 1955, the American Economic Association awarded him the John Bates Clark Medal, given to one economist under age 40. He has been a member of the National Academy of Sciences since 1972. In 1981, he received in Stockholm the prize in Economic Science, established by the Bank of Sweden in memory of Alfred Nobel. He is author or editor of 13 books and more than 300 articles. His main professional subjects have been macroeconomics, momentary theory and policy, fiscal policy and public finance, consumption and saving, unemployment and inflation, portfolio theory and asset markets, and econometrics. James has written both for professional readers and the general public.

Women ascending courthouse steps to register to vote.

ARTWORK BY

SHARON RILEY

MIKE MILLER

The Mississippi Freedom Democratic Party

"Race Has Kept Us Both in Poverty"

Only one year old, the Mississippi Freedom Democratic Party (MFDP) is one of the most exciting political phenomena of the country. Born of the voter registration drive initiated in Mississippi by the Student Nonviolent Coordinating Committee (SNCC), the MFDP now is an independent organization, claiming before the nation its right to be recognized by the national Democratic Party as the Democratic party of Mississippi. The MFDP first came to the attention of the nation when it challenged the seating of the so-called "regular" Democrats at last summer's Atlantic City Democratic Convention. Again the country was aroused by the Mississippians when, on opening day of Congress, they challenged the right of Mississippi's five congressmen-elect to sit as the representatives of the state of Mississippi. Behind these national confrontations is a quiet, but even more dramatic, story of people in Mississippi creating their own statewide political organization, an organization growing up from the grass roots, expressing the demands of the Movement in Mississippi and reflecting the problems of poverty and deprivation faced by the vast majority of Mississippians, both black and white.

To Rally Against Fear

Beginning in 1961, Negro citizens increasingly sought to register to vote. For SNCC, two basic problems had to be faced. First, the overwhelming fear based on the experience of beatings, killings, home bombings, evictions, and firings that confront Negroes who seek their constitutional rights in the state; second, more subtle and more difficult to work with, was the feeling shared by many Negroes in the state that politics wasn't their business. The phrase commonly used was, "politics is white folks' business." The oppression of the caste system leaves its mark on the consciousness of those who must live under it. Behind that phrase was a sense of inferiority, a sense of being "unqualified," that was shared by many of the Negroes in Mississippi.

For two years, first one at a time, then in tens, then in hundreds, Negroes went to the county courthouses seeking to register to vote. In some cases, they were not even allowed to fill out the application form that precedes registration. In most cases, they were told they failed to successfully complete the application. Two questions were generally used to flunk the applicant: (1) interpret the following section (chosen from 383 sections of the Mississippi Constitution) of the Constitution; (2) interpret the duties and obligations of citizenship under a constitutional form of government. Whether the applicant passed or failed was determined by the registrar of voters, usually a member of the White Citizens Council.

Mike Miller directs the San Francisco-based ORGANIZE Training Center (OTC) from which he continues to work as an organizer with community, labor, and religious organizations and projects. He was a participant in the Mississippi Civil Rights Movement.

The First Ballots Cast

Early in the summer of 1963, a Yale law student who had come to Mississippi to work with SNCC discovered a statute which allowed any person who believes he is being illegally denied the right to vote to cast a ballot along with an affidavit stating that he is an elector in the state. In a statewide meeting with local Movement leadership, the statute was described and discussed. It was decided that a concerted effort would be made across the state to get Negro voters to the polls with affidavits and that they would seek to vote. In the 1963 state primary election, thousands of Negroes in Mississippi went to the polls for the first time. The response across the state varied. In some places, like Greenwood, ballots and affidavits were accepted and later disqualified by local officials. In other places, like Ruleville, Negro voters were met with guns and forced away from the polling places. Despite the fact that no votes counted, the confrontation was an important one. State officials became apprehensive over the national publicity around the voting and in some cases Negroes had their first polite treatment by a white official.

Equally important, the primary election Negro turnout demonstrated to civil rights workers in the state that their painstaking door to door, church to church, bar to bar work was paying off. Morale was bolstered, both among the full-time SNCC workers and among the Negroes in the communities where election challenges took place.

83,000 for Freedom

Out of the summer election came new discussions about politics in Mississippi—and a new concept, the "Freedom vote." Excluded from the official elections in the state, Negroes in Mississippi decided to hold their own election. The Council of Federated Organizations (COFO) met on October 6, 1963, and named Aaron Henry and Rev. Ed A. King as Freedom candidates for governor and lieutenant governor of the state. (COFO, probably the most misinterpreted civil rights organization in the

country, is a loose coalition of local movements in the state of Mississippi, including some branches of the NAACP, and full-time staff workers from SNCC, CORE, and SCLC). A Freedom ballot was printed, which named the "regular" candidates—Democrat Paul Johnson and Republican Rubel Phillips—and the freedom candidates. Freedom registration forms were used to enroll voters. The first experiment with northern college students coming into the state as volunteers was initiated as some thirty students from Stanford and Yale joined regular staff and local community activists in the circulation of the Freedom registration forms and the election day collection and tabulation of ballots. When all the ballots were turned in, eighty-three thousand Negroes had cast Freedom votes, with the overwhelming majority cast for Aaron Henry and Ed King.

A Parallel Political Force

The Mississippi Freedom Democratic Party was a logical extension of the concept of Freedom votes and Freedom candidates. That the new party should be a Democratic party was a matter of some discussion in the state. Following the November 1963 Freedom election success, another statewide meeting of civil rights activists in Mississippi, held April 26, 1964, discussed the future. Their decision was to create a parallel Democratic party—one that would, in every respect, comply with the rules and regulations set down by the Mississippi Constitution for the conduct of political parties, and that would be Democratic because it was in the Democratic party that significant decisions about the lives of the people in the state were made. However, the MFDP was independent in the sense that it owed no patronage or appointments to the national or state party. This double character of the Freedom Democratic Party, at once inside and outside the system, is a major source of its national strength and the fear that it later caused the "pros" of the national Democratic Party.

Underlying the Atlantic City Convention challenge were three basic considerations. A special MFDP report named them as:

> (1) the long history of systematic and studied exclusion of Negro citizens from equal participation in the political processes of the state; (2) the conclusive demonstration by the Mississippi Democratic party of its lack of loyalty to the national Democratic Party in the past; (3) the intransigent and fanatical determination of the state's political power structure to maintain the status quo.

At its founding meeting, the MFDP stated, "We are not allowed to function effectively in Mississippi's traditional Democratic party; therefore, we must find another way to align ourselves with the national Democratic Party." So that such an alignment could be established, the MFDP began organizing meetings throughout the state to send delegates to the Atlantic City Democratic National Convention.

The People Came to Atlantic City

Beginning at the precinct level, moving then to county meetings and congressional district caucuses, and ending with a state convention on August 9, 1964, in Jackson, Mississippi, the Freedom Democrats went to work. The meetings were conducted under the leadership of a temporary state MFDP executive committee which had been chosen on April 26. Out of the meetings came a full delegation, ready to go to Atlantic City claiming the right to sit as the Democrats of Mississippi.

Nationwide Support: But Not from the White House

At the same time as work was being done in the state, representatives of the MFDP were traveling across the country seeking support from Democratic Party delegations for the challenge. As the opening of the convention drew near, the following states were among those whose state Democratic executive committees or state conventions had passed resolutions (some of them not binding) supporting the MFDP's challenge: New York, Massachusetts, District of Columbia, Minnesota, Wisconsin,

Michigan, Oregon, California, and Colorado. A SNCC worker who traveled across the country seeking support for the MFDP later described the convention experience. Writing in the October 1964 *Liberator,* an independent Negro monthly, Frank Smith said:

> ... By the time the convention started, there were eight state delegations which had passed resolutions supporting the seating of the Mississippi Freedom Democratic Party, but word had come down from Washington that President Johnson wanted the regulars seated and the FDP ousted. The word from the president came as an unexpected shock to the FDP, because their basic strategy had been built around the idea that the president would either be on their side or be neutral. There were, however, political considerations involved, and there is an old political adage that says "whenever there is cake to be cut, never fail to get your two cents' worth." With this in mind, it now seems foolish that the FDP could have ever expected the president to be either on their side or neutral.

> The hearing at the Credentials Committee added more brush to the fire. The FDP had developed a strategy of getting the required twelve signatures out of the Credentials Committee to file a minority report, and thus get their fight to the floor of the convention, and to get the required eight state caucuses to sign a petition to get a roll call vote on the floor. So that when Washington decided to bring pressure, it first started on the credentials people from the states that had already passed resolutions in support of the FDP. By Sunday, the second day of the Credentials Committee hearings, there were reports of threats of bank charters and judgeships being denied and various kinds of appointments being in jeopardy.

Smith notes that FDP delegates learned a great deal at the convention. "it was clear," he said, "that at the convention the delegates did not vote on anything. . . . It seems, however, that the delegates were satisfied to have their right to vote usurped and the decision handed down to them." He points to the contradiction between this and the FDP position. "The FDP philosophy was one man, one vote, a philosophy born of the democratic process and fostered in the faith that if the people are allowed to decide they will make the right and just decisions.

No to the Compromise

The Credentials Committee, reflecting the Johnson Administration, offered a series of compromises. The "best" compromise they offered was to give Aaron Henry and Rev. Ed King votes as delegates-at-large, to require the regular Democratic party of Mississippi to pledge support for the national Democratic ticket, and to establish a committee to work on requirements for ending racial discrimination in the party by the 1968 convention. Liberal spokesmen across the country could not understand why the FDP refused to accept the compromise. Among other things, they called the decision "apolitical." The FDP answered its critics—though the press never saw fit to carry the answer. In its reply to critics, the FDP said:

> . . . In analyzing why the FDP did not accept this compromise, it is important to understand first what the FDP delegation represented and what it accomplished at the convention. The FDP delegation was not simply an alternative delegation chosen by Negro instead of white Mississippians. The FDP is not a Negro party, but an integrated party, open to all whites. It grows directly out of the Civil Rights Movement in Mississippi. It came to Atlantic City demanding, not simply that Negroes be represented, but that racism be ended—in Mississippi and in the Democratic Party.
>
> Moreover, the conditions under which the FDP delegation was chosen were certainly unique. Though the FDP delegation was chosen according to the laws of Mississippi, its role was only partially political. This is so because simply to take part in political pro-

cesses of the state makes the Negro in Mississippi automatically a rebel against the segregated society. This means that he is in immediate and grave danger of losing his job, his home, and possibly his life. Many of those who represented the FDP at Atlantic City have suffered the most brutal and continual reprisals ever since they began working for their political rights. This lends a peculiar and unique air to their efforts to attend the convention, and means that they were literally gambling their lives against the right of being seated in Atlantic City.

> The third thing that must be understood is that the FDP had the support it needed to win the fight at Atlantic City. Within the Credentials Committee there was sufficient support to get the FDP's demands on the floor, there was sufficient support to force a roll call vote. Once a roll call was allowed, most observers agreed that the FDP would have been seated. What prevented this was the massive pressure from the White House, through the mediation of Hubert Humphrey. The FDP delegation was aware of all of this, and it therefore knew that the leadership of the party and the convention was denying it what in fact it had the popular support to win. This kind of dictation is what Negroes in Mississippi face and have always faced, and it is precisely this that they are learning to stand up against.

The Freedom Primers

The FDP has launched a major new educational program in the state through the use of Freedom Primers. The Freedom Primers are short, simple booklets on different phases of politics, economics, and civil rights as they affect Mississippians. The first primer concerned the convention challenge and the Freedom Vote.

The primers will be distributed to MFDP activists and to students in the Mississippi Project's Freedom Schools. As much as possible, MFDP distribution will be made through local officers of the party. In this way they will serve an organizational as well as an educational function.

The primers will be used as the basis of discussion at precinct and county meetings and at voter registration meetings. It is hoped that the primers can be published once every ten days for a full year, each issue on a different topic. It is hoped the primers will provide a breadth of facts and concepts more vital to the growth of political understanding than a more rigid educational program.

Decisions Rise to the Top

The basic tool of political education and decision making in the FDP at the local level is the workshop. Workshops are designed to do two things: (1) to share information; (2) to open discussion and begin to break through the feeling of being unqualified that still exists among many Negroes in the state. In most places, workshops are now led by members of the MFDP. Only in new, unorganized areas do staff members organize initial workshops and these are soon led by people from the local community. Workshops deal with real problems confronting the FDP, like organizing in the next community or county, or developing a program for coming county elections, or circulating Freedom registration forms, or selecting local Freedom candidates to run for council, sheriff, and other local posts.

The Moderate Opposition

Atlantic City represented a major new stage in the development of the FDP. Conservative civil rights spokesmen joined with conservative—and some liberal—Democrats in questioning this new maverick party. Since Atlantic City, FDP leaders have been warned against starting a third party. They are told to be "realistic." They are urged not to move too fast. These warnings are reflected in the behavior of the NAACP national staff person in Mississippi, Charles Evers. The NAACP said it was pulling out of COFO (though the National was never really in) and Evers became the spokesman within the state on this position. Despite Ever's

position, branches of the NAACP in Mississippi remained active in the FDP, some of them providing the party with active members. In other places, local people had their first real internal political fights. It is interesting to note that national columnists, like Evans and Novak, recently have sought to use these internal debates as a lever to split the FDP and to weaken its northern support. In their nationally syndicated column, Evans and Novak spoke of three known Communists in the FDP delegation. Mrs. Fannie Lou Hamer, former sharecropper and now a major spokesperson for the FDP whose testimony before the Atlantic City Credentials Committee stirred the nation, was recently called "demagogic." More interesting and important than the attacks has been their apparent lack of success in changing the minds of either Negroes in Mississippi or people across the country who are tired of the Eastlands and Whittens, who have for so long represented the Magnolia State in Congress.

With Atlantic City behind them, the Freedom Democrats went back to Mississippi to begin work on two new endeavors. First, and by this time almost a routine, was a Freedom election, with Freedom candidates from the FDP running for office and supporting the national Democratic ticket. Second, and now the major national effort of the FDP, was the congressional challenge.

Rocking the Boat from the Bottom

The congressional challenge is based simply on the idea that the congressmen of Mississippi have been illegally elected and should, therefore, not sit in the House of Representatives.

On the opening day of Congress, acting in close contact with the MFDP but using a different legal base for the challenge, Congressman William Fitz Ryan of New York introduced a "Fairness Resolution" which stated that in all due fairness to the challenging MFDP candidates and in recognition of the discriminatory practices of the Mississippi Democrats, the Mississippi congressional delegation should not be seated and the contestants, Mrs. Fannie Lou Hamer, Mrs. Victoria Gray, and Mrs. Annie Devine, should be given floor privileges through the session of the House so that, should their challenge be successful and should they later be named congresswoman, they would have the opportunity of knowing the history of that session of Congress.

Again the Freedom Democrats stirred the nation—and rocked the political boat. Working through ad hoc committees in many congressional districts, through friends of SNCC groups, CORE chapters, some NAACP branches, ACLUs, ADA chapters, and other organizations, the FDP was able to build a movement that led, finally, to 150 votes in support of the challenge. While the final result is impressive, it was not enough to win. Equally impressive was the way in which the coalition backing the challenge was built. Many of the national organizations that were to finally back the FDP's challenge only did so after they began to receive pressure from their own members at home. The final January 4 grouping that was around FDP was built from the bottom up, beginning first with maverick chapters, branches, and locals of national organizations that only began to move after questions from below.

The California vote for the January 4 Fairness Resolution is a clear indicator of how congressmen may be expected to vote on the statutory challenge when it comes to the floor of the House again. It should not be taken for granted that congressmen who voted for the opening day Fairness Resolution will also vote for the challenge. The voting record of the California congressmen follows:

(R) Republican; (D) Democrat; (Number of Congressional District)

Against seating the Mississippians; supporting the MFDP:
Robert L. Legett (D) (4th)
Phillip Burton (D) (5th)
William S. Mailliard (R) (6th)
Jeffery Cohelan (D) (7th)
George P. Miller (D) (8th)

Don Edwards (D) (9th)
John F. Baldwin, Jr. (R) (14th)
Chet Holifield (D) (9th)
Augutus F. Hawkins (D) (21st)
James C. Corman (D) (22nd)
Ronald Brooks Cameron (D) (25th)
James Roosevelt (D) (26th)
Alphonzo Bell (R) (28th)
George E. Brown, Jr. (D) (29th)
Edward Roybal (D) (30th)
Ken W. Dyal (D) (33rd)
Lionel Van Deerlin (D) (37th)
For seating the Mississippians; opposing the MFDP:
Don H. Clausen (R) (1st)
Harold T. Johnson (D) (2nd)
John E. Moss (D) (3rd)
Charles S. Gubser (R) (10th)
J. Arthur Younger (R) (11th)
Burt L. Talcott (R) (12th)
Charles M. Teague (R) (13th)
John J. McFall (D) (15th)
B.F. Sisk (D) (16th)
Cecil R. King (D) (17th)
Harlan Hagen (D) (18th)
H. Allen Smith (R) (20th)
Del Clawson (R) (23rd)
Genard P. Lipscomb (R) (24th)
Ed Reinecke (R) (27th)
Charles H. Wilson (D) (31st)
Craig Hosmer (R) (32nd)
Richard T. Hanna (D) (34th)
James B. Utt (R) (36th)
John V. Tunney (D) (38th)

The statutory challenge to the seating of the five Mississippi congressmen now is supported by the American Civil Liberties Union (ACLU), the Southern Christian Leadership Conference (SCLC), the Congress of Racial Equality (CORE), the Students for a Democratic Society (SDS), the Student Nonviolent Coordinating Committee (SNCC), the Americans for Democratic Action (ADA), The National Council of Churches (NCC), and the Louisiana Committee of Concerned Citizens. In addition, numerous organizations at the state and local level have given support to the challenge, as well as many lesser-known national organizations.

The MFDP: Cannot Be Bought and Sold

Within this national coalition and within the state of Mississippi, a quiet struggle goes on over the Freedom Democratic Party. Two central issues are involved. One has to do with the militant stance of the FDP, especially in regard to the national Democratic administration. No state Democratic party is as independent as the MFDP would be if it were to become the Democratic party of Mississippi. Despite the fact that our civics books tell us that the national parties are weak, there is a web of presidential power that keeps most state Democratic parties in line. The web is held together by powers of patronage and appointment, by the discretionary powers involved in the awarding of contracts and the selection of sites for public spending. The tools of national power that can be mobilized against recalcitrant congressmen and maverick state parties are many, and they are manipulated by a master in the arts of politics. Lyndon Johnson's Great Society does not seem to include room for the MFDP; nor does his style of consensus politics allow the sharp raising of fundamental questions that has been so characteristic of the MFDP in its short history.

The MFDP: Belongs to Itself

This quiet struggle goes on, perhaps even more intensely in Mississippi. Here is the second aspect of the fight over FDP. Just as the FDP raises fundamental questions and issues, so does it also function in a way that is frightening to the manners of polite society. The FDP is genuinely a party of the grassroots people in Mississippi. They participate in and run the party. Sharecroppers and domestics, laborers and unemployed, they make up and control the destiny of their party. Because this kind of participation has become so alien to American political thinking (the Town Meeting was alright then, but after all . . .), many Doubting Thomases have questioned its existence. Generally, they advance a conspiracy theory regarding the FDP. It is, they say, manipulated from someplace else—most frequently it is alleged that SNCC manipulates the FDP. And the more SNCC staff pulls out of Mississippi to begin work in other places where the Movement has not yet begun to take hold, the more sinister is SNCC's control over the FDP.

Two qualities of MFDP—its rank and file participation, and its ability and desire to raise basic issues and questions—are related. It is, after all, those who are hungry, ill-housed, and ill-clothed, those who are denied the right to vote and who are beaten and abused by local police who are most likely to raise questions of poverty and civil rights. And because they have nothing to lose, having nothing to begin with, they are also least likely to "sell out." Thus their participation in and control of the MFDP is intrinsic to its ability to remain a voice of honesty, dealing with central issues, refusing to substitute rhetorical gains for substantive victories. And it is here, in this area, that the day-to-day politics of the MFDP are fought out.

For some time it was argued that the Mississippi Movement ought to be guided by a national board of directors that would include representatives of the major liberal and civil rights organizations in the country. It was always SNCC's position—and others came to share it—that such an idea was a direct violation of the spirit of one man, one vote. SNCC workers took the position that people who lived and worked in the state of Mississippi would have to be the ones who made the decisions. This did not mean that everyone had to automatically accept these decisions. It did, however, mean that control of decision making would have to be in the hands of the people of the state.

This decision has now been accepted—in part because it is a reality, and in part because some have come to see the merit of the view.

There tends to be a correlation between social status in the Negro community and the militancy advocated for the Movement and the issues to be raised. The moderates tend to be the people with more status in the community, whether this be the status of money or education or position. The moderates also tend to be the traditional leaders (or non-leaders) of the community, and this relates to the whole question of qualifications and who can participate in politics. There is now a new leadership in the state built around people like Mrs. Hamer. Some of the people of status in the Negro community have joined with this new leadership in raising basic questions. Most have not.

The issue is particularly painful as the voting bill nears passage. Even on its face, the bill has serious inadequacies. In particular, it offers no protection against economic harassment against Negroes who seek to vote, nor is it clear why this bill will be any more forcefully executed than the many good laws already on the books. It is clear, however, that some Negroes are going to register to vote and that this number may, in some cases, be a key bloc vote able to carry primary elections or even general elections one way or the other. So basic questions are raised. Will Negroes continue to support the MFDP and its present positions? Will Negroes support white "moderates" when they run against blatant racists?

The "Regulars" Feud

Within the state's Democratic party, a split appears to exist just below the surface of racist unity. One wing of the party seems to be ready to concede that the days of Southern-style racism are done. They are the realists who recognize that de facto segregation will have to be tried now, and they are learning how to do that from the North. The white patriots who defend "the Southern way of life" to the end are now on the defensive. With the voting bill, the national party will be able to align itself with the realists in the state. This means that tremendous resources will suddenly become available to those who will make some concessions toward joining the rest of the country in its more subtle forms of discrimination and prejudice. The realists are joined by a tiny number of white Mississippians who are committed to racial justice

but who have been silent. Generally these are churchmen, professionals, and others in the middle class.

The Negroes May Split

The Negro moderates see in the development of the white realists an ally. Since their major concerns have to do with civil rights and not poverty, they do not demand a program of social reform along with a promise of legal reform. To the extent that their voices are still respected in the broad Negro community, their advocacy of moderation may well be extremely powerful. They might even take the position that the MFDP ought to be allowed to die and that Negroes ought to join in the formation of a new Democratic Party which would force the rabid racists into the state's Goldwater Republican party.

Needed: A Wider Insurgent Movement

The moderates' position is strengthened by two other facts. First, the MFDP, as it is now constituted, has no counterparts anywhere in the country. There are local movements, such as the county movements in Louisiana, Virginia, Alabama, and other places in the South; there are small pockets of insurgency in poverty-stricken areas, such as Appalachia, the California farm valley, and the urban ghettos. But nowhere is there a full-fledged insurgent Democratic party. The reform Democratic movements in the North tend to be led by professionals—lawyers, businessmen, and professors. Thus poor Negroes in Mississippi who now lead a political party must feel themselves quite alone and must, indeed, wonder at times whether they really can do what they are doing. Secondly, within the state there is no movement among poor whites which could be a counterpart to the realists who have emerged within the Democratic Party.

The white community project, initiated well over a year ago by COFO under the slogan "Race has kept us both in poverty," remains more an organizing goal and political strategy than a reality. Efforts to bring whites together to discuss their problems of poverty have invariably failed because of the identification of the white COFO workers who were in the project with the Negro-based movement.

Freedom Labor Unions, Co-Ops

COFO staff in Mississippi are beginning to deal with some of these problems. A Mississippi Freedom labor union is being organized specifically to raise issues of wages, hours, and conditions. Farmers' Leagues are growing in the state and are making demands for just treatment for the small farmer. Small co-ops are being talked about and, in Ruleville, the first start to building them is underway. Federal programs, such as those under the Department of Agriculture, the Housing and Home Finance Administrations, the Department of Health, Education, and Welfare, and the Office of Economic Opportunity are being investigated. Still a weak point in the COFO program is its white community project.

The Challenge

For MFDP the problems of the immediate future now take priority. Calls to the country for support of the challenge are now out. SNCC Chairman John Lewis recently called the challenge the most important political event in 1965. To support the challenge and to raise the issue of home rule in Washington, D.C., SNCC is calling for students from across the country to come to the capital from June 13 to July 4. During that time there will be a student lobby for the MFDP. Subsequent to the lobby, some students will be asked to return home to engage in lobbying activities in their home districts; others will go south to join in summer projects.

Whatever the future for MFDP, it constitutes in the eyes of many the most exciting political event of the post-World War II era. Whether the MFDP will be able to maintain itself as a movement of the poor or whether it is only the first in the development of new movements at the grassroots level that are soon to join in the development of a program that addresses itself to the basic problems of the society can only, at this point, be a question.

Reprinted with permission from *The Movement,* Spring 1965. ❖

Ella Baker addressing Mississippi Freedom Democratic Party delegates at boardwalk rally during 1964 Democratic Convention at Atlantic City.

PHOTOS BY

GEORGE BALLIS

Mississippi Freedom Democratic Party delegates singing at rally on Boardwalk. Women from right: Fannie Lou Hamer, Eleanor Holmes Norton, Ella Baker.

Fannie Lou Hamer reacts with anger to compromise offered MFDP delegates seeking to be seated at Democratic Convention. Her comment: "I didn't come all this way for no two seats!"

Rally on boardwalk. Portrait of Mickey Schwerner, murdered civil rights worker, with Fannie Lou Hamer, Aaron Henry, and the Schwerners.

Martin Luther King testifying before Democratic Party Credentials Committee as to why Mississippi Freedom Democratic Party delegates should be seated at convention.

COFO demonstrators on Atlantic City boardwalk outside convention headquarters.

Mississippi Freedom Democratic Party delegates stage sit-in in seats of loyalist Mississippi Democratic delegates.

Weeks in Rebuttal of Joseph L. Rauh, Jr., Counsel, Mississippi Freedom Democratic Party Before the Credentials Committee of the Democratic National Convention

August 22, 1964

Mr. Rauh: Mr. Chairman and members of the Credentials Committee: We have just heard from Mr. Collins that the Freedom Party was like the Ku Klux Klan. I did not believe that I would ever hear that those who have been beaten were like those who did the beating.

What did Mr. Collins say was the reason for that similarity? He said that we had secret files of our voter registration. There they are, ladies and gentlemen, sixty-three thousand human beings registered in the Freedom Party, right there, available for every member of the Credentials Committee to come up afterwards and look at.

Mrs. Moses is there and she will show the files to you. We will not give them to the Mississippi people for a very simple reason. You heard Aaron Henry, you heard Mrs. Hamer, you

Joseph L. Rauh, Jr. was a lawyer for the United Auto Workers Union and a long time civil rights activist. He represented the Mississippi Freedom Democratic Party during the 1964 convention.

heard the others say what would happen to these people. Men's lives would be at stake if those files were given. But, ladies and gentlemen of the Credentials Committee, you may come and see them—sixty-three thousand people in Mississippi signed up for the Freedom Party, went to precinct meetings, went to county conventions, went to the state convention.

Mr. Collins said we only had precinct meetings in thirty-five counties. Isn't it terrible that we were too scared to hold one in Neshoba County, where three boys were murdered, one of whose wife testified here? Isn't it terrible we couldn't have a precinct meeting there? But we did have them in thirty-five counties. You heard the representative of the National Council of Churches tell you that this was the greatest grassroots political action of modern times.

Yet they say we don't have a party. But we do have a party—a party one can be proud of—thousands of people who came and registered with us.

Senator Collins said he never heard of anyone in Mississippi who had been denied the right to vote. Yet only 6 percent of the Negroes are registered—more than that are in those files. They want to vote but they can't get the right to vote. It is only this Credentials Committee, by seating the Freedom Party, that can make the right to vote a reality in Mississippi.

Now, ladies and gentlemen, you get a kind of sweet talk here. They talk one way in Mississippi and they talk another way here.

The governor and Senator Collins say in Mississippi, "We will fight segregation no matter what it costs in human lives," and they sweet talk here.

What do they say in Mississippi? Here is what the governor says, "Our Mississippi Democratic Party is entirely independent and free of the influence or domination of any national party."

Why do they want to come here if they are independent of the party? What are they here for at all? I will tell you why they are here. They are here to warm the seats and keep the Free-

dom Party out of them—because if the Freedom Party is once seated, Mississippi will change. You have it in your power to make the greatest change in Mississippi in the history of modern times by making the Freedom Party the real Democratic party in Mississippi.

(Applause.)

What else do they say down there? Listen to this wonderful Governor Johnson. This is in 1963: "My determination is to do anything I can to get the Kennedy dynasty out of the White House."

Our great John F. Kennedy—yet Governor Johnson's major ambition was to see that John F. Kennedy did not return to the White House. And he called him, and I say this reading from the record, Governor Paul Johnson called John F. Kennedy a "dimwit."

Is that the kind of people you are going to seat at this convention?

What does Paul Johnson's co-leader of the party, Ross Barnett, who is also his co-defendant in a criminal contempt case for violating a court order, say? What about Ross Barnett, co-leader of this "regular" party? Only this very month he called our great president, Lyndon B. Johnson, "a counterfeit Confederate who resigned from the South."

And what else do they say? Ladies and gentlemen, the Democratic Party is the party of minorities. As I look at the Credentials Committee, we are half minority ourselves, first generation Americans. We are some of us Negroes. We are some of us Jews. We are all a minority. And what does this Johnson-Barnett crowd say about Negroes? Last year Johnson campaigned up and down the state of Mississippi saying, "You know what the NAACP stands for: Niggers, alligators, apes, coons, and possums."

Are you going to seat the delegation sent by a man like that? I don't believe so.

And then you know about this recessed "regular" convention. Who was temporary chairman? He was the present Democratic National Committeeman—not Mr. Collins who becomes national committeeman next week. The present national committeeman and temporary chairman of the state convention is Judge Thomas Brady who compared Negroes to chimpanzees and caterpillars. Is that who we are going to seat in this convention? Is that who counts here?

Then, I heard them say we could come to all their precinct meetings. I have got a stack of affidavits this high of people who were kept out of precinct meetings.

Of course, Fannie Lou Hamer had the nerve to go there. She had the nerve to lay her life on the line. You heard her here—the beating she took in that prison because she went to a voting school. She had the nerve to go to a precinct meeting, and they say, "See, it is all open. Fannie Lou Hamer was there"—Fannie Lou Hamer, who lost her job and then was beaten for the privilege of voting.

They say we concocted these things. Do you think Aaron Henry concocted his story? Do you think Fannie Lou Hamer concocted her story? Do you think Edwin King, a Reverend of the Gospel, concocted his story? I don't believe you believe that at all.

They said our party is not a legal party.

What does it take to be a legal party in Mississippi? Theirs is certainly not a legal party. They did not have a Negro at their entire state convention. Not only is no Negro on their delegation; there wasn't a Negro at the whole state convention. They excluded them all. That illegalizes their delegation; on that ground alone they ought not be seated.

What about us? I hope you members of the Credentials Committee will spend Saturday night in Atlantic City reading the legal part of my brief. But I haven't that much faith in you, so I may just say a word about it.

The law is clear that when there are two groups with substantial membership, and that is what we have here, you have the right to choose those who work for you, those who are for your platform.

The "regular" platform says repeal the Civil Rights Act. The national platform will say en-

force it. They can't possibly support that platform, and we all know it. They know it, too.

The sweet talk you hear is to keep the Freedom Party from the Mississippi seats. If the Freedom Party gets the seats here, when they go back to Mississippi they will build a new Mississippi that will make the Democratic Party proud of it.

(Applause.)

Sometimes it is the best advocacy not to point out some things that have happened. But I think this ought to be highlighted. Time and again this afternoon they were asked to pledge support to our great President Lyndon Johnson, and they would not do it.

You know what they are going to do on September 9. The questions that were asked by the delegate from Indiana and the delegate from Wisconsin leave no question about this.

On September 9 they are coming out for Barry Goldwater. If we seat them, we have just been made monkeys of once again.

Bob Kastenmeier pointed this out to them. He read to them what happened in '60. They had a convention. They recessed. They came here. They went back. They rejected the president of the United States, John Kennedy. They rejected Lyndon Johnson.

History is repeating itself. They had a convention. They are going back. They are not going to like our platform. We are going to have a great liberal platform that they are not going to like in Mississippi. If we adopt a platform they did like in Mississippi, we would get licked throughout the United States of America.

The Freedom Party is a legal party. You can't follow the laws of Mississippi if you are a Negro. The laws are made to keep Negroes out of everything in Mississippi. All you can do in a legal way in Mississippi is to do the best you can. And we have done the best we can.

We have built registration. We have held precinct meetings where we could, even at great risk. We held county conventions. We held a state convention. We pledged loyalty—what they won't pledge.

The biggest hand I got speaking to the Mississippi Freedom Party Convention was when I said this: "The biggest difference between us at this integrated convention and their lily-white one last week is not that we are largely Negroes and they were all white. It is that we are for Lyndon Johnson and they are for Barry Goldwater."

And when I said "Lyndon Johnson" the house came down because they want to work for him so much.

(Applause.)

Are you going to throw out of here the people who want to work for Lyndon Johnson, who are willing to be beaten in jails, to die for the privilege of working for Lyndon Johnson? Are you going to seat people who come in here and won't even get up and say "I will try to see that Governor Paul Johnson and Governor Ross Barnett support Lyndon Johnson?"

Why don't they say it? Because they know the answer. Only last week Governor Paul Johnson, that great moderate, called the Lyndon Johnson administration "weak, vacillating crawfish." Is that support for our party?

We are here because we love the Democratic Party. We will work for its candidates.

There is no legal problem. If I can get you to read the brief, I am sure you will agree. But even if you don't read it, I assure you as an attorney that under law you don't have to do things that are impossible. We did everything humanly possible to follow Mississippi law and even more because there was a grave risk.

And so, ladies and gentlemen, the case comes down to some pretty fundamental things.

Will the Democratic Party stand for the oppressors or for the oppressed? Will it stand for loyal people like those who testified, or for the disloyal, "regular" party?

And remember, they had their chance. They had their time to rebut. They made no effort to

contradict our people. They made no effort to contradict the statements of Johnson, Barnett, Brady. Of course they can't. The statements are out of their own mouths.

I have the two minute warning from the chairman. Life is like that when you have so much to say.

This is the one moment when we may save Mississippi from a dictatorship as bad as that in any totalitarian country of the world.

I have so much in my heart to say. And the time is so short.

The Democratic Party cannot fight the white backlash by surrendering to it. The seating of the Freedom delegation is legally and equitably right. The liberal principles upon which the Democratic Party has grown great demand that it stand with the Freedom Party at this convention.

The Democratic Party has won over the years when it stood fast for principle. It cannot win this time by hauling down the flag.

And let me say one thing more. The "regulars" represent the power structure of Mississippi. Senator Collins is here representing Governor Johnson and the power structure of Mississippi. Your choice comes down to whether you vote for the power structure of Mississippi that is responsible for the death of those three boys, or whether you vote for the people for whom those three boys gave their lives.

And so I give you in all seriousness and all earnestness these concluding feelings. We will not win this election by hauling down the flag of principle. And what is much more important to me, and I believe to this wonderful Credentials Committee, is this: Unless we stand up for principle and seat these people who have given so much for our party and our president, what is worse than the fact that we won't win is that we won't deserve to win. Thank you.

(Applause.)

PHOTO BY

GEORGE BALLIS

Joseph Rauh, labor lawyer, Democratic party personality, and MFDP supporter. He gave advice to the delegation, but ultimately accepted the DNC compromise on the seating issue.

JULIUS LESTER

(ADAPTATION OF TRADITIONAL SONG)

Ain't Gonna Let Nobody Turn Me 'Round

"Ain't Gonna Let Nobody Turn Me 'Round" *was generally the third song I would do because it was easily adaptable to any town with the names of the local mayor, sheriff, etc., being substituted for "nobody." I remember one night in Meridian, Mississippi, I think, when Len Chandler, Cordell Reagon, and I led this song for half an hour with people in the audience putting in names of who or what was not going to turn them around.*

Well, ain't gonna let nobody, Lordy, turn me 'round,
turn me 'round, turn me 'round,
Ain't gonna let nobody, Lordy, turn me 'round,
I'm gonna keep on a walkin', keep on a talkin',
Marching up to freedom land.

Well, ain't gonna let segregation, Lordy, turn me 'round,
turn me 'round, turn me 'round,
Ain't gonna let segregation, Lordy, turn me 'round,
I'm gonna keep on a walkin', keep on a talkin',
Marching up to freedom land.

Well, ain't gonna let no police dogs, Lordy, turn me 'round,
turn me 'round, turn me 'round,
Ain't gonna let no police dogs, Lordy, turn me 'round,
I'm gonna keep on a walkin', keep on a talkin',
Marching up to freedom land.

Well, ain't gonna let no sheriff, Lordy, turn me 'round,
turn me 'round, turn me 'round,
Ain't gonna let no sheriff, Lordy, turn me 'round,
I'm gonna keep on a walkin', keep on a talkin',
Marching up to freedom land.

Well, ain't gonna let nobody, Lordy, turn me 'round,
turn me 'round, turn me 'round,
Ain't gonna let nobody, Lordy, turn me 'round,
I'm gonna keep on a walkin', keep on a talkin',
Marching up to freedom land.

ARTWORK BY

SHARON RILEY

THE STUDENT VOICE

McCOMB SHAKEN BY OVER 20 BOMBINGS

UNION ARMS AGAINST KKK

'DEMOCRATIC' OUT SAYS MISS. JUDGE

COP POLLS MOST NEGRO VOTES IN ELECTION

THE NEGRO VOTE: AN ANALYSIS

Front page of newspaper put out by the Student Nonviolent Coordinating Committee (SNCC).

CONGRESSMAN JOHN LEWIS

Freedom Summer Remembered

In the spring of 1964, the Student Nonviolent Coordinating Committee recruited more than one thousand young people to come south to participate in what was called the "Mississippi Summer Project." That spring, I had traveled north with my fellow activists to campuses all throughout the Northeast and the Midwest.

At that time, the state of Mississippi had a black voting-age population of more than four hundred fifty thousand, but only about eighteen thousand were registered to vote. Almost two hundred thousand people turned out to participate in a mock election that SNCC had sponsored, and that election spurred us to organize the Mississippi Summer Project. After the election, we started recruiting students to come and be a part of the project. Our goal was to get more blacks registered to vote.

I had mixed emotions about helping to organize the Mississippi Summer Project. Along with other SNCC leaders, we had been told that almost anything could happen. We worried about the potential for violence, because Mississippi was considered a dangerous place for social activists. There was a history of violence in the Delta where many of us would be. We also considered the possibility that friction would develop between some of the black and white workers. After I had gone around the campuses recruiting students, I felt a heavy responsibility for a lot of the people because I convinced them to come to Mississippi.

As the summer got underway, we moved the SNCC office from Atlanta to Greenwood, Mississippi, and I spent most of the summer working out of Greenwood. Soon after getting there, we had the disappearances and deaths of three civil rights workers. Two young Jewish men from New York and a young black man from Mississippi—Andrew Goodman, Michael Schwerner, and James Chaney—became heroes in the eyes of many Americans. These three young men gave their lives to advance the cause of freedom for every American. We must never forget these three men and their deaths.

After the murders, we lived in Mississippi with the constant possibility that something could happen to any of us. During the summer, many churches were bombed and burned, particularly black churches in small towns and rural communities that had been headquarters for Freedom Schools, voter registration rallies, and workshops. There were shootings on homes, so we lived with constant fear.

At the same time, we tried not to become too preoccupied with the fear. You came to feel as if you were part of a nonviolent army, and, within the group, you had a sense of solidarity. You knew you had to move on in spite of the fear. I will never forget some of the problems and trauma that some of the SNCC people went through. It was a trying time for all of us. Somehow, we made it through the summer. I really don't know how, but we made it. What happened that summer helped to change the direction of the Movement. It forced a great many

John Lewis was born the son of sharecroppers on February 21, 1940, outside of Troy, Alabama. He holds a B.A. in Religion and Philosophy from Fisk University and is a graduate of the American Baptist Theological Seminary in Nashville, Tennessee. From 1963–66, Lewis was Chairman of the Student Nonviolent Coordinating Committee. In 1977, he was appointed by President Jimmy Carter to direct more than 250,000 volunteers for ACTION and in 1980, became Community Affairs Director of the National Consumer Co-Op Bank in Atlanta. Lewis's first electoral success came in 1981 when he was elected to the Atlanta City Council. He was elected to Congress in 1986 to represent Georgia's Fifth Congressional District where he currently serves as a member of the House Ways and Means Committee; Chief Deputy Minority Whip; and Co-Chairman of the Congressional Urban Caucus.

people to rededicate themselves to the Movement. I often think of the mothers of those three guys that died helping us.

I think for many of us that summer in Mississippi was like guerilla warfare. You knew that you had to prepare yourself, condition yourself, if you were going to be there. You knew that you were going to stay for a period of time, and there were going to be disappointments and setbacks. What we tried to instill, particularly in the SNCC staff and also into the young people coming down, was that even as they came there, we weren't going to change Mississippi in one summer or one year, that it was a much longer effort. In a sense, we went down to help the people there, but no doubt they helped all of us a great deal; there's no question about that. Some of us, no doubt, literally grew up overnight because of being in positions of responsibility where we had to make decisions, we had to act. Our main purpose was empowering the local, indigenous black people of Mississippi.

I think Freedom Summer helped many of us to reaffirm our commitment to nonviolent struggle. While nonviolence was, for some, merely a tactic for social change, for many of us it became a philosophy of life—a way of living. When we suffered violence and abuse, when we were arrested and jailed, our concern was not for retaliation. We sought to understand the human condition of our attackers and to accept suffering in the right spirit.

As I worked throughout the South during the 1960s, I saw civil rights workers and indigenous people whom we were trying to help with their heads cracked open by nightsticks, lying in the street weeping from tear gas, calling helplessly for medical aid.

I saw old women and young children in peaceful protest, who were run down by policemen on horses, beaten back by fire hoses, and chased by police dogs. Yet these people were still able to forgive, understand, and sing *Ain't gonna let nobody turn me 'round.*

One of the most important things I tell people today is that you must believe in the possibility of positive change. I have worked all my life to make my community and our country into a better place for everyone. I have always had a firm belief in the idea that people of goodwill could work together and bring about positive change.

The Mississippi Summer Project gave many of us hope that positive change was possible even under the most adverse and daunting conditions. The Civil Rights Movement instilled in me and many others the dream that we could, through disciplined nonviolent action, transform this nation into the Beloved Community. This has been a conscious goal, and, though it may be a distant one, the Mississippi Summer Project strengthens my conviction that we can make that dream a reality. ❖

Registrar's Office

ARTWORK BY

SHARON RILEY

CAROLYN GOODMAN

Andrew Goodman 1943-1964

Dr. Carolyn Goodman Eisner's career has been distinguished by her dedication to public service on the local, national and international levels. She was the former President of the Pacifica Foundation; is on the board of Directors of Symphony Space; and is Chair of the North American Advisory Committee of Interns for Peace. Carolyn holds a doctoral degree in Psychology and has worked as a Clinical Psychologist in schools and outpatient psychiatric clinics. Her son Andrew Goodman was murdered with two fellow civil rights worker, James Chaney and Michael Schwerner, in Mississippi during the Freedom Summer of 1964.

The story of Andrew Goodman is the story of youth activism. In critical times, when justice and inequality become intolerable, it is the young people who are prepared to face the consequences of challenging the status quo. In the last half century young men and women, often in nonviolent protests against injustice, have been gunned down in South Africa, the United States, China, France, and elsewhere. Their efforts led to revolutionary changes. Today in South Africa the system of apartheid is crumbling, and in our country, the superstructure of segregation and white supremacy, if not dead, is in a state of decay.

Andy Goodman was born in 1943 on the cusp of a student movement. At the time of his birth, our country was waging a war against fascism in Europe. In the 1940s, millions of Jews, labor leaders, and cultural minorities in Western Europe were slaughtered by a self-styled "master race." They were exterminated in gas chambers and tortured in concentration camps because of their religion, political activity, and race. In our own country, congressional committees censored, investigated, and jailed political and social dissidents who stood on their constitutional rights and refused to testify. It was a dark period for freedom when our constitutional guarantees were threatened by the very men who were charged with upholding them.

In contrast to a national atmosphere of mistrust and divisiveness, where people informed on former colleagues and segregation prevailed throughout the nation, Andy was raised in a racially mixed community of white, black, and Hispanic families. He played on the street and in the playgrounds with children who came from different cultures and races. He became aware at an early age of the differences in lifestyle and comfort between himself and his neighborhood friends. Even as a young boy, Andy had questions about these disparities. He saw the hopelessness and frustration of the "newly arrived" immigrants from Puerto Rico who had emigrated to the mainland to seek employment and a better life for their children. In discussions at home and in school he learned that language, color, and religion closed doors of opportunity to people already burdened by second-class education and poverty.

As he grew into adolescence, Andy tried to understand the political and social forces that governed life in the late 1950s and early 1960s. The questions he raised grew out of the values and experiences he learned within his family, in a school where teachers welcomed diversity, and from his own observations in a multicultural community. He wondered why people were afraid to express opinions if they represented minority viewpoints. He asked why people were put in prison for refusing to inform on friends. He questioned how workers such as coal miners could organize themselves for better living conditions when they were dependent on their bosses for jobs, and he asked why citizens were denied the rights and protections granted them

Andy Goodman at a meeting in Oxford, Ohio, on June 15, 1964, prior to leaving for Mississippi to take part in a voter registration drive. He, Schwerner, and Chaney were last seen alive on June 21, 1964, in Philadelphia, Mississippi. Photo submitted by Carolyn Goodman.

under our constitution.

Andy was not satisfied to read or hear about the world he was growing up in. He was a born activist and wanted to learn by direct encounter and personal experience. At fifteen, he and a friend went to West Virginia to live in a coal mining town. They were disturbed by the working conditions and decided to call the governor but were not able to find a phone booth! At seventeen Andy traveled to farming communities of Western Europe where he saw how large-scale agribusiness was displacing small farmers; at nineteen he spent the summer as a dramatics counselor at a camp for inner-city children. That summer he was attacked by a gang of men who opposed the presence of interracial children in their community. In his college years, Andy

worked on a construction crew and as a helper to a truck driver. His knowledge deepened in a school without walls.

But for Andy life was not all work and study. He played with the same zest and intensity that he devoted to his work. As an ardent Brooklyn Dodger fan, he arranged for his neighbor, Dodger star Jackie Robinson, to speak at his school. Jackie, the first black man to play in the major leagues, was a hero to the students. As a clarinetist, Andy's interest in music ranged from jazz to classical, but practicing the clarinet did not always mean concentration on the music. One day, lost in a fantasy, his clarinet became a baseball bat, he the great Duke Snyder playing in Ebbets Field. He swung for the ball, hit a door knob, and his "guaranteed unbreakable" instrument lay in pieces at his feet!

The theater was Andy's passion and the means through which he expressed his creative gifts. He participated in every school play beginning at an early age and continuing through high school. He wrote plays and stories, one of which was performed by his classmates at graduation. His English and dramatic arts teacher, Richard Crosscup, who fostered Andy's love for the theater, wrote these words in a book on drama and self-discovery in children.

> . . . It was Andy we were talking about when we described the sensitive human insights by which a twelve year old was able to get below the surface of a harsh and superficially rude person and make him as tenderly funny and as loved and—in a deep, essential way—as loving as everyone else. In his sophomore year, Andy was Marc Antony in an informal dramatization of *Julius Caesar.* His gifts were subtle and his Antony was not the flamboyant man who hardly knows where real emotion leaves off and histrionic emotion begins. He was an Antony whose quiet delivery and cunning emphases were as much an incitation to riot as though he had blown up a storm. In his junior year, Andy was the Covey in *The Plow and the Stars.* It was his marvelous face which, in the tragic moment, expressed a more disquieting self-revelation than what O'Casey had written seemed to demand. In his senior year he was the author of the stream-of-consciousness story some of his classmates dramatized with readers and a pantomimist. His own role in the senior dramatics program was strangely prophetic. It is best described by one of his classmates in the words she spoke at the dedication of his tombstone:

> Four years ago I wrote a play in which Andy had the role of a prince who lived life and died to preserve his integrity. Andy gave the part a vitality and impact which my self-conscious attempts at poetic drama did not deserve, and I knew then that this work

was one of the most beautiful gifts I would ever receive.

It would be a great over-simplification to claim that Andy's participation in creative dramatics shaped the humanity which dictated his decision to go South. But it would be to mistake him altogether not to know that this decision was the direct result of the sensitivities, insights, and integrity which characterized both his personal relationships and his creative work.

One time when Andy was in sixth grade, a lonely boy got himself involved in a wrangle with the other boys and found himself so overwhelmed he ran home and said he would never come to school again. The boys discussed the problem very earnestly, and it was Andy whom they dispatched to the boy's house, feeling that he alone among them could reassure the boy and bring him back— and Andy did. . . . It can be said that what Andy Goodman took to Mississippi when he was twenty was the perceptiveness, the integrity, and the humanity which his boyhood had shaped.

—Richard Crosscup, *Children and Dramatics,* Charles Scribner's Sons, New York, 1966.

Andy entered college with a major in dramatic arts which he later changed to sociology, yet he always maintained his love for the theater, and throughout his college days he acted with an Off-Broadway repertory company. Real-life issues and the creative arts were joined in the short span of Andy's life and allowed him to drink deeply from his political, social, and cultural heritage. He knew the pain of those less fortunate than he and gave much tenderness and love to his family and friends.

Andy's father, a poet, humanist, and engineer, wrote a poem to his three sons when Andy was only five and a half years old. It expressed, with unusual sensitivity, the depth of his understanding toward his children.

And Andy—as the strength of my own excur-

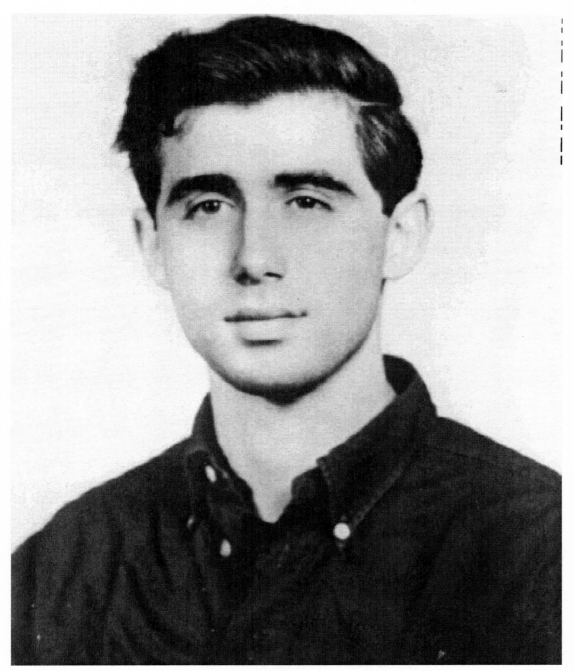

Andy Goodman

sions

Into the realm of jubilee and laughter

Into the peace of love and beloved

Into the frost of bruise and hurt

Into the fantasy of idols above him

Into the knowledge that good is for him

And from him flows a tide of belonging

That gives to the giver his own desirings.

These lines written by Robert Goodman caught the essence of Andy, and like his father, he too expressed insight and feelings in poetry. The year before the 1964 Mississippi Summer Project, Andy wrote this poem in an English class at Queens College. It was based on A.E. Housman's "To an Athlete Dying Young":

How dismally the day

Screams out and blasts the night.

What disaster you will say,

To start another fight.

See how heaven shows dismay

As her stars are scared away;

As the sun ascends with might

With his hot and awful light.

He shows us babies crying

We see the black boy dying

We close our eyes and choke our sighs

And look into the dreadful skies.

Then peacefully the night

Puts out the reddened day

And the jaws that used to bite

Are sterile where we lay.

In the spring of his junior year at college, Aaron Henry and Fannie Lou Hamer, two veteran black Mississippi activists, spoke to the students about the oppressive conditions in their state. They presented plans for a summer project and were recruiting students who, if they were under twenty-one years of age, required their parents' permission to sign up for the project. Andy saw the Freedom Summer 1964 Project as an opportunity to participate in a movement that could have positive ramifications on race relations and the rights of black people. It was inevitable that he would decide to join with others to register voters, teach in Freedom Schools, and work in community centers. Andy's friend, Ralph Engleman, who spoke at his memorial service said, "Andy's decision to go to Mississippi was the result of a simple ability to perceive and feel the reality of the social evil which pervades our society. And for Andy the step from conviction to action, made quietly but firmly, came naturally."

The young activists who took part in the 1964 project and the three who lost their lives—Andy Goodman, James Chaney, and Michael Schwerner—were brave men and women. They are part of a long tradition of youth committed to justice and equality. The poet Stephen Spender memorialized and paid tribute to young men and women who were committed to the cause of justice and democracy. In 1938 young people came from all over the world to form an International Brigade that would join with the Spanish people in a fierce struggle to preserve their democratic society and defeat an infamous dictator. They were drawn to Spain just as young activists thirty years later answered a call to go south because they believed, as Abraham Lincoln did, in a government "of the people, by the people, and for the people." The last verse of Spender's poem, "I Think Continually of Those Who Were Truly Great," although written for the Freedom Fighters in Spain, is a tribute to committed youth at any time in history.

Near the sun, near the snow, in the highest field
See how these names are feted by the waving grass
And by the streamers of white cloud
And whispers of wind in the listening sky.
The names of those who in their lives fought for life
Who wore at their hearts the fire's center.
Born of the sun they traveled a short while toward the sun
And left the vivid air signed with their honor.

Youth activism has been, is now, and will continue to be a flexible but unbreakable fiber in the fabric of today's society. We who are part of the tradition of activism can continue to play a role in perpetuating youth participation in social change. At this writing, the Andrew Goodman Foundation will make that effort by working with young people to develop Freedom Summer '94. The legacy of Andy Goodman, James Chaney, and Michael Schwerner can be an inspiration to the youth of the late 20th century. They can stand on the shoulders of their predecessors and continue to struggle for a just society. ❖

Portraits of Andrew Goodman, Michael Schwerner, and James Chaney.

ARTWORK BY

SHARON RILEY

J. WASHINGTON LANDRÓN

Song For Ben Chaney

I'm sitting here remembering all the things I learned in school
'bout how so many fought and died to call their lives their own
and carved them out a nation strong where freedom is the rule
I wonder now, has Freedom's Eagle Flown?
'Cause the words sound so hollow
Hear how they echo
"Land of Equality, Justice, and Liberty"
If there were truth in what you say
Evers would be alive today
Black men wouldn't live in fear
Three men couldn't disappear
Four little girls would not have died
The world could never say to us,
"America, You Lied."

I'm listening to you tell me that I'll get my due in time
I'm watching you ignore me saying, "No! The time is now."
Change places with me for awhile. Your place in life for mine
and let me grind your children 'neath my plow

Now don't the words sound a little hollow?
Hear how they echo
"Land of Equality, Justice, and Liberty"
If there were truth in what you say
Evers would be alive today
Black men wouldn't live in fear
Three men couldn't disappear
Four little girls would not have died
The world could never say to us,
"America, You Lied."

Portrait of Ben Chaney singing.

ARTWORK BY

SHARON RILEY

BEN CHANEY

They Came Up Missing

Ben Chaney is president of the James Earl Chaney Foundation, a human and civil rights organization established in April 1988, in memory of his brother James Chaney. Born in Meridian, Mississippi, he grew up in the Civil Rights Movement and was arrested in nonviolent demonstrations more than 21 times before he was 12. Ben is a former member of the Black Panther Party, Republic of New Africa, and former Minister of Defense for the New York City High School Coalition.

The quilt lay unfinished in its wooden frame. Three weeks ago she started this quilt. The Saturday before J. E., Micky, and Andy disappeared, Mama trimmed a lot of old hand-me-down clothes that other folks had given her, clothes that were too small for her children, which she arranged into decorative color patches. She then stitched the color patches together in a beautiful arrangement to make the quilt's top. Next she took the leftovers from the patches and pieced them together to make the back. Mama would then stretch the bottom on the floor where she would put an even layer of cotton over it. Then she would put the colorful top on and roll the entire thing up on a long wooden pole. She would put the pole into the wooden frame and hand stitch the entire quilt, inch by inch, as she unrolled it off the pole. It usually took Mama four days and plenty of scraps to make a queen-sized quilt. But this quilt has been in the frame ever since J. E. came up missing, thirty days ago.

Mama had to quilt. Separated from Daddy for several years, she had always worked long hours on white folks' jobs just to have the money needed to raise five children. But ever since J. E. became a "civil righter," white folks stopped giving Mama work. They said she let her son "slanderize Mississippi whites." So now to feed her children, she had to fall back on the skill taught to her by her grandmother—making quilts. Before J. E. went with Mickey and Rita to Ohio, Mama said that she wanted to make as

many quilts as she could by fall, that way she'd have plenty to sell when the weather turned cold.

Looking at the colorful unfinished quilt you would never know it was only patches made from scraps. "When Mama gonna finish this quilt?" I mumble to myself. "Hush-up boy," Mama's voice came from the kitchen, where she was mopping the floor for the fourth time today. Being only twelve nobody ever paid much attention to anything I said or did. Now, since J. E. has disappeared, Mama pays attention to every word and gesture. She won't let me go out to Davis Street Park down the street to play ball. I can't play in the house because it's too clean. Mama cleans it four to five times a day. Just yesterday, after breakfast and after my sister had washed the dishes, Mama took every dish, pot, pan and washed them again. Not once, but three times. My sister tried to help her but Mama wouldn't let no one in the kitchen. This old house will never get dirty again.

Mama gets little rest now that everyone is looking for J. E. If she is not cleaning, she's walking. But she doesn't go anywhere. She just walks in the yard in circles around the house. There was grass growing in the backyard. J. E. was captain of his high school football and track teams. Sometimes he would take me and my cousins to the backyard and show us how to get out of the blocks fast, make a tackle, or throw a block. Mama would scream for us to get off the grass. Now, with all the walking she does around the house, she has worn the grass down and created a little path. Mama does a lot of walking around the house. While everybody is asleep Mama walks. One morning I woke up at the time when there is not enough darkness for night and too little light for daybreak and heard Mama humming a spiritual and walking. I looked out of my window and saw her walking around the house. She had passed my window so I hung my head out of the window and felt the warm wet summer air on my face. "I'm gonna cook biscuits this morning," Mama said when she returned to my window. "Go back to bed, I'll get you up when they're ready." With that she had passed my window and was walking around the side of the house. I heard the hum of *Rock of ages, cleft for thee, let me hide myself in thee.*

The other day Mama came in the house from walking and she wasn't tired. A news bulletin was on T.V. "For thirty days three civil rights workers have been missing in Mississippi." Pictures of J. E., Mickey, and Andy came across the screen. Everybody sat quiet and still, as we have done for the past four weeks whenever the news or a special bulletin came on T.V.

"They came up missing just like Grandpa Jim," Mama said from the sofa where she sat. I had never considered Mama an old woman until that moment. She was short and stoic with a light complexion, thick straight hair, and well-defined proud features. To me her clear complexion was without wrinkles until now, while she talked about Grandpa Jim. When Mama was six years old, he had owned a lot of land with plenty of cows and was a successful farmer. Mama told us that Grandpa Jim's neighbors were white and wanted his farm. Mama said they felt no yellow nigger should be more successful than whites, and they tried to get Grandpa Jim to undersell his farm. But Grandpa Jim didn't want to sell at all. He was saving the land and farm to pass on to his children. After many threats from those white neighbors, Grandpa Jim warned that he would shoot anybody who came on his land unwelcomed and started sitting every night on the porch with a shotgun in his lap. His wife, Grandma Lauria, being worried for Grandpa Jim's life, persuaded him to go visit one of his daughters in Mobile, Alabama—until things quieted down. He agreed. A few days later Grandpa Jim's family saw him to the train depot where he boarded a train headed for Mobile, Alabama. The train was late arriving in Mobile and when it did arrive Grandpa Jim was not on it. His daughter found out that some white men had stopped the train and took Grandpa Jim off. Weeks later a white neighbor brought Grandpa Jim's watch and his folded shirt to Grandma Lauria.

Grandma had to sell the land and cows to a white neighbor for pennies. Mama told us.

"Why?" I softly asked from my spot on the floor in front of the T.V.

"I declare boy," Mama screamed so loud that everyone in the room stopped watching T.V. and turned to her. "Listen, for your own good," she screeched out from tight lips, her face tighter than a rubber band. "Like Grandpa Jim and J. E. and his friends," she pointed to the picture of the missing three that was still on the T.V. screen, "Grandma would have came up missing."   ❖

Portrait of Mrs. Chaney and Ben at James Chaney's funeral.

ARTWORK BY

SHARON RILEY

Excerpts from an interview with Dick Gregory

January 8, 1994   Transcribed by Susie Erenrich

Susie: Tell me about your involvement in the Mississippi Civil Rights Movement.

Dick: To go back to talk about Mississippi Summer, from my standpoint, I have to go back to when I was a child and say what Mississippi meant to me as Northern black folk. We used Mississippi as the whipping boy for all of our horrors. We knew in Mississippi if you looked at a white woman you could be lynched. If a white woman didn't like you and you looked at her, you could be lynched.

At no time when I was growing up did you ever consider going to Mississippi. There was no such thing as South Africa as long as Mississippi was like it was. You were in awe when you knew someone who went to Mississippi and made it.

You were told that Mississippi had first grade, second grade, third grade, fourth grade through eighth grade all in one room with a pot belly stove. That's what you grew up with. Even if you were eating out of garbage cans you always justified what they did to you because it would be worse in Mississippi.

It never dawned on you that there were real people in Mississippi that were dealing with the problem, that lived underneath that twenty-four hours a day.

And when the Civil Rights Movement hit, they called me to come to Mississippi. I was in show business. I wasn't nonviolent, but I wasn't about to confront a Mississippi sheriff who was 6'3" and would kill you.

So when I went down I went down to die. Not that I wanted to die, but that was the ultimate test of John Wayne. And the only difference between me and John Wayne was that I couldn't fight back but had a way out because they [SNCC] said nonviolence.

I thought, what am I doing? But I loved it. I said, bring me Mississippi. I couldn't wait to get to Mississippi. It's like going down into a pit ten thousand feet down into the ground where nobody in their right mind would go. So when I finally got to Mississippi I was just stunned that it didn't look the way that I thought hell should look. People looked normal. The black doctors looked just like medical doctors. People didn't seem to be afraid. People didn't seem to be getting an okay from white folk before they could do something.

People from Mississippi had a special hatred for the Civil Rights Movement that they didn't have for black folk. They would disrespect me but those are two different things.

And then you'd see that God force because I look back now and it was very interesting how black folks lived on the farm, white folks paid them and sold them their goods. They never had no money on them.

Dick Gregory is a comedian, author, nutritionist, businessman, recording artist, actor, philosopher, anti-drug crusader, and activist. Credited with opening many doors for black entertainers, Gregory found comedy an expedient avenue for getting people's attention, to make them think as well as laugh. He became a household name in the '60s for his outspoken and provocative humor. Once he achieved success in the world of entertainment, Gregory shifted gears and used his talents to work for social change. His participation in the Civil Rights Movement is well documented, as are his efforts for world peace, against hunger and on behalf of the American Indians. Gregory's devotion to causes have cost him dearly, for he was virtually barred from the entertainment industry, and he has been jailed numerous times for taking part in demonstrations. But his unflagging sense of justice has led him from Louisiana to Iran, and from Ireland to Detroit, always working for human rights, and always for "people." Gregory's books include, Dick Gregory's Natural Diet For Folks Who Eat, and his acclaimed autobiography, Nigger.

But I never understood why the Elks Club, black folk, was downtown, across the street from the police department. I didn't know that they were running bootleg whiskey for the sheriff. They were the only black folks that had a business or club downtown.

And so I knew up north, your sleek hiphustlers, your school teachers, really had something on Mississippi. But it never dawned on me that there must be something going on in Mississippi. And so the horror of Mississippi was like no horror in the world.

I'll be thrilled until the day I leave this planet that I went in spite of thinking that I wouldn't. I went in spite of that fantastic fear.

And then when I got there, there were white women at a rally next to me. It was unbelievable. That's the horror that was in me.

You knew you couldn't go to the bathroom. You knew you couldn't eat at a restaurant. You knew that if a white lady looked in your direction, you looked away. These are all the things you just knew you did.

You heard of Emmett Till as a little boy that had gotten lynched in Mississippi. In spite of that I went and the more I went the more it freed me from fear. I liked it more than from the standpoint of an entertainer. The feeling I got going down south terrorizing white folk reached anything I ever felt in my life. So it was a joy for me. And it superseded death.

Susie: Tell me about some of your experiences in Mississippi.

Dick: One night I was sitting in a church. They threw a bomb in the church. I would have run but by the time I was ready to run the exit was blocked. So I threw the bomb back outside and then went outside to cause havoc.

In Greenwood, Rap Brown and Stokely Carmichael told me that if I couldn't behave myself I would have to leave. But who would ever believe, listening to them now, that they would tell me I was too violent. It was kind of interesting because in Mississippi that was a whole youth movement.

One night in Greenwood, they arrested ev-

erybody but me. I knew they planned on killing me. They left me in the street. There was a guy with a double-barrelled shot gun. I kept walking. I just felt everything one would feel when you are going to die. I walked across the street, and I just turned around. It took me so long to get across the street. I got to the alley. I looked back. Then I hid in the bushes until daytime. By that time some Justice Department people were out.

My life in Mississippi was real interesting because I wasn't there but just for a few minutes. I did what I had to do. It's like a kicker. You come out, put your shoe on, and kick the ball. You go sit in the stands.

I wasn't there for twenty-four hours a day under that madness. I could come back and articulate it and got fantastic space from the white folk. And I could come back to Chicago the folk hero. The press would ask, what was it like?

Susie: Tell me about "Christmas for Mississippi."

Dick: Then one day I decided to have Christmas in Mississippi. I was going to send twenty thousand turkeys to Mississippi for Christmas day. I had to raise $150,000. It was the week of the Clay–Liston return match in Boston. I called Sonny Liston, I'm fixing to send twenty thousand turkeys to Mississippi for Christmas. Thought it would be wild if you and Cassius would buy ten thousand apiece from the gate of the fight. Mohammed Ali said it sounded great. Then I called Drew Pearson. He became co-chairman of a committee called "Christmas For Mississippi." The project became tax exempt.

Then complications developed. Mohammed Ali discovered a hernia and the fight was canceled. I decided on street donations in Chicago and a big benefit show on the same front. I needed a big star, Sammy Davis, Jr. Sammy agreed to appear at the Arie Crown Theater in Chicago on December 20. On the streets of Chicago, a few of us dressed up as Santa Claus and collected donations. Everyday we would go on a different corner from 6:00 A.M.

The day of the show Charles Evers and Drew Pearson flew into Chicago. Charles was in charge of setting up the distribution of turkeys in Mississippi. Drew, the co-chairman, had been collecting donations from his contacts in high places. Drew started pulling all this money from his coat pocket.

Besides Sammy, other performers helped with the benefit—Eartha Kitt, George Kirby, Red Saunders' band, and the Four Step Brothers. The show was a big success.

We got to Mississippi and over eight hundred people were jammed into Pratt Memorial Methodist church. All the press was there. At least 90 percent of the people never had a turkey before. The trucks were late. When the turkeys arrived I jumped on the back of the truck and started handing out turkeys. I said find me a white guy to get the first turkey. That story went all around the world. The first turkey, the biggest turkey we had, went to a white man.

I really felt bad later because I fed them on Christmas what I wanted. But that is what it was about.

Susie: What did you do when you found out about the disappearances of Goodman, Schwerner, and Chaney?

Dick: I was in Russia with a friend of mine when the UPI guy came early that morning and told us about the three missing civil rights workers in Mississippi. So we canceled everything; we got on a plane that morning, went to Paris, London, from there to New York, and because of the time difference, at eight o'clock that night I was shaking my finger at Sheriff Rainey and Deputy Cecil Price, in their face. They were nervous. And after talking to them I knew they did it and that they were scared. They just never knew the whole world would react the way they did. I came back home, and it was the biggest news.

So I had to go to San Francisco to borrow $25,000 from Hugh Hefner to put up a reward to help find the bodies. Then the Justice Department and FBI announced it was putting up $30,000.

The guy who went and told them where the bodies were to collect the reward for some strange reason told me too. I guess he wanted to collect it twice.

So I had the identical information. I knew three weeks ahead of time where they were. I held a press conference and said J. Edgar Hoover knows where those bodies are. And those bodies were discovered. I think that is what broke Mississippi. ❖

Move On Over
Or We'll Move On Over You

Mine eyes have seen injustice in each city town and state
The jails are filled with black men
And the courts are white with hate
With every bid for justice someone whispers to us wait
But the Movement's moving on

Move on over or we'll move on over you
Move on over or we'll move on over you
Move on over or we'll move on over you
For the Movement's moving on

They conspire to keep us silent in the field and in the slum
They promise us the vote, then sing us we shall over come
But John Brown knew what freedom was and died to win us some
And the Movement's moving on

Move on over or we'll move on over you
Move on over or we'll move on over you
Move on over or we'll move on over you
For the Movement's moving on

The dove of peace with bloody beak sinks talons in a child
They bend the olive branch to make a bow then with a smile
They string it with the lynch rope they've been hiding all the while
But the Movement's moving on

Move on over or we'll move on over you
Move on over or we'll move on over you
Move on over or we'll move on over you
For the Movement's moving on

I declare my independence from the fool and from the knave
I declare my independence from the coward and the slave
I declare that I shall fight for right and fear no jail nor grave
For the Movement's moving on

Move on over or we'll move on over you
Move on over or we'll move on over you
Move on over or we'll move on over you
For the Movement's moving on

Many noble dreams are dreamed by small and voiceless men
Many noble deeds are done the righteous defend
We're hear today John Brown to say
We'll triumph in the end and the Movement's moving on

Move on over or we'll move on over you
Move on over or we'll move on over you
Move on over or we'll move on over you
For the Movement's moving on

TOM PAXTON

Ain't That News!

It is a distinct honor to be asked to contribute to any remembrance of the Mississippi Freedom Summer. That summer proved to be a defining moment for many in my generation. Some of us sat in at lunch counters in the South; some of us picketed corporations in the North that kept to a segregated policy elsewhere. Some went to Mississippi to register voters. Three young civil rights workers were murdered there by white supremacists in league with the police.

In 1965 I wrote a ballad called "Goodman, Schwerner, and Chaney," which told that story. When I found the recording of that song I reread the liner notes for the album on which it appeared. The notes, an open letter to a black friend in my home town of Bristow, Oklahoma, represent, more truly than even my memory would allow, the quality of idealism and hope that persisted despite the terrible losses the Movement had already suffered. I offer it, along with the song, as a portrait of a time when anger at injustice co-existed with the conviction that right would prevail.

Now, when all the ills the 1990s are heir to, are blamed on what some are pleased to call the excesses of the '60s, we would do well to think of those who faced—and suffered—death to keep democracy's promise. Let us especially remember the Mississippi Freedom Summer and its legacy of courage, commitment, and hope.

The night air is heavy, no cool breezes blow.
The sounds of the voices are worried and low,
Desperately wondering and desperate to know
About Goodman and Schwerner and Chaney.

Calm desperation and flickering hope;
Reality grapples like a hand on the throat,
For you live in the shadow of ten feet of rope,
If you're Goodman and Schwerner and Chaney.

The Pearl River was dragged and two bodies were found,
But it was a blind alley for both men were brown,
So they all shrugged their shoulders and the search it went on
For Goodman and Schwerner and Chaney.

Pull out the dead bodies from the ooze of the dam.
Take the bodies to Jackson all according to plan.
With the one broken body, do the best that you can—

It's the body of young James Chaney.

The nation was outraged and shocked through and through.
"Call J. Edgar Hoover; he'll know what to do,
For they've murdered two white men and a colored boy, too:
Goodman and Schwerner and Chaney."

James Chaney, your body exploded in pain,
And the beating they gave you is pounding my brain,
And they murdered much more with their dark, bloody chain,
And the body of Pity lies bleeding.

The pot-bellied coppers shook hands all around,
And joked with the rednecks who came into town.
They swore that the murderers soon would be found,
And they laughed as they spat their tobacco.

Sheriff Rainey and other accused at the trial of Goodman, Schwerner, and Chaney.

ARTWORK BY

SHARON RILEY

TOM PAXTON

A Letter for John Cherry

Dear John,

I've been twenty years in the writing of this letter. I hope you haven't minded the waiting, but there were things that required time to straighten themselves out. But now I guess it's time to say what's on my mind.

When I met you in June of 1945, John, my Uncle Cal, and Aunt Clara had brought me back with them to Bristow to spend the summer in Oklahoma. Having lived my first seven years in Chicago, you can imagine how excited I was to get down where the cowboys were.

You and your friend Charlie were working for Uncle Cal at the D-X station at 10th and Main, and my summer was spent mostly in the station, at Cal's house next door (the old hospital), or out at the Circle J ranch. Out at the ranch I ran wild with Charlie's boy, Harper (where is he now?).

I know that you liked me right away, as I liked you, because you started right in teasing me. You got a kick out of my Chicago accent and never got tired of hearing the way I said "cow."

But when I got my set of cowboy cap guns and my straw cowboy hat and decided it was high time I launched my career of crime, you didn't act your part too well. When I sauntered into the station, coolly looked the situation over and said "Reach for the sky!" or something like that you just broke out laughing and couldn't stop. It was a pretty rough beginning for a hardened gunfighter.

But, John, do you know the one thing about that summer that I remember best, some twenty years later? It was our night at the movies. You and your wife took me to the Walmur to see some shoot 'em up and I was happy all the way to the theater. When we got inside, though, you and your wife started up the stairs into the balcony so, naturally, I followed. But you turned around and told me I had to sit downstairs. That upset me, and I wonder now whether or not you debated telling me *why* we couldn't sit together; but I guess you figured I was too young and you didn't want to have to be the first to tell me how it was, so you just scooted me downstairs into a seat and went back to the balcony. I was pretty unhappy about it, John, but the sad truth is that two minutes after the show started I was lost in it and forgot all about being alone.

And then Mom, Dad, and Nancy came down from Chicago for their vacation. World War Two ended, Bristow went mad, and we all went back to Chicago.

In 1948 we came back to stay. My father passed away three months later. You were at the Firestone store now, still with Uncle Cal and still my friend. You stayed my friend all the way through school and never quit teasing me. Once when I was home from college we went out to the Vaughn's place to fish, but I don't recall that we had much luck.

But in all those years, John, do you know something that we never did? We never had one single cup of coffee together. It never occurred to us, I suppose. I mean, where could we have gone? In all of Bristow, was there a restaurant that would have served us? And that's how I came to see that the freedom I always thought I had was a farce. We spent years as friends and were never free.

But all that is changing now, John. A bunch of kids we don't even know started changing things in 1960 when they sat down at lunch counters and wouldn't get up until they were served. They let themselves be beaten and spat on and some of them were killed. Some of the dead were black and some were white, and if the white deaths aroused the nation's conscience more strongly it's just one more thing we'll have to try to understand.

They've been fighting for years and they've won some very important battles. We owe them a great deal, more than we can repay, in fact, because even though I've never been jailed or beaten in a civil rights demonstration and even though you've never sat-in somewhere, it looks like now we're going to be free. And even though there's much more to freedom than a cup of coffee, still, that's one cup of coffee that is going to taste just fine.

Tom

FRANCES TAYLOR

Those Three Are On My Mind

I think of Andy in the cold, wet clay
Those three are on my mind
With his friends beside him on that final day
Those three are on my mind.

But I breathe yet, and for some the sky is bright
I cannot give up hoping for a morning light
And so I ask the killers, "Do you sleep at night?"
Those three are on my mind
Those three are on my mind

There lies young James in his mortal pain
Those three are on my mind
So I ask these killers, "Can you sleep again?"
Those three are on my mind

But I breathe yet, and for some the sky is bright
I cannot give up hoping for a morning light
And so I ask the killers, "Do you sleep at night?"
Those three are on my mind
Those three are on my mind

I see blue-eyed Michael with his blue-eyed bride
Those three are on my mind
And three proud mothers weeping side by side
Those three are on my mind

But I breathe yet, and for some the sky is bright
I cannot give up hoping for a morning light
And so I ask the killers, "Do you sleep at night?"
Those three are on my mind
Those three are on my mind

I see the tin roofed shanties where my people live
Those three are on my mind
And the burned-out churches where they sang, "We forgive"
Those three are on my mind

But I breathe yet, and for some the sky is bright
I cannot give up hoping for a morning light
And so I ask the killers, "Do you sleep at night?"
Those three are on my mind
Those three are on my mind

While on the backwards road ride the hooded bands
Poisoning the air throughout the southern lands
So I ask the killers, "Can you ever wash your hands?"
Those three are on my mind
Those three are on my mind

There sit the mighty judges handing down the law
Those three are on my mind
In their marble courthouse we are filled with awe
Those three are on my mind

But I breathe yet, and for some the sky is bright
I cannot give up hoping for a morning light
And so I ask the killers, "Do you sleep at night?"
Those three are on my mind
Those three are on my mind

I know the price of liberty
But I must ask the question that must burn in me
Did they also burn the courthouse when they killed those three
Those three are on my mind
Those three are on my mind
Those three are on my mind

Rita Schwerner after disappearance of her husband, Michael, 1964.

ARTWORK BY

SHARON RILEY

JERRY MITCHELL

Confession

The scenes from the Holocaust haunt us all. The cool calculated violence. The unbridled hatred that stripped citizens of their dignity. The bitter betrayal of neighbor against neighbor.

These images cause Americans and others around the globe to rise up in righteous indignation. How could this happen, we ask. How could other Germans sit by and let the Nazis carry out such heinous acts? Shouldn't the people who performed such acts be tracked down and prosecuted if they somehow escaped punishment?

These are among the questions we ask as we tour the National Holocaust Museum in Washington or watch *Schindler's List* at the movies.

While the extermination of six million Jews appears unequaled in world history, most Americans have lived through a period that also involved horrific scenes.

The cool calculated violence of lynchings and firebombings. The unbridled hatred that stripped black Americans of their dignity. The bitter betrayal of neighbor against neighbor.

For many Americans, those scenes during the Civil Rights Movement seem as remote as the big screen, as distant as Europe. Perhaps it is because we are uncomfortable with the questions that such images instantly raise: How could this happen? How could other Americans sit by and let white supremacists carry out such heinous acts just three decades ago?

Most importantly, we need to ask,

"Shouldn't the people who performed such acts be tracked down and prosecuted if they somehow escaped punishment?"

The successful reprosecution in 1994 of Ku Klux Klan member Byron de la Beckwith for the June 12, 1963, assassination of Mississippi NAACP field secretary Medgar Evers proves that it can be done. So do the Alabama convictions in the 1970s against Ku Klux Klan members, successfully sought by Attorney General Bill Baxley.

Those efforts, however, represent but a small percentage of such killings. Consider this fact: more than 3,449 black Americans lost their lives in lynchings in the U.S. in the century following the Civil War.

In the 1960s, businessman Sam Bowers served as imperial wizard for the White Knights of the Ku Klux Klan in Mississippi, whose organization the FBI blamed for at least ten killings. Testimony showed that Bowers masterminded the January 10, 1966, fatal firebombing of Mississippi NAACP leader Vernon Dahmer and the June 21, 1964, murders of three civil rights workers popularly known as the "Mississippi Burning" case.

Yet Bowers continues to walk the streets a free man.

If oral votes had counted the night in 1968 that a dozen white men deliberated Bowers' fate in the Dahmer trial, he would have been put behind bars for life. Juror Douglas Herring stood and argued strongly in favor of convicting the

Jerry Mitchell, a longtime reporter for The Clarion-Ledger *in Jackson, Mississippi, wrote the story in 1989 that caused authorities to reprosecute white supremacist Byron de la Beckwith. He is currently writing a book on Mississippi and that era for the Times division of Random House titled,* Blood Corruption.

imperial wizard. Other jurors nodded in agreement. One by one, each man around the wooden table agreed that Bowers was guilty of ordering the firebombing.

Jurors went through the official process of placing their votes onto secret ballots. As they readied to leave the room in anticipation of the unanimous verdict, they shockingly heard that one ballot read, "Not guilty."

That deception repeated itself throughout the night, resulting in a mistrial. Jurors then watched helplessly as the man they orally agreed had ordered the fatal firebombing walked out of the courtroom a free man. "We felt he was guilty, and he was getting away," recalled juror Wayne R. Walters.

It was not the only murderous accusation that Bowers would dodge. Although he and seven other Klan members did serve a brief stint in prison on federal conspiracy charges in the Mississippi Burning case, the state of Mississippi never prosecuted them for murder—a charge that appropriately carries no statute of limitations.

What this nation needs is its own Nuremberg-like trials to see that those who killed with impunity are finally punished. What the South needs is a chance at redemption, to purge the past that has long plagued its present.

The following confession by one Klan member about the Mississippi Burning killings should outrage us enough to bring any of these men before the bar of justice. ❖

FEDERAL BUREAU OF INVESTIGATION

Date_____11/24/64_____

1

    The following is a signed statement which was
furnished by HORACE DOYLE BARNETTE on November 20, 1964:

          "Springhill, La
          November 20, 1964

    "I, Horace Doyle Barnette, do hereby make
this free and voluntary statement to SA Henry
Rask and SA James A. Wooten, who have identified
themselves to me to be special agents of the Federal
Bureau of Investigation and SA Henry Rask <u>have</u>
informed me that I do not have to make a statement,
that any statement made by me can be used against
me in a court of law and that I am entitled to
consult with an attorney before making this
statement and that if I can not afford an attorney
and I am required to appear in court, the court
will appoint one for me. That no force, threats
or promises were made to induce me to make this
statement.

    "I presently reside at Cullen, La. I am 26
years old and was born on September 11, 1938, at
Plaindealing, La.

    "On June 21, 1964 about 8:00 P.M., I was having
supper at Jimmy Arledge's house, Meridian, Mississippi.
Travis Barnette called Arledge on the telephone and
told Arledge that the klan had a job and wanted to know
if Arledge and I could go. Arledge asked me if I
could go and we went to Akins trailer park on
Highway 80 in Meridian, Miss. We did not know what
the job was.

On __11/20/64__ at _Springhill, Louisiana_ File#____JN 44-1____

by __SA HENRY RASK &
SA JAMES A. WOOTEN :bjm__ Date dictated____11/23/64____

    - 2 -

JN 44-1
2

"Upon arriving at Akins trailer Park we were met by Preacher Killin, Mr. Akins, Jim Jordan and Wayne. I do not know Wayne's last name, but I do know his brother is a police officer in Meridian_ Miss. Killin told us that three civil rights workers were in jail in Philadelphia, Miss., and that these three civil rights workers were going to be released from jail and that we were going to catch them and give them a whipping. We were given brown cloth gloves and my car was filled with gas from Mr. Akins gas tank. Jim Snowden, who works for Troy Laundry in Meridian came to Akins trailer Park too.

"Arledge, Snowden, and Jordan got into my car and we drove to Philadelphia. Killin and Wayne left before we did and we were told that we would meet him there. Killin had a 1962 or 1961 white Buick.

"When we arrived in Philadelphia, about 9:30 P.M., we met Killin and he got into my car and directed me where to park and wait for someone to tell us when the three civil rights workers were being released from jail.

"While we were talking, Killin stated that 'we have a place to bury them, and a man to run the dozer to cover them up.' This was the first time I realized that the three civil rights workers were to be killed.

"About 5 or 10 minutes after we parked a patrolman from Philadelphia came to the car and said that 'they are going toward Meridian on Highway 19. We proceeded out Highway 19 and caught up to a

- 3 -

JN 44-1
3

Mississippi State Patrol Car, who pulled into a store
on the left hand side of the road. We pulled along
side of the Patrol car and then another car from
Philadelphia pulled in between us. I was driving
a 1957 Ford, 4 door, 2 tone blue bearing Louisiana
license. The Philadelphia car was a 1958 Chevrolet,
2 door and color maroon. It also had a dent on front
right hand fender next to the light. No one got out
of the cars, but the driver of the Philadelphia car,
who I later learned was named Posey, talked to the
patrolmen. Posey then drove away and we followed.

"About 2 or 3 miles down the Highway Posey's car
stopped and pulled off on the right hand side of the
road. Posey motioned for me to go ahead. I then
drove fast and caught up to the car that the three
civil rights workers were in, pulled over to the side
of the road and stopped. About a minute or 2 later,
Deputy Sheriff Price came along and stopped on the
pavement beside my car. Jordan asked him who was
going to stop them and Price said that he would and
took after them and we followed. The Civil Rights workers
turned off Highway 19 on to a side road and drove about
a couple of miles before Price stopped them. Price
stopped his car behind the 1963 Ford Fairlane Station
Wagon driven by the Civil Rights Workers and we stopped
behind Price's car. Price was driving a 1956 Chevrolet,
2 door and 2 tone blue in color.

"Price stated 'I thought you were going back to
Meridian if we let you out of jail.' The Civil Rights
Workers stated that they were and Price asked them
why they were taking the long way around. Price told
them to get out and get into his car. They got out of
their car and proceed__ to get into Price's car and
then Price took his blackjack and struck Chaney on the
back of the head.

- 4 -

JN 44-1
4

"At the junction of Highway 19 and where we
turned off, I had let Arledge out of the car to
signal the fellows in the Philadelphia car. We
then turned around and proceeded back toward
Philadelphia. The first car to start back was Price
and he had Jim Jordan in the front seat with him
and the three civil rights worker_ in the back seat.
I followed next and picked up Arledge at the junction
of Highway 19. Snowden drove the 1963 Ford, belonging
to the Civil Rights Workers.

"When we came to Posey's car Price and Snowden
pulled over to the left side of the Highway and
stopped in front of Posey's car. I stopped behind it.
Wayne and Posey and the other men from Philadelphia
got into the 1963 Ford and rode with Snowden. I do
not know how many men were from Philadelphia. Price
then started first and I pulled in behind him and
Snowden driving the 1963 Ford came last.

"I followed Price down Highway 19 and he turned
left on to a gravel road. About a mile up the road
he stopped and Snowden and I stopped behind him,
with about a car length between each car. Before I
could get out of the car Wayne ran past my car to
Price's car, opened the left rear door, pulled
Schwerner out of the car, spun him around so that
Schwerner was standing on the left side of the road,
with his back to the ditch and said 'Are you that
nigger lover' and Schwerner said 'Sir, I know just
how you feel.' Wayne had a pistol in his right hand,
then shot Schwerner.

"Wayne then went back to Price's car and got
Goodman, took him to the left side of the road with
Goodman facing the road, and shot Goodman.

- 5 -

JN 44-1
5

"When Wayne shot Schwerner, Wayne had his
hand on Schwerner's shoulder. When Wayne shot
Goodman, Wayne was standing within reach of him.

"Schwerner fell to the left so that he was
laying along side the road. Goodman spun around
and fell back toward the bank in back.

"At this time Jim Jordan said 'save one for
me.' He then got out of Price's car and got
Chaney out. I remember Chaney backing up, facing
the road, and standing on the bank on the other
side of the ditch and Jordan stood in the middle
of the road and shot him. I do not remember how
many times Jordan shot. Jordan then said 'You
didn't leave me anything but a nigger, but at least
I killed me a nigger.'

"The three civil rights workers were then put
into the back of their 1963 Ford wagon. I do not
know who put the bodies in the car, but I only
put Chaney's foot inside the car.

"Price then got into his car and drove back
toward Highway 19. Wayne, Posey and Jordan then
got into the 1963 Ford and started up the road.
Snowden, Arledge and another person who I do not
know the name of got into my car and we followed.
I do not know the roads we took, but went through
the outskirts of Philadelphia and to the Dam site
on Burrage_s property.

"When we arrived at the Dam site someone said
that the bulldozer operator was not there and Wayne,
Arledge and I went in my car to find him. We drove
out to a paved road and about a mile down the road

- 6 -

JN 44-1
6

we saw a 1957 Chevrolet, white and green, parked
on the left side of the road. Wayne told me to
stop and we backed up to this car. Burrage and
2 other men were in the car. Wayne said that they
were already down there and Burrage said to follow
them. I followed the 1957 Chevrolet back toward
the Dam site, taking a different road, until the
Chevrolet stopped. Burrage said 'it is just a little
ways over there,' and Wayne and the bulldozer
operator walked the rest of the way. The bulldozer
operator was about 40 years old, 6 ft_ 2 inches tall,
slim built and a white male. He was wearing khaki
clothes. Arledge and I then followed Burrage and
the other man back to Burrage's garage. The other
man was a white male, about 40 years old, 5 feet 8
or 9 inches tall, stocky built. Burrage's garage is on
the road toward Philadelphia and he had tractors and
trailer parked there. His house is across the road.

"We were there about 30 minutes when the other
fellows came from the dam site in the 1963 Ford.
Burrage got a glass gallon jug and filled it with
gasoline to be used to burn the 1963 Ford car owned
by the three civil rights workers. Burrage took
one of the deisel trucks from under a trailer and
said 'I will use this to pick you up, no one will
suspect a truck on the road this time at night.'
It was then about 1:00 to 1:30 in the morning.

"Snowden, Arledge, Jordan, Wayne and I then
got into my car and we drove back toward Philadelphia.
When we got to Philadelphia a city patrol car stopped
us and we got out. Sheriff Rainey, Deputy Sheriff
Price and the City Patrolman, who told us which way
the civil rights workers were leaving town, got out
of the patrol car. The patrolman was a white male,
about 50 years old, 5 feet 8 to 9 inches, 160 lbs_,

- 7 -

JN 44-1
7

and was wearing a uniform. This was about 2:00 AM.,
June 22, 1964. I do not know his name, but I have
met him before and would know him again.

"We talked for 2 or 3 minutes and then someone
said that we better not talk about this and Sheriff
Rainey said 'I'll kill anyone who talks, even if it
was my own brother.

"We then got back into my car and drove back
to Meridian and passed Posey's car which was still
parked along side the road. We did not stop and
there was one or two men standing by Posey's car.
We then kept going to Meridian. I took Wayne home,
left Jordan and Snowden at Akins Mobile Homes, took
Arledge home and when home myself.

"I have read the above Statement, consisting
of this an_ 9 other pages and they are true an_
correct to the best of my knowledge and belief. I
have signed my initials to the bottom of the first
9 pages and initial__ mistakes. No force_ threats
or promises were made to induce me to make this
statement_

"/s/Horace Doyle Barnette

"Witnessed:

"/s/Henry Rask, Special Agent, F. B. I. Nov_ 20, 1964.

"/s/James A. Wooten, Sp. Agent, FBI, New Orleans, La.,
    11-20-64."

- 8 -

Mr. and Mrs. Goodman at Newark Airport after their son, Andy, was murdered 1964.

ARTWORK BY

SHARON RILEY

MIMI FARIÑA

Tribute to Richard Fariña

I was always so deeply impressed by Richard's skill as a poet to capture an emotion or political event. While performing this song the effect on me as well as the audience was always chilling.

It was natural for Richard to write this song because the murders of Goodman, Schwerner, and Chaney affected our lives so personally. Richard was approximately the same age as the three civil rights workers. Two years after these tragic deaths, Richard was killed in a motorcycle accident in California.

After pursuing a musical career, I founded a non-profit organization, Bread & Roses, whose purpose is to uplift the human spirit through the performing arts. The organization brings free live entertainment to people confined or isolated in institutions such as homeless shelters, convalescent homes, psychiatric facilities, AIDS wards, prisons, and other institutions. My convictions were cemented by the dramatic incidents of the early 1960s. ❖

Mimi and Richard Fariña captured national attention as a folk duo in the early 1960s, becoming one of the first groups to fuse folk material with a rock rhythm theme. Richard was the author of Been Down So Long It Looks Like Up To Me *(Random House), a poet, composer, and musician. Both Richard and Mimi's voices harmonized to create a unique sound accompanied by their dulcimer and guitar. They recorded three albums on Vanguard Records before Richard's death in a 1966 motorcycle accident.*

RICHARD FARIÑA

Michael, Andrew, and James

It's hard the klansmen galloping down
Red the dust their hooves have blown
Loud the lashing of their steel
Never more to know the day
Never to be growing old but
Dim the terror they conceal
Mad was the moon when Michael died
Chilled were his thighs against the clay
Dry was his tongue against the mold
Once his manhood riding tall now
All is blood upon our hands.

It's woe, woe, woe, and woe I'm calling
Twelve wild winds are loudly raging
Three cold graves are numbly wailing
Nine salt seas are deeply boiling
Six dark swans are fiercely reeling
Three cold graves are numbly wailing.

Blue the hooded eyes that blind
Blonde the sour eyes that bind
White the mushroom faces leer
Red the flaming cross they bear
Black was the sun when Andrew died
Chilled were his eyes against the clay
Never more to see the day
Cold were his loins against the loam
Never to be going home
But once his manhood riding tall
Now all is blood upon our hands.

It's woe, woe, woe, and woe I'm calling
Twelve wild winds are loudly raging
Three cold graves are numbly wailing
Nine salt seas are deeply boiling
Six dark swans are fiercely reeling
Three cold graves are numbly wailing.

It's one the Wizard high on his throne
Two the whispers he has known
Three the bodies underground
Four the freedoms none of them found
Five their senses never more
Six their parents on the shore
It's foaming bells for James who died
Chilled was his groin against the clay
Never more to feel the day
But once his manhood riding tall
Now all is blood upon our hands.

It's woe, woe, woe, and woe I'm calling,
Twelve wild winds are loudly raging
Three cold graves are numbly wailing
Nine salt seas are deeply boiling
Six dark swans are fiercely reeling
Three cold graves are numbly wailing.

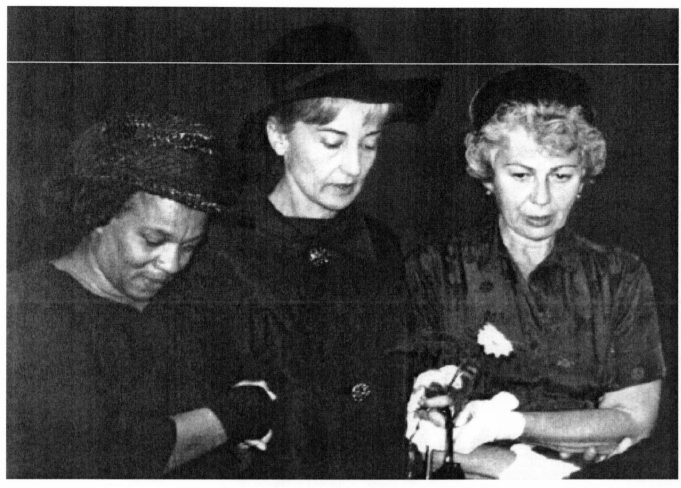

Mrs. Chaney, Mrs. Goodman, and Mrs. Schwerner after their sons James, Andy, and Michael were murdered during the Freedom Summer 1964.

PHOTO SUBMITTED

BY CAROLYN

GOODMAN

This May Be The Last Time

Arrangement by Bernice Johnson Reagon.

This may be the last time
This may be the last time
This may be the last time
May be the last time, I don't know

This may be the last time
This may be the last time
This may be the last time
May be the last time, I don't know

May be the last time we'll all meet together
May be the last time, I don't know
May be the last time we'll all meet together
May be the last time, I don't know

This may be the last time
This may be the last time
This may be the last time
May be the last time, I don't know

May be the last time we'll all sing together
May be the last time, I don't know
May be the last time we'll all shout together
May be the last time, I don't know

This may be the last time
This may be the last time
This may be the last time
May be the last time, I don't know

Bernice Johnson Reagon, composer, singer, mother, historian, author, and founder and artistic director of Sweet Honey In The Rock, lives in Washington, D.C., where she also works as a curator for the Smithsonian Institution. Her latest book is We'll Understand It Better By and By: Pioneering African American Gospel Composers; *she has completed "Wade In The Water," a Smithsonian Institution and National Public Radio production on the history of African American sacred music.*

May be the last time we all pray together
May be the last time, I don't know
May be the last time we all bow together
May be the last time, I don't know

This may be the last time
This may be the last time
This may be the last time
May be the last time, I don't know

I don't know, Lord
I don't know
May be the last time, I don't know
I don't know, Lord
I don't know
May be the last time, I don't know

This may be the last time
This may be the last time
This may be the last time
May be the last time, I don't know

DAVE DENNIS

Oration for Funeral of James Chaney

David J. Dennis Sr. was an early member of the Congress of Racial Equality (CORE) in New Orleans. In May 1961, he was one of the first Freedom Riders to reach Jackson, Mississippi, where he stayed to become a senior representative for CORE in that state. By April of 1962, Dave became the project Co-Director of the Council of Federated Organizations (COFO) and later co-directed Freedom Summer with Bob Moses. He graduated cum laude from Dillard University and received his Juris Doctorate from the University of Michigan. Presently, Dave serves as director of the Algebra Project's Southern Initiative where he administers programs in Mississippi, Alabama, Louisiana, Arkansas, North Carolina, South Carolina, and West Virginia. He is also actively involved in the formation of the National Algebra Project Network.

Sorry, but I'm not here to do the traditional thing most of us do at such a gathering. And that is to tell of what a great person the individual was and some of the great works that the person was involved in and etc. I think we all know it because he walked these dusty streets of Meridian and around here long before I came here. With you and around you. Played with your kids and he talked to all of them. And what I want to talk about is really what I learned to grieve about. I don't grieve for Chaney because the fact is I feel he lived a fuller life than many of us will ever live. I feel that he's got his freedom and we are still fighting for it. (AMEN)

But what I want to talk about right now is the living dead that we have right among our midst, not only in the state of Mississippi but throughout the nation. Those are the people who don't care (THAT'S RIGHT), those that do care but don't have the guts enough to stand up for it (THAT'S RIGHT), and those people who are busy up in Washington and in other places using my freedom and my life to play politics with. (ALL RIGHT) That includes the president on down to the governor of the state of Mississippi, you see. In my opinion, as I stand here, I not only blame the people who pulled the trigger or did the beating or dug the hole with the shovel (ALL RIGHT), or buried the people, not buried, sorry . . . But I blame the people in Washington, D.C., and on down to the state of Mississippi for what happened just as much as I blame those who pulled the trig-

ger. (AMEN) Because I feel that a hundred years ago, if the proper thing had been done by the federal government of this particular country and by the other people responsible or the irresponsible people, we wouldn't be here to mourn the death of a brave young man like James Chaney, you see. (AMEN, ALL RIGHT)

As I stand here a lot of things pass through my mind. I can remember the Emmett Till case (YES), what happened to him (ALL RIGHT), and what happened to the people who killed him. (ALL RIGHT) They're walking the streets right now and the brother of one is a police officer here in a place called Ruleville, Mississippi. (THAT'S RIGHT) I remember back down here, right below us here, a man by the name of Mack Parker and exactly what happened to him and what happened to the people who beat, (UMM, UMM), killed him (UMM), and drug him down the streets and threw him in the river. (THAT'S RIGHT) I know that those people were caught but they were never brought to trial. (OH NO) I can remember back in Birmingham of the four young kids (RIGHT) who were bombed in the church (RIGHT) and had just went to service and I know what has happened to the people who killed them—nothing. (THAT'S RIGHT) Remember the little thirteen-year-old kid who was riding a bicycle and who was shot in the back? (THAT'S RIGHT) And the youth who shot him, who was a white guy from Birmingham, got off with three months. (ALL RIGHT, SHAME) I can remember all of that right now. Or I can remember the Medgar Evers case in Beckwith. (YES) The person who was governor of the state at that particular time going up and shaking his hand when the jury said that it could not come to a verdict. (YES) I can remember all of that. (YES) And I can remember down in the Southwest area where you had six Negroes who'd been killed, and I can remember the Lees and all these particular people who know what has happened to those who have been killing them. I know what is happening to the people that are bombing the churches, who've been bombing the homes, who are doing the beatings around this entire state and country. (YES, ALL RIGHT)

Well, I'm getting sick and tired. (THAT'S RIGHT) I'm sick and tired of going to memorials, I'm sick and tired of going to funerals. (YES) I've got a bitter vengeance in my heart tonight. (SO HAVE I) And I'm sick and tired and I can't help but feel bitter, you see, deep down inside, and I'm not going to stand here and ask anybody here not to be angry tonight. (YES)

Yeah, we have love in our hearts, and we've had it for years and years in this country. (ALL RIGHT) We've died on the battlefield to protect the people in this country. (THAT'S RIGHT) We've gone out in World War I and in 1942 millions of us died too, you see. (YES) Meanwhile, you understand, there are people in this country with no eyes, without a leg, without an arm, to defend this country and to come back and do what? To live as slaves you see, and I'm sick and tired of that. (I AM TOO) Yeah, I'm probably supposed to stand here . . . (YES) Got a lot more I want to say. (YES, GO ON)

You see, we're all tired. (YES) You see, I know what's gonna happen. I feel it deep in my heart. When they find the people who killed these guys in Neshoba County, (ALL RIGHT) you've got to come back to the state of Mississippi and have a jury of their cousins, their aunts and their uncles. (ALL RIGHT) And I know what they're going to say—not guilty. Because no one saw them pull the trigger. I'm tired of

that. (YES, GOD HELP US. I AM TOO; I'M SICK OF IT!)

See another thing that makes me even tireder though, and that is the fact that we as people here in this state and the country are allowing this to continue to happen. (THAT'S RIGHT) Even us as black folk. So I look at the young kids here—that's something else that I grieve about. For little Ben Chaney here and the other ones like him around in this audience and out on the streets. I grieve because sometimes they make me feel that, maybe, they have to go through the same thing, you see. (YEAH) And they are gonna have to go through the same thing. (GOD HELP US) Unless we as individuals begin to stand up and demand our rights and a change in this dad-blasted country, (RIGHT) you see. (THAT'S RIGHT) We have to stand up and demand it because tomorrow, baby, it could be your child. (YES, THAT'S RIGHT)

And one thing that I'm worried about is just exactly what are we going to do as people as a result of what happened, for what this guy died for and the other people died for. (RIGHT) We're going to come to this memorial here, say, "Oh, what a shame," go back home and pray to the Lord as we've done for years. (THAT'S RIGHT) We go back to work in some white folks' kitchen tomorrow (ALL RIGHT) and forget about the whole God-blasted thing, you see. (RIGHT, SPEAK) (Applause from congregation)

Don't applaud! Don't applaud! Don't get your frustration out by clapping your hands. Each and every one of us as individuals is going to have to take it upon ourself to become leaders in our community. (THAT'S RIGHT) Block by block, house by house, city by city, county by county, state by state, throughout this entire country. Taking our black brothers by the hand, (THAT'S RIGHT) one at a time, stepping across with our feet through the mighty oceans to the mighty country of Africa. Holding our hands up high, telling them that if they're not ready for us, "Too bad, baby, 'cause we're com-

PHOTO BY

GEORGE BALLIS

CORE leader Dave Dennis gives funeral oration.

ing anyway." (THAT'S RIGHT) So we have to do as people. (THAT'S RIGHT)

We can't take it any longer and be wiped off of the face of the earth. I look at the people of gray hair down here, the tiredness in the face and think about the millions of bolls of cotton that you picked, the millions of actions it took to chop it for $10.00 a week, for $25.00 a week, or whatever you could get to eat. (THAT'S RIGHT. AMEN. SICK AND TIRED OF IT.) I watch the people here who go out there and wash dishes and you cook for them. For the whites in the community and those same ones you cook for, wash and iron for, who come right out and say, "I can't sit down and eat beside a nigger," or anything like that. I'm tired of that, you see. (YES) I'm tired of him talking about how much he hates me (YES, THAT'S RIGHT), and he can't stand for me to go to school with his children and all of that. (HERE YOU GO) But yet, when he wants someone to babysit for them, he gets my black mammy to hold that baby. And as long as he can do that, (ALL RIGHT) he can sit down beside me, (YES) he can watch me go up there and register to vote, and he can watch me take some type of public office in this state, and he can sit down as I rule over him just like he's ruled over me for years, you see. (ALL RIGHT)

This is our country, too. We didn't ask to come here when they brought us over here (AMEN, RIGHT), and I hear the old statement over and over again about me to go back to Africa. Well, I'm ready to go back to Africa, baby, when all the Jews, the Poles, the Russians, the Germans and they all go back to their country where they came from too, you see. (RIGHT, SPEAK) And they have to remember that they took this land from the Indians. (YES, AMEN) And just as much as it's their, it's ours too now. (ALL RIGHT) We've got to stand up!

The best thing that we can do for Mr.

Chaney, for Mickey Schwerner, (YES) for Andrew Goodman is stand up and demand our rights. (ALL RIGHT) All these people here who are not registered voters should be in line Monday morning from one corner of this county to the next, demanding, don't ask, if I can become a registered voter. Demand! Say, "Baby, I'm here." (THAT'S RIGHT, ONE MAN ONE VOTE, RIGHT)

People, you've got relatives in places like Neshoba County, talk to them. They're at a disadvantage. They only have 12 percent of the population that's black over there. So that man thinks he's going to run over us over there. But we're going in there, baby. (ALL RIGHT) We're going to organize in there, (ALL RIGHT) and we're going to get those people registered to vote and organized. I don't care if we are just 12 percent. Because that 12 percent is part of that almost 50 percent of this whole entire state, you see. (AMEN)

Don't just look at me and the people here and go back and say that you've been to a nice service, (AMEN) a lot of people came, there were a lot of hot-blasted newsmen around, anything like that. But your work is just beginning. (THAT'S RIGHT) I'm going to tell you deep down in my heart what I feel like right now. (TELL IT) If you do go back home and sit down and take it, God damn your soul! (THAT IS THE TRUTH)

(Some audience applause)

Stand up! (STAND UP!) Your neighbors down there were too afraid to come to this memorial, take them to another memorial. (AMEN) Take them up and take them down there. Make them register to vote and you register to vote. I doubt if one fourth of this house is registered. Go down there and do it. (YES) Don't bow down anymore. (THAT's RIGHT) Hold your heads up! (THAT'S RIGHT, RIGHT, ALL RIGHT, AMEN, AMEN) ❖

WILLIAM M. KUNSTLER

Freedom Summer

William Kunstler was an activist attorney who dedicated his life to human rights and social justice. He represented the Freedom Riders, the Chicago 8, members of the Black Panther Party, and the American Indian Movement. He also worked with Martin Luther King, Jr., Medgar Evers, Malcolm X, Lenny Bruce, and the Kent State families, to name a few. Bill had a first-rate intellect and could match knowledge in court with the best litigators. He was the Founder, Vice-President, and volunteer staff attorney of the Center for Constitutional Rights, New York, N.Y. His daughter, Karin, was one of the volunteers in the Mississippi Freedom Summer Project. William Kunstler died on September 4, 1995, from heart failure at th age of 76. He was the first participant to submit materials for the Freedom Is A Constant Struggle *anthology.*

The summer of 1964 marked the third year of my representation of Dr. Martin Luther King, Jr., and his Southern Christian Leadership Conference (SCLC), and the Student Nonviolent Coordinating Committee (SNCC). I had come into the struggle for civil rights in the Deep South through my involvement, as an attorney, with the Freedom Riders who, in 1961, had begun streaming into Jackson, Mississippi, where they were promptly arrested by Captain William Ray, the police officer in charge of what was then referred to by the authorities as "Operation Mix." At that time, my oldest daughter, Karin, a Connecticut College student, was starting her one-year exchange program at Tougaloo Southern Christian College, just outside of Jackson.

Three years later, she had volunteered to spend the summer of 1964 in Mississippi, together with one thousand other northern students, in a massive effort to register black voters. Before the project began, we, along with a number of other parents, were invited to an orientation session at New York's Riverside Church. I can't remember who addressed us but I do recall that he pointed out that the Council of Federated Organizations (COFO), the loose coalition of civil rights groups in charge of what came to be known as the Freedom Summer, could not guarantee the safety of the volunteers. As he was giving this ominous warning, a woman behind me whispered, "They always say that, but I'm sure that nothing will happen to anyone." I later

learned that her name was Carolyn Goodman and, ironically, her son, Andy, became one of the three civil rights workers murdered by Neshoba County law enforcement officials a month or so later.

In the middle of June, the volunteers reported to Miami University in Oxford, Ohio, for further orientation. I was invited to speak to them on June 19, their last day before they left for Mississippi. After I had delivered my remarks, I met Mickey Schwerner, who, with his wife, Rita, ran a biracial community center for the Congress of Racial Equality (CORE) in Meridian; James Chaney, a local black plasterer; and Andy Goodman, a white Queens College anthropology major, who planned to drive to Mississippi the next day. I can't remember what we talked about, but I am sure that it had to do with the Freedom Summer program. I then said goodbye to my daughter and returned to New York.

Three days later, on the morning of June 22, I received a frantic call from a man who told me that his name was Nathan Schwerner. "My son, Mickey, and two other young civil rights workers are missing in Mississippi," he said. "They left Meridian in Mickey's car yesterday morning for a trip to Neshoba County, and they have not returned or called in. Can you find out for me where they are—my wife and I are worried sick." I called COFO in Jackson and was informed by Bob Moses, its director, that there had been no word from Schwerner and

William Kunstler

his two companions, James Chaney and Andrew Goodman, since they had left early in the morning to inspect the remains of the Mount Zion Baptist Church, the hub of civil rights activities in Neshoba County, which had been mysteriously burned to the ground a week earlier.

I then contacted the Neshoba County Sheriff's Office in Philadelphia, Mississippi. A drawling voice informed me that the trio had been arrested by a deputy the previous evening. The three youths, part of COFO's advance party, had been picked up, the voice said, for driving sixty-five miles per hour in a thirty-mile-per-hour speed zone and held at the county jail "for investigation" until 10:30 P.M. They had been released when Chaney, who had been driving

Schwerner's late-model Ford station wagon, paid a $20.00 fine. They had last been seen leaving town on State Highway 19.

Later that day, Deputy Sheriff Cecil Ray Price, who had arrested the three, said that after their release he had ordered them "to leave the county." His boss, Sheriff Lawrence A. Rainey, a burly, tobacco-chewing man, told a newspaper reporter that, "If they're missing, they just hid somewhere, trying to get a lot of publicity out of it, I figure." A year later, both officials, along with sixteen other defendants, would be indicted by a federal grand jury and charged with a conspiracy to intercept and murder Schwerner, Goodman, and Chaney.

On June 23, Schwerner's burned-out station wagon was found in a swamp on Bogue Chitto Creek, fifteen miles northeast of Philadelphia and some fifty feet off State Highway 21. In the ensuing weeks a nationwide search for the three men was conducted. On August 4, after paying $25,000 for a tip from an informer, the FBI found their bodies buried fifteen feet apart under a newly erected earthen cattle pond dam in a thickly wooded area, six miles southwest of Philadelphia. Each had been shot to death at point blank range.

Before COFO's Freedom Summer ended, some sixty thousand new black registrants had been added to Mississippi's voting rolls. This accomplishment, won at such cost, prompted enactment of the Voting Rights Act of 1965, legislation that eventually altered forever the balance of political power in the South. Within nine years after its passage, the number of blacks registered in Mississippi and four other Southern states had increased by almost 50 percent. Mickey Schwerner, Andy Goodman, and Jim Chaney may have died on a rural back road in pain and terror, but hardly in vain.

At summer's end, COFO's student volunteers returned to their campuses with the sure knowledge that they had indeed wrought a major miracle. The murders of their three comrades had shocked and terrified most of them, as well as their worried parents, but they had worked

on and hoped for the best, somehow managing to sublimate their fears of the worst. That they endured was undoubtedly because their slain friends had become for them, as Rabbi Arthur J. Lelyveld had put it at Andy Goodman's memorial service in New York on August 10, 1964, "the eternal evocation of all the hosts of beautiful young men and women who are carrying forth the struggle for which they gave their lives."

Years later, on the twentieth anniversary of the murders, I tried to memorialize the three civil rights workers in a sonnet which eventually found its way into one of my books, *Trials and Tribulations,* published by Grove Press in 1985. It went as follows:

> *They had no thought in mind except to try*
> *To change the world in one short season's flight;*
> *They did not think that they would ever die*
> *For doing what their instincts said was right.*
> *They perished on a backwoods country lane,*
> *These integrated victims of the past;*
> *The bullets that destroyed each youthful brain*
> *Were meant to make a dying system last.*
> *Their bodies lay, just fifteen feet apart,*
> *Beneath an earthen dam for forty days,*
> *Until a bonus bought a change of heart*
> *In one who knew their killers' hidden ways.*
> *At summer's end, their comrades left the field*
> *With sixty thousand registrants their yield.*

When local black burial grounds refused to inter James Chaney's body because of fear of reprisals, he was finally laid to rest in an isolated grave in the Okatibbee Baptist Church Cemetery in remote southwest Lauderdale County. Over the years, vandals frequently desecrated the site and, at one time, threw his headstone into a nearby lake. On the twenty-fifth anniversary of his murder, a four-foot tall marble monument was erected at the grave. However, one of the two marble flower pots was soon broken and a small photograph of Chaney at the top of his tombstone defaced. His brother, Ben, who had been serving as Ramsey Clark's paralegal in New York City, has returned to Mississippi, determined to prevent any further damage to the site.

On James's tombstone are engraved the words:

There are those who are alive
Yet will never live,
There are those who are dead
Yet will live forever,
Great deeds inspire and
encourage the living.

Ben is determined that "The desecration of James Earl Chaney's grave must stop. . . . The knowledge that, in death, James can find no peace, nor reprieve, from the vicious assembly-line bigotry which he fought against and sacrificed his life to stop is painful." It can only be hoped that the thirty years that have passed since the murders have neither deadened the sensibilities of all of us who once pledged that the memory of our three dead comrades would illuminate the road of our lives, nor sapped our determination that the Freedom Summer of 1964 would not be relegated to a tragic historical footnote but would continue to inspire all people of good will to continue to give of themselves so that, someday, somehow, the cancer of racism could, at long last, be excised from the body politic. Then, and only then, will the Freedom Summer have perpetuated itself and the lonely shades of Michael Schwerner, James Chaney, and Andrew Goodman found peace at last. ❖

A year after the deaths of three civil rights workers near Philadelphia, Mississippi, demonstrators hold memorial service at site of Mt. Zion Baptist Church, burned the day the three were killed. CORE leader James Farmer (center) singing "We Shall Overcome".

PHOTOS BY

MATT HERRON

A year after the deaths of three civil rights workers near Philadelphia, Mississippi, marchers carry signs memorializing the event.

SI KAHN

I Have Seen Freedom

I missed Mississippi Summer.

How it happened, I'm still not sure. Looking back at that period in my life, it certainly seems that everything had been moving me in that direction, southward toward the Civil Rights Movement. After all, I had been involved at least peripherally since high school days in Bethesda, Maryland, when members of our class had picketed the Woolworth's on Wisconsin Avenue and, across the street, the Baronet Theater, which in 1961 was still segregating its audience, no more than fifteen miles from where the United States Supreme Court sat in solemn judgment. The next spring, I had ridden a bus from Cambridge, Massachusetts, to Maryland, where Race Street running down the center of the town divided black from white, to march and picket with Gloria Richardson and the Freedom Movement in that city.

But then I dropped out of college for a year, trying (I now understand) to figure out who I was and where my life was going. By the time I returned to school, it was already early 1964, and I felt disconnected from much of my previous life. Now a year behind, I felt the pressure to graduate, if not with my class, at least not too far behind it. So, while others went to Mississippi, I went to summer school. I watched the news on TV, I listened, I was inspired, I worried, I was sick at heart—but I wasn't there.

That's the story. But I wonder: is this story true? Or was it just that I didn't have the courage, the vision, the commitment that others had?

Did I really want to go but just talked myself out of it, because I was scared, because other things seemed more important to me at the time? Was it, for reasons I'll never know, simply not the right time—in the same way that, a year later, in the summer of 1965, it was very much the right time for me finally to head south, to Forrest City, Arkansas, to the Student Nonviolent Coordinating Committee, to a life of Southern organizing from which I've never gone back.

So maybe, though "a dollar short and a day late," I got there after all. My Mississippi Summer happened a year later, in the summer of 1965, when I was finally ready to go. And it wasn't in Mississippi after all, but across the Mississippi River in Forrest City, Arkansas. The crowds, the cameras, were gone, but the heart of the Movement—the African American citizens of the South, who had inspired us and me by risking everything on the highway to freedom, were still there, willing to tolerate and teach yet one more northern kid who was trying to find his own road.

Better a year late than never.

My hands are as cracked as an August field
That's burned in the sun for a hundred years
With furrows so deep you could hide yourself
But I ain't planting cotton no more this year
I'll just sit on the porch with my eagle eye
And watch for a change of wind
The rows are as straight as a shotgun barrel
And long as a bullet can spin

Si Kahn is an organizer and songwriter who has worked in the South since the Civil Rights Movement. Since 1980, he has been the director of Grassroots Leadership in Charlotte, N.C., a team of African Americans and whites who provide strategic organizing assistance to Southern poor and working communities. His 10 albums of original and traditional songs are available on Flying Fish and Rounder Records.

You know how hot it gets in Mississippi
You know how dry it gets in the summer
sun
The dust clouds swirl all down the Delta
I just hope that I don't die 'fore the harvest
comes

Black clouds gathering on the edge of town
But no rain's gonna fall on us
Hoes rise and fall in a distant field
Earth takes a beating for all of us
I thought I heard the angel of death overhead
But it's only the crop duster's plane
Hoes rise and fall like the beating of wings
Lord send us freedom and rain

You know how hot it gets in Mississippi
You know how dry it gets in the summer
sun
The dust clouds swirl all down the Delta
I just hope that I don't die 'fore the harvest
comes

There was neither rain
nor freedom in Forrest City, Arkansas
the place where I spent
the summer of 1965.

It was a stopping place
first on the railway
then on the road
that runs from Memphis to Little Rock.

A farming town
set down in the furrows and dust
of the Mississippi River delta
in the heart of what was in those days called
the "Black Belt"
that crescent of black land and black people
that stretched from Virginia to East Texas
that once marked the boundaries
of cotton
and of slavery.

The town had in fact been founded
by the Confederate cavalry leader
General Nathan Bedford Forrest
and in the summer of 1965
that town was doing its best
to live up to its name
and namesake.

I have not been back to Forrest City
since I left twenty-eight years ago
so I don't know what has changed.
But in that summer of 1965
it was a typical Southern county seat:
a red brick courthouse in the center,
fields of cotton and soybeans
radiating out from the town square
in rows as long as the eye cared to see
in the deadly sun
of an Arkansas summer.

There was the usual assortment
of small-town, farm-town businesses:
cotton gin, feed store
truck lot, tractor dealer
even, in a gesture to changing Southern times
a factory that made fork lifts.

And the usual assortment of small-town officials
a police chief named Gunn
a city attorney named Sharp
even a resident FBI agent named Smart
and then two of almost everything else:
a black high school
and a white high school;
white restaurants
where blacks couldn't go
and black restaurants
where whites wouldn't go;
black barber shops, bars, and beauty parlors;
white barber shops, bars, and beauty parlors;
a white funeral home
and a black funeral home.

a river of hatred and fear
ran down the social center of town
sharply dividing black and white
as certainly as the Mississippi River
forty miles to the east
divided the state of Arkansas
from the states of Mississippi and Tennessee.

But in that summer of 1965
Forrest City had something else
something new
which was beginning to chip away
at the stone walls

of ignorance and fear
of segregation and discrimination
of racism and violence
that had been built up
along with the town.

Forrest City
had a freedom movement
a field office
of the Student Nonviolent Coordinating Com-
    mittee
comfortably and commonly known by its ini-
    tials as SNCC
the militant student wing
of the Southern freedom movement.

SNCC and that freedom movement
were centered and headquartered
in the black funeral home
where Mrs. Florence Clay
ministered to the living and to the dead
and where we SNCC volunteers
slept fitfully at best
all too aware of the living dangers
in the night outside
cruising by in cop cars and pickup trucks
and of the recently deceased
lying in their satin-lined caskets
in the chapel downstairs.

I had grown up
in a Pennsylvania mountain town
not much bigger than Forrest City
and had gone to a consolidated high school
where I'd learned carpentry
along with a teenage taste for auto mechanics

and so I had been recruited
by the northern friends of SNCC
and of the black freedom movement
to help build freedom centers
in places like Forrest City.

So there behind the new funeral home
built of brick and block
in the old wood frame building
which had been abandoned for years
we put up siding and sheet rock
rolled out roofing and Romex cable

ran water and sewer lines
built school tables and library shelves
so that the black children of Forrest City
could come to the freedom center
to study and learn the history which had been
    denied
them their own history
so that they could learn what freedom was all
    about

Outside the freedom center
in the unpaved streets and shotgun shacks
in the beauty parlors and barber shops
in the churches and restaurants
in the bars and pool halls
where the black community of Forrest City
lived and breathed

There in the stubborn heat
of an Arkansas summer
something else was being pieced and pulled
planned and measured
hammered and honed
built and born:
A black movement for freedom.

And though the white folks talked
of "outside agitators"
of "communists" and "race mixers"
this movement for freedom
was bred and born in the bone
imagined, shaped, and formed
lived, loved, and led
by local folks
like Mrs. Clay at the funeral home
keeping watch from her upstairs window
as the pickup trucks and police cars
sped by in the night

By people like Mervin Barr
born and raised in Forrest City
where there was not much of a future
for a bright young man
whose skin was black

So Mervin Barr
seeking a better future for himself
had enlisted in the United States Marines
and was sent to boot camp at Parris Island

where, because he was black and outspoken
he was beaten so badly
that his kidneys never worked right again.

Mervin Barr would die
before the year 1965 ended
refusing to go for treatment
yet another time
to the Veterans Hospital in Memphis
because that would have meant
not marching through the streets of Forrest City
with his sisters and brothers
after he had asked them, begged them,
pleaded, cajoled, preached, agitated, talked,
walking the streets day after day, night after night
in the heat and dust of an Arkansas summer
raising his voice
talking his heart out
giving his life for freedom.

> *Have you heard of General Nathan Bedford*
> *   Forrest*
> *For five years he fought the Yankees hand to*
> *   hand*
> *But after Appomatox he got lonesome*
> *So he went and organized the Ku Klux Klan*
> *His ex-soldiers crossed the Mississippi River*
> *And they founded Forrest City, Arkansas*
> *I never got to meet old General Forrest*
> *But then he never met my old friend Mervin*
> *   Barr*
>
> *All along the bars and grills of Forrest City*
> *Talking to the people where they are*
> *"I think it's time for us to get together*
> *There's no need to be afraid" says Mervin Barr*
> *Shooting pool to supplement the pension*
> *From injuries he got in the Marines*
> *When he talked you couldn't help but listen*
> *He was the gentlest man I've ever seen*
>
> *Some days he was too sick to leave the south*
> *   side*
> *Where he lived with his momma in a little*
> *   old shotgun shack*
> *So they'd send him to the V.A. home in Mem-*
> *   phis*
> *Where the sheets were white but Mervin's face*
> *   was black*

> *But he knew that he was needed by his people*
> *And he marched them up and down that Delta*
> *   town*
> *The doctors tried to send him back to Mem-*
> *   phis*
> *But he wouldn't leave until the fight was won*
>
> *They say that on the day that he was buried*
> *Five hundred people stood beside his grave*
> *I don't like funerals, but I kinda wish I'd been*
> *   there*
> *Though I couldn't say just why I feel that way*
> *The nightriders' shotguns didn't kill him*
> *Nor the people that had sworn they'd do him*
> *   in*
> *He died because he wouldn't go to Memphis*
> *And I don't expect to see his like again*

But while in one sense it is true
that I have never again seen the like
of this person, this time, this place

It is also true
that what I learned in the summer of 1965
I have learned again and again
in my daily work
as an organizer
in the Southern United States
for what is now almost thirty years
surprisingly still here
hopefully still working and fighting
for freedom

the memories, the images, the stories
of that time and place
are my guideposts, my highway signs
on this long and winding road
I keep trying to walk
together with you.

I remember Reverend Sherman Jones
preaching at the Salem Baptist Church
on the west side of Forrest City
and telling us,

"Whenever you have a birth
you have three things that go with it:
blood, pain, and water.

Some folks want the birth

but they don't want the blood
or the pain or the tears;

but if you want the one
you've got to take the other with it."

I remember this story
and I remind myself, I tell myself:
There are no easy answers,
no promises, no guarantees
sometimes not even a good long shot
but because the road is hard and long
and there are stones in our pathway
we have no choice
except to get started right now.

And this reminds me of a story
from my own Jewish tradition:

A very old man is sitting with a friend
in front of his house.
And he tells the friend:
"Tomorrow I'm going to plant a fig tree."

His friend looks at him and says,
"You're crazy.
A fig tree doesn't bear fruit for generations.
You'll die years before that ever happens.
Maybe your grandchildren will eat the fruit—
but not you."

The old man turns, looks at his friend and says:
"In that case,
I'd better plant the tree today."

And I remind myself, I tell myself
another saying from Jewish tradition:
"It is not your responsibility
to finish the job;
but you are also not free
from the responsibility to begin
and to do your part."

And because after so many years
memory runs together
like small rivers feeding the Mississippi
I also remember the story told by a poor white
        lay preacher
from the Appalachian mountains
Clinton Patrick of Cob Hill, Kentucky:
"They say one night Roosevelt couldn't sleep.
Well, his wife asked him what was the matter

and he said:
'I keep hearing the hungry children crying.
You know, I ordered them to plow under all that
        wheat
and I can't sleep
for hearing the children crying for bread.'
She said, 'Well, why don't you put cotton in your
        ears?'
He said, 'I can't.
I had that plowed under too.'"

And I remind myself, I tell myself:
People without power
can only rely on themselves
and not on those who have power
however well-intentioned.

I remember sitting in the Salem Baptist Church
the church where Reverend Sherman Jones told
        the story
of birth, blood, pain, and tears
listening to the Freedom Singers
(one of whom was Bernice Johnson Reagon
founder of Sweet Honey in the Rock
who is still singing for freedom after all these
        years)
I remember listening and singing
as those voices joined in powerful unity lifted
        us
not just out of our seats
but out of ourselves
out of our everyday lives
out of our insecurities, out of our fears
and into a dream, into a vision
of the harmony of freedom.

And I remind myself, I tell myself:
Power alone is not enough.
Even as we struggle to change
who owns, who rules, who decides
we must also open up the human heart
to the freedom to love
whomever one chooses
to the freedom to live
however one needs to live
to the freedom to laugh
in the voice that is uniquely our own
no matter who is listening.

I sometimes remember, too,
how hopeless it all sometimes seemed
how impossible, how foolish
to dream of freedom
having been enslaved so long

And I tell myself, I remind myself:
Be careful
as you organize with people
not to sell them short
with "strategies" and "tactics"
based on "what is winnable"
or "what is possible"

but rather let yourself be guided
by *their* vision
of what is right
of what is just
of what is true
however far off or impossible
that vision may seem

because freedom
always has been
and always will be
a far off and impossible dream.

And finally
I tell myself, I remind myself:
On the one hand, it's simply not true
that because of the Southern freedom movement
everything changed overnight.

Drive down any Southern highway today
turn to the right and to the left
anywhere the gravel meets the blacktop
turn again when the gravel changes
to dirt or sand or mud
and it is still the summer of 1965
the sagging porches the broken lives
the bitter shacks the barren yards
old cars and dreams stripped bare
the legacy of racism and segregation and slavery.

Down too many Southern roads
time has stood as still
as the air on an Arkansas summer night
in the cotton and soybean fields
along the Mississippi River.

But on the other hand
it's also not true

that nothing has changed
because freedom is truly
as the old hymn and freedom song tells us
"a constant struggle"
a daily act
a way of everyday life.

Freedom is a "habit of resistance"
an acquired taste for saying "no" to injustice
a conditioned reflex
for helping others
stand up and speak out.

Freedom is not
the safe harbor
at the end of the journey

Freedom is the journey itself
every day of our lives
every step of the way.

When our lives that follow fields of cotton
Burn and crack like sun-baked clay
We will gather at the deepest river
Longing for a new day

Though the night divides us from each other
Though the days are hard and long
When we walk along this road together
We are strong
We are strong

When the years of dust have choked our voices
'Til there's not a word to say
We will look to where the plow is turning
Longing for a new day

Though the night divides us from each other
Though the days are hard and long
When we walk along this road together
We are strong
We are strong

When we look to each other for courage
Strong when we tear down the stone walls between us

In the silence of a world gone crazy
Truth and justice lose their way
We are gathered at the edge of midnight
Longing for a new day

Though the night divides us from each other
Though the days are hard and long

When we walk along this road together
We are strong
We are strong

In the end
what I learned almost thirty years ago
in the dust and heat of an Arkansas summer
continues to be that core of values and beliefs
that still shapes my everyday life and work:

I believe that ordinary people
are in fact often quite extraordinary
capable of remarkable wisdom
unusual stubbornness
and great courage

but I also believe
that often these same ordinary people carry
    within them
the capacity for outrageous violence
for doing great damage and harm to others
for undoing what love and care
what courage and wisdom have built

and that whether any of our lives
are lived for good or for evil
depends at least in part
on whether we have a vision of a better world
in which to trust and believe
and a chance to act in ways
that bring that vision
that better world
a step or two closer
to where we stand today;

I believe that the most profound leadership
(as well as the most effective)
is that which flows up
from the grassroots
rather than down from the top;

I believe that a person's capacity for leadership
is often in inverse proportion
to the discrimination and exclusion
they have personally experienced—
which explains why, in our time
so much visionary and transforming leadership
has come from African Americans
and other people of color
from women of different colors and classes
from poor and working people of different races;

I believe that in the end
those who are now excluded and exploited
will get what they deserve
only through their own action
by organizing together
by building collective power
and by demanding change;

Because freedom
cannot be given
but must be taken

Equity and parity
cannot be appropriated
but must be negotiated

Respect
cannot be requested
but must be demanded

Dignity and self-esteem
cannot be bestowed
but must be earned.

Finally, I believe
that it is in the very process
of working and fighting for freedom
that a person
or a people
becomes free.

It is not
when we arrive at our destination
but when we take the first step
on our journey
that liberation begins;

It is when we join with others
in an irrevocable decision
that all people must be free
that we ourselves
can see freedom.

I read in the paper, I watched on the show
They said that it happened a long time ago
The years had gone by, I just didn't know
    Working for freedom now
The songs that we sang still ring in my ears
The hope and the glory, the pain and the fear
I just can't believe it's been twenty-five years
    Working for freedom now

    Been a long time, but I keep on trying

For I know where I am bound
Been a hard road, but I don't mind dying
I have seen freedom

Sometimes we stumble, sometimes we fall
Sometimes we stand with our backs to the wall
This road will humble the proudest of all
   Working for freedom now
Though the road up ahead may stretch out far
   and long
We must always remember the roads that we've
   gone
Memory will help us to keep keeping on
   Working for freedom now

   Been a long time, but I keep on trying
   For I know where I am bound
   Been a hard road, but I don't mind dying
   I have seen freedom

Those who have fallen and given their last
Have passed on to us what remains of their
   task
To fight for the future and pray for the past
   Working for freedom now
The song of their laughter, the step of their feet

The voice of their pain that cries out in our
   sleep
Will be judged in the end by the faith that we
   keep
   Working for freedom now

   Been a long time, but I keep on trying
   For I know where I am bound
   Been a hard road, but I don't mind dying
   I have seen freedom

The wind in the winter is bitter and chill
The cry of the hunted is heard on the hill
I just can't believe there's such suffering still
   Working for freedom now
The wind blows the summer from fields far
   away
We stand in the dust in the heat of the day
Our hearts stopped so still that there's nothing
   to say
   Working for freedom now

   Been a long time, but I keep on trying
   For I know where I am bound
   Been a hard road, but I don't mind dying
   I have seen freedom

BOB MOSES

Legacies of the Civil Rights Movement

The Civil Rights Movement of the 1960s left two movement legacies. The legacy which is more widely known is associated with Dr. Martin Luther King, Jr., and the idea of mass demonstrations to achieve particular local and/or national civil rights goals and objectives. That very powerful legacy includes the Albany and Birmingham demonstrations, the March on Washington, the Selma to Montgomery Voter Registration March, and the Memphis Sanitation Workers Movement during which Dr. King was assassinated. The other legacy, which is hardly known at all, is associated in my mind with Ella Baker. For it was Ella who provided in her life a model and a message that the Movement should focus its attention and energy on the organizing of grassroots people to help them develop their leadership potential.

Tens of thousands of students were the grassroots people that set fire to the South with their sit-in movement of the early 1960s. Ella alone of the national civil rights leadership argued for, and prevailed in, the establishment of an organization (The Student Nonviolent Coordinating Committee) which provided a vehicle for the student leadership to emerge and take control of the sit-in movement. In so doing, she gave many of us a living lesson in organizing. Namely that one central task of the organizer is to help bring about structures that provide opportunities for local, state, and national leadership around movement issues. Those of us who worked on voter registration in Mississippi instinctively put this lesson to work in organizing the Mississippi Freedom Democratic Party which provided a political structure for the emergence of black grassroots political leaders such as Fannie Lou Hamer, Mrs. Annie Devine, Victoria Gray, Aylene Quinn, Hazel Palmer, Unita Blackwell, and others.

It was this tradition which provided the implicit philosophy for the work which laid the foundation for an event such as the Mississippi Freedom Summer. It is a tradition which we all need to study more and to know more about.

❖

Robert (Bob) Moses was a field secretary for the Student Nonviolent Coordinating Committee (SNCC) and director of its Mississippi project. He also served as co-director of the Council of Federated Organizations (COFO). From 1969–1975 he worked for the Ministry of Education in Tanzania, where he was chairperson of the Mathematics department. Upon his return to the U.S. in 1976, Bob returned to Harvard, where he received his M.A. in Philosophy, to pursue his doctorate in the same field. He founded the Algebra Project in 1982, where he serves as a mathematics educator, curriculum developer, and teacher trainer. Bob resides in Cambridge, Mass., with his wife, Dr. Janet Moses. They have 4 children.

Ella Baker addressing MFDP meeting at the Democratic National Convention in Atlantic City, 1964.

ARTWORK BY

SHARON RILEY

HARRIET TERRY TANZMAN

Ella Baker: Mother Of The Civil Rights Movement

Ella Baker, godmother of the Civil Rights Movement, exerted a profound effect upon everyone who came to know and work with her. In over fifty years of working to develop people and organizations geared towards creating a just society for all people, Ms. Baker used her invaluable experience and understanding to mentor several generations of activists in the South and in the North over her lifetime.

Ms. Baker's values were shaped by her childhood in rural North Carolina. She was born in Norfolk, Virginia, in 1905 and grew up with her family near her grandparents' farm in North Carolina. Her grandfather was a minister who had been a slave, as had her grandmother. When she was quite young, he sat Ella next to him before the congregation and called her, "Grand Lady." Ms. Baker's mother cared for the ill and needy in the community; she was a woman who was known to be there for anyone who needed help. Her father shared these values but worked away from home as a waiter on the ferry between Norfolk and Washington, D.C., and was therefore only home between trips.

Ms. Baker grew up hearing her grandparents talk of their lives under slavery. They bought the land on which they had been slaves, land that was rightfully theirs through their years of unpaid toil. They purposely grew more than enough food than they needed, feeding anyone in need in their community. When the nearby Roanoke River periodically overflowed on neighbors' land, her grandfather mortgaged their land to feed needy families in the community.

Ms. Baker remembered: "We had a garden much too big for the size of the family. I'd pick a bushel or more of peas, so you'd give them to the neighbors who didn't have them. That's the way you *did*. And so, you share your *lives* with people.

". . . Where we lived, there was no sense of hierarchy, in terms of those who have, having a right to look down upon, or to evaluate as a lesser breed, those who didn't have. Part of that could have resulted, I think, from two factors. One was the proximity of my maternal grandparents to slavery. They had known what it was to not have. Plus my grandfather had gone into the Baptist ministry, and that was part of the quote, unquote, Christian concept of sharing with others. . . . Your relationship to human beings was more important than your relationship to the amount of money that you made."

"The sense of community was pervasive in the black community as a whole, I mean especially the community that had a sense of roots. . . . I think these are the things that helped to strengthen my concept about the need for people to have a sense of their own value, and *their* strengths, and it became accentuated when I began to travel in the forties for the National Association for the Advancement of Colored People (the NAACP). Because, during the period, in the forties, racial segregation and discrimination were very harsh. . . . As people moved to towns and cities, the sense of com-

Harriet Terry Tanzman was an active member of CORE at the University of Wisconsin. After John F. Kennedy was assassinated, she quit the school of social work to volunteer for SNCC's national office in Atlanta, before moving on to work in Mississippi and Alabama through COFO, MFDP, and SCLC. In the late 1960s she migrated to New Orleans where she wrote publicity for an interracial neighborhood poverty center and was active in women's groups. For 20 years, Harriet has focused on using the media, guest speakers, and whatever means possible to educate, organize, and empower people. In her spare time she writes poetry and civil rights movement history and dances.

munity diminished. . . . They lost their roots. When you lose that, what will you do next? You *hope* that you begin to think in terms of the *wider* brotherhood."[1]

When Ella Baker left North Carolina in 1928, two years after graduating from Shaw, she came to New York. It was the height of the Depression and jobs were hard to find, even harder if you were black. She waitressed and did factory work, unable to afford realizing a dream of studying sociology at the University of Chicago. The sight of thousands of people on breadlines had a strong impact on her, and she became active in helping to organize and lead the Young Negroes Cooperative League. The group worked locally and nationally to organize consumer cooperatives. Ms. Baker went on the staff of the federal government's Works Progress Administration, one of the New Deal agencies, thereby continuing her speaking, writing, and teaching about consumer affairs.

New York and the nation were in ferment during the thirties; a range of organizations were founded composed of workers, employed and unemployed, tenants, elderly, veterans, students. It was an era of street corner speakers, rallies, demonstrations, marches on Washington, and the beginning of unions in mass industries. Harlem took its place as one leading community in these currents. During this period, Ms. Baker began to write for several black newspapers. "When I came here, there was a greater participation in the Harlem area than now. You see, New York was the hotbed of—let's call it radical thinking. You had every spectrum of radical thinking in the W.P.A. We had a lovely time! The ignorant ones, like me, we had lots of opportunity to hear and to evaluate whether or not this was the kind of thing you wanted to get into. Boy, it was stimulating!"[2]

Ella Baker went to work for the NAACP in 1938 as a field organizer in the South, and later as national director of branches. It was an extremely dangerous time to join the NAACP in the South; members were risking their livelihood, their safety, and sometimes their lives for

taking this courageous step. Organizing under these conditions took a great deal of courage and sensitivity to people's conditions and needs. Ella Baker unfailingly brought these qualities to her work. She spent four or five months each year traveling across the South and became the mentor of many organizers in the region. She taught people that their power lay within, and that by uniting with others in their community and linking up with other communities in a national framework like the NAACP, they could change oppressive conditions.

Ms. Baker led organizing workshops which included people like Rosa Parks and E. D. Nixon, later of the Montgomery Bus Boycott, and Amzie Moore, who played a key role in organizing the NAACP statewide after World War II, and served as mentor and enabler for SNCC in Mississippi through working with their key Mississippi organizer, Robert Moses.

In the mid-1940s, Ella Baker left the staff of the NAACP and moved to New York to raise her niece, Jacqueline. She worked at fundraising for several national health organizations and the National Urban League Service Fund. However, she continued to participate actively in the NAACP's New York chapter, serving as its president. She was instrumental in revitalizing the chapter, in part through moving it into the Harlem community from a distant office, and through working on issues of burning interest to the community at the time. One key focus after the 1954 Supreme Court decision on school desegregation was dealing with New York's de facto segregation. She worked with the NAACP, Dr. Kenneth Clark, and with the Mayor's Commission on School Integration. During the summer of 1957, she helped to organize Parents in Action for Quality Education.

Twenty years later, Ms. Baker evaluated the results of the organization's work with her usual keen sense of perspective: "I don't think we achieved too much with the committee except to pinpoint certain issues and to have survived some very sharp confrontations with the superintendent and others on the Board of Education. But out of it came increased fervor on the part of black communities to make some changes. One of the gratifying things to me is the fact that even as late as this year I have met people who were in that group and who have been continuously active in the struggle for quality education in the black communities ever since."[2]

Ms. Baker saw her own role as functioning where there was a need. Her involvement with the Southern Christian Leadership Conference illustrates her style of work: "Come 1957, I went down South a couple of times in connection with the formation of the Southern Christian Leadership Conference (SCLC). At the end of '57 there was the need for someone to go down to set up the office of SCLC in Atlanta and to coordinate what it considered its first South-wide project, which was the holding of simultaneous meetings on February 12 in twenty different cities. I went down with the idea of not spending more than six weeks there. . . . I stayed with SCLC for two and a half years. . . . My official capacity was varied. When I first went down, I didn't insist on a title, which is nothing new or unusual for me; it didn't bother me. . . . And then there was nobody, and of course there was no money in those days, so I kept on until the summer of 1960. And prior to that, of course, the sit-ins had started, and I was able to get the SCLC to at least sponsor the conference in Raleigh."[3]

The student conference, convened Easter weekend of 1960, was attended by over three hundred people, primarily from the Southern sit-in movement, but including northern students and representatives from several civil rights organizations. Organizing and convening the historic conference was Ms. Baker's response to the sit-ins; she understood the need to connect student sit-in activities from different areas of the South to solidify the gains they were making. The meeting gave birth to the Student Nonviolent Coordinating Committee (SNCC); Ella Baker served as its midwife. Her refusal to cooperate with the SCLC leaders' insistence on

forming an SCLC youth chapter composed of student leadership from sit-ins, ensured the creation of an independent framework run by and for the youth. Ms. Baker once again used her extensive experience and belief in people's right to take control of their lives to encourage the formation of a key civil rights group, according to the felt needs and wishes of the youth themselves.

Ms. Baker continued to play a key role as mentor to SNCC: "After SNCC came into existence, of course, it opened up a new era of struggle. I felt the urge to stay close by. Because if I had done anything anywhere, it had been largely in the role of supporting things, and in the background of things that needed to be done for the organizations that were supposedly out front. So I felt if I had done it for the elders, I could do it for young people."[4]

Ms. Baker's sharing of her wide range of contacts with local NAACP activists in the South was crucial to the later work of SNCC in the 1960s. Many of these older men and women taught SNCC (and, also CORE organizers in several states) to understand the communities and the oppressive conditions faced daily by people trying to survive and to work for change. They also housed organizers, helped them to find meeting places, and reached out to their neighbors to participate in the Movement.

Communication across the generations was a skill Ella Baker possessed all of her life; more than many others of her generation, she did not patronize or lose patience with youth. SNCC organizer Muriel Tillinghast described Ms. Baker to me: "At endless meetings, I found her always listening. . . . She never ignored a comment regardless of how irrelevantly (and irreverently) it might have been tossed. She was years ahead of me in age and experience, but I never felt that what I had to say, what I saw, was boring or useless. . . . She wanted to hear what everyone had to say. She would move from group to group listening, perhaps raising a question or two. . . . They were for the group to mull over. . . ."

Muriel Tillinghast continued, ". . . Oddly, the distance of years never was a negative factor in our political work and in our friendship. . . . Many years later, Ella Baker became a family friend—we would meet and talk at length about SNCC. . . . It was then that I learned that Ms. Baker had a plan. She believed that people were the best source of their own release, their own freedom. Therefore, people had to take on the various tasks, express their thoughts, act—they had to learn to handle the weight of their own lives. . . . And, more importantly, they needed experiences which would help them get better and do better. They could do so only if they had opportunity."[5]

SNCC organizers were deeply influenced by Ella Baker in their style of organizing. The group's goal was empowerment of the people, rather than dependence on a leader. They perceived that empowerment took place within the struggles for issues like voting rights, public facility and school desegregation, and ending discrimination in all areas of life. SNCC organizers lived in communities with local people, who included farmers, sharecroppers, maids, and retirees, developing local leadership and building organizations. Despite the massive resistance of the state and local elected officials and the indifference of the federal government in the early '60s, young and old black Mississippians increasingly involving themselves in the Movement, along with black community people in states from North Carolina to Alabama, due in large part to the courageous organizing by youth of SNCC.

Jailings, violence, and economic reprisals were used to intimidate local communities. The press gave scant coverage to everyday organizing—not considered "media events" like marches were. These were key factors leading to the development of the Mississippi Summer Project, initiated by SNCC in the summer of 1964. The campaign brought in one thousand students from the North, most of them white. The hope was, in part, that this would make the nation take notice, as it was *not* doing previously, of the violence against blacks in the South, and that this would result in federal protection of the rights of black Mississippians.

In the Spring of 1964, the Council of Federated Organizations was created; it encompassed SNCC, the Congress of Racial Equality (CORE), the NAACP, and SCLC. COFO was the official umbrella for the summer project and continued to exist for the period following that project. A major statewide grassroots organization, the Mississippi Freedom Democratic Party (MFDP), was also created that spring, and once again, Ella Baker was a key advisor, inspirer, and friend. The MFDP was formed while blacks were totally excluded from the Democratic Party and nearly completely excluded from voting. It encouraged thousands of people to try to vote despite reprisals and impossible "literacy" tests given only to blacks by frequently illiterate registrars. MFDP sponsored "freedom votes" which demonstrated the strong desire of black people to vote. Unlike the regular Democratic Party in the state, the MFDP was open to everyone, black or white.

Sponsoring meetings in beats, counties, districts and statewide conventions, the MFDP elected delegates to the 1964 Democratic National Convention and sent its own representatives to Atlantic City in August 1964. Once there, they demanded the unseating of the illegally elected Democratic congressmen from their state and the seating of the MFDP by the national party. Ms. Baker worked closely with the organization's leadership, Fannie Lou Hamer of Ruleville, Victoria Gray of Palmers Crossing, Annie Devine of Canton, its chairman, SNCC organizer Lawrence Guyot from Pass Christian, as well as many other community leaders in MFDP on the Challenge. Democratic Party delegates were contacted all over the country before they went to Atlantic City; the case for seating the MFDP was documented and strongly presented to them.

Support for the Challenge grew among the delegates, and this historic development was considered dangerous by Lyndon Baines

Johnson, then president of the United States. He wanted to keep the support of the powerful congressmen from the South, all of whom came from states which also denied the right to vote to black people, though sometimes not as totally as Mississippi did. Johnson told his vice president, the liberal Hubert Humphrey, that he would have to engineer the defeat of the Challenge. The president also called a hastily improvised press conference to take television and radio attention away from Mrs. Fannie Lou Hamer, who was testifying to the nation about the vicious and debilitating beating she suffered at a Winona, Mississippi, jail on her way back from a voter education workshop in 1963.

The offer to the MFDP from the Democratic Committee was only two seats, to be picked by the Democrats; the two the party picked were Dr. Aaron Henry of Clarksdale and Rev. Ed King, a white Mississippian, chaplain at Tougaloo College. The Freedom Democratic Party, after extensive discussion, stood together and voted *not* to accept the Committee's decision. They stated that they were tired of tokens and wanted all sixty-eight votes they were entitled to, and to choose their own leaders. Despite pressure from liberal friends up north and leaders of several national civil rights groups, they came to this principled decision knowing that they were risking losing much-needed northern support for the organization's work. Bob Moses and James Forman made it clear in speaking with them that it was MFDP's own decision to make; no one outside the organization had the right to influence them in their decision.

By taking this stand, the Freedom Democratic Party retained its integrity, courage, and responsiveness to the needs of the Mississippi people it represented. Today, the MFDP continues to live—as an organization in Holmes County, Mississippi, and as an inspiration to those who never stopped organizing in their own communities in the state. Thanks to their Challenge, by 1968 the Democratic Party democratized its ranks nationally to include more people of color and more women. Along with the

Selma, Alabama, march of the 1965 Voting Rights Bill which made possible massive voter registration in the South, the MFDP and Ella Baker included clauses against discrimination in voting useful all over the country.

Once again, Ella Baker saw the fruits of her behind-the-scenes labor . . . in the Mississippi Movement.

After the 1964 Challenge, Ms. Baker returned to live in New York; however, she continued her relationship as advisor to those who sought her help, from southern and northern organizers to solidarity workers who were building support for liberation struggles in Southern Africa and Puerto Rico. Her long term relationship with the Southern Conference Education Fund (SCEF), an interracial group involving white Southerners alongside the black community in struggles against racism, continued for another decade. Ms. Baker remained in many active areas as long as her health permitted. Her spirit remained strong all the rest of her life, inspiring any lucky person who came to see her. She was close to neighbors of different ages and many others in the Harlem community where she lived a good part of her adult life.

I cherish my last visit with Ms. Baker, which took place at Harlem Hospital a year before she passed away, at age eighty-three. She was her usual warm and welcoming self, despite illness, and we talked for awhile. . . . She then introduced me to her neighbor in the next bed, who was in pain, and sang a spiritual for both of us. I joined in singing. I left, lifted in spirits as always. (After coming to visit a sick friend!)

In 1979, a tribute to Ms. Baker on her seventy-fifth birthday brought hundreds of people in from all over the country who knew her in different areas and organizations. We came to honor the Mother of our Civil Rights Movement. *Fundi: The Story of Ella Baker*, a film by Joanne Grant, has brought knowledge of Ms. Baker's life to a broader audience in the last decade.

Ms. Baker shared with all of us her gift of a sense of history, perspective on present freedom struggles, faith in our ability to realize our own gifts, and deep friendship. She passed away on her birthday in December of 1986, leaving a daughter, granddaughter, and hundreds and more of her Movement children to "Carry it On" . . .

Ella Baker will always live and be with us in our hearts. ❖

Footnotes

[1]Susan Gushee O'Mally and Ellen Cantarow, *Moving the Mountain.* New York: Feminist Press, 1980. pp: 57–61.

[2]Ibid. p. 64.

[3]Gerda Lerner, ed., *Black Women in White America: A Documentary History.* New York: Pantheon Books, 1972. pp: 349–350.

[4]Ibid., p. 350.

[5]Muriel Tillinghast, interview, November 1993.

BERNICE JOHNSON REAGON

Ella's Song

We who believe in freedom cannot rest
We who believe in freedom cannot rest until it comes

Until the killing of black men, black mothers' sons
Is as important as the killing of white men, white mother's sons

That which touches me most is that I had a chance to work with people
Passing on to others, that which was passed on to me

To me young people come first, they have the courage where we fail
And if I can but shed some light, as they carry us through the gale

The older I get the better I know that the secret of my going on
Is when the reins are in the hand of the young, who dare to run against the storm

Not needing to clutch for power, not needing the light just to shine on me
I need to be one in the number, as we stand against tyranny

Struggling myself don't mean a whole lot, I've come to realize
That teaching others to stand up and fight is the only way my struggle survives

I'm a woman who speaks in a voice and I must be heard
At times I can be quite difficult, I'll bow to no man's word

HARRIET TANZMAN

Ella Baker "Guide My Feet, While I Run This Race..."

I met Ella Baker in 1963 when I quit graduate school at the University of Wisconsin to volunteer full-time at the Atlanta headquarters of the Student Nonviolent Coordinating Committee. In Madison, Wisconsin, a group of us—African American and white Southerners and Northerners—established a chapter of the Congress of Racial Equality (CORE) that September. We focused on racism in the community and encouraged the participation of local residents. At the same time, I was very restless in my social work studies, feeling like I was only learning to apply Band-aids to victims of social injustice instead of working to change the whole racist and inhumane system.

SNCC's Dion Diamond was a student in 1963-1964 at the university. A few months after he and some other students founded a Madison Friends of SNCC chapter, his studies were rudely interrupted by the loss of an appeal in Louisiana concerning a civil rights related conviction. Dion was forced to leave school to serve time in a brutal Southern jail. This injustice, coupled by news of repression and violence against the Movement and the courage of local people and SNCC organizers (brought home to us by Diane Nash of SNCC and other organizers who visited campuses), presented us with a

choice. Do we continue to study and choose a middle-class lifestyle, demonstrating on weekends at a segregated Sears store, or do we join the Movement full time and work daily for what we believe in? Several of us chose to go south, including Silas Norman, our CORE chair, and myself. We didn't return to school for many years.

I quit graduate school twice that year, the first time, right after President Kennedy was assassinated in November 1963. I headed to Atlanta, moved in with Wisconsin friends living there, and asked to work for SNCC. Ruby Doris Robinson, SNCC's executive secretary, used my talents (such as they were) in typing, and I went to work in the office. Listening to the field workers report back on conditions from southwest Georgia to Arkansas, reading WATS line reports of freedom days at the courthouse, of the murder of Louis Allen in Mississippi, I felt like I had just begun my education into the realities of this country.

Ella Baker, as I came to learn, was a close friend, advisor, nurturer of SNCC, an organization she founded from scattered sit-in student protesters around the South in 1960. I first met her at a disappointing lecture given by James Silver, the University of Mississippi professor who wrote *Mississippi, the Closed Society*. Dick Krooth and I drove Ms. Baker home and were invited in to talk at length about Mississippi and the movement for change. Though we were peripheral to the Movement, in a way, Ms. Baker was warm, gracious, and interested in our reactions to Professor Silver. Most of all, I remember that she took us seriously, unlike many older people I had met over the years who acted patronizing towards young participants in movements.

At the one SNCC staff meeting I attended, in December 1963, I remember Ella Baker sitting next to a quiet person insuring that his or her voice was heard by the group by pointing out that this person had something to say. She was sensitive to the many different personalities she encountered over many decades of organizing; Ms. Baker could talk with anyone and put them at ease as well as encourage them to realize the talents they possessed within.

Many years later, after I organized in different frameworks in Mississippi, Alabama, and Louisiana, I migrated to California where I worked with a documentary film cooperative, Newsreel, and I studied Women's history and literature in graduate school. After ten years, I felt increasingly like I was too far from east-coast family and from Movement friends in the southeast and in New York. In 1977, I returned for a visit to Mississippi and to attend the funeral of Fannie Lou Hamer. Despite the sadness of losing one of the great leaders and human beings of the Mississippi Movement (at only age fifty-nine), it was very moving to see old friends come together from Minnesota to Guinea, from the Mississippi Delta to Washington, D.C., to pay tribute to Mrs. Hamer.

Ella Baker's speech in the overcrowded Ruleville church service has stayed with me. She spoke of Mrs. Hamer's lifelong commitment to change, her continuing involvement in organizing and speaking into the '70s at great personal risk. Mrs. Hamer, a leader of the Mississippi Freedom Democratic Party in the '60s, co-organized a Freedom Farm which fed poor folk—

black and white—in the Delta in the later part of her life.

Ms. Baker reminded us that the MFDP's finest hour was when its delegation at the Democratic National Convention in 1964 refused a "compromise" of two non-voting seats rather than the full seating of the delegation as the legitimate party representing all Mississippians. She pointed to the courage of this decision, made despite enormous pressure by liberal "friends" from civil rights leaders of other organizations to union heads to politicians.

Ms. Baker pointed out that Fannie Lou Hamer kept the faith and continued to work for change even when it wasn't always clear what the best tactics or strategies were for ending racism and creating a just society. I felt that Ms. Baker was speaking to each of us, knowing that we sometimes got discouraged and wanted to give up and just make a life for ourselves, personally. Once again, Ella Baker inspired us to stay in for the long haul and lend our talents to the struggle all of our lives, as Ms. Hamer and she had done.

When Ella Baker was advisor to the MFDP, she gave the address to its state convention in August of 1964. Her words were put to song by Bernice Reagon in "Ella's Song," and Ms. Baker was moved by this. Some of these words are: "We who believe in freedom cannot rest . . . until the murders of a black man, a black mother's son, is as important as the murder of a white man, a white mother's son." Since this is still true in 1995, we have a great deal of work to do. I felt then and now that we continue to need the wisdom of our elders to guide our feet along the path, as well as the wisdom of the youth who are beginning to organize.

When I returned to live in New York in 1980, I was committed to not only work in tenant rights and on other local issues, but also to find a way to produce films, radio programs, or books based on oral histories I wanted to do with our elders in the Southern Movement. I decided to visit and talk with Ella Baker, particularly, in Harlem as well as local people in

Holmes County, Mississippi, and others I knew from the past. We were losing more and more people whose lives could teach our generation and the young people a great deal. I wanted to record them while it was still possible. At the time, Joanne Grant was finishing an excellent film on Ms. Baker's life, *Fundi, The Story of Ella Baker,* and hundreds of us had celebrated Ms. Baker's life at a memorable gathering in the late 1970s.

I visited Ms. Baker on my fortieth birthday that year and enjoyed wide-ranging conversations about her childhood, my life and, of course, the Movement—past and present. On her birthdays, some old friends came together and had small parties, occasionally bringing children, too. Ms. Baker enjoyed it and could talk to any age person, as usual. Though Alzheimers affected her memory and other ailments confined her to her home more than she wanted to be, Ms. Baker's spirit continued strong, and she delighted in friends, family, and neighbors. She always was eager to know what her visitor was working on in the community and had insights about the present day, as well as a keen historical sense of past struggles.

In the late '70s, Joanne Grant brought Ms. Baker to Mississippi for a historical conference on COFO's Mississippi Summer anniversary. Once on the stage, Ella Baker rose to the occasion and shared her knowledge with us. During conference breaks, she visited with old friends including Hazel Palmer of the MFDP, John O'Neil of SNCC and the Free Southern Theater, and Arthur Kinoy, our lawyer for the MFDP Congressional Challenge (with William Kunstler).

I visited Ms. Baker in 1985 at Harlem Hospital, where she was a patient. It was Saturday night and my last visit with "Ma Baker." As I entered the room, her face lit up, then she joked with me, asking why I wasn't out somewhere having fun on Saturday night. Her spirits were strong, as usual.

I hope that I (and all of us who knew her, and read or see a film about her now) will take her example and help to nurture the next generation who will "carry it on." I believe that if we show them respect and interest, they may let us on the freedom bus with them. The strong spirit of Ella Baker, Medgar Evers, Herbert Lee, Fannie Lou Hamer, Carl Braden, and so many others will be on that bus, and always—in our hearts. ❖

Ella Baker, Mississippi Freedom Party delegate, addressing Democratic Party convention at Atlantic City, 1964.

PHOTO BY

GEORGE BALLIS

VICTORIA GRAY ADAMS

Ella Josephine Baker: Communicator, Initiator, Enabler, and Prophetess

. . . and the word became flesh and dwelt among us . . .

When I think of Mrs. Baker, when I attempt or am asked to describe her, the above cited words come to mind, and for me they say it all. For many, the writings of the Bible are perceived as stories about people and other beings from other times and places, but for me (self-described as a Christian activist) it is a guidebook, a handbook, a blue print on Becoming. Consequently, the opening statement is an attempt to give context to this offering on and about Ella Jo Baker.

I'm not really sure when or where I first met Mrs. Baker (she was always "Mrs. Baker" to me), but it seems that I've always known her. What is clearly remembered is the mutual respect and affection that we shared and the knowledge of our being kindred spirits. Remembered too, is the tremendous admiration I had for her and the equally tremendous inspiration she was and continues to be for me.

As a communicator, Mrs. Baker was second to none. She clearly understood the importance of effective communication and its elements—speech, attitudes, and actions—and had the ability to relate both appropriately and positively to the target audience/human environment. Mrs. Baker said it so well in referring to her experi-

ence with the Student Nonviolent Coordinating Committee (SNCC): "I had no difficulty relating to the young people. I spoke their language in terms of the meaning of what they had to say. I didn't change my speech pattern, and they didn't have to change their speech pattern. But we were able to communicate."[1]

Mrs. Baker was equally proficient in communicating with whatever segment of the society with which she was interacting. Her secret was having the ability to talk with people and not at or about them. As Mrs. Baker put it in an interview, "Your success depends on both your disposition (personality) and your capacity to sort of stimulate people—and how you carry yourself, in terms of not being above people. . . ."[2] Truly, she was a great communicator.

As an initiator, Mrs. Baker exhibited again and again her ability to move ideas, dreams, strategies, and people from paper and rhetoric to realities. Each of the major civil rights organizations and many other significant groups and agencies were beneficiaries of her unique ability to define the need, develop the strategies, and implement the actions to meet the need. She was a savior and redeemer to the National Association for the Advancement of Colored People

(NAACP) at all levels, at one time or another; she inspired and prodded Dr. King to call the meeting of the South's key black leaders, which resulted in the formation of the Southern Christian Leadership Conference (SCLC), the first Southern-based, Southwide civil rights organization; she was the key person in support of the formation and organization of the Student Nonviolent Coordinating Committee (SNCC), the student organization that energized and inspired Southern black communities from the Mississippi Delta and across the South to stand up and take responsibility for their lives; she was there when the idea of organizing an alternative political party evolved following the 1963 successful Freedom Vote (a mock election set up in Mississippi to protest the barring of black participation in the then official elections in Mississippi), the Mississippi Freedom Democratic Party (MFDP), which became a model for effective independent political organizing and action, and it effected the abolition of the all-white Democratic Party in Mississippi thereby altering the direction of the Democratic Party in the state and all across America. The list goes on. Mrs. Baker the initiator was called into service in many diverse communities of our society, to include federal government agencies.[3] As an initiator she had few peers and left as a legacy untold numbers of emulators.

I believe that Mrs. Baker's most profound contribution was that of enabler. She had the ability to inspire people of every imaginable ilk. This genius flowed from her deep faith in people's capacity to do what is necessary to respond to their needs and to resolve the contradictions in their lives once they obtain the understanding, acquire the information and the support person or system to work and share with them. Mrs. Baker believed, insisted that the salvation of a person and a people must come from within. That the struggle must be engaged by the struggler in cooperation with significant others having the compassion and needed elements which they, themselves, do not possess. She was equipped by training, experience, courage, and

compassion to offer and share the missing elements where indicated. Thus, she assisted people in discovering their own gifts and talents and to release these into the larger community. This deep conviction and belief in giving of oneself to the development of the larger community was her way of "Being." In so doing she inspired and created a broad body of leadership that spans the country and reaches into every segment of the society. Mrs. Baker, the enabler, dedicated her life to the premise that "A strong people have no need for a strong leader."

Finally, Mrs. Baker was a prophetess, one who envisioned the future, predicted possible outcomes of situations, conditions, and events, and called to accountability all whose lives touched hers, imploring us to vision the impossible—the not yet; to define the contradictions; to develop proposals and strategies to overcome and eliminate the blocks or contradictions; to determine the tactics required to actualize the proposals; to implement the tactics that will release the impossible dream into the possible, the "IS." Today, Ella's prophesy, her conviction of a strong enabled people standing up and taking responsibility for their destinies is taking place in communities around the globe, such as the people of Eastern Europe.

The great civil rights campaign of the '50s and '60s inspired people under oppressive regimes to take heart and deliver themselves by their own collective actions in unbelievable time frames. I do not consider it an exaggeration to say that the long and wide shadow of Mrs. Baker may very well have influenced the actions taking place in South Africa, even now, as we celebrate in these, sharing our impressions and experiences of living in her time and her world.

It seems to me that the one word which ties it all together is "educator." In all of the different areas that Mrs. Baker served, under all of the different hats that she wore, she taught. She taught a new set of the three R's: relationships that respect differences, responsibility for ours and all life, and risk-taking so as to free, rather than control people.[4]

The greatest tribute that we can pay Mrs. Baker is to—like her—commit our lives to becoming the embodied words of love, justice, freedom, and peace.   ❖

Footnotes

[1]Gerda Lerner, Ed., *Black Women in White America: A Documentary History*. Pantheon Books, 1972. Cited in *Ella Baker, A Leader Behind the Scenes*, Shyrlee Dallard, Silver Burdett Press. p: 79.

[2]Ibid. p: 46.

[3]Ibid. pp: 49–50.

[4]Shirley Farlinger, *The Crete Conference: Celebrating Minoan Partnership*. Edges, Summer 1993. p: 21, col.3.

FAITH RINGGOLD

The Sunflowers Quilting Bee at Arles

The National Sunflower Quilters Society of America are having quilting bees in sunflower fields around the world to spread the cause of freedom. Aunt Melissa has written to inform me of this and to ask me to: "Go with them to the sunflower fields in Arles. And please take good care of them in that foreign country, Willia Marie. These women are our freedom," she wrote.

Today the women arrived in Arles. They are Madame Walker, Sojourner Truth, Ida Wells, Fannie Lou Hamer, Harriet Tubman, Rosa Parks, Mary McLeod Bethune, and Ella Baker, a fortress of African American women's courage with enough energy to transform a nation piece-by-piece.

Look what they've done in spite of their oppression: Madame Walker invented the hair-straightening comb and became the first self-made American-born woman millionaire. She employed over three thousand people. Sojourner Truth spoke up brilliantly for women's rights during slavery, and could neither read nor write. Ida Wells made an *exposé* of the horror of lynching in the South.

Fannie Lou Hamer braved police dogs, water hoses, brutal beatings, and jail in order to register thousands of people to vote. Harriet Tubman brought over three hundred slaves to freedom in nineteen trips from the South on the Underground Railroad during slavery and never lost a passenger. Rosa Parks became the mother of the Civil Rights Movement when she sat down in the front of a segregated bus and refused to move to the back.

Mary McLeod Bethune founded Bethune Cookman College and was special advisor to Presidents Harry Truman and Franklin Delano Roosevelt. Ella Baker organized thousands of people to improve the condition of poor housing, jobs, and consumer education. Their trip to Arles was to complete "The Sunflower Quilt," an international symbol of their dedication to change the world.

The Dutch painter Vincent Van Gogh came to see the black women sewing in the sunflower fields. "Who is this strange looking man," they asked. "He is *un grand peintre*," I told them, "though he is greatly troubled in his mind." He held a vase of sunflowers, no doubt *une nature morte,* a still life for one of his paintings.

"He's the image of the man hit me in the head with a rock when I was a girl," Harriet said. "Make him leave. He reminds me of slavers." But he was not about to be moved. Like one of the sunflowers, he appeared to be growing out of the ground. Sojourner wept into the stitches of her quilting for the loss of her thirteen children, mostly all sold into slavery.

One of Sojourner's children, a girl, was sold to a Dutch slaver in the West Indies who then took her to Holland. "Was that something this

Faith Ringgold is a painter, mixed media sculptor, performance artist, and writer, and is an art professor at the University of California, San Diego. Faith's "The Sunflowers Quilting Bee At Arles" is part of the French Collection, Part I, series, which is a tribute to her mother, Madame Willi Posey, and other African American women for their life long dedication to work, family, culture, and community.

The Sunflowers Quilting Bee at Arles

Dutch man might know something about? He should pay for all the pain his people have given us. I am concerned about you, Willia Marie. Is this a natural setting for a black woman?"

"I came to France to seek opportunity," I said. "It is not possible for me to be an artist in the States."

"We are all artists. Piecing is our art. We brought it straight from Africa," they said. "That was what we did after a hard day's work in the fields to keep our sanity and our beds warm and bring beauty into our lives. That was not being an artist. That was being alive."

When the sun went down and it was time for us to leave, the tormented little man just settled inside himself and took on the look of the sunflowers in the field as if he were one of them. The women were finished piecing now. "We need to stop and smell the flowers sometimes," they said. "Now we can do our real quilt-

ing, our real art—making this world piece up right."

"I got to get back to that railroad," Harriet said. "Ain't all us free yet, no matter how many them laws they pass. Sojourner fighting for women's rights. Fannie for voter registration. Ella and Rosa working on civil rights. Ida looking out for mens getting lynch. Mary Bethune getting our young-uns' education, and Madame making money fixing hair and giving us jobs. Lord, we is sure busy."

"I am so thankful to my Aunt Melissa for sending you wonderful women to me. Art can never change anything the way you have. But it can make a picture so everyone can see and know the history and culture of a people. That is one of the ways we know our true history and culture, from the art. Someday I will make you women proud of me, too. Just wait, you'll see."

"We see, Willia Marie," they said. "We see."

Fannie Lou Hamer at the National Democratic Convention in Atlantic City, 1964.

ARTWORK BY

SHARON RILEY

BERNICE JOHNSON REAGON

Women as Culture Carriers in the Civil Rights Movement: Fannie Lou Hamer

First published in *Women in the Civil Rights Movement: Trailblazers and Torchbearers 1941–1965*, edited by Vicki L. Crawford, Jacqueline Anne Rouse, and Barbara Woods; Indiana University Press.

Understanding Fannie Lou Hamer and her role as a cultural carrier becomes clearer when we recognize that she opened many mass meetings by pulling the congregation into a community of singing.

Remember me
Remember me
Oh Lord, remember me.

Father, I stretch
My hands to thee
No other help I know.

You remembered my mother, remember me
You remembered mother, remember me
Oh Lord, remember me.

There is something I feel when sound runs through my body. I cannot sing without experiencing a change in my mood, a change in the way I feel. In the African American culture, that is a major function of singing. People come to singing because of how they feel in it and on the other side of the song. The aim is to be sure that whatever shape you were in before you started to produce this sound is transformed when the singing is over. There are cultures where one can engage in singing without having one's inner self aroused, but this is not the case with the African American congregational song tradition.

Fannie Lou Hamer was an activist and a cultural leader who assumed major responsibility for the creation and maintenance of the environment within which those who struggle for freedom lived and worked. She positioned herself so that she was constantly in great danger; she operated in the open, above ground, confronting an entire system that was organized to keep her and all black people subjugated. When Mrs. Hamer found her voice as a fighter, she became a transmitter of the culture of that struggle. Her work as an organizer was grounded in her own testimony. She called and urged others to join in battling racism, poverty, and injustice. A natural and fearless community leader, master orator, and song leader, she used her stories and songs to nurture the air we breathed as fighters.

The first time I saw Fannie Lou Hamer she came up to me and thanked me for everything we had done for her. I couldn't figure out why this giant was thanking me. I struggled a long time to figure out whom she was talking about. She was talking about the young people who made up the staff of the Student Nonviolent Coordinating Committee (SNCC).

I was in the Atlanta SNCC office, and she was a SNCC field secretary by then, primarily organizing in Mississippi, but increasingly traveling throughout the South and the nation telling stories about what it took for a citizen of the United States of America of African descent to vote in the state of Mississippi. In expressing her thanks to SNCC, Mrs. Hamer was defining and validating the work of the Movement from a new perspective. She was saying that the Movement was the best thing that had ever happened to her. She sounded as if we in SNCC had rescued her. When I thought about it, I understood what she meant. The Movement gave all of us choices about how we would live, and it gave us the chance to act as people with power.

Fannie Lou Hamer was expressing thanks— as I have done many times since—for the opportunity to become, for her time and her community and her people, more like herself. We all have souls, an inner voice that wants to find its essence through the expression of our living. Often we feel that the world would not tolerate us if we followed our hearts. The Movement provided a nurturing ground that encouraged us to open up and move beyond our fears and become who we were in our hearts. One who answered that call was Fannie Lou Hamer.

Fannie Lou Hamer was born in Montgomery County, Mississippi, in 1917. She was the youngest of twenty children born to Jim and Lou Ella Townsend, who worked as sharecroppers. From the age of two, she lived in Sunflower County and she began to pick cotton at six. Of her childhood years, she said: "Life was worse than hard. It was horrible! We never did have enough to eat, and I don't remember how old I was when I got my first pair of shoes, but I was a big girl. Mama tried to keep our feet warm by wrapping them in rags and tying them with string."[1]

One year after a good season, her father cleared enough to rent land and buy stock and a car. A white neighbor envious of this progress struck a devastating blow by poisoning the stock with Paris green, an insecticide. This plunged the family back into poverty, from which they never recovered. The family's situation was complicated by an accident that left her mother blind. As the plight of the family worsened, Fannie Lou Hamer was forced to leave school at twelve years of age, just able to read and write. So in 1962, when the Movement came to Ruleville, Mississippi, she was working weighing cotton and serving as timekeeper for B. D. Marlowe, a job she held for eighteen years until she made her first attempt to register to vote.

We know about Fannie Lou Hamer because of her tireless efforts to change the conditions of African Americans in Mississippi in particular and the country in general. We know about her because of the price that she paid to participate in the struggle for change. We know about her because of the power of her voice. Everywhere she went she spoke, sang, and shared her life and her vision of a better world. It was a powerful message; her delivery was Southern, black, and riveting.

The first time I heard her speak was in Town Hall in New York City. It was the first time I had ever been in Town Hall. I owe a lot to the Movement that the first time I entered this hallowed hall of the land was to hear Fannie Lou Hamer tell the stories of our fight for justice. Walking into Town Hall, New York City, for the first time to hear Mrs. Hamer, E. W. Steptoe, and Hartman Turnbow, all from Mississippi, was the way to learn about that place and others like it. Because of the Movement, such places became ours, to use for our forums and our messages. They were never beyond our lives and our reach. The first time I ever heard about Carnegie Hall, I was invited to sing there as a Freedom Singer.

Listening to the story of Fannie Lou Hamer took me to a place I had witnessed so many times in black church services. Someone rises and through her or his offerings begins to charge up the air. Sometimes after a service has begun somebody will just come out of a corner and with the support of the congregants will do something to bring the space under his or her power. This refocusing and transforming spaces goes beyond content and data; it deals directly with the power to establish the tone and tenor of the environment. Within the African American oral tradition our stories and our legacies travel through time in a bed of rich cultural sound. I am not talking about simply starting something in a room and changing the space the people in the room have to deal with. It goes much farther because the oral tradition requires the transmission of its lode across generations. When you are a part of such an environment the experiences that are passed in that space become forever a part of who you are. In order to serve and extend the process and keep alive these treasures for others living in your time and beyond, you walk out of that space with responsibility for the stories you now carry within your soul. For example, I know

Walk with me, my Lord, walk with me
Walk with me, my Lord, walk with me
While I'm on this tedious journey
I want Jesus to walk with me.

I cannot tell you when I learned that song. I did not get it out of a book, and I did not learn it in a classroom. It was traveling to me through time, an integral element of the cultural world into which I was born. I know the song and the singing because when I was surrounded by it, its power moved me and became a comfort to me, and I now continue its life in sharing it.

Make a way for me, now Lord, make a way
for me
Make a way for me, now Lord, make a way
for me
While I'm on this tedious journey

I want Jesus to walk with me.

It is important to talk about cultural transmission, how ideas, analysis, social stances, and world views move through communities and across time. A lot of us do not understand what it really would take to make our work available to the next generation—not only for those who follow us to read about what we believed and valued and tried to do with our living, but also to receive our stories as models and the base from which our children may move in the world they struggle to shape. The idea that the world you live in is one you should work to shape moves across time only if it is a part of the cultural environment you create and put in motion.

This work within African American culture—the work of passing on the stories of life in song, in ceremonies, in games, in the sounds around us—has been carried to a large extent by the women. You know who you are before you remember that you don't know who you are. And you know that from the women. They whisper it to you in the cracks between feeding and the air you breathe. Fannie Lou Hamer understood that what she experienced was not for her alone but for those who would be moved by the sound of her voice and the power of her living.

That night at Town Hall, Mrs. Hamer told the story of her arrest and the severe beating she and Annelle Ponder received because of their efforts to register voters in Mississippi. It was a story I was to hear many times, but that night it was engraved in my heart. I was transformed by the intensity of her identification with struggle. There was no separation; she had stepped onto a path and found joy amid unspeakable danger. As a young woman beginning to find my own voice, it was crucial that I sat in an environment created by the life and struggle of Fannie Lou Hamer.

She began, "My name is Fannie Lou Hamer. I live in Ruleville, Mississippi. . . ." She told how she and five other people had been returning from a voter registration training session in Charleston, South Carolina. Their bus was stopped in Winona, Mississippi, and they were arrested. From her cell, Mrs. Hamer could hear Annelle Ponder, a student from Atlanta who worked with the Southern Christian Leadership Conference (SCLC), screaming as they beat her. When Annelle Ponder, her face swollen, walked past Mrs. Hamer's cell, she whispered, "Pray for me."

Then Mrs. Hamer heard her own name called and they came and got her and made her lie down on a bench. She was beaten by two black men, prisoners called trustees, who were charged to beat her by two white guards who held guns on them to make sure they gave her a good whipping. As they lashed her about her legs, her dress started to move up her thighs and as she reached to try and pull it down, one of the guards pulled her dress over her head. They beat her with leather straps until her thighs were as hard as a board, until pain came and went. When they told her to get up she didn't think she could move. When she finally was able to get up, she knew that although they had whipped her body, they had not whipped her soul. She knew that freedom was when you understood that not even an attempt to kill you would determine what you did or said.

Fannie Lou Hamer's participation in the Movement seemed to come from a long-held desire to do something about the way her people had been forced to live. This pride was instilled in her by her mother: "Sometimes when things were so bad and I'd start thinking maybe it would be better if we were white, she'd [Hamer's mother] insisted that we should be proud to be black, telling us, 'nobody will respect you unless you stand up for yourself.'"[2]

Growing up believing in God and being taught not to hate, Mrs. Hamer discovered that there were many things "dead wrong" with the lives of blacks and whites in Mississippi. "I used to think . . . let me have a chance, and whatever this is . . . I'm gonna do somethin' about it."[3]

Her chance came one night when she went to a mass meeting at a church in Ruleville, where she heard James Forman and James Bevel speak

about voter registration. Reverend Bevel told those gathered about how many black people there were in the county and how, if they were voters, they could remove from power the racist politicians who controlled their state. They also learned that in Washington, many of the senior members of the House and Senate were from the South because they were able to hold on to their seats for the most terms. Their longevity was directly related to blacks not participating in the political system; they did not have to be accountable to the majority of people in their districts since most of them were not allowed to vote.

Mrs. Hamer was one of those who volunteered to try to register, and she was made the leader of the group. This resulted in her losing her job and her family being kicked off the plantation. She often told this story in mass meetings to encourage others to join the Movement.

> It was 1962, thirty-first of August that eighteen of us traveled twenty-six miles to this place to the county courthouse to try to register to become first-class citizens. When we got here to Indianola to the courthouse, that was a day I saw more policemen with guns than I'd ever seen in my life at one time. They were standing around, and I never will forget that day. One of the policemen called the police department in Cleveland, Mississippi, and told him to bring some type of big book back over there. Anyway, we stayed in the registrar's office—I was one of the first persons to complete, as far as I knew how to complete, my registration form and I went and got back on the bus. During the time we were on the bus, the policeman kept watching the bus and I noticed a highway patrolman watching the bus.

> After everybody had completed their forms and after we started back to Ruleville, Mississippi, we were stopped by the policeman and highway patrolmen and was ordered to come back to Indianola, Mississippi. When we got back to Indianola, the bus driver was charged with driving the bus the wrong color. This is the gospel truth. This bus had been used for years for cot-

ton chopping, cotton picking, and to carry people to Florida to work in the wintertime to make enough to live on to get back here in the spring and summer. But that day the bus had the wrong color. We got to Ruleville about five o'clock.

Reverend Jeff Sunny drove me out to the rural area where I had been working as a timekeeper and a sharecropper for eighteen years. When I got there I was already fired. My children met and told me, "Mama, this man is hot! Said you will have to go back and withdraw [your registration application] or you will have to leave." . . . It wasn't too long before my husband came and he said the same thing. I walked in the house, set down on the side of my little daughter's bed, and then this white man walked over and said, "Pap, did you tell Fannie Lou what I said?" I said, "He did." "Well, Fannie Lou, you will have to go down and withdraw or you will have to leave." And I addressed and told him, as we have always had to say, "Mr., I didn't register for you; I was trying to register for myself." He said, "We're not ready for that in Mississippi." He wasn't ready, but I been ready a long time. I had to leave that same night.[4]

While organizing in Mississippi, Mrs. Hamer never hesitated to speak of the cost and danger of entering a life of activism against racism: "On the tenth of September in 1962, sixteen bullets were fired into the home of Mr. and Mrs. Robert Tucker for me. That same night two girls were shot at Mr. Herman Sissan's, in Ruleville. They also shot Mr. Joe McDonald's house that same night."[5] She then moved from her personal testimony to sharply focused analysis: "Now the question I raise: Is this America? The land of the free and the home of the brave? Where people are being murdered, lynched, and killed because we want to register and vote!"[6]

As a good organizer, she never failed to return to the immediate goals of the project. "You know I feel good. I never know what's gonna happen to me tonight. But you see, you know the ballot is good. If it wasn't good, how come he trying to keep you from it and he still doing

it? Don't be foolish, folks. They go in there by the droves and they had guns to keep us out of there the other day, and dogs. And if that's good enough for them, I want some of it too."[7]

Mrs. Hamer was much more than a talker, organizer, and singer; her efforts brought results. She failed the literacy test the first time she tried to register to vote. She told the registrar she would return every thirty days until she passed the test. And she did. She wore them out with her living and became one of the first African Americans to register to vote in the Sunflower County voting campaign.

It was perhaps these two stories—Mrs. Hamer and Annelle Ponder being beaten in jail and her first efforts to register to vote—that pushed me to write this song when I heard that she had passed.

Fannie Lou Hamer, Fannie Lou Hamer
Fannie Lou Hamer, Fannie Lou Hamer

This Little Light of Mine
Her song would fill the air
She rocked the state of Mississippi
Now a few more black people stand there.

For twenty years she weighed cotton
Down on a white man's farm
She received threats on her life, fired from her
 job
Scorned and kicked off the farm.

We're sick and tired of being sick and tired
That's what the lady would yell
Her body was beaten and she walked crippled
Trying to vote, she was thrown in jail.

Land of the tree and home of the slave
She criticized the law of this land
For hundreds of years blacks had lived in fear
Now we marched, took our lives in our hands.

She came by here and she didn't stay long
Helped to turn a few things around
Cancer took her body, the struggle's got her soul
Now we've laid her body in the ground.

When I look at the words of Fannie Lou Hamer, I am always struck by how she defined who she was. She was a religious woman, and whenever she got up to speak she took a text or she quoted from the Scripture. In this case, she defines the work she felt she was called to do. The first thing she did was to lead out on "This Little Light of Mine." Then right out of the song she said:

> From the fourth chapter of St. Luke, beginning at the eighteenth verse: "The Spirit of the Lord is upon me because he hath anointed me to preach the gospel to the poor; he hath sent me to heal the broken-hearted, to preach deliverance to the captives, and recovering of sight to the blind, to set at liberty them who are bruised, to preach the acceptable day of the Lord."
>
> Now the time have come, that was Christ's purpose on earth, and we only been getting by paving our way to hell, but the time is out. When Simon Cyrene was helping Christ to bear his cross up the hill, he said, "Must Jesus bear this cross alone and all the world go free? No, there's a cross for everyone and there's a cross for me. This consecrated cross I'll bear, till death shall set me free. And then go home a crown to wear, for there's a crown for me."[8]

When she finished quoting that hymn (and I understood that Simon Cyrene had not said those particular words), she added, "It is not easy out there. We just got to make up our minds and face it, folk, and if I can face the issue, you can too." In this sermon, she is saying that she is charged to do the work from the highest source she has operating in her life. The preaching of the gospel, and the anointing, and the giving of sight to the blind are activities that Jesus did. She claims that territory where seemingly impossible changes are brought forth, for herself. And before she finishes, she calls the congregation to action by saying, "If I can do it, you can too."[9]

Fannie Lou Hamer placed Jesus where his experiences, as passed through the traditions of the black church, could be used in the freedom struggle. She used all of this material, and she brought its full force to bear on the work she had to do.

There was the time in the mass meeting in Greenwood when Mrs. Hamer talked about how long she had been concerned about the system she was now risking her life every day to challenge.

> And brothers, you can believe this or not—I been sick of this system as long as I can remember. Heard some people speak of the Depression in the thirties; in the twenties it was always "pression" with me! Depression! I been as hungry . . . You know it's been a long time, people, I have worked, I have worked as hard as anybody. I have been picking cotton and would be so hungry and one of the poison things about it, wondering what I was gone cook that night, but you see, all of them things were wrong? And I asked God, and I have said, "Now Lord," and it ain't no need a lying and saying you ain't, "open a way for us. Please make a way for us, Jesus, where I can stand up and speak for my race and speak for my hungry children," and he opened a way and all of them mostly backing out.
>
> It's a funny thing since I started working for Christ—it's kinda like in the Twenty-third Psalm, He said, "Thou preparest a table before me in the presence of my enemies; thou anointeth my head with oil; and my cup runneth over," and I have walked through the shadows of death, because it was on the tenth of September in 1962 when they shot sixteen times in a house—and it wasn't over a foot over the bed where my head was—but that night, I wasn't there. Don't you see what God can do? Quit running around trying to dodge death, because this book says, "He that seeketh to save his life is gonna lose it anyhow."[10]

Mrs. Hamer walked the ground that was the Twenty-third Psalm as a fighter. These Bible stories became concrete in her attempt to register to vote. She always drew on this source in her speeches. For instance, she used the Israelite story of Moses to describe Bob Moses, the head of the Mississippi Freedom Project: "You see, He made it so plain for us: He sent a man to

Mississippi with the same name that Moses had to go to Egypt and tell them to go down in Mississippi and tell Ross Barnett to let my people go."[11]

She directly addressed the fear of the black people in that church. After telling everyone that they might get killed if they joined the Movement, she used this story to show them how that was exactly what they were supposed to do. She was telling black people that this was the time. How do we know it? Bob Moses was the sign of Moses. And though Bob Moses was not always comfortable with this analogy, Fannie Lou Hamer the organizer used it like a guarantee that the time had arrived. She believed that the Movement was an unmistakable door that the people had opened in their own lives and now must be fortified to walk through. Whenever she talked, you felt that she was processing material that had come to her and was analyzing it and blending it with the challenges of the day.

She became a national voice, moving throughout the nation, speaking to the issues of the day. In one speech she was asked to talk about women. In the opening part of the speech, she speaks to white women:

> You know I work for the liberation of all people, because when I liberate myself, I'm liberating other people. But you know, sometimes I really feel sorrier for the white woman than I feel for ourselves because she been caught up in this thing, caught up feeling special, and folks, I'm going to put it on the line, because my job is not to make people feel comfortable. You've been caught up in this thing because, you know, you worked my grandmother, and after that you worked my mother, and then finally you got a hold of me.[12]

The irony of the issue, still before us today, was the widening of the historic gulfs between white women and their nonwhite servants. As "liberated" women increasingly chose professional careers outside the home as well as motherhood and homemaking, they turned to poorer women to provide the services to make their lives

possible. Often these women were not paid enough by their sisters to provide adequate care for the children they had to leave at home so their employees' children would be well cared for.

In speaking to issues like this, Mrs. Hamer was and is timeless and relentless in her honesty. She insisted that the relationships between maids and nursemaids and their employers be a part of any discussion about sisterhood. She acknowledged her experiences, including the mixed families she grew up in, and how many blue-eyed black people she knew, and how many cousins she had who said they were white in Mississippi who never "sistered" or "cousined" her.

For Mrs. Hamer, black women were in partnership with black men in the interest of the family and the future of their people. She was uneasy with the radical edge of feminism that seemed to say that if you are going to fight for your freedom as women and you are going to fight against sexism, it may become necessary and appropriate to separate yourself from your fathers, your brothers, your male lovers, and your sons. Mrs. Hamer took a strong position on what she felt was divisive and destructive to black American organizing: "I'm not hung up on this about liberating myself from the black man, I'm not going to try that thing. I got a black husband, six feet three, two hundred and forty pounds, with a fourteen shoe, that I don't want to be liberated from."[13]

Mrs. Hamer's view on the partnership between black men and women was not a romantic one. As a leader in the Movement and in her community, she did not hesitate to criticize men who wanted to lead but were unable to confront their fears. She believed that leadership came from actual work and commitment and was not preordained by sex. She clearly stated her position on this when urging people to face the danger: "You see the thing what so pitiful about it, the men been wanting to be the boss all these years, and the ones not up under the house is under the bed."[14]

Coming out of the poorest state in the nation, from one of the poorest classes, Mrs. Hamer was harsh and frank about the way some college-educated black women had difficulty embracing her as their sister.

Fannie Lou Hamer had a realistic sense of how she was perceived by her community. She understood and spoke about the power of class in paralyzing people to organize against their own oppression.

> You see in this struggle, some people say, well she don't talk too good. The type of education that we get here, years to come, you won't talk too good. The type of education that we get in the state of Mississippi will make our minds so narrow, it won't coordinate with our big bodies. We know we have a long fight, because our leaders like the preachers and the teachers, they are failing to stand up today. But we know some of the reasons for that. This brainwashed education that the teachers have got.[16]

> We have a job as black women, to support whatever is right, and to bring in justice where we've had so much injustice. Some people say, well I work for $24 per week. That's not true in my case, I work sometimes for $15 per week. I remember my mother working for 25 and 30 cents a day. But we are organizing ourselves now, because we don't have any other choice.

> Sunflower County is one of the few counties in the state of Mississippi where we didn't lose one black teacher. Because I went in and told the judge, I said, "Judge, we're not going to stand by and see you take a man with a master's degree and bring him down to janitor help. So if we don't have the principal . . . there ain't going to be no school, private or public."[17]

Looking at the economic reality of slavery and racism, Fannie Lou Hamer blended a familiarity with God with her personal history and testimony to make her point.

> A house divided against itself cannot stand. America is divided against itself and without they considering us as human beings one day America will crumble! Because God is not pleased! God is not pleased with all the murdering and all the brutality and all the killing for no reason at all. God is not pleased that the Negro children in the state of Mississippi [are] suffering from malnutrition. God is not pleased, because we have to go raggedy and work from ten to eleven hours for three lousy dollars! And then how can they say that in ten years' time we will force every Negro out of the state of Mississippi. But I want these people to take a good look at themselves, and after they have sent the Chinese back to China, the Jews back to Jerusalem, and give the Indians their land back, they take the Mayflower back from where they came, the Negro will still be in Mississippi! We don't have anything to be ashamed of in Mississippi and actually we don't carry guns, because we don't have anything to hide.[18]

Fannie Lou Hamer, standing among a chorus of black women leaders like Ella Baker and Septima Clark, taught something else about being a leader in the Movement. These women made their political and social stances primary in their lives. They had jobs of a sort, somebody sometimes paid them wages, but the work never changed. By being in the atmosphere they created and listening to the talk, I learned that it is possible to live in this society and be a radical and always be ready to fight. Sometimes you would get killed, but a lot of times you wouldn't. There was in the midst of pain and effort and the real dangers also a sweetness about struggle that no human being should go through life and not experience.

There is another story Fannie Lou Hamer tells, this one about the 1964 Democratic National Convention in Atlantic City. She described being in a room with Hubert Humphrey, who explained that in his heart he really supported their struggle. The Mississippi Freedom Democratic Party was challenging the seats of the all-white Mississippi delegation on the grounds that blacks were not allowed to exercise their rights as citizens to participate in electoral politics in that state. However, Humphrey's chance to be on the ticket with Lyndon Johnson would be jeopardized if the issue reached the floor. Mrs. Hamer said:

> I was delighted even to have a chance to talk with this man. But here sat a little round-eyed man with his eyes full of tears, when our attorney at the time, Joseph Rauh, said if we didn't stop pushing them and fighting to come to the floor, that Mr. Humphrey wouldn't be nominated that night for vice president of the United States, I was amazed, and I said, "Well Mr. Humphrey, do you mean to tell me that your position is more important to you than four hundred thousand black lives?" And I didn't try to force nobody else to say it, but I told him I wouldn't stoop to no two votes at large.[19]

It takes a fresh vision to raise that question and then stand on your position and say that's your ground. Mrs. Hamer refused the compromise offered by the convention—to seat the regular all-white delegation and give the MFDP two seats at-large. "Now they thought they had us sewed up, bag sewed up, but I told it everywhere. You can kill a man, but you can't kill ideas. 'Cause that idea's going to be transferred from one generation 'til after a while, if it's not too late for all of us, we'll be free."[20]

It was this Fannie Lou Hamer who, when I actually met her, said, "I want to thank you all for what you are trying to do for us." I will always stand in her shadow charged by the power of her work.

> *I wandered far away from God*
> *Now I'm coming home*
> *The path of sin too long I've trod*

Now I'm coming home. This is a favorite hymn in the black church. If you are not a Christian, go beyond the specific text and think about being lost from yourself. You cannot understand what the Civil Rights Movement means or what you did if you don't have a space like this where out of the heat of the activity you can sit and ponder it. Fannie Lou Hamer's reality of representing six hundred thousand people in the state of Mississippi was her home base. No matter where she was, she knew that if she moved with

integrity from that reality she would be on solid ground. Committing one's self to long-time struggle requires the search for one's self and the embracing of your vision of the world and yourself in it at your fullest development as "home." Then from that place you can move and return as you struggle to make a way for the life you have to live.

> *Coming home, Coming home,*
> *Never more to roam.*
> *Open wide, thine arms of love*
> *Now I'm coming home.* ❖

Notes

[1]Phyl Garland, "Builders of the South: Negro Heroines of Dixie Play Major Role in Challenging Racist Traditions," *Ebony,* August 1966, p. 28.

[2]*Ibid.*

[3]George Sewell, "Fannie Lou Hamer," *Black Collegian,* May/June 1978, p. 18.

[4]Fannie Lou Hamer, mass meeting, Hattiesburg, Mississippi, 1963, Moses Moon Collection, Program in African American Culture, Archives, National Museum of American History, Smithsonian Institution, Washington, D.C.

[5]*Ibid.*

[6]*Ibid.*

[7]*Ibid.*

[8]Fannie Lou Hamer, mass meeting, Greenwood, Mississippi, © 1963, Moses Moon Collection.

[9]*Ibid.*

[10]*Ibid.*

[11]*Ibid.*

[12]Fannie Lou Hamer, speech, NAACP Legal Defense Fund Institute, New York City, May 7, 1971, in Gerda Lerner, ed., *Black Women in White America* (New York: Vintage, 1972).

[13]*Ibid.*

[14]Hamer, Greenwood meeting.

[15]Hamer, NAACP speech.

[16]Hamer, Hattiesburg meeting.

[17]Hamer, NAACP speech.

[18]Hamer, Hattiesburg meeting.

[19]Fannie Lou Hamer, interview, *Southern Exposure,* 9, 1 (Spring 1981).

[20]*Ibid.*

PHOTO BY

MATT HERRON

Fannie Lou Hamer marching in voter registration demonstration outside Forest County Courthouse, Hattiesburg, Mississippi, 1963 (hand-lettered sign reads: "Freedom Now, SNCC")

Fannie Lou Hamer at the Democratic National Convention in Atlantic City, 1964.

ARTWORK BY

SHARON RILEY

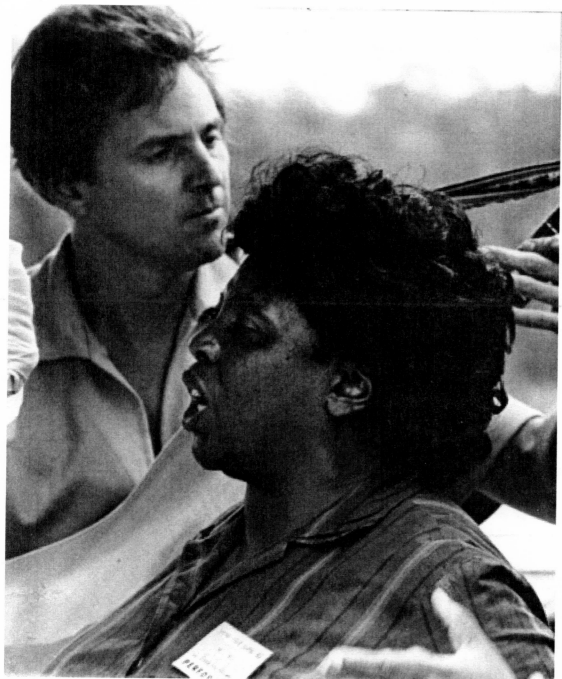

Guy Carawan with Mrs. Fannie Lou Hamer of Mississippi at the Newport Folk Festival, 1964.

PHOTO BY

JOE ALPER

Joe Alper's photographs have appeared in Life, Fortune, Downbeat, Jazz, *and* U.S. Camera, *to name a few. In 1962, he was a prize winner in the International Jazz Photography Competition in Poland and in 1967 he became a lecturer in photography in the State University at Albany. A devoted fighter in the struggle for human rights all his adult life, Joe died in June, 1968 following a long and complicated kidney operation.*

Fannie Lou Hamer with Len Chandler, Newport Folk Festival, 1965

JOANNE GRANT

Not in Mississippi

Standing on the lawn at Tougaloo on a sunny day in June 1984, I was chatting with the two students—one a young black man from Tougaloo and the other a white woman from Millsaps—who had been assigned to escort me from the airport to the 20th anniversary celebration of the Mississippi Summer. The blues singer Barbara Dane and I were reminiscing about the way it had been way back in 1964 and were explaining to our escorts how exhilarating, but how terrifying, it had been. We went on to describe how interracial groups drove around the state. If there were more whites than blacks in the car the blacks rode on the floor and vice versa. This was so that night riders or the police would not see that whites and blacks were riding in the same car—a sure sign that the occupants were "outside agitators," "freedom riders," and such. The immediate reaction to our account from both students was almost in chorus: "Not in Mississippi!"

Such disbelief was an amusing eye-opener to veterans of the Civil Rights Movement of the 1960s. We remembered well what the state had been like at that time.

The situation is indeed different now. If the students could not even recognize the Mississippi which we were describing, obviously there had been some changes, and one wonders what kind of history is being taught? Those students ought to know from whence they came. It would have been absolutely unheard of twenty years earlier that a white woman and a black man

would have been assigned to shepherd guests to their respective colleges. It is as simple as that.

For me, knowing that Millsaps, a formerly all-white college, and Tougaloo, a formerly all-black college, were now integrated institutions, was somewhat less important than the experience of seeing black reservation clerks at the desk of the motel, black bank clerks, black cashiers at local restaurants and in retail establishments.

This was a new Mississippi, decidedly different from the days of driving along a Mississippi highway with Bob Moses, who commented that even the kudzu vines rapaciously twining up the sides of the ditches towards the trees, spreading everywhere, seemed malevolent. Different from the time when he and I and some others were seated at a restaurant in Jackson and the police walked in. A black policeman said that he knew me. He'd seen me get off the plane at the Jackson airport. It gave me an eerie feeling, being watched.

Decidedly different from the nights when we turned on the shower and all of the faucets, the air conditioner, and the television in our motel room to override the microphones that we were sure were in place to catch our every word. We were talking about clues to the disappearance of the three civil rights workers, James Chaney, Andrew Goodman, and Michael Schwerner. We were talking about Movement efforts to find out what had happened, because we didn't trust the Justice Department, the FBI, and certainly not the local police to find out the

Joanne Grant, a 1960s Movement participant is the author of Black Protest *and* Confrontation On Campus *and producer/director of the documentary film* Fundi: The Story of Ella Baker.

409

truth.

That night I was so traumatized that I couldn't sleep in my motel room with its sliding glass doors leading out to a walkway where anyone could lurk. I called my friend, Michael Standard, an attorney and Movement participant, and said: "Come get me." I was too terrorized to walk down a flight to his room. I suppose that this is too bizarre to fathom for a young person accustomed to the new Mississippi. The point is that there *is* a new Mississippi. It is a Mississippi with which we have to deal in a new way, but it is different from the time thirty years ago when violent death stalked the nonconformists, the outsiders, the people who were fighting for change.

The prospect of death, the dangers faced, welded us together. We were there, basically, to struggle for black people's access to the seats of power. In order to do that we were forced to fight for seemingly trivial things like the right of blacks and whites to ride in the same taxis, let alone in private cars.

We had a system for keeping tabs on field secretaries—people organizing in local communities in the rural areas. Workers were required to call in to the central office to report activities, harassment, arrests, and above all, their whereabouts. When traveling from one area to another they were required to call in their time of departure and to report on arrival. I was present one sunny afternoon when Rita Schwerner—for whose missing husband an intense search was in progress—reported to a group of us that Chuck McDew, the former SNCC chairman, was overdue for a scheduled arrival in Natchez. The tension was palpable, relieved only when Chuck reported that a flat tire had delayed him.

Experiences like that bound us together. We spoke of ourselves as "a band of sisters and brothers" determined to establish the "beloved community." In a certain sense we did that. But we did something else: we helped people to realize their own potential unafraid to stand up for their rights. We helped scores of people learn how to

organize, and they continue to organize, to fight. Not everything is fine now; people are still struggling, but in a new way.

There is a valuable legacy of the 1960s Movement. It was a catalyst for other movements which followed: the free speech movement, the anti-Vietnam War movement, the women's movement, the gay liberation movement. The Civil Rights Movement did create change. Movement activist Vincent Harding pointed out at Ella Baker's seventy-fifth birthday celebration: "If you don't think that things have changed, then you just don't know what had gone before." He went on to say that we must understand that because of this change "we have to change, change our goals, change our methods, perhaps even change our way of thinking, for the changed situation requires changed attitudes and changed methods."

The Civil Rights Movement changed the conditions. And it altered the relationships. Many black plantation workers were no longer afraid to stand up for their rights. The Movement fostered the development of scores of local black leaders, for example Unita Blackwell, a SNCC worker in the Mississippi Delta who became the mayor of Mayersville, Mississippi, and in 1992 received a MacArthur Foundation "genius" award, and Mae Bertha Carter, of Drew, Mississippi, who, empowered by the Movement, chose to send her seven children to the local all-white school in the Mississippi Delta. Though her family was harassed and deprived of livelihood because of this choice, her children did attend the white school and went on to the University of Mississippi. One of her daughters became a member of the Drew school board.

The fight for empowerment began decades before the Civil Rights Movement of the 1960s and was and is an on-going process. Nevertheless, despite the progress the creation of indigenous leadership represents, there is a long way to go.

Black elected officials came out of the Movement to become sheriffs or members of county boards of supervisors. Such local officials can make a difference—sometimes. Sometimes they cannot. Often the real power remains in the same hands as before: the white plantation owners, or the local factory owners, the bankers, the real estate developers. Many black local officials are the hand-picked choices of the white power establishment and therefore are ineffective.

Innumerable problems remain. In education, for example, the hard-fought battle for integration of the schools has resulted in the flight of white students into private academies leaving the public schools in the South predominately black and poor as is the case in much of the rest of the country. On the economic front poor blacks, particularly in the South, attempted to raise their living standards by establishing producer cooperatives, most of which have failed due to the financial squeeze of the banking establishment and, in some cases, some financial mismanagement.

By 1993 there were over seventy-five hundred African American elected officials in the United States, some of whom had real power.

Yet gains in the political sphere are not reflected in the economic arena. Nearly 33 percent of African Americans still lived below the federally defined poverty level in 1991, compared to 11.3 percent of whites. The income of African American families represented only 57 percent of white family income. Unemployment among blacks was double that of whites. Poverty rates of persons under eighteen was 45.9 percent for blacks as compared to 11.3 percent for whites. Unemployment among black teen-

agers was 36.3 percent as compared to 16.4 percent for whites, according to government statistics. But more to the point, the National Urban League's "hidden" unemployment index which factors in discouraged and involuntary part-time workers showed 57 percent of black teenagers out of work compared to 30 percent of white youths.

Other disparities are even more outrageous. The African American infant mortality rate is more than twice that of whites. Death rates for homicide including killings by law enforcement officers were at 61.1 percent for African Americans and 8.2 percent for whites per one hundred thousand population. And 40 percent of all prisoners on death row are African American.

The figures tell a part, but not the whole story, of the destruction and degradation which racism wreaks on our society. Despite the enormous gains which the Civil Rights Movement of the 1960s made, we must recognize that the goal of racial equality is still far out of our reach.

Note: All statistics (except those for black elected officials which are from the Joint Center for Political Studies, Washington, DC) are from *The State of Black America, 1993,* published by National Urban League, Inc., January, 1993; from statistics of the U.S. Census Bureau; U.S. Department of Labor, Bureau of Labor Statistics; and U.S. Department of Justice, Bureau of Justice Statistics. ❖

James Meredith March, 1966

Marchers on the highway north of Canton, Mississippi.

PHOTOS BY

MATT HERRON

Marchers prepare to erect tent for overnight stay in Canton, Mississippi, school yard. Visible are James Meredith (second from left), Stokely Carmichael (center), and Martin Luther King Jr. (center, wearing dark shirt). Shortly after, they were tear gassed and beaten by Mississippi National Guard.

Marchers reacting to tear gassing by Mississippi National Guard in Canton, Mississippi, school yard.

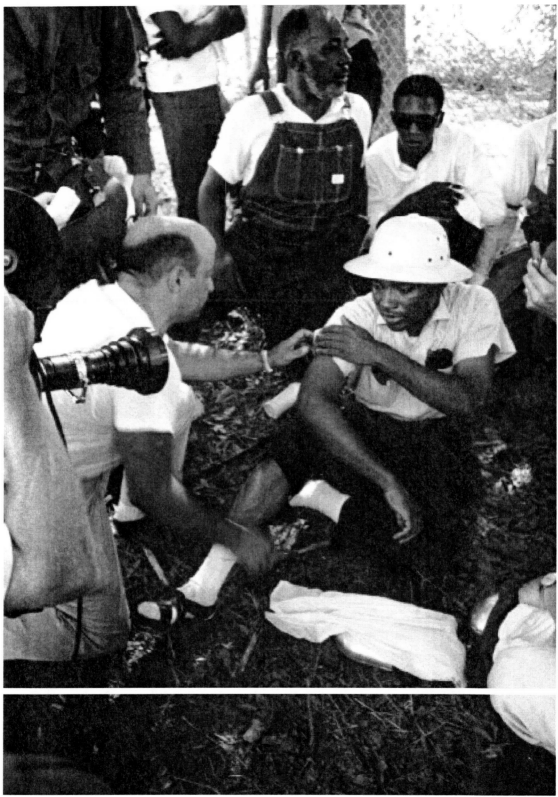

Doctor dresses wounds of James Meredith during roadside rest stop. Action is witnessed and photographed by press.

RITA SCHWERNER BENDER

Comments Upon Twenty-Fifth Anniversary Commemoration At Statuary Hall U.S. Congress, June 23, 1989

We are here today at what has been designated as a commemoration of the anniversary of the murders of three men, but I do not believe that there is much significance in the mere recognition of the twenty-fifth anniversary of their deaths.

This is not to say that J. E.'s family, or Andy's family, or our family has not felt grief—overwhelming at first, quieter with time—at our loss. But many families have suffered personal losses, and they, like us, have gone on with life.

These men were part of a continuum of history. They were not alone in their efforts or their fate. There have been so many participants and too many victims. Medgar Evers, whose labor and commitment brought death for himself, but whose work helped to ensure the changes in Mississippi and America which were destined to occur. Fannie Lou Hamer, who was arrested, beaten, and abused over and over again for daring to demand that blacks in the Mississippi Delta would vote. Victoria Gray and Annie Devine, who ran for Congress on the Missis-

sippi Freedom Democratic Party ticket. John Lewis, Dave Dennis, Bob Moses. And all the brave men and women whose names are not part of the history books but who dared to risk their lives and honor for a most overwhelming and simple concept—all men and all women are born to be free, to live with dignity, respect, and hope.

When my children were little, they repeatedly asked a question which defies answer—why should anyone be mistreated, abused, tossed aside in poverty? Why should anyone suffer beatings or death?

Perhaps because we as a nation have yet to purge ourselves of the cultural and institutional racism which was certainly a part of the fabric of society years ago, but continues to be a part of this country today. I believed at the time, and I continue to believe today, that if all three of the men killed in Neshoba County had been black, the nation would have taken little notice. This is a society which values white lives more.

During the years of the Civil Rights Move-

Rita Schwerner Bender lives with her family in Seattle, Washington where she is an attorney. She was an active participant in the Mississippi Movement and was married to Mickey Schwerner at the time of his murder.

ment, governments brought their power to bear to deny rights—to vote, to education, to jobs, and ultimately to life itself. The preservation of a society of white privilege was deemed so important that police arrested, jailed, and beat men and women who dared to stand in line outside the county registrar's office to register to vote, and the FBI itself engaged in deliberate activities to discredit and destroy the Civil Rights Movement. It cultivated informants and provocateurs, and conducted wiretaps of civil rights workers, while at the same time the president of the United States assured the country that the government would protect the rights of all citizens. And in this climate of institutional racism, violence thrived. And a sheriff and his deputy joined a Klan plot to murder three men—one black, two white—for their involvement in voter registration in Neshoba County. And the world noticed what it should have seen and understood long before.

I've been told that Congress made June 21, 1989, a commemorative day to the three men. Members of Congress are here with us today. The president met with us earlier this morning.

None of this is itself a suitable or fitting memorial to the many men and women who have been part of the struggle for equality. So long as the Justice Department argues before the Supreme Court for a narrowing of the laws whereby discrimination can be recognized and remedied, so long as the Congress and the president fail to commit themselves to the needs of the poor— housing, education, medical assistance—there is no honor shown the civil rights participants. Congress must return to the unfinished business of this country. The president must commit himself to judicial appointments of men and women who understand that the constitutional guarantees of the 13th, 14th, and 15th Amendments cannot be eroded. This society of white privilege must end.

And we too must continue the struggle, looking both outward and within ourselves for the causes and cures.

The backward slide of the last several years must be reversed. The only appropriate honor to the many men and women who have participated in this struggle is its continuation. ❖

CHUDE PAMELA ALLEN

Watching The Iris

It is June and the one iris is blooming. On sunny days I've been sitting outside my door watching the buds form, waiting for them to open. At first I thought there was only one bud growing straight and tall. I urged it along, impatient for the bearded iris to show itself. But slowly I noticed protrusions on the side of the stem. Then there were four buds in various stages of development plus the topmost one in full bloom. I tell myself this is a lesson about patience. If I'd had my way the stalk would have bloomed its one bud and been gone by now. Instead I've had blooms for weeks.

I used to think buds opened slowly, one petal at a time—a ballet in slow motion. But the friend who gave me the bulb says no. She was on retreat once, meditating, and sat before an iris bud. It went "pop," she said, "pop, pop, pop." Little explosions and there was the iris in full bloom.

I've harbored hopes of being here in my chair just as a bud goes "pop." It would be a sign, I think, that I am right to spend time staring at this iris when there is so much to do for the civil rights reunion I'm helping to organize. Twenty-five years ago I was one of a thousand volunteers who went to Mississippi for the summer to assist the Freedom Movement in the struggle to end racism in that bastion of white supremacy. We taught in Freedom Schools, organized community centers, and encouraged people to register to vote. We registered people into the Mississippi Freedom Democratic Party,

the Movement's interracial alternative to the segregated state Democratic Party.

What does an iris have to do with Mississippi and terror and freedom? What does an iris have to do with the pain in my heart, that sense of deep loss that never goes away? How can I explain this need to sit and contemplate a flower?

People say we should be proud of ourselves—those of us who went south in 1964 to work for equality and justice. The younger activists who are helping with the reunion say they envy our having the opportunity to be a part of a movement that changed history.

But when two of us put out the mailing announcing the reunion in the San Francisco Bay Area, I asked my co-worker, who'd also gone south, what he remembered most about that summer. His answer has remained with me. "Terror," he said. "I felt terrified all summer long."

He'd been beaten in a "safer" area of the state where he was working until the leaders felt it was possible to send volunteers into southwest Mississippi, where local people had been killed for working with the Movement. The freedom house in McComb was bombed before he ever got there. He never stopped being frightened.

I'd been sent to a "safer" area. My parents thanked me when I called from the orientation session to tell them of my assignment. This was four days after the three workers disappeared: James Chaney, a local Mississippian, Mickey Schwerner and Andrew Goodman, both New

Chude Pamela Allen (Pam Parker) works part time as an Administrative Assistant. She lives simply, spending the rest of her time writing and leading workshops that focus on political memoir. Chude is interested in the dialectical relationship between personal life and political experience, that is, the integration of the personal and political.

Yorkers—Andy, a volunteer like myself, who arrived in the state the day before he disappeared. "Thank you," my parents said, never mentioning one of their senators had called Dad at work and told him to get me the hell out of there. That was the senator's response to my good Republican father's letter asking for federal protection for us.

"Safe" was a relative term in Mississippi. Last year I read an interview with the man who'd been director of my "safer" project. "Now that was a town," he'd said. "Talk about terror!"

No one was shot in our town. But one black worker was killed in a mysterious car accident, his partner awakening on the pavement with a gun at his head and a cop saying, "Stay real still or you'll get what your buddy got." There were numerous false arrests and car chases, not to mention the night the sheriff in Oxford stopped three carloads of workers leaving a mass meeting and there was almost a riot. He'd stopped them right where a white mob had formed.

That was the same sheriff who'd stopped four of us that afternoon. Another Freedom School teacher and I had hitched a ride with the voter registration workers to Ole Miss. We spoke in a couple of sociology classes about why we northern volunteers had come to Mississippi. The sheriff followed us out of town, held us by the side of the road until a truckload of white men rode up, their rifles prominently displayed on a gun rack. Then admonishing us to tell him if we came to town again so he could be sure we were "protected," he let us go and we flew down the road at ninety miles an hour with the armed men chasing us.

That was one of the "safer" projects, and I still am afraid when I see police. I still have fears of dying in an automobile accident. I still have fears, and I wonder if it is this terror that lingers in my bones that causes me to sit hour upon hour in front of the iris.

I've been reading all the books I can find about the Movement in Mississippi. Horrors have come to my attention I'd never known. I can't understand how people could be as cruel

and sadistic as those racist whites. Beating people in jail—women as well as men. Putting loaded guns to people's heads and playing Russian roulette. One activist said when he couldn't take it anymore, he went back to college in the Midwest and met a white woman he'd known in the South. A sheriff had played Russian roulette with her. She worked at the library as part of her therapy at the mental hospital.

Our project director had had a gun put to his head. He'd been held incommunicado in jail for days with broken ribs from a beating. He had migraine headaches. I learned all this in books I read. I now understand his temper tantrums.

"He has trouble relating to white women," we used to say when he would blow up at the Freedom School teachers. More than once the voter registration guys came home late, tired and dirty, after driving all day on dusty roads and there was nothing in the project to eat. He was right, of course. We who'd been at the project all day teaching in the Freedom School needed to make sure there was food. We all lived on peanut butter sandwiches that summer.

But our director's temper flared all the time—over insignificant things, too. In the interview he said if you couldn't handle the terror you got out. He said you didn't stay if you couldn't take it. But what were the temper tantrums and migraines?

I think about the tensions on our project—the overwork, poor food, and fear. I think of the anxiety that accompanied the workers who drove those back roads wondering when they'd come across some armed "crackers" or be stopped by the police, possibly arrested or "just" subjected to insults or intimidation. I remember the horror when we knew for sure those first three, Goodman, Chaney, and Schwerner, were dead.

At the start of the reunion we want to remember those who died, to begin our program with their names. Some of the planners wanted to read the names off a list; others to let participants call out names spontaneously. The question was would anyone get forgotten if there was no list? Could we trust ourselves to remember everyone? Spontaneity won this time. But the anxiety about forgetting someone created a tension that never went away.

Come to think of it, there's always an anxiety. Will there be enough food? Have we done enough publicity? What if we've missed someone? If the news media is present, will it inhibit dialogue? Do we need to structure workshops or will people talk naturally? Where will we get the money?

At one planning meeting a man who'd come to my project late in the summer of '64 spoke about our inability to mourn the deaths. He said he arrived on our project the day after Wayne Yancey was killed in the car accident. Someone pointed out an empty bed and told him he could have it since the guy had died the day before. That's all he ever heard about this worker.

It wasn't that we didn't care. We were on overload—the accident and then the news that the bodies of the three missing men had been found buried in a dam. I didn't know what else to do but keep on teaching and registering people into the Mississippi Freedom Democratic Party.

I started looking for people with whom to organize a twenty-fifth anniversary reunion because I wanted the human contact. Reading all those books brought everything up, but without any of the human element, the sharing. So far all I seem to have found is other people's hurts and fears to compound my own.

Watching the iris bloom is what keeps me steady and has allowed me to go back week after week to the planning meetings. I need its clarity of purpose and focused energy. It's not easy to break one's covering and burst into bloom. Is that what we're doing with this reunion—trying to burst protective shells that let us get on with our lives? Opening up again to remembering and feeling the pain? I realize it's about timing, not trying to rush things, and trusting that the reunion really will be nourishing, really will move us past the pain.

I'm having a brunch here Sunday, the morning after the reunion. Bob Moses, the man who'd directed the Mississippi Summer Project, said it would be a good idea. People will need an opportunity to share feelings that come up at the reunion, he said. He's had some experience with reunions on the East Coast since he came back from Africa.

It will be the first time I'll have seen him since he stood before us at the orientation the night before we left to go into Mississippi. He said he knew the three were dead, and he didn't know how many more of us would die, but all he could say was he'd be there too. He kept looking at his feet while he talked, and I swear I would have gone anywhere he said.

A woman began singing in the back of the room that night after Bob finished speaking. *"They say that freedom is a constant struggle . . ."* Her voice pulled us from our seats. We stood singing with our arms around each other, not knowing which of us would live, which of us would die. I felt a profound unity and knew it was worth dying for, black and white together—and even a few Latinos and Asians, although back then we thought in terms of black and white.

Black and white together. Only I hadn't bargained on tempers and mistrust; had no idea how hard it would be to keep that sense of loving unity in the face of racist harassment. And I hadn't planned on the Harlem riots that ripped my world apart.

It was the day after the riots and some of us sat out on the grass, Freedom School teachers and voter registration guys. The white volunteers, Northerners, many from New York City, said the violence in Harlem was wrong. The black workers, volunteers too, and some Northerners, said they were glad, it was about time something happened to force America to wake up to racism in the North.

I was horrified, I was devoted to the philosophy of nonviolence. But I'd been in the South longer than the other white volunteers and learned the black workers had a better read on things. I kept silent that afternoon, but the project was polarized. I found it didn't matter that I never condemned the riots. I hadn't supported them. *And* I was white.

It was difficult not to blame myself, as if skin color somehow made me complicit with the racist white cruelty, the overt violence and the deep, deep poverty. I left Mississippi thoroughly ashamed of what white America had created, the disparities of wealth and poverty. And then I saw the opportunism at the Democratic Convention in Atlantic City, where President Lyndon Johnson made sure the white supremacist delegates from Mississippi kept their seats despite clear evidence that the Movement's Mississippi Freedom Democratic Party was the only open and democratic party from Mississippi.

I voted for Johnson anyway that fall, my first time voting. I voted for Johnson because Barry Goldwater, the Republican candidate, said he would bomb Hanoi and President Johnson said he wouldn't. Only Johnson went right ahead and ordered the bombing of North Vietnam and that was enough of electoral politics for me.

The reunion is tomorrow. I'm scared and excited. We all scattered after that summer in Mississippi. There was no coming back together, no closure or evaluation. SNCC, the main group behind the summer project, was moving inexorably towards becoming an all-black organization. The twenty-fifth anniversary is our first major attempt at bringing white volunteers as well as black activists together. There are events on the East Coast as well as here, including in Mississippi where the three were murdered.

I took the day off from work and walked all around the park. I walked in a quiet state noting the last of the rhododendron blooms are falling. Where there's no watering, the grasses have died. Flowers are seeding. Nature is going dormant as the dry season moves into full gear. Now I'm sitting in front of my iris, all its blooms gone except the last. I am sitting and watching and waiting for tomorrow. ❖

CATHY CADE

Mississippi Summer Twenty-five Years Later

A Photo Essay

Introduction:

On June 17, 1989, Mississippi veterans, friends, supporters, and their families convened in Tilden Park in the hills above Berkeley, California, for the West Coast commemoration of the twenty-fifth anniversary of the Mississippi Summer Project. It was an afternoon of talk, singing, and inspiration. Bob Moses, director of the Summer Project, came from Cambridge, Massachusetts, to engage in a discussion with Summer Project participants. We were welcomed by Elizabeth Sutherland Martinez, former SNCC staff person and editor of the book *Letters from Mississippi.* We began by remembering the people who died during or since that summer. Wazir (Willie) Peacock, one of the original SNCC Song Leaders, led us in singing Freedom Songs. The following are photographs from the reunion and selected quotes from the discussion at the early part of the day. For most of the project participants this was the first time to gather since the summer of 1964.

ELIZABETH SUTHERLAND MARTINEZ:

I find it very exciting and significant that this reunion is happening right in the middle of the events in China (the pro-democracy demonstrations). The spirit in resisting repression that we've seen in China of students and people like yourselves when you went to Mississippi, in resisting repression, has been pretty terrific. . . . This gathering tells me that the myth that everybody who was an activist in the sixties has either burned out, dropped out, or copped out simply isn't true.

BOB MOSES:

I always think of Mississippi and the Freedom Summer as it was "damned if you do and damned if you don't." There just wasn't any space to maneuver in there, so we didn't quite get through it whole. We all came out with damaged parts of ourselves. The Movement never really recuperated from that summer, and the price of sort of freeing Mississippi was the destabilization of SNCC. People have weighed, in I don't know how many debates, whether that was worth the price. . . . As many times as I've gone through it, I've never come out in a different place. . . .

There wasn't space enough in the black community to hold the whole. When we got you folks down in those communities with the workers from SNCC and CORE, we couldn't all be in that one little space. So we asked you to go home.

We didn't try in those times to get you together, or to get you to form something out of what that experience was because . . . we didn't see any way to strike a consensus so that you

*Cathy Cade worked with SNCC in Albany and Atlanta, Georgia; North Gulfport, Mississippi; and New Orleans from 1962 to 1964. She has been a lesbian feminist photographer for the last 20 years. Her initial photography lessons were from Bill Light, who had been taught by Matt Herron. She lives in Oakland, California.
Cathy has 2 sons and is working on a photography book about lesbian mothering. Her day job is Administrative Assistant at the Wheeled Mobility Center, which coordinates wheelchair riders/ builders in developing countries.*

could all be together . . . that wouldn't tear people apart. It's taken twenty-five years to feel right about coming together. . . . I hope some kind of healing process can take place within ourselves and maybe we can figure out ways to help each other to begin that.

STEPHEN BINGHAM:

. . . People in Mississippi gave us an incredible part of their lives to create a space so that we could learn and be changed forever from it. It hurts me that white progressives, for all the creative work we do, have not been as able to return that experience and allow people to be comfortable working with us.

CHUDE ALLEN:

I appreciate, Bob, you talking about wounds. I've come to feel that we need to talk to each other from all our perspectives, that none of us will ever know the totality of what happened in Mississippi until we hear each other's stories.

When I was in Mississippi and the South, I learned about love in a way I had never known love before. Somehow in having to break through so many barriers, both personal barriers and the violence and resistance in society, when we did connect, when we did it, it was more meaningful and more powerful than I had ever experienced. I know that people in Holly Springs, Mississippi, greeted me with love. Yet some part of me keeps denying that, saying that can't be true because I am white and I did at times do things that were arrogant and insensitive. You know everybody says in the literature that black women didn't love white women, and white women couldn't love black women. *It wasn't true.* Even though we also had trouble with each other.

FRAN BEAL:

Obviously there was some pain and hurt feelings, but people didn't go home and stick their heads in the ground. They went on and got involved in various things. I can make a link between the women's movement and the anti-war movement and a lot of the women who had

been in SNCC. Remember, McCarthyism had had its grip on the country. The whole concept of nonviolent direct action was seen as against the law. We were saying sometimes there's a morality higher than the law and we are going to take part in making a change. I've tried to pass this on to my kids. The one area where I feel a little bit sad is that it is very difficult to pass on our experience. My kids are black so it keeps them conscious, but they're still not activists in the sense that we are. We have a morality that goes beyond our individual careers, our individual wants. I think a lot of us still have those sentiments no matter what we are doing.

MATT HERRON:

I share the pain, but I think that Mississippi succeeded in ways that none of us could ever possibly imagine at the time. I have pictures of Mario Savio in the backyard of a Freedom House in Holmes County, Mississippi, taking a sitz bath. Nobody had ever heard of Mario Savio (who became one of the leaders of the Student Free Speech Movement, which started at the University of California in Berkeley and swept the country.) I think a lot of the Vietnam War protest grew out of Mississippi. . . .

Mississippi was an incredible moment in history, an opportunity. Some people stepped out of themselves and seized that moment and were able to do something with it. Then history changed and here we are . . . with Reagan and Bush. . . . I just want to say that history is very, very long. It doesn't go on for twenty years, it goes on for thousands of years. In those hard times when there isn't a moment that you can seize and really move things, you've got to sit there and deal with your neighbor. You have got to be who you are and take that sense of wonderful oneness and just live it with the person who's next door to you.

HARDY FRY:

I had the opportunity to go back and study politics in Alabama and Mississippi, in particular in west Alabama. I don't see anything we did as a failure at all. . . . You should go back and see what the difference is. . . . Mississippi has more elected black officials than any state in the union. They might not be governors or senators, but they are officials. . . . There is a way you can cross Alabama to the Mississippi border and you'll never be in a county where the sheriff is not black. . . . I saw a big change.   ❖

Hardy Fry

PHOTO BY
MATT HERRO▮

Chude Allen and Belvie Rooks

PHOTOS BY

CATHY CADE

Bob Moses

Matt Herron

PHOTOS BY

CATHY CADE

*(Left to right) Elizabeth Martinez,
Bob Moses, Wazir (Willie) Peacock,
Stephen Bingham*

BEN MOYNIHAN

Rainbow Babies

Ask us where we come from
Wonder where we've been
Trying to make sense of
This world we live in
We come from Senegal, or out on the Plains
We come from Ecuador, or down by the river
*   Seine*
Rainbow Babies—Shine—
Let everybody see
All the beauty you carry
The beauty of your ancestry

While COFO workers and student volunteers sent waves of change through Mississippi and the rest of the United States of America during that Freedom Summer of 1964, there were many others who would be greatly influenced by those events who were yet to be born. It would be years before these waves would roll onto the shores of the hearts and minds of those of us who were not there. It would be years before I came to know and feel a connection to the people who drove those events. It is this connection that brings me to write these words, and again it is this connection which I seek to understand. My hope is that in sharing my thoughts I can reflect on those events and also address issues that are very much with us today.

I believe that one of the most important things we can do while on this planet is to find out why we're here, how to make ourselves useful, and do this in a context of growing and learning. As an African Rainbow European American adoptee, I am compelled to discover my past history. (The Rainbow for the spectrum of beings that we are, with the infinite potential of each life's expression.) I desire to learn of the past, not to live in it, and to be really alive in the present and meet the future with an open heart and balanced mind.

Looking for a place in the heart
That's what I want to call home
I have been home
and by the grace of the universe
I will be again.
I have strayed
Wandered from my inner child—This inner
*   person I want to be home with—*
Ignored, forgotten, even scorned
But the inner child's patience is longer than
*   the mind's restless inventions*
Even desecration has not altered the depths of
*   the sincere goal*
To be useful to life on-flowing.
The challenge is persistence and,
possibly more importantly,
patience.

I was born on April 29th, 1965, at Grace New Haven Hospital. I lived at the Children's Center in Hamden, Connecticut, near New Haven, until April of 1967, except for one short, unsuccessful placement. I was listed on the state's adoption registry under a "special needs" category, both for my age, almost two by 1967, which was beginning to be old for adoption,

Ben Moynihan lives with Becca Emigh and their two sons, Jaam Jibril and Joshua Tobias, in the Boston area. He works with the Algebra Project, Inc., founded by Bob Moses, participating in the development of an African Drums & Ratios mathematics curriculum for middle school students. He also enjoys playing African Diasporic hand drums and composing songs.

and because of my ethnicity: my birth father is African American and my birth mother is European American. In 1967, a social worker at the Children's Center told my, then prospective, adoptive parents not to tell anyone that my birth parents met while working with the Civil Rights Movement in Mississippi during the summer of 1964.

Ruth and Bill Moynihan wanted to adopt a child, even though they already had six children. Like many people, they wanted to contribute to the healing of the country, but were unable to work directly with the Movement due to prior commitments of family and employment. They decided that by adopting a child, they could help one person, and in turn, our society. At the time, they were interested in adopting a Korean child or an African American child. My parents like to say they decided to adopt me because I had the loudest voice in the place and the nicest smile. I lived with my new family for one year before the adoption was finalized in Hamden Probate Court in May of 1968.

It was a "closed adoption," which means that all "identifying information" was sealed in records kept at the Children's Center, Hamden Probate Court, and the local Catholic Charities branch—who had facilitated my parents' introduction to the Children's Center. This policy of secrecy explains why the original social worker had told my parents not to reveal the information about my birth parents' involvement in the Movement: it rode the border between identifying, truthful information and non-identifying, truth—denying information in this American institution of closed adoption. The identity of my birth parents is sealed from me and my identity is also sealed from them. A reunion can only take place upon mutual consent.

Amazingly however, birth parents and adoptees are not allowed to communicate directly with each other, which makes a reunion quite difficult because they must negotiate this through a social worker who may or may not be in support of a reunion. The Children's Center policy regarding this is such that an adoptee is only allowed to communicate with her/his birth parents by sending letters to her/his own sealed record, which a social worker will then read. If deemed acceptable, through an unrevealed process, the social worker will then write another letter to the birth parents, to be sent through another intermediary such as an alumni office explaining that there is a letter on file from their birth child which could be sent on to them.

It is my intention to one day contact both of my birth parents. The Children's Center has stated that they only have sealed identifying information regarding my birth mother. In 1990, I placed a letter in my file at the Children's Center which was addressed to my birth mother. For a fee, a social worker reviewed my letter and then wrote another letter to my birth mother, informing her that I had written her a letter, which was being held at the Children's Center. My birth mother declined to receive the letter I had written her. Following these results, I asked the social worker for a copy of the letter the Children's Center had drafted to my birth mother—with any identifying information deleted—so that I could ascertain how the Center had presented my intentions to my birth mother. Even though I was charged for the service of contacting my birth mother, the social worker at the Children's Center determined that to send me even an edited copy of their letter would qualify as "identifying information." My request was refused and the Children's Center now considers my case closed.

It seems the interpretation of "identifying information" is left up to the discretion of the social worker handling a particular case. It is clear to me that the laws governing the institution of closed adoption in the state of Connecticut and the United States of America are extremely arbitrary and very likely unconstitutional.

I think there is an information-access issue here, which has moral and constitutional questions tied up in it. Does a human being have a right to know her/his identity? Does a human being have a right to know who her/his birth parents are (particularly after the age of majority)? Can a social worker "objectively" mediate contacts and exchanges of information between birth parents and birth children? Should state-run or privately owned institutions be given the authority to mediate these contacts? Surely, we cannot legislate a required interpersonal relationship between birth parents and their children, but I propose that all people must have the right to be able to choose to know their geneological history. One person's right to privacy must not include erasing the history of another person. Currently, this situation is a very real part of the lives of many Americans and their families, and I think there should be an open debate about this.

The weight of the denial of rights and opportunities to citizens in the present and the past United States of America hinders hopes of building for the future. We are no longer in a position to wait for a "nationally recognized" leader to tell us how to work for change. The challenge remains: how do we create environments in which we support every individual's development and participation in the rights and responsibilities of living in our country and on the planet.

To my birth parents: Sometimes I wonder what I would tell you if I ever were to meet you. Thoughts fill and crowd my mind. What would be of interest to you? What would let you know who I am, what I feel, where my interests lie? How do you talk to people you have thought about all your life but have yet to meet? I want you to know that I am not trying to recover time passed, or a family situation or relationship that wasn't to be. Besides, I have my own family now. I would like information, understanding, and if possible, an opportunity at getting to know who you are now and who you were thirty years ago. I would like to say it's okay, we're okay. Love, Forgiveness, and Healing. Whether our paths ever meet or not, I will continue on my way, trying to keep my eyes open.

To Rainbow People reading this: What have I learned since I began this search and study of the Movement? Examples of lives which keep

singing despite every obstacle. That it will be better if we light our lights and work together for positive change. That to work for change together we must make commitments to develop and explore our own potential. I ask myself, what is America? This nation whose foundations have been built on stolen land, unfree people, and contradictory idealism. Amidst this odd mixture I am learning of people still living, breathing, and working among us today that are committed to realizing our proclaimed democracy by developing situations for all individuals to light their lights, whether in a mathematics classroom, a city hall, a voting booth, or their own homes.

Cycles of Freedom Summer waves continue to roll in on heartshores around the globe; waves now also flow back again into the ocean. . . .

Postscript:

Since I have written my reflections above, I have contacted my birthparents. And, in a twist of fate, it turns out that my birthparents were not involved in the '64 Summer Project in Mississippi, contrary to what I had been told while growing up. Instead, they were involved in a Goodwill summer camp for disadvantaged, inner-city children from Boston during that same summer.

There were some aspects of my parents' situation that were similar to that of the Summer Project, such as an interracial effort during the summer of '64 to improve the lives of others; moments at the camp when race became less of a primary issue for the workers as their striving together for change echoed the "freedom high" I've read about in some history books about the Movement; and other struggles waiting after that summer was over. So much was different in Massachusetts from the experience in Mississippi in '64—as witnessed by the testimonies in this anthology. Yet in learning the story of my parents' lives since that time, I am struck by the similarities. . . . I am grateful to know my birthparents, and I recommend this highly to anyone who has considered searching. Knowing your soil and roots can help you grow whole and healthy.

I feel fortunate to have connected with the people that were part of SNCC. I am thankful to all those who encouraged me along the way, in particular to Bob Moses and Chude Pam Allen. I have heard about aspects of the Summer Project that never made it into the history books; both those which confirm it as a high water mark in recent human history and those told through anecdotes which help de-mystify it for me. In Senegal the people have a proverb that says "when an old person dies, it is like a library burning." Perhaps one of the greatest gifts that SNCC staff and volunteers give now is a balanced telling of their experiences in the '60s. May those with ears listen well. ❖

CONSTANCE SLAUGHTER-HARVEY

WITH CHRIS GILMER

To Endure or to Prevail: The Human Rights Question for Our Generation and Beyond

Constance Iona Slaughter-Harvey is a Mississippi African American female, mother, sister, daughter, attorney, Assistant Secretary of State and General Counsel, Girl Scout Troop Leader, Boy Scout Scoutmaster, and Tougaloo College adjunct professor. She recounts painful memories and experiences in connection with her college graduation and her first major civil rights wrongful litigation. Her dedication and commitment to her daughter Constance Olivia Harvey and to the Mississippi youths are reflected in the article where she struggles to determine if African Americans will endure or survive.

Are we doing for the next generation what our parents did for us? It is a question formed of simple words, but only the words are simple. The implications are complex and far reaching, stretching from the white sand coastlines of tribal Africa to the cotton plantations of the old South, from the graveyards where lie the bodies of those who died because they spoke to a white woman or dared to defend a black child, to the shores of the Potomac, where all races of Americans now work to forge a new world order, and from the automobile plants of Detroit to the classrooms of Tougaloo College and the University of Mississippi. The question deserves an honest answer, and though honesty sometimes causes pain, our people—all people—can no longer afford the luxury of self-deceit. The truth hurts less in the long run.

It is a short distance in miles from the rural Scott County, Mississippi, community of my youth to the Heber Ladner State Office Building in Jackson, Mississippi, where I sit behind my desk today in a corner office overlooking the state capitol—a short distance in miles, but a lifetime journey walking uphill for my spirit and for the generations now at rest who gave

me sustenance for the trip. I often muse about the real progress which this state and nation has made during the last decades in delivering on the promise that we are all created equal, but almost without exception my reverie is interrupted by a chorus chanting in my mind the question which must be answered—are we doing for the next generation what our parents did for us, or are we resting on their laurels which we have come to think of as our own?

My sisters and I are known to many simply as the Six Cees, because my parents had six daughters and gave all of us names which start with the letter "C." That was our earliest "claim to fame" in the small town of Forest, where my parents, W. L. and Olivia Slaughter, were educators and merchants. My father would later become Forest's first African American elected official, elected to two terms as alderman against a popular white opponent. My mother, after her own children were reared to her satisfaction and my father preceded her in death, gave her life to founding the W. L. Slaughter Memorial Library, where she combined her great loves for children and for learning. I write of my beginning because wherever I end will be directly related to it, and I cannot plot my future without recalling my past—a past profoundly shaped by two parents who taught me, first and foremost, to be true to myself and my ideals.

Daddy taught me to fight for what is right with my head, my heart, my voice, and my body, and during the turbulent years which followed my upbringing I did all of this. Mama taught me that, on some occasions, it is better to speak softly than to shout. Even when we whisper, there can be strength and passion in what we say. Her lessons took me longer to learn, but they have also served me well. I sometimes think that Daddy's fire got me into the courtroom and later the halls of state government, but it has been Mama's diplomacy which has kept me here.

In 1963, I graduated as valedictorian from E. T. Hawkins High School, a segregated school at that time, which now serves as the integrated junior high school for the Forest Municipal School District. My daughter, Constance Olivia Harvey, is now a graduate of this school, but I think that her years spent there as an equal with African American and Caucasian friends were much different from my own.

From Forest, where I witnessed my first racial injustice but was somewhat sheltered from it, I journeyed to Tougaloo College in 1963, where I met Medgar Evers six days before his life was abruptly ended in its prime. During six days which I now think were pivotal in my life, I heard him say what my parents had been saying all of my life—right is right. There may be a double standard for justice, but there is a single definition. He was committed and compassionate, and I would have followed him almost anywhere. Medgar Evers felt what he was saying; there was no show, no quest for glory. When he spoke, we saw directly into his soul. It was really that simple. Six days after I met him, I participated in the Medgar Evers funeral march; in November of that same year, President John F. Kennedy was assassinated. My freshman year was one during which the philosophy of "We Shall Overcome" was shaken and tested—and finally burned indelibly into the fabric of my spirit.

If 1963 was the defining year of my adulthood, then I would have to say that 1967 and 1970 were the most disheartening years for a proud, young African American woman who still experiences great pain reliving those years, even though more than two decades have passed. This is my first public account of that period. After completing requirements for graduation at Tougaloo and being accepted to the University of Mississippi School of Law, I was denied the right to take part in the 1967 Tougaloo College graduation ceremony, though I was eventually awarded my diploma in 1976. As president of the Tougaloo student body, I had arranged for a group of students to be transported by professors in their cars to a rally in downtown Jackson in support of the student body at Jackson State College, now Jackson State University.

Tougaloo is a private, historically African American college, and Jackson State is Mississippi's largest state-supported historically African American university. This was during a time when some older African American educational leaders thought it better to "soft peddle civil rights," as one would later tell my father, but many of my generation did not have it within us to soft peddle. I had arranged for the professors to transport us back to the college, but the Jackson chief of police threatened to arrest all of us if we were not off the streets before 6 P.M. The curfew imposed did not correspond with the transportation schedule planned, so another student and I took the Tougaloo College bus after we were denied emergency use of the bus by Tougaloo's transportation manager. When the bus loaded with students pulled up to the Tougaloo gate, my heart sank. The college president was personally blocking the entrance, and he demanded that all of the students file off of the bus. I refused to comply because I knew that all of the students would be penalized for taking part in the protest, so we drove through the gate to the back of the campus and allowed the students to get off of the bus without their identity being known. One African

American man, Benjamin Brown, had been killed at Jackson State by a highway patrolman that day in what I considered an officially sanctioned act of murder. Two of our identities the president knew very well. I was the first. The second was the driver of the bus. His name was Bennie Thompson, and he currently serves as the second African American elected since Reconstruction to the U.S. House of Representatives from Mississippi. After being told that I would not graduate, the college—because of student support of my plight—finally allowed me to graduate without marching. I was devastated because I could not understand the actions and behaviors of some of my own leaders, those to whom I had entrusted my educational future. In 1970, after what I and many others consider the Jackson State massacre, the university administration would again make the attempt to muzzle me and construct obstacles preventing effective representation of my clients. I was hurt by their actions to impede my efforts, but I was more hurt by their inaction which, in my mind, reflected their lack of outrage over the killings.

When the incident at Tougaloo occurred, I was just a college student. I had no degrees, no credentials, not even a complete grasp of my own civil rights, but when the young men were killed at Jackson State I came back armed with a law degree. It was my intention to fight my battles with dignity in the courtroom instead of taking to the streets, which I considered my only option in 1967, but the university officials issued an order that I was to be barred from campus. Even though I was the legal representative for the families of the two male students killed at Jackson State, a federal court order had to be obtained for me to enter the campus and review the evidence at Alexander Hall, sight of the barrage of gunfire that resulted in the deaths of Phillip Gibbs and James Earl Green and the wounding of at least ten others. Phillip Gibbs was a twenty-year-old junior from the small Mississippi town of Ripley, and James Earl Green was a seventeen-year-old high school student from Jackson who made the innocent, but fatal,

decision to cut through campus on his way home from work. At one point during my investigation, I was even intimidated by being placed in a police car and threatened with arrest, a frightening experience indeed for any person of color at that time, but I persevered and overcame this obstacle in filing the lawsuit Burton vs. Williams on behalf of Mrs. Myrtle Burton, the mother of James Earl Green, and Mrs. Dale Gibbs, the widow of Phillip Gibbs. The name "Williams" refers to one of the defendants, the former segregationist Governor John Bell Williams. When we lost the trial in federal court in 1972, I was saddened, but not surprised. When my own people stood in my way of winning, however, it pierced my heart just as the incident at Tougaloo had done. Many other events in my legal career have made me very angry, but few have made me cry. Over this, I shed tears—tears for a society which would officially sanction murder and tears for those of my own race who refused to call it what it was.

In retrospect, I judge that these events strengthened me, for I became adamantly determined that no other student would feel my sense of betrayal. I also know now that, had certain actions been explained to me, I would not have agreed at that time as I do not agree today; however, knowing why they acted as they acted would have greatly lessened my pain. A person can agree to disagree peacefully when she knows what page another person is on, but neither of these educators—both of whom did a great deal of good for their respective institutions—bothered to even tell me from what book we were reading. From those experiences which gave me purpose, I also learned that communication is one of the most important gifts which we can share with our children. We must always take time to tell our children why.

Since those painful days, I have put these incidents behind me and forged many fond memories at Tougaloo, where I have served as an adjunct faculty member free of charge for more than twenty years and where I now serve as a member of the board of trustees. I have also witnessed great progress at Jackson State. Shortly before my mother died in 1991, I took part in the graduation ceremony of Tougaloo College at her request. Both she and my father are buried in the cemetery at Tougaloo College, an alma mater which they revered as something larger than themselves or any person. What a reward it has been over the years to watch the successes of such former students as Denise Sweet-Owens, who is now Hinds County Chancellor, and Robert Gibbs, who is now Hinds County Circuit Judge, accomplishments that African Americans could only have dreamed of when I was the first African American woman to graduate from the University of Mississippi School of Law in 1970. In later years, my mother confided to a friend that during my law school days she feared greatly for my life. In retrospect, I know that her fears were not unfounded. I kept a rebel flag as my doormat and never ran away from a confrontation. Indeed, my pride and my hope for a better world often led me to seek confrontations, such as when our protests forced the Ole Miss campus to be closed in 1968 after Dr. Martin Luther King, Jr., was assassinated.

I learned a great deal very quickly during my years (1970–1972) with the Lawyers Committee for Civil Rights Under Law (LCCRUL) and my years of private practice (1972–1978) that began with my first trial in Simpson County, during which I did not even know to stand when the judge entered the courtroom; through Burton vs. Williams and a discrimination lawsuit, Morrow vs. Crisler, which ultimately desegregated the Mississippi Highway Safety Patrol. In 1979, I became deputy director and then director of East Mississippi Legal Services, working out of the Forest and Meridian offices. In 1980, former Governor William Winter appointed me to serve as executive director of the Governor's Office of Human Development, and in 1984 incoming Secretary of State Dick Molpus appointed me assistant secretary of state for Lands and Elections. That appointment was significant to me for many reasons, not the least of which was the fact that in 1979, during an open house

at East Mississippi Legal Services in Forest, Dick Molpus had been the only white business person to attend. He did not even live in Forest, but he did live in adjoining Neshoba County and worked nearby in the city of Morton. Even then, well before Dick entered the political arena, he was already a strong proponent of quality public education for all children. His wife, Sally, was a teacher in the Scott County public school system, and they encouraged white parents to keep their children in the public schools. Since joining Dick in the secretary of state's office, my title has changed to assistant secretary of state for Elections and General Counsel, and I have had the opportunity not only to take part in the government of my home state, but also to serve on the national level as president of the National Association of State Election Directors.

I believe that the most gratifying progress of which I have been a part, possibly because I have been able to see it evolve with my own eyes, has occurred in my home state, where we currently have African Americans serving in these elected offices: 1 representative in the U.S. Congress from Mississippi, 1 supreme court justice, 8 chancery and circuit court judges, 32 members of the House of Representatives, 10 senators, 8 sheriffs, 6 circuit clerks, 3 chancery clerks, 5 tax assessors and/or collectors, 6 coroners, 11 superintendents of education, 2 county attorneys, 1 surveyor, 85 supervisors, 32 justice court judges, 39 constables, 85 election commissioners, 103 school board members, 39 mayors, and 399 alderpersons. That translates into 1 federal official, 49 state officials, 388 county officials, and 438 municipal officials for a total of 876 African Americans serving in elected office in Mississippi alone, the state which prior to the Voting Rights Act of 1965 had the worst record of minority registration and voting, and as recently as 1970 had only one African American legislator. In 1992, the total number of African American elected officials in the state was 826, so our progress appears to be consistent.

The statistics for women are not quite as gratifying, but we have indeed come a long way.

In Mississippi, we currently have women serving in these elected offices: 1 supreme court justice, 4 senators, 15 representatives, 1 district attorney, 6 chancery, circuit and county court judges, 67 chancery or circuit clerks, 10 coroners, 2 constables, 3 county attorneys, 74 county school board members, 152 election commissioners, 34 justice court judges, 3 superintendents of education, 7 supervisors, 37 tax assessors and/or collectors, 33 mayors, and 278 alderwomen. That translates into 20 state officials, 7 district/county officials, 389 county officials, and 311 municipal officials for a total of 727 female elected officials, up from 706 in 1992. Of course, quite a few of the African American and female office holders overlap, and to those special people—my sisters who are overcoming both racial and sexual prejudice—I offer my highest praise. Indeed, the people of my home state have much of which we can be proud. Nonetheless, I keep my desk turned away from the picture window in my office which overlooks the capitol, not because the breathtaking view keeps me from concentrating on my work, but instead because my still unrealized expectations of those elected to serve in that building, coupled with scars from my many battles there, make me sad when I dwell on them for too long. But from time to time I turn around for a brief reminder to fuel my determination and direct my sense of hope. I do indeed have great hope.

Many people—black and white, female and male, young and old—have influenced my life for the better, but two particular role models come to mind. The lives of the late Fannie Lou Hamer, a civil rights leader whose voice rang out across America from the cotton fields of Mississippi, a leader in the voting rights movement who helped found the historic Mississippi Freedom Democratic Party (MFDP), and Dr. Johnnetta B. Cole, noted anthropologist and current president of Spellman College in Atlanta, have quietly yet firmly inspired what has become my primary mission—helping others, particularly our young people, to live up to their individual potentials. General Colin L. Powell, re-

tiring chairman of the Joint Chiefs of Staff, captured their words and actions when he recently said: "As we climbed on the backs of others, so must we allow our backs to be used for others to go even higher than we have." Although I am unclear as to where he fits into the political landscape, General Powell knows what he is talking about, because he climbed on the backs of several generations of civil rights leaders to become the first African American named to the military's most prominent post. It is again time for all of us to bare our backs and bend down. We must teach our children that I is a word which has worth, but that we is a pearl of even greater price. To teach any lesson, we must first learn it. We must accept that I is not an end unto itself, but a valuable, indeed intrinsic, part of we—we being African Americans, we being women, and finally we being the entire family of people. I have joined hands and sung "We Shall Overcome"—black hands and white hands, male hands and female hands—but We shall overcome is not the same as We have overcome. That is a song the time for which has not yet arrived, though some of us are mistakenly trying to sing it now. There are too many vines left to tend in too many vineyards, and we must all own the problems which continue to plague our society—the increasing availability and use of drugs, a faltering educational system, teenage pregnancy, inadequate health care and child care for a staggering block of the population, violence which knows no racial, geographic, or socioeconomic boundaries, black-on-black crime, and the continuing, abhorrent discrimination against and disenfranchisement of women and people of color.

One of my sisters gave me a plaque which simply says, "Some leaders are born women." It now hangs on the wall in my office, and it reminds me of an important lesson learned long ago. Prejudice is a word with many definitions, all of them heinous. It does not necessarily involve white people hating and persecuting black people. In many ways, some large and others rendered large by their cumulative weight, our society has conspired to deny women the right to know our self-worth and plot our self-direction. Women are not a minority group in sheer numbers, but we have always been and still are a minority group when judged by political, educational, and economic standards. As surely as African Americans, Native Americans, Latinos, and other minority groups have been treated and judged with prejudice, so have women of all races. I cannot begin to count the times when I have been the only woman working in a group of men. They simply say, "But Connie, you are the exception." I no longer wish to be regarded as an exception, but rather as a part of the rule. Esteemed American poet Maya Angelou once told someone who had just finished introducing her not to label her the foremost African American woman poet in America, but simply to think of her as a good poet. That must be our battle cry as women continue the long march toward our own version of civil rights.

Until we all own the problems of our society, we cannot truly work to solve them; and if we are not part of the solutions, then ultimately we become part of the problems. We must renounce immediate gratification and await our rewards in the form of meaningful progress in the lives of our children and even more meaningful progress in the lives of our grandchildren. The fact that we acquire a Mercedes-Benz and a country home will not even make it into our obituary, but what a legacy to leave my daughter's children if their only exposure to prejudice comes as a history lesson or a vocabulary word. Our generation must work, so that their generation can breathe easier. Our sins of omission could prove as dangerous to our posterity as the sins of commission committed against us which comprise so much of our past.

Nobel laureate William Faulkner, hardly considered progressive when it came to depicting African Americans and women in his work, nonetheless made a statement in one of his many speeches which is equally challenging for all humanity. Faulkner said that mankind will not only endure, but that it will also prevail. There are those who would say that endurance is an end unto itself, that in fact enduring is a form of prevailing. While that may be true to a degree, we must not be satisfied with endurance alone because with that resignation comes our worst enemy—complacency. We dishonor the memory of those who died giving women and African Americans the right to vote when we do not go to the polls; we dishonor those who bravely refused to ride in the backs of the buses when we see injustices around us and turn our heads in an attempt to preserve what we perceive as harmony. We must continue to live the dream of "We Shall Overcome" while working toward the goal of "We Have Overcome." When we can all sing the latter chorus together in perfect harmony, then alone will we have prevailed.

I prepare to leave you with some words from American poet Robert Frost taken from "Stopping By Woods on a Snowy Evening." This is a favorite quotation of Dr. Aaron Henry who has diligently and wisely served as president of the Mississippi State Conference of the National Association for the Advancement of Colored People (NAACP) for more than twenty-five years. Dr. Henry is a Mississippi state legislator, and he was a close friend of Medgar Evers. We would all do well to heed these words. Frost writes: "The woods are lovely, dark, and deep, but I have promises to keep, and miles to go before I sleep, and miles to go before I sleep." What we have accomplished is indeed much more than lovely. It is real, lasting, and abiding. It will be here to tell our story when we are gone, but the challenges, the unrealized potential, the unrighted wrongs, are dark and deep. I believe that, if left unmet, the challenges which remain could one day overtake the good to which my parents and their parents dedicated their lives. I am unwilling to stand idly by and watch that happen, and I hope that my sisters and brothers of all races will join me in moving forward. We cannot tread water for long; either we swim, or we drown. If we drown, our foremothers and forefathers sink with us. That is why I have promises to keep—promises to my child, bonds with my parents, commitments to generations of slaves, pacts with my sisters who are just now learning to use the voices we are rediscovering, and a covenant between my Creator and myself not to waste what I have been given. That is why I have miles to go before I sleep. ❖

PHOTOS BY

MATT HERRON

Girls dormitory window showing police bullet holes and spectators outside on street after Jackson police and Mississippi highway patrolmen fired on a crowd of black students at Jackson State College, 1970.

Sign scrawled on stairway wall of girls' dormitory at Jackson State College after the shootings, 1970.

ACIE BYRD, JR.

Mississippi—USA A Special Case for the Tolerance of Apartheid and Fascism in a Constitutional Democracy

Political analyst Acie L. Byrd, Jr., specializes in African American politics, American government, and the political economy. Acie has a B.A. in Economics and African American Studies from the University of Maryland and graduate degrees in Political Science from Howard University. Currently, he works as a political analyst and consultant on a range of issues, including civil rights, peace, electoral politics, international affairs, and African American politics. Acie was appointed Chair of the Nuclear Weapons Freeze Commission of the District of Columbia. He also served as Deputy Mobilization Director for the 30th Anniversary Civil Rights March on Washington in August, 1993. Acie participated in numerous presidential, gubernatorial, mayoral, and senatorial campaigns. In 1994, he served as Deputy Field Coordinator against VA senatorial candidate Oliver North. He frequently is called upon by the media for his analysis on current affairs.

Introduction

The Preamble to the Constitution of the United States:

> *We the people of the United States, in order to form a more perfect union, establish justice, insure domestic tranquility, provide for the common defense, promote the general welfare, and secure the blessing of liberty to ourselves and our posterity, do ordain and establish this constitution for the United States of America.[1]*

The aim of this paper is to outline a brief frame work for future public debate by activists and scholars on the need to liberate our constitutional democracy from the "devil of racism" and all forms of human exploitation. This brief outline is drawn from the experiences of activists, scholars, and legal experts, in addition to the Nuremberg trials of 1946, the World War II experience, and the Civil Rights Movement for democracy during the 1960s, and the present.

I believe that others who are participating in this work will provide a penetrating and insightful view, which will guide us all in our common struggle to elevate the standard for a progressive human kind. My role here is to attempt to place Mississippi in a historical context. May I congratulate Susie Erenrich for undertaking this historic task, and Angelia Smith for her administrative support to me in this endeavor.

The Roots of White Supremacy Governance in the United States

The core foundation of the violent history of Mississippi and other Southern states, as it relates to African Americans, is rooted in the socio-political history of the U.S. itself.[2] Its legacy derived from the formation of the U.S. as a colony, the revolutionary establishment of the nation-state, and the constitutional structure designed in 1787 which "proclaimed the rule of law" as the foundation of governance for the new republic of the U.S.

Dr. Mary Francis Berry, preeminent constitutional scholar and historian, argues in her works *Black Resistance White Law* and *History of Constitution Racism in America* that:

"Constitutionally sanctioned violence against blacks and violent suppression of the black resistance [is] the outgrowth of a government policy based on essentially racist, not legal, concerns throughout the American experience.

"Black people have been a disquieting presence in America since the arrival of the first twenty Africans at Jamestown in 1619. To most blacks, their status, usually as slaves until 1865 and as second class citizens thereafter, has been unacceptable; to some it has been intolerable. Before 1865, in addition to aiding in the suppression of slave revolts, the national government ignored or approved—on constitutional grounds—white mob violence directed at blacks and their few white supporters even when local officials participated in the violence. Those blacks who did not become involved in conspiracy and rebellion before the Civil War were not necessarily 'docile'; they lived in the grip of a system of violent control institutionalized under the Constitution. The years since Reconstruction, when blacks became nominally free, are littered with incidences of white riots against blacks, burning of black homes and churches, and lynchings, while federal and local law enforcement agencies stood idly by."[3]

Hence the early colonial period saw the seeds being sown for what Dr. Berry describes as "the foundation of repression" of the African American. She argues that "the colonialists' principle instrument of slave control was the local militia."[4] The establishment of the colonies demanded it to be revived as the primary military organization in America, clearly institutionalizing violent repression as the method by which the behavior of blacks was to be regulated. Further established was the importance of slavery to the economic interest of the British crown and the royal governing class during the period of British rule over the colonies in America. The American slave holders, even after British colonialism ended in 1776, continued the violent and legal repressive tradition embraced by their colonial masters. The British colonialist, in recognition of the economic boon of slavery, established "a body of customs, radical sanctions, and statutory laws evolved to institutionalize the system. Slavery was officially recognized as an institution in colonial laws by the 1660s. In 1697, the British parliament expressed the view that blacks were property of great value to the kingdom, and ten members of the Court of the King's Bench agreed that slaves were merchandise—that could be regulated under the Navigation Act."[5]

The continuation of the legacy of violent control of African slaves received no relief with the Declaration of Independence from British colonial rule in America in 1776, nor at the founding Congress on September 29, 1789.

"In the second Congress, a bill was passed on May 2, 1792, which provided that the state militias could be called out to execute the laws of the 'union,' suppress 'insurrections,' and repel invasions. Thus granting the president power to federalize the state militias, and suppress domestic violence. . . ."[6] This, of course, included slave uprisings.

This fact illustrates the legal basis for the national government to use its powers to control slavery. Dr. Berry states that "these debates lend credence to the view that the Southern states would not have ratified the Constitution without the pro-slavery compromises." The Fugitive Slave Clause and the commitment of the national government to protect slavery, but not to interfere with it, were indispensable parts of the Constitution."[7]

The role of the national government clearly reveals the complicity and tolerance for the repression and economic exploitation of African-Americans from the time of their arrival in 1619 to the present day. Berry noted "from 1877–1957 federal troops or marshals were not used to prevent pre-advertised lynchings or other kinds of violence directed against African Americans when state officials refused them protection."[8]

Mississippi—United States of America

"On April 17, 1963, the U.S. Civil Rights Commission [USCRC] expressed alarm at the open and flagrant violation of constitutional guarantees in Mississippi which precipitated serious conflict; [which on several occasions] has reached the point of crisis. The [USCRC] has become increasingly alarmed at the defiance of the Constitution. Each week brings fresh evidence of the danger. A complete breakdown of law and order, citizens of the U.S. have been shot, set upon by vicious dogs, beaten, and otherwise terrorized because they sought to vote."[9]

The USCRC report cited above reflects what most regarded in a historic context as a page in Mississippi's violent and ruthless history. It is important to note that while the U.S. was openly fighting fascism abroad, it long tolerated and permitted its own subordinate jurisdictions to function as "outlaw states." These states, Mississippi among them, were ruled by an oligarchical elite, in open defiance of U.S. and international laws.

Mississippi is acknowledged by most observers to be one of the most violent and barbaric states in the union. However, it is my contention that Mississippi cannot be separated from its socio-historical origins—the United States society itself. Nevertheless, because of its violence prone oligarchy and its strict ideology of theocratic white supremacy, along with the super-exploitative nature of its economy, it presents a unique picture of America at its worse.

Mississippi's means of governance was more akin to the apartheid system of oppression in South Africa and the fascist system in Hitler's Nazi Germany. There are significantly similar political elements in all three systems and the U.S. government's policy relationship to them all.

Author Frank Parker argues that the "Mississippi white supremacy machinery was warned by Mississippi's leading newspaper, the *Jackson*

Clarion Ledger (the ideological organ for white supremacy) to "take a serious look at the racial composition of the state's congressional districts in view of the NAACP's vigorous drive for negro voting rights."[10]

Parker further stated that "from 1966–1982, the Mississippi legislature gerrymandered Mississippi's five congressional districts to prevent the election of a black member of Congress by dividing the predominately black Delta region among three of the five districts, denying black voters a majority district."[11] To demonstrate the ability of Mississippi's ruling oligarchy to dominate and oppress African Americans in the political, economic, and social spheres, "almost half of Mississippi's eighty-two counties were gerrymandered in order to dilute the black voting strength and to prevent the election of black county officials. Most of these vote dilution strategies were products of the 1966 regular and special sessions of the Mississippi legislature, referred to as the massive resistance session."[12]

The dynamics of slavery, race, and economic exploitation have shaped Mississippi's socio-economic life. Historically, the systematic use of brutal tactics including murder, rape, forced eviction, and fire burning have all been utilized by the Mississippi ruling oligarchy to maintain power.

There is profound prima facie evidence of the alienation of Mississippi's violent oligarchy from the Constitution and the principles governing the U.S. society: the brutal and savage killing of Emmett Till for the alleged advance toward a white female; the barbaric assassination of Andrew Goodman, Michael Schwerner, and James Chaney; and the brutal murder of one of the United States' most patriotic heroes. This was a patriot who had gone to war on behalf of the U.S. to protect the territorial integrity of the nation, to defend the world against Adolph Hitler's Nazi's and the Fascist take over of Europe; a patriot who fought and risked his life for his home state of Mississippi. But this patriot was murdered for struggling to secure democracy and justice in his own country, for fighting against tyranny, fascism, and racism, and endeavoring to establish the rule of law in his home state of Mississippi. That American patriot is Medgar Wiley Evers. His legacy must be kept in the present for generations to emulate down through the centuries. Justice will demand no less for the United States and the world.

Ms. Myrlie Evers is yet another bold and courageous freedom fighter, patriot, a daughter of Mississippi, and the wife of Medgar Evers, who led a gallant and unequaled thirty year struggle to "instill justice on the soil of Mississippi" and to honor the legacy she and Medgar Evers sacrificed and built for the cause of democracy and justice in America. Ms. Evers said "that the last book which Medgar was seeking to complete was *Mein Kampf,* the autobiography of Adolf Hitler, in order to gain insight and develop strategies to dismantle that evil from Mississippi for the nation." What a profound irony.

Nazi Germany was a racist and barbaric political oligarchy whose ideology and purpose was to establish a world order based upon ranking the whole of human kind according to race by making all races and ethnic groups subordinate to the "pure Germanic stock." The Nazi regime was responsible for the murder of over fifty million people, for squandering vast quantities of human resources such as houses, farms, art works, rails, bridges, cities, and technologically developed projects, thereby disrupting the cultural life of millions of human beings. The emergence of Nazi Germany on the world stage represented a barbaric and backward step for human civilization. Medgar Evers returned to Mississippi, only to find a smaller but determined barbaric oligarchy, equally as racist, as violent, as anti-human as the one he helped to defeat in Nazi Germany.

Mississippi's ruling oligarchy has its roots anchored in the slavery system. The slave holding class formed the ruling elite in the old Southern Confederate states. Even though the slave holding insurrections, through the Civil War,

were decisively defeated in their attempts to overthrow the U.S. government and to establish a slavocracy government, they nevertheless found a way of reentry into U.S. society with renewed respect and a minimum degree of punishment for their armed aggression against the people of the United States and their duly established constitutional government. One glaring example is that the leader of the rebellion and president of the Confederacy, Jefferson Davis, was never tried for treason against the United States. This is a factor which plagues United States society today, with the continuing legacy of racism directed against African Americans and other persons of color, notwithstanding the impact this great historic phenomenon had on the functions of U.S. democracy! For example, Reconstruction after the Civil War (1866–1877) resulted in the Hays-Tildmen compromise, which prematurely withdrew federal troops from the rebellious and treasonous Confederate states. This infamous decision was made with the full knowledge that the flood gates would be opened to massive and brutal repression against African Americans, who risked life and limb with profound sacrifice and courage, who gave their lives to free themselves and the nation from the shackles of slavery and to "insure domestic tranquility, provide for the common defence," all for the preservation of a unified nation, and most of all the preservation of the "rule of constitutional law."

As president, Abraham Lincoln declared that without African American participation, the war could not have been won. Fellow Americans, regardless of race, creed, or color need only to ask one fundamental question to appreciate the magnitude of the sacrifice by African Americans during the Civil War: What would the nation be like if Lincoln had lost the war? The consequences would have been (a) the Bill of Rights nullified; (b) the Constitution nullified; (c) white men without property disenfranchised; (d) white women's suffrage would not have been possible; (e) black men and women continued in enslavement; (f) Jewish Americans continuously oppressed; (g) other persons of color most likely enslaved or in subservient conditions. The aim of the slave holders was to extend slavery, not to abolish it.

President Lincoln said on August 26, 1863, "some of the commanders of our armies in the field who have given us our most important successes believe the emancipation policy and the use of colored troops constituted the heaviest blow yet dealt to the rebellion. . . . You say you will not fight to free Negroes, some of them seem willing to fight for you. . . . There will be some black men who can remember that, with a silent and clenched teeth, and steady eyes, and well poised bayonet, they have helped mankind on to this great consummation; while I fear there will be some white ones unable to forget that with malignant heart and deceitful speech, they have strove to hinder it."[13]

Two hundred eighteen years after the Declaration of Independence, we can still experience both state and national government sanctioned violence directed against African Americans. One need only look at the estimated forty-eight thousand police brutality cases against African Americans pending in the Justice Department awaiting resolution and the fact that African Americans compose more than 40 percent of the prison population in the U.S. while constituting only 15 percent of the population as a whole." Enforced poverty and, hence, enforced ignorance and psychologically crippling conditions all contribute to domestic violence. We have witnessed violence become the primary mode of resolving conflicts, particularly in poverty stricken neighborhoods (ghettos) and poor rural areas of the country.

The 1994 Crime Bill before the Congress reflected the historical pattern described by Dr. Mary Francis Berry when she states "white oppression and black resistance have been a part of the American scene since the colonial period."[14] The Crime Bill was heavily weighted toward prisons and police. An estimated $9 billion for police and $8 billion for prison construction were allotted out of a total budget of $30 billion—almost two-thirds. Hence, the proposed remedy for poverty and lack of opportunities, the underlying cause for crime, is more prisons and police. This model is part of the continuing repression that began as slavery for African Americans.

One hundred ninety-eight years (1776–1964) after the formation of the United States, "whether its policy was action or inaction, the national government has used the Constitution in such a way as to make law an instrument for maintaining a racist status quo."[15] Thus the turbulent and violent summer of 1964 was indeed a glaring reminder of the continuing legacy of violent, barbaric methods of governance in Mississippi and the sluggish response of the U.S. government despite the fact that the U.S. Constitution, The United Nations charter (i.e. treaty), the Nuremberg trials, and principle were all "operative." "Though the Bill of Rights, the Civil Rights Act of 1866, and the Fourteenth Amendment purport to protect individuals in their lives, liberties, and property, these ringing phrases have in fact afforded little protection to black people as a group. Law and the Constitution in the U.S. have been a reflection of the will of the white majority [the governing/ruling elite] That white people have and shall keep superior economic, political, social, and military power, while black people shall be the permanent mudsills of American society."[16]

The thirtieth anniversary commemoration of the infamous summer of 1964's historic struggle for democracy and justice in Mississippi and the nation saw Mississippi's ruling oligarchy display modern forms of warfare techniques. A strategy of "enforced ignorance," the assault on the ability of African Americans to have equal access to education and technology, is being attempted. Many African Americans are denied the right to participate in the educational process designed to guarantee quality education, compatible with the national goal of educating and preparing American people to compete in the global economy. This is being accomplished by assaulting one of the great, historically viable institutions which has facilitated the successful production of highly qualified, educated, and skilled individuals of African American heritage—i.e. the historic black colleges.

In the case of *United States Ayers vs. Fordice*, Mississippi Governor Kirk Fordice attempted to render impotent these historic institutions, which would in effect scatter to the winds the great treasures of knowledge and experience that could be shared by African American educators and students. Governor Fordice, as the statutory leader of the Mississippi governing elite, is responding negatively to a demand by African American institutions for greater resources to enhance the historically black schools in Mississippi. The governing elite of Mississippi is equally engaged in continuing a historic battle to contain and dismantle any and all attempts by African Americans to gain political empowerment.

Some Lessons Drawn from Nazi Germany

Hitler's Nazi Germany offers a mirror to constitutional democracy. It allows the American people to see clearly what it means to establish a "racist regime," with the full powers of the national government, i.e., the control of the White House or any of the three branches of our government. Add to that state governments, like Mississippi, and our own history has reflected elements of Nazism, tolerated and openly condoned by both state and national governments. Some examples of Nazi Germany's method of governance include its philosophy of white supremacy, its rule by terror, murder, intimidation, psychological warfare, political subordination, racism, torture.

The central foundation of the Nazi/fascist structure under Hitler was (a) racism, (b) Social Darwinism, and (c) socio-biology. The oligarchical dictatorial regime's structure was designed to facilitate the establishment of a superior race, of a special type. A type that would be ethnically clean and pure "Aryan" German, a blue-eyed and blond prototype free from seven-eighths of the planet's population which hap-

pens to be of color. The structure involved a continuous purification process among the different ethnic Europeans who are ranked below the Hitler created prototype. In Adolf Hitler's political autobiography, *Mein Kampf*, he postulates the following: "The consequence of this racial purity, universally valid in nature, is not only the sharp outward delimitation of the various races, but their uniform character in themselves. The fox is always a fox, the goose is a goose, the tiger is a tiger, etc. And the difference can lie at most in the varying measure of force, strength, intelligence, dexterity, endurance, etc. of the individual specimens. But you will never find a fox who in his inner attitude might, for example, show humanitarian tendencies toward geese, as similarly there is no cat with a friendly inclination toward mice." He further states that, "historic experience offers countless proofs of this. The result of all racial crossing is therefore in brief always the following: (a) lowering of the level of the higher race; (b) physically and intellectually regressive and hence the beginning of a slowly but surely progressing sickness. To bring about such a development is, then, nothing else but to sin against the will of the eternal creator."[17]

In countless recordings and documentation of the modern civil rights era and the preceding era, there are clear illustrations of racist philosophical views strikingly similar to those expressed by Hitler. They were expressed by elected officials including white citizens councils, members of Congress, state-level officials, supreme court justices, and presidents. These views carried the force of law, the force of culture, and the force of customs in the society of the United States.

The following are selections from the War Crimes trials after the defeat of Nazi Germany, as exhibited by the Nuremberg documents. These excerpts will reveal the striking similarity between Germany under Hitler's regime and the method of governance in the state of Mississippi.

The Nuremberg Trials

Order of the President of the United States,

21 July 1950, Executive Order 10144, Defining the Responsibility of the United States High Commissioner for Germany in Connection with Sentences Imposed on War Criminals at Nuremberg, and Related Matters.

Executive Order No. 10144

The High Commissioner, as representative of the United States, shall share the four-power responsibility for the study, care, and execution of sentences and disposition (including pardon, clemency, parole, or release) of war criminals confined in Germany as a result of conviction by military tribunals established by the United States Military Governor pursuant to Control Council Law No. 10.

The Nuremberg trials were more than the trials of individual defendants for individual crimes. They were group trials of men who, while participating separately, were engaged in a vast criminal enterprise against international law and humanity. We think that three things of equal importance should eventuate from these trials and be pointed up in this report.

(1) Recognition of laws of humanity which no people or state can flaunt and the certain knowledge that the individual engaged in their violation will be held accountable to society and punished.

(2) Education of the people of the world as to what took place under the Third Reich, that they may become ever alert to guard against the risks of repetition.

(3) Individual justice for defendant. He must not be assimilated to the government, party, or program. His individual action and circumstances must be scrupulously observed to the end that he be held accountable only for his own misdeeds and not have visited upon him the misdeeds of others.

The 12 trials were separate proceedings, each concerning a segment of the Nazi program: the SS, the army, the concentration camps, the courts, the government, the industrial front. All were integrated in a massive design which despite its madness was thoroughly worked out to incorporate every endeavor. The concept which underlay the design and aggressive action was the idea that the Germans were a master race destined to conquer, subjugate, and enslave inferior races of the East, but that even the master race must be ruled by a dictator who would have complete control over their lives.

[Some] parts of the master plan all carried out in unison were:

—The elimination of all actual and potential opposition, by the extermination of political leaders and those who had any promise of becoming political leaders in opposition, or their collection and removal to concentration camps.

—The elimination of Jews, occasionally by deportation, but generally by outright slaughter. This organized business of murder was centered in SS groups which accompanied the army for purposes of eliminating Jews, gypsies, and all those even suspected of being partisans. No less that 2 million defenseless human beings were killed in this operation. (New estimates over 6 million people.)

—The pillage of property and enslavement of the population of the invaded eastern territories to feed the machine of war.

—The resettlement program which had the dual purpose of permanently ousting non-Germans from their homes, eliminating their culture and even their existence, and settling Germans in their place. Included in this program were . . . the deportation or reduction of non-Germans to a position of virtual slavery, an elaborate program to end the propagation of the inferior races by means of sterilization, abortions, and the imposition of the death penalty for forbidden sexual intercourse. All this was done in a systematic basis of racial examinations which determined the disposition of all the people involved. This gigantic uprooting of people regardless of ties to home, family, or their wishes was carried out in thoroughly businesslike ways by agencies of the government set up for the purpose.

Hence it was a necessary part of the program to eliminate law, and the law was eliminated. There was an outright substitution of Nazi ideology for law. Judges were frankly instructed that in dealing with non-Germans they were not expected to apply or observe the statutes, but were to be guided by Nazi ideology.

London Agreement, 8 August 1945

In Witness Where of the Undersigned have signed the present Agreement. Done in quadruplicate in London this 8th day of August 1945 each in English, French, and Russian, and each test to have equal authenticity.

For the Government of the United States of America

Robert H. Jackson

To the Provisional Government of the French Republic

Robert Falco

For the Government of the United Kingdom of Great Britain and Northern Ireland

Jowitt, C.

For the Government of the Union of Soviet Socialist Republics

I. Nitkitchenko

A. Trainin' [18]

(Also see Appendices 1–9)

Conclusion

The primary issues raised in this paper are as follows:

(a) The introduction of slavery in North America by the British Crown from the first landing at James Town, Virginia, of the African slaves gave rise to the introduction of repressive methods of violence employed to control and regulate African slave behavior throughout this period and throughout the post-colonial and slave period. This has been the case since January 1863—the official date of the Emancipation Proclamation to free the slaves—and the 134 years post emancipation.

(b) The roots of Mississippi's violent history derive from the history of the U.S. itself and the level of violent repression the national leadership of America has willingly tolerated.

(c) The gentlemen's agreement to tolerate Jim Crow in the South and the acceptance of racial and economic exploitation of blacks as the natural state of affairs.

(d) The acceptance of African Americans as property, to be exploited at will. The exploitation of African Americans as property remains the paramount issue preventing a solution to the crisis of poverty and crime today.

(e) While the U.S. government participated in a military tribunal designed to rightfully prosecute German Nazi leaders for war crimes including racism and anti-Semitism, genocide, and economic exploitation, they maintained a double standard by refusing to apply the same laws and principles to American citizens who committed these same crimes against African Americans. This was especially true in Mississippi.

The violent decade of the 1960s in Mississippi must be placed in the historical context of our nation's evolution. As Martin Luther King, Jr., observed the violent behavior of the governing elite of U.S. society, he said, "I could never again raise my voice against the oppressed in the ghetto without having first spoken clearly to the greatest purveyor of violence in the world today—my own government."[19] These words ring true today. The women and men who gave their lives and who confronted death and physical and psychological harm to their persons in Mississippi in 1964 and throughout the decades of the '50s and '60s acted for all Americans, then and for future generations, to strengthen the foundation for democracy and justice for our country. These daughters and sons of the United States deserve today to be honored by the nation with the medal of freedom, the country's highest civilian medal, for their great contribution to the nation and toward raising the progressive standard for human civilization. Great progress was made as a result of their sacrifices in the fields of business, politics, cultural accomplishment, and race relations. Nevertheless, stagnation in all the fields cited has emerged as a major cancer on the body of the nation's social progress for African Americans in the U.S.

What, then, is the solution for our country? I am compelled to draw from the profound wisdom of Dr. Martin Luther King, Jr., when he asserted on April 4, 1967, "I am convinced that if we are to get on the right side of world revolution, we as a nation must undergo a radical revolution of values, we must rapidly begin the shift away from a 'thing oriented' society to a 'person oriented' society. When machines and computers, profit motives, and property rights are considered more important than people, the giant triplets of racism, materialism, and militarism are incapable of being conquered."[20] This statement summarizes the essence of our society and the essence of our dilemma as a society!

I shall forever remain optimistic that the progressive majority of the American people can, with unity, realize a new epoch, characterized by full democracy and justice for all in our land, and will proudly embrace the reputation as world peace makers. ❖

Footnotes

1. Preamble of the Constitution of the United States.

2. Berry, Mary Francis. *Black Resistance—White Law.* Penguin Press-Allen Lane, 1994, Preface, pp. 1–2.

3. Ibid., p. xi.

4. Ibid., p. 2.

5. Ibid., p. 8.

6. Ibid., p. 7.

7. Ibid., p. 242.

8. *Eyes on the Prize.* Penguin Books, 1987, p. 179.

9. Parker, Frank. *The Black Vote Counts.* University of North Carolina at Chapel Hill, 1970, p. 24.

10. Parker, p. 36. Also see Appendix 9.

11. Parker, p. 36.

12. McPherson, James M. *The Negro's Civil War.* Ballantine Books, University of Chicago Press, 1945, p. 195.

13. Berry, p. xii.

14. Berry, p. xii.

15. Hitler, Adolf. *Mein Kampf,* p. 286.

16. The Nuremberg Trial material is drawn from Volume 15 of the Trial Series. For page numbers see listing of Apendix 1–3 under the London Agreement, August 8, 1945, signed by the United States, Great Britain, France, and the Union of Soviet Socialist Republics. And President Harry Truman, June 6, 1945, Executive Order 10062, Establishing the Position of the United States High Commissioner for Germany.

17. King, Dr. Martin Luther. "Beyond Vietnam." Clergy and Laity Concerned. Riverside Church. Speech delivered on April 4, 1967.

18. King. "Beyond Vietnam."

19. Information on Medgar Evers—Interview with Myrlie Evers-Williams.

MARIAN WRIGHT EDELMAN

Progress and Peril: America's Unfinished Symphony

The overture of our nationhood—the Declaration of Independence—is awaiting its next movement.

Abraham Lincoln's Emancipation Proclamation and the 13th, 14th, and 15th Amendments completed the first movement of America's symphony of freedom and justice.

Charles Houston, Thurgood Marshall, Martin Luther King, Jr., Rosa Parks, Ella Baker, Fannie Lou Hamer, and thousands of unsung white and black heroes and heroines, who tore down the walls of legally sanctioned American apartheid, composed the second movement.

In the 1990s, you and I must create the third movement by putting the social and economic underpinnings beneath the millions of African American, Asian American, Latino, white, and Native American children left behind when the promise of the civil rights laws and the progress of the 1960s in alleviating poverty was eclipsed by the Vietnam War and changing national leadership and priorities.

Like Thurgood Marshall and his gifted team of colleagues, you and I, individually and collectively, can cause and not just witness change. We can close the gaping hole of opportunity between black and white and rich and middle-class and poor children in America before the new century dawns. We can prod our great nation to choose whether our racial diversity will be its greatest strength or fatal weakness and whether our democratic ideals will be a banner of hope or a profile of hypocrisy.

In the face of the savagery of Bosnia-Herzegovina, the ethnic tensions tearing nations asunder, and pandemic suffering among children who die by the thousands every day from preventable disease and poverty, holding high America's founding principle that all human beings possess God-given rights never has been more important.

One Day in the Life of Black Children in America

3,374 black students are suspended each school day from public school.

1,418 black students are corporally punished each school day in public school.

1,334 black teenagers become sexually active for the first time.

1,253 black infants are born to unmarried mothers.

910 black infants are born into poverty.

827 black teenage girls get pregnant.

548 black infants are born to mothers who were not high school graduates.

544 black students drop out of school.

448 black infants are born to teen mothers.

256 black infants are born at low birthweight (less than 5 pounds, 8 ounces).

220 black infants are born to mothers who received late or no prenatal care.

133 black infants are born to teen mothers who already had a child.

126 black children are arrested for violent crimes.

80 black children are arrested for drug offenses.

Marian Wright Edelman is founder and president of the Children's Defense Fund, a national voice for children, and a founding leader of the Black Community Crusade for Children. A native of Bennettsville, South Carolina, she graduated from Spelman College and Yale Law School and was the first black person admitted to the Mississippi State Bar.

56 black infants are born at very low birthweight (less than 3 pounds, 5 ounces).

34 black infants die.

19 black children are arrested for alcohol-related offenses.

6 black young adults, age 20–24, are murdered.

5 black young adults, age 20–24, die by fire-arms.

5 black children are murdered.

4 black children die by firearms.

3 black children die in auto accidents.

2 black young adults, age 20–24, die in auto accidents.

1 black child or young adult under 25 dies from HIV.

1 black child commits suicide.

1 black young adult, age 20–24, commits sui-cide.

At his inauguration, President Clinton stated that what is right with America is strong enough to cure what is wrong with America. Our history has taught us this. Our progress has shown us this. So let a new spirit of struggle spread across our land today to stop the killing and neglect of children and heal our racial and class and gender divisions. Every American leader, parent, and citizen, led by our president and Congress, must personally and collectively struggle and sacrifice to reclaim our nation's soul and give our children back their hope, their sense of security, their belief in America's fairness, and their ability to dream about, envisage, and work towards a future that is attainable and real.

We must struggle together again to be more caring, more tolerant, and to replace "I" with "we" and "them" with "us." We have no choice if we are to realize the promise and premise of our American democratic experiment; if we want to be a moral and economic leader in the competitive twenty-first century global village; if we want to stop the civil war raging in our cities—and spreading to our suburbs, small towns, and rural areas—fueled by guns, gangs, drugs, joblessness, and hopelessness; if we want to stop our taxes being consumed by prisons; sickness,

remediation, and welfare; if we want to increase our current and future productivity.

In the aftermath of the unjust 1992 Rodney King verdict and the ensuing Los Angeles riots, like many Americans I was stunned by how vibrant racism remains in American life, how far negative and national leadership in the 1980s fed our regression, and how prone we are to historical amnesia and despair. How surprised I was to hear many people—young and old alike—say "nothing has changed." Nothing could be further from the truth. And nothing indicates more the need both to remember how far we have come and must still go to confront our remaining racial divisions.

Now is the time to finish our national quest for inclusion and fairness as we face a new century and millennium.

Progress . . .

Black leadership has permeated a range of mainstream institutions. At the time of this writing, there are more than seventy-five hundred black elected officials—almost five times the number in 1970. Colin Powell chaired the Joint Chiefs of Staff; Frank Thomas heads the Ford Foundation; Donald Stewart is president of the College Board. The late Reginald Lewis broke into the Fortune 500 ranks by purchasing Beatrice Foods. Clifton Wharton, after heading TIAACREF, the world's largest pension fund, has become Undersecretary of State. Four blacks sit in the Clinton administration cabinet. The 17 African Americans among the 120 new members of the 103rd Congress bring the total black caucus to 39. Carol Moseley-Braun is the first black woman senator, Eva Clayton is president of the freshman class in the House of Representatives, and Ron Dellums chairs the Research and Development subcommittee of the U.S. House Armed Services Committee.

The three courageous black civil rights attorneys who practiced law in Mississippi when I moved there in 1964 are all dead now. But their legacy lives on in the almost four hundred black lawyers in Mississippi today, one of whom sits on the Mississippi Supreme Court. Unita

Blackwell's rise from sharecropper to mayor of Mayersville, Mississippi, and MacArthur Prize Fellow shows how many rungs of the racial ladder we have climbed. Mae Jemison's flight into space shows how high we can soar with the right opportunity.

Bill Cosby is America's favorite daddy, Oprah Winfrey is queen of the talk show circuit, Michael Jackson and Whitney Houston are perennials on the top-10 charts, and Michael Jordan is the idol of millions of American children and youths.

Spelman College, my alma mater, looks toward its future with a stronger endowment and student body than ever before. There are tens of thousands more black lawyers, doctors, engineers, and professionals than there were in 1960. Thousands of blacks have entered corporate and academic circles. Black infant mortality rates were halved over the 1960s and 1970s. Childhood hunger was greatly reduced while the black middle class grew. Black child poverty decreased by 40 percent during the 1960s and black elderly poverty decreased 20 percent.

But there is another side to this extraordinary progress which propels this call for urgent and sustained action today.

And Peril

Although black per-capita income is at an all-time high and many blacks have moved up the corporate ladder, many of the ladders we climb don't reach the pinnacle of corporate power. Black purchasing power, now over $250 billion annually, exceeds the combined gross national product of Australia and New Zealand. But all our spending has not translated into commensurate black economic influence and concrete results for the masses of black Americans. Despite greater black representation in political life, white economic power still controls our city and rural area tax bases. And many political leaders, rather than call for a fair sacrifice from privileged Americans and powerful special interests, still hide behind a $4.1 trillion mountain of national debt, resulting from tax breaks for the rich and a huge military buildup, to deny chil-

dren the investment needed for them to live and learn today and pay back that debt tomorrow.

Amidst a sea of American affluence, during a period when our real gross domestic product grew by more than $1 trillion in the 1980s, child and family poverty increased dramatically. Today one in five of all American children is poor and two in five black children are poor. Among black children in single-mother families, two in three are poor. Four of five black children in families with single mothers under twenty-five are poor.

Black members of the middle class are disproportionately dependent on two workers to stay above water and many are one job away from poverty. Black families without a second worker are falling further and further behind. Tens of thousands of young black males in their twenties whose real annual earnings fell by 24 percent between 1973 and 1989 are unable to find jobs to form or support stable families. They frequently succumb to despair or the underground economy and crime—too often the only door opened to them by their skills and our above-ground economy.

In 1989, 19 percent of young black males reported no income. Therein lies a, if not the, principal cause of pervasive out-of-wedlock births in the black community. Marriage is influenced not only by personal values but by hope and the self-respect that comes from gainful employment that enables one to support a family.

Today, almost two-thirds of all black children are born to unmarried mothers and 54 percent of all black families with children are headed by females. Thousands of black children are growing up in homes other than their own. The gap between black and white infant mortality has widened. Nonwhite one-year-olds are less likely to be fully immunized against polio than children in sixty-nine other nations. Black U.S. infants are more likely to die than babies in Cuba, Bulgaria, or Kuwait.

Although the threat of lynching no longer hangs over black people in America, death by gun and preventable sickness and poverty remains a daily reality. More young black men die from homicide each year than we lost in all the horrible decades of lynching. A black child is murdered every four hours. Black children make up more than half of all reported cases of AIDS in children under thirteen and more than three in five deaths among children with AIDS. America's prisons are bulging with our young men, many of whom see them as better alternatives than the streets and premature death. Thousands of young black boys and girls no longer say "when I grow up," but "if I grow up."

Millions of black children and youths—unprepared to seize mainstream opportunities in our inner cities, small towns, and rural areas—are growing up in a Third World within America—without dreams, without hope, without stable families, without enough respect and love, and without an extended black community family, and nation, that views all children as community property, affirms their worth, and buffers them against and provides them the tools to challenge and overcome the hostile messages and barriers of the external world.

Never has America or the black community seen the wanton killing of children that we see today. Never have we known such a plague of drugs and sexually transmitted diseases. Not since slavery have we suffered the family breakdown and out-of-wedlock births we see today. Never has America or the black community permitted children to rely on guns and gangs rather than parents and neighbors and community institutions for their protection and love to the extent we do today. Never have we exposed our children so early to cultural messages that glamorize sex, alcohol, tobacco, and violence with so few mediating influences from family, religious, and community leaders. Never have we seen such incessant advertising that creates demand for more and more material things that are replacing the spiritual and civil values that give purpose and meaning to life.

What We Can Do

"You have no right to enjoy a child's share in the labors of your fathers unless your children are to be blest by your labors."

—Frederick Douglass
"The Meaning of July Fourth
for the Negro"

As Americans we can decide and act with faith and determination together to save our children and all children, to repair the breach between our communities, and to restore the streets we live on. In every black organization in every community, we can reach out in multiple ways to help our children regain their moral footing, self-esteem, and ethic of achievement.

And we can insist that others do their part: the white community, the private sector, government at all levels, and the media and cultural leaders since they did their part in creating and permitting the problems our children and nation face. Black leaders, however, must reconnect personally with our children through a variety of self-help efforts while fighting for their just treatment by American society—"their right is to get the same thing in the same place at the same time as other people's children," as one African American preacher recently said.

When, as a student at Spelman College, I took my first airplane ride to Shaw University, a historically black college in Raleigh, North Carolina, for the organizational meeting of the Student Nonviolent Coordinating Committee (SNCC), I was excited by the possibilities of working in the Civil Rights Movement and apprehensive about the challenges before us. But I was fortified growing up in a world where adults cared for us, demanded our best contributions, and supported us every step of the way. Most of all, they provided inspiration.

Ella Baker left us a legacy of inspiration and tenacity; of faith and determination; of struggle and triumph; and of profound respect in the ability of the young to make a difference. She and the other adults in my life left me with an enduring sense of possibility, something too few of our young people have today. So today, black adults must help youth find a sense of community, a sense of possibility and hope, and provide them the leadership tools for effective social change, just as Ella Baker and so many others did for America during the Civil Rights Movement.

And we must work together. We cannot win for our children unless we involve all of America. We cannot win unless we change the cultural signals, values, and priorities of America. So we must seek policies that benefit all children while targeting them in appropriate ways to black and other minority children. Similarly, America cannot claim the title of "just" society or win the race for the future without helping black, brown, and all children succeed.

While the responsibility to ensure fair treatment for all children and to close the opportunity gap between white and black, rich and poor children rests with all Americans, history and reality make clear that the black community has borne, and must continue to bear, a disproportionate burden of personal and political action to eliminate racial and class injustice in America.

Many black leaders have accepted that burden and challenge and are working to build a massive and sustained Black Community Crusade for Children (BCCC). Coordinated by the Children's Defense Fund (CDF), the BCCC has many actions underway, including:

A massive public education/media and consciousness raising campaign. A number of publications, posters, and television and radio ads are available.

The Ella Baker Child Policy Training Institute and Black Student Leadership Network (BSLN). A key BCCC goal is to train at least one thousand new black leaders for the 1990s and to strengthen existing leadership for children and youths. A student network is growing nationwide.

Summer Freedom Schools run by black college students in a number of sites combining child feeding programs with academic and cultural enrichment, recreation, and child advocacy.

A first-step policy agenda—to be revised annually—to get all children fully immunized and every disadvantaged child ready for school by ensuring a high quality Head Start experience for every eligible child. We seek to make a high quality Head Start experience available on a full-day, full-year basis for those parents who need it. We also seek to ensure that black child and family needs are heard as major health, family support, economic, and education policies are developed.

National policy and community mobilization strategies to prevent the violence that is ravaging our children and communities.

A Religious Action Network (RAN) with targeted materials and technical assistance that helps strengthen youth and family ministries inside and outside church walls.

A clearinghouse for the collection and dissemination of successful models making a difference for disadvantaged children, youths, and families in a variety of networks.

We are committed to implementing a range of complimentary strategies to strengthen all children meeting the special needs of black children. We urge you and our nation to do the same. Most of all, we urge a new overall vision and commitment to preventing child poverty, suffering, and neglect through creative experimentation, and persistent and integrated actions that address the needs of the whole child within a family and community framework.

We do so guided by the example and the spirit of people like Ella Baker for the future of our young people. As the African proverb says, "Children are the wisdom of a nation." Let's work together to make sure we're giving our children all they need today, tomorrow, and for generations to come. ❖

Excerpted from *Progress and Peril: Black Children in America, A Fact Book and Action Primer* published by the Children's Defense Fund, 1993. All rights reserved.

PHIL OCHS

How Long?

How long, how long can we go on?
How long, how long can we go on?
This troubled land may never last;
There is not future if we forget the past.

How far, how far have we gone?
How far, how far have we gone?
So many struggles we have lost;
So many people on the cross.

Why the fear of the coming of the morning?
Why the trembling at the call?
Can't we hear the final warning?
Can't we see the writing on the wall?

So many years before the dawn.
So many years before the dawn.
So many children have never grown;
So many seeds of hatred sown.

So many rains had to fall.
So many rains have had to fall.
So many storms before the flood;
So many rainbows red with blood.

MARSHALL POMER

Economic Opportunity

Marshall Pomer is a visiting scholar at the University of California at Berkeley and director of the Macroeconomic Policy Institute. Pomer taught previously at the University of California at Santa Cruz. He co-authored with Nobel Economists James Tobin and Robert Solow the influential open letter on the economy that was endorsed in March of 1992 by 100 prominent economists. Working with economists at the Institute of International Economic and Political Studies of the Russian Academy of Sciences, Pomer organized the Economic Transition Group, which has been advocating a "middle of the road" strategy for the transformation of the economies of the former Soviet Union. He is currently an economic advisor to Eritrea and is hopeful that this new African nation can set an example for equity and efficiency. Pomer has a B.S. from Yale and a Ph.D. in economics from Harvard.

It was late October in New Haven, 1963. An exuberant civil rights organizer from New York, Allard Lowenstein, and an activist college chaplain, William Sloan Coffin, were appealing for volunteers. At the time an impressionable college sophomore, I was one of about fifty Yale students listening to their pleas for help. Lowenstein and Coffin asked us to drop out of school for a week and go off to Mississippi to help get out the vote in the Freedom Ballot Campaign, a mock election for governor that was being staged by blacks to draw attention to the denial of their right to vote. Though I had not previously been involved in the Civil Rights Movement, I decided to go.

Nothing could have prepared me: "Whites Only" signs on drinking fountains and restrooms, harassment from the police, and people being told they must not linger after rallies lest they be shot at. Not only was I appalled by the blatant racism, but also I was struck by Mississippi poverty, both white and black.

I was horrified by what I saw in the South, but was told that racism was just as bad in the North. Robert Moses, a northern black hero in the struggle against segregation in the South, explained to me that northern whites were terrified by the prospect of black migrants taking their jobs away.

My experience in Mississippi taught me that racial justice requires economic change and inspired me to become an economist.

Thirty years later, most African Americans still confront oppressive economic circumstances. While legal remedies and social programs are important, they have limited value in the absence of a vigorously expanding economy. Unfortunately, errors in economic policy since the mid-eighties resulted in economic stagnation in the early nineties that obstructed progress toward racial equality.

The purpose of this essay is to explain how economic policy in the nineties could be changed to enlarge economic opportunity, particularly for African Americans. Economic policy has been more concerned with inflation than with unemployment, putting at a disadvantage those struggling to gain entry into the economic mainstream.

Expansion in the Eighties

In response to the 1981–82 recession, President Reagan won congressional approval for strong remedies. Tax cuts on personal income and corporate profits were combined with large increases in federal expenditures on defense and health care. Although skewed toward the rich, the stimulus was beneficial. It propelled the economy out of recession. Starting with the second quarter of 1983, output rose by 8 percent in one year's time. Over twelve million jobs were created by 1986.

Table 1. Employment Growth

	'80s Expansion	'90s Stagnation
Black	32.2%	-1.6%
White	16.5%	-0.3%

Note: Data indicate change in civilian employment for blacks and for whites for the six years and seven months from October 1983 to May 1990, and for the two years and seven months from May 1990 to December 1992. Source: Bureau of Labor Statistics. Seasonally adjusted monthly data.

The Federal Reserve Bank (the "Fed") reluctantly supported this expansion. It gradually lowered interest rates, but still kept rates high out of concern that rapid expansion could ignite inflation. The high rates help to explain why productivity did not increase much during the eighties. Businesses were slow to keep pace with technological advances and reduced their rate of investment in new facilities and equipment. Also, high interest rates caused an artificial rise in the value of the dollar until 1986, which hindered exports and aggravated the much lamented shrinkage in manufacturing jobs.

The vigorous expansion of the eighties greatly increased employment for African Americans despite a lack of well-paid jobs in manufacturing. Table 1, comparing job gains for blacks and whites, shows the number of employed blacks rose by one third, which was double the rate for whites. Between March 1983 and May 1990, the number of employed blacks increased by over three million.

The Onset of Stagnation

In the summer of 1987, with unemployment low and inflation beginning to increase, the Fed began pushing interest rates up. The collapse of the stock market in October of 1987 caused the Fed to relent, but only temporarily. Within six months, the Fed not only resumed but also intensified its policy of restraint. By 1989 the higher interest rates had a major impact—cooling the real estate fervor, dampening construction, and stalling equipment purchases by businesses.

If it had not been for the Iraqi invasion of Kuwait, a temporary slowdown (a "soft landing") might have been achieved. Instead the economy crashed. The surprise invasion caused oil prices to soar, jittery consumers turned very

cautious, and the real estate slump intensified. Thus, the summer of 1990 marked the end of the long expansion that had been launched in early 1983.

In hindsight, it seems incredible that the Fed maintained restraint for six months after the recession began, rather than promptly lowering interest rates to invigorate the economy. Compounding this serious error, President Bush broke his "read my lips" pledge against higher taxes in a mistimed effort to reduce the deficit. The president and Congress belatedly agreed to do what should have been done years before, thus providing restraint at precisely the wrong time.

Not until December of 1990 did rising unemployment make it obvious to the Fed and the Administration that a recession had begun. Yet complacency prevailed. A recession had not occurred for almost a decade, and it was wrongly believed that slightly lower interest rates would quickly spur the economy.

Employment began falling in June of 1990 and remained below its pre-recession level into 1993. Table 1 compares the decline in employment for blacks and whites over the two-and-a-half years from mid-1990 to the end of 1992. On a percentage basis, job losses were substantially higher for blacks. Differential rates of population growth made matters even worse for blacks relative to whites. During this period, the number of adult blacks grew by more than 1.5 million, while black employment fell by almost two hundred thousand.

Macroeconomic Policy

The U.S. economy thus suffered unnecessarily in the early nineties due to policy errors. If we are to do better in the future, the public will need a better understanding of aggregate demand, monetary policy, and fiscal policy.

The key concept is aggregate demand for goods and services. This is the level of overall demand in the economy, as opposed to the level of demand for a particular product. It is measured by the total amount of spending on new output. Shortage of aggregate demand implies a general scarcity of jobs and an abundance of trained but unemployed workers. This concept of demand shortage, first popularized in the thirties by John Maynard Keynes, who showed that it was essential for combatting the Great Depression, is crucial for understanding unemployment.

Monetary policy is determined by the Fed, primarily through short-term interest rates. The Fed controls short-term interest rates by buying and selling government securities and by changing the interest rates charged member banks when they borrow from the Fed. Short-term rates are not only a determinant of the cost of borrowing but also an indicator of the availability of funds to borrowers. Monetary policy intended to make it easier to borrow is called "monetary ease"; policy to reduce borrowing is called "monetary restraint."

Fiscal policy is defined by the size of the federal deficit. The combination of higher government spending and lower tax rates that propelled the economy out of the 1981–82 recession is an example of "fiscal stimulus"—a widening of the deficit that invariably stimulates the economy. While changes in the federal budget to boost spending or cut tax rates provide fiscal stimulus, a decrease in the deficit indicates "fiscal restraint."

Shortage of aggregate demand can be remedied only by more spending, brought about either by fiscal stimulus or monetary ease. Fiscal stimulus in the form of increased government spending directly increases the amount of spending in the economy. Less sure and immediate in its effect on aggregate demand than the use of either fiscal or aggregate demand is the use of either fiscal or monetary policy to increase private spending, either by tax cuts or interest rate reductions. Monetary ease is appealing, however, because it does not require Congressional deliberation, and lower interest rates can spur investment and reduce the interest expense on the federal debt.

Thus there are two levers of macroeconomic policy, monetary and fiscal. Either can be used to remedy demand shortage and speed up the economy, creating new jobs and reducing unemployment. During the late eighties, the fiscal lever was overutilized, causing large deficits and provoking monetary restraint and high interest rates. In the early nineties, both the fiscal and monetary levers were underutilized.

When the number of unemployed falls, businesses are forced to pay higher wages in order to attract the workers they want. Higher labor costs are passed on to consumers in the form of higher product prices. At the same time, higher product demand enables businesses to raise their prices.

The Fed has traditionally been more concerned with inflation than with unemployment. Like the recent recession, most past downturns are attributable to monetary restraint intended to control inflation.

The Limits of Monetary Ease

Most economists underestimated the power of the recession that began in August 1990. They did not realize that the speculative excesses of the late eighties unbalanced the economy and rendered it prone to contraction, reducing the impact of monetary ease.

Excesses in real estate markets were foremost in destablizing the economy. Soaring real estate prices fed on unsavory liaisons between developers, politicians, and financial institutions—including banks, insurance companies, and especially savings and loan associations (S&Ls). At the same time, rising home prices fueled housing demand as homeowners traded up to more expensive homes in the belief that housing investment was a sure path to large capital gains. Overbuilding of office buildings continued well after the recession began.

Corporate America embarked on a spree of acquisitions and buyouts that often were motivated by short-term gains from selling off corporate holdings of real estate at inflated prices. These activities were financed by massive bank lending as well as by an exploding volume of junk bonds. Personal debt also rose to new heights as consumers, embracing the yuppie mentality, relied on home equity loans made possible by inflated home prices.

Because of the unprecedented increase in private debt that accompanied the speculative surge in real estate prices, monetary restraint had drastic effects in parts of the country as early as 1989. Declining real estate values not only bankrupted developers but also led to the S&L debacle. Mortgage-holding banks and insurance companies still face the possibility of additional losses as expired commercial leases are renegotiated at reduced rates.

In the past, the construction industry had been the engine of recovery: lower interest rates spurred building, especially of housing, which in turn stimulated the rest of the economy. But the real estate sector was not positioned in 1991 to pull the economy quickly out of recession. Office, retail, and multifamily vacancies were high due to overbuilding. Demand for real estate was also weakened by the aging of the baby boomers and the drop in the number of young adults. Furthermore, prodded by regulators and Wall Street analysts, financial institutions curtailed their real estate lending. The government and financial institutions still have a substantial inventory of foreclosed properties yet to be sold off at firesale prices.

Concerned about liquidity and safety, banks and other financial institutions invested heavily in government bonds and cut back on loans. Stable businesses had their credit lines canceled, at times with devastating consequences. In addition, still deeply in debt and wary of the economic outlook, many businesses and households were either unable or unwilling to borrow.

Thus high consumer and business debt, shaken financial institutions, and overbuilding made monetary ease less potent than it had been during previous recessions. The power of the Fed to slow the economy in 1989 was not matched by willingness and ability to produce a prompt and full recovery. Although more vigorous action by the Fed would have helped, it was unwise to reject fiscal stimulus and rely solely on monetary ease.

The economic stagnation of the early nineties was avoidable. Fiscal stimulus in combination with monetary ease could have maintained aggregate demand at the level required to maintain a robust economy.

The shortage of aggregate demand was prolonged by recession in Europe and Japan, which depressed demand for U.S. exports. Not until late 1993 did continued monetary ease finally bring on a sustained recovery led by home building and auto manufacturing. The recovery would have occurred sooner and been more robust if fiscal stimulus had been forthcoming earlier.

The Value of Fiscal Stimulus

Fiscal stimulus may well be needed in the future, especially since the Fed is likely to be overly zealous in its efforts to control inflation. The fiscal stimulus could help redress the poverty caused by economic stagnation and make the investments in human capital and infrastructure needed for long-run improvement in the economy.

A major increase in public investment, strongly advocated by Bill Clinton during the presidential campaign but deferred amidst the fervor for immediate deficit reduction, could be embodied in a fiscal stimulus. In contrast, the Reagan stimulus boosted military spending and personal consumption by the wealthy.

One approach is federal grants to state and local governments. State and local budgetary difficulties have caused spending cutbacks at a time when increasing numbers of Americans are in need of public services. Worsening student-teacher ratios, reduced job training, and even deteriorating prison conditions have long-run effects. Short-sighted reductions in public spending, combined with reduced job opportunity, will be reflected in future statistics on homelessness and crime, as well as in unsatisfactory rates of productivity growth for the economy as a whole. To counter the depressing effects of military cutbacks, grants could be targeted to affected areas.

As part of a stimulus package, there is a place for tax reductions to encourage business investment. Increased spending on new equipment and facilities would raise the productivity of American workers.

Fiscal stimulus should be designed to have a sure and rapid impact. An essential requirement for anti-recessionary grants, for example, is that the money be spent rather than saved. Personal tax cuts might be ineffectual since they may be used by consumers to pay off debt rather than to make new purchases. Furthermore, it is politically difficult to rescind tax cuts once implemented.

Example

If the economy were to falter, a fiscal stimulus of 1% of gross domestic product (GDP), about $60 billion at an annual rate, would give a substantial boost. Due to its effect on inducing additional spending, the 1% stimulus should produce a 2% overall increase in GDP. This would generate noticeable gains in employment that would raise consumer income, increase government revenue, and stimulate business investment. Economic expansion would likely be self-sustaining so long as monetary policy did not turn restrictive. The deficit would subsequently shrink on its own accord. As the recovery strengthened, action to speed deficit reduction would be beneficial.

For illustrative purposes, posit a $60 billion fiscal stimulus: $40 billion of public investment and grants to state and local governments, and $20 billion of tax reductions to encourage business investment. A very conservative estimate is that the stimulus would increase GDP by $90 billion. Assuming receipts at a rate of 15% of GDP, federal tax revenues would rise by $13.5 billion. Employment growth caused by the stimulus should lower government payouts for unemployment and related social benefits by a couple of billion. This implies a net cost of less than $45 billion.

While fiscal stimulus when needed is beneficial, such a program lacks political support. The rub is the federal deficit.

Fear of the Deficit

Fear that the federal deficit is out of control paralyzed fiscal policy during the recession. Although concern is warranted, it is urgent to put the deficit in perspective.

The deficit in 1992 was widely misinterpreted as indicating substantial fiscal stimulus. But excluding interest payments and deposit insurance outlays, the 1992 deficit was only about $30 billion, or about half a percent of GDP. In contrast, the comparable figures for the recovery years of 1975 and 1982 were deficits of about 3% of GDP.

Most of the federal debt is attributable to unnecessary deficit spending during the eighties. Ballooning military and medicare spending was accompanied by a consumer binge spurred by tax cuts for the affluent. The result was unprecedented. In times of war, federal debt as a percentage of national output typically increases, as it does during recessions. But federal debt as a percentage of output rose year after year during the eighties despite robust expansion. This string of large deficits roughly doubled the federal debt as a percentage of GDP. Although federal debt is still far below the percentage after World War II, it could eventually threaten the viability of the social security system once the baby-boom generation retires. Indeed, interest payments on the debt might soon exceed the defense budget.

The debt run-up discredited the conservative thesis that tax cuts would lower the deficit. Nevertheless, it strengthened conservatives. Railing against the deficit is a potent tactic for eliminating programs designed to redress inequality.

Much attention has been given to the effect of deficit spending on investment and productivity. Deficit spending supposedly "crowds out" business investment in new equipment and facilities, thereby undermining the productive capacity of the nation. The logic behind this contention is that investment must always equal private savings, minus deficit spending, plus net capital inflows from abroad. Thus, everything else remaining the same, increased deficit spending implies lower investment. But everything else does not stay the same. Reviving an economy by deficit spending will increase the total of private savings and possibly also increase capital inflows.

When there is little unemployment and industry is operating close to capacity, the economy can "overheat," in which case crowding out would occur. The process involves the impact of inflation, inflationary expectations, and monetary restraint. These three factors drive interest rates upward, inhibiting investment, although increased capital inflows from abroad, as in the eighties, can moderate the rise in interest rates and support continued investment despite low national savings. An increase in the deficit would not cause crowding out as long as inflation is low and there is excess capacity and wide availability of workers. The constricting effect of moderately higher interest rates would be more than offset by the stimulative effects of higher sales on investment.

In the long run, a vibrant economy is key to sustained deficit reduction. Thus, fiscal stimulus when needed is part of a prudent approach to reducing the federal debt. However, the long run is inherently uncertain and fast economic growth invariably increases the risk of inflation. Opponents to fiscal stimulus may really be primarily concerned with this risk.

The burdens of inflation and unemployment are not equally shared. Despite persistent high unemployment, the early nineties were highly profitable for Wall Street. Slow economic growth is compatible with the myopic self-interest of the financial community, since strong recovery could increase inflation and lower prices of stocks and bonds. High unemployment reassures the financial community because it quells inflation and discourages the Fed from pushing up interest rates.

State and Local Financing

A targeted stimulus program is feasible despite rigid opposition to deficit spending. Teamwork among different levels of government is required.

The national economy as a whole may experience prosperity while recessionary conditions may linger in some areas, most likely in California and in the Northeast. Particularly vulnerable are large cities buffeted by manufacturing decline, stagnant construction, and reductions in public services.

State and local governments, unlike the federal government, have capital budgets that permit them to finance infrastructure spending without increasing their operating deficits. The federal government could pay the debt service temporarily on anti-recessionary public investment. Through its contribution to economic growth, such capital spending should produce revenue gains sufficient to enable state and local governments to take responsibility for debt service once recessionary conditions are over. Funding sources for the federal contribution could include monies already allocated for military conversion and economic development programs.

The Myth of the Self-Adjusting Economy

The federal deficit is not the only obstacle to rational fiscal policy. Also critical is the belief that the economy will automatically adjust on its own, quickly remedying any temporary shortage of aggregate demand. The three mechanisms (in italics) are:

Wage and Price Adjustment: When there is a shortage of aggregate demand, lack of customers forces product prices down. The surplus of job seekers likewise causes wages to decline. Sales and hiring will both increase because of the declines in prices and wages. But this mechanism can take years to work, since prices and especially wages are slow to fall. Also telling, lower prices and wages imply lower incomes, which in turn aggravates any shortfall in aggregate demand.

Automatic Stabilizers: As the economy slows, tax receipts decline and government expenditures for unemployment benefits and welfare programs increase. These automatic stabilizers counter any shortage of aggregate demand by pumping money into the economy. The current system of unemployment compensation covers fewer workers than it did during earlier recessions. During the first part of the recession, it provided benefits over a shorter period. On the state and local level, stagnation also takes a large toll on tax receipts, forcing tax hikes and cutbacks in public services, siphoning money out of the economy.

Pent-Up Demand: Slack consumer spending builds pent-up demand. Likewise, rising population continually pushes aggregate demand upward. But shaken consumer confidence can nullify pent-up demand. The consumer's primary identity is as a worker, and workers, both employed and unemployed, remained anxious in the face of anemic recovery. Prospects for a strong revival of consumer spending were also undercut by a decline in the number of adults under age thirty-five.

The tendency toward self-adjustment is also hindered by the integration of the U.S. economy into the world economy. U.S. exports expanded markedly following the decline in the value of the dollar after 1986, leaving the U.S. highly dependent on export markets. Because of the growing reliance of Americans on imported goods, increases in consumer spending are now translated into more imports and therefore fewer domestic jobs than before.

The recovery that eventually took firm hold in late 1993 was not simply a consequence of automatic self-adjustment. It is attributable to the gradual effects of monetary ease. Low interest rates, which sank to levels not seen since the sixties, finally spurred strong sales of new homes and cars.

Two-Phase Fiscal Program

A two-phase fiscal program is required to manage the economy effectively over the long run. The program would provide fiscal stimulus when needed without the kind of misuse of deficit spending that occurred in the mid and late eighties. The fiscal-stimulus phase would expand the economy and create jobs when aggregate demand is insufficient, and the deficit-reduction phase would be triggered automatically when justified.

Table 2. Deficit-Reduction Measures

1. Suspension of temporary tax reductions
2. Gasoline taxes (10 cents per gallon per year)
3. Taxation and means-testing of entitlement benefits
4. Limits on deductibility of home mortgage interest
5. Age requirements for entitlements
6. Restrictions on deductibility of business expenses
7. Changes in cost-of-living adjustments for entitlements

Without automatic deficit-reduction, fiscal stimulus, even if sorely needed, could aggravate inflationary expectations. Also, since the Fed is inclined to apply monetary restraint to eradicate inflationary expectations, fiscal stimulus could provoke monetary restraint that would counter the stimulus.

Once demand shortage is remedied, deficit-reduction would be triggered. The goal is to lower the growth of the federal debt to below the growth rate of the economy. Thus federal debt, relative to the capacity of the economy to service that debt, would shrink over the long run. This would encourage the Fed to keep interest rates low.

Deficit reduction requires painful political choices. Which programs and whose benefits should be cut? Whose taxes should be increased? Table 2, meant to be illustrative, proposes deficit-reduction measures. First on the list is suspension of the tax cuts implemented to provide stimulus. The other measures include higher gasoline taxes, restrictions on and taxation of entitlements, and reductions in tax write-offs. The measures must be prioritized and are to be implemented gradually in accordance with phase two of the fiscal program.

Deficit reduction is triggered unless the economy is beset by high unemployment, and even then deficit reduction would be triggered if inflation is high. More precisely, deficit reduction is automatic whenever the economy is not in a state of "non-inflationary stagnation."

This condition is defined as high unemployment coupled with low inflation as determined by specified targets.

A reasonable specification of the unemployment target is 6% (4-month moving average of the total civilian unemployment rate, seasonally adjusted). A reasonable target for inflation is 4.5% (4-month moving average of the core inflation rate, seasonally adjusted CPI-U index). Thus deficit reduction is mandated whenever: (1) inflation rises above 4.5%, or (2) unemployment falls below 6%.

Deficit reduction that is too rapid would push the economy back into recession. Accordingly, the deficit-reduction phase mandates deficit reduction at a moderate rate of $40 billion per year (1994 dollars), roughly two thirds of 1% of GDP. The $40 billion requirement, to be a meaningful measure of fiscal constraint, should exclude asset sales by the government and receipts and outlays associated with the S&L debacle.

The deficit-reduction measures would be triggered as needed to achieve the deficit-reduction target. The number of measures implemented depends on the budgetary impact of spending and revenue changes not included in this fiscal plan (for example, spending changes due to health care reform). Unless the growth in entitlement spending were to slow, most of the deficit-reduction measures are likely to be triggered.

Table 3. Deficit Projections

	Scenario A	*Scenario B*
FY 1995	$200 Billion	$200 Billion
FY 1996	$150 Billion	$245 Billion
FY 1997	$100 Billion	$195 Billion
FY 1998	$60 Billion	$155 Billion

Scenario A: No stimulus required through 1998.
Scenario B: Stimulus required in fiscal year 1996.
Note: Values in 1994 dollars. Mandated deficit reduction is $40 billion per year plus the amount of net inflows from deposit-insurance transactions. It is estimated by the CBO that net inflows will be about $10 billion in 1996 and 1997.

The fiscal plan relies on the CBO as an impartial source for deficit projections. The deficit-reduction measures would be activated at the beginning of each calendar year on the basis of the CBO projected deficit for the fiscal year already begun. The amount of deficit reduction is determined by the gap between the projected deficit and the deficit limit. For example, suppose that in December 1995 the CBO estimates that the deficit for fiscal year 1996 will be $10 billion greater than the mandated limit. Then deficit-reduction measures amounting to $10 billion would be triggered unless the economy is in a state of non-inflationary stagnation.

Scenarios

Table 3 shows the implications of the two-phase fiscal program under two different scenarios. It is assumed that at the outset of 1995 the estimated deficits for both fiscal 1995 and 1996 are $200 billion.

Scenario A is optimistic. It projects sustained employment growth without the need for fiscal stimulus. Scenario B, in contrast, assumes fiscal stimulus of 1% of GDP will be needed in fiscal year 1996. Adding the $45 billion cost of the fiscal stimulus, as discussed above, yields a projected deficit of $245 billion for fiscal year 1996. Both scenarios assume that unemployment will go below 6% in 1997, and that the economy will not fall back into non-inflationary stagnation after that year. Scenario A projects a deficit of only $60 billion by FY 1997, compared with $155 billion under Scenario B.

If the threat of inflation were to become severe, then the deficit should be reduced more quickly than specified by the mandated deficit limits. Otherwise inflationary expectations and Fed reaction to those expectations would likely elevate interest rates, which could impede business investment on equipment and facilities, restrict purchases of new homes and cars, and raise the cost of servicing the federal debt. Indeed the reason to enact both phases of the fiscal plan at the same time is to prevent such an occurrence.

Once enacted, the proposed program of deficit reduction is likely to stick. Suspension would require the joint agreement of both Congress and the president, or a two-thirds majority of both the House and Senate. Unforeseen developments, however, could justify modifications. For example, it would not be prudent to try to reduce the deficit solely because inflation is above 4.5% on account of a temporary factor such as an oil embargo.

Conclusion

Too many African Americans continue to confront severe economic circumstances. A critical reason, apart from racial prejudice and class stratification, is economic policy that favors the haves over the have-nots.

A low unemployment rate is essential to reduce the gap between the rich and the poor and resume progress toward racial equality. Also, a robust economy with low unemployment will help generate the government revenues required for public investment, including inner-city programs that would assist many African Americans. But we are faced with an inflexible program of deficit reduction, which means that fiscal stimulus will not be forthcoming even if economic expansion falters. Since fiscal stimulus has been ruled out, the Fed controls the pace of economic activity.

The Fed is legitimately concerned with inflation but gives too little attention to unemployment. This is demonstrated all too well by its role in bringing on recession in 1990 and its reluctance to spur a timely rebound. Highly sensitive to Wall Street sentiment, the Fed will maintain high unemployment to assure low inflation.

Pressuring the Fed should be high on the agenda in the struggle for racial justice. We should support Congressional efforts to make Fed policy committees more democratic. Public clamor might restrain the Fed from the fanciful ideal of zero inflation.

Contrary to conventional wisdom, temporary increases in the federal deficit are beneficial when the economy is slack. A two-phase program, with automatic triggers for both stimulus and deficit reduction, is needed. The Administration, operating within parameters set by Congress, would set explicit targets for unemployment and inflation. If unemployment is high and inflation below its target, then fiscal stimulus would be automatic. Conversely, if inflation is above its target, then deficit reduction would be mandated.

Such a program would force the Fed to comply with the unemployment target set by the Administration. It would make little sense for the Fed, for example, to try to slow the economy unless the targets prescribed such action. If the Fed did so anyway, then its monetary restraint would automatically be reversed by fiscal stimulus.

Without these changes, the Fed will have free rein. This poses a threat to African Americans wanting to enter the economic mainstream. To move us closer to the goal of racial justice that we embraced thirty years ago, low unemployment must be made a higher national priority. ❖

The Reminiscences of Lawrence Guyot

Oral History Research Office, Columbia University, 1993

Introduction

I first met Allard Lowenstein in Jackson, Mississippi, in 1963. At the time, I was a member of SNCC. The following interview presents a side of Allard Lowenstein which is not ususaly discussed in American history textbooks or amongst Civil Rights Movement participants. I believe that Lowenstein was an evil man whose primary goal was to take control of the movement.

Preface

The following oral history memoir is the result of a tape-recorded interview with Lawrence Guyot. The interview took place in Washington, D.C., on March 29, 1989.

The interview is one in a series documenting the life of Allard K. Lowenstein. The interviews in this series were conducted by William Chafe of Duke University in preparation for a biography of Allard K. Lowenstein. Processing of the interviews was made possible by a grant from the Allard K. Lowenstein Fund, Inc.

Mr. Guyot has reviewed the interview but did not return a corrected copy; the transcript is a verbatim record of the conversation with only minor stylistic changes. The reader should bear in mind that he or she is reading a verbatim transcript of written rather than spoken prose.

Interviewee: Lawrence Guyot
Session #1
Interviewer: William Chafe, Washington, D.C.
Date: March 30, 1989

Lawrence Guyot: 507 U Street, Washington, D.C. 20001.

Q: Just for the record, state your name.

Guyot: My name is Lawrence Guyot.

Q: I guess the best place to start is just to ask when you first recall coming into contact with Lowenstein, the nature of your experience with him over the years.

Guyot: I first met Lowenstein in 1962 at an NSA meeting, and I saw him pretty much controlling things then. I also met Connie [Constance] Curry at that time. Lowenstein, to me, was always an anti-communist liberal provocateur. His role in Mississippi was to be involved in the discussions that led to the Freedom Vote. It wasn't his idea. It flowed from a discussion in a Freedom house, talking about research that Timothy Jenkins had done on the right of people who were not registered to vote to cast votes in Mississippi. This was passed by the Mississippi legislature before Reconstruction to protect whites who might not be registered to vote at the time. There were some of us who wanted to use that—

Lawrence Guyot was born in Pass Christian, Mississippi, where he was always politically active. In 1957 he entered Tougaloo College, which he considered to be an intellectual feast and an advocate's heaven. In 1962, he joined SNCC, where he worked in Greenwood, Greenville, and Hattiesburg. Guyot organized the first Freedom Day in Mississippi in which there were no arrests. This led to the creation of the Delta Ministry. Guyot was elected Chairman of the Mississippi Freedom Democratic Party in 1964, but was unable to attend the National Democratic Convention in Atlantic City due to his arrest in Hattiesburg for disturbing the peace. In 1965, he actively supported the attempt to unseat the congressional delegation from Mississippi which he believes led to the strengthening and passage of the 1965 Voting Rights Act. Guyot led the struggle to extend the voting rights act in 1970, helping to prevent it from being terminated. Today, Guyot is an elected Advisory Neighborhood commissioner. He continues to speak out on political issues, register voters, and assist people in empowering themselves. He believes that the most pressing concerns are racial polarization and the preservation of the hard fought victories such as medicaid, medicare, and the voting rights act.

and we did. The extension of that was, "Why not show that if given the vote, blacks would vote," which led to the Freedom Vote, which led to his involvement in bringing in students from Yale, Stanford.

What we found was that totally independent of him, the reaction from the FBI was to provide almost an agent for every student. I was operating in Hattiesburg.

Q: This is the fall of 1963.

Guyot: That's right. We had FBI protection like you would never believe. It was unparalleled. A volunteer—there was so much scrutiny that the violence depreciated, and any violence that occurred was immediately reported, and calls were made by the Department of Justice. Well, this led to an intense realization of, "Why not the 1964 Summer Project? If national attention can be generated like this, and if governmental activity can be brought which can protect the lives of us and of other people that we're trying to organize, why not do it on a larger scale?"

Well, the problems that Lowenstein had been involved in and created in the summer of 1963 led to his attempt to take control of the entire operation beyond the Freedom Vote. He wanted to control SNCC—you know, specifically telling us which jails to fill, when to fill them. What he failed to realize—and I read an interview of his to prepare myself for this—when he looked at a situation and we looked at it, we were looking at the same fact pattern from a totally different frame of reference and sense-value relationship. He talks about the relationship of COFO and the NAACP as though we were aligned against the NAACP and we somehow forced them out of the Freedom Vote and the 1964 Democratic Challenge and the 1965 Congressional Challenge—none of which is true. Aaron Henry in 1964 took all the propaganda that we had for the Freedom Summer and brought it to the NAACP convention, had them adopt it, his theory being since he was the president of COFO, and COFO as you know was a combination of NAACP, CORE, SNCC, SCLC, and the NAACP, he wanted their in-

volvement in the summer project. We'd gotten their involvement—both Lowenstein and Henry had spoken at the 1963 NAACP state convention in support of the Freedom Vote.

So this flow of cooperation where possible flowed from the beginning of COFO to the 1968 Democratic Convention and beyond, where possible. For instance, Vernon Dahmer was a member of the NAACP, but also one of the guys who supported me coming into Hattiesburg. As you know Vernon Dammer was killed in 1965. E. W. Steptoe had been a long-time NAACP member, but also a fervent supporter of SNCC. [Hollis] Watkins, the treasurer in McComb. Clearly NAACP was a supporter of Moses and his entre into Mississippi. Amzie Moore, the Godfather of Mississippi politics, NAACP, COFO. We stayed in his house, thirteen of us, when we first started organizing the Delta.

The reason I'm going into this is I think Al Lowenstein was one of the most effective provocateurs in America. Let's look at some of the things he did. He recruited for the Freedom Election in Mississippi. He pretty much organized the [Eugene] McCarthy campaign himself. Right before Robert Kennedy was shot, the last words he said publicly was, "Call Al Lowenstein, we're trying to bring him into that election, into that campaign." His ability to move freely and without question between Aaron Henry. [Robert] Moses, all the other civil rights leaders, Joe Rauh [Jr.], the college campuses. One of his continuing characteristics was his energy, and his intensity, and his commitment to what he was about. When we, I mean, a lot of us in SNCC were astounded that Moses could be, I guess the most non-benevolent word to say is co-opted by someone like Lowenstein. I mean, I remember me talking in casual conversation with the guy. I mean, it was always an attempt to find out "What are the differences between SNCC?" Not only "What are they," but "How can they be played upon?" There was just never an attempt at, "How do you really build power in order to reach people with it?" which is what

SNCC was about. Lowenstein was about, "How do you formulate a policy that is consistent with the American credo and can be controlled?" Lowenstein was one of the participants in the leadership meeting held in New York.

Q: In October.

Guyot: You're familiar with that?

Q: Yes, but I want to hear your version too.

Guyot: Courtland Cox was in the city—you should talk to him bout it—he was in the meeting, and it was a meeting of Courtland Cox, Robert Spike from the National Council of Churches, Roy Wilkins, Gloster Current, Joe Rauh, Al Lowenstein, and others. The basic thrust of the meeting was, "How do we"—which was nothing new, because I want to go back to another type of this meeting that occurred earlier—"How do we deal with getting rid of the underbrush?" People like Steptoe. How do we establish a committee that really decides what's going to happen in Mississippi—which again is contrary to everything we'd ever worked for. We felt the decisions should flow up rather than down.

But in 1962 the AFL-CIO came to a SNCC conference here on Jobs and Peace at Howard University and said, "Look, we will contribute money to you. We're going to set up this committee, though, to guide you along." In an instant—we didn't have any money at that time—we said, "No." So there had been more and more attempts by labor and others to say, "Look, now that SNCC has been unleashed in this voter registration"—see, because the Kennedys, Robert Kennedy specifically said, "Okay." John Kennedy was quoted recently as referring to SNCC as, "those son of a bitches, they love blood," while Robert Kennedy's approach was, "Look, let's concentrate on voting, and this way you stop the Freedom Ride, just stop the bus whatever." It is clear now to me that Lowenstein was a part of that, an effective part of it.

There are two wings in SNCC. I always identified with the political wing, the voter registration. I never said anything. I was only a

member. But there was that dichotomy in SNCC between demonstrations and—what we found in the real part of reality there was no difference. They were just as threatening, but the vote was more threatening and more deliverable and more permanent and more people would bring about change.

To get back immediately, then, to Lowenstein. After the 1963 vote, Lowenstein then began to Red-bait us, across the country. There were Maoists in SNCC. There was no concern about structure, no concern about order, who made the decisions. They were being influenced by the Left. Now, we very clearly [telephone rings; tape stops and starts].

Q: The Red baiting.

Guyot: Right. Now this was, this wasn't effective as it would have been, because we had established by holding—when I held the Freedom Day in Hattiesburg I invited all the major religions. All of them came, which led to the organization of the Delta Ministry. So we'd established our own contacts independent of Lowenstein, thank the Lord. But people then had begun to see [telephone rings; tape stops and starts].

Q: When you had Freedom Day.

Guyot: Right. We'd established our contacts with the National Council of Churches, which paid off for us because then when we moved to—once they got established in Mississippi, when we then moved to the 1964 Summer Project, they were very supportive as far as money, training, recruiting—you name it, support. This flowed also in the 1965 Congressional Challenge, which was tremendously effective for us. It's interesting. There's only one author who has really developed how closely the Congressional Challenge was to the passing of the 1965 Voting Rights Act, and that's Mary King in her book, *Freedom Song*. But [Anne] Romaine is going to do the same thing in her piece.

My concern is that both Joe Rauh and Al Lowenstein were both involved in supporting activities that they could not control, and once they could not control them they set out to destroy them. I mean, Bob Moses's agreement on the Freedom Democratic Party was you go to Atlantic City and then you disbanded, either win or loose there. My position was, "There's no party registration in Mississippi. We can make the fight here on a day to day"—for every election after. I won that argument. But 1964, we now know that Lyndon Johnson had FBI agents there, went on television to stop, Fannie Lou Hamer put pressure on individual delegates, because it was just that important to make sure that you don't have plantation workers determine a public policy nationally. If that would have been, if we had succeeded then, why couldn't urban blacks and the urban poor be doing the same thing as it relates to forcing the Democratic Party to be something other than a mechanism simply to hold elections every year, every four years.

One of my college professors, Doctor Barinsky—

Q: Ernest Barinsky.

Guyot: You know Ernest Barinsky?

Q: Yes.

Guyot: Ernest Barinsky had been very supportive of SNCC early on, but even before SNCC—the first time I saw Martin Luther King was in Tougaloo Chapel, but I also saw in there people from the Klan, speakers, people from the White Citizens Council, black conservatives who openly supported white people. All kind of thought was brought into Tougaloo. I mean, that was understood. But he made one good point. He said, "Look, when you talk about politics you've got to talk about bread, butter, the interests of people that you're trying to organize." It's something that a lot of us in SNCC never forgot.

So what we were concerned about in developing leadership was leadership that could not be controlled, that was issue oriented, that was indigenous, that was going to be there. So the whole question of opening up WLBT, A.A. Branch, the dean of Tougaloo, was one of the litigants in filing a law suit that challenged the

FCC (Federal Communication Commission) on WLBT. As you know, Aaron Henry later became an owner in this sort of way. But, every possible avenue in which there could be an attack on leveling opportunity for blacks in Mississippi was done from the Free Southern Theater to you name it. Parallel institutionalism.

Now, how does this fit into Lowenstein? Well, it fits because the more we opened up, the more there were new forces that had to be dealt with that could not be contained. I think you know—if you don't, I'll tell you—the Mississippi Freedom Democratic Party came out against Vietnam before Martin Luther King, before Julian Bond, and before Allard Lowenstein. We were attacked by people like Hodding Carter, Bob Boyd, who's now on the school board here—you might want to talk to him. We were freely open on the question of associating with people regardless of their spectrum on the Left, Right. Arthur Kinoy, Ben Smith, [William] Kuntsler—we had no problems. I remember our first meeting with them; myself, Moses, Dave Dennis met with Kuntsler, Kinoy, Ben Smith and we said, "Look, our only concern is we make the decisions." To their credit, they always stuck to it. We couldn't have gotten better legal representation. We made the decisions, they defended them, and the country is better for it.

Lowenstein's, as far as I'm concerned, greatest achievement was organizing the [Eugene] McCarthy campaign. I think the way he did it, and the timing of it, was very well done. You know, the frightening thing to me is that given his relationship to Bob Kennedy, given his relationship to—all of whom Mississippi would have galvanized around in 1968, had he not been assassinated, but after his assassination a lot of us went with McCarthy. The Aaron Henry wing went with [Hubert] Humphrey—and you can see how that vote broke down in that delegation.

But it's a bit saddening that somebody with the energy and the talent of a Lowenstein, who could have contributed so much more to this country, felt it—I'm sure he felt that he was justified in protecting this country from what I consider anathetically its greatest resource—the vitality of people moving around their self-interests, creating institutions where necessary, and supplanting those that aren't working. You don't have to be a political junkie, like I am, to know and be concerned about empowerment, to know the political parties in this country are not functioning. You see, and when we talk about function we've got to look at more than simply conducting elections. We've got to look at formulating policy, almost day-to-day activities—making sure that rent is paid, making sure that medicine is provided, and see, I think while I have shared Lowenstein's concern for anti-communism, I've always found that there's enough flexibility in capitalism to do whatever is necessary. Given the economic problems of this country, and of the world right now, we're going to see so many fluctuations within the next six years we won't be able to separate the two.

But you know, Dennis [Sweeney], the guy who shot and killed Al Lowenstein, did a movie called *Black Mattress*. Have you seen that?

Q: No, I haven't seen that. I know about it, but I haven't seen it.

Guyot: You ought to get it. It shows the difference in the organizational style between the NAACP and COFO. I think that's important, because here was a force that was at times very cooperative and at times totally removed. Sometimes their analysis was so close to Lowenstein's, whether or not he was involved it was just as juxtaposed. For instance, Charles Evers refused to become a part of the 1964 Summer Project and of the 1964 Challenge to the Democratic Party. His position was, "Look, we need to go down to those small counties, take those over." He told me this, which is what he did. But his whole question was, "Look"—I was his campaign manager when he ran for Congress in 1966. He said, "Look, you've got to understand something. I'm in politics to make money. You're in politics to help people." He said, "Look, when I was in Chicago no one ever paid me to sleep

with someone after they slept with them." I said, "What does that have to do with this?" He said, "You've got to understand that basically this is a country of money, and I want as much of it as I can get." So I'm saying that not to attack Chuck, because he would admit to every word of it, but to show that there was a different interest guiding the time and the energy put in by people who organize and who were moving.

I would like to have something kind to say about Al Lowenstein. I can, despite his motivation and his destructiveness, he was a tremendous force in American history, and may the Lord forgive him.

Q: Can I go back to some of these things?

Guyot: Sure.

Q: Your use of the word provocateur is an interesting one, and Ed [Edward] King uses it all the time also to talk about Al.

Guyot: Really? I find that surprising.

Q: Yes. But you know what would be helpful to me is if you could just tell me, provocateur on whose behalf? Do you think it was a connection between what he was doing and the CIA or the FBI or the administration?

Guyot: I think it was clearly, I think he was clearly associated with the CIA, but I think his association was more with Robert Kennedy, who was, in my opinion, just as concerned with containing SNCC early. I mean, he sowed the seeds. Now, a lot of people began to really openly, the open attack was after Atlantic City, beginning with Bayard Rustin's *Commentary* article, the whole COINTEL program was then beginning to be put in place by, coincidentally, John Doar, who was the assistant attorney general, who was a hero to civil rights workers. John Doar got me out of jail a lot of times, okay? But, the Church Committee investigation hearings clearly show that John Doar is the guy who organized the COINTEL program. So, you know, you have to say, "Okay." These guys opted for voter registration without looking at the fact that if we'd really gotten the vote then, 1984 proved what could have happened. So you talk about really getting representation and really turning that thing around, we'd have had another country. See, the interesting thing too is, you have to understand, the liberals must have been very frightened, because the case of the *United States versus Mississippi* was before the Supreme Court. The solicitor general, Archibald Cox, who later gained fame because of, as you know, the Saturday Night Massacre, did not want the court to rule on the merits of the case. Had they done that, all of the voter registration laws in Mississippi would have been declared unconstitutional, we'd have had new elections, immediate registration. Just look at what that would have done to South Carolina, Alabama, Texas, Louisiana, *ad infinitum.*

So, you know, Mississippi was—plus, all of the organizing that was done that was threatening, every scintilla of it was opposed by Roy Wilkins. See, Roy Wilkins's position was, you don't do any organizing in Mississippi. You raise money there, you raise membership, you thrive on the atrocities, but no, anyone who would go in there to organize would automatically be a fool. Well, we did that. I mean, I was born there. I was born in Harrison County, the county that adjoins Hancock County. Hancock County was the home of Theodore Bilbo. The lieutenant governor under Bilbo was a guy named Biddle Adams, who was a personal friend of my father's—who defended me—who was chairman of the Democratic Party, of the regular democrats, who supported John Kennedy in 1960, who defended blacks who were accused of raping white women. This was the lieutenant governor under Bilbo. This same gentlemen was a longtime friend of mine who said to my father, "Look, why don't you get that boy of yours to stop working for the Freedom Democratic Party and come work for us?" He also said, at the 1968 convention he said, "Look, unless you deal with desegregating this delegation, you're wasting your bus fare to Chicago." He said that at the podium, as the chairman of that party.

I can understand why liberals would have been frightened at that time. You had people like Marge Kuret popping up, talking about desegregating the schools. You had Bill [William] Higgs, a native Mississippian, Harvard graduate, bringing in young people. You had a lot of action in the Methodist Church. You had King. A lot of other white ministers were kicked out. So you had the ferment—and if it could happen in Mississippi it could happen anywhere. Of course you had the [James] Meredith desegregation, which we all know how that played.

Then when you start going to the most vulnerable, the most patriotic, the most acceptable duty of citizenship, the vote, you had expanding African freedom—countries coming in and emerging. So what's this contradiction here? Not only am I proud to have been a part of it, but I'm proud to, in retrospect, to look at what was all that was arrayed against us, that we not only survived but thrived. Participatory democracy is the very essence of democracy. Either you're in, or you're out. To be out of a democracy is to make democracy in America a non sequitur. I mean, I don't mean to sound trite on that, but I firmly believe that. It's that deep faith in the people of this country that has allowed me to fight and spend my life fighting, to open it up, empower, and then accept the consequences.

Q: It sounds to me as though when you first met Al in 1962 at the NSA convention you already had some suspicions.

Guyot: No I didn't, I really didn't. I just saw him—and I left the 1962 convention feeling that, "Here's a guy who's a political dynamo in that organization." That was it. I didn't have any preconceived—but when I saw him in Mississippi in 1963 and the way he operated, I mean I just told Moses bluntly, "Why are you dealing with this guy? I mean, this is contrary to everything we operate with. What's with this?"

Q: What did he say?

Guyot: Moses, as usual, said, "Well, you know, he's got a lot of contacts. I think we can work with him. Let's try it."

Q: Take advantage of what he can do for us and then we'll take care of the problems.

Guyot: Yes.

Q: So do you see Moses as having been pivotal to Lowenstein's being able to do whatever he did do? Not Moses' acquiescence—

Guyot: Let me put it this way. Moses was key to getting Lowenstein into SNCC, okay. Otherwise, I don't think he would have made it. But as to what was done subsequently, no, because there were enough checks and balances once we saw him operate that we were all responsible after that.

Q: This discussion where the Timothy Jenkins research was, that took place early 1963, something like that? I hadn't heard that, I mean I probably read it somewhere but I—

Guyot: You may not have read it anywhere, but I know it happened because I was involved in it.

Q: I'm sure. Was it Timothy Jenkins's research, that was just being done then or it had been done before? In other words was the work that was going on going back to the Reconstruction stuff?

Guyot: No, no. Jenkins found the laws. They were still intact on the books.

Q: So this is being done at the time. It had not been done before this.

Guyot: That's right.

Q: Okay, fine. And it was being brought in this group for discussion?

Guyot: Right.

Q: And it is in this context the discussion eventually evolved the notion of the Freedom Vote, or actually a series of freedom votes in the spring and then the big one in the fall.

Guyot: Right.

Q: So that, what you're saying is this whole thing evolves out of a multifaceted discussion in which eventually the ties between all these things—the Jenkins research and everything else—comes together into this plan.

Guyot: That's right.

Q: I should know this and I don't. Is this before or after the episode with Lowenstein and Yazoo?

Guyot: This is—I'm not sure. That I don't know. It's hard to place that.

Q: Were you involved in that directly, that controversy?

Guyot: I just knew about it. I knew about it when it was going on.

Ivanhoe Donaldson was involved, Lowenstein, and Moses.

Q: Those are the three primary actors?

Guyot: Right.

Q: My recollection, at least my sense of it—mostly from Jim Forman's book—was that this was the classic example of someone coming in and trying to tell people what to do.

Guyot: Precisely. That's how it was viewed at the time.

Q: It was widely talked about?

Guyot: Yes, oh yes.

Q: Was that sort of the beginning point of the suspicion?

Guyot: Yes, for a lot of people. For others it had happened earlier. The way he approached people. It was, you know, it was so negative. It was almost—"what can you say bad about the NAACP today? You know, I talked to those guys. They're really good guys. You all just don't understand them."

Q: The interesting thing—of course, would you say that, you did seem to say at the beginning that the presence of the students made an important difference in the politics of—

Guyot: Very positive. There's no question.

Q: Dennis was one of those people—

Guyot: right.

Q:—as were, not a whole lot more but maybe eighty or 100 students, altogether, that fall. As you see it, that then leads directly to the discussions about Freedom Summer.

Guyot: The time we're talking about, you had a very small circle of people who were the moderate establishment at the time. Eleanor Roosevelt, Joe Rauh, Arthur Schlesinger [Jr.], Fred Graham, and Lowenstein. These people never really broad based commonality of leadership. They saw themselves as the intellectual and the ethical justification and epitome of what leadership was. So the clashes were quite predictable, in retrospect. Here we were talking about "Every man a leader," and they were talking about, "Every man must be lead."

Q: A very accurate, short description! When did the discussions start about Freedom Summer?

Guyot: I'll be glad to tell you. There were two meetings about it. Dave Dennis headed the first one. We met in Greenville, and the vote was against it—there would be no Freedom Summer. The reasons being: We were bringing in well-trained, articulate people to uproot our base. We had people who couldn't read and write, but who could organize the town. We had done the work. Moses' position—and that was the first day. The second day Moses came into the meeting and said, "Look, I want this done. I'm putting my reputation on the line on it. I don't want to be a part of an all black thing. We have to bring the nation into Mississippi to settle this, to protect us and the people we're trying to get to register to vote. The Summer vote has proven that that's what happens, and that's what I want you all to do." So we did it. Now I want to be clear. Moses had a lot of support because he was Moses, but the Summer Project—I supported the Summer project in both meetings. But you know, that's the way that happened.

Q: I was just wondering—obviously Lowenstein was not part of these meetings, but had he been part—I have to ask Bob Moses this also—but do you know if he was part of prior conversations with you or with Moses or other people before these decisions were made?

Guyot: No. No, I would hardly think so. See because he was red-baiting us in 1963.

Q: Or at least after the Freedom Vote.

Guyot: That's right.

Q: Not before the Freedom Vote.

Guyot: That's right—not before, but immediately after.

Q: One of the interesting things to me—I'm trying to sort of pinpoint this—is because, at least, the correspondence files show his being involved in recruiting all during the early spring of 1964.

Guyot: I heard that. I heard that, but I find that hard to believe. I did hear that. Ed King told me that he was recruiting students for 1964, but I just, you know I didn't—

Q: But you were also hearing about red-baiting.

Guyot: Most definitely. You see, and you know, when you look at the way he operated, the two are not mutually exclusive at all. He always thought about the possibility of the NAACP taking this program over at any time, that you just—after all SNCC was unstructured, how decisions were made, who made the decisions—this sort of foolishness.

Q: How about the idea, the suggestion of Bill [William Sloan] Coffin as the new head of the whole thing. Did that ever come up?

Do you remember hearing about that?

Guyot: The head of the whole—

Q: Sort of imposing Bill Coffin as the director of the whole project.

Guyot: Oh yes, I heard discussions, short discussions, about that. But that was it.

Q: It never would go anywhere.

Guyot: No.

Q: But you do recall that as being something that was at least mentioned during that time.

Guyot: Yes. But you see, the reason it was dismissed so quickly is no one could have done that. Because see, in 1962 we had met with R. L. T. Smith, Aaron Henry—we'd organized COFO again, and we fought that fight right then, that Moses would be the executive director, that R. L. T. Smith would run, that Aaron Henry would be the president of COFO. We fought that out in Clarkstead—myself, Dave Dennis, Dary Ladnes, Aaron Henry, R. L. T. Smith, Wiley Branton, who was a hero to all of us. Then, see, because the whole question of decision making was key to everything we did, so there would have been no way that anyone could have been interjected.

Q: It wouldn't have happened, obviously.

Guyot: No. Now, you see, I remember in late 1962, we had a COFO meeting, and we had a couple hundred people from all over the city, all over the state. I rode to the airport with a guy from the Civil Rights Commission. He told me, "I'm going to tell you something. This kind of stuff cannot be allowed to continue." I said, "What do you mean?" He said, "The government can't allow for this to be continued." I said, "What are they going to do, kill us all?" He said, "No, but you've got to understand—this cannot be allowed to be continued." It wasn't like he was angry or anything. It was just a certainty of life with him. Even at that time—we were talking about re-apportionment of the state. We were bringing in people who could barely afford to live into a statewide meeting, paying their own gas, their own transportation. We had no salaried individuals. SNCC at that time was paying ten dollars a week. So, you see the potential.

Q: Now, Lowenstein's relationship with Henry goes back a long way. How tight was that?

Guyot: Extremely. Extremely tight. After all— you've got to understand. They had a lot of things in common. They were both very concerned about being accepted in the establishment milieu, and had connections, good connections there. Who were both tied to the Kennedys, and both were law and order sort of folk. "Let's run things right."

Q: So that Lowenstein might have thought that that connection, that tie, would help him prevail.

Guyot: Well let me tell you something. Let me show you how well—I was at Aaron Henry's house when Lowenstein called, on a couple of occasions. They were intensely tied because they needed each other.

Let me give you an example. Aaron Henry supported the compromise in Atlantic City. After that was over and people rejected the compromise, not only did Aaron Henry leave early but Joe Rauh and Al Lowenstein came to Mississippi after Atlantic City and publicly announced that they had created the Mississippi Freedom Democratic Party, that it had succeeded, and now what it needed was new leadership. Okay? Joe Rauh really—I have good

things to say about Joe Rauh now in retrospect— says, "Look, I had two bosses—Guyot and Aaron Henry." I was in jail in Hattiesburg, but I was chairman of the party. Aaron was head of the delegation to Atlantic City, and after Atlantic City his role evaporated. Now, there's just so much difference in what we were trying to do politically. I think the best thing I can say about Aaron Henry is when Alan Dulles came to Mississippi representing the CIA and the president and were searching for the bodies of [Michael] Schwerner, [James] Chaney, and [Andrew] Goodman, that with us in the capitol, told us, "You're going to stop over this. We're going to do everything we can to stop this." Aaron Henry said, "Look. You're talking to the wrong people. We're not going to stop. What we're doing is right. We're going to continue to do it, and that's it, and we're going to continue to encourage everyone else to do it. You should be supporting us rather than trying to calm us down."

So, I have a lot of respect for Aaron Henry. I mean, he made a major contribution in the state. I remember asking him to come down to Hattiesburg—he came! Had to walk through the police and the firemen, but he came. Again, I don't mind the fight that is—Aaron Henry and I said to one another, "Look, let's work together to register the voters, and then we're going to both try and take them different ways." We did that. So I don't have a problem with Aaron Henry because of his association with Al Lowenstein. What concerns me is when we look at the contribution. In a democracy I think we owe it to one another to be as least destructive as possible. If we were going to differ on terms and intensity around parameters, let's let that be the fight. I don't want to feel that I have the obligation to destroy you because of what you believe.

Q: How about Bob Spike?

Guyot: Bob Spike—a saint. Bob Spike got committed in 1963, around the Freedom Day in Hattiesburg. He was key. He opened up the church to us, and opened the church up to us— made it work both ways. We trusted him. There was nothing that he ever could do for SNCC that he didn't do. He was good on the Vietnam question. He was good on providing the money for the training at Oxford. I'm trying to think of two other guys. Art Thomas, who was the first director of the Delta Ministry, and a guy named Ben something who headed the Center for Community Change for a long time. I think the role of organized church was indispensable.

Guyot: I remember attending an ECRU meeting—Episcopalians for Cultural and Racial Unity—and talking to them about the congressional challenge, telling them how they should support it, and some of them standing up and saying, "You know, we have our tax exemption to do." Others standing up saying, "Hey look, we know how to get around that. We'll set up"— so I mean that kind of access we couldn't have created.

Q: Did Lowenstein have a close relationship with Spike?

Guyot: Well, let's put it this way—when they were subject institutionally to the same pressures—I mean Lowenstein knew how to get to the leadership of the churches, the business interest—to get to them. But I'd say unless there was pressure really applied from the top, universally, Bob Spike could be counted on.

Q: Wasn't he part of the meeting at the God house, as it's called?

Guyot: Yes.

Q: So that at least to that extent there was, obviously not everyone who was part of that meeting shared the same point of view, but in retrospect the people who were part of that meeting who were associated with New York powers were all—as I understand it, it was a situation of Mississippi folk being pretty well isolated and having to all be under attack. I don't remember what Spike did in that meeting.

Guyot: Neither do I. See, in that particular—I think, as I remember, he was sort of ambiguous. But, given his relationship to SNCC, his consistent relationship to SNCC, he would have to go way overboard for us to have broken with him. The interesting thing about Spike is SCLC

felt the same way about him that we did. I remember talking with Hosea [Williams] about Spike after his assassination—that's what we called it, that's what we thought it was.

Q: By the summer of 1964, no matter what's going on and certainly in Atlantic City, what I hear you saying is that there was almost no one left in SNCC who had any confidence in Lowenstein.

Guyot: That's right.

Q: Yet, he's at the convention, and he's in some meeting. What's your sense of what's going on there, and of what his role is?

Guyot: Well, just look at the forces that were brought to bear. UAW, National Council of Churches, White House. Everyone now had to say, "Look, we can't go any further." The question was just that intense. So I have no doubt about what his role was. His role was, "Split them all." I mean Aaron Henry and Ed King supported the compromise. Fannie Lou Hamer told me that—and were prepared to go out and announce it to the press. Fannie Lou Hamer stopped it.

Q: Now, you were in jail during this period?

Guyot: For thirty days.

Q: Thirty days. Now, my understanding from, I guess at least from Rauh, and I think from, I have to talk to Moses about this, is that Moses and Lowenstein and Humphrey were part of the critical meeting—two or three people were part of that meeting who are no longer with us, and I haven't talked to Moses about it. Have you heard any stories about that session? It was a session that preceded the announcement of the "false" acceptance of the compromise.

Guyot: What I know about that meeting was that Moses was in the meeting. There were other people other than those three—it was a larger meeting than that. Moses saw on television that the announcement had been made and then he left the room right then, accusing, talking about Humphrey like a dog—as he should have. But that meeting will be described—Romaine describes it in her book. I wasn't there, so I don't want to—

Q: Right [Walter F.] Mondale was there, I think. Mondale plays a critical role in this whole thing.

Guyot: Mondale is very, very clear. Mondale's—that's why I said to people when we had a SNCC meeting in Trinity, "Look, you've got to understand. Jesse Jackson's campaign is the continuation of 1964." In 1964 SNCC had to fight for empowerment, involvement, and changing the policy and the direction of the Democratic Party, but it had to get in to do something. Who do we have to fight with? We have to fight Mondale, Andy Young, and the White House. Who is Jesse fighting? Mondale, Andy Young, Aaron Henry—on both of those. Aaron Henry was on the opposite side on both of those. Conceptually this was—now some of them agreed with it. James Forman wanted to take him on, because of obvious leadership things. I think that's true, and I think the reaction in 1984 of the Joint Center for Political Studies when the run-off elections were made an issue and they were asked, "Do you think this is discriminatory?" Their position was, "After study and careful analysis, we have no position." Well!

Q: Pretty clear.

Guyot: Yes.

Q: Wow! Who was seen—were there any people seen in Mississippi as being, by 1964 as being, allies or associates—friendly associates—of Lowenstein?

Guyot: Ed King. Ed King, Aaron Henry, occasionally Hodding Carter.

Q: And Moses would stay in touch? You wouldn't characterize him as an ally, but you'd characterize him as someone who would stay in touch.

Guyot: Yes.

Q: Now Forman never had anything good to say about Lowenstein.

Guyot: Never. Never. Forman organized his position on Lowenstein in NSA meetings.

Q: Back in the 1950s.

Guyot: There you go.

Q: Did Ed retain the confidence?

Guyot: Oh yes. I was astounded when you said what you said about Ed using the term "provocateur." I mean, Ed was a supporter, protector, and defender, and Ed was one of the people Lowenstein usually checked with when he came to Mississippi.

Q: During most of this period, his correspondence of course is almost all with—there are some interesting letters with Bob Moses, back and forth.

Guyot: Is that right?

Q: But most of the correspondence is with Stanford and Yale and other people.

Guyot: See you're privy to things that I haven't seen.

Q: Sure. But it's very interesting stuff, and it's clear that there's a very ambivalent relationship developing, as you say, during the winter and spring. Now there's no evidence that's for—I mean there's evidence, verbal evidence. I don't see any writing yet about the red-baiting, but I know it happened. There's no question about that, as you say. But there is this very kind of approach-avoidance thing with the whole movement.

Guyot: You've got to understand. Let me tell you some of what Lowenstein was thinking, and I won't tell you the basis of where I get my source for that. He said, "Look, there are thousands of dollars tied up in bond money." Nobody had been registered to vote. The Birmingham killings had happened. Things were just not moving. That's his description of that period. My description of it would have been, "We're building leadership. We're organizing around the vote. We're identifying and recruiting and training leadership. We're utilizing the churches, getting them opened up on the question of voter registration. We've been able to withstand, we've been able to tear down the terror and bring it just into normal fear, given the conditions we're operating in Mississippi. That we have survived from 1961 to 1963 was a political achievement." So it's a question of how you look at it. I mean, we'd been getting—the Fifth Circuit Court of Appeals could not have been better, and we could not have survived as a political movement without it. I litigated for the right to distribute leaflets, *Guyot versus Thornton. NAACP versus Jackson,* where the Fifth Circuit declared, developed this policy of Iron Clad Segregation, which was the policy of Jackson that occurred. So you had things moving. *United States versus Mississippi* was on the way to the Supreme Court.

Q: So there were a lot of important things that were in process.

I think you're right—the key issue is control. It's the bottom line.

Guyot:—this involved. One at some college in, some liberal white college in Jackson, and the other at Tougaloo. At Tougaloo people didn't want him to speak, and I was the one who asked them to let him speak because I didn't want him to use the press and to go out and say he was denied to speak and this sort of thing. Millsaps— at Millsaps, he played the role openly of trying to provoke the people on the panel with him and the audience around the whole question of foreign policy and the left and the credentials of people who had been involved in the movement, and this sort of thing. So I understand, see. But again, I think what he did was good. I have no qualms about his red-baiting anything that he couldn't control. I understand that. That was his reality. I mean if he or someone like him couldn't control it, it had to be communist.

Q: Mistrusted.

Guyot: That's right.

End of interview

JACK LANDRÓN (JACKIE WASHINGTON)

I Thought We'd All Be Friends By Now

Social change is often amazing. When trying to affect a long-term change, I wonder if you can ever predict with any accuracy how things will turn out. In school my nine-year-old daughter learns about Rosa Parks, Ralph Abernathy, Martin Luther King, Jesse Jackson, and Fannie Lou Hamer. These are all great people who have helped make significant changes in this country. I have been privileged to have known them all and with the exception of Ms. Parks, on more than one occasion I have had informal or private conversations with each of them. At no time do I recall any of these people saying anything that would indicate that they thought thirty years ago that the racial climate of this country would be what it is today. I believe they each thought as I did, that conditions would simply be nicer than they were in the childhoods each of us had. Vida, my daughter, asked why things had to be changed. She wanted to know what it was like when I was her age. I tried to tell her but I don't think she got it. It is hard to understand if you didn't live through it. Not only is social change hard to predict, it's also difficult to reassemble an accurate picture of what the society was like before the change occurred.

America before the Civil Rights Movement of the sixties was quite a different place. For the most part, anybody of any consequence had to be white. Nobody else did anything truly im-

portant or worthwhile. You couldn't pick up a magazine from a mainstream national publisher and read about accomplishments of non-whites. Nothing in newsreels, on billboards, radio and television commercials, nothing in any human interest pieces that appeared in newspapers of the time gave the impression that blacks and other non-whites were anything more than exotic trifles whose main purposes were to serve, entertain, or otherwise enhance the quality of white people's lives. Schools taught young people a history that suggested it had always been that way and probably always would. Although church and state were separate, America presented itself as a Christian country and universally recognizable portraits of Jesus were everywhere. It was common knowledge that Jesus and the Father were one, so the assumption that God is a white man didn't come under attack. Being a white man was on the level of divine heritage. It was not enough, therefore to *be* a white man, one strove to be the *image* of a white man. It seems practically everyone was swept up in that endeavor, especially the middle to lower middle class. It was as though the white man was a concept advanced by Plato. It was an idea—a single, original entity hovering just above reality. "White man" was an image, and its nearest manifestation was as he was portrayed in the movies, on television, and in advertisements. This image was the criterion for our lives. "White man" was wise, he always wore a tie, often smoked a pipe, and he was handsome. He could be found seated in the living room of a single family house that he owned in some picture perfect small town. He had two children (this number could vary) and his wife was coiffed to a fair-thee-well, busily doing something in a neat well-appointed kitchen wearing high heels, a nice cotton frock, and a pert little apron. "White men's" taste and behavioral preferences informed the middle-class America of my formative years. It was a time when black youngsters were not encouraged to choose a field and become the best in it. One was instead urged to be a credit to the race.

Black people did not seem to find their own invisibility a cause for anger. To be sure, they were keenly aware of the unfairness of second-class citizenship, they deplored the hideousness of cases like that of Emmett Till, and they disliked Jim Crow. But for the most part, blacks lived through this time with a good-natured disdain for racial injustice. Rage was not a consideration. Like their Caucasian counterparts, emulating "white man," not criticizing him, seemed to be the priority job. This was a time when a light-skinned colored girl with "good hair" was considered pretty even if she wasn't. Up until the sixties racism was so insidious that even black people looked down on the black race. Negroes seemed to insist that those who would lead them had to be light, bright, and damn near white. As well as for his many other achievements, Dr. Martin Luther King is owed a debt of gratitude for having successfully challenged this custom. He did it just by being himself and having the courage to champion a cause whose time had come. His dark skin, full lips and hair like watch springs, along with the musicality of his eloquent, colored preacher style of oratory were in sharp contrast to the crisp articulation of Adam Clayton Powell, the erudite sophistication of W.E.B. Dubois, the fair skin of Walter White, and the flaxen hair of Thurgood Marshall. Without in any way attempting to minimize the outstanding accomplishments of these fine men, I have to point out that to some degree their ac-

cess to positions of influence had something to do with the way they looked and sounded. Their images were more like "white man" than the average Negroes for whom they were spokesmen. Dr. King was a hero that looked like us! On proud, flat feet he marched through the land changing our country and changing our minds. The spell of "white man" was broken! Everybody—young and old, black and white (and all shades in between), rich and poor have learned to see black people differently. Since this revelation, changes have taken place with lightening speed. Blacks are mayors of major cities, they run for president and sit in the supreme court. There are lots of black millionaires and black captains of industry. Black folks practically run the music business and black actors and directors are not only finding work but they regularly win top honors in their field.

With these advances has come evidence of the intense anger that has lain dormant for so many years. This deep-seated anger among blacks occasionally flares up and reveals, in some cases, the existence of full-blown racism. It is especially evident and widespread among the young. One might wonder what have these kids got to be so angry about? They never had loved ones needlessly bleed to death outside hospitals that wouldn't admit Negroes. They never experienced the demoralizing effect of the low self-esteem we lived with back when we were induced to love "white man" better than we loved ourselves. They were never drafted into an army that told them that segregation was needed in the armed forces because although they were good enough to fight for the country, they weren't good enough to die alongside white soldiers. They never lived through these and many hundred more degradations. What are they so angry about? All of it! Psychology teaches us that though they may be suppressed, human emotions don't go away. The anger, rage, and resentment has been there for years. The old folks swallowed it yesterday, the young are spitting it out today because at last it seems safe to do so. I think it is healthy. But at the same time there is cause for alarm.

America is a racist country. Racism is a convention that begets itself. It should not be startling, therefore, to learn that there is a new racism lurking in the justifiable anger of a long oppressed people. But it seems to have a physical nature and is spawning a popular culture with a violent core. Rap music is performed by fist-shaking artists and often features hateful lyrics. The burgeoning wave of gifted young black comedians includes performers whose well received routines deal with violence as an acceptable resolution of differences. There are those who say these are violent times. It's not just the black kids. To be sure, I see anger among young whites too. But my lack of surprise at the numbers of white youths who are active in Neo-Nazi, skinhead, reactionary, ultraconservative groups is because, although I am well aware that all white people are not racists, I have to say that I am accustomed to finding overtly racist sentiments among whites. I view this thinly veiled malice, this violent undercurrent of the popular culture among blacks, as a new occurrence. The alarming thing is that blacks have a responsibility that as yet is not being met. The responsibility is that, quiet as it is kept, black people have long been the driving force behind the design and style of the broad spectrum of American popular culture. One has only to look at the far reaching, profound influence blacks have had over the years on music, sports, fashion, language, and what it means to "be cool" and/or socially correct among the young in this country. While battling the intolerable stigma of second-class citizenship, black people have nonetheless had a lot to do with the shaping of America's popular culture. God forbid that we make fashionable the polarization of America's peoples.

When as a young man I took off for Mississippi in the spring of 1964, there was no doubt in my mind that I was off to join a mighty army that would bring about the end of bigotry and racial intolerance. Not only were we going to wipe out disenfranchisement among rural black people in that state, but we would help take the national fascination with "white man" and lay it to rest. This would allow all Americans to become receptive to other images and that would open the way for blacks and other non-whites to assume positions of universal respect and admiration. There would finally be powerful role models for kids like the one I used to be.

Most of that stuff happened. It is a good feeling to know that the great adventure of my young life met with a commendably high level of success. Of course we did not end racial intolerance. Racism is part of the fabric of this country. My conviction that its threads must be pulled out remains as strong today as it was thirty years ago. I continue to urge others to take up the task. However, racism has changed, and we must devise new plans of attack. That business of white and black Northerners standing side by side in some Southern place like the Mississippi of thirty years ago, warbling hopefully that we shall overcome someday—that's played out. Ironically, our fighting today will mostly be done in separate but equal ranks. Blacks aren't near helpless victims anymore. We're very much stronger. We have our own racists now, and black racists are more effectively discredited by other blacks. It's funny, but I think the army that we send out today to defeat racism should be segregated. One can never see Dr. King's dream as he dreamed it, and unfortunately he is not here to describe it more vividly. There is no doubt as we look around these days at Bensonhurst, Los Angeles, Howard Beach, and Miami . . . This ain't it! Let's get busy. Freedom Summer of 1964 was just the dramatic beginning of an on-going quest. ❖

Father's Grave

Cordell Reagon and I traveled together during the summer Caravan through Mississippi and other areas of the South. We visited the house where Cordell grew up in Waverly, Tennessee. Cordell had talked often about not getting to his father's funeral on time. We went to the graveyard and cut the weeds down over the grave. We talked about freedom and about whether our children in the next generation would have to go through the difficult changes we were going through.

This is a personal song, yet its chorus speaks for many in the Movement.

With my swing blade in my hand, as I looked across the land
And thought of all the places that I'd been,
Of that old house that I called home,
Where I'd always been alone
And of that weedy grave that held my closest kin.

And as I cut the weeds from o'er my father's grave, father's grave,
I swore no child I bore would be a slave.

Oh, the old house was a shell, there were weeds around the well,
And I touched the rusty hinge that held no door
And the roof was caving in, It was always sort of thin,
And I found the place where the ash pan burned the floor.

And as I cut the weeds from o'er my father's grave, father's grave,
I swore no child I bore would be a slave.

I thought of all the glad and the good times that I had
With my pockets full of purple plums each fall
When the yard was wide and clean and the grass was short and green
Now the underbrush has laid its claim to all.

And as I cut the weeds from o'er my father's grave, father's grave,
I swore no child I bore would be a slave.

It made me feel so bad, lost the best friend that I had
And I didn't get to hear the preacher pray
Yes, and I was only eight, no, I can't recall the date
Nor the reason I was late, but a funeral just can't wait
And when I got to church they were rolling him away.

And as I cut the weeds from o'er my father's grave, father's grave,
I swore no child I bore would be a slave.

STEPHEN BINGHAM

Looking Back

Being asked to look back on the Mississippi Summer Project of 1964, I am struck by the irony in the request: the interest in marking the thirtieth anniversary of that event arises in part out of the central reason the summer was organized: the involvement of white Northerners in the project. The silent work of African American civil rights activists which came before and after that summer is remembered less well, if at all.

COFO organizers of the Summer Project felt that white participation would bring attention from the northern press, so important in forming opinion in the white political institutions of America. It was hoped America's leaders would wake up to the outrageous injustices occurring in the Deep South.

The most atrocious example of the press's attitude during the '64 Summer itself occurred when a headless torso of an African American was discovered floating down the Mississippi River, near Natchez as I recall. The story became instant national news because the press thought it might be the body of Jim Chaney, killed with northern whites Mickey Schwerner and Andrew Goodman. Once the press learned the body was someone else, the commonplace incident became a non-story.

It is a sad commentary on the times that it was the discovery of those three civil rights workers' bodies which probably contributed more to the passage of the Voting Rights Act of 1965 than all the collective work of staff and summer

volunteers.

While this Act has led to the election of hundreds of African Americans throughout the nation, it is striking how segregated the United States remains thirty years later. All legal Jim Crow barriers are gone, yet the vast majority of African American children go to schools as different in quality from white schools as the segregated schools in Mississippi were in 1964. While America still tends to express genuine outrage at civil rights discrimination, most African Americans cannot afford to live in any of the middle-class communities of this country where most whites live. So de facto segregation remains, its roots being more economic than political.

The Los Angeles uprising after the Rodney King verdict was the costliest civil uprising since the Civil War. It was as much due to atrocious economic conditions as outrage over the verdict. Sixty percent of South Central Los Angeles survives on welfare. The value of AFDC has decreased by 42 percent over the past three decades. Most astonishing was the failure of the federal government to respond in any meaningful way to such tinderbox conditions. Clinton's seventeen billion dollar economic stimulus package—small to begin with but symbolically important as an effort to help the inner cities—ended up as a paltry one billion dollar program, with no hope of addressing the abject poverty consuming this country. While vastly larger percentages of people of color are poor, in absolute

Stephen Bingham since 1990 has been a staff attorney at the San Francisco Neighborhood Legal Assistant Foundation, the local legal aid program. He specializes in the areas of general assistance benefits, homelessness, and employment.

numbers more whites are poor. Ultimately, therefore, poverty is caused by economic forces but exacerbated by racism.

As a legal aid lawyer in San Francisco specializing in public benefits issues, I see the misery every day. AFDC benefits in California were cut 4.5 percent in 1991, 5.8 percent in 1992 (1.3 percent of which was later declared unlawful) and another 2.7 percent in 1993. General Assistance (GA) benefits, given to poor adults who qualify for no other assistance, were eliminated in Michigan in the winter of 1991–92, leaving eighty thousand without anything. Illinois and Ohio followed suit. Many other states, including California, severely reduced the GA benefit levels. African Americans were disproportionately hard hit. Astoundingly, there has been no national reaction and little local reaction.

Even more surprising is that these draconian assaults on poor people pass almost unnoticed by liberals/progressives who should care. I was struck two years ago that nearly one hundred thousand people marched in San Francisco on two consecutive weekends to protest the war in Iraq yet, a few months later, welfare rights organizers were able to assemble a courageous crowd of only three hundred to demonstrate in Sacramento against AFDC cuts, which were clearly going to create homeless families.

The United Nations Declaration of Human Rights guarantees the right to shelter, the right to economic survival. Yet, in the United States, the richest nation on earth, millions of children go to bed hungry every night. An estimated three million people are currently homeless in this country. They have become the latest pariahs in a country which supposedly prides itself on so-called Christian values. The hypocrisy of it all is celebrated annually at Christmas, the story of a little boy, Jesus, whose mother had to give birth in a stable for lack of a room.

Perhaps, as a nation, we don't feel the same need to protect the poor. Race discrimination in one way is worse: one has no control over one's skin color while, theoretically at least, the

poor can always get a job and become middle-class. Yet, all economists, whatever their political stripe, will agree that this country's economic system, capitalism, requires that a large number of people are unemployed at any one time. Economists used to say that 4 percent unemployment was really "full employment." Now many say it's 7 percent unemployment. Insurance benefits, which in the late '70s covered 80 percent of unemployed workers, now only cover two in five. The minimum wage has lost over a dollar in value over the past two decades. It is so low that single parents cannot afford to work at $4.35 an hour because child care and medical expenses leave them with almost nothing to live on.

And so the permanently unemployed and the mentally disabled, thrown out onto our streets and parks in the Reagan years to fend for themselves, grow in number every day. AFDC children are made to pay for savings-and-loans scandals whose perpetrators usually do not even get arrested, let alone serve time. Neighborhoods continue to deteriorate as a tax structure which rewards keeping buildings empty pushes greedy investors to construct more office buildings rather than invest in housing. And all of these injustices against the poor hit people of color especially hard.

Part of me wanted to write about my precious memories of black and white solidarity in the sixties: clear-cut battles which we sensed at the time were at the cutting edge of political progress. Sounds of freedom songs in my ears. Yet it all doesn't feel right. We won a battle for political expression but are losing the war.

Ironically, the South in many ways may be a better place for African Americans to live today than the North. A few years ago, I spoke to a largely African American high school class in Oakland about my experiences in Mississippi in 1963–64. I asked a girl who had visited relatives in Mississippi what the biggest difference was between Oakland and Mississippi. "The violence in Oakland," she told me.

Illustrative of the secondary place economic

rights plays in our national dialogue was a meeting last year of a civil rights group in the San Francisco Bay Area with the powerful speaker of the California Assembly, Willie Brown. He came to express his support for an omnibus civil rights bill, protecting the rights of people of color, women, and gays and lesbians. When asked how hard he would fight against proposed welfare cuts, he equivocated completely. In fact, he has done virtually nothing in the last three years to stave off the wave of welfare bashing being done in the name of budget balancing. The public outcry against welfare recipients has reached a fever pitch and is somehow reminiscent of the hidden racist message in the Bush campaign's successful Willie Horton strategy in 1988.

As progressives are constantly forced to fight reactionary anti-poor proposals, I wonder if we will ever have the time to propose meaningful, positive change that would guarantee work for those who want it and address the worst of the inequities, typified by tax loopholes enjoyed by the rich in every state. My wish is that the energy which brought us through the civil rights years of the sixties will reemerge, that once again we will find common ground, but that this time around we will fight for economic rights, not merely political rights. For, until we do so, the political rights won in the sixties have limited meaning to those who are poor, as shown by their extremely low voter turnouts. We can do better. We simply need the will. ❖

GREG TRAFIDLO AND NEAL PHILLIPS

Summer '64
Oh Freedom!

"Summer '64"

Were you sittin' on the sidelines?
Were you really in the fight?
Helpin' people raise their voices
All together, black and white

Were you preachin' civil rights?
Teachin' door to door?
In Mississippi, in that summer '64

Did we learn from Mississippi
When hatred burns today?
Can we keep the dream of Martin's
From ever fadin' 'way

It's been thirty years and countin'
But that march ain't over yet
Oh Freedom! Let 'em know we won't forget.

"Oh Freedom"

Oh freedom. Oh Freedom.
Oh freedom over me
And before I'd be a slave,
I'd be buried in my grave
And go home to my lord, and be free.

Greg Trafidlo and Neal Phillips wrote Summer 64/Oh Freedom *specifically for "Freedom Is A Constant Struggle: Songs Of The Mississippi Civil Rights Movement." They are multi-talented, award winning singers/ songwriters based in Virginia's Blue Ridge Mountains.*

STAUGHTON LYND

Freedom Summer: A Tragedy, Not A Melodrama

I was director of Freedom Schools in the Mississippi Summer Project. This gives me no special claim to insight. I was in Mississippi only about two months. It is true that I "directed" by traveling around the state rather than sitting at a telephone in Jackson, but inevitably my perspective was to some extent from above, not from below. Finally, I was white, male, and at thirty-four somewhat older than the typical volunteer or SNCC field secretary.

With all these caveats, I want to offer an analysis of Freedom Summer that I have not seen elsewhere. Media and historical treatment of the Mississippi Summer Project has been nostalgic, romantic, oversimplified. The dominant image is that of black and white young heroes engaged in melodramatic struggle with the dragon of Mississippi racism. I see things a little differently. The analysis I offer is based on facts that I think we all know, but I have tried to indicate my sources. I hope others will respond and carry the analysis further.

There was a long and serious debate among civil rights workers in Mississippi during late 1963 and early 1964 about whether Freedom Summer was a good idea. One position was that in more than two years SNCC had succeeded in registering very few black voters in Mississippi; that black Mississippians who had responded to SNCC's call had been killed (Herbert Lee), injured, imprisoned, expelled from school,

and otherwise harmed, without a great deal to show for their sacrifices; and that if white volunteers were to come to the Magnolia State in large numbers, the nation's attention would be drawn to Mississippi, and helpful intervention by the federal government might follow.

The opposing position was that SNCC activity in southwest Mississippi and the Delta from 1961 to 1963, while it might not have registered many voters, had begun to build an indigenous black movement. Older leaders consulted by Bob Moses when he came to the state, like Mr. Steptoe, had been joined by younger leaders: Fannie Lou Hamer, Curtis Hayes, Brenda Travis, and countless others. The concern of those opposing Freedom Summer was that a flood of articulate, white, middle-class Northerners would cause these new leaders of the black community to become unsure of their skills in organizing, public speaking, and writing; that in the presence of the volunteers these local black leaders might revert to deference to white folks; and that, whatever the short-run gains, Freedom Summer might disorient and even destroy the self-organization of the Mississippi black community.

It seems that in internal SNCC discussion about Freedom Summer, Bob Moses was at first neutral. Anyone who knew him then will recall the self-effacing style that he habitually assumed. If asked to speak, he would stand in place rather

Staughton Lynd taught at Spelman College in Atlanta from 1961 to 1964. He is the author of Nonviolence in America: A Documentary History *(revised edition to be published by Orbis Books) and other books.*

than come to the front of a room. Rather than lay out his own ideas he tended to ask questions. His characteristic manner was that of one who facilitates the empowerment of others. So it was, apparently, at the beginning of SNCC's internal debate on the proposed Summer Project.

According to Taylor Branch in *Parting The Waters*, a messenger interrupted one of the SNCC staff debates in Hattiesburg with news that Louis Allen, who had witnessed the murder of Herbert Lee, had himself been killed. Bob Moses went to see Mrs. Allen. On returning to the Hattiesburg meeting, Bob said "We can't protect our own people," and threw his moral authority behind the Summer Project.

Indeed, it appears that Bob used his personal influence to override rejection of the Summer Project by SNCC and CORE staff. In 1967 I had a conversation with Dave Dennis, who coordinated all CORE work in Mississippi during the summer of 1964. Dave said that SNCC and CORE workers took a vote defeating the Summer Project proposal. He added that Bob (with, as I understood it, Dave's support and assistance) then insisted on a second vote, and obtained a different outcome. The Summer Project went forward.

The hard question that needs answering is: Who was right in the internal SNCC and CORE debate? Was the Summer Project a good thing or a bad thing?

My conclusion is: *Both* sides were right; the Summer Project was *both* good and bad. It was therefore a tragedy, in the classical Greek sense, wherein the tragic flaw in a good thing produces a bad thing, as well.

On the one hand, it cannot be doubted that the Summer Project helped to bring about the passage of the 1964 Civil Rights Act and the 1965 Voting Rights Act, and played a major part in creating a South in which black persons can vote. This might or might not have been true had James Chaney, Mickey Schwerner, and Andrew Goodman not been killed. And no one expected the Freedom Democratic Party's bid

to be seated at the Democratic Party convention in Atlantic City to be so nearly successful. The fact is that a voter registration strategy based on the Summer Project succeeded after the failure of a voter registration strategy based on years of sacrificial organizing by SNCC cadre.

But on the other hand, can there be any question that the Summer Project helped to break up the interracial Civil Rights Movement that SNCC was until 1964?

There were whites in SNCC before 1964, among them Bob Zellner, Mary King, Casey Hayden, Howard Zinn, Jane Stembridge, Betty Garman, and Jack Minnis. They were a minority in the organization and took direction from black leaders like Jim Forman, Julian Bond, and Bob Moses. The summer of 1964 created a new situation. Unexpectedly, many volunteers decided to remain in Mississippi. Thus one white Freedom School director (myself) was succeeded by another (Liz Fusco). More importantly, after the Atlantic City events, white Northern lawyers like Arthur Kinoy continued to make or try to make fundamental decisions about long-run SNCC strategy.

Perhaps the SNCC opposition to Freedom Summer was wrong in one respect. Perhaps it was not so much indigenous black organizees who resented the white volunteers from the North as it was SNCC organizers, SNCC *staff*. (This had a sexual aspect that I have been chastised for trying to discuss. There was a great deal of sex between black males on SNCC and CORE staff, and white female volunteers, during the summer of 1964. Sex happened, as Doug McAdam's book recounts, despite constant public pronouncements that it should *not* happen because it would endanger the Summer Project. A great deal of personal confusion and disorientation happened along with it.)

Sometime in the 1970s I had a conversation about all this with a former student of mine at Spelman, Gwen Robinson, now Zaharah Simmons. After volunteering for the Summer Project, Zaharah dropped out of college and became a full-time SNCC organizer. She worked in the Vine Street project in Atlanta. This group drafted what I believe to have been the first Black Power statement by members of SNCC. Zaharah sent me a copy in, I think, spring 1965.

When I saw Zaharah in the 1970s, I asked: "What was Black Power all about?" Her immediate answer was that Black Power responded to the fact that after the summer of 1964 decisions about SNCC strategy began to be made by white people in the North. Zaharah pointed to the fact that after Freedom Summer, SNCC came to have a much larger budget, including, for example, a fleet of rental cars. A larger fundraising operation in the North, and greater dependence on that operation, resulted. Moreover, after Freedom Summer SNCC's local organizing languished as attention focused on the effort to seat Freedom Democrats in Congress. This too was an effort headquartered in the North, rather than in the South.

Cause and effect in these developments may be difficult to untangle. It does seem clear that SNCC decision making tended to shift northward and into the hands of whites, and that, if Zaharah's testimony is credited, this was a major stimulus to the ascendancy of Black Power in SNCC.

I hope I am not understood to be pointing a finger of blame at anyone. We were all protagonists in the play. I am not even blaming myself: actually, after I was asked to be Freedom School director, I tried very hard to find a black person to share the job with me, but failed.

No, my thesis is that the Mississippi Summer Project was a tragedy, not a simple contest of good guys and gals on the one side, and bad guys on the other. The Summer Project was a tragedy because a strategy effective in winning the right to vote also disempowered blacks at the same time. Both sides in the Movement still debate about whether the supporting arguments to have a Summer Project were proved correct. The casualties of the summer included not only the individuals who died, but the idea of an interracial movement for fundamental social change. ❖

DOUG MCADAM

"Let it Shine, Let it Shine, Let it Shine"

When I was asked to write a piece for this thirtieth anniversary volume on the 1964 Freedom Summer Project, I again felt the deep ambivalence that the Project has always aroused in me. Let me be clear on the source of my ambivalence. I have nothing but praise for the Project itself. Quite simply, Freedom Summer was one of the most audacious, courageous, inspirational, and ultimately successful campaigns to take place in arguably the most audacious, courageous, inspirational, and ultimately successful social movement in recent American history. I refer, of course, to the Southern Civil Rights Movement.

But I cannot persuade myself that the attention lavished on the Summer Project, today no less than in 1964, owes only to the admirable qualities noted above. For if audacity, courage, and inspiration were enough to generate attention then many more Americans would know of Bob Moses's audacious first year of organizing in Mississippi; or Charles Sherrod's courageous three decades of civil rights work in southwest Georgia; or the inspirational life and times of Fannie Lou Hamer. No, I suspect that the Freedom Summer Project continues to generate interest now for the same reason it made headlines in 1964: white Americans were central to the story. And therein lies the source of my ambivalence and the first of several ironies connected with the Project. To celebrate the

Project while ignoring the countless other campaigns that made up the Movement is to perpetuate a subtle form of racism that places a higher value on white rather than black experience.

Now for the irony; it was precisely this double standard that Project organizers sought to exploit and which must be credited for much of the campaign's success. A bit of background is in order. The Project was born of SNCC's frustration at the stalemate it faced in Mississippi after three years of grueling and extremely dangerous organizing there. Despite the predictable string of atrocities by segregationists over that period of time, SNCC had been unable to persuade federal officials to intervene in the state. Nor had the national news media shown the same level of interest in events there as they had in the actions of Martin Luther King. Lacking the glare of media coverage or any real federal presence in the state, SNCC came to realize it had little chance of effecting change in what remained the most recalcitrant of Southern states. The Summer Project was a response to this dilemma. The logic ran as follows: if the murders, beatings, and jailings SNCC workers had endured in Mississippi had not been enough to stir public attention, perhaps the media—and, in turn, the general public and the federal government—would take notice if those being beaten and jailed were the sons and daughters

Doug McAdam is professor of Sociology at the University of Arizona and author of Freedom Summer *and* Political Process and the Development of Black Insurgency, 1930–1970.

of white America. In short, Project organizers sought to exploit the very racism they hoped ultimately to eradicate.

The success of the Project, then, was testament not only to the strategic genius of the SNCC staff and the unquestioned courage of Project participants, but to the depths of American racism as well. The media *did* come, compelled less by the issues at stake—which after all had been constant for decades—than by the inherent appeal of the specter of "idealistic college students aiding the impoverished Negroes of Mississippi." In turn, the media's doting coverage of the Project generated the desired public support and helped prod a reluctant federal government into more forceful civil rights action. But the psychological linchpin underlying the Project was American racism pure and simple.

Given this history, it is perhaps inevitable that public celebrations of the Project such as this anniversary volume or the movie *Mississippi Burning* would leave me feeling a bit ambivalent. More accurately, there is something both encouraging and depressing about the attention lavished on Freedom Summer. The encouraging thing is the apparent willingness of the American people—whites as well as blacks—to reexamine the civil rights struggle and embrace it as part of their history and their American heritage. This acceptance, grudging and slow, is nonetheless significant. It marks a kind of cultural triumph for the Civil Rights Movement and a marked departure from its past reception.

During its heyday in the early to mid 1960s, the Movement encountered massive opposition from whites in every region. Public opinion surveys became a kind of broken record: black leaders were consistently judged to be "pushing too hard" for civil rights. Nor was the opposition merely attitudinal. In 1966 rock-throwing mobs of whites greeted Martin Luther King when he inaugurated his open housing campaign in the Chicago suburb of Cicero. Court-ordered busing triggered spasms of white violence in countless Northern and Western cities, including that

bastion of American liberalism, Boston.

America is no stranger to such marked shifts in public sentiment. Indeed, the history of this country is the history of such shifts. If we can believe the historians, the percentage of Colonists who actively supported the American Revolution was fairly small, certainly less than the majority of the total citizenry. Yet soon after the Revolution—certainly by 1800—virtually all Americans had come to identify with the glorious defeat of British tyranny.

The Civil War received much the same treatment. It may be hard for us to imagine the Civil War as unpopular outside of the South. But, in fact, it was, with the North beset by conscription riots, high rates of desertion, and marked violence against blacks. But in time the Civil War, too, came to be embraced as an inspirational page in our national history. It was recast as a heroic period, a time in which all liberty-loving Americans rallied around Honest Abe to free the slaves and preserve the Union.

Most recently, the Vietnam War has been the subject of this reinterpretive process. The spate of recent films on Vietnam, the twelve-part PBS series on the subject, even the much acclaimed (though now defunct) television series, "China Beach," attest to the reality of this process. While the war may still be viewed by most as a foreign policy fiasco, retrospective accounts have increasingly imbued the conflict with a certain heroic and noble quality that was decidedly absent from most contemporary views of the war.

For all the distortions and inaccuracies associated with this kind of collective reconstruction of history, the process is probably inevitable and not without its positive side. Through its retelling and acceptance of history, America rededicates itself—at least symbolically—to the values associated with particular chapters in its past. And so, one might hope, the hard won gains of the Civil Rights Movement might be cemented all the more by the current retrospective acceptance of the struggle, as reflected in the spate of recent favorable retellings of the

Freedom Summer story. By casting the Project, and the Movement, more generally, as a part of our heritage and history, it would be nice to think that most Americans would be ever more vigilant about practices that contradict the aims and ideas of that struggle.

All well and good. But, as noted above, there is a down side as well to the current attention accorded the Movement and especially the disproportionate interest in the Summer Project. That concerns the relative lack of attention being paid those who most deserve it: the black activists and black Southerners who bore the brunt of the struggle. For white Americans to embrace and accept the Movement as part of *their* heritage it seems they need to place themselves at the center of the story. And so from among the countless struggles that comprised the Movement, Freedom Summer gets singled out for special attention for precisely the same reasons the media flocked to Mississippi thirty years ago: whites—and class privileged whites at that—*were* central to the drama.

The continuing interest in the Project is thus a reminder both of how far we have come—at least culturally—and yet how far we still have to go. All of this calls to mind a little known incident that took place during the Summer Project. In the days following the disappearance of James Chaney, Andy Goodman, and Mickey Schwerner, the attention of the nation was riveted on Mississippi. Each new rumor or development received extensive coverage. So you can imagine the kind of interest that greeted news that two headless torsos had been pulled from the Mississippi River during the search. The media descended on the site of the discovery in droves, only to melt away when it was determined that the bodies were those of two young black males from Mississippi who had been missing for several days. Sadly, in the eyes of the nation's press, there was nothing newsworthy about the murders of black males in Mississippi.

The continuing interest in the Freedom Summer Project coupled with the relative disinterest accorded other equally important campaigns in the civil rights struggle suggest that the same double standard is very much alive and well. Apparently thirty years later, the courage, heroism, and sacrifices of the scores of blacks who birthed and sustained the Movement that we now seem so willing to celebrate remain less noteworthy than the important, yet clearly subordinate, contributions made by whites to the Movement.

End of sermon; beginning of testimonial. In criticizing what I see as the subtle form of racism inherent in the ongoing and disproportionate attention accorded Freedom Summer, it is not my intention to demean the Project. My displeasure is entirely with the popular and media attention accorded the Project and what that suggests about underlying racial attitudes in this country. The Project itself is another matter. At a personal level, I know what drew me to study the campaign. Though considerably younger than those who took part in the Project, I too came of age in the 1960s. And from the vantage point of my life during those years, I always regarded the Summer Project as a kind of high-water mark for the New Left as a whole. Social movements, as any number of observers have noted, are important not merely for their concrete achievements, but for the broader social and cultural possibilities which they suggest or "prefigure." And, for me, the "possibilities" glimpsed that summer remain among the richest and most revolutionary of any to emerge during an era dedicated to the exploration of new possibilities.

For, at its most ambitious, the Summer Project was not merely an effort to redemocratize voting rights in Mississippi, or even to dramatize the continuing operation of a brutal and inhumane racial caste system. In its prefigurative politics the Project also represented the purposive negation of a wide range of divisions that had long crippled social relations in America. The most obvious of these divisions was, of course, race. But there were a good many others as well. In recruiting nearly one thousand primarily upper-middle-class students to live and work with some of the most impoverished representatives of "the Other America," Project organizers sought to bridge the yawning chasm that defines class relations in this country. Then there is the matter of gender divisions. For all the criticism aimed at the Project's sexual politics, the fact remains that the majority of female participants found their summer experience profoundly empowering. Simply taking part in the Project required a certain transcendence of the narrow definition of what it meant to be female—especially a white middle-class female—in 1964. The Project contradicted the prevailing conception of femaleness in at least five ways. The Project was interracial, coeducational, unchaperoned, dangerous, and, perhaps most important, explicitly political. What's more, in the opportunities accorded its female members, SNCC was among the most egalitarian organizations operating in 1964. If the organization did not always practice what it preached, the contrast only encouraged the development of a nascent feminism all the more.

The Project also sought consciously to integrate across regional lines, bringing participants to the deepest South from every other part of the country. For most, it was their first exposure to the region's distinctive charms and decided deprivations. Finally, owing to SNCC's stubborn and principled insistence that *anyone* willing to aid the fight for racial equality was welcome, the Project became host to a diverse array of political types. Socialists mingled with conservative young Christians intent on actualizing the social gospel. Young Democrats stood shoulder to shoulder with the SNCC veterans. The organizations listed on the applications betray the diversity which informed the Project: Catholic Worker, Job's Daughters, Future Farmers of America, SDS, Phi Eta Sigma, Women Strike for Peace, Bronx Reform Democrats. The Project marks that shining, but ultimately fleeting, moment at which the possibilities for communion and coalition in American society—or at least among American youth—seemed virtually unlimited.

This is not to say that all of this diversity merged into a loving, seamless whole over the course of the summer. Far from it. The Project was beset by very real class, racial, gender, and regional tensions. But despite these tensions, a very real effort was made to actualize what remains for me a wholly positive vision of a social order founded on equality, justice, and individual dignity rather than the artificial and divisive constraints of ascribed categories. Alas, SNCCs commitment to this effort did not survive the summer. That the Project's prefigurative politics failed to take hold, however, owed less to any flaw in the vision itself than to the depths of the divisions SNCC sought to confront.

Understandable as the ultimate collapse of the "beloved community" may have been, we can still lament its passing and the subsequent direction taken by SNCC, the Movement, and the New Left following the summer. From a commitment to blurring divisions and emphasizing shared values, the Left came to stress sectarian differences and to magnify seemingly tractable points of disagreement. Today's oftentimes shrill and corrosive "politics of diversity" is the legacy of the sea of change that accompanied the abandonment of the prefigurative politics that informed the Summer Project.

There is, of course, another irony in all this. For all its emphasis on blurring divisions and promoting integration, the Summer Project embraced and nurtured diversity far more than the current politics of diversity, whose stress on preserving and celebrating differences often masks a narrow and defensive form of tribalism. But the beauty of the prefigurative content of a movement is that it never really dies. Having once been expressed, it remains available as an alternative template to be rediscovered and adopted by future generations of activists.

And so I end with one final irony. The very attention to the Summer Project that I earlier characterized as excessive and expressive of a subtle form of racism, is exactly what will insure the ongoing availability of the Project as a prefigurative model not only of what might have been, but of what might yet be. It is clear that the summer continues to serve as precisely this kind of reminder and resource for those who took part in it. One volunteer put it this way:

> The thing I remember most is . . . the courage of the Mississippi citizens that we were working with. . . . They were a great source of inspiration for me then and they are still a great source of inspiration to me now. I mean, when I get really into a bad situation or . . . [when] I'm real worried about my internal fortitude, I . . . dip back into that time and . . . my knowledge of what I saw people doing.

Another participant allowed as how:

> the memories of that summer are very important to me because they redeem me personally and they redeem this country. [They serve] as a reminder that there are qualities in me that are worth . . . something and that people are capable of quite remarkable things. It's the single most enduring . . . moment of my life. I believe in it beyond anything.

Finally, one other Project veteran put it this way. She said:

> I know that I exaggerate the importance of that summer . . . and especially my role in it. But those memories have served me well. The . . . purest moment in my life was in that little church in Hattiesburg, sweating like a pig and crying like a baby, singing "This Little Light Of Mine." Do you know the words? One part goes:

> *The light that shines is the light of love,*
> *lights the darkness from above.*
> *It shines on me and it shines on you,*
> *shows what the power of love can do.*
> *This little light of mine, I'm gonna let it*
> *   shine,*
> *Let it shine, let it shine, let it shine.*

> Somehow the fact that I once had that experience is very important to me . . . It's like that little light still shines in my life a bit.

And through the lives of those who experienced that summer and retrospective tributes such as this volume, I can hope that the exemplary politics of that special time and place will continue to shine a bit in American culture, and be available as a model for any with sufficient courage who may seek to apply its lessons in the future. Let it shine, let it shine, let it shine! ❖

DORIE A. LADNER

Band of Brothers

Dorie Ladner gave me this poem in 1964 when I was living in Greenwood. I put it in an old briefcase that Rick Tuttle gave me when he left Mississippi—a place where I stored all of my keepsake things. The last time I saw it was in 1975 and then it mysteriously disappeared. I recently received my files from the Mississippi State Sovereignty Commission and the poem was in my files.

Wazir (Willie) Peacock

Come gather round people while I tell you of a tale
About a Band of Brothers who worked in Mississippi, a living hell.
They were ninety-nine in number
Some old, some very young
And from each of their mouths a song was sung.

This Band of Brothers was led by Bob Moses
Who was fought by all of the official forces.
He was silent in manner
But his strength and determination were like a waving banner
In his work he was persistent
And met his opposition with nonviolent resistance.

This little Band of Brothers worked in north, south, east, and west
Sometimes not knowing which direction for them was best
Yet they met their foes in each of these directions
Trying to erase their evils with love and humane correction.

Among this group were the Sam Blocks and the Willie Peacocks
Who worked in what is known as Greenwood
An area that was tough and hard as timberwood.
They went without food and sleep each day
Trying to pave for their black brothers a Freedomway.

This Band of Brothers worked in Voter Registration
Which made their character targets of defamation.
Oh, no, this did not stop them.
They paid no attention to their foes vicious whims.

This Band of Brothers even initiated the idea of a Summer Project
Which met with opposition and was subject to rejection.
Included in it was such things as the Community Center, Freedom School, Voter
Registration and the Federal Program
Which some tried to cancel and shouted goddamn!
But to this Band of Brothers surprise
This small idea did rise and rise
It became known nation-wide as a huge success
To each and everyone joy and triumph was all they could confess.

Now don't get me wrong
The Brothers homes were faced with many a bomb
Especially in that great city of McComb.
Oh, of course nine arrests were made for the bombings
The nine pled guilty on their part
The fatherly judge set them free and the nation alarming.
Yes, to him, doing this deed came from the mercy of his heart.

Yes there was the horrible killings of the three
Which by now is known to everyone throughout the Country.
It was done by men trying to uphold sovereignty
In the grand state of Mississippi.
This triple murder Mississippi will never erase
So she'd better get her face set for more disgrace.

There was organized within this group a Freedom Democratic Party
Which brought praise and respect from the majority
At her most of the opposition found themselves pointing a finger.
Of course she would speak and sing louder than ever,
Making her enemy wish they could lower the lever.
This little Party journeyed to the Democratic Convention;
The idea of being seated was their one intention.
Of course, they met good and bad
This seemed not to make them sad only glad.
Now you know they were approached with bargains
But being seated was what they were trying to gain
Rather that bargain, unseated they did remain.

This Band of ninety-nine is still leading the Freedom line
With no intentions of stopping ever crossing their minds
Their one ambition is Freedom and Equality
For their Black and White Brothers in this land of Democracy
This is the Band of Brothers.

12/22/64

CLEVELAND SELLERS

Holly Springs: Gateway to the Beloved Community

Cleveland L. Sellers is a political activist, civil rights pioneer, educator, and administrator, who has had a profound impact on American history, life, and culture. As a young man, Dr. Sellers aligned himself with the veterans of the Civil Rights Movement. Joining the Student Non-Violent Coordinating Committee, he traveled the South in the 1960s urging African Americans to register to vote and worked as an advocate for justice and human rights. Today, Dr. Sellers is Associate Professor of African American Studies at the University of South Carolina and is an elected member of the South State Board of Education, Second Judicial District. He serves on the Board of Directors of Voorhees College. He is a

In June 1994, thirty years after my first introduction to Mississippi's "Closed Society," I boarded an airplane for a flight back to Jackson, Mississippi. I traveled to participate in a reunion for the 1964 Mississippi Summer Project. There was anxiety and uncertainty. There was also sadness, because I knew that three of the people I'd worked with in Holly Springs, Mississippi, would not be there—Ralph Featherstone, Rita Walker, and Wayne Yancey, each a Freedom Fighter, had met their maker while on the battle field for civil rights. The rest of us were now graying, balding, heavier, (but still idealistic) middle-aged veterans of the Mississippi Summer, who traveled from all regions of this country and represented all professions, to participate in the thirtieth anniversary celebration. Unlike the "welcome" three decades prior, this time we were met by a large banner hanging from the ceiling of the Jackson airport—"Metro Jackson Welcomes Mississippi Homecoming, June 23-26, 1994." The next sign, "Welcome 30th Reunion—Mississippi Summer 1964" looming high above the freeway was in sharp contrast to the deadly violence that welcomed us when we came to Mississippi in the summer of 1964.

This time some of us would travel together to the communities where we had worked. Those of us who worked in the Holly Springs Project would be presented the key to the city by its African American mayor at a special awards ceremony. In 1964, I merely hoped that I could survive Holly Springs with all of my faculties intact. Never did I imagine that thirty years later we would be given a key to the city.

Karin Kunstler-Goldman likened the reunion to "a college reunion, a funeral, a family gathering, and a political caucus." There were so many people to memorialize, so much to remember and talk about, so many ironies, so many contrasts, and in the end, so far to go. I wondered if so much had truly changed that the despised Freedom Fighters of 1964 were now the VIPs of 1994.

The Holly Springs Project would have the largest number of Freedom Fighters back. That shouldn't have been a surprise because in 1964 the Holly Springs Project, with Ivanhoe Donaldson as its director, was a true reflection of the "beloved community." This project became a fervent, collective spirit born out of the hearts of many caring, committed, and diverse individuals. The unsurpassable sense of love and hope among us created such an unbreakable bond that for one brief period in history the "band of brothers (and sisters)," the circle of trust felt invincible, even in the face of relentlessly imminent danger. Never has any experience paralleled the intense exhilaration and passion that we felt for our work, the local people, and one another. Together our body was impenetrable;

victory our only option.

The Holly Springs Project where we worked operated voter canvassing, Freedom Schools, preventive health clinics and seminars, and registered members for the Mississippi Freedom Democratic Party (MFDP) in eight counties, (Marshall, Benton, Desoto, Tate, Layfayette, Tippah, Ripley, and Union) making it the largest geographic and populated project in the 1964 Summer Project.

The project tried union organizing (organizing a Hod Carriers union) and community organizing activities in an effort to empower the poor. The project utilized women in community organizing. The project was active in towns like Blue Mountain, New Albany, Byhalia, and Oxford (the home of the university). The office/residential center for the project was located on the corner of heavily traveled Highway 78 and the Highway 78 bypass. Our white frame house faced Rust College, and across the street to the left was Mississippi Industrial College.

Holly Springs was in the northern part of the Delta and in the then 2nd Congressional District. This area of Mississippi was the area where both the large agricultural plantations and the largest number of the state's African American population were located. The 2nd Congressional District was known as the Black Belt because, among other reasons, many of the counties in the district had African American populations of 50 percent or better. In the eight counties a total of zero African Americans were registered to vote. There were no black elected officials.

The communities in the project areas were extremely close knit yet they extended open arms to the new young Freedom Fighters who were filing into their midst. These communities radiated with an idealism that, with the right amount of faith and hope, building a just social order was indeed possible. At times we observed little children and tired old men pointing and smiling. Sometimes you could hear them say, "Those are Martin Luther King's brothers and sisters in town, and things are gonna change."

While we knew something was different, we never knew that we were walking onto the pages of history. The names Amzie Moore, Fannie Lou Hamer, Annie Devine, Aaron Henry, Euvester Simpkin, Roy Deberry, Ella Baker, Bob Moses, Wayne Yancey, and Ralph Featherstone would go down in history as those who fought for justice and peace.

As a young man of nineteen, I was introduced to Mississippi through a special assignment to investigate the disappearance of James Chaney, Andrew Goodman, and Michael Schwerner. Eight of us left the summer project training session to travel to Philadelphia to search for the bodies of the missing men. Under the cover of darkness, in teams of two, we searched the backwoods, swamps, and hillsides for sign of these friends.

There I would get to know Ralph Featherstone, Donna Moses, and Gwen Gillon on intimate terms. The other searchers were Charlie Cobb and Stokely Carmichael, who were members of the Howard University contingency. We had already become very close friends. There is something very special that happens to an individual when he observes, continuously, his own immortality. During the orientation, Featherstone appeared to be a carefree hip-hop kind of guy. He had a portable record player, and in the breaks at orientation sessions he would play Aretha Franklin and dance. In the darkness of night in Philadelphia, Mississippi, we admitted our fears, our expectations, and our hopes. There was no separation by class or gender. After four nights of searching without success, we returned to Philadelphia and were dispatched to our assigned areas throughout the state. We later discovered that Chaney, Schwerner, and Goodman were murdered under the watchful eye of the county sheriff. Their bodies were found buried under an earthen dam on the opposite side of the county.

Even though our investigation had been unsuccessful, this experience left a lasting impression in my mind regarding the character and commitment of the participants in the Move-

junior warden at St. Phillip's Episcopal Chapel, Denmark, South Carolina, and serves as president of the Bamberg County Black Association for Political Programs. Dr. Sellers is program volunteer for the Denmark Community Center. He is also the chairman of the South Carolina State Department of Education; African American Male Institute Task Force. Dr. Sellers is a graduate of Shaw University (B.S.), Harvard (M.A.), and the University of North Carolina-Greensboro (Ed.D.)

ment. I often think of the idealism that motivated us. We had a compelling urge to risk our lives, transcend fear, and walk proud in the footsteps of other freedom fighters and abolitionists like Tousaint L'Overture, Frederick Douglass, William Lloyd Garrison, and Sojourner Truth. The Movement consisted of young people who turned away from school, job, family, and all the tokens of success in America to take up new lives. We were hungry and hunted in the name of justice and equality.

When I arrived in Holly Springs, I was greeted by our core of master teachers (Marjorie Merril, Aviva Futorian, Gloria Xafarius, Ralph Featherstone); field organizers (Robert Fullilove, Hardy Fry, Larry Rubin, David Kendall, Pam Parker, Karin Kunstler, Carl Young, Charlie Scales, Wayne Yancey); a registered nurse (Kathy Dahl); and a graphic artist, Frank Cicciorka. Our staff, a multi-talented group, remained steadfastly vigilant. We tried not to intimidate local organizers or turn them away with our particular skills. We always knew that one of our jobs was to develop a group that could take over when we left.

Ivanhoe Donaldson served as the project director. Though small in stature, he was endowed with such an awesome presence and interminable leadership ability that his position guaranteed the utmost respect. Donaldson, who had a knack for testing limitations, continuously stressed the importance of commitment, diligence, and personal focus. His explicit rules and policies ranged from avoiding outdoor lights at night and not standing in front of windows, to the rigidly enforced code of never leaving the office/residence without someone knowing the destination and expected time of return. Ivanhoe discouraged interracial couples fraternizing in public, which was not to be confused with mixed race and mixed gender teams doing project work. Ivanhoe discussed how the freedom struggle might limit personal relationships. Furthermore, he stressed the components of training local people as organizing leaders and administrators. Ivanhoe insisted that Kathy Dahl apply for her

RN and driver's license in Mississippi. By doing so, Holly Springs had a professional nurse present on the project.

Ivanhoe always expected the staff to monitor their behavior, because philosophically we did work for the local people of Mississippi, who deserved our resolute dignity and respect. If our demeanors indicated otherwise, the community would lose faith in us and not support the "cause." We were all matched into teams of two which recruited local blacks to provide additional man power. They would also help us with the logistical work and familiarize us with the network of rural roads and communities. On one occasion we were asked to observe the body of a black man who had died mysteriously along a heavily traveled road.

The most traumatic experience for all of the Holly Springs staff was the mysterious death of Wayne Yancey. Wayne and Charlie Scales were driving a 1964 white Ford when they collided head-on with another vehicle en route to Holly Springs from Memphis, Tennessee. Yancey was a twenty-one-year-old black male who had come to Holly Springs from Chicago, where he graduated from Cooley Vocational School and then became an active participant in SNCC's local Chicago chapter. He was reared in Paris, Tennessee, where his parents lived. Wayne was lively, energetic, outwardly loud and tough yet warm and gentle inside. While always sporting his signature cowboy hat, he had the uncanny ability to lighten up the darkest room and inspire others to give their ultimate effort. Such dauntless charisma seemed to cloak any fears he may have harbored, but he was mindful and cautious, and always warning us of ever present hostility and impending danger.

I remember a black man, someone I had never seen before, rushed up to us and said, "A Freedom Rider has been killed up the road in a car crash!" We had not seen an ambulance nor any emergency vehicle. We began to scout around to see what was going on. We found the badly damaged car at a service station and then went to the hospital. Oddly, the police were already at the hospital. We were shocked to find Wayne's body lying in the back of the ambulance/hearse with blood dripping into a puddle beneath. We could not tell how long the body had been there or if Wayne had died at the scene or while still in the ambulance waiting for medical attention. Charlie was inside the hospital when we took Kathy Dahl, the project nurse, inside to check on him. Even though the hospital had not provided extensive medical treatment to Charlie, the chief of police was trying to put him under arrest for vehicular homicide. Immediately Ivanhoe asked Kathy to work on getting Charlie to a Memphis hospital. Kathy, in her authoritative voice, said that Charlie was in need of immediate medical attention and if he didn't get to Memphis quickly he may die. The police chief was reluctant to let Charlie go. More negotiations were required for the sheriff to finally release Charlie, who was driven to Memphis and then flown to Chicago. Charlie maintained that he was lying on the ground immediately following the wreck, some white men walked over to him and said, "Stay still or you will get the same as your buddy." Charlie assumed that they may have been responsible for not allowing the car to return to the appropriate lane.

That night the undertaker called and asked if we wanted to be there while he prepared Wayne's body. I went along with Ivanhoe, and we stayed with Wayne until his body was made ready for his coffin.

Wayne's death had a profound impact on those of us in Holly Springs, not only because we loved him like a brother, but because for some they saw first hand how the lives of poor black males were not valued in Mississippi. There was no fanfare, no FBI, no investigation, no massive press coverage. No named civil rights leader rushed down to Paris. Just us, the family, and our brother. We all climbed into cars and drove to Paris for the final homecoming of Wayne Yancey, a Freedom Fighter like so many others who had given their lives for freedom, justice, and equality. When we returned to Holly

Springs, we hung the cowboy hat in the living room where it remained for the rest of the summer—as did Wayne's spirit.

Stokely Carmichael, a veteran of Mississippi's Parchman Penitentiary, worked in Greenwood, Mississippi, as the district's project director. Stokely had recruited many of the workers in the 2nd Congressional District. Two of the projects were directed by black women from the Howard University contingency. The Howard University group was the largest group of African Americans recruited for the Summer Project. All of the Howard recruits were placed in the 2nd Congressional District. Muriel Tillinghast was project director in Greenville, while Cynthia Washington headed up the Cleveland project. These women were seasoned organizers and excellent administrators, who performed with distinction in their projects.

Midway through the summer, Ivanhoe was transferred to Jackson to help secure the statewide efforts to build the Mississippi Freedom Democratic Party (MFDP). I became the project director in the Holly Springs project. I followed the policies left by Ivanhoe, and under his tutelage I learned a lot of lessons that would make me become a seasoned organizer, even though I was younger than all of the other directors and all of the volunteer staff.

There were organizers in each of the counties. Most of our time in Tippah County was spent working on arrangements for the "Freedom Vote," a mock election run by the MFDP. We tried to do this with long term plans in mind. We spent more than three weeks working on one area to get the people to allow us to use their church for a polling place. Much time was spent explaining the Freedom Vote and the Freedom Democratic Party as a political party. We had a big rally to kick off the Freedom Vote. We had Freedom Schools and MFDP meetings in the Antioch Missionary Baptist Church for the past two months. We were all delighted that we had Mr. Henry Reaves (from Benton) and Mrs. Fannie Lou Hamer (from Ruleville, running for Congress on the Freedom Vote) as speakers.

Great preparations were made. Some of the local high school girls decorated the church with streamers and posters. The local women prepared sandwiches and cookies and punch for refreshments. Our only concerns that afternoon were whether our speakers would arrive and whether there would be a big crowd to greet them. We stepped back to look at the work we had done. The recently redecorated church really looked good—spanking clean, red, white, and blue streamers and pictures of President Johnson and the Freedom Party candidates adorning the walls. The girls had practiced freedom songs while decorating. They were going to lead the songs at the rally. They had each made a banner decorated with ribbons to wear from shoulder to waist saying "Hamer." They were to be the "Hamer Girls." Mr. Reaves spoke until Mrs. Hamer arrived. She was presented with a corsage (the first she had received in Mississippi), and then she spoke to an enthusiastic crowd that interrupted her at nearly every sentence with applause. There was a wonderful feeling in the church that night. Everyone stood straight and talked excitedly of the truths Mrs. Hamer had spoken about. We left at about 11:00 P.M. feeling that the rally had been a tremendous success. Being slightly exhausted from the hectic week preparing for the Freedom Vote, we fell asleep easily after an hour or so of office work. We woke up hearing, "Wake up! Antioch Church has been burned to the ground."

We went out to the site and spent most of the day there. How pitifully small the foundation looked. Could this really be the place that was so alive last night? A small table and bench were set up with a ballot box for the Freedom Vote. More than fifty people voted there that first day while the sheriff, his deputies, the Mississippi state inspector, the FBI, and the fire inspector milled around and questioned all those who had been present the night before or lived nearby.

Now the people of Antioch had to meet in a tent. They had no insurance on the church and still owed for materials they used to redo the interior of the one-hundred-year-old structure. Churches in the area started to take up collections for rebuilding.

Several of the summer volunteers were forced to mature quickly, especially with the awesome responsibility that went along with the job. I tried to purge myself of bias and chauvinism and take advantage of the diversity of our volunteer staff. I viewed the position as requiring more coordination, planning, and support than giving orders and making demands. I understood what was expected of me and supported a less authoritative, power hungry leadership style. Now we realized that this was a special moment in history.

During the summer, we registered approximately fifty voters where there were none before, enrolled eighty-five hundred members into the MFDP, set up successful, well-attended Freedom Schools, provided political education, created community-based organizations, established youth centers, and began to train the local leaders to take our places. We believed that ordinary people could do extraordinary work. We also believed that, if given a chance, poor people would take control of their destiny.

In Benton County in 1964, there were five agricultural stabilization committee districts (the ASC regulated cotton allotments and the soil bank). For the first time, black candidates ran for seats on these committees. L. B. Paige, Calhoun Jackson, and Sarah Robins won the top three seats in one district. Blacks won seats in three of the five districts. This was a first in Mississippi. Mrs. Robins was the first female, black or white, to win a seat in an ASC election.

Five MFDP delegates and three alternates from the Holly Springs Project traveled with the state MFDP delegation to the Democratic National Convention in Atlantic City. For most of them, this was a once-in-a-lifetime experience. They would return with no seat but with tremendous dignity and self-determination.

Rita Walker first, then Bud, became project director. After a couple of years in the position, Rita and Bud would be forced to relocate. Declining contributions and fading interest made continued survival impossible even in their hometown. The Walkers moved to Illinois. There Rita would die a short time later because of an undiagnosed aneurysm. The family was devastated by her death.

Many of us have continued communication and contact with the families we worked with in 1964. Marg and Gloria have spent extended time in Benton County. Laura Strong and Charlene Hill continued to be active in the Benton County community. As teenagers they published a newsletter and organized anti-discrimination demonstrations. They are now passing the legacy to their own beautiful families.

The strength to survive was tested, but the members experienced a surge of renewal. The Freedom School concept would continue to grow and expand in Holly Springs. The cadre of teachers (Marg, Aviva, Gloria, Feathers, and others) developed portable models, improved curricula, and expanded pedagogy. The school became the model for the Child Development Group of Mississippi and would later become the prototype for the National Head Start Program. The first Negro history supplement for school children, "The Negro in American History," was illustrated by Frank Cicciorka and produced by SNCC and the Holly Springs Project. Antioch Baptist Church was rebuilt with assistance from people across America. Mississippi now has the largest number of African American elected officials than any state. A large number of the officials are female.

We became empowered by both experience and process. Many of us who had worked the dusty back roads lost some of our idealism. The Movement took a decisive turn. It became apparent that the elusive "Beloved Community" we experienced momentarily was still far off in the distant future. The real issue was power: who has it? how is it used? to whose benefit? The Movement focus changed to community empowerment, building independent political organizations (as opposed to relying on the liberal, labor Democratic Party) and self-determination. Many of us continued in the freedom struggle. There were some who never got over the disappointment of Atlantic City. They were crushed by the rejection of our moral imperative by the national Democratic Party. For others it would be a transitional experience. For some it would take years to talk about the anger and pain. Some will never talk.

I was glad that I put aside my anxieties and attended the reunion. I was able to feel the presence of our missing comrades. We played records and danced. I was glad to know that some of the idealism remained. I was also glad to be able to pass on to the next generation of activists the Freedom Torch. Maybe now the lessons of Mississippi can be shared to reveal a glimpse of the "Beloved Community." The next generation may just have the passion, commitment and determination to experience it for more than just a fleeting moment . . .   ❖

BOB ZELLNER

Thoughts on the Thirtieth Anniversary Reunion

Thursday morning we slept late at my apartment before having coffee with Peter and Annetta, who lived on the first floor; then it was off to Jackson, Mississippi, for the thirtieth anniversary of the 1964 Summer Project. The most extensive civil rights gathering in years, the reunion can best be described by who was not there. SCLC and NAACP were under-represented, whereas SNCC and CORE veterans were legion and very much in charge. When Linda and I entered the reception hall, we were engulfed in the legendary, Movement love embraces. Boisterous pandemonium was marred only slightly by the ubiquitous movie lights and cameras. During an early session on the music of the Movement (conducted by SNCC leader Bernice Johnson Reagon, founder of Sweet Honey in the Rock and Smithsonian factotum, Boo said hello to the CBS reporter who later narrated the reunion segment on "Sunday Morning."

Avoiding public sessions, we visited quietly with long-absent friends and comrades-in-(non)-arms. I went around disguised in a linen suit, dark glasses, and a big straw hat. We ran into Dottie Miller Zellner as soon as we arrived. I introduced her to Linda, and we had a nice chat. Julian Bond, John Lewis (U.S. congressman), Bob Moses, Clayborne Carson (Stanford prof and author of *In Struggle: SNCC and the Black Awakening of the 1960s*), and Tom Hayden were

participants in the one session we attended. Where were the women?

Hayden observed that Movement lives may be seen as journeys of self-discovery and improvement similar to the stages of development in native American culture. Individuals move from coyote to eagle and on to wisdom, symbolized by the bear. He claimed modestly that he was still trying to leave the category of coyote.

Julian Bond was moderating when a volunteer of 1964 asked the panel what they would do differently if SNCC and COFO had the Summer Project to do over again. John Lewis, who had answered the previous question, started to walk away from the podium, when Julian called him back. "John, you can help answer this question." The packed hall laughed because they recognized a loaded question. A debate has raged over the years concerning the advisability of bringing white Northerners into remote corners of the burning state of Mississippi that summer. (SNCC staff opposing the summer project thought their position was vindicated when many volunteers remained to become staff and some Mississippians felt pushed aside by the hotshot college students. Events proved SNCC's belief that news media, the government, and the public were moved to action only when middle-class white kids were killed and brutalized. Two summers later, most whites were gone; by 1967, all whites had been removed from the organization.) Julian took a stab at the question, then turned to Lewis, who also studiously avoided the implications of the question. I was disappointed; my hope that Movement heavies were ready to deal with the question of whites in the struggle was apparently unfounded. Julian and John seemed relieved to recognize my hand when I stood up to speak.

It was alright with me, I said, if they chose to shuck and jive but the issue was important. The efficacy of bringing whites into Mississippi and the resulting changes in the Movement were central to ongoing historical debate, a subject of scholarly books and articles. Outsiders were beating the question to death, I pointed out, while the people who had made the decisions appeared unwilling to address the pros and cons of white participation in the Civil Rights Movement. I argued that the summer soldiers of '64 deserved some discourse on a controversy that affected their lives and the course of the Movement. Despite my emotional outburst, the question was never seriously addressed. During the subsequent discussion, Hayden said something about him and me in McComb in 1961, but the commotion in the auditorium and poor hearing kept me from comprehending the statement. Later, no one could reconstruct much beyond Tom's assertion that I was notorious among Southern judges and was considered a very radical fellow by sheriffs and other (out)law men of the South.

Linda and I enjoyed a quiet lunch with Clay Carson discussing Tulane and plans for my memoir-dissertation-book of the SNCC years. I noted with pleasure that John Dittmer's book on Mississippi, *Local People,* was selling out rapidly. I told Carson that Dartmouth historian,

Bruce Nelson, had raved about the book when I saw him and Dittmer at the wedding in the Hamptons. Bruce called it the best ever written on the Movement. Before leaving the reunion, my new wife and I had a good visit with Julian and Pam and Julian's patrician Mother, Mrs. Bond, and his brother, whom I introduced to Linda as "Bond, *James* Bond," which is his name. Others had come from our wedding to the reunion. John Dittmer attended the wedding and the reunion. Joanne Grant Rabinowitz came. Victor stayed home. Jo Martin came, while her mate Bob Swartz remained at home. Connie Curry made the reunion and not the wedding, as did Marion Barry, who apologized for not coming—the mayor's race was heating up, etc. Hayden regretted passing up the hitching ceremony; he was running for governor. What's new?

As we were leaving Jackson State, an enjoyable event occurred. Hollis Watkins and Mike Sayer, a salt and pepper pair of Movement stalwarts, brothers in crime, spied Linda and me slipping out to the car. They set up a cry, "You're not leaving? You can't leave yet." Yeah, sorry, we have to go to Alabama to get married again.

"But we haven't sung yet!" And they would not let us go until we had belted out a half dozen freedom songs at the top of our lungs. The whole campus was aroused when our impromptu trio got going on "Been Down into the South," which I had copyrighted years ago when SNCC tried to sort out who wrote which songs. It was hard to leave, but we ripped ourselves away. Then it was on to the Heart of Dixie; but in order to get from Jackson to Mobile, one must traverse some out-back areas of deepest, darkest Mississippi. On the way, Boo and I had some adventure, but I'll let her tell the story. ❖

CHUDE PAMELA ALLEN

Thank You

He will not be there. His wife took his ashes to Africa twenty-four years ago. He did not want to be buried in this land of oppression; he wanted to return to his ancestors.

I am thinking about him as I return to Mississippi. Thirty years ago we met, both of us Freedom School teachers in the Mississippi Summer Project, what everyone now calls Freedom Summer. Over a thousand of us, black and white, though mostly white, converged on Mississippi in support of the local freedom movement's attempts to break the racist stranglehold in the state.

I'm sure I wasn't the only white woman to fall in love with a black man during that summer of 1964. There've been things written about interracial sex, but little about love. I fell in love. Oh, we kissed and held hands, but ours was an innocent romance. The night before he left for the most dangerous part of that violent, racist state, I lay on his cot with him. He held me tight, kissed my face and I wondered if I would ever see him again. I knew he might die.

I could have died too. All of us faced danger. But everyone agreed that southwest Mississippi was the worst. The project house where he was going had already been bombed.

It has been thirty years since that summer romance in the freedom school; thirty years since we sat with other activists in the local black cafe eating our lunch and flirting across the table; thirty years since he held me close and then left to start a Freedom School in southwest Missis-

sippi. He did survive the summer. He was killed later by a bomb. He'd only just married.

He was a man of unique caliber. He wanted me to be the best Freedom School teacher I could be. More important than being with him was that I prepare my lessons well. I'd been raised to serve a man. Women in my hometown quit their jobs when they married to serve their mates and raise the children. No man I'd known would have thought a woman's teaching was more important than he was.

The racist whites were wrong. It was not black men's sexual prowess they needed to fear. It was rather the idea that men and women working together could change things. It was the dignity of human beings in the face of vicious discrimination, men and women standing up and saying no to state sanctioned abuse.

In that powerful movement for social change I fell in love, and if I were to see him at this reunion, if he were not dead but returning himself to Jackson, I could meet him with my head held high. I have stayed true both to myself and the struggle. There have been pitfalls, confusions, and mistakes, but I have stayed true.

How I wish I could look him in the eyes and say thank you. Thank you for believing in me and thank you for never trying to use me. Thank you for the gentle love we shared and for showing me a new type of man who wanted women as partners in the struggle, not servants or playthings. I have carried you in my heart.

PHOTO BY

MATT HERRON

Three civil rights volunteers from the summer of 1964 and a former student gather at ruins of a Freedom House near Mileston in the Mississippi Delta, where they lived that summer. L to r: Volunteers Robbie Osmond, Martha Honey, student Eddie Carthan, Harriet Tanzman.

MATTHEW JONES

When I Was Young

When I was young, I fought for freedom.
When I was young, I fought the Klan.
Who would have thought, I'd still be fighting
Thirty or forty years down the line.

When I was young, I fought for justice.
When I was young, I fought for peace.
Who would have thought, I'd still be fighting
Thirty or forty years down the line.

Freedom, fighting for freedom;
Thirty or forty years down the line.

When I was young, I fought for unions.
When I was young, I fought to vote.
Who would have thought, I'd still be fighting
Thirty or forty years down the line.

When I was young, I fought for housing.
When I was young, I fought for jobs.
Who would have thought, I'd still be fighting
Thirty or forty years down the line.

Freedom, fighting for freedom;
Thirty or forty years down the line.

When I was young, I fought segregation.
When I was young, I fought Jim Crow.
Who would have thought, I'd still be fighting
Thirty or forty years down the line.

Freedom, fighting for freedom;
Thirty or forty years down the line.

When I was young, I fought for children.
When I was young, I fought for love.
Who would have thought, I'd still be fighting
Thirty or forty years down the line.

Freedom, fighting for freedom;
Thirty or forty years down the line.
Thirty or forty years down the line.
Thirty or forty years down the line.

ANTHONY SEEGER, SMITHSONIAN INSTITUTION

Sounds of the Struggle: Folkways Records and the Civil Rights Movement

Anthony Seeger is an anthropologist, ethnomusicologist, archivist, and record producer. He received his B.A. from Harvard University and his M.A. and Ph.D. in Anthropology from the University of Chicago. A specialist in Amazon Indian societies and their music, he has taught at the National Museum in Rio de Janeiro (1975-1982), served as Director of the Indiana University Archives of Traditional Music (1982-1988) and is currently Curator of the Folkways Collection and Director of Smithsonian/ Folkways Records.

Thirty years ago home video, CNN, and cable television were unimagined. Then, as now, money, power, and certain definitions of "newsworthiness" controlled or at least oriented the mass media. Certain groups of people systematically found themselves deprived of a voice. Yet then, as now, some individuals and small companies used new technology to provide a forum to the all too infrequently heard voices. Then, as now, emerging technology enabled individuals to bring positions and events directly to the rest of the country without the approval of the mass media giants. One of the individuals was Moses Asch, one of the companies was his Folkways Records, and the new technology employed was the portable tape recorder.

Moses Asch wanted to provide a document of the world of sound in the 20th century. And by sound he meant not just music, but also literature, current events, technologies, and other sounds that expressed the aspirations and struggles of peoples around the world. He wanted to make all these sounds available to the world as a kind of public archive, through a commercial company. Every recording had a booklet giving background on the music, speech, or events being documented. Asch founded Folk-

ways Records in 1949 and ran it until his death in 1986, by which time he had produced nearly two thousand recordings—an average of more than fifty titles a year.

During the 1960s Moses Asch issued a number of important recordings that captured the events, social and political processes, and dramatic sounds of the times. He published another group of Civil Rights Movement recordings in 1980. Asch issued these on Folkways Records and kept them in print until the day the Smithsonian acquired the collection. And as curator, I have kept them in print ever since.

Probably the most famous Folkways recording of the period is the "authorized recording, produced for the Council for United Civil Rights Leadership" of the 1963 march on Washington, *We Shall Overcome: The March on Washington* (Folkways 5592). It opens with Joan Baez singing "We Shall Overcome" on the Washington mall, includes a short piece of a statement by John F. Kennedy inviting "anyone who feels concerned" to come to Washington for the march. The full text of Martin Luther King, Jr.'s, "I have a dream" speech follows, supported by billowing waves of sound from the assembled masses. The brilliant oratory is followed by

Marian Anderson's "He's Got the Whole World In His Hand"; Odetta's "Oh, Freedom"; Rabbi Joachim Prinz's words, prefaced by his observation "I wish I could sing!"; performances by Bob Dylan, Brother John Lewis, and Peter, Paul, and Mary; as well as demands from Bayard Rustin, and a pledge by A. Philip Randolph. It is a fiery recording, filled with masses and well known people and performers.

The strength of the Civil Rights Movement may have been expressed in the huge march on Washington, but the struggle was fought and won in countless small cities throughout the South, among them Selma, Alabama (Folkways 5594); Greenwood, Mississippi (Folkways 5593); Nashville, Tennessee (Folkways 5590); and Birmingham, Alabama (Folkways 5487). Events in these cities were documented by Carl Benkert, Guy and Candie Carawan, Edwin Randall, and others. In most cases the projects involved a close collaboration between the documenters and the protesters. The recordings were one of the expressions of struggle—like the songs themselves. The poetry, the rich cadences of political speeches and sermons, the humor in the midst of oppression, and the brave sounds of marchers singing as they were led off to jail were all part of the political process captured on the Folkways recordings.

The U.S. Civil Rights Movement was one of the most musical political movements in history. While union songs have been known to enliven picket lines, and nationalist anthems have quickened the steps of soldiers, the church-based Freedom Songs of the Civil Rights Movement were unlike anything that had come before. The music, like the institutions themselves, provided a strong underpinning to the political processes. The songs were documented on Folkways also, performed both by the original groups and by performers like Pete Seeger who brought them to a wider audience.

Moses Asch, whose family had escaped 19th century pogroms in Poland, was a strong believer in human rights and civil liberties. He had published documentaries long before the Civil

Rights Movement began, including *Berthold Brecht Before the Committee on Un-American Activities* (Folkways 5531), *House Committee on Un-American Activities, Hearing in San Francisco* (Folkways 5531), *The Investigator, Political Satire in Documentary Form* (Folkways 5451), and other titles documented the McCarthy era; *From the Cold Jaws of Death: Inmates and Ex- Inmates from Attica, Rikers and the Tombs* documented the prisons; *Angela Davis Speaks* (Folkways 5401), and *Huey!: Listen Whitey* (Folkways 5402) gave voice to black political leaders in the 1960s; *Berkeley Teach-In* (Folkways 5765) and others presented the Vietnam protests. Years later, Asch would document the Watergate Hearings (Folkways 5551, 5552, 5553, 5554, 5555).

When documentation was impossible, Moses Asch would sometimes commission it. Long after the Sacco and Vanzetti affair, he hired Woody Guthrie to visit the area and to write a series of songs commemorating the trials and the lingering feeling of injustice (*Ballads of Sacco and Vanzetti*, Folkways 5485). Asch published revolutionary songs from around the world because he believed that great art could grow out of struggle, and because he thought the struggles themselves were important. The voices should be heard.

Moses Asch marketed his Folkways Records to libraries and sold them through the independent record company distribution system as well as by mail order out of the Folkways offices in mid-town Manhattan. By popular music industry standards, Folkways sales were insignificant; but they often had influence far beyond their relative numbers. Folkways apparently did not make much money on its documentary publications of the Civil Rights era, but the sounds did get around. Asch had a policy of keeping everything he issued in print. He was known to justify this policy by arguing "Would you stop publishing the letter 'B' of an encyclopedia just because people used other letters more?" Throughout the later struggles of the 20th century, the sounds, speeches, and music of the 1960s movements continued to be found and continued to be heard.

Thirty years ago you could hear the sounds of the evolving political struggle in the South on Folkways Recordings. Today you can hear them still. They have lost little of their power and continue to provide inspiration.

In 1987 the Smithsonian Institution acquired Folkways Records. Moses Asch had been negotiating with the Smithsonian for the transfer of the company at the time of his death in 1986. The Smithsonian agreed, as part of the acquisition, to keep every title in print, and they are. Demand does not justify putting them all on compact disc, but they are all available on high-quality cassettes. If you would like The Whole Folkways Catalogue, it is free. And if you want to see what we have been publishing on the new Smithsonian/Folkways Recordings label, look in a good record store or ask for them. Among the new releases is a compilation prepared by Guy and Candie Carawan from their earlier Folkways recordings: *Sing for Freedom: The History of the Civil Rights Movement in Song* (Smithsonian/Folkways Recordings SF 40032, CD and Cassette).

How to get a catalogue:

Write to Folkways Catalogue, Center for Folklife Programs, 955 L'Enfant Plaza Suite 2600, Smithsonian Institution MRC 914, Washington D.C. 20560, USA. Or call 202/287-3262, or fax 202/287-3699.

Short Discography

FOLKWAYS 5486

Movement Soul: Sounds of the Freedom Movement in the South, 1963–1964. Lest We Forget Volume 1. Songs, sermons, shouts, prayers, testimony. Compiled by Moses Moon. Published 1980.

FOLKWAYS 5487

Birmingham, Alabama 1963, Mass Meeting: Lest We Forget Volume 2. Martin Luther King, Jr., Ralph Abernathy, Birmingham Choir. Recorded and Produced by Guy and Candie Carawan of the Highlander Center. Published 1980.

FOLKWAYS 5488

Sing for Freedom: Lest We Forget Volume 3. Workshop 1964 with the Freedom Singers, Birmingham Movement Choir, Georgia Sea Island Singers, Doc Reese, Phil Ochs, Len Chandler. Produced by Guy and Candie Carawan—Highlander Center. Published 1980.

FOLKWAYS 5502

The Sit-In Story: The Story of the Lunch Room Sit-Ins. Edwin Randall, Narrator. Including Dr. Martin Luther King, Jr., Ralph Mcgill, Greenfield Pitts, Peggy Alexander, Kelly Miller Smith, Philip Howerton, Dr. John Cunningham and Rev. Ralph Abernathy.

FOLKWAYS 5590

The Nashville Sit-In Story. Conceived, coordinated, and directed by Guy Carawan. Narration written (and partly ad lib) Rev. C. Tindell Vivien, Vice-President NCLC.

FOLKWAYS 5591

We Shall Overcome: Songs of the "Freedom Riders" and the "Sit-Ins." Spirituals, gospels and new songs of the Freedom Rider and Sit-In Movement sung by The Montgomery Gospel Trio, The Nashville Quartet, and Guy Carawan. Published 1965.

FOLKWAYS 5592

We Shall Overcome! Documentary of the March on Washington. Authorized recording, produced by the Council for United Civil Rights Leadership. In order of appearance: John Baez, President J.F. Kennedy, Dr. Martin Luther King, Jr., Marian Anderson, Odetta, Rabbi Joachim Prinz, Bob Dylan, Whitney M. Young, Jr., John Lewis, Roy Wilkins, Walter Reuther, Peter, Paul, and Mary, Bayard Rustin, A. Philip Randolph. Published 1964

FOLKWAYS 5593

The Story of Greenwood, Mississippi. Featuring Bob Moses and SNCC workers, Fannie Lou Hamer and Greenwood citizens, mass meetings, hymns, prayers, freedom songs, Medgar Evers, Dick Gregory. Recorded and produced by Guy Carawan for the Student NonViolent Coordinating Committee (SNCC). Published 1965.

FOLKWAYS 5594

Freedom Songs, Selma, Alabama: A Documentary Recording by Carl Benkert. Documentary of dramatic events. Published 1965.

FOLKWAYS 5595

WNEW's Story of Selma. With Len Chandler, Pete Seeger, and the Freedom Voices. Produced by Jerry Graham and Mike Stern. Published 1965.

SMITHSONIAN/FOLKWAYS SF 40032

Sing for Freedom! The Story of the Civil Rights Movement Through its Songs. A compilation of a number of the albums above.

SMITHSONIAN COLLECTION OF RECORDINGS

Voices of the Civil Rights Movement. 3 LP set, compiled by Bernice Johnson Reagon. Currently out of print. Now available as a 2-CD set.

The Folkways documents of struggle continue to be available to the public.

Thirty years ago you could hear the sounds of the Civil Rights Movement on Folkways Records, compiled and annotated by thoughtful activists and published by Moses Asch; now you can still hear them, published by the Smithsonian Institution. ❖

CHUDE PAM ALLEN

Bibliography: The Mississippi Summer Project

Last year I decided to write about my experiences as a white freedom school teacher in Holly Springs in 1964. I began by reading whatever I could find on the Summer Project. I went to the San Francisco Public Library and to used and new bookstores. This list is not complete, nor does it necessarily include some good works. I was especially interested in books which would help me reclaim the feel of that time as well as an understanding of SNCC.

Chude Pam Parker Allen
June 1989

I. The Bottom Line

The three books listed below will help ground a reader. They allow the reader to identify with individual blacks living in Mississippi. The first two are novels based on the life of the author's father. The third is an autobiography. I think this bonding is important. One can stay untouched by statistics and facts; seldom from human experience.

1. *Roll of Thunder, Hear My Cry*
    Mildred D. Taylor, Bantam Starfire Books, 1976.
    This novel is excellent and won the Newberry Award. It can be read by teenagers as well as adults. It also reads well out loud, if you want to read it to your children. The story is told from the point of view of a young black girl living in Mississippi in the 1930s. Her fam-

ily owns land and organizes a boycott against white storekeepers who kidnapped and burned two black men. Taylor shows how difficult it was for a black family to keep its land, but at the same time how much more difficult it was to be a sharecropper.

Taylor is willing to address complex issues, including the idea that sometimes you fight even though you know you can't win, in order to be an example to the next generation. She also shows how the son of a sharecropper sets himself up to be used by unscrupulous whites. It's a painful story; all the more so because the boy who is victimized is not likable. This book speaks about integrity and struggle and will ground a reader in what it was like to live in Mississippi.

There are descriptions of the segregated school, which makes a good introduction to why freedom schools were necessary in 1964.

2. *Let the Circle Be Unbroken*
    Mildred D. Taylor, Bantam Starfire Books, 1981.
    In the sequel to *Roll of Thunder,* Taylor deals with the hardships of the Depression and organizing among white and black sharecroppers and small farmers. The Logan children go to the trial of TJ, the sharecropper boy who is blamed for killing a white store owner. He is found guilty; the two white men who were responsible are not charged. The children never see him again.

Cassie, the young girl who tells the story, teaches an elderly woman to read so she can try to register to vote. The woman and her family, who are sharecroppers, are thrown off the land. Blacks were not passive before the Civil Rights Movement. These two novels show they tried to resist and the repression and economic discrimination they faced.

3. *Coming of Age in Mississippi*

Anne Moody, Dell Publishing Company, 1968. My copy was printed in 1980.

I don't know of any other book like this one. It adds a deeply personal view of what it was like to grow up poor, black and female in Mississippi and to join the Civil Rights Movement, in spite of terrible fear and resistance on the part of one's family.

This book is gripping and even nonreaders might be induced to read it. As with the Taylor novels (#1 and #2), this book can be read by teenagers and makes a good introduction to understanding conditions in Mississippi.

Moody left Mississippi in the summer of 1964 and was not involved in the Summer Project. She had, however, worked with CORE in Canton and details the white terrorism against both civil rights workers and local people, including blacks who were not involved in any agitation. Moody had a strong consciousness of the differences facing women and men in the Movement.

II. From the Sixties

You may have to ask your library to get some of these books through interlibrary loan, but the effort will be well worth it. The books written in the 1960s, have an immediacy and passion that's missing from much of the later work.

The books listed in this section need to be supplemented with Anne Moody's book, *Coming of Age in Mississippi*, which was written in the mid sixties (see #3 above) and with Cleveland Seller's chapter on "The Long Hot Summer" in his autobiography, *The River of No Return* (see #16). His is the only personal account I know from a black participant in the Summer Project.

4. *Our Faces, Our Words*

Lillian Smith, W.W. Norton & Company, 1964.

Our Faces, Our Words was published before the 1964 Summer Project. I read it before going to Mississippi. It is a collection of photographs and first person stories written by Smith, focussing on racism and the Movement in the South. The characters range from a southern white girl trying to deal with her father's unwillingness to take a stand against racist atrocities to a black militant's disgust with whites. Smith, who is herself a southern white, does an especially good job with the southern white girl.

These are monologues and can be used in presentations. I worked on a program of readings for KPFA, the listener sponsored radio station in the Bay Area. We ended the program with the southern white girl's monologue, read by a woman who grew up in the South. It was very moving.

5. *Killers of the Dream*

Lillian Smith, W.W. Norton & Co., 1961.

Smith wrote her autobiography, *Killers of the Dream,* in the 1940s; it was republished in the early sixties with a new introduction. I reread it recently and found it very thought provoking.

The book is both personal and analytical. Smith examines the sexual repression and racist programming to which she and other white children were subjected. She describes the South as a totalitarian society in which none of its members were allowed to step out of their assigned roles.

Lillian Smith was a progressive middle class white woman, who was a role model for many of the southern white women who joined the Civil Rights Movement. She also had strong feelings about communism; saying it was just another form of totalitarianism. Since she was writing in the 1940s, I assume she was referring to Stalin.

6. *SNCC, The New Abolitionists*

Howard Zinn, Beacon Press, 1964.

I read this book in 1964 and was inspired

by Zinn's descriptions of the heroism and commitment of the student activists in the Student Nonviolent Coordinating Committee (SNCC). Zinn was a northern white professor who taught at Spelman College in Atlanta during the early sixties and was active in the Freedom Movement in Atlanta.

Zinn's treatment of the Movement is idealistic, but it accurately reflects the feelings and ideas I encountered in the Movement in Atlanta in the spring of 1964, when I was an exchange student at Spelman College. The litany of white violence in this book is overwhelming, but I think if you read it in conjuction with other studies of the Movement, you'll find it valuable.

7. *Black Like Me*
   John Howard Griffin, Houghton Mifflin, 1961.

   I read this book in my Christian Ethics class in college in January, 1964. I remember the students (all white) argued that the Civil Rights Movement was moving too fast and the feelings of the southern whites had to be taken into account. I was the minority voice saying white feelings weren't the point; justice and equality were.

   The following month I went to Spelman College in Atlanta for a semester as an exchange student. I learned that the black students were very offended by *Black Like Me.* They felt it was racist for a white man to color his skin for a short time and then claim he knew what it was like to be a Negro.

   I reread this book last year and feel that it belongs in any study of racism in the South, not because Griffin learned what it meant to be black, but because Griffin learned how southern whites acted when they perceived a person to be black. This distinction is important. This book is about white racism and white pathology. It is also about the solidarity and help Griffin experienced from blacks, who perceived him as Negro. Griffin and his family were run out of his hometown.

8. *Freedom Summer*
   Sally Belfrage, The Viking Press, 1965.

   Sally Belfrage's account of her experience as a volunteer in Mississippi is well written and full of information. She was the project librarian in Greenwood, Mississippi. Her book is quite moving in parts, especially in its discussion of the McGhee brothers' attempt to integrate the local movie house. (These were local people who were acting out of their own convictions. The statewide leadership of the Summer Project determined that it was too volatile to try to test the public accommodations bill that had passed Congress that summer).

   Belfrage keeps a certain emotional distance in her account, however, and this book would best be read in conjuction with Sutherland's *Letters from Mississippi* (see #9 below).

9. *Letters from Mississippi*
   Elizabeth Sutherland, ed., McGraw-Hill, 1965.

   Volunteers were encouraged to write letters from Mississippi to family and friends and to their local newspapers. By August 1964 my parents were distributing 80 copies of my letters. After the summer we were asked to send copies of our letters for inclusion in this book.

   I reread this book last year and found that it held together very well. Sutherland did an excellent job of editing. Sometimes first names are used, but essentially the letters are anonymous and a collective impression of the summer project is achieved.

   Since 90% of volunteers were white and the letters are printed anonymously, this book reflects a mostly northern white experience.

10. "The Stresses of the White Female Worker in the Civil Rights Movement in the South, by Alvin F. Pouissant, M.D., *American Journal of Psychiatry,* 123, no. 4, pp. 401-5.

    Pouissant was the only black psychiatrist in Mississippi in the summer of 1964. He discussed the fact that blacks as well as whites looked upon the white women volunteers as having "a perverse sexual interest in Negro men." Sara Evans (*Personal Politics,* see #19) referred to his article as being "a hostile, but useful analysis." I found him very supportive and affirming, for he acknowledged how difficult it was for the volun-

teers and staff to function within this environment of sexual obsessiveness.

11. *Mississippi, The Long, Hot Summer*
William McCord, W.W. Norton & Co.,
1965.
The Summer That Did Not End
Len Holt, Morrow, 1965.

These books, written at the same time as
Letters from Mississippi and *Freedom Summer,*
complement those books and give some useful
information. They would be good background
reading and will provide some overview statistics, especially about the educational system in
Mississippi. I wasn't touched by them as I was
by the Sutherland and Belfrage books, but that
might not be true for others.

12. *So the Hefners Left McComb*
Hodding Carter, Doubleday, 1965.

I read this book one day in the library and
found it helpful in understanding the pressures
on whites in Mississippi. This family was not
for integration; they merely agreed to having
their Episcopal minister bring two of the white
workers to their home for dinner. They were
harassed by whites who drove around their house
at all hours. Mr. Hefner, who was a salesman,
lost the lease to his office and could not get anyone to do business with him. They eventually
left Mississippi.

Interestingly, the elder daughter was Miss
Mississippi, but that didn't protect the parents
from harassment. She disassociated herself from
her parents while the younger daughter, who was
attending school in the North, supported them.
Mr. Hefner was given a job; I believe with the
Episcopal Church.

Anne Moody's book, *Coming of Age in Mississippi* (#3), tells in a personal way what happened to a black family when one member
(Moody) took a stand against racism.

III. Recent Books on the Mississippi Sum-
mer Project

These books were published in 1988. They
should be available in bookstores and libraries.
13. *Freedom Summer*

Doug McAdam, Oxford University Press,
1988.

McAdam was drawn to the Mississippi
Summer Project while working on a broader
study of the Civil Rights Movement. His book
is infused with a personal commitment to understanding the human side of the experience
while at the same time attempting a sociological study. This white sociologist genuinely cared
about those of us he interviewed. I found parts
of his book very moving.

This study deals with how the volunteers
feel about their experiences now. In that it is
quite unique. It also contrasts what happened
to the volunteers with people who applied to go
to Mississippi but then did not go. The major
weakness of the study, in my opinion, is its failure to differentiate between the experiences of
white and black volunteers. (About 10% of the
volunteers were black.)

This book has the same title as Sally
Belfrage's 1965 account of her experiences as a
summer volunteer. (See #8.)

14. *We Are Not Afraid, The Story of Goodman,
Schwerner and Chaney and the Civil Rights
Campaign for Mississippi*
Seth Cagin & Philip Dray, MacMillan Pub-
lishing Company, 1988.

The publisher commissioned this study. The
authors, both white, had no prior commitment
to or knowledge of the Mississippi Summer
Project or the three men who were killed. Interestingly, this is a strength as well as a weakness
in this study. I found their overview of the Movement one of the clearest and easiest to grasp. I
think the fact that the authors had no prior
knowledge meant that they didn't assume their
readers did either. Also, the authors were able to
interview Bob Moses, who headed the Summer
Project.

At times the authors' assumptions about
people's motives or feelings do not ring true.
More importantly, they fail in at least two cases
to tell us information which would allow us to
make an independent judgement.

They do not tell us Dick Gregory's story about having to force the FBI to find the bodies of Chaney, Goodman and Schwerner after the informant had told where they were. This story appears in Howell Raines's *My Soul Is Rested* (See #18).

They tell us they do not agree with those who think that James Chaney was viciously beaten before he was killed. But they don't tell us who did think that he was and what their sources were. One such person was James Farmer, executive director of CORE,who says eyewitnesses saw Chaney being beaten. (*Lay Bare The Heart,* see #21.)

What is significant about these omissions is that Gregory and Farmer are long time black activists and the authors are uninvolved, although very sympathetic, white writers. There have been complaints that the Civil Rights Movement is being "white-washed." I would have to say these omissions are an example of such. The issue here is not that the authors should agree with Gregory and Farmer, but that they needed to tell us what these men said.

IV. Studies of the Civil Rights Movement, Autobiographies and Oral Histories

There's a wealth of material available now on the Movement. I haven't included in my listings any on Martin Luther King, Jr., SCLC or the NAACP. My own experience was with student groups and SNCC in Atlanta and the Mississippi Summer Project. Thus this section is not an overview of the whole Movement, but rather includes books which focus on SNCC or Mississippi or include such material.

15. *In Struggle, SNCC and the Black Awakening of the 1960s*
    Clayborne Carson, Harvard University Press, 1981.

This book would be appropriate to read along with Howard Zinn's (*SNCC, The New Abolitionists,* see #6) as it has a historical perspective and puts the Mississippi Summer in a context.

The Student Nonviolent Coordinating Committee (SNCC) provided the major leadership and energy for the Summer Project. But the Summer Project was controversial within the organization. Many of the SNCC workers did not want us white volunteers coming to Mississippi. This study gives some background into the debates and different opinions surrounding the Summer Project.

If you want to learn about SNCC's history, this book is important reading. Carson is a black academic, who has written a sympathetic analysis of SNCC. I advise reading this book with some of the autobiographies. They balance each other.

16. *The Making of Black Revolutionaries*
    James Forman, Open Hand Publishing, 1985. This book was first published by McMillan Company in 1972.

James Forman was a significant leader of SNCC. (He refers to the organization as the SNCC.) His book is a comprehensive study of his political development and there is a great deal of information and analysis about SNCC. Forman specifically does not write about the Mississippi Summer, since so much had already been written about it. But he does give some history about SNCC's early activities in Mississippi and he goes into detail about events leading up to the summer. He discusses the Mississippi Freedom Democratic Party's challenge at the 1964 Democratic Convention, and subsequent events in SNCC.

Forman discusses what went on behind the scenes with other civil rights groups and the Kennedy and Johnson Administrations in Washington, including the pressure on SNCC to refuse help from people who were or might have been connected to the Communist Party. It's easy to portray the Freedom Movement as a struggle between idealists and violent racists, but it was much more complex and Forman helps fit in the missing pieces.

17. *The River of No Return, The Autobiography of a Black Militant and the Life and Death of SNCC*
    Cleveland Sellers with Robert Terrell, Will-

FREEDOM IS A CONSTANT STRUGGLE

iam Morrow & Company, 1973.

Reissued by the University Press of Mississippi, 1990.

Cleve Sellers headed the voter registration project in Holly Springs, Mississippi in the summer of 1964. A black southerner who worked with Stokely Carmichael at Howard University, he described the summer as "the longest nightmare I have ever had." I worked in the freedom school in Holly Springs, so his chapter on the summer has a particular immediacy for me.

Cleve described being part of a group of SNCC workers who went looking for the bodies of James Chaney, Michael Schwerner and Andrew Goodman when they disappeared at the beginning of the summer. I've never read of this search anywhere else.

18. *My Soul Is Rested, The Story of the Civil Rights Movement in the Deep South*
Howell Raines, Putnam's Sons, 1977. My copy is a 1986 printing from Penguin Books.

This book of oral histories gives a broad range of experiences (including that of white racists) while maintaining a sense of immediacy and involvement. There is a section on Mississippi. I never had the opportunity to meet Dave Dennis, who worked with CORE in Mississippi, but I highly recommend his interview in this book.

Raines has a most interesting interview with Dick Gregory regarding the FBI and the finding of the bodies of the three missing civil rights workers. Gregory says that he originally borrowed $25,000 to put up a reward for information. Only then, he says, did the FBI put up a reward for $30,000. Also, Gregory says that the informant came to him as well as to the FBI. When Gregory passed on his information to the FBI and they did nothing, he held a press conference and announced that the FBI knew where the bodies were. J. Edgar Hoover called him a liar. Gregory held a second press conference where he said "if the bodies ain't up in eighteen hours, I will lead the press down there." He said the FBI found the bodies that day where his

informant said they were.

19. *Personal Politics, the Roots of Women's Liberation in the Civil Rights Movement and the New Left*
Sara Evans, Alfred A. Knopf, 1979.

Sara Evans studied how the struggle against sexism first manifested in the Movement. She interviewed many women activists, both black and white and some men as well. She showed how important black women were as role models for white women activists.

Evans and many other white women defined as sexist the assigning of women in the Summer Project to freedom schools and men to voter registration. Although sexist thinking undoubtedly played a part, I don't feel Evans gives enough respect to the threat of racist white violence as the reason for limiting white women's activities.

Anyone examining the questions of white women and sexism, will find it helpful to include Septima Clark's comments about northern white women not listening to her advice (*Ready From Within,* see #22), Anne Moody's discussion of being a woman in the Movement (*Coming of Age in Mississippi,* see #3), and Mary King's discussion of women (*Freedom Song,* see #20). Doug McAdam (*Freedom Summer,* see #13) discusses sexism in the recruiting and assigning of the volunteers. I thought I was immune to being shocked about sexist attitudes, but his examples of recruiters commenting on the women applicants' looks made my skin crawl.

20. *Freedom Song, A Personal Story of the 1960s Civil Rights Movement*
Mary King, William Morrow & Company, 1987.

Mary King, a white activist who worked with SNCC in the early sixties, worked in communications and collected a wealth of material on which she bases her study. This book is both a personal story and a history of early SNCC. One white activist told me she felt Mary's book had given her back a part of her life.

King was an author of the 1964 SNCC position paper on women, submitted anonymously at the Waveland meeting. Be sure you read her account of Stokely Carmichaels's joke, "The position of women in SNCC is prone." That statement has been used over and over again as an example of sexism in SNCC. King has a different interpretation, saying it was said in a monologue where Stokely was poking fun at everyone, including himself.

21. *Lay Bare the Heart*
James Farmer, Arbor House, 1985.

Farmer's focus is the Congress of Racial Equality (CORE) which was responsible in the summer of 1964 for the district in which Schwerner, Chaney, and Goodman were working. Both Schwerner and Chaney were on the CORE paid staff.

I was impressed with Farmer's attempt to be personally honest in this book, as he is an organizational man and could easily have left out the more personal aspects of his life. He tells us he was shamed by a young activist into going on the Freedom Ride to Mississippi, where he and others were arrested and imprisoned. He'd planned to organize the action and then use the excuse of work back at the office for not going himself.

22. *Ready from Within: Septima Clark and the Civil Rights Movement*
Cynthia Stokes Brown, ed., Wild Trees Press, 1986.

Septima Clark's life and work were not centered in Mississippi, although she did work there. Her experiences give a breadth and depth to our understanding of the Movement. She was a southern black woman who was fired from her teaching job for refusing to renounce her membership in the NAACP. She spent a lifetime working with the poor and illiterate, teaching them to read and preparing them to try to register to vote. Her views on the Movement are very perceptive and informative. Her comments on Martin Luther King, Jr. (whom she loved) and SCLC's male chauvinism are quite interesting.

Because it focuses on the life of a southern black woman who worked consistently with the poor, this book balances the fetish on stars and organizational politics. It is an excellent way to be introduced to the Civil Rights Movement, if you're looking for a book to share with someone who knows little or nothing about the Movement.

23. *They Should Have Served That Cup of Coffee*
Dick Cluster, ed., South End Press

This book includes essays and interviews on the black struggle, the women's movement and the antiwar movement. Its first section is on the Civil Rights Movement and includes interviews with John Lewis, Bernice Reagon and Jean Smith. It is not specifically about Mississippi, but the perspective is important. Bernice Reagon notes that you cannot have an accurate picture of the movements of the 1960s and 1970s unless you understand that they rest on the foundation of the Civil Rights Movement.

24. *Dreams Die Hard: Three Men's Journey Through the Sixties*
David Harris, St. Martin's, 1982.

I am ambivalent about this book. The impetus for the study was Dennis Sweeney killing Allard Lowenstein in 1980. Harris was trying to make sense of the killing and, using that as a starting point, sense of Lowenstein's, Sweeney's and his own experiences in the Sixties.

Sweeney, a white working-class student from Stanford who worked in the McComb project in 1964, had become paranoid. He heard voices and felt driven to kill Lowenstein. Allard Lowenstein was a controversial liberal Democrat, whom many SNCC workers distrusted. He had recruited a lot of people for the Mississippi Summer Project and indeed, claimed the idea was his own.

I don't know if the information about Lowenstein is accurate. I have heard that not everything about Sweeny is correct. But what concerns me about the book is its treatment of the Movement in Mississippi and its lack of feeling about the individuals involved.

If you want to look at an example of how a white writer can distort the Movement by focussing on one white activist, then take a look at how Harris deals with McComb. There's a conspicuous absence of history and little mention of black activists in the Movement. Harris is a capable researcher. He could have corrected this distortion.

At the 1989 Mississippi Summer Project reunion in the San Francisco Bay Area, Bob Moses spoke of Dennis as someone whom the Movement had failed. He spoke with such caring. It was in marked contrast to how Harris writes of Dennis Sweeney—or Mary King. (*Freedom Song,* see #20.)

Books I Haven't Read Yet, But Should Be on the List

25. *Mean Things Happening in This Land: The Life and Times of H.L. Mitchell, Cofounder of the Southern Tenant Farmers Union*
H.L. Mitchell, Allanheld, Osmun & Co., 1979.
Against the Grain, Southern Radicals and Prophets, 1929-1959
Anthony P. Dunbar, University of Virginia, 1981.

A historical perspective is missing from most treatments of the Civil Rights Movement. It is very easy to hate all poor and working class whites without having any real understanding of their history of struggle against exploitation and the attempts that were made to transcend racism.

26. *Down To Now: Reflections on the Southern Civil Rights Movement*
Pat Watters, Pantheon, 1971.

The library couldn't find a copy of this book in the Bay Area and hasn't tracked one down for me yet. I mention it because Doug McAdam told me about it. Watters is, if I remember correctly, a southern reporter who was transformed by the Movement and particularly regretted the loss of the vision of the "beloved community."

27. *A Death in the Delta: The Story of Emmett Till*
Stephen J. Whitfield, The Free Press, 1988.
Emmett Till was brutally beaten and killed in 1955 for speaking to a white woman at a store in Mississippi. (Some say he whistled. He sup-

posedly had a speech impediment that made him speak with a whistle.) Emmett Till was a 14-year-old black youth visiting relatives from Chicago. After his body was found and shipped back to Chicago, his mother insisted the casket be opened so the world could see what had been done to her son. The white murderers were found not guilty in a Mississippi court.

This book is a scholarly study by a white academic. I have only skimmed it. It looks dry but thorough.

28. *Sturdy Black Bridges, Visions of Black Women in Literature*
Roseann P. Bell, Bettye J. Parker and Beverly Guy-Sheftall, ed., Anchor Press/Doubleday, 1979.

I bought this book one day while browsing in a local bookstore. It includes four interviews with elderly women in Mississippi, who speak about herbal medicines and relationships with men. In the last interview, however, Melina Wango talked of Emmett Till's murder, saying the white men cut off his genitals and forced him to eat them before they killed him. She went on to say that they cut his body open after he was found and his genitals were in his throat.

I've not found that story about Emmet Till's murder anywhere else and don't suggest that it is true. I did call a friend who grew up in the South and asked if she remembered that story. She said yes. Whether or not Emmett Till was forced to eat his genitals, I think it's important to know that this story existed in the black community.

29. *Eyes on the Prize*
In addition to books and articles, the television series covers Emmett Till's murder in the first program and would be an important segment to watch as well as the program on Mississippi.

A 1994 Postscript

I. Suggestions and Books That Have Come My Way:

I want to remind readers that this is not an exhaustive review of the literature but rather the books I found in the public library and bookstores in the San Francisco Bay Area. When I distributed this bibliography in 1989, I did ask for suggestions and received the following for books on Mississippi published in the Sixties:

Three Lives for Mississippi
William Bradford Huie, WCC Books, 1966.
A Case of Black and White: Northern Volunteers and the Southern Freedom Summers, 1964-1965.
Mary Aickin Rothschild, Greenwood Press, 1982.
Mississippi Notebook
Nicholas Von Hoffman, D. White, 1964.

Another person told me about a classic study of southern whites. If I were redoing this bibliography, I would put this book in the section with Lillian Smith (see #5 above). The person who told me of this book shared the following:

The Mind of the South
W.J. Cash, originally published by Vintage Books in 1941; Reissued sometime in the 1980s.

Cash was a white journalist who wrote this book as a dialogue with his people. (He knew North and South Carolina and Kentucky best.) He saw white southerners as fearful, rigid, and unable to change. Although he was strongly attached to his people and especially loved the farmers, he felt they were totally in denial and committed suicide soon after completing this book.

A fellow freedom school teacher told me of this recent study of what happened to people who were children during the Movement. She said it's wonderful:

Freedom's Children
Ellen Levine, Putnam.

Here are some books that have come my way since I wrote the bibliography. I've leafed through them, but don't feel I'm able to assess them:

Like a Holy Crusade, Mississippi 1964—The Turning of the Civil Rights Movement

Nicolaus Mills, Ivan R. Dee, 1992.
This Little Light of Mine, The Life of Fannie Lou Hamer
Kay Mills, Dutton 1993.
Memories of the Southern Civil Rights Movement
Danny Lyon, The University of North Carolina Press, 1992.

I'd like to alert you to a couple of articles and a paper:

"To Transform a Murder into Life," by Dorothy Friesen
The Other Side, November-December 1991, pp. 26-29.

This article is on Emmett Till's mother, Mamie Till Mobley.

"Teaching Freedom: SNCC and the Creation of the Mississippi Freedom Schools," by Daniel Perlstein
History of Education Quarterly, Vol 30, N. 3, Fall 1990, pp. 299-324.

"Mississippi Freedom Schools as Model for Social Studies Instruction," by George W. Chilcoat and Jerry A. Ligon.

This paper was presented at the College and University Faculty Assembly, at the annual meeting of the National Council of the Social Studies, November 20, 1992. I know it has been revised. Contact Professor Chilcoat at the College of Education, Brigham Young University, Provo, Utah for information.

II. Politics, Spirit, and Song:
(A Personal Note About What's Missing)

In rereading this bibliography I'm aware that many of the books listed fail to capture a feel for the spirit that permeated the Southern Freedom Movement. Somehow this quality doesn't translate well, especially in terms of the academic and historical books. I think it was about making a commitment to life, whether or not one believed in God. In Danny Lyon's book listed above, Prathia Hall is quoted in SNCC minutes (Wednesday, June 10, 1964) as saying: "We are fighting because we want life to be worth living. When I discovered I was dead already I decided that I'd die to gain life."

Two books which capture the importance of singing to the struggle include photographs and personal stories as well as songs:

We Shall Overcome, Songs of the Freedom Movement
Compiled by Guy and Candie Carawan, Oak Publications, 1963.
Everybody Says Freedom, A History of the Civil Rights Movement in Songs and Pictures
Pete Seeger and Bob Reiser, W. W. Norton & Co., 1989.

Also, there are albums and CDs of freedom songs which will enhance anyone's feel for the Freedom Movement. But I don't know whether they can capture the dialectical relationship between singing and struggle. Perhaps that's only possible in times of collective mass action when people are putting their lives on the line and even those of us who can't carry a tune are encouraged to sing louder! ❖

LAWRENCE GUYOT

Books With Which to Fight

The following books will begin to unravel the mystery of how and why we brought the United States to Mississippi. The next step for us is to bring the best of Mississippi to the United States, which is now as racially polarized as Mississippi was in 1964. We did not fail then, we will not fail now.

List of books:

Political Participation: A Report of the United States Commission on Civil Rights, 1968.

This book gives an excellent description of the role of the Mississippi Freedom Democratic Party; the racist policies of political parties in Mississippi; and the strategies used to circumvent the 1965 Voting Rights Act.

The Summer That Didn't End: The Story of the Mississippi Civil Rights Project of 1964
Holt, Len
New York: Da Capo Press, 1992.

This documents the participants, the literature, and the thinking of the Summer Project, the '64 Convention Challenge, and the '65 Congressional Challenge.

Like A Holy Crusade: Mississippi 1964—The Turning of the Civil Rights Movement in America
Mills, Nicolaus
Chicago: I.R. Dee Publishers, 1993.

An excellent description of the origin and contours of the collective thinking process that led to this decision.

Mississippi Challenge

Walter, Mildred Pitts
New York: Bradbury Press, 1992.

An excellent account of the Freedman's Bureau and the strategy of building support for the Congressional Challenge.

Mississippi's Defiant Years 1953–1973: An Interpretive Documentary with Personal Experiences
Johnston, Erie
Forest, Mississippi: 1990.

An outsiders view to justify State tyranny.

This Little Light Of Mine—The Life of Fannie Lou Hamer
Mills, Kay

The power of this book lies in the fact that it is not only about the most well known Mississippi fighter but it actively depicts what she was doing; who she was doing it with. This is the first documentation of the roll of Lawrence Guyot, Harrie Bowie and Armand Derfner in raising money and sponsoring a conference at Mary Holmes College to extend the Voting Rights Act.

Black Votes Count
Parker, Frank
Chapel Hill, N.C.: University of North Carolina Press, 1990.

A clear map of how the vote was fought for and how the fight to maintain it was waged. The best history of Whitley vs. Johnson and Allen vs. The Board of Elections.

We Are Not Afraid: The Mississippi Murder of Goodman, Schwerner, and Chaney—The

Dramatic Story that Shocked the Nation
Cagin, Seth, and Philip Dray
Political and Civil Rights in the United States:
Student Edition Vol. II
By Emerson, Haber, and Dorsen
A complete discussion of Hamer vs. Campbell; the Congressional Challenge; and it's legal manifestations. A history of voting rights laws from the 1957 Voting Rights Acts to 1965 Voting Rights Act.

My Soul Is Rested: The Story of the Civil Rights Movement in the Deep South
Raines, Howell
New York: Viking Penguin Press, 1983.
A series of interviews of the individuals who made the fight.

Rights On Trial: The Odyssey Of A People's Lawyer
Kinoy, Arthur
Cambridge, Ma.: Harvard University Press, 1983.
The Attorney General of the Civil Right's Movement is named Arthur Kinoy. He has written the best description of the Congressional Challenge; the fight for federal protections and the role of advocacy by lawyers for advocates.

Local People
Dittmer, John
Urbana, Ill.: University of Illinois Press, 1994.
An excellent description of the independence of MFDP, COFO, and SNCC.

Racial Matters
O'Reilly, Kenneth
New York: Free Press, 1989.
This book is the bible that we must thoroughly dissect. This book identifies who the infiltrators were; where they worked; and who they answered too. To read this book is to understand the fear that this country has of an issue oriented indigenous mobilization of people around their own self interest. To not read this book is to do battle unarmed.

Freedom Song
King, Mary
New York: William Morrow and Company,

1987.
The best use of the SNCC telephone log ever put into print. The first book to make the connection between the Summer Project of '64; the Congressional Challenge of '65 leading to the passage of the 1965 Voting Rights Act.

Church People of the Civil Rights Movement
Findley, James
New York: Oxford University Press, 1993.
Describes the role of the National Council of Churches in the Civil Rights Movement in Mississippi, from freedom day in Hattiesburg; the founding of the Delta Ministry; the financing of the training of the summer volunteers, as well as the support of the National Council of Churches for the Challenge to the Mississippi delegation in 1965.

Letters from Mississippi
Sutherland, Elizabeth (ed.)
New York: McGraw Hill, 1965.
Edited letters of COFO summer volunteers during the summer of 1964.

Mississippi Notebook
VonHoffman, Nicholas
New York: D. White, 1964.
A light human interest approach to COFO activities in Mississippi written by a Washington journalist.

Who Speaks for the Negro?
Warren, Robert Penn
New York: Random House, 1965.
A series of interviews with civil rights leaders and valuable to this study for the interviews with Bob Moses and James Forman.

Climbing Jacob's Ladder
Watters, Pat and Reese Cleghorn
New York: Harcourt, Brace and World, 1967.
The most thorough study of the black voter registration drive of the 1960's.

SNCC: The New Abolitionists. (2nd Edition)
Zinn, Howard
Boston: Beacon Press, 1965.
An account of the development of SNCC throughout the South from 1960 through 1964. There are three useful chapters on Mississippi

COFO activities and preparations for the Challenge.

Freedom Summer
Belfrage, Sally
Viking Press, 1965.

A detailed account of the 1964 COFO Summer Project written by a summer volunteer.

The Magnolia Jungle
East, P.D.
New York: Simon and Shuster, 1960.

A background source on segregation in Mississippi written by a former Mississippi white newspaper editor, critical of Mississippi segregation. An autobiography.

Lyndon B. Johnson: The Exercise of Power
Evans, Rowland and Robert Novak
New York: The American Library, 1966.

A political biography of Lyndon Johnson, including a section on the MFDP Challenge. The account of these journalists, long-term SNCC foes, is replete with factual inaccuracies but useful as a reflection of the way the general media received the MFDP Challenge.

Three Lives for Mississippi
Huie, William Bradford
New York WCC Books, 1965.

A journalistic account of the deaths of the three COFO workers in June, 1965. It is heavy on emotion and lacking thoroughness.

Mississippi: The Long Hot Summer
McCord, William
New York: W.W. Norton and Company. 1965.

A detailed account of the MFDP Challenge with a useful documentation of the Convention proceeding in Atlantic City.

Stranger at the Gates
Sugarman, Tracy
New York: Hill and Wang, 1966.

A light account of the COFO summer activities written by a summer volunteer. It is important for its sketches of the Freedom Schools

and of Mrs. Hamer. The introduction is written by Mrs. Hamer.

VI Articles

"Allen's Army," *Newsweek,* February 24, 1964, p. 30. A description of the Jackson police force's efforts to build up its reserve pool of deputies, state troopers, and neighborhood citizen patrols and equipment in preparation for the 1964 COFO Summer Project.

Herron, Jeannine. "Underground Election." *Nation,* December 7, 1963, pp. 387-389. An account of the 1963 Freedom Vote in Mississippi.

Jencks, Christopher. "Mississippi: When Law Collides With Custom," *New Republic,* July 25, 1964, pp. 15-18. A description of Mississippi civil rights violence including an analysis of the circumstances surrounding the death of Herbert Lee. He is critical of Mississippi state law enforcement and of the reluctance of the FBI to interfere.

Kempton, Murray. "Conscience of a Convention," *New Republic,* September 5, 1964, pp. 5-7. A critical analysis of President Johnson's attempts to deal with MFDP Challenge at the 1964 Convention. Kempton stresses the conflicts between legal and moral considerations.

Minnis, Jack. "The Mississippi Freedom Democratic Party: A New Declaration of Independence," *Freedomways,* Spring, 1965. An excellent factual defense of the decision of the MFDP delegation to reject the compromise at the 1964 Convention in Atlantic City, written by the former Director of the SNCC Research Department.

Sitton, Claude. "Inquiry Into the Mississippi Mind," *New York Times Magazine,* April 28, 1963, pp. 13, 104–107. Useful on the attitude of white Mississippians toward the Civil Rights Movement. He describes briefly the history and economy of the state with emphasis on the relationships between black and white.

❖

A Selected Reading List

"Allen's Army." *Newsweek,* February 24, 1964, p. 30.

Belfrage, Sally. *Freedom Summer.* Charlottesville, Va.: University Press of Virginia, 1990.

Bell, Roseann P., Bettye J. Parker, and Beverly Guy-Sheftall, eds. *Sturdy Black Bridges: Visions of Black Women in Literature.* Anchor Press/Doubleday, 1979.

Berry, Mary Frances. *Black Resistance—White Law.* New York: Penguin Press-Allen Lane, 1994.

Branch, Taylor. *Parting the Waters: America in the King Years, 1954–1963.* New York: Simon & Schuster, 1988.

———. *Pillar of Fire.* New York: Simon & Schuster, 1998.

Brown, Cynthia Stokes, ed. *Ready from Within: Septima Clark and the Civil Rights Movement.* Wild Trees Press, 1986.

Burner, Eric. *Robert Parris Moses: And Gently He Shall Lead Them.* New York: New York University Press, 1994.

Cagin, Seth, and Philip Dray. *We Are Not Afraid: The Story of Goodman, Schwerner and Chaney and the Civil Rights Campaign for Mississippi.* Indianapolis: MacMillan Publishing Company, 1988.

Carawan, Guy and Candie, eds. *We Shall Overcome: Songs of the Freedom Movement.* Oak Publications, 1963.

Carson, Clayborne. *In Struggle: SNCC and the Black Awakening of the 1960s.* Cambridge, Mass.: Harvard University Press, 1981.

———, ed. *Eyes on the Prize Civil Rights Reader: Documents, Speeches, and Firsthand Accounts from the Black Freedom Movement, 1954–1990.* New York: Viking Penguin Books, 1991.

Carter, Hodding. *So the Hefners Left McComb.* Doubleday, 1965.

Cash, W. J. *The Mind of the South.* New York: Vintage Books, 1941.

Chilcoat, George W., and Jerry A. Ligon. "Developing Democratic Citizens: The Mississippi Freedom Schools As a Model for Social Studies Instruction." *Theory and Research in Social Education,* vol. XXII, no. 2, Spring 1994, pp. 128–175.

Children's Defense Fund. *Progress and Peril: Black Children in America: A Fact Book and Action Primer.* Children's Defense Fund, 1993.

Cluster, Dick, ed. *They Should Have Served That Cup of Coffee.* Boston: South End Press.

Cohen, Bob. "The Mississippi Caravan of Music." *Broadside,* vol. 51, October 20, 1964.

Colmar, Penny. *Fannie Lou Hamer and the Fight for the Vote.* Brookfield, Conn.: Millbrook Press, 1993.

Corbin, Carole Lynn. *The Right to Vote.* New York: Franklin Watts Publisher, 1985.

Crawford, Vicki Lynn. "Grassroots Activists in the Mississippi: Civil Rights Movement." *Sage* 5, No. 2 (Fall 1988).

———, et al, eds. *Women in the Civil Rights Movement: Trailblazers and Torchbearers, 1941–1965.* Brooklyn, N.Y.: Carlson Publishing, 1990.

Dallard, Shyrlee. *Ella Baker: A Leader Behind the Scenes.* Englewood Cliffs, N.J.: Silver Burnett Publisher.

Dent, Thomas C., et al., eds. *The Free Southern Theater.* The Bobbs-Merrill Company, 1969.

"Dismissing the Five Mississippi Election Contests and Declaring the Returned Members

Are Duly Entitled to Their Seats in the House of Representatives." *Congressional Record— House,* 88th Congress, volume 111, September 17, 1965, pp. 24263–24292.

Dittmer, John. *Local People: The Struggle for Civil Rights in Mississippi.* Urbana, Ill.: University of Illinois Press, 1994.

Dunbar, Anthony P. *Against the Grain: Southern Radicals and Prophets, 1929–1959.* Charlottesville, Va.: University of Virginia Press, 1981.

East, P. D. *The Magnolia Jungle.* New York: Simon and Schuster, 1960.

Evans, Rowland, and Robert Novak. *Lyndon B. Johnson: the Exercise of Power.* New York: The New American Library, 1966.

Evans, Sara. *Personal Politics, the Roots of Women's Liberation in the Civil Rights Movement and the New Left.* New York: Alfred A. Knopf, 1979.

Faber, Doris. *Petticoat Politics: How American Women Won the Right to Vote.* New York: Lothrop, Lee, and Shepard, 1967.

Farmer, James. *Lay Bare the Heart.* Arbor House, 1985.

Findlay, James. *Church People in the Struggle: The National Council.* New York: Oxford University Press, 1993.

Forman, James. *High Tide of Black Resistance.* Seattle: Open Hand Publishing, 1994.

———. *The Making of Black Revolutionaries.* Seattle: Open Hand Publishing, 1985.

Friesen, Dorothy. "To Transform a Murder into Life." *The Other Side,* November–December 1991, pp. 26–29.

———. Sammy Youngs, Jr.: *The First Black College Student to Die in the Black Liberation Movement.* Seattle: Open Hand Publishing, 1986.

Fusco, L. "The Mississippi Freedom Schools: Deeper Than Politics." *Liberations,* vol. 9, no. 10, pp. 17–19.

Garland, Phyl. "Builders of the South: Negro heroines of Dixie Play Major Role in Challenging Racist Traditions." *Ebony,* August, 1966,

p. 28.

Gillette, William. *The Right to Vote: Politics and the Passage of the Fifteenth Amendment.* Baltimore: John Hopkins Press, 1965.

Grant, Joanne. *Black Protest History: Documents and Analysis, 1619 to the Present.* New York: Ballentine Books, 1968.

———. "Freedom Schools Open a Door to the World." *National Guardian,* August 29, 1964, p.5.

Griffin, John Howard. *Black Like Me.* Boston: Houghton Mifflin, 1961.

Grisham, John. *The Chamber.* New York: Doubleday Publisher, 1994.

Guyot, Lawrence, and Mike Thelwell. "The Politics of Necessary and Survival in Mississippi." *Freedomways* 6, No. 120 (Summer 1966).

———. "Toward Independent Political Power." *Freedomways* 6, No. 246 (Fall 1966).

Hampton, Henry, and Steve Fayer. *Voices of Freedom: An Oral History of the Civil Rights Movement from the 1950s Through the 1980s.* New York: Bantam Books, 1990.

Harris, David, Sr. *Dreams Die Hard: Three Men's Journey Through the Sixties.* New York: St. Martin's, 1982.

Herron, Jeannine. "Underground Election." *Nation,* December 7, 1963, pp. 387–389.

Hilton, Bruce. *The Delta Ministry.* New York: Indianapolis: MacMillan Publishing, 1969.

Hoffman, Nicholas Von. *Mississippi Notebook.* D. White, 1964.

Holt, Len. *The Summer That Didn't End: The Story of the Mississippi Freedom Summer.* New York: Da Capo Press, 1992.

Howe, F. "Mississippi's Freedom Schools: The Politics of Education." *Harvard Educational Review,* vol. 35, no. 2, 144–160.

Howell, Leon. *Freedom City: The Substance of Things Hoped For.* Richmond, Va.: John Knox Press, 1969.

Huie, William Bradford. *Three Lives for Mississippi.* New York: WCC Books, 1966.

James, Joseph A. *The Ratification of the Four-*

teenth Amendment. Macon, Ga.: Mercer University Press, 1984.

Jencks, Christopher. "Mississippi: When Law Collides with Custom." *New Republic,* July 25, 1964, pp. 15–18.

Jones, F. "Freedom Teacher." *New Zealand Listener,* September 18, 1964, p. 5.

Johnston, Erle. *Mississippi's Defiant Years, 1953–1973: An Interpretation.* Lake Forest, Miss.: Lake Harbor Publishers, 1990.

Kempton, Murray. "Conscience of a Convention." *New Republic,* September 5, 1964, pp. 5–7.

Kinoy, Arthur. *Rights on Trial: The Odyssey of a People's Lawyer.* Cambridge, Mass.: Harvard University Press, 1983.

King, Mary. *Freedom Song: A Personal Story of the 1960s Civil Rights Movement.* New York: William Morrow and Company, 1987.

Lake, A. "Last Summer in Mississippi." *Redbook,* November 1964, pp. 64–65, 112–117.

Lauter, D., and Daniel Perlstein. "Mississippi Freedom Schools: Introduction." *The Radical Teacher,* vol. 40, pp. 2–5.

Lawson, Stephen F. *Black Ballots: Voting Rights in the South, 1944–1969.* New York: Columbia University Press, 1976.

Lerner, Gerda, ed. *Black Women in White America: A Documentary History.* New York: Pantheon Books, 1972.

Lester, Julius. *And All Our Wounds Forgiven.* New York: Harcourt Brace & Company, 1994.

———. *Look Out Whitey! Black Power's Gon' Get Your Mama!* New York: The Dial Press, 1968.

Levine, Ellen. *Freedom's Children.* Putnam.

Lynd, Staughton. "The Freedom Schools: Concept and Organization." *Freedom Ways,* vol. 5, no. 2, pp. 302–309.

Lyon, Danny. *Memories of the Southern Civil Rights Movement.* Chapel Hill, N.C.: The University of North Carolina Press, 1992.

Mabee, C. "Freedom Schools, North and South." *The Reporter,* September 10, 1964, pp. 30–32.

McAdam, Doug. *Freedom Summer.* New York: Oxford University Press, 1990.

McCord, William. *Mississippi: The Long Hot Summer.* New York: W. W. Norton & Co., 1965.

McDowell, Jennifer, and Milton Loventhal. *Black Politics: A Study and Annotated Bibliography of the Mississippi Freedom Democratic Party.* San Jose, Cal.: Bibliographic Information Center for the Study of Political Science, 1972.

McLemore, Leslie B. "Protest and Politics: the Mississippi Freedom Democratic Party and the 1965 Congressional Challenge." *Negro Educational Review* 34, nos. 3 and 4 (July and October 1986).

———. "The Effect of Political Participation Upon a Closed Society—A State in Transition: The Changing Political Climate in Mississippi." *Negro Educational Review* 23 (January 1972).

———. "The Mississippi Freedom Democratic Party: A Case Study of Grass Roots Politics." Ph.D. thesis, University of Massachusetts at Amherst, 1971.

———. "Fannie Lou Hamer: An Unfinished Political Portrait." Paper presented at the Sixth Annual Meeting of the National Council for Black Studies, Chicago, March 17–20, 1982.

McPherson, James M. *The Negro's Civil War.* Chicago: University of Chicago Press, 1945.

Mills, Kay. *This Little Light of Mine: The Life of Fannie Lou Hamer.* New York: Dutton, 1993.

Mills, Nicolaus. *Like a Holy Crusade: Mississippi 1964—The Turning of the Civil Rights Movement.* Chicago: Ivan R. Dee Publishers, 1992.

Millstone, J. "Mississippi's Freedom Schools to Remain on Permanent Basis." *St. Louis Post-Dispatch,* August 18, 1964, pp. 6–7.

Minnis, Jack. "The Mississippi Freedom Democratic Party: A New Declaration of Independence." *Freedomways,* Spring 1965.

Mitchell, H. L. *Mean Things Happening in This Land: The Life and Times of H. L. Mitchell, Cofounder of the Southern Tenant Farmers Union.*

Allanheld, Osmun & Co., 1979.

Moody, Anne. *Coming of Age in Mississippi.* New York: Dell Publishing Co., Inc., 1968.

Newfield, Jack. *A Prophetic Minority: The American New Left.* New York: The New American Library, 1966.

O'Mally, Susan Gushee, and Ellen Cantarow. *Moving the Mountain.* New York: Feminist Press, 1980.

O'Reilly, Kenneth. *Racial Matters: The FBI's Secret File on Black America, 1960–1972.* New York: Free Press, 1989.

Parker, Frank. *Black Votes Count: Political Empowerment in Mississippi After 1965.* Chapel Hill, N.C.: University of North Carolina Press, 1990.

Paynes, Charles M. *I've Got the Light of Freedom: Organizing Tradition and the Mississippi Freedom Struggle.* Berkeley, Cal.: Berkeley University of California Press, 1994.

Perlstein, Daniel. "Teaching Freedom: SNCC and the Creation of the Mississippi Freedom Schools." *History of Education Quarterly,* vol. 30, no. 3, Fall 1990, pp. 299–324.

Pouissant, Alvin F. "The Stresses of the White Female Worker in the Civil Rights Movement in the South." *American Journal of Psychiatry,* 123, no. 4, pp. 401–5.

Raines, Howell. *My Soul Is Rested: Movement Days in the Deep South Remembered.* New York: Viking Penguin Press, 1983.

Rothchild, Mary Aickin. *A Case of Black and White: Northern Volunteers and the Southern Freedom Summers, 1964–1965.* Westport, Conn.: Greenwood Press, 1981.

Rubel, David. *Fannie Lou Hamer: From Sharecropping to Politics.* Englewood Cliffs, N.J.: Silver Burnett Publisher, 1990.

Salter, John R., Jr. *Jackson Mississippi: An American Chronicle of Struggle and Schism.* Melbourne, Fla.: Krieger Publishing, revised edition 1987.

Sellers, Cleveland. *The River of No Return: The Autobiography of a Black Militant and the Life and Death of SNCC.* Jackson, Miss.: University Press of Mississippi, 1990.

Sewell, George. "Fannie Lou Hamer." *Black Collegian,* May/June 1978, p. 18.

Silver, James. *Mississippi: The Closed Society.* New York: Harcourt Brace, 1966.

Smith, Lillian. *Killers of the Dream.* New York: W. W. Norton & Co., 1961.

Stavis, Morton. "A Century of Struggle for Black Enfranchisement in Mississippi: From Civil War to the Congressional Challenge of 1965—And Beyond." *Mississippi Law Review Journal* 57 (1987).

Stoper, Emily. *The Student Nonviolent Coordinating Committee.* Brooklyn, N.Y.: Carlson Publisher, 1989.

Seeger, Pete, and Bob Reiser. *Everybody Says Freedom: A History of the Civil Rights Movement in Songs and Pictures.* New York: W. W. Norton & Co., 1989.

Sitton, Claude. "Inquiry Into the Mississippi Mind." *New York Times Magazine.* April 28, 1963, pp. 13, 104–107.

Spofford, Tim. *Lynch Street: The May 1970 Slayings at Jackson State.* Kent, Ohio: Kent State University Press, 1988.

Student Nonviolent Coordinating Committee. "Mississippi Freedom Schools." *The Student Voice,* August, 1964, pp. 2–3.

———. *The Student Nonviolent Coordinating Committee Papers, 1959–1972.* Stanford, N.C.: Microfilming Corporation of America, 1982.

Sugarman, Tracy. *Strangers at the Gates: A Summer in Mississippi.* New York: Hill and Wang Publishers, 1966.

Sutherland, Elizabeth (editor). *Letters from Mississippi.* New York: McGraw Hill Press, 1965.

Taylor, Mildred D. *Roll of Thunder, Hear My Cry.* Bantam Starfire Books, 1976.

———. *Let the Circle Be Unbroken.* New York: Bantam Starfire Books, 1981.

Thelwell, Michael. *Duties, Pleasures, and Conflicts: Essays of Struggle.* Amherst, Mass.: University of Amherst Press, 1987.

U.S. Congress. House. Challenge to the

Mississippi Delegation Unnecessarily Delayed. 88th Congress. *Congressional Record* (29 July 1965) vol. 111.

———. Elections in Sunflower and Moorhead, Mississippi. 90th Congress. *Congressional Record* (3 May 1967) vol.113, p. 4981.

———. Brief of the Mississippi Freedom Democratic Party. 87th Congress. *Congressional Record* (20 August 1964) vol. 110, pp. 29742–29753.

———. Mississippi Freedom Democratic Party Wins Historic Decision. 88th Congress. *Congressional Record* (17 September 1965) vol. 111, pp. 24263–24292.

Van Hoffman, Nicholas. *Mississippi Notebook.* New York: D. White, 1964.

Warren, Robert Penn. *Who Speaks for the Negro?* New York: Random House Publishers, 1965.

Walter, Mildred Pitts. *Mississippi Challenge.* New York: Bradbury Press, 1992.

Waskow, Arthur I. *From Race-Riot to Sit-in: 1919 and the 1960s.* Garden City, N.Y.: Doubleday and Company, 1966.

Watters, Pat. *Down to Now: Reflections on the Southern Civil Rights Movement.* New York: Pantheon, 1971.

———, and Reese Cleghorn. *Climbing Jacob's Ladder.* New York: Harcourt, Brace, and World, 1967.

Weisbrot, Robert. *Freedom Bound: A History of America's Civil Rights Movement.* New York: Plume, 1991.

Whitfield, Stephen J. *A Death in the Delta: The Story of Emmett Till.* New York: The Free Press, 1988.

William, McCord. *Mississippi: The Long Hot Summer.* New York: W. W. Norton and Company, 1965.

Williams, Juan. *Eyes on the Prize: America's Civil Rights Years, 1954–1965.* New York: Penguin Books, 1988.

Zinn, Howard. "Schools in Context: The Mississippi Idea." *Nation,* vol. 199, November 23, 1964, pp. 371–375.

———. *SNCC, the New Abolitionists.* Boston: Beacon Press, 1965.

———. *Student Nonviolent Coordinating Committee: The New York Abolitionists.* Westport, Conn.: Greenwood Press, 1985.

———. *You Can't Be Neutral on a Moving Train: A Personal History of Our Times.* Boston: Beacon Press, 1994.

Song Credits

List of *Freedom* Photos, Artwork, and Graphics

Index

Britt, Travis 89–90, 90
Broadside magazine 7, 9–10, 11, 12, 147, 180,
    182, 216, 231, 232, 242, 244
Broadside Records 180
Bronx Reform Democrats 490
Brooks, Gwendolyn 175
Brooks, Katherine 155
Brooks, Paul 155
Broonzy, Big Bill 183
Brown v. Board of Education 107

Brown, Benjamin 432
Brown, James 214
Brown, John 334, 335
Brown, Rap 332
Brown, Willie 482
Brown, Wilson 167, 168
Bruce, Lenny 364
Brumfield, Judge 91
Bryant, C. C. 88
Bryant, Roy 5, 6
Burrough, Margaret 123
Burton, Myrtle 432
Bush, George 422, 455, 482
Butler, Angeline 155
Byrd, Acie, Jr. 439

C

Cade, Cathy 421
Cagin, Seth 514
Callender, Gene 21–22
Caravan of Music. *See* Mississippi Caravan of
    Music Project
Carawan, Candie 143, 181, 507, 508
Carawan, Guy 143, 169, 181, 407, 507, 508
Carmichael, Stokely 332, 412, 495, 497, 516, 517
Carson, Clayborne 500, 501, 515
Carter, Hodding 86, 466, 473, 514
Carter, Jimmy 317
Carter, Mae Bertha 410
Carthan, Eddie 138, 503
Carthan, Nancy Jane 4
Cash, W. J. 519
Caston, Billy Jack 88–89
Catholic Worker 490
Center for Community Change 472
Chafe, William 463
Chaffee, Lois 32
Chambers, Ruth Howard 170
Chance, William Claude, Sr. 159
Chandler, Len 146, 151, 182, 185, 192, 195, 196,
    208, 220, 223, 224, 231, 242, 314, 408, 478
Chaney, James 91, 93, 95
Chaney, Fannie Lee 330

Chaney, Ben 326, 327, 328, 330, 361, 366
Chaney, James 9, 81, 91, 93, 95, 154, 166, 169,
    170, 175, 177, 190, 191, 192, 223, 225, 243,
    253, 259, 285, 292, 317, 324, 325, 328, 329,
    330, 333, 337, 354, 363, 364, 365, 366, 367,
    409, 417, 418, 441, 471, 485, 489, 495, 515,
    516, 517
Chavez, Cesar 95
Cherney, Lafayette 209
Cherry, John 339–340
Chicago 8 364
Chilcoat, George W. 107
Church People of the Civil Rights Movement 522
Cicciorka, Frank 496, 499
Civil Rights Act, 1960 58
Civil Rights Act, 1964 57, 485
Civil Rights Bill, 1963 113, 116
Civil Rights Commission 471
Civil Rights March, Washington 53
Civil War, U.S. 488
Clancy Brothers 198
Clark, Kenneth 380
Clark, Ramsey 366
Clark, Septima 136, 403, 516, 517
Clarksdale Freedom Press 119
Clay, Cassius 332
Clay, Florence 371
Clayton, Eva 449
Climbing Jacob's Ladder 522
Clinton, Bill 449, 457
Closed Society 99
Cluster, Dick 517
Cobb, Charlie 82, 108, 110, 118, 129, 134, 145,
    169, 224, 495
Cochran, Adam 182
Cochran, Paula 182
Coffin, William Sloan 454, 470
Cohen, Bob 12, 87, 147–148, 171, 182, 190,
    191, 195, 201, 231, 242
Cohen, Susan Beecher 178, 178–179, 182, 186,
    187, 191, 201
Cole, Johnneta B. 434
Collins, [Senator] 309, 310, 312
Collins, Judy 3, 63, 182, 186, 223, 231
Collins, Lucretia 155
Coming of Age in Mississippi 514
Congress of Racial Equality 25, 78, 79, 107, 135,
    160, 190, 214, 296, 300, 364, 382, 386, 421,
    464, 485, 500, 512, 515, 516, 517
Congressional Black Caucus 137
Congressional Challenge, 1965 521, 522
Conner, Bull 161
Convention Challenge, 1964 521
Cordier, Robert 248